FROM
SLAVE
SOUTH
TO NEW
SOUTH

THE
FRED W.
MORRISON
SERIES IN
SOUTHERN
STUDIES

From Slave South to New South

PUBLIC
POLICY IN
NINETEENTH-
CENTURY
GEORGIA

PETER
WALLENSTEIN

UNIVERSITY

OF NORTH

CAROLINA

PRESS

CHAPEL HILL

AND LONDON

© 1987 The University of North Carolina Press

All rights reserved

Manufactured in the United States of America

Library of Congress Cataloging-in-Publication Data

Wallenstein, Peter.

From Slave South to New South.

(The Fred W. Morrison series in Southern studies)

Includes bibliographies and index.

1. Fiscal policy—Georgia—History—19th century.

2. Finance, Public—Georgia—History—19th century.

3. Georgia—Race relations.   4. Reconstruction—Georgia.

I. Title.   II. Series.

HJ384.W34   1987   336.758   86-19359

ISBN 0-8078-1717-1

in memory of

Henry Wallenstein

(1886–1983)

and

Crandall R. Wallenstein

(1919–1985)

CONTENTS

MAPS,
FIGURES,
AND
TABLES

ACKNOWLEDGMENTS

AT LAST I get to thank the people and institutions that have made this book possible. Chief among the repositories on whose holdings I have relied are the Georgia Department of Archives and History, the Georgia State Library, and the Emory University Libraries. Others include the Library of Congress, the National Archives, the Boston Athenaeum, the Atlanta Historical Society, and the libraries of Atlanta University, Duke University, the University of Georgia, and Harvard University.

Columbia College provided a scholarship that enabled me to attend the school where I discovered that history could make sense and be fun. The Johns Hopkins University awarded me a National Defense Education Act Fellowship, and Ford Foundation funds paid the costs of my initial research in Georgia. Later, Sarah Lawrence College gave me a reduced teaching load the term I completed the dissertation, and the University of Toronto provided a summer travel fellowship. The University of Maryland's Asian Division took me far from my sources, and left me little time for "my own work," but kept me a teacher and then let me return to the States to resume research and writing with the assurance that I had a classroom to go back to. Finally, the American Historical Association awarded me an Albert J. Beveridge Research Grant, and Virginia Polytechnic Institute and State University supplied travel funds, secretarial assistance, and word processing facilities to finish the book.

Completion of a first book provides an appropriate time to acknowledge teachers who contributed even when they had no specific role in its creation. At Columbia, Orest Ranum gave me a wonderful introduction to the study of history, and Walter P. Metzger, David J. Rothman, James P. Shenton, Alden T. Vaughan, and Alan F. Westin opened new vistas. At Johns Hopkins, Charles A. Barker, Alfred D. Chandler, Jr., Robert Forster, and Jack P. Greene nurtured my developing ideas of the discipline of history and of myself as a historian. So did David Herbert Donald, who directed my dissertation and thus helped me craft an earlier version of this work, and Louis C. Galambos, who served as second reader.

Other people, too, shaped my work. From our undergraduate days to a winter in the White Mountains, David Osher and I talked history to the point that I remember wondering where his ideas left off and mine began. Harold C. Livesay, graduate school colleague long ago and department colleague and chairman more recently, wielded wisdom and forceful comments on work in progress. Other historian friends—particularly J. William Harris and Anastatia Sims—offered suggestions and encouragement and helped craft the final version.

The history secretaries at Virginia Tech—Rennie Givens, Patty Mills, and Debbie Rhea—helped in many ways. At the University of North Carolina Press, my editor, Lewis Bateman, and copyeditor, Pamela Upton, played crucial roles. The editors of the *Journal of Southern History* and the *Georgia Historical Quarterly* granted permission to include material that has previously appeared in articles.

For my several sanctuaries, where I did much of the writing, I am much indebted to Mama Bouvette in Georgia and Mama Ho in Malaysia, the Herseys in New York, and the Wallensteins in New Hampshire. The dedication is for two gentlemen, my father and his father, who did not live long enough to see the book they trusted would someday appear and would, they were willing to believe me, be better for the wait. Finally, to Sookhan Ho, *terima kasih.*

Kuala Lumpur
5 July 1986

INTRODUCTION

LIFE, LIBERTY, and the pursuit of happiness largely depend, as the Declaration of Independence stressed, on the behavior of public authority, the texture of public policy. Yet, steeped in the myth of a "laissez-faire" past, most Americans conceive of their history as having been shaped with few governmental constraints. This study illustrates the central importance of public authority in the American past and reveals some of the ways in which governments shaped people's lives in nineteenth-century America. At the same time, it demonstrates ways in which citizens sought to use government as a tool to achieve their objectives.

Nineteenth-century Americans, unlike their twentieth-century descendants, typically were more involved with state and local government than with federal affairs. This study of public policy in nineteenth-century Georgia traces the development of state power in the United States. In 1800 Georgia spent no state money on education or transportation and had no penitentiary or mental institution. Like other states, Georgia changed all that in the years that followed, preparing the way for the 1920s, when schools and highways absorbed the bulk of greatly increased state spending. To view Georgia in broader southern and national perspectives, I have related developments there to those in neighboring states and in New York.

Georgia reflected many of the trends of nineteenth-century America; it exemplified the Old South and its transformation. Before the Civil War, Georgia comprised part of both the settled Old Southeast and the frontier Old Southwest. In the 1840s, only Virginia and South Carolina counted more slaves, and only Alabama and Mississippi grew as much cotton. War and Reconstruction forced Georgians to adjust abruptly to emancipation. I have reexamined such problems in southern history as the comparative constituencies, ideas, and programs of Whig and Democratic politicians in the Old South; the patterns of conflict and cooperation that characterized the political relations of planters, merchants, and small farmers; the importance of cities in nineteenth-century life; and the significance of race and slavery in politics and government.

This book seeks to accomplish a number of things. Where most studies of politics focus on party organization and electoral politics, I have related power to policy objectives. Rather than write only of common schools or higher education, or of mental institutions or penitentiaries, I have discussed all those, as well as schools for the deaf and the blind. Most studies of public policy focus on either social *or* economic affairs, in most cases for only a few decades; instead, I demonstrate the connections among education, transportation, and tax policies, and I track each of these through the entire nineteenth century.

Rather than examine only state policy, or the affairs of a single community, I have combined federal, state, and local developments in one analysis.

Moreover, I have integrated social and political history to point out the social sources of political conflict *and* the social consequences of public policy. Working at the intersection of social and political history, I have attempted to delineate the public policy context of the social history of the nineteenth-century South. Laws shaped lives, in no case more clearly than in racial policy. I relate the law of black freedom in the Old South to the mandates of slavery, and I show how social policy for black Georgians shifted in the years after emancipation.

In exploring the workings of public authority, I have emphasized taxes and spending by Georgia's state and local governments. Issues of public finance— policy relating to demands for public spending and the availability of public revenue—reflected both what government sought to accomplish and the underlying economic conditions and political attitudes. I have broadly distinguished among three major categories of public spending—economic programs, such as the promotion of railroads; social spending, such as support for schools; and government costs, such as legislative expenses. Similarly, I have distinguished among public revenue from taxes, borrowing, and earnings from public investments (a particularly important category).

Viewing the public budget as an instrument of policy, I have treated government as a distributive mechanism that absorbs and then redirects part of a society's resources. My study locates the chief sources of public revenue, weighs the tax burdens of various social groups, ranks the objects of government spending at state and county levels alike, and identifies the social groups that benefited most, and least, from that spending. In economic terms, it suggests the relative costs and benefits of public operations to various social groups at different times, while in the language of political science it focuses more on policy outputs than on inputs, more on the outcomes of policymaking than on the process. The story is one of economic conditions, political conflict, and the social consequences of government actions.

Some of the more pressing questions in the history of the American South concern change and continuity in the period of the Civil War and Reconstruction. Important as these questions are, studies of the nineteenth-century South typically end with secession or begin at Appomattox. In the absence of systematic comparisons of prewar and postwar life, studies of the post–Civil War South tend to exaggerate the significance of differences separating one postwar regime from the next. Thus the conventional division of the postwar period into Presidential Restoration, Congressional Reconstruction, and Bourbon Redemption has impeded as much as it has contributed to an understanding of public policy in the South.

Bridging the Civil War, I have surveyed public policy across the entire nineteenth century in order better to assess the impact of the war and comprehend the Reconstruction of the region. If slavery dominated all aspects of prewar southern life, as has been generally thought, then its elimination had transforming consequences. Makers of postwar public policy—Republicans and Democrats alike—had to operate in dramatically changed circumstances. Emphasizing the period from the 1830s to the 1880s, particularly the 1850s and 1860s, I have divided this study into three parts—the antebellum period, the Civil War, and the postwar years. This structure reflects the central role of war and emancipation in contorting prewar patterns of public authority and in providing the backdrop for very different postwar patterns.

Part 1

RAILROADS,
SLAVES, AND
PUBLIC POLICY

1 SOCIETY AND POLITICS

BY THE TIME James Edward Oglethorpe died in 1785, the colony he had founded was firmly established. Already, however, Georgia was becoming very different from its founder's vision. Established as a refuge where poor Englishmen might become independent farmers and where slavery was prohibited, it had become a home to slaves and planters. Formed as a part of the British Empire, it had just gained independence from England in the American Revolution. However, it had not yet outgrown its origins as a military outpost against hostile Indians and England's imperial rival, Spain. As a colony under Oglethorpe—even as a new state at the time he died—Georgia was small in territory, population, wealth, and power.[1] Georgia's rapid growth in the years between the American Revolution and the Civil War was matched, and facilitated, by the growing powers of its state government.

King Cotton to the Throne

Georgia's population in the 1830s differed radically from that of a century earlier. Europeans planted their first permanent settlement in Georgia at Savannah in 1733. At that time Indians, with their hunting grounds and scattered villages, occupied the entire area. In the 1750s, African slaves became a significant part of the new colony's social and economic system. As late as 1787, when Georgia ratified the U.S. Constitution, the state controlled only a small portion of the area it eventually encompassed. In fact, the state's need for assistance against the Creek Indians provided a major reason for ratifying the Constitution. White Georgians and their slaves had settled little more than a narrow strip of territory along the Atlantic coast and up the Savannah River. The first federal census in 1790 enumerated only 52,886 whites and 29,264 slaves. But by 1840, white Georgians numbered 407,695, their slaves 280,944, and together they had extended their settlements to Georgia's modern boundaries. The Creeks and Cherokees, having ceded the last of their tribal lands, had almost entirely disappeared from Georgia.[2]

Meanwhile a comparable revolution occurred in Georgia's agriculture. Where the characteristic farm in the 1740s was small, largely self-sufficient, and worked by free or indentured labor, a new pattern developed in the decades that followed. Large, commercially oriented plantations worked by slave labor became dominant along the Coast.[3]

New crops accompanied the changes in population and agricultural organization. Corn and timber have remained important products from the eighteenth century to the present; even today, a traveler driving from Macon to Savannah sees seemingly endless stretches of pine trees and corn fields. But with the rise of plantation slavery, rice and indigo became important export crops. As migrants from Virginia and the Carolinas settled upcountry Georgia in the 1780s and 1790s, tobacco became the area's chief commercial crop.[4]

Then came cotton. On the coastal islands, Sea Island cotton took the place of indigo soon after the American Revolution. Textiles, the Industrial Revolution's first industry, generated a voracious demand for raw cotton. Eli Whitney's cotton gin, developed near Savannah in 1793, enabled Southerners to meet that demand. For a time, the bottleneck in the production of short-staple cotton, the upcountry variety, had been the separation of the cotton fleece from seeds. The advent of the cotton engine, a spiked cylinder (or sawtooth)— cranked by hand, horse, or water power—that snatched the fluff through narrow slits, leaving the seeds behind, solved that problem. Middle Georgia soon became cotton country as tobacco was reduced to a minor commercial crop.[5]

King Cotton now began his imperious rule. The new monarch mandated expropriation of more Indian lands. Then he dictated development of improved transportation facilities to move to market the product of the new lands. Cotton could be cultivated in piedmont as well as coastal Georgia, in large quantities or small, with slaves or without. But slave plantations became an increasingly important part of Georgia's newly settled areas, as Indian land, black slavery, and white cotton fused into the antebellum cotton plantation. Beyond transforming Georgia's agriculture, King Cotton began to reshape its society and politics.

Given the availability of land and the market for cotton, the demand for slaves increased. Who else would work all that land for someone else? In part, new recruits came through additional imports of slaves, particularly around the turn of the century. Although they were few relative to the total American slave population, they added measurably to the number in Georgia. Mainly, however, southern slaves grew in numbers through natural increase. The growing demand for slaves, together with the end of importation, led to better treatment and longer lives. Slave deaths lagged far behind slave births.

Regardless of whether farmers raised cotton or corn, they also raised bumper crops of young farmers, who needed land of their own. Census takers counted the harvest as the numbers of residents in the South Atlantic states grew at rapid rates. Between 1790 and 1820, the combined populations of Virginia, the Carolinas, and Georgia, together with Tennessee and Kentucky, increased sharply—slaves by 128 percent, whites by 119 percent. Where could whites go to find land? Where might slaves be sent to work it? Increasingly, in the early republic, they went to the lands that became Kentucky, Tennessee, and the cotton states of the Deep South. Last settled and least populated among the original states, Georgia grew particularly fast; its population doubled in the 1790s and more than doubled again by 1820.[6]

In the 1790s, Georgia claimed, but could not control, abundant land. The young state reached west, far beyond its modern boundary along the southern reaches of the Chattahoochee River, all the way to the Mississippi, and it included land that comprises most of today's Alabama and Mississippi. But Creeks and other Indians inhabited the region, and Spain claimed it as well. Alone, Georgia lacked the power to pacify its western lands. By 1795 Spain had relinquished claims to the disputed land, but thousands of Indians remained.[7]

Regardless of Spain, Indians, and even political probity, land fever flourished. Speculators and prospective landowners alike wanted that Georgia land. Moreover, many Georgians hoped to convert some of it from public domain to public revenue. Speculators and legislators combined in 1795 to produce the Yazoo Act, which offered to transfer huge chunks of western territory to four land companies for a total of $500,000. Cries of outrage greeted the act—too much land to monopolists, too little money for the state, too much corruption of members of the legislature. Pro-Yazoo legislators were swamped in the next elections, the act rescinded, and the repeal placed prominently in a new state constitution.[8] Georgia still shared its western lands with Indians, its treasury remained bare, and its landless citizens multiplied.

In 1802 the governments of Georgia and the United States reached an agreement that promised to change those conditions. Georgia became the last of the original states to surrender western land claims. In return the Georgia Cession agreement stipulated that the U.S. government would pay the state $1,250,000, an amount that would be realized as the lands were sold. Moreover, the federal government assumed all claims arising out of the abortive Yazoo sale, as third parties who had made purchases from participating land companies sued to recover their investments. Finally, the United States undertook the responsibility of extinguishing Indian titles to all the land that remained inside Georgia's boundaries.[9]

The Louisiana Purchase provided the United States with a huge territory west of the Mississippi River. Writing to Georgia's Governor John Milledge in November 1802, President Thomas Jefferson declared that "the acquisition of Louisiana will, it is agreed must, put in our power the means of inducing all the Indians on this side to transplant themselves to the other side of the Mississippi before many years get about." [10] As a rule, the United States now forced the exchange of Indians' eastern lands for portions of those western lands, while it granted annuities, derived from the sale of the eastern lands, in return for improvements that Indians had to leave behind when they emigrated to Indian Territory.

After the Georgia Cession of 1802 and the Louisiana Purchase the following year, Indian removal from the South was a certainty. The process of removal, though not concluded until the late 1830s, began almost immediately. Insatiable land hunger led to unremitting pressure on the Indians, and on federal officials to force new treaties on them. Georgia and federal authorities differed, at times heatedly, over the urgency of Indian removal. Georgians called on the national government to redeem its promise of removal, while federal agents felt themselves restrained by promises to Indians and by a condition in the agreement that called for peaceful extinction of their claims. As Indian spokesmen pointed out repeatedly—but in the end fruitlessly—the promise to extinguish Indian titles violated treaties in which the United States had guaranteed the Creeks and Cherokees perpetual possession of all their remaining lands in Georgia.[11]

Town and Country

The transfer of lands from Indians to the state of Georgia led to the state's most significant function of the first third of the nineteenth century—distribution of that land to whites. In general, the state sold the land, at prices much lower than those charged by the federal government, to white Georgians who entered lotteries to obtain 202.5-acre lots. Successive waves of settlers followed successive Indian land cessions and public land lotteries. Fresh lands meant landownership for thousands of white families, those that had been landless and those that sought richer or more abundant land.[12]

A human stream of migrants flowed southwest along the Atlantic Seaboard and then west along the Gulf of Mexico. Southerners, when they migrated, acted much like Americans elsewhere; they moved from one farm to another, whether in the next county or the next state, in a generally westerly direction. Of whites who had migrated to Georgia and still lived there in 1850, 78 percent had come from North or South Carolina and more than nine out of ten had been born in the Carolinas, Tennessee, or Virginia. Similarly, among whites born in Georgia who had moved away by 1850, 62 percent had moved to Alabama or Mississippi and more than nine out of ten now lived there or in Florida, Tennessee, Louisiana, Arkansas, or Texas.[13]

At midcentury Georgia remained overwhelmingly rural, and some parts of the state had been only recently and sparsely settled by whites. Yet by that time, Georgia was no longer a frontier society. In 1850 more than three-fourths of the white residents of Georgia had been born there, and the number of native Georgians who had moved away from Georgia slightly exceeded the number of people who had moved to Georgia from elsewhere. One of the more striking aspects of Georgia's society at midcentury was that, among its entire free population, 97.5 percent were whites born in the Slave South. All

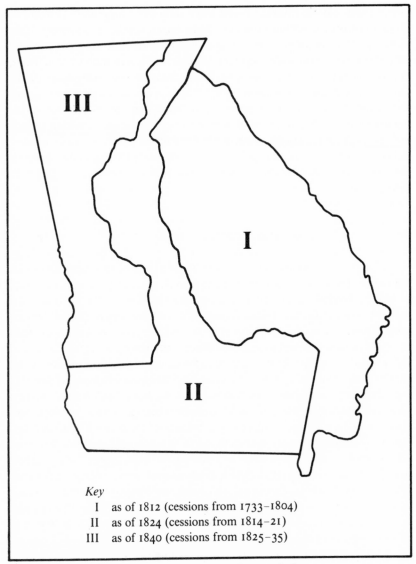

Key
  I   as of 1812 (cessions from 1733–1804)
  II as of 1824 (cessions from 1814–21)
  III as of 1840 (cessions from 1825–35)

MAP 1. *Indian Land Cessions as of 1812, 1824, and 1840*

Source: Phillips, *Georgia and State Rights*, plate 1.

others—free blacks, immigrants from Europe, and migrants from the free states—comprised only one in forty free Georgians in 1850.[14]

In contrast to rural Georgia, the city of Savannah was peopled with free blacks, Yankees, and immigrants. The flow that swept farmers in antebellum America from one farm to another did not bring many to the towns. Like other American cities, Savannah depended for much of its growth on an influx of people from Europe. Georgia's largest town was not very large; its population—14,622 in 1850—included a scant 1.6 percent of Georgia's slaves and 1.7 percent of its free residents. Yet Savannah's population included 18 percent of the Americans from free states living in Georgia, 23 percent of all Georgia's free blacks, and 41 percent of all foreign-born free residents of Georgia. Among whites in Savannah, only 4,774 were natives of Georgia and another 720 were from neighboring South Carolina, while 1,555 had been born in Ireland, 383 in the German states, 305 in New York, and 287 in England, Scotland, or Wales. The smaller cities, too, had notable, though smaller, concentrations of immigrants. In the towns, far more than in rural Georgia, native whites competed for status and income directly with immigrants and free blacks, as well as with slaves.[15]

Towns provided an occupational structure more diverse and a social structure more complex than did rural areas. Fewer than one-tenth of Georgia's people lived in towns in 1850; aside from Savannah, only Augusta, Columbus, and Macon had as many as 3,000 residents, and barely a dozen other towns had as many as 1,000. But towns grew rapidly in the 1840s and 1850s, as railroads pushed into western counties and as commerce and manufacturing quickened. Savannah had a deep harbor at the mouth of the Savannah River and, like Charleston and Mobile, was one of the larger port cities between Baltimore and New Orleans. Augusta, Macon, and Columbus were situated near transportation breaks at the fall lines of the Savannah, Ocmulgee, and Chattahoochee Rivers. As railways began to rival waterways in Georgia's transportation system, they gave rise to new urban centers. Atlanta, in particular, grew rapidly where major railroads met. Settled only in the 1840s, Atlanta had become Georgia's fourth largest city on the eve of the Civil War. Serving as political home to railroad men, merchants, bankers, and other retainers to King Cotton, Georgia's towns offered the legal, commercial, and other professional services that the plantation economy required.[16]

Class and Region

Public policy in antebellum Georgia always reflected, and generally reinforced, a very unequal distribution of wealth, power, and status. While the overwhelming majority of Georgians resided in rural areas, derived their livelihoods directly from agriculture, and had been born in the Slave

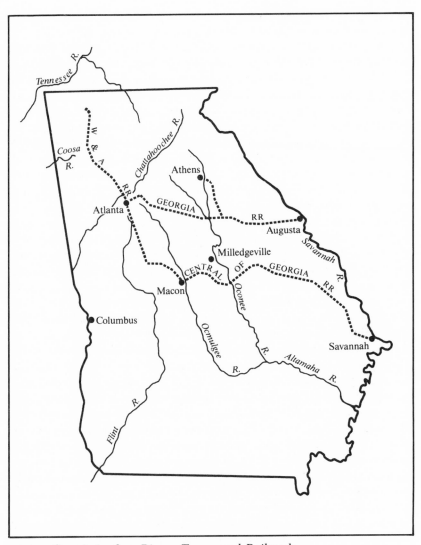

MAP 2. *Georgia in 1850: Rivers, Towns, and Railroads*

South, no such homogeneity could mask enormous differences in race and class. More than two-fifths of the residents of antebellum Georgia—462,198 of 1,057,286 in 1860—were slaves. Public policy denied slaves their freedom, refused them property rights, and excluded them from political activity. Two other groups of nonwhites—similarly denied political rights yet subject to public authority—were much smaller; free blacks were never numerous in Georgia before 1865, and Indians had virtually vanished by 1839.[17]

On the white side of the great racial divide, only men possessed political rights. A few white women enjoyed full property rights—some even managed their own plantations—and in Georgia, as elsewhere in nineteenth-century America, all married white women slowly acquired greater property rights.[18] But regardless of civil rights or property holdings, white women could not participate in the political system.

White men in Georgia were divided by both region and class. Men of wealth —planters and merchants—often differed among themselves, but together they dominated the social, economic, and political structures of antebellum Georgia. Wedged between the wealthy and their slaves were large groups of small property holders and propertyless poor whites. The four main groups in the political system, in brief, were planters, merchants, yeomen farmers, and poor whites. Numerically dominant were the yeomen; economically and politically dominant, the planters.

Slave ownership provided the clearest single indicator of the social and economic position of a white individual or family in pre–Civil War Georgia. Slaves comprised nearly half of all the wealth in Georgia, yet a majority of white families owned none at all. Among those families, the lowest three-fifths (in fact, 62.6 percent in 1860) owned no slaves; the next quintile owned 9.9 percent of the slaves in Georgia (none of these families owned more than four or five, or one family of slaves); and the top one-fifth owned the remaining 90.1 percent. At midcentury, planters—conventionally defined as farmers owning at least twenty slaves—headed only 6.5 percent of the free families and yet counted among their property 57.6 percent of all the slaves in Georgia.[19]

Tax lists and census returns tell of the concentration of other wealth, too, in the Slave South. The majority of free families owned at least some land and other property. Yet landownership, though more widespread than slaveholding, was roughly proportional to slave ownership. The majority of Georgia's free families (or voters, or taxpayers) who owned no slaves also owned no land; few slaveholders were without land; and, as a rule, the more slaves a person owned, the more land he held. The disparity of wealth and the relationship of landholding to slaveholding prevailed throughout the state, both in predominantly white regions of largely subsistence farms and in heavily slave areas of rice or cotton plantations. In cotton-belt Columbia County in 1851, for example, one-fourth of the taxpayers possessed at least twenty slaves and 500 acres of land, while, at the other extreme, nearly another fourth held no taxable property at all and were subject only to a poll tax.[20]

Submerged in the white social structure were those families owning neither land nor slaves. Many heads of such families worked as overseers on plantations, as laborers on others' farms, or even (increasingly in the 1840s and 1850s) as low-paid factory workers. Herdsmen needed to own neither land nor slaves to raise hogs and cattle on the open range, particularly in South Georgia, and some tenants had much more autonomy than would their postwar counterparts. As a rule, however, the structure of opportunity in the Old South made limited space for the many landless whites.[21]

In some parts of antebellum Georgia, a majority of white families held ten or more slaves; in others, opportunities were more limited, and few families had much wealth. Planters were concentrated in the black belt.[22] Shaped like a lopsided horseshoe, Georgia's black belt hung from Hancock County in Middle Georgia, reached east and west to the South Carolina and Alabama borders, and rested at both ends on the Florida border. Most black-belt counties lay in a 150-mile-wide band that stretched from Augusta in Middle Georgia, through Macon and Central Georgia, to Columbus in Southwest Georgia. At midcentury the densest concentrations of planters and slaves were in the rice counties below Savannah and in the cotton counties of Middle Georgia (see map 3).[23]

Fresh, fertile land in Southwest Georgia, between the Flint and Chattahoochee rivers, was opening up to cotton culture by the early 1850s. Attempting to compete more successfully on the world cotton market, planters were moving west from the relatively less fertile lands of the old cotton counties. As Savannah merchants competed for trade otherwise drawn to the Gulf ports, railroads reached into Southwest Georgia and made it increasingly accessible to markets. Much of the region was therefore in transition to the plantation system, and by 1860 Dougherty County's population was only 27 percent white.[24]

Neither planters nor slaves lived in large numbers in North or South Georgia. The eastern half of North Georgia included the southern tip of the Blue Ridge Mountains. Small farmers in the Blue Ridge produced little surplus and remained largely outside the market economy. For some years after a gold rush that began in 1829, however, considerable mining persisted in the area, and a federal gold mint operated at Dahlonega. In other northern counties, land was less rugged and less isolated; the Coosa River flowed west into northern Alabama, and the Western and Atlantic Railroad pushed north from Atlanta. Cotton cultivation in the northwest had begun, but most commercial farmers concentrated on grain production; North Georgia's counties included the state's leading per capita producers of corn.[25]

A predominantly white region of pine barrens and wiregrass country pushed

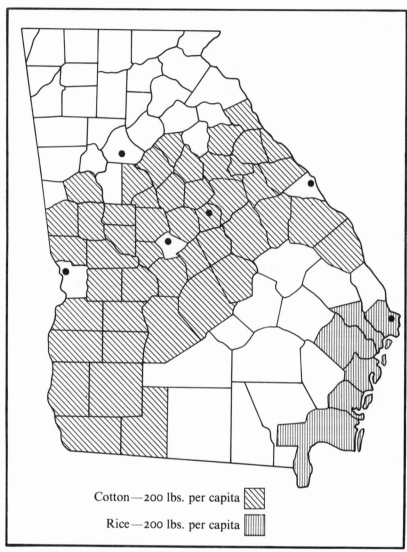

MAP 3. *Rice and Cotton Production, 1849*

Source: Seventh Census, 364–65, 378–81.

northward from the middle of the Florida border. Much of the land in South Georgia remained uncleared and sparsely settled, but the area's counties boasted the highest per capita values of livestock in the state. As one observer recalled of antebellum South Georgia, "most of the people . . . lived by raising stock."[26]

The Issues

The most important issues in Georgia politics, whether before or after the Civil War (and whether latent or manifest), related to race policy and federal power. Long before the "Solid South" that followed Reconstruction, public officials and their constituents in Georgia stood united in their attitudes toward the federal government. In fact, in an almost unbroken line from the 1790s to the 1860s (indeed, to the 1960s) Georgia presented a united front in national politics. Prewar politics differed from postwar in that, while Democrats presided over a one-party state between Reconstruction and the 1960s, two parties stood on equal footing in Georgia in the 1840s. Historian William J. Cooper has written of "the politics of slavery," which prevailed from the 1830s to the 1850s. While competing ardently for power within the state, Whigs and Democrats alike vigorously extolled the virtues of slavery and the right of white Georgians to decide their future without interference from outsiders.[27] What preceded "the politics of slavery" might well be termed "the politics of Indian removal."

Georgia's four major white social groups were in fundamental agreement on the permanence of slavery and the removal of Indians. Whatever the objective interests of poor whites or small farmers in slavery as an economic institution, they joined with planters and merchants in perpetuating slavery as an essential instrument of social control. All four groups, too, promoted Indian removal. Early in the nineteenth century, much of the best agricultural land in Georgia remained in the hands of the Creeks, and farmers wanted that land. Many merchants favored removal of the Cherokees from North Georgia to make way for transportation links with the Tennessee River. Whites used violence and the threat of violence against Indians to secure the desired territory.

Georgians were prepared to employ violence against the national government should it interfere with the state's policy regarding Indians or blacks. Governor George M. Troup set the tone in 1827, a few years before South Carolina's more celebrated nullification of a tariff law. He threatened a defensive war against the United States should the national government attempt to prevent the extension of Georgia's sovereignty over Indians who inhabited lands not yet ceded to the state.[28] A generation later, Georgia went to war over slavery, and poor whites and yeomen farmers fought alongside planters in a war for southern independence.

In practice, the two issues differed. They could be as different as Georgia's actions in 1789, when it ratified the U.S. Constitution and joined in the new government, and 1861, when it left the Union and joined the Confederacy. Particularly in the early years, Georgia needed federal assistance to remove Indians, and the interests of the two governments tended to be complementary. But when the national government violated what Georgia citizens perceived as their rights, they protested vigorously. As the Spanish threat receded and white Georgians no longer felt that they garrisoned an outpost on a hostile frontier, they could behave more obstreperously on Indian policy, as in 1827. As the Indian problem vanished, assistance from the national government became less essential to Georgia's race policy, which increasingly hinged on slaves and slavery—as investment, as labor supply, and as a means of race control.

Although white Georgians presented a united front to the nation's capital, they differed with animation over political questions at home. On issues negotiable among themselves, the four groups followed divergent imperatives. By the late 1830s, almost all the Cherokees had been driven west and the last land lottery had taken place; thus land was no longer directly at issue in the formation of state policy. The major questions now related to state finance, particularly tax policy and transportation policy. On these matters, planters sometimes opposed merchants, and both these groups often opposed small farmers and landless whites.

Georgians' political behavior differed according to their wealth and their involvement in the market economy. Those with large landholdings generally owned large numbers of slaves as well, and their economic purpose was to produce a surplus of agricultural goods. To move that surplus to market, planters promoted transportation improvements, whether by river, road, or railway. Merchants' primary concern with state policy was the promotion of commerce. Through transportation improvements, they sought to reach new territory whose trade they could control.

Small farmers and poor whites, by contrast, had little commerce with a world larger than their neighborhoods. As a rule, they had little interest in governmental promotion of transportation facilities. Access to Savannah, the price of cotton—what did such things matter to a Blue Ridge farmer in the 1840s? As for social welfare, literacy could not compare in importance with land, and a state university offered little to a subsistence farmer when neither he nor his child would ever attend.

As a rule, the proponents of positive government in antebellum Georgia were planters and merchants, not small farmers. Planters and merchants provided most of the political support for state spending on economic growth and social welfare alike. They could better afford to pay any taxes that positive government might require, and they had more reason to expect benefits from the expenditures those taxes made possible. When planters opposed merchants, it was black belt versus towns. When they opposed small farmers, it was black belt versus upcountry.

Power

According to the Constitution of 1798, which provided the framework of state and local government in pre–Civil War Georgia, the state legislature and the counties' inferior courts comprised the centers of public authority. The legislature established the boundaries of legitimate behavior for individuals and for private and public corporations. It defined corporate powers when it chartered towns, banks, railroads, and academies. It created counties and could change their boundaries, and it established ceilings for local taxes. More important for purposes of this study, it determined state taxes and state expenditure benefits.

Each county's inferior court, consisting of five members elected to four-year terms, acted both as a court of law and as a board for the administration of county affairs. In that latter role, the inferior court had jurisdiction over county taxes (within the limits allowed by state law), poor relief, local schools, and the construction and maintenance of roads and bridges, courthouses and jails.[29]

The structure of formal politics reflected the great racial divide in Georgia's society. While nonwhites were excluded from participation in politics, whether as voters or as officeholders, political democratization proceeded apace for white men. No differences among white men could be so great, the structure implied, as to preclude their jointly creating and maintaining public policy. White men might agree and cooperate, they might differ and compete, but such differences as they might display would not likely jeopardize fundamental values that any of them held.

Formal political equality among white men increasingly characterized politics in early nineteenth-century Georgia. Property restrictions against voting and officeholding vanished. The 1798 constitution, unlike the 1777 constitution, stipulated no property requirements for voting, though it did require voters in any given election to have paid any poll or property taxes due for the preceding year. Constitutional amendments in 1835 and 1847 eliminated property requirements for election to the state legislature and governorship. Other changes extended the electoral principle, and voters began to elect other officials in addition to members of the general assembly. According to the Constitution of 1798, the general assembly (on joint ballot) appointed governors to serve two-year terms and justices of the inferior courts to serve during good behavior. By 1812 all county offices were elected by popular ballot, and an amendment in 1824 provided for direct election of the governor as well.[30]

Most white men could vote for state legislators, but some votes carried more weight than others. Legislative apportionment determined how much

the State: forgetting all sectional interest, all local divisions, all dissonance of political feeling, in the one aim of raising our State to the position which her size, her resources and her wealth entitle her." [38]

As a guideline for public policy, "the good of the State" was neither wrongly conceived nor universally ignored. It was, in fact, a central component of antebellum Georgia's most ambitious and successful public enterprise, the Western and Atlantic Railroad. The sectional, partisan, and other disunity that the editor decried, however, reflected sharply divergent interests. Wealth was distributed very unevenly, both by class and by region. Georgia towns, sections, and classes competed for state assistance to projects that would give them relative advantages. They obstructed projects that promised them little benefit or that threatened, at their expense, to profit their rivals. Each sought also to pay as little as possible of the costs of all public functions.

Appeals to state pride and promises of general prosperity could not easily shunt aside such obstacles to unity. Competition among various white social groups, based largely on differences in prospective costs and benefits, worked sometimes to prevent, often to postpone, and always to shape state legislation. Public policy would inescapably bear the distinctive stamp of Georgia's social, economic, and political systems.

2 STATE POWER AND TAX-FREE FINANCE

GROWTH IN state power characterized the early republic. Soon after the War of 1812, American states—both northern and southern—began great new projects in economic growth and social welfare. No longer did state governments undertake to do little more than protect each citizen's life, liberty, and property. By successfully tapping new and richer means of financing public activities, states released themselves from the more restricted roles that had marked their earlier behavior. With state support, canals flourished, as did railroads and then schools.

The "rise of the common man" and the spread of political democracy sum up the dominant perceptions of the Age of Jackson. Just as important as the extension of suffrage or the hoopla of electioneering, however, was a remarkable growth in the range of government activities—the behavior that the growing electorate could shape.[1] Focusing on state finance in antebellum America permits the integration in one analysis of such disparate facets of the period as public schooling, railroad development, Indian removal, and relations between the federal government and the states.

An American System

Historians have told how states promoted economic growth and development in pre–Civil War America. They have written of widespread state investment in banks, canals, and railroads. Some ventures were jointly public and private, such as the mixed enterprise of Virginia. Some, on the other hand, like New York's Erie Canal and Georgia's Western and Atlantic Railroad, were exclusively public enterprises. But such accounts of the "American System," as historian Robert A. Lively termed it, tell only part of the story.[2]

The American system of public investment in banking and transportation sought twin objectives. Not only should citizens benefit from the general prosperity that state-fostered economic growth would bring, but those investments should also generate profits for their shareholders, the taxpayers. The profits could be realized, and the dividends distributed, in the form of lower tax bills. In 1836, for example, Indiana legislators authorized an indebtedness of $10 million for railroad and canal construction. They did so with the expectation that operating revenue from the new facilities would service the debt and, better yet, within a few years profits would become great enough to permit the abandonment of taxation.[3] Not only might the transportation improvements turn out to cost the taxpayers nothing, but they might also unburden citizens of tax obligations to pay for other services they wanted government to provide. Here was a form of abolition—the abolition of taxes—that North and South alike eagerly pursued in the first half of the nineteenth century.

Nor did these state programs of public investment stop at seeking economic growth and nontax revenue. The American system promoted schools as well as railroads; it sought solutions to social problems as well as to economic underdevelopment. Contemporaries saw direct connections between the two types of state programs, one designed to promote economic growth, the other, social welfare and social control. Jacksonian efforts to develop public schools, as well as what David J. Rothman has termed "the discovery of the asylum,"[4] could not help but cost public funds. Those funds might come from revenues other than taxes.

In short, if a state government managed to accumulate surplus funds and invested those funds in profitable enterprise, it might succeed both in enhancing the private sector economy and in generating abundant nontax revenue for the public sector. If successful, the state could then choose among several attractive options: plow the profits back into more public enterprise; use the profits as a substitute for tax revenue; transfer the funds from programs of economic growth to programs of social welfare; or some combination of those options. The state's citizens might, in fact, benefit from more railroads, lower taxes, *and* more schools. To begin this process, the state had to have substantial monies for investment. Georgia's experience illustrates how it could all happen, as the public domain supplied seed capital.

Three objectives, then—education, transportation, and lower taxes—were central to American state finance between the War of 1812 and the Civil War. After the discovery of gold in North Georgia in the late 1820s, for example, Governor George R. Gilmer argued that the state government should operate the gold mines. The resulting public revenue, he suggested, might permit the state "to relieve the people from taxation, improve all the roads, render its rivers navigable, and extend the advantages of education to every class of [white] society."[5]

Relying not on gold mines, as it happened, but on land revenue and on investment of that revenue in banking, Georgia successfully suspended state taxes in the late 1830s, at the same time launching major efforts in both education and transportation. Hard times forced cutbacks in spending and a resumption of taxes through the 1840s. The quest for a tax-free system of state finance continued, however, as did efforts to promote economic growth and social welfare through state action. Ambitious new adventures in social spending and railroad promotion, together with declining tax rates, characterized the 1850s.

The national government provided much of the seed money for state investments in banking and railroads. Twice, in the generation after the War of 1812, the federal government made substantial sums available to Georgia, and the state's quest for a continuing nontax source of public revenue lurched forward at both times. So did state spending on economic growth and social welfare. Without the infusions of nontax revenue from the national government, Georgians could not have conceived, let alone inaugurated, their three-pronged program. The key to the sequence was the abundant land that Americans found in the West. They employed the machinery of national government to convert that land to their own use—to obtain it by purchase or conquest, to pacify and depopulate it, and to redistribute it from Indians to whites. Along the way, they turned it into a public revenue bonanza.

The federal role was related to tensions between advocates of "state rights" and proponents of federal power. While state power grew in Jacksonian America, various steps to limit the growth of federal power, or even to diminish that power, surfaced in Jackson's veto of the Maysville Road Bill, his attack on the Second Bank of the United States, and the fate of Henry Clay's American System. Clay's package of proposals to promote American manufacturing included a protective tariff, federal aid for transportation improvements, and a central bank to provide credit and a uniform national currency. Though portions of the American System became law, by the early 1830s Clay's program was in disarray—the bank denied a renewal of its charter, tariffs on their way back down, and a transportation program never effectively enacted at all.

Such measures as Jackson's led to a displacement of governmental power, functions, and funds from the central government to the states.[6] The destruction of the Second Bank increased the significance of state banks. Opposition to the use of federal funds for transportation led to state sponsorship of internal improvements. Moreover, in distributing a federal treasury surplus among the states in 1837, the national government provided large shares of the funds the states invested in banking and railroads. Thus the defeat of Clay's American System at the national level led to its enactment, in part, at the state level. Similarly, the federal government provided much of the money that the states spent on schools.

Historians of American law have recently reinterpreted the relationships of public policy and economic growth in antebellum America. Seeking to encourage economic growth without relying on taxes, state legislatures granted powers of eminent domain to railroads and other corporations. Such uses of public authority often benefited "large-scale capitalist organizations" "at the expense of small property holders."[7] All groups, however, wished to avoid taxes, and race often overshadowed class as public policy displaced many of the costs of economic development. The central role of expropriated western lands in the public finances of various states shows that, in many cases, what American citizens saved in taxes, Indians paid in land.

What Can Be Done

In the nineteenth century, as always, public funds seemed scant. Georgia's policymakers sought to balance citizens' needs against public resources. As an 1851 report to the legislature noted regarding elementary education, "What the State actually needs is one thing; what can be done . . . is another."[8] The observation applied to the entire spectrum of public spending.

More than anything else, the availability of funds determined what antebellum Americans could accomplish through public authority. Because they tried to avoid direct taxation, social spending depended almost entirely on the availability of nontax revenue. Thus it was that major new undertakings in social welfare in Georgia can be dated from 1817–21, 1835–37, and 1856–59, three periods in which the state received extraordinary amounts of tax-free revenue.

Georgia's quest for schools, transportation, and lower taxes first became a possibility in 1802, the year of the Georgia Cession agreement with the U.S. government. In return for Georgia's surrender of its western land claims, the agreement required the United States to pay the state $1.25 million. Georgia would receive that money, not all at once, but in installments as the federal government sold the lands and thus converted them to cash. The Georgia Cession agreement also obligated the federal government to extinguish Indian title to all the lands that remained in Georgia. Indian removal from Mississippi Territory made Georgia's receipt of the $1.25 million imminent. Removal from Georgia supplied the state with public land to convert to private farms and public revenue.[9]

In 1802 the Treaty of Fort Wilkinson secured a portion of the Creeks' lands. As a special session of the legislature that year demonstrated, no issue in Georgia politics was more important than how the land should be distributed —whether the state should offer inexpensive land or should secure public revenue. Proponents of a revenue policy, though divided in their specific objectives, agreed that Georgia's public domain should be converted into some type of public investment that could supply continuing revenue. One group, seeking tax relief, hoped to use that revenue as a substitute for state taxes. Another, hoping to promote social and economic development, planned to use it to finance education and transportation improvements. Georgia resolved the debate by adopting a policy directed more toward free land than toward public revenue. Consequently, though the state treasury gained nontax funds from the land distribution program, the sums were smaller than proponents of a revenue policy had sought.[10]

The seizure and redistribution of Indian lands in Georgia led to the availability both of inexpensive land and of state revenue far exceeding the costs of administering the land program. Most of the newer areas of settlement had little access to river transportation, however, and cotton had little value unless it reached a market. Acquiring the land pleased Georgians, but better transportation would make their land more valuable to them; they called on the state to use land revenues to supply that transportation. By the 1830s, Georgia had netted more than $1.7 million from the sale of its public domain.[11]

Georgia's new posture in public finance remained only a promise until 1817. One reason was a delay in realizing much revenue from land sales, either by the United States in the western territory Georgia had ceded or by Georgia in its own territory. A related reason was the War of 1812. When the U.S. government levied a direct tax to help finance the war, Georgia's share of the $3 million tax each year amounted to $94,936. The tax act gave each state the option of assuming its citizens' obligations under the act, paying the sum into the federal treasury by an early date, and receiving a reduction of 15 percent. Georgia opted for assumption and reduction but, instead of sending the money north, requested the federal treasury to credit its tax account by debiting its account for the western lands.[12]

When Congress established the Second Bank of the United States in 1816, the national bank was expected to make money for the government. Senator John C. Calhoun of South Carolina, in his early incarnation as a nationalist, proposed that the profits be set aside as a permanent fund for the construction of internal improvements. Georgians favored their neighbor's proposal. Though Georgia's Senators were divided, its Congressmen voted 3–0 for the bill, with Georgia providing the difference in the House vote of 86–84. President James Madison, however, vetoed the bill, and the House failed to override the veto. States then had to look elsewhere for funds to finance internal improvements. New York led the way by financing the Erie Canal, a showpiece in public enterprise that encouraged other states to make comparable efforts.[13]

For most states, the alternative to taxes as a source of funds for internal improvements turned out to be public lands. In the late 1810s, Georgia began to gain large sums from the sale of its lands. In 1817 and 1818, moreover, Georgia collected a final $756,000 from the federal government for the ceded lands. Governor William Rabun told the legislature in 1817 that Georgia could not expect "a more favorable opportunity to commence internal improvements on an extensive scale." In response the legislature appropriated considerable sums for river improvements, and it also created a permanent internal improvements fund as well as a "poor school" fund, each with $250,000. Four

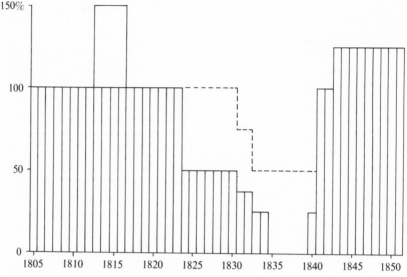

FIGURE I. *State Tax Rates, 1805–1851*

Sources: Cobb, *Digest*, 1065–71; Lamar, *Compilation*, 877–87.
Notes: The state rate is displayed as a percentage of the rates for 1805 (1805 = 100%).
Also displayed are 1) an extra tax (1813–16) levied to pay expenses of the War of 1812; and
2) state taxes collected solely for county purposes (1824–40).

years later, it established a similar fund for "academies" and doubled the size
of the internal improvements fund. That money, invested in bank stock, produced annual dividends available for schools, roads, and riverways.[14] With
receipts from public lands, Georgia had inaugurated substantial and continuing state support for both education and transportation. As the state continued
to gain revenue from land sales, it continued to invest funds in bank stock.

Nontax revenue from banking and land sales led to large tax cuts. Beginning in 1824, Georgia cut state tax rates by one-half. Rates remained at half
their previous levels through the end of the 1820s, and rate changes in the
1830s took taxes even lower (fig. 1).[15]

The chronic treasury surpluses led to another financial decision as well.
Instead of investing further in the stock of private banks chartered in Georgia,
the general assembly created the Central Bank in 1828. Completely state
owned, the Central Bank served as the state's fiscal agency. At the same time,
by channeling public funds into long-term bank loans to citizens, it enabled
the state to promote economic growth.[16]

A major reason that Georgians supported the Central Bank related to their
hopes of an end to state taxes. In 1823, for example, Governor John Clark
called on the legislature to withdraw the state's investments from private banks
and establish a state bank. Its profits, he predicted, would soon "be sufficient,

if not entirely, measurably to relieve the citizens from taxation, enable the state to progress advantageously in internal improvement, and perfect its system of public education." Similarly, in 1829 Governor John Forsyth (of the opposition Troup party) anticipated the time, "not remote, if the institution should be prosperous, when the agriculture of Georgia, like that of Pennsylvania, will be relieved of all direct contributions for the payment of State expenses." [17] Forsyth's prediction, like Clark's, proved realistic.

Increased income from banking more than made up for a decline in revenue from land sales following Georgia's last land lottery in 1832. From the half-rates that prevailed from 1824 through 1830, taxes declined to three-eighths in 1831 and 1832, one-fourth for 1833 and 1834, and, finally, nothing at all beginning in 1835 (fig. 1).[18] Having permitted the abandonment of state taxation, however, Georgia's revenue system did not yet supply ample new funds for social spending or transportation. Nonetheless, appropriations for higher education bulged in the early and mid-1830s, and Georgia began to provide funds for the schooling of deaf white children. In addition the state purchased slaves to work on river improvements and other transportation projects.[19]

An act of Congress furthered Georgia's three fiscal objectives: greater spending on education and transportation, with no additional taxation. In the 1830s, the U.S. government received unusually large sums from land sales, while tariff revenue continued to suffice for federal expenditures. Confronted with strenuous arguments against federal spending on internal improvements, Congress devised a means in 1836 whereby the federal government might constitutionally allocate funds to the states for purposes of transportation and education. Apportioned to the states according to Congressional representation, the federal treasury surplus was to be deposited (technically as a loan, not an outright grant) in the treasuries of the states. In this way, Georgia received $1,051,422 as its share of the distribution in 1837.[20]

Like many other states, Georgia deposited its share of the surplus in its state bank and allocated large portions to social spending and transportation improvements. In 1837 Georgia began construction of a state mental institution. At the same time it placed $350,000, one-third of its share of the distribution that year, in a "common school" fund, to which it added the assets of the old poor-school fund of 1817 and the academy fund of 1821. Interest from the fund was to be distributed to the counties each year to pay teachers.[21] Most important of all, the state turned its attention to constructing a railroad.

Georgians had been investigating the feasibility of establishing a great public enterprise that, like the Erie Canal, might eventually finance itself as well as promote economic growth. Soon after construction of the Erie Canal, the age of railroads had begun, and North Georgia's rugged topography argued against a canal. A rail system promised increased trade for the merchants of Augusta and Savannah, more freight traffic on lines connecting those cities with what became Atlanta, and—contingently and at a more distant time—profits for

Georgia's treasury. In addition it would open North Georgia to settlement. In 1836 the state embarked on its own great public enterprise, the Western and Atlantic Railroad—the key to the state budget for a generation following the end of land revenue.[22]

Georgia began to transfer its investments from the Central Bank to the Western and Atlantic, but, as it financed the railroad, the state also accumulated a substantial debt. By forgoing taxes in the middle and late 1830s, the state required the bank to pay roughly $1 million for ordinary appropriations; the bank also provided $1.4 million to finance the state railroad. The federal treasury surplus, and its distribution to the states, ended abruptly in the depression that began in 1837. Instead of remaining a permanent fund for the redemption of liabilities and a source of nontax revenue, the Central Bank's capital stock was largely exhausted.[23] One result was depreciation of the bank's currency. Meanwhile Georgia sold state bonds to finance the railroad. To pay for current appropriations, finance the Western and Atlantic, restore some of the bank's capital, and deflate its currency, the state needed to overhaul its system of public finance.

In 1839, Georgians reluctantly resumed taxation as a major source of state revenue. Subsequent changes in the tax system took the rates up, not down. Rates peaked in 1852, however, and through the 1850s they drifted back down.[24]

As Governor Forsyth realized in 1829, Georgia's fiscal experience in the Age of Jackson resembled that of many American states. Nontax means of financing government enabled a number of states to parallel Georgia's policy of avoiding state poll and property taxes. Alabama, for example, abandoned state poll and property taxes between 1836 and 1842 and sought to finance the state government solely through the earnings of the state bank. Maine suspended general taxes from 1837 through 1840, New York from 1827 through 1842. Between 1831 and 1843, Massachusetts followed a similar path, to which it returned occasionally even in later years.[25]

State Power and Tax-Free Finance

The policy initiatives of 1817 proved only the beginning of state promotion of economic growth and social welfare. Building on that foundation, citizens undertook ever more ambitious projects. Public policy in antebellum Georgia progressed from investing land revenue in bank stock, to using bank profits to finance a state railroad, and finally to siphoning railroad earnings into social programs.

State power and tax-free finance grew together. Priorities, like the sources and amounts of nontax revenue, varied from time to time and from one person or party to another, but the linkage persisted. James Camak, president of the

Central Bank, looked forward to the time when the bank's earnings could finance all the ordinary expenses of government, and in fact the bank permitted the state to suspend poll and property taxes for a time. Camak's successor, Tomlinson Fort, directed the bank as it helped finance the state-owned Western and Atlantic Railroad.[26]

State power and nontax revenue also shrank together. Social spending, in particular, depended on the availability of nontax funds. Hard times, cost overruns, and diminished revenues meant that it was the 1850s before the Western and Atlantic began to prove profitable. When at last it did, public policy shifted in emphasis. The state concentrated its resources less on economic programs and more on common schools and other social programs.[27]

More often than not between the War of 1812 and the Civil War, annual taxes produced less state revenue than did sales of public land or investments in banking or the state railroad. Infusions of nontax revenue permitted Georgia to spend more, tax less, or even do both at once. Federal payments for Georgia's western lands, of course, constituted the most striking example of nontax revenue, but such revenues recurred through the antebellum years. Georgia's share of the federal treasury surplus in the 1830s helped the state, despite the suspension of taxes, to embark on major new efforts in economic growth and social welfare. Similarly, in the 1850s, earnings from the Western and Atlantic Railroad enabled the state to double its annual spending without an increase in taxes.

By 1860 the Western and Atlantic produced more state revenue than did all taxes combined. With revenue from the railroad, the state quintupled its public school appropriations, expanded the mental institution, and began investing in another great railroad, the Atlantic and Gulf. Before addressing the fiscal changes of the 1850s, however, we must survey the operations of public authority in antebellum Georgia. Some of these—no less important, though less often noted—were not fiscal in nature and did not grow or shrink with treasury receipts.

3 THE ACCOMMODATION OF THE PUBLIC

LUTHER ROLL, prosperous owner of a carriage shop in Augusta, suffered considerable damage to his property and his business in the 1850s when a railroad and two roads were constructed adjacent to his shop. When he sought $24,000 in damages from the city council for authorizing such destructive improvements, the Georgia Supreme Court ruled that the city was not liable for consequential damages: "If the Legislature think proper to award damages under such circumstances, let them say so; otherwise, the parties who suffer are without remedy—the Legislature considering that the interests of individuals must give way to the accommodation of the public." [1]

Lingering images to the contrary, antebellum Americans did not worship at the altar of laissez-faire. Although they opposed government-sponsored actions that damaged them, they sought to use public authority for a broad range of their own purposes. Public authority gave them leverage, far beyond their individual means, to effect improvements in society and the economy. Those improvements entailed costs as well as benefits, but men possessing both political power and economic resources had reason to feel confident that they could control the process and deflect the costs. If Luther Roll's interests could "give way to the accommodation of the public," however, perhaps anyone's could.

Unlimited Power

In the early republic, Americans employed public authority as an increasingly powerful tool to enhance their liberty and their property. By facilitating migration and the acquisition of land, governments promoted the individual independence that landownership brought. Governments contributed further to citizens' economic well-being by sponsoring transportation improvements that increased the value of that land. As early as 1806, the federal government promoted the National Road west from Maryland. New York embarked in 1817 on construction of the Erie Canal, which became a model of public enterprise in large-scale transportation facilities. Georgia began a similar venture in 1836, when the legislature authorized construction of a state-owned railroad, the Western and Atlantic. [2]

Like Janus, America's increasingly active public authorities showed two faces—one beneficent, one harsh—as various costs accompanied the increasing benefits. The extractive and regulatory functions of government marched arm-in-arm with the disbursive and promotional roles. A New York lawyer, arguing in 1831, reflected a significant current of public thought in antebellum America: "The states, representing the whole people, are sovereign and possess unlimited power except where they are restricted by either the federal or their own constitution." As Georgia's supreme court had occasion to lecture plaintiffs in an 1857 decision, the Fifth Amendment's prohibition against taking private property for public use "without just compensation" restricted the powers of the federal government only; no such restriction limited the powers of a state.[3]

Public Investment

Georgians enlisted public authority to supply their transportation needs. Particularly in the case of internal improvements that required large sums of capital as well as engineering expertise, they turned to all levels of government for leadership and funds. Of approximately $25.2 million in state, local, and private capital invested in Georgia's railroads between 1833 and 1860, only half came from private sources.[4]

Of the $12.75 million in private investment, railroad companies themselves contributed $4.6 million. They applied earnings to further construction and made stock subscriptions in other railroads. The Central of Georgia Railroad, a line extending from Savannah to Macon, offers an example. Seeking to expand its tributary area, the Central helped finance the extension of the Southwestern Railroad from Macon into the newly developing black-belt region of Southwest Georgia.[5]

Other private sources contributed $3.2 million in cash and $5.0 million through stock subscriptions in labor, land, or materials.[6] Much of private investment came from planters (most of them from along the route of a railroad). A planter might contract with a railroad—to be paid perhaps one-fourth in cash and three-fourths in stock—to supply a gang of slaves and land or timber. In this manner, planters obtained railroad stock and subsequent dividends without investing any cash. In turn the railroad company obtained a graded roadway, while reserving much of its cash for the purchase of rails and rolling stock.

Playing a leading role, the federal government contributed in several major ways. In 1826, for example, Congress appropriated $50,000 to build a lighthouse near Savannah and remove obstructions from the river there. In 1855 Congress provided $161,000 to remove further obstructions from the channel. Nor were these appropriations for rivers and harbors the only federal contributions. After the General Survey Act of 1824, the national government financed and conducted surveys for railroad construction. To three Georgia railways it remitted tariff duties on iron amounting to $204,985. Still larger were its outright payments to Georgia—compensation for the cession of Mississippi Territory and distribution of the federal treasury surplus—which the state then allocated to transportation.[7]

Aside from direct grants, the state materially assisted corporations by delegating its power of eminent domain—the right to seize private property for public use. As a result, not all private investment was voluntary. The charter of the Central of Georgia Railroad, for example, required the company to compensate landholders for losses incurred when the railroad either built on their land or appropriated building materials such as stone and timber. The charter established a procedure whereby a landholder, if dissatisfied with the Central's offer, could appeal it. Appraisers would calculate the "loss or damage" he suffered, and they would also calculate any "benefit and advantage" he might derive from the railroad. The compensation awarded would be the difference between the two figures. The act provided that: 1) the work would, regardless of appeal, be "continued without interruption"; and 2) in no case might the appraisers' arithmetic result in a landholder's becoming "indebted to the corporation."[8]

The state invested somewhat more ($6.7 million) in railroads than did the counties and cities combined ($5.8 million). The counties were insignificant in financing railroads until the late 1850s, and even then they subscribed to a combined total of only about $400,000 in railroad stock. The cities of Savannah, Augusta, Macon, Columbus, and even little Thomasville each invested larger amounts. Georgia's largest city, Savannah, invested about $2.7 million —as much as all other cities in Georgia combined. It supplied seed capital for the Central of Georgia Railroad and then, when that line could stand independently, transferred its investment in the 1850s to the Atlantic and Gulf.[9]

Railroads and cities played vital roles in each other's finances. Beginning in 1835, for example, Savannah contracted a substantial debt in order to invest in the stock of the Central. In 1842 the Central suspended the payment of dividends on its stock. Because it was receiving no dividends, the city had to resort to taxes to service its debt; it increased all its tax rates that year by half. In 1847 the legislature authorized the mayor and council of Columbus to collect extra city taxes, including a tax of 2 percent on the value of all real estate. Columbus needed the additional revenue to pay interest on bonds it had issued to pay a stock subscription in the Muscogee Railroad Company. Taxpayers actually received stock in the railroad proportional to the extra city taxes they paid.[10]

Savannah and Columbus illustrate the fiscal role of local government in promoting antebellum Georgia's railroads. On the basis of their taxable wealth, the cities sold municipal bonds in distant money markets and thus were able to import capital to finance railroads. By their powers of taxation, they absorbed local private capital and made it available for the promotion of railroads. Georgia's state government behaved in much the same way.

In the last quarter-century before the Civil War, financing the Western and Atlantic Railroad took the bulk of state spending. Because railroads required enormous sums of capital, private citizens could finance only part of their construction. Cities, seeking to expand their commercial spheres of influence and avoid being outflanked by merchants in rival towns, led the way in Georgia in providing public assistance to railroads. Widening markets and competition between cities and across state lines also induced the state government to take an active role. Moreover, the Western and Atlantic, like the state's Central Bank, was expected to serve a significant fiscal function by eventually providing the treasury with nontax revenue from earnings. As Georgians exploited the new technology, however, the results were neither solely nor immediately those that the promoters promised.

A Railroad System

Georgia's three largest railroads comprised an integrated system, no portion of which was intended to stand alone. In the 1830s, Augusta and Savannah each began to push a railroad west through Georgia's cotton belt. The Georgia Railroad, which connected Augusta with adjacent black-belt counties, could support itself as it pushed westward. As the Charleston and Hamburg Railroad threatened to carry the Augusta trade away from Savannah to Charleston, Savannah pushed its own line, the Central of Georgia Railroad, toward the towns and cotton belt of Central Georgia. Internal cotton-belt towns like Macon and Athens vigorously supported such efforts, for they sought external commercial connections. The lines from Augusta and Savannah pushed west toward what would become Atlanta, where they intersected in 1845 at "Terminus." Meanwhile the state was building the Western and Atlantic Railroad north from that point toward the Tennessee River (see map 2).[11]

Just as there was little purpose in extending the Georgia and Central lines to Terminus unless they met the Western and Atlantic there, so the state railroad would have proved unprofitable had it merely ended in a corn field near the Chattahoochee River. The central developmental purpose of the Western and Atlantic Railroad was to tap, not the area it passed through, but rather the grain-producing Tennessee and Mississippi river valleys beyond, and thereby to funnel more trade through both the Central and Georgia railroads to Augusta and Savannah. The sale of state bonds, largely in the New York and European money markets, enabled Georgia to build a section of the rail system that other capital could not have financed so soon. The state thereby encouraged the Georgia and Central of Georgia railroads in two ways. Private and municipal resources concentrated on the more profitable eastern routes, and the Western and Atlantic's promise of expanded trade opportunities encouraged the extension of those eastern lines to Atlanta.

When construction of the Western and Atlantic took longer and cost more than anticipated, the railroad's management had to remind Georgians of the benefits that awaited completion according to plan. As the line's chief engineer, Charles F. M. Garnett, contended, the state must push the line all the way to Chattanooga "in fulfillment of her implied pledge to the whole people," for "no adequate return can be expected from the work until it reaches the Tennessee River." Requesting $375,000 in 1847, he argued that completion would take eight years if, denied such funds, the line were financed solely through the meager earnings of the finished portion. During that period, the $3.3 million investment would remain largely unproductive, and the state would be deprived of the railroad's potential benefits.[12]

In addition to requiring further appropriations, through the 1840s the Western and Atlantic had to deflect threats of being sold or leased to private enterprise, if only an acceptable bidder would step forward. (None could; none did.) The chief engineer urged retention of state control and emphasized the possibility that the state would soon receive a direct return on its investment: "It is now evident that a work, which was looked upon by many as valuable chiefly for its indirect effect on the agricultural, commercial and political prosperity of the State, is destined to become a great source of revenue." In case the promises of trade to merchants and relief to taxpayers proved inadequate attractions, Garnett's search for additional legislative support led him to describe a symbiosis of railroad and region and to promise Northwest Georgia prosperity in return for votes: "No part of the State should be more sensible of . . . [the need for the railroad] than the Cherokee region, with its great mineral wealth and its vast powers of production heretofore valueless for want of a market."[13]

Even as the state railroad's management struggled both to avert a lease to private parties and to gain further appropriations, other rail lines sought state assistance. In 1850, for example, the Southwestern Railroad, running southwest from Macon, confidently requested that the state invest $500,000 in its stock. Spokesmen for the railroad received the legislature's refusal with apparent disbelief: "The inhabitants of Southwestern Georgia have patiently borne their share of taxation for the benefit of their more fortunate brethren of the Northwest." The cotton-belt area of Southwest Georgia, they argued, held the key to "the commercial wealth and prosperity of the State" and required only transportation of "the valuable product of her soil to market to develop her immense resources." Now, they complained, the region was "doomed to neglect and disappointment, or to a reliance on her own means." Two years later, the Southwestern again protested "the injustice of the Legislature, in withholding all aid from this enterprise at its last two sessions, while millions are lavished on another section of the State." [14]

The Southwestern Railroad was a victim both of unfortunate timing and of Georgia's antebellum policy of assisting only trunk line railroads that, traversing great expanses of sparsely populated territory, could not become profitable until completed. With the state treasury already fully extended, many legislators were unwilling to add to the burden until the Western and Atlantic began to produce at least a portion of the state revenue absorbed by the public debt. Even then, the state held off efforts to aid a variety of railroads and chose instead to assist only the Atlantic and Gulf Railroad, a trunk line that ran through South Georgia from the coast. As it happened, the denial of state assistance caused little interruption of the Southwestern's progress. Capital from private and municipal sources—the city of Savannah, the Central of Georgia Railroad, and planters in Southwest Georgia—proved sufficient to finance construction.

State railroad policy produced discontent even in the Cherokee region. The management of the Western and Atlantic, in a remarkable statement on "The Policy of the Road" in 1855, attempted to justify its denial of preferential rates to North Georgia farmers. "There are those," the statement noted, "who . . . contend that the policy of the road should be so shaped as to foster the local at the expense of the 'through' business." The report continued:

They insist that the Road was constructed for the purpose of promoting the agricultural and industrial interests of one peculiarly favored section of the state, and protest against the efforts of its managers to make it a source of direct pecuniary profit; they are willing to tax the whole population of Georgia for its construction, but when the time comes to reimburse its owners for their outlay, . . . they seek to . . . deprive the Road of all profit from its way business.

Those who would commit the Road to such a policy have certainly lost sight of the enlarged controlling views of its projectors, who undertook its construction because they were convinced it would offer the best and easiest connection between the Ocean and the West. [T]hey saw New York, Pennsylvania, Maryland and Virginia all reaching out to attract through their Territories and to their seaports the trade of the Great West. [B]elieving that Georgia possessed natural advantages for the competition, they put forth her energies also to secure a perpetual participation in the prize. Will not any policy which keeps out of view this great original intention of the *Western* and *Atlantic* Railroad, as indicated by its very name, prove fatal to its best interests and defeat the prominent purposes for which it was designed. [15]

The Western and Atlantic's lengthy official response to its North Georgia critics frankly told citizens of that region to consider themselves lucky to be near a railroad that the state had built for purposes other than to make isolated subsistence farmers into prosperous commercial farmers. Tying Georgia together was an important consideration, to be sure. But the Western and Atlantic was out to make money—in this case profits for its investors, the taxpayers of Georgia—as surely as any privately owned and privately managed transportation enterprise. Its primary purpose was to compete successfully for the trade of the West. In Georgia, as throughout the United States, struggles pitted way rates against through rates and shippers against railroads. Later in the century, Populists railed against corporations and threatened them with government takeovers. Clearly, however, public rather than private ownership promised no sure difference in the origins or outcomes of such controversies.[16]

The Rewards

Georgia's rail system in general, and the Western and Atlantic in particular, produced many benefits, whatever the claims of critics. The state railroad provided access to markets for North Georgia grains and other products. It increased passenger and freight traffic on the Georgia Railroad and on the Central of Georgia, thereby increasing the trade of merchants in Augusta and Savannah. Moreover, the construction, operation, and maintenance of the Western and Atlantic and other railroads created many jobs. Finally, one of the stronger appeals for railroad construction was an anticipated increase in the value of otherwise less productive property. A Whig newspaper in Macon made this argument to promote a railroad spur to Thomaston. Not only would the branch "make Thomaston at once a successful rival to Griffin in the cotton business," but "the expense of its construction would be more than paid by the increased value given to real estate in the county."[17]

Yet the aggregate rewards from railroads comprised only part of the story in antebellum Georgia, because the diffusion of those rewards proved so uneven. Many of the jobs went to slaves and not, as in the North, to free labor. Wages —or shares of railroad stock—went to planter-capitalists, not to workers.[18] For example, a large portion of the operating expenses of the state railroad each year consisted in the "hire of negroes, provisions, clothing, etc., for same." The Central of Georgia Railroad described its work force of 500 as mostly black and spoke of contracts with planters as a fine way of "diffusing the benefits" of construction. Planters along the route of a railroad, whether it was under construction or in operation, had the choice of planting cotton or of hiring out their slaves to the company. As one newspaper noted of the Southwestern Railroad: "Contractors can earn from $15 to $20 per hand per month, payable one-half cash, and one-half stock. That is decidedly better business than planting cotton, and ought to satisfy any reasonable man."[19]

Rising real estate values, too, primarily benefited the wealthy—the planters and merchants.[20]

Many yeomen, too, benefited from the state railroad. As parts of North Georgia became accessible to markets, slaves and planters appeared in greater numbers. In Cass and Gordon counties, for example, the numbers of slaves grew by about 20 percent between 1857 and 1860. Production figures of corn, wheat, and even cotton, together with data concerning way freights south on the Western and Atlantic, indicate increasing exports from formerly insular farms.[21] In some cases, the planter who crowded out the farmer was only the same man grown more wealthy. Even in North Georgia, though, landholdings were concentrated in a few hands; even there, the preponderance of benefits from railroad development went to people in the upper portion of the white social structure.

4 TAX
UPON THE
TIME AND
LABOR
OF OUR
CITIZENS

COMMITTED AS Georgians were to the expansion of state power, they refused to predicate it on greatly increased taxes. Like antebellum Americans elsewhere, they attempted to avoid direct taxation whenever possible. Expenditures varied according to the total amount of revenue available —tax and nontax—and in more years than not between the War of 1812 and the Civil War, taxes paid for less than half the state's spending. Nonetheless, revenue had to match expenditures. Whether derived from land sales, investments, or the federal government, nontax revenue fluctuated, so taxation carried varying proportions of the burden of public expenditures. Even when the state borrowed, it had to find the money to service its debt.

State Taxes

The Georgia tax system at midcentury rested directly on the tax act of 1804. That act taxed some property not at all, some according to value, and most at various specific rates regardless of precise value. The tax structures of 1804 and the 1840s were basically identical, except that the state uniformly increased all rates by one-fourth in 1842.[1]

As might be expected in an agricultural society with roughly half of its wealth invested in slaves, the bulk of state tax revenue came from levies on rural property. In 1849, 49 percent of state property taxes came from the levy on slaves (the characteristic form of planter wealth) and another 20 percent came from agricultural land (owned by yeomen as well as planters). Other important sources included town real estate (14 percent), pleasure carriages (6 percent), and merchants' stock-in-trade (6 percent).[2] At that time, Georgia did not tax crops, livestock, furniture, or such occupational necessities as wagons and tools. Nor did it tax income or sales, the staples of its revenue system today. And the only tax on corporations was a tax on bank stock.[3]

The dominant role of the tax on slaves must be stressed, given that most historians have overlooked it. According to one, a tax on real estate constituted "practically the sole source of [state] revenue" in Georgia.[4] Because the state derived the bulk of its revenue before the Civil War from returns on various investments, land sales, or the federal government—and not from any particular object of taxation—such emphasis on real estate taxes is doubly misleading.

Although the tax on slaves produced the bulk of tax revenue, the rate on slaves was lighter than that on some other forms of property. At midcentury Georgia taxed merchandise and town real estate at $3.91 per $1,000 value. Because each slave under age sixty was taxed $0.39 regardless of market value, at an average value of $500 the effective rate on slaves amounted to only one-fifth as much, or $0.78 per $1,000.[5]

The tax on rural real estate applied only to acreage and not to such improvements as houses, outbuildings, and fencing. The 1804 tax act had roughly determined the value of land according to location and quality—using such classifications as "pine lands" or "oak and hickory lands"—and taxed each class at a fixed rate per acre. Because specific taxes remained constant, land, like slaves, bore progressively lighter effective tax rates as values increased. On the average, rural real estate carried a tax of $0.55 per $1,000 in 1850, less than any other rate.[6]

Aside from property taxes, the state levied poll and professional taxes. In the 1840s, the state taxed each white man aged twenty-one to sixty at $0.39; in 1850 the figure was cut to $0.25. By contrast, free blacks between the ages of twenty-one and sixty—men and women alike—were required to pay $5.00 each. In their case, the tax was clearly regulatory and punitive in intent, not a revenue measure. An identical $5.00 tax was exacted from each doctor, lawyer, dentist, factor, or broker.[7] In contrast to the tax on free blacks, the professional tax constituted a traditional means of indirectly taxing income in cases where property ownership failed as a proxy for income.

Plantation and urban counties paid the highest per capita state taxes.[8] While a propertyless white family was subject only to the poll tax on men, a planter paid $0.39 for each of his slaves, including women and children. Though Georgia's planters headed only one white family in fifteen, the taxes on their slaves alone accounted for one-fourth of the state's revenue from property taxes. As for urban counties, not only did they contain much wealth, but much of it—real estate and merchandise—was subject to discriminatory taxes. Moreover, professionals and free blacks alike, taxed $5.00 each, tended to live in large towns. In 1850 Richmond County, a Middle Georgia county containing the city of Augusta, paid a per capita tax of $1.20, the highest in the state. North Georgia's Gilmer County, 98 percent white and almost entirely rural, paid the lowest at $0.09 per person.[9]

A different pattern emerges if one relates each county's total state taxes to the value of its residents' property. Much of planters' property was taxed lightly or not at all; the cotton counties of Central and Southwest Georgia paid the lowest state taxes relative to the value of their property. In the predominantly white counties, by contrast, where poll taxes comprised a larger portion of tax liabilities and people also owned less untaxed property, the burden tended to be heaviest.[10]

Wealthy Georgians paid much more in state taxes than poor people paid. Therefore, urban and plantation counties supplied higher per capita tax revenue. Relative to their property, however, large slaveholders typically paid less than did the poor. Cotton planters paid the least.[11]

Throughout the Old South, in fact, planters paid the bulk of the taxes. Like Georgia, neighboring states derived the bulk of their tax revenue from the wealthy. Like Georgia, they did so not because they taxed planters' property at discriminatory rates, but because planters held most of the wealth.[12]

County and Town

Georgians' other tax liabilities resembled their state taxes. In the aggregate at midcentury, county taxes and town taxes roughly equaled those the state collected.[13] State law required that county taxes each year be levied as a percentage of that year's state poll and property taxes. Because the same officials handled both sets of taxes, the administration as well as the apportionment of county taxes depended on the state system.[14]

Within each county, the burden of county taxes, regardless of the rate, was distributed in precisely the same way as state taxes. Jefferson County's rate in 1850, at 100 percent of the state tax, meant that each Jefferson resident paid identical state and county taxes. Without special legislation, counties at midcentury were limited to ceilings of 50 percent of the annual state tax for general county purposes, 12.5 percent to support paupers, and an unspecified tax for schools.[15]

Unlike state taxes, county taxes fluctuated from year to year and varied widely from county to county. Despite almost annual changes, however, county rates bore a loose relationship to the burden of state taxes. Wealthier counties could obtain any given amount of revenue with lower rates than a county with a smaller tax base on which to draw; so could counties paying high state taxes relative to their property valuation. Though five counties levied rates at 125 percent of the state tax, most counties at midcentury imposed taxes at closer to 50 percent. Burke County taxpayers were fairly typical; they paid county taxes of 37.5 percent for general purposes, 12.5 percent for schools, and another 12.5 percent for paupers.[16]

In many cases town taxes, like county rates, were levied simply as a percentage of the state tax. When the legislature incorporated the towns of Griffin and Albany, for example, it authorized them to levy general taxes not to exceed one-half of the state tax. Cassville was permitted to impose poll taxes of $0.50 on whites and $2.00 on free blacks, while the ceiling on property taxes was one-third the state rate.[17]

Service Obligations

Just as taxes were not the sole source of public funds, cash payments from the public treasury were by no means the only method by which governments in Georgia conducted their business. Some county officials, for example, received fees from individuals for services rendered rather than salaries from the county treasury. Although taxes comprised a large portion of the public obligations to which residents might be subject, authorities demanded labor payments as well as cash. Various service obligations—militia, patrol, and road duty—went uncompensated; they enabled authorities to conduct important functions without levying cash taxes or disbursing cash payments. Jury duty, however, was compensated (typically at $1.00 per day) in jury scrip, which was acceptable in payment of county taxes.[18]

Militia and patrol duty shared security objectives—one against Indians, the other against blacks. The militia served as a citizens' military force in time of intermittent warfare on the frontier. As late as 1837, Hancock County was still fining citizens $3.00 "for failure to perform at Muster," but the militia's objective largely disappeared with Indian removal in the late 1830s.[19] During the frontier stage, even road duty could be viewed as a security requirement. In his charge to the Liberty County grand jury in 1794, Judge George Walton observed of a road to St. Mary's that, "although it does not immediately affect this County, [it] ultimately does, as [the County's] future security against the savages will increase in proportion to the extension of settlements beyond it."[20]

White Georgians depended on the patrol to monitor and control slaves' behavior, especially at night and off the plantation. According to the law, in each district of a county a company consisting of a maximum ten men went on patrol at least one day or night every two weeks. All white male inhabitants aged sixteen to sixty made up a pool from which each district's patrol members were periodically appointed, although those selected had the option of employing substitutes.[21]

Nineteenth-century Georgians lived in a world without chain saws or bulldozers, but they still needed adequate transportation facilities. Because neither rivers nor railways could satisfy all local transportation requirements, roads had to be constructed and maintained. To that end, counties demanded "statute labor," or road duty, an American incarnation of the *corvée* system. Road duty in antebellum Georgia threaded through the web of men's obligations, private as well as public. When John S. Dobbins hired Eaton Brown in 1857 as an overseer, their contract stipulated that Brown would have pay deducted for all lost time "except general election day and the time he may be lawfully required to work on the public road."[22]

Some black-belt counties exempted white men from road duty. Glynn County, only 14 percent white in 1850, exempted white men but subjected all male blacks aged sixteen to forty-five (whether slave or free) to road duty for six days a year. Slaveowners in Glynn could exempt their workers by paying $0.50 per work day into a fund for erecting and repairing bridges. Putnam County used publicly owned slaves on the roads. After a time, however, "the county hands having been sold," the grand jury of the Putnam superior court announced that "an additional tax upon the time and labor of our citizens is indispensable."[23]

Most white men found road duty more onerous than patrol duty. In most counties, all men aged sixteen to forty-five—whites and slaves alike—were subject to road duty for as many as five days at a time and, as a rule, a maximum of fifteen days per year. Road duty was not always enforced. No doubt less than the maximum time was usually demanded, though in emergencies it could be exceeded. Nevertheless the road commissioners might call for 5 percent of many residents' annual labor.[24]

Equality of Burdens

These various public obligations are best evaluated in terms of antebellum Georgians' own criteria. What, for example, did Governor George W. Towns have in mind in 1847 when he called for "the adoption of a system of Finance equal in its operations upon all"?[25] Public attitudes went on display when state taxes generated controversy in the 1840s. Whig planters favored heavier poll taxes than did Democratic farmers, yet these two groups agreed on fundamentals.

Georgians perceived governments' primary responsibility to citizens to be the protection of life, liberty, and property. Living in a slave society, white Georgians valued their own liberty at a premium, and they shared "a personal interest entirely independent of property" in the privileges and responsibilities of white men in the young republic. Relating liberty to such central aspects of public life as schooling and suffrage, Georgians justified a poll tax—a tax that "all are equally bound to contribute; the poor, no less than the rich"—on grounds that citizens shared an equal interest in the availability of elementary education and in the exercise of political rights.[26]

All voters paid a poll tax, but they believed that most tax revenue should come from a property tax. Government in Georgia protected property as well as liberty. As property among white Georgians was "most unequally distributed," the benefits received from public authority's protection of it could not be construed as equal. Wealth created both the obligation and the ability to pay; property should "bear its equal and just proportion of the burden of Government." Thus, as advocates of a uniform tax rate argued, "equality of burdens" required a tax directly proportional to wealth. "Governments were instituted to protect persons and property; and property requires more protection than persons," contended one antebellum Georgia citizen who concluded that "every one should pay in proportion to the amount he has at stake." [27] The accepted measure of fiscal fairness among white Georgians, then, combined a small poll tax on all voters with a more or less uniform rate according to value applied to most property.

The burden of road duty and patrol duty, together with poll taxes, suggests that poor whites incurred public obligations disproportionate to their wealth and to the benefits they received. Planters and merchants had a much greater interest than poor whites in adequate roads. The road tax, though proportional to rural wealth in that a planter's obligation depended on the number of his slave men, was nonetheless uniform in that commutation cost the same for a poor white as for a wealthy one.

Small as the poll tax on whites might appear, it represented a heavy burden on people with little or no cash income or property. The poll tax in the 1840s was identical to the tax on a slave worth hundreds of dollars. In every county, some poor whites failed to pay the poll tax and, having no property for the tax collector or sheriff to seize, were listed simply as "insolvents." They thereby lost the right to vote in that year's elections.[28] It may not have entirely escaped planters' notice that the poll tax could either deny poor whites the franchise or make their votes available to the party or politician who paid the tax. In the web of class relationships in the Old South, one can readily envision a landless white—dependent on a planter patron for credit and employment—who held up a portion of his side of the relationship through a combination of road and patrol duty and political support.

Neither the poll tax, the general property tax, nor any service obligation was progressive; none required that the wealthy pay a greater percentage of their wealth or income into the public treasury. Yet the general property tax, the major source of tax revenue at each level of government in Georgia, was roughly proportional to wealth. Georgia's general property tax required a planter with twenty slaves to pay a state tax on his slaves ten times greater than a farmer with only two. The wealthy—planters in the country and merchants in the city alike—paid the same state property taxes on each domestic servant they owned. On the other hand, merchants paid state taxes roughly five times as high on much of their wealth as planters typically paid on agricultural property of equivalent value.

In sum, planters paid a large portion of the taxes in antebellum Georgia, because they were much more numerous than merchants and possessed much more wealth than did yeomen farmers or poor whites. Yet, measured in terms of their wealth—the nineteenth-century measure of benefits received and ability to pay—planters paid less than did either merchants or poor whites.

Discrimination against urban property, together with the service obligations and the poll tax, suggests who ruled Georgia. Planters had to tax their own wealth because the other classes possessed so much less. Georgia's state and county governments comprised, in effect, corporations in which the wealthy owned most of the stock and tended to make the decisions. On those corporations' boards of directors, merchants and planters sometimes divided, and rice planters sometimes opposed cotton planters.

From a survey of the tax side of the public ledger, one might easily conclude that taxes may have impeded the growth of towns in antebellum Georgia. Through the entire first half of the nineteenth century, the state taxed town lots and stock-in-trade—aside from slaves the main forms of tangible urban property—at rates much higher than it taxed rural land and slaves, the dominant forms of rural property.[29] County taxes replicated such tax rate differentials. Without a doubt, that discrimination dampened growth in some of the smaller towns. No matter what the state might do to promote urban growth, certainly the cost to towns would have been lighter had all taxable property been subject to identical rates.

Yet while the state taxed town property at much higher rates than it taxed rural property, it also fostered urban growth through the promotion of internal improvements. The spending side of the public ledger served to reduce the imbalance. Legislators from the major urban centers consistently supported higher state taxes than rural legislators would allow. They also worked to eliminate rate discrimination, but their primary objective was to promote the railroad system's growth. Besides Savannah's direct investment in railroads, a city newspaper declared, its property owners "paid towards the State Road . . . in [state] taxes as much as the whole of Southwestern Georgia and the Cherokee country together."[30] Urban merchants sought railroads, invested in them in return for tax receipts and/or shares of stock, and benefited from the increased trade that rail lines brought to their cities.

In the 1850s, two changes promoted the growth of Savannah and other Georgia cities. A change to uniform rates on all taxable property eliminated the discrimination against town lots and merchandise. More important, the Western and Atlantic Railroad finally reached Chattanooga and brought the long-promised trade to Georgia's cities. During this decade, Georgia's two greatest corporations—the privately managed Central of Georgia Railroad and the state-owned Western and Atlantic—unleashed a population growth in Savannah from 15,312 to 22,292 and in Atlanta, a child of the railroads, from 2,572 to 9,554.[31]

Benefits

The private and public spheres in social spending remained undifferentiated in antebellum Georgia. At the institutions for the insane and the deaf, the state paid for the support of penurious patients or students. But those who could were required to pay their own way.

Elementary schooling operated in a similar fashion. To the extent that private and public schools were separate institutions, "academies" were schools supported through tuition or endowment, and "poor schools" served students who could not afford tuition. By apportioning the poor-school fund among the counties, which in turn distributed it to the teachers—often pro rata, when the money ran short—the state paid tuition for the children of poor families. In some cases, the children of paying, part-paying, and nonpaying parents attended school together, and the teacher simply billed the county rather than the parents for tuition payments.

Because the state's contribution did not stretch very far, many students at poor schools paid tuition to supplement the public payments. To obtain public funds in addition to the small amount from the state, many counties levied school taxes. In 1849, for example, Chattooga County supported eleven common schools, each with one teacher and an average of thirty students, by means of $140 from a county tax (amounting to 10 percent of the state tax) in addition to $130 from the state fund.[32]

Among county governments' major responsibilities were the construction and maintenance of roads and bridges, courthouses and jails. Construction of public buildings was a major, though only occasional, expense to counties. For such extraordinary expenditures, the legislature generally passed special acts authorizing higher county taxes until the building was paid for. The 1847 general assembly, for example, enabled each of four counties to collect an extra tax, not to exceed the state tax, for the purpose of building a new courthouse.[33] The counties' inferior courts determined what roads were public roads and at what locations to maintain bridges. Road duty by adult males kept roads more or less in repair, even with unskilled and irresponsible labor, but bridges required skilled labor and continuing responsibility. Therefore, by levying taxes and paying cash, counties contracted to have bridges built and kept in repair.

Most counties spent a portion of their budgets for the support of a very few white people, particularly aged widows too poor to provide for themselves. Paulding County, for example, levied a pauper tax of 12.5 percent of the state tax in 1849 in addition to a tax of 50 percent for other county purposes. One-fifth of Paulding's budget that year supported the very poor. The county helped to keep paupers alive and, when that effort failed, it paid for their burial. Perhaps as many as one-third of Georgia's counties—including those containing the cities of Savannah, Augusta, Macon, Athens, and Columbus—

established poorhouses, termed "asylums for the invalid poor," before the Civil War. Most counties engaged in outdoor, or non-institutional, relief; they provided cash or supplies to needy individuals. According to the census of 1850, a total of 1,036 paupers in Georgia had received the sum of $27,820 during the previous year; Paulding County's 1849 tax produced $151.50 to support six of them.[34] The pauper tax shifted a bit of the wealth of the propertied to Georgia's poorest citizens.

Conclusion

How did Georgia's major social groups fare, then, at the hands of public authority? In general the well-off fared well and had cause for satisfaction. On the other hand, there were men like Luther Roll, who felt sufficiently aggrieved to bring suit against the city of Augusta and carry his case all the way to Georgia's supreme court. In general, Georgia's yeomen and poor whites fared reasonably well, too. Yet some poor whites subsidized the wealthy in their communities; they paid poll tax and road duty, but derived no benefits from the poor-school fund or the pauper tax.

Planters and merchants benefited far more than did other social groups from public financing of railroads, much the largest item of state expenditure in late antebellum Georgia. Minor items of public expenditure, however, allocated considerable portions of state and county budgets to the families of poor whites and yeomen farmers. Because Georgia's welfare institutions—the school for the deaf and the mental institution—charged those who could afford their own support, such state spending proved most helpful to families that could not afford to pay. State spending on elementary education came from nontax sources; neither planters nor yeomen paid state taxes for schools, which nonetheless benefited the families of poor children. County spending on schools, by contrast, came entirely from taxes and represented a shift downward in the social structure from those who paid to those who benefited. By no means, however, did all counties levy school taxes.

Clearest in its redistributive role was the county tax for pauper support. Supplying roughly 20 percent of an average county's budget, the pauper tax clearly shifted a portion of the wealth of the propertied to the penurious. Through counties' spending on schooling and paupers, poor whites as a group, like the wealthy, received benefits that outweighed their tax costs.

5 CREATING A NEW REVENUE SYSTEM

I N 1838 the state tax system began to emerge as a significant issue in Georgia politics. That system rested squarely on the tax act of 1804 and had changed little in format since the eighteenth century, but Georgians had been paying state taxes at reduced rates for many years. Beginning in 1824, the state had slashed its tax rates in half. Further reductions had followed, and since 1835 Georgians had paid no poll or property taxes to their state government (see fig. 1).[1]

By the late 1830s, however, a return to taxation seemed unavoidable. Tax-free sources of revenue had dried up. Moreover, Georgia had embarked on the Western and Atlantic Railroad, a giant experiment in public enterprise that drained capital from the state's Central Bank and resulted in a growing public debt.[2] That debt threatened to grow much larger before the railroad could be completed and could begin to pay its own way and perhaps even contribute profits to the state treasury. While nontax revenues vanished, expenditures rose for debt service.

Thus it was that in 1839 Georgia's newspapers went to press with some words about state finances. The *Augusta Constitutionalist* acknowledged widespread aversion to direct taxes and anticipated "strong opposition" to any substantial tax hike. Nevertheless, it contended, Georgians must "make up their minds to pay sufficient taxes for the support of the government, until such taxes can be dispensed with, without injury to the public interest." Taxpayers might find solace, however, in the prospect that they "would have to submit to additional burdens only a few years; after which all taxes may be removed, when the people will enjoy the fruits of their sacrifice." Meantime, as the *Milledgeville Federal Union* expressed the hope, the "deranged state of our finances" might "give rise to a revision of our system, which has always been one of the worst in the world."[3]

Toward Tax Revision

The quest for a tax-free system of state finance was a central feature of antebellum America, yet tax revision, in particular the adoption of ad valorem taxation, was widespread as well. State after state, in North and South alike, finding that reliance on taxes could not be avoided, adopted an ad valorem tax. Replacing the previous systems of specific taxes, which had featured various rates for each carriage, slave, or 100 acres, ad valorem systems taxed according to value. Everywhere tax reform resonated to rhetoric of "equality of burdens."[4] In the South, the debate was energized by prospective gains and losses in tax revenue derived from slaves, the characteristic property of planters, and from land, that of yeomen. Not only did small farmers oppose planters, but in Georgia urban interests clashed with rural, as spokesmen for the cities sought to remove from the tax laws serious inequities against urban property. Moreover, Georgia had to confront the problem of securing an income that did not rise and fall like a barometer measuring the condition of the economy.

Tax policy remained a central issue in Georgia politics through the 1840s and into the 1850s. Of several efforts to renew, and then increase, state tax revenue, three were successful. Despite continuing efforts, however, not until 1852 did Georgia adopt an ad valorem system. All groups but the city people had something to lose by breaking free of the moorings of the basic 1804 act. Throughout the 1840s, efforts to adjust the tax burden would reach an impasse, broken only when someone suggested simply retaining the old tax system, which legislators then rushed to adopt as the most workable compromise.

Even when no changes were enacted, voting patterns on fiscal issues displayed significant splits among legislators by region, political party, and social group. Democratic representatives, pursuing a general bent toward only limited governmental activity—particularly if that activity required taxes—tended to vote against higher rates. Whigs, on the contrary, though they shared a statewide regard for low taxes, were committed to a program of internal improvements; when safeguarding the state's credit seemed to compel it, they were willing to vote higher taxes.

Party and constituency operated in tandem. Most Whig legislators came from commercially oriented districts, whether black belt or urban, planter or merchant.[5] Democrats came mostly from predominantly white, subsistence-farming districts. Urban Whigs favored appropriating larger amounts for internal improvements, and they sought to remove the tax inequities against town property and to shift more of the tax burden to rural property. Democrats, too, tried to translate their interests into tax policy. Whenever it became clear that more tax revenue must be collected, they attempted to obtain it from slaves, railroad stocks, income, and other property of the wealthy. Democrats favored and Whigs opposed cuts in poll taxes.

Whigs and Democrats differed little in political power in the 1840s; they supported contrasting fiscal policies. Democrats representing North Georgia's yeomen farmers sought lower taxes than did Whig legislators from planter and urban counties. By contrast, urban legislators promoted the higher taxes that would pay the public debt, protect the state's credit, and promote rail-road construction.[6] Though greatly outnumbered by rural delegates, they also worked consistently, and finally with success, to reduce their constituents' shares of the tax burden. Regardless of party affiliation, all legislators were forced to fit their priorities to new circumstances that constrained their choices, and their decisions in the 1840s necessarily differed from those of the previous decade.

Though Georgians handed over ever-larger sums to tax collectors, they could console themselves with the prospect that an increase in nontax revenue would again ease their burdens. Georgia, like other states, found itself com-pelled to resume taxation, but, more than other states, it pushed doggedly on in its quest for a revenue system that would not depend primarily on taxes. Considerable success, though belated and only temporary, finally rewarded its efforts. By the late 1850s, the policy environment in Georgia differed as much from that of the 1840s as the latter had from the mid-1830s. Investments in the Western and Atlantic Railroad began to generate the long-awaited revenue, and tax rates turned down again. Georgia's degree of success in its quest for nontax revenue—not the quest itself—proved unique among American states.

The Commissioners' Report

When the 1838 legislature convened, Georgia had collected no poll or general property taxes since 1834. During that time, the state had levied taxes at half the rates established by the basic 1804 act, but it had relinquished all proceeds to the counties in which they were collected. The only state tax revenue came from the separately administered tax on bank stock, and even it was levied at half-rates.

The 1838 session continued the suspension of taxes for another year, but it left open the likelihood of an early return to general taxation. It directed the governor to appoint three commissioners, who should suggest "a system of finance for the State, which calling into action all her resources . . . [would] sustain, as in the present age they should be sustained, the great interests of Public Education and Internal Improvement." According to the legislature, the state had in the past "relied chiefly, for the means of meeting the ordinary expenses of Government, of Public Education, and of the public works under-taken by her, on the revenue drawn from her public lands, and her Bank Stock." As these traditional resources dwindled and public works expenditures continued, Georgia needed a new system of public finance.[7]

The commissioners' report outlined the arguments employed by supporters of fiscal change during the next dozen years. Though railroad construction might best be financed through deficit spending, the sale of state bonds re-quired that the treasury have a dependable source of income. Potential bondholders demanded assurance that the state could redeem its promise to pay semiannual interest. Because nontax revenue could no longer be depended on, property taxation now had to provide the bulk of state treasury revenue. However, renewed interest in taxation made Georgians, already burdened by a depression, increasingly aware of major inequities in the state's tax laws. Citizens had a right, the commissioners declared, that taxation "be fair and equal, in proportion to the value of property, so that no one class of individuals, and no one species of property, may be unequally or unduly assessed." Pending consideration and adoption of a broad new scheme of taxation, the commissioners urged a return to the old tax system.[8]

Observing that "equity requires that each citizen should contribute equally according to his property," the commissioners suggested that an ad valorem general property tax replace the miscellaneous specific taxes. Property should be subject to a uniform tax according to its value; the commissioners proposed a rate of $1.25 per $1,000 valuation.[9] Such a tax would reduce rates on merchandise and town real estate by three-fifths.[10] At the same time, it would raise slightly the average tax on slaves and would redistribute the burden on slave property according to value. In most cases, it would substantially raise taxes on rural real estate, for not only was land the most lightly taxed form of property, but rural buildings and other improvements had previously escaped all taxation. Money and solvent debts would become liable to taxation, as would cattle, horses, and mules above a number to be specified by the legislature.

The ad valorem tax, together with the poll tax, bank dividends, and the tax on bank stock, would satisfy Georgia's revenue requirements. Moreover, as state-aided railroads reached completion, the treasury would no longer suffer a drain on its resources. Rather, it would once again profit from public investments, this time as profits from investments in railroads "convert[ed] expenditure into income."[11] Renewed nontax revenue would permit Georgia to resume its quest for a tax-free fiscal system.

Resuming Taxation

The legislature responded to the need for revenue and the report on finances by resuming state taxation. Though the legislative wrangling at each session seemed interminable, the results are readily summarized. The 1839 session maintained the previous year's half-rates but voted to divide the proceeds equally with the counties. The 1840 session revived the basic 1804 tax act; by returning to full rates and no longer sharing the proceeds with the counties, the legislature expected to quadruple state tax receipts. Newspaper response to the latest rate hike varied according to party connection. Though the *Milledgeville Southern Recorder*, Whig voice of the state capital, deemed the act "inadequate," the Democratic *Milledgeville Federal Union* castigated the higher taxes as "useless and oppressive" and the Whig legislators responsible for levying them as men who "would not if they could" relieve the people.[12] Two years later, the legislature raised all tax rates by another fourth (see fig. 1).[13]

With three increases in four years, the tax burden had become much greater, but it remained distributed in the traditional manner. Despite continued efforts to terminate the old tax system, it persisted through the end of the decade. So did the new rates, as no further tax increases were enacted through the remainder of the 1840s.

Governor George W. Towns, though a Democrat, championed a change to the ad valorem system. To force the issue, in 1847 he vetoed the legislature's tired handiwork, but the general assembly had its way. "Viewing as an evil of no ordinary magnitude the present system of specific taxation," Governor Towns tried again at the next session, in 1849–50, to effect its repeal. He condemned the "patchwork" character of the tax system as a "capricious, ill-digested, and miserable expedient," whose "gross inequality" was "universally acknowledged." Not only would an ad valorem system equalize rates among all property currently taxed, it would also tax all other property and thereby "make the available or productive property of the State bear its equal and just proportion of the burden of Government." Seeking to banish the specter of angered constituents, he admonished legislators: "Place your tax act upon the plain principles of equality of burdens and equality of benefits, and the people will sustain you."[14]

Governor Towns stressed the problem of predictability as well as "equality of burdens." He warned that "a degree of uncertainty and doubt must ever attend the present mode of raising revenue." Fluctuations in the value of property, together with "the elasticity of conscience," constantly threatened either a surplus of revenue, which was "grossly unjust to the People," or "the still more perilous hazard" of insufficient funds. Such "uncertainty in providing adequate means to meet all demands" upon the state treasury depreciated the state's credit, and capitalists who sought investments in state securities would look elsewhere than Georgia.[15]

Towns tied the need for a reliable income directly to the new role in state finance that the Western and Atlantic would soon play. Until such time as the railroad began to produce profits for the treasury, he noted, the state would have to continue depending almost entirely on taxes. Even then, those profits could not be reliably estimated; but as they increased, they would lend strength to the rationale behind a switch to ad valorem. If nontax sources produced $250,000, for example, then "it would be necessary only to raise by taxation a sum sufficient to supply the deficiency" that remained.[16] As nontax revenue grew, taxes could decline.

Meanwhile, the cities were becoming increasingly restive under their inequitable share of the tax burden. For a decade they had sought relief in an ad valorem system. As the Bibb County (Macon) superior court grand jury remonstrated in 1849: "Believing as we do, that the present tax law is unequal and oppressive in its operations, we would most respectfully request our Senator and Representatives . . . to use their best endeavors to have an ad valorem tax bill passed." The *Milledgeville Southern Recorder* was more outspoken in its effort to attract the legislature's attention: "the present system is . . . partial, unequal, unfair, oppressive, and tyrannical." Seeking to exploit the Democrats' own rhetoric, that Whig paper went on: "The Democratic party having the control of the Legislature, will have on this occasion an admirable opportunity of illustrating their much boasted principles of equality to all, and special privileges to none. There never was a more unequal system than the present one of taxation." [17]

During the 1849–50 session, a bill to perpetuate the traditional tax system directly confronted a bill to establish an ad valorem tax system. The ad valorem bill proposed to tax all property at a uniform rate, except that it would continue to exempt all farm tools as well as household furniture worth up to $500 per taxpayer. Even though the amount of revenue was not an issue, rural Democrats were notably unreceptive to the ad valorem bill, particularly because it would exempt no property other than tools and furniture. Conversely, because the existing system discriminated against urban property, legislators from Chatham, Richmond, Muscogee, Bibb, Clarke, and Baldwin counties voted consistently against the traditional bill and for the change to ad valorem. [18]

Other tax issues separated Whigs from Democrats, urban legislators from rural ones, and representatives of black-belt counties from those with small-farmer constituencies. In 1850 black-belt Whigs defeated a proposed elimination of the poll tax on white men, for example, but they could not prevent its being lowered from $0.39 to $0.25. Before midcentury, railroads in Georgia, newly completed, were exempt from taxation. Democrats, using their small majority to replace the lost revenue from poll taxes with a corporation tax, forced the enactment of a tax of 0.5 percent on the net annual income of the Georgia and Central Railroads. Urban representatives supported retention of the poll tax, opposed even reducing it, and voted against taxing railroads. [19]

This Radical Measure of Reform

The 1851–52 legislature faced calls for a more predictable and more equitable tax system. "If we are not *highly* taxed," one citizen asserted, "we are more *unequally* taxed than any people in the civilized world." [20] Legislators also faced the need for increased tax revenue. As the Finance Committee put the case for using more state funds to hasten completion of the

Western and Atlantic Railroad: "The State has millions of dead capital invested in that great enterprise which must remain comparatively unproductive, until its final completion. Its *rapid* progress is therefore closely connected with the successful management of our finances, as its completion will be an important aid to the Treasury, and thus for a relief to every tax payer in the State."[21]

By far the most important spending bill in 1851–52 called for funds for the construction and equipment of the Western and Atlantic Railroad. Considered a final appropriation, the bill would complete the state railroad and establish it as a revenue-producing public utility. Subsequent costs of repairs or equipment would come from current revenue, and surplus revenue would be deposited in the general funds of the state treasury. In both the house and the senate, the bill met sufficient opposition, particularly from white counties remote from the railroad, to necessitate cutting the appropriation from $750,000 to $525,000; even then, the senate passed the bill by a single vote.[22]

Upcountry and cities clashed bitterly that session over an ad valorem bill. That measure proposed no change in the poll tax but called for $375,000, an increase of one-third, in total poll and property tax revenue. As urban Georgia began to anticipate the fruits of its long struggle for a new tax system, North Georgia legislators, in a final effort to block passage of the ad valorem bill, offered as a substitute the tax act of the previous biennium. Black-belt representatives, led by urban members, overcame the opposition and rejected the old tax system. The ad valorem bill would now pass, the *Augusta Daily Chronicle and Sentinel* guessed, "although it is exceedingly unpalatable to the up-country people." The Milledgeville correspondent to the *Savannah Republican*, less sympathetic to North Georgia, observed testily that "I cannot understand, how gentlemen representing counties that do not pay into the State Treasury, taxes enough to meet the actual expenses of their representatives in the legislature, can complain about inequality, injustice, oppression and the like. Their notions carried out, amount to this—that they are oppressed exactly in proportion as they are taxed at all."[23]

When the house finally approved the measure, legislators voted according to the wealth of their districts. Representatives from the poorer counties, where white subsistence farmers predominated and almost the only property was land, voted 14–30 against a bill that threatened both to raise state taxes and to shift proportionately more of the total tax burden to their constituents' property. Representatives from planter counties, on the other hand, voted 36–11 for the bill, because it offered greater state revenue without significantly changing the taxes on slaves. Urban legislators, supplying the narrow margin of victory, voted unanimously for the bill, because it promised both increased tax revenue and substantial tax relief on merchandise and town lots.[24]

Having passed the house, the measure faced the senate. The senate cut the furniture exemption from $500 to $300; more important, it slashed the standard exemption from $500 back to $200, though it defeated an effort to remove even that. When a substitute bill narrowly failed, the future of the ad valorem bill appeared precarious, and a Savannah paper warned that "some Senators express strong doubts of its success." Nevertheless the bill passed 22–18 and, after house approval of the amendments, went to the new governor.[25]

Governor Howell Cobb expressed his "cordial concurrence with the judgment of the Legislature, in this radical measure of reform in our Tax laws," but he declared the bill inadequate. New appropriations, together with payments on the public debt, would amount to the stipulated figure, $375,000. He doubted, however, that the designated property tax of $0.83 per $1,000 would produce the required amount. On the grounds that the general assembly had prohibited collection of more than $375,000, Cobb characterized the rate ceiling as redundant and proposed a supplementary bill to remove it.[26]

Both houses of the legislature rejected, reconsidered, and finally passed the requested supplementary bill. In the house, representatives from predominantly white counties voted 19–31 against a measure that would allow still higher rates. Legislators from the black belt had more interest in producing the revenue they had voted to appropriate and supported the bill 40–19. Urban representatives supported it unanimously.[27] The measure opened the way to a further tax increase, to $1.00 per $1,000 valuation for 1852 and 1853.[28]

Having led the struggle for ad valorem taxation, Georgia's cities supplied the margin of victory in both houses of the 1852 legislature. Throughout the previous decade, legislators from Georgia's few cities had usually voted as a bloc on tax issues, but with scant success when rural legislators voted as an opposing bloc. When rural Georgia divided, however, the towns could sometimes swing a legislative majority to their side. Representatives from counties containing towns with at least 750 residents voted for the 1852 tax bill 16–0.[29]

Winners and Losers

The *Savannah Republican* greeted the enactment of the "great reform" with superlatives of approval. It flung one last barb at the tax system now happily replaced: "The citizen should contribute to the support of the Government according to his *means* and not according to the *kind* or description of those means."[30]

Enactment of the 1852 tax act simultaneously increased property taxes and redistributed the larger tax burden. Regardless of changes in the distribution of the burden, aggregate property taxes increased by nearly one-half. With the advent of a uniform rate, some types of property bore tax burdens substantially different from their shares under the previous system. There were local differences, of course, but most rural real estate bore much higher taxes, while urban real estate obtained significant tax relief (see table 1).

TABLE I. *The State Property Tax Burden before and after Adoption of Ad Valorem, Selected Counties*

County	Type of Property	1851	1852	Change
Baldwin	Slaves	43.0%	43.6%	1%
	Rural land	14.4	18.7	30
	Town lots	18.2	4.9	−73
	Miscellaneous	24.5	32.8	34
Hancock	Slaves	64.1%	53.2%	−17%
	Rural land	12.6	22.6	79
	Town lots	8.0	2.3	−72
	Miscellaneous	15.4	22.0	43
Walton	Slaves	55.2%	43.6%	−21%
	Rural land	19.1	26.2	37
	Town lots	6.3	1.4	−78
	Miscellaneous	19.4	28.8	48

Source: Tax lists for Baldwin, Hancock, and Walton counties (mfm, GDAH).
Notes: Miscellaneous objects of taxation included carriages, livestock, merchandise, and money loaned at interest.
Baldwin County (includes Milledgeville)—43% white
Hancock County—36% white
Walton County—64% white

The changes least affected both the wealthy and the poor in rural Georgia. The average tax on slaves—the largest portion of planters' wealth and also the largest source of tax revenue—amounted to little more in 1852 than it had in 1851. Therefore, though state taxes on many planters increased by about one-third, planters' share of the total tax burden changed little. Slave property, in fact—though it continued to be the largest source of tax revenue—bore a reduced share of the property tax burden.[31] At the base of the white social structure, the propertyless were unaffected. And the standard exemption of $200 worth of property provided limited tax relief to the poorest of the property holders, or, if they owned small amounts of previously untaxed property, left them virtually unaffected.

The two social groups most influenced by enactment of ad valorem taxation were yeomen farmers and holders of urban property. Because of the 75 percent cut in state taxes on town lots and merchandise, the tax changes proved most advantageous to owners of urban property. The votes of urban legislators made possible the enactment of a uniform ad valorem tax system, and the new system in turn facilitated the growth of towns in the 1850s. By 1857 urban

TABLE 2. *The State Property Tax Burden, 1849 and 1857*

Type of property	1849		1857	
	($)	(%)	($)	(%)
Slaves	130,311	49.1	179,152	42.3
Rural land	52,559	19.8	109,346	25.8
Town lots	35,937	13.5	24,030	5.7
Merchandise	16,601	6.3	9,466	2.2
Money at interest	9,949	3.8	—	—
Money, solvent debts	—	—	67,116	15.9
Pleasure carriages	15,201	5.7	—	—
Stallions	2,986	1.1	—	—
Furniture ($300+)	—	—	1,616	0.4
All other	1,889	0.7	32,418	7.7
Total	265,433	100.0	423,142	100.0

Sources: "Taxes in Georgia," *MSR*, 18 Nov. 1851; CG (1857), 23–25.
Notes: Dollar amounts are rounded to the nearest dollar. See chapter 5, note 32.

landowners and merchants reported more than triple the 1849 value of town lots and more than double the 1849 value of stock-in-trade. Yet state taxes on these two important types of urban property in 1857 totaled less than two-thirds the amount of a decade earlier (see table 2).[32] Many yeomen, by contrast, making up the savings that urban dwellers now enjoyed, paid double or even triple the taxes in 1852 that they had paid previously.[33]

As before the advent of ad valorem taxation, the wealthy counties continued to generate most of the state's tax revenue. The lowest per capita state tax in 1860 ($0.11), as in 1850 ($0.09), was collected in North Georgia's Gilmer County, 97 percent white. Southwest Georgia's Dougherty County, only 27 percent white, paid the highest per capita taxes in 1860 ($0.82). The burden in urban Richmond County dropped from $1.20 in 1850 (the highest in the state that year) to $0.73 a decade later. If urban counties produced higher-than-average per capita state taxes, it was because they contained substantial wealth and not because, as under the pre-1852 tax system, urban property suffered discriminatory rates. If, on the other hand, the predominantly white counties still paid very low per capita taxes, it was because their people were poor, not because their property was lightly taxed.[34]

Fulfilling the Promise

The Western and Atlantic began to fulfill its fiscal promise in the 1850s. After receiving its last antebellum appropriation in 1852, the railroad was able to finance all subsequent maintenance and improvements in the 1850s out of operating revenue. In addition, it began in 1854 to make payments to the state treasury. The $50,000 payment in 1854 grew to more than $100,000 in 1857 and 1858. Under the energetic governorship of Joseph E. Brown, a North Georgia Democrat, the railroad netted the state over $400,000 in each of the years 1859 and 1860. In fact, state revenue from the Western and Atlantic Railroad in 1860 ($450,000) exceeded that from all taxes combined ($430,614).[35]

Ever since Georgia reluctantly revived state taxation in the late 1830s, citizens had anticipated tax relief whenever the Western and Atlantic finally began to produce profits.[36] Indeed, renewed efforts to cut taxes materialized even before the Western and Atlantic began to show a profit. In the 1853–54 session, for example, a North Georgia Democrat submitted a bill to revive the 1850 act—a proposal designed not only to wipe out the tax increase of the previous session but also to revert to the system of specific rates. In general, legislators from urban and planter counties supported retention of the ad valorem system, while representatives from farmer counties sought a return to the 1850 act. Eventually the legislature reenacted the ad valorem system and raised from $375,000 to $400,000 the sum to be produced.[37]

Georgia's new tax system received little challenge after 1854, and even the $400,000 figure remained unchanged until the secession crisis in late 1860. Beginning in 1854, the more important changes in Georgia's revenue system involved the long-awaited combination of rising railroad profits and declining tax rates. Wealth in Georgia doubled during the prosperous 1850s, from $335 million in 1850 to $672 million ten years later. That increase enabled the state to reduce the property tax rate and still obtain a constant tax revenue. Between 1852 and 1860, the rate declined by more than one-third: $1.00 per $1,000 valuation in 1852 and 1853; $0.90 for the next three years; $0.80 in 1857; $0.75 in 1858; and $0.65 in 1859 and 1860.[38]

The decline in state rates after 1853 left intact the *redistribution* of the tax burden that the ad valorem system effected. It also left unchanged the increases in general property tax *revenue* introduced in 1852 and 1854. The decline wiped out the 1852 boost of average property *rates*, however, and it reduced the average rate in 1860 to little more than it had been in 1841 or even 1805.

Fiscal responsibility and administrative ability were two keys to the success of Georgia's revenue system in the 1850s. The state did not prematurely relinquish tax revenue, as it had in the 1830s when it lived off its capital and destroyed the Central Bank. Moreover, unusual administrative ability characterized the men in charge of the revenue system, especially Governor Joseph E. Brown, elected to the first of his four terms in 1857.[39] As the editor of the *Sumpter Republican* wrote in 1859, "Governor Brown's stern official integrity has endeared him to the people, and his successful management of the State Road has made him thousands of friends. As long as he pays in $35,000 per month [to the state treasury] from that source, it were vain to oppose his election." In 1865, when the Civil War had ended—and with it Brown's tenure as governor—Sidney Andrews, a visiting northern journalist, discovered that Brown had "more personal popularity than any other man in Georgia. Everybody seems to concur in the assertion that he managed her finances better than any other Governor they ever had."[40]

6 WHAT DISPOSITION SHALL BE MADE OF THE MONEY?

AFTER FOCUSING on economic growth in the early nineteenth century, the states increasingly turned their attention to social spending. In this area, too, the experience of the Empire State of the South resembled that of the Empire State of the North. In 1836 and 1837, New York and Georgia made initial appropriations to establish state insane asylums; in 1842 and 1843, both institutions opened. New York took a major step toward securing tuition-free elementary schooling when it levied a state property tax to raise $800,000 for common schools in 1851.[1] Relying on profits from the Western and Atlantic Railroad, Georgia quintupled its spending on elementary schools from $30,000 in 1859 to $150,000 the following year.

In the late 1850s, Georgia came within reach of its longtime financial utopia. In 1854 the Western and Atlantic began to contribute to the state treasury; by 1860 the railroad's profits led to a doubling of state revenue with no increase in taxes. At the same time, rising per capita wealth permitted cuts in tax rates without reductions in tax revenue. As in the 1810s and the 1830s, the surplus income allowed Georgians to choose between further tax cuts or increased spending.

The 1855–56 general assembly was the first to face the flow of new revenues. Legislators at that and subsequent sessions had to decide, as Governor Joseph E. Brown put the question in 1858, "What disposition shall be made of the money?"[2] Rather than cut tax revenue, Georgians chose to spend more, and they began to divert their investments from transportation to social welfare. By the late 1850s, as in the 1830s, the state cut its tax rates and yet expanded its support of education and welfare institutions, as nontax revenue facilitated a much more active state government.

Until the advent of railroad revenue in the 1855–56 session, legislative behavior patterns on spending issues in the 1850s echoed those on taxes in the previous decade. Representatives from black-belt and urban counties had tended to seek greater tax revenue in the 1840s. In the following decade they resisted efforts to reduce tax revenue and, often despite opposition by North Georgia legislators, managed to increase state spending. But as nontax revenue took pressure off taxpayers, those differences in willingness to spend grew less pronounced.

The Western and Atlantic Railroad was central to state finance in the 1850s. The state continued to spend the larger portion of its budget to pay principal and interest on debt incurred in financing the railroad. Increasingly, moreover, the state derived the larger portion of its revenue from the railroad's profits. In fact, earnings of the Western and Atlantic provided the entire difference between aggregate state revenue in the half-decade 1851–55 ($3.0 million) and the total for 1856–60 ($4.1 million).[3]

Thus, the Western and Atlantic provided funds for new spending programs at the same time that it belatedly justified Georgia's policy of using state financial backing to promote railroads. In 1855–56 the legislature committed the state to a major role in financing a new trunk line, the Atlantic and Gulf. That railroad would connect Savannah and Brunswick, Georgia's Atlantic ports, with Pensacola, the Apalachicola River, and the Gulf of Mexico. The state did not, however, directly tap the Western and Atlantic's profits to finance the Atlantic and Gulf. It sold bonds to cover most of its investment, as it had done to pay an 1851–52 appropriation to the Western and Atlantic. Spending on the Atlantic and Gulf reached $500,000 by 1860, compared with the $750,000 spent earlier in the decade on the Western and Atlantic.[4]

Western and Atlantic earnings enabled Georgia to make higher payments on the public debt without resorting to higher taxes. Until the late 1850s, the debt continued to increase as a result of bond issues to finance the two railroads. At the end of the decade, however, able to make still larger payments, the state began to prepay portions of the debt and thereby save interest.[5]

The administrative costs of government, always a major item in the state budget, rose during the 1850s. When Georgia reverted to its pre-1843 legislative system, each county again sent at least one senator and one representative to the legislature, which again met annually rather than biennially. Together with an increase in the number of counties from 93 in 1849 to 132 in 1860, these changes more than doubled the average annual costs of the general assembly, from $104,301 for the 1849–50 biennial session to $115,850 for the 1859 session. As a retrenchment measure, the state had slashed its legislative costs in the early 1840s, and the availability of nontax revenue facilitated the changes of the 1850s.[6]

Debt service, together with the administrative costs of government, took only half the $1.1 million in profits of the Western and Atlantic Railroad. Meanwhile, tax receipts remained constant after the tax hike of 1852. Thus a half-million dollars became available in the late 1850s to support new or expanded social welfare programs for white Georgians: elementary schooling; higher education; and institutions for the blind, the deaf, and the insane. From 1851–55 to 1856–60, state spending on elementary schooling increased by

$157,681, higher education by $65,500, and the three welfare institutions by $215,045—a total of $438,226 (see fig. 2).

An Aristocracy of Color and of Conduct: Elementary Education

The history of state aid to elementary education in Georgia before the Civil War was one of general neglect interrupted by occasional bursts of generosity. Georgians made frequent allusions to the social, economic, and political benefits of having an educated citizenry. As long as state spending on education hinged on revenue from taxes, however, they were willing to leave schooling at the bottom of the approved list of state expenditure priorities. Georgia's first state constitution (1777) provided that "schools shall be erected in each county, and supported at the general expense of the State." Yet three-quarters of a century later, one-fifth of Georgia's white adults were illiterate. In the early 1850s, the state contributed less than 4 percent of its budget to education.[7]

Shortly after the War of 1812, Georgia created a fund for education. As was characteristic of Georgia's support of schools before the Civil War, the education fund derived from nontax revenue, in this case payments from the United States for Georgia's western territories. Between 1817 and 1821, the state set aside $250,000 for county academies and another $250,000 for free schools ("poor schools"). Both funds were invested in bank stock, with the dividends distributed each year. At that time, the poor-school fund was available to students whose parents paid no more than $0.50 in annual state taxes in addition to the poll tax. Such children could benefit from the poor school fund for no longer than three years, and, if they had already learned reading, writing, and arithmetic, they were not eligible at all.[8] The fund did not establish schools. Rather, poor students attended whatever schools were available, and their teachers billed the poor school fund, just as they charged the parents of paying pupils.

When the U.S. government distributed its revenue surplus in the late 1830s, Georgia attempted to establish a single system of publicly supported common schools. Critics had charged that, though less than one-tenth of Georgia's school-age children were educated in academies, those academies received fully half the state's contribution to education. Seeking to discontinue this inequitable dual system of schools, a legislative committee declared that state funds should be applied "to the elementary education of *the whole community*."[9] The 1837 legislature consolidated the academy and poor school funds, which, together with one-third of Georgia's share of the federal revenue distribution, became a fund for common schools.

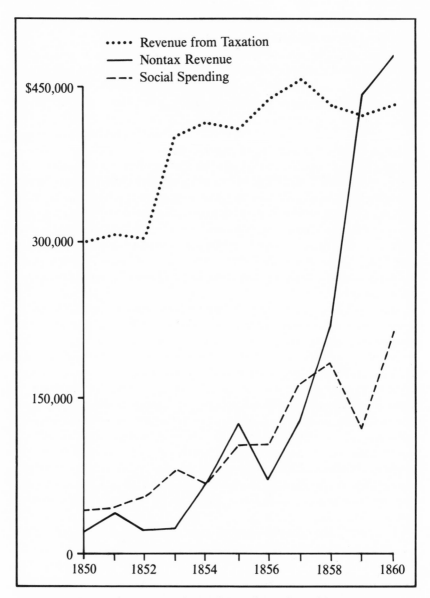

FIGURE 2. *Nontax Revenue and Social Spending, 1850–1860*

Sources: Annual Reports of the Comptroller General.
Notes: The three lines display (respectively): 1) revenue from taxation; 2) income from investments in bank stock and the Western and Atlantic Railroad; and 3) spending on social welfare (that is, on elementary schooling, higher education, and the institutions for the deaf, blind, or insane).

The new fund was to be apportioned to counties according to the number of white children aged five to fifteen, though older youths under twenty-one could also attend. For a county to receive any state aid, its schools had to operate for at least three months of the year in each militia district. State money was supplied to pay teachers, or to purchase books and stationery for the children of indigent parents, not to erect schools. An 1838 act authorized each county to supplement its share of the state fund by levying a school tax of up to half the state tax.[10]

Before the new system could be established, a long depression set in. Cotton prices sank from seventeen cents a pound in 1836 to seven cents four years later. Much of the school fund was diverted to the Central Bank and the Western and Atlantic Railroad. The 1840 legislature repealed the 1837 act and converted what little remained of the common-school fund into another permanent poor-school fund, approximately the size of the 1817 fund. The 1821 academy fund had vanished, as had the schools' share of the federal treasury distribution. All that remained of the 1837 and 1838 acts establishing a publicly supported school system was the authority for counties to levy an extra tax for schools.[11]

Though Georgia citizens opposed the use of state property taxes to support schools, they increasingly felt that the state should take a larger role in providing education. As the legislature's Committee on Public Education reported in 1847: "Those now growing up in ignorance will in a few years hold the power to decide the most important questions. . . . All will agree that education cannot be made general without the aid and direction of the State. It is an enterprise too great to be accomplished by individual efforts." Even avid supporters of schools were anxious not to appear radical; a Savannah editorial, protesting that "we mean no agrarianism," recommended a poll tax of $1.00 per voter for education instead of a higher property tax. Two years later Joseph E. Brown, state senator and future pro-education governor, introduced a resolution to upgrade the education system, "provided, it can be done without cost to the State"; the legislature passed it.[12]

Two major reports on elementary education in Georgia, both published in 1851, opened a campaign, eventually successful, to adopt a statewide system of common schools. Viewing the state as fettered by lack of funds, however, the writers of both reports fell short of recommending changes that could be immediately implemented. As directed by the general assembly, three commissioners appointed by the governor reported to the legislature on Georgia's educational needs. "What the State actually needs," they observed, "is one thing; what can be done legitimately and effectually to meet those necessities, is another thing. A regular, uniform, perfect system, adapting itself with equal facility to the densely and sparsely settled counties, to our towns and cities, and to remote and obscure neighborhoods, would require an outlay of money vastly exceeding the resources of the State, in view of other imperative demands." [13]

The other report resulted from a state educational convention and urged "wholly abolishing the odious distinction of 'poor scholars.'" State law at mid-century defined poor children as those "unable, from the poverty of themselves or parents, to procure a plain English education without public assistance." Arguing for a state-supported system of common schools, the report denigrated the poor-school system as constituting a "gross injustice to the poorer counties, where there is the greatest number of poor children, and the least ability to bear taxation." [14]

Seeking to dismantle obstacles to legislative action, the report directed one argument to the poor and another to the wealthy, a two-pronged appeal typical in antebellum America. To citizens whose children would not "have money and family influence to raise them to distinction among their fellows," the report declared: "The plan of educating all the children of proper age at common schools, free of charge, must commend itself to all classes; but most especially to those who cannot spare both the labor of their children and the money necessary for their instruction." At the same time, the report offered comfort to any aristocrats inclined to view state action with suspicion: "Far be it from us, to excite the envy or the prejudice of the poor against the rich; we would rather extinguish these hateful feelings, for by educating the poor—by increasing their intelligence, and improving their condition, we would remove all temptation to the exercise of such feelings." [15]

Both reports looked to the Western and Atlantic Railroad to finance a more ambitious school system. Because much of the common school fund of 1837 had been spent on that railroad, the privately sponsored report asserted, "the cause of education has a lien upon the State Road." Similarly, the commissioners' report anticipated that, with the Western and Atlantic's net income, the state could someday pay the full costs of a system of universal education for whites, a system that would require neither state nor even local property taxes to finance it. [16]

As the Western and Atlantic's profits rose in the late 1850s, the financial impediment to establishing a school system gradually disappeared. But what would result from a trade-off between lower taxes and increased aid to education?

In 1855, when Representative Joseph Pickett of North Georgia's Gilmer County submitted a bill to apportion profits of the Western and Atlantic Railroad to a common school system, even an upcountry newspaper greeted it with mixed feelings: "The Road has been constructed by taxation of the people of the State, and now that this great work has been completed, and yields an income, there can be no disposition made of the same that will benefit the large class of our citizens more than to set it aside as a school fund." [17] Such a fund could "enable us to carry out a common school system which will give all classes—both the rich and the poor, an opportunity to gain a good education." But too much of a good thing, the paper objected, would cost too much. "The bill, we believe, proposes to appropriate the whole of the proceeds to a school fund, when, in our opinion, a portion of the same should go to defray the expenses of the State, and thereby lessen the taxes." Though the paper earnestly hoped "that our law-makers will . . . not adjourn without providing for a general system of education," it advised that only one-third or one-half of the Western and Atlantic's profits be set aside for a permanent school fund, for "it would be but a short time before the present rapidly increasing income would raise an amount sufficient to support a general system of common schools." [18] In any case, Pickett's bill failed.

When North Georgia's Joseph E. Brown became governor in 1857, he turned his energies to education as well as to the state railroad. He scrapped his predecessor's plan for a state-assisted, matching-funds educational system tied to local taxation, which would have tended to allocate the most money where it was least needed. According to Brown's plan, the state would make its contribution from a portion of the net earnings of the Western and Atlantic, regardless of local finances—though each county could also impose a school tax. Abolish the system of poor schools, he thundered: "Let the teachers be paid by the State, and let every free white child in the State have an equal right to attend and receive instruction in the public schools. Let it be a Common School, not a Poor School System. Let the children of the richest and the poorest parents in the State, meet in the school-room on terms of perfect equality of right. Let there be no aristocracy there but an aristocracy of color and of conduct." [19]

Nontax revenue, gubernatorial leadership, and widespread support for educational reform all strengthened the likelihood that the legislature, for the first time in two decades, would act to increase state spending on elementary education. Various proponents, however, supported competing measures. Upcountry legislators wanted increased state funding, but they were unconvinced of the need for a state superintendent to direct the new system or a normal school to supply it with teachers, and a bill incorporating these elements lost in the senate. Nor were they satisfied with a proposal that would have increased public funding but left it targeted on the poor, and that measure lost in the house. They embraced a third measure, however, that created and funded a new common-school system but eliminated the normal school and the state superintendency.[20]

With only scattered opposition, the legislature enacted the essentials of Brown's proposal. The act provided that, in addition to the old poor school fund, $100,000 of the Western and Atlantic Railroad's net earnings be appropriated annually for education. The new common school fund would be distributed among the counties according to the total number of white school-aged children reported each year. As under the old system, county and town governments could supplement their shares of the state fund with local taxes.[21]

Without the income from the railroad, there would have been no education act of 1858. Unlike other social spending measures of the 1850s, the education act met more opposition from planter representatives than from North Georgia legislators. Compromising between tax cuts and more aid to schools, legislators from the poorer areas chose to use a portion of the Western and Atlantic's increased profits for elementary education. In the votes on passage (79–32 in the senate and 96–29 in the house), only two negative votes in each chamber came from yeomen counties.[22]

Thus, on the eve of the Civil War, the state quintupled its annual spending on elementary education, from $29,569 in 1859 to $149,565 in 1860.[23] At last, it seemed, Georgia had laid the financial foundation for a school system that, funded primarily by nontax revenue and not at all by state taxes, would provide a free basic education for all white children. In the 1850s, as in the 1810s and the 1830s, initiation of significant state spending on education required the advent of substantial nontax revenue. Continued spending depended on continued prosperity, which alone could assure that the school fund would not be diverted to more pressing needs.

To Multiply Doctors and Lawyers: Higher Education

Higher education at midcentury, like elementary schooling, had changed little from a generation earlier. College was for the wealthy; state aid, minimal. In the 1830s, Governor Wilson Lumpkin had decried the "most pernicious effect" of a "general impression which pervades the public mind, that the almost exclusive object of a college education is to multiply lawyers and doctors" and complained that "none but the wealthy [are] able to incur the expenses incident to classical education."[24]

As Lumpkin perceived, higher education in Georgia seemed designed to provide a leadership class of well-schooled professional men from elite families. Among students attending the University of Georgia in the late 1850s, those from the wealthier portions of the state—the cities and the black belt—outnumbered those from predominantly white counties four to one. The university required a knowledge of Greek and Latin for admission; after terminating the academy fund, however, the state provided no money for schooling beyond three years of a rudimentary English education. The spotty system of elementary education thus precluded attendance by large numbers, and even among those who managed to meet the entrance requirements, tuition and living expenses put the university well beyond the financial means of most.[25]

Though Georgia relied heavily on private resources to supply higher education, state funds, too, were tapped and, in the 1850s—particularly after the Western and Atlantic began to produce profits—appropriations increased. Such expenditures, though they exceeded 2 percent of the state budget in only one year during the decade, played a vital part in financing several schools. State spending on higher education may better be gauged by the importance of such assistance to those schools and their students than by its portion of the annual budget. Most beneficiaries, all of them white males, came from comfortable backgrounds in the black belt and the towns. To the extent that the state conditioned its aid on institutions' offering scholarships to the poor, however, state spending offered some chance for enterprising young men from families of little wealth to obtain training as engineers, doctors, soldiers, or teachers.

When the legislature chartered the University of Georgia in 1785, it exempted the university's property from taxation and excused its students and faculty from militia, patrol, and jury duty. An 1820 act exempted the real estate of academies from taxation. Finally, the legislature extended the privileges of the university to all other schools in Georgia—elementary, secondary, and higher. The state sometimes demanded specific conditions for these concessions. For example, when the legislature incorporated the Atlanta Female College, it exempted the school's property "from all taxation so long as the same is used for the purposes of education, and for this exemption one young lady from any part of Georgia, fit for a teacher and unable to pay her tuition, may at all times be educated in Atlanta Female College, free of tuition fee."[26]

The state endowed the University of Georgia with 40,000 acres of land at the time of its chartering in 1785. The endowment was subsequently converted into $100,000 worth of bank stock, on which the state, in 1821, guaranteed an annual income of $8,000; if dividends sank beneath that figure, the state made up the difference. On occasion the treasury had to make good that 1821 promise, as annual deficiencies between 1839 and 1849 totaled $33,500.[27]

In the 1830s, the university also received $6,000 a year from the Central Bank. In return the school was required to educate free of charge one young man per county, whom the inferior court justices were "to select from among the poor of their county." But the bank fell victim to the 1830s depression, and in 1841 the act requiring the additional payment was repealed. Not until after the Civil War did the University of Georgia again receive any state aid other than the annuity from bank stock, the "constitutional debt" of $8,000 per year. Income from the endowment provided one-third to one-half of the university's annual revenue in the 1840s and 1850s.[28]

Efforts were made in the 1850s to use railroad earnings to increase the university's endowment. After a bequest of $20,000 by Dr. William Terrell in 1854 to endow a professorship in agriculture, the university sought more funds. The Senate Committee on Education proposed a $10,000 appropriation to support "a liberal scheme for the diffusion amongst our people of scientific information upon the subject of farming, and the application of manures and fertilizing agents." The committee also requested $25,000 for a new library. Because "the Western & Atlantic Railroad . . . ought to be made to bear the expenses of our systems of public education," and the net earnings of the next year could cover the requested appropriation, there need be no addition to the tax burden. In an attempt to gain legislative support, the university offered to absorb the expenses of five students per congressional district each year in return for state assistance; but the effort failed.[29]

Unlike the state university, four medical schools obtained new state funds. In an early precedent, between 1833 and 1835, Augusta's Medical College of Georgia had received appropriations totaling $24,800. In 1852 the state provided $5,000 to the Southern Botanico Medical College at Macon, and it duplicated the grant in 1856 after fire destroyed the school. Between 1857 and 1860, it supplied $15,000 each to the Atlanta Medical College and the Savannah Medical College and $10,000 to the Medical College of Georgia.[30]

In return for state aid, the schools were to provide a free medical education to a certain number of students. The legislature directed that such benefits be distributed evenly throughout Georgia. The Medical College of Georgia, the largest, agreed to teach twenty students each year "who may be unable to pay their own expenses"—two from each of the eight congressional districts and four from the state at large. The other three medical colleges were to educate free of charge, each year, one student per congressional district.[31]

In the three decades between Nullification and secession, southern citizens looked with increasing favor on military education.[32] The Georgia Military Institute at Marietta was incorporated as a private school in 1851. The legislature provided an annual appropriation of $2,000, with which the school was to educate as many as ten "state cadets" each year, one from each congressional district and two from the state at large.[33] State cadets, who must be unable to pay their own expenses, were provided free tuition and board. In return they pledged to teach in a Georgia school for two years after graduation.[34]

As railroad revenue grew, and sectional tensions increased, the legislature provided the Georgia Military Institute with more funds. The school's board of visitors reported in 1855 that facilities were inadequate, which "state of things must necessarily continue so long as the Institution remains entirely dependent on the precarious profits of a private establishment." Desiring that the school approach the rank of West Point, and noting the great necessity for engineers and architects as well as military officers, the board labeled it an "indispensable necessity, that the State alone should control" the institute. The legislature appropriated $15,000 to discharge the school's debts, erect additional buildings, and purchase books and other necessities.[35]

At the 1857 session, the general assembly appropriated $14,000 to purchase and enlarge the institute. Describing the state's purpose in taking control of a private institution, the bill declared it the legislature's "duty" to secure a militia able at any time "to repress insurrections or repel invasions," or even "to perform the more arduous duties of soldiers in regular and steady war." To accomplish this purpose, the legislature declared "the wisest and best plan" to be "for the State to assume, direct and superintend the military education and training of men who are to form the future reliance of the country in times of such exigencies."[36]

Legislators displayed a clear-cut sectional pattern in votes on appropriations for higher education. Planter representatives tended more strongly than yeomen representatives to support such spending. They thereby reflected their constituents' greater wealth, more cosmopolitan views, and disproportionate benefits from Georgia's system of higher education. North Georgians, on the other hand, less impressed with the potential benefits of opening college doors to their young men, tended to work against state spending projects. Some farmer representatives, however, attracted by provisions that would enable needy students from their areas to attend the schools, provided the margin of support necessary to pass a number of spending bills.

With the advent of profits from the Western and Atlantic, state aid for higher education no longer required tax revenue, and farmers proved more willing to support aid bills. Though GMI was located in North Georgia, representatives from the upcountry voted 17-36 against assisting it at the 1851-52 session, and the bill passed by only one vote. In 1857, by contrast, farmer representatives supported the bill to purchase and enlarge the institute 39-21, and they split almost evenly (23-26 against) over assistance to the Savannah Medical College. Black-belt representatives, who remained more willing to spend public money, voted 53-18 to purchase the military school and 37-16 to help the Savannah school.[37]

As the Western and Atlantic's profits mushroomed in the late 1850s, Georgia's governors attempted to elicit more generous support for some of the state's larger colleges. By aiding those schools, they advised the legislature, the state could curtail Georgians' patronage of northern colleges and reverse the economic drain by attracting more out-of-state students. Even more important, by imposing obligations on the recipients of scholarship aid, the state could supply its elementary schools with enough competent teachers.

Governor Herschel V. Johnson, in his annual message to the legislature in 1857, noted: "We have several denominational colleges in Georgia, founded by private enterprise. Why should not the Legislature endow an Agricultural Professorship in one of each denomination, upon the condition that it will educate gratuitously, a specified number of young men, in each congressional district, to be selected as the Legislature may direct, who shall pledge themselves to teach a given number of years after their graduation, in the District from which they were selected? This will rapidly supply educated teachers, native born, and sympathizing with Southern interests and institutions." In addition,

Johnson suggested, the state should educate at the University of Georgia one young man from each county who would make a similar pledge.[38]

Governor Joseph E. Brown refined and expanded his predecessor's recommendations. Proposing that the state issue bonds on which the Western and Atlantic Railroad would pay the interest, Brown suggested in 1858 that the state provide $200,000 in bonds to the University of Georgia and $50,000 each to the three larger denominational male colleges and to the Georgia Military Institute. In return each of the five schools was to educate as a state student one young man for every $200 of annual interest that it derived from the bonds.[39] The proposed bond issue of $400,000, at 7 percent interest, would thus support the education of 140 young men every year. If the state adopted Brown's proposals, its larger colleges would receive substantial assistance; at least one young man from each county would annually be provided with all the expenses of a college education except clothing; and, finally, each student would be pledged to teach in the county from which he was chosen for as many years as he was provided a free education.

Such proposals by Georgia's governors suggested the potential value of the Western and Atlantic in financing higher education. Inaction by unreceptive legislatures, however, revealed a limited popular commitment to large-scale aid to the state's colleges. Aside from granting appropriations to buy and enlarge Georgia Military Institute and to assist several medical schools, the general assembly focused its attention on other matters.

As it happened, the state of Georgia used its financial resources for purposes other than either higher education or tax reductions in the next five years. During that time, school buildings became military hospitals, prospective students received their education in battle, and graduates found another occupation than teaching. The commissioners' proposal of 1851 was finally enacted following the Civil War, as a method of simultaneously supplying teachers, supporting colleges, and assisting disabled Confederate veterans.[40]

Nontax Revenue and Social Spending

Georgia's state treasury received large sums of nontax revenue each generation in the years between the War of 1812 and the Civil War. In the 1810s, the federal government conveyed funds for western lands that Georgia had relinquished and Indians had ceded. In the 1830s, the state's Central Bank, together with land sales, produced public revenue sufficient to negate the necessity of state taxes, and in addition the federal government distributed its treasury surplus in 1837. Finally, in the 1850s, the state railroad's sharply rising earnings permitted higher expenditures at the same time that taxes grew lighter.

Thus it was that at three points in the years between 1815 and 1860 Georgia launched major new undertakings in social welfare. Significant spending on elementary education, for example, resulted from laws enacted in 1817–21, 1837, and 1858. Because Georgians attempted whenever possible to avoid direct taxation, and nontax funds were frequently unavailable, their wants—which proved much more consistent than their means—often went unsatisfied. Administrative costs of government, like the interest on public debt, had to be paid. But social spending, though important, seemed less urgent. More readily adjustable than the costs of government or the debt, social spending was tied to nontax revenue; it bulged only when a windfall arrived at the treasury. In the 1840s, when the Western and Atlantic was still absorbing state funds, not generating them, Georgians found their state budget too cramped to permit generous appropriations for social welfare. The late 1850s, by contrast, displayed much greater spending on elementary schooling, higher education, and (as shown in the next chapter) such institutions as schools for the deaf and blind.

The education act of 1858 offered the strongest evidence of Georgia's increasing commitment to social spending, and not only because of the size of the new annual appropriation for schools. After decades of emphasis on investment in banking or transportation, state spending began to shift from economic growth to social welfare. Following Governor Brown's suggestion, the act provided that, as the state paid off its debt on the Western and Atlantic, it would increase its spending on schools.[41] Total spending on the two items would remain constant, but as one declined, the other would increase.

7

GREAT
OBJECTS OF
THE STATE'S
CHARITY

A S T H E Western and Atlantic Railroad's net earnings increased, Georgia grew more generous with state institutions. In 1852 Governor Howell Cobb proposed that "one-third of the large revenue of the State Road shall be devoted to the maintenance of the three great objects of the State's charity: the Lunatic Asylum, [the school for] the Deaf and Dumb, and the school for the Blind." And it was. In the second half of the 1850s, the state supplied the three institutions with nearly twice as much support ($446,720) as during the first half of the decade ($231,675).[1] More than in the 1810s or the 1830s, in the late 1850s Georgia could and did increase its spending on institutions of social welfare and social control, just as it did on education. The penitentiary, too, reflected changes in the state's finances, although many Georgians wished it would pay its own way.

Some institutions embodied more coercion than benevolence. Social welfare best characterized those whose inmates were voluntary, social control those that involved force. Most people entered Georgia's insane asylum no more voluntarily than those incarcerated in the penitentiary. Chronology suggests the priorities of antebellum Americans: The most coercive institutions opened first, the more benevolent ones last. Thus Georgia's penitentiary opened in 1817, its insane asylum in 1842, and its schools for the deaf and the blind at about midcentury.

From Europe to Georgia

The development of Georgia's social welfare facilities demonstrated the diffusion of men, institutions, and ideas in the late-eighteenth and early-nineteenth centuries. Therapeutic institutions for the deaf, the blind, and those considered mentally ill had their genesis principally in France in the late eighteenth century, though pioneer efforts also occurred in England, Germany, and the United States. In 1775 Abbé Charles Michel de l'Epée founded a school for the deaf, where he matured a system of sign language to enable his students to communicate. Ten years later, Valentin Haüy adapted some of de l'Epée's ideas when he founded a school to render blind people both literate and self-supporting. Haüy gave public demonstrations to obtain first private donations and then public support. During the French Revolution, the national government took over both schools and opened them to the poor. Another French citizen, Philippe Pinel, had the greatest influence in Europe in propounding "moral treatment" for the mentally afflicted. His methods called for institutions that were therapeutic and not merely custodial. Sharing many ideas with Pinel, but more directly important in America than he, were a British Quaker, William Tuke, who established the York Retreat in 1796 and had many Quaker contacts in the United States, and Benjamin Rush, a leading physician in Jeffersonian America and for thirty years a professor of medicine at the University of Pennsylvania.[2]

European institutions and ideas called some Americans' attention to the needs of the mentally troubled and the physically handicapped; they also provided examples of what could be done for such people. Schools for the deaf and the blind, however, needed teachers and funds. Private citizens in New England paid to send Thomas Hopkins Gallaudet to Europe to study at the school founded by de l'Epée, where he learned methods for teaching the deaf. Gallaudet's training, along with a $5,000 appropriation by the state of Connecticut, made possible the first permanent institution for teaching the deaf in America. The American Asylum at Hartford for the Education and Instruction of the Deaf and Dumb opened in 1817. By 1823 similar schools had opened with state support in New York, Pennsylvania, and Kentucky.[3]

Within a few years, the story was repeated with schools for the blind. Samuel Gridley Howe visited schools in Edinburgh, Paris, and Berlin in 1831, and the next year the New England Asylum for the Purpose of Educating the Blind opened in Boston. By 1833 similar institutions opened in New York City and Philadelphia. Like the schools for the deaf, all three depended on both private contributions and state appropriations.[4] These early northern institutions contributed to the founding, about a generation later, of their counterparts in Georgia.

Asylum

In the quarter-century before the Civil War, the state of Georgia developed institutions for the insane, the deaf, and the blind. Georgia's welfare expenditures began in the prosperous mid-1830s, when the state received most of its revenue from nontax sources. Then, dependent on tax revenue for a time, social spending held at a low level through the 1840s. In the 1850s, as the Western and Atlantic Railroad again made large amounts of nontax revenue available for public use, Georgia enlarged its welfare facilities and further extended their benefits. The three institutions absorbed 10 percent of state spending in the 1850s, more than education did.

Until the 1830s, local governments provided the only public assistance available to the blind, deaf, or insane in Georgia. Some such people received support from county or town "pauper" funds, and the legislature authorized Gwinnett and Talbot counties, for example, each to establish an "asylum for the lunatic and invalid poor." But in 1833 a deaf man named John J. Flournoy petitioned the legislature to inaugurate schooling for the deaf, and at the same time Tomlinson Fort, who had attended Benjamin Rush's medical school, led an effort to launch a state mental institution. Governor Wilson Lumpkin endorsed both causes in 1834, and social welfare in Georgia soon began to follow the lead set elsewhere in the country.[5]

The general assembly appropriated $44,000 between 1837 and 1841 to erect an asylum at Milledgeville for insane white residents. When the institution first opened, the legislature authorized the county inferior courts to commit persons they deemed "dangerous," but inmates were to be supported either by the counties that sent them or by private funds. In 1842 the legislature authorized the state to support, for the duration of their sentences, any lunatics sent from the nearby state penitentiary. Finally, in 1843, it declared that the state would pay up to $50 per year for the support of each pauper patient. By 1850 the annual appropriation for the maintenance of indigent inmates was $6,000, and annual salaries at the asylum cost another $6,000.[6]

Revenue from the state railroad permitted much higher expenditures for the asylum in the 1850s. During that decade, Georgia spent about $280,000 for building improvements, and total spending on the institution amounted to 8 percent of all state spending in the years 1856–60. The legislature appropriated $3,000 for "purchasing individual servants for the Asylum, who have been long employed and found to possess such qualities as render them particularly valuable to the Institution." The asylum grew rapidly; by 1861 it had 322 inmates (187 men and 135 women). By 1860 the state spent an annual $15,000 for pauper patients and $14,400 for salaries and help.[7]

Despite increased appropriations, the state bore less than two-thirds of the costs of maintaining the asylum. The institution received over one-third of its revenue in 1859, for example, from patients who paid all or part of the costs of their keep; fifty-eight patients (one-fourth of the total number of inmates) paid from $10 to $450 each that year. In addition, the asylum's inmates produced much of the soap, clothing, vegetables, poultry, eggs, and milk used at the institution.[8]

Dorothea Dix was a major advocate, in the South as well as the North, both of insane asylums, which she called "my chief work," and of penitentiary reform, her "secondary one." She influenced developments in states from Massachusetts to Mississippi, although she had little specific impact in Georgia. Still, she visited the state briefly a few times and was warmly received. In 1846 she found the Georgia mental institution "very bad" but the penitentiary "excellently ordered."[9]

Unlike most northern reformers, Miss Dix shunned the antislavery movement and thus retained her legitimacy in the South. As she wrote in 1850 from Mississippi, where she found legislators distracted from her cause by sectional politics, "I have *no* patience and no sympathy either with Northern Abolitionists or Southern agitators." In January 1859, the Georgia insane asylum's superintendent, Dr. Thomas F. Green, wrote her that he kept a "Dix room" in the institution's Centre Building "in the sincere hope, that it might be often occupied by the lady, whom it will be our peculiar pleasure always to honor." The next month, she visited Milledgeville, and soon afterwards she procured various materials in the North for the institution. Dr. Green reported happily to her in July that the asylum was prospering. The number of patients had continued to increase, yet "we have sent fifteen home, well, since you were with us." [10]

Schooling the Deaf

In 1835 the state began to supply schooling for deaf white Georgians. At first it set aside funds to educate students for no longer than four years each at the American Asylum in Connecticut, and it paid $600 a year for a commissioner to make all the arrangements for applicants' education and to convey them to the Hartford school. Six Georgia students attended in 1835. By 1838 the legislature had established a standing annual appropriation of $4,500 for the education of the deaf. [11]

In the 1840s, the state prepared for their education in Georgia. The state commissioner arranged for the Hearn Manual-Training School at Cave Spring in Floyd County to establish a department for them. After one of the school's teachers, Oliver P. Fannin, attended the Hartford institution to learn its methods of teaching the deaf, Georgia rescinded its authorization for students to attend out-of-state schools at state expense. The 1847 legislature required that a portion of the annual appropriation be used to establish a new institution near the Hearn School, and two years later it appropriated an additional $4,000 to pay for new buildings. [12]

The Georgia Asylum for the Deaf and Dumb opened in 1849. The school sought higher appropriations by sending students to Milledgeville to demonstrate their "proficiency" in exhibitions before the general assembly, and in 1852 the annual appropriation was increased from $4,500 to $8,000. Additional appropriations enabled the school to increase the variety of its facilities; to extend, from four years to six, the maximum period of its support for each student; and to expand its enrollment from twenty-five students in 1851 to forty-four by 1856. [13]

The Georgia Asylum for the Deaf and Dumb was not intended merely as a place to impound children unable to hear, but as a place to educate them to self-sufficiency. On every day but Sunday, students spent six hours on academic studies and three hours at work—males in shops, females in a "domestic" department. To support a request for a $2,000 appropriation to provide additional workshops, the institution observed that its shoe shop more than paid for itself: "We do not ask for means to support the trades; set them afloat and they will sustain themselves." It received the requested funds.[14]

The school accepted both paying and state-supported students. Tuition for paying pupils was $175 a year; prospective state beneficiaries had to be unable to pay that amount. The school reportedly attempted to treat both nonpaying and paying students alike: "All who are admitted, those who pay their own way as well as beneficiaries, are to compose one family, and be placed on a level [of] equality as to attention, dress and labor."[15]

Schooling the Blind

Though the 1850 census enumerated 224 blind white residents of Georgia, no institution existed at that time to help them. After a blind teacher's arrival in Macon from Philadelphia in early 1851 energized the local community, private citizens subscribed $802 to begin schooling four blind children, two of them indigent. The teacher, Walter S. Fortescue, had graduated from the Pennsylvania Institute for the Blind and the University of Pennsylvania.[16]

Organizers of the Academy for the Blind in Macon sought state support and, to impress legislators with the educability of blind youths, emulated the Asylum for the Deaf in sending students to Milledgeville to display their proficiency. The organizers' petition to the legislature reported that twenty-five states had appropriated public money for educating the blind. Noting that the more successful schools were "private corporations founded in the charity of a community, governed by elective trustees, and sustained by aid from the State," they requested that the academy be "placed on a permanent basis with liberal advantages as well for indigent as for paying pupils." The Macon press supported the effort: "Let Georgia then add to existing institutions for the Deaf and Dumb and the Insane, another for . . . the Blind, that her beneficence may be dispersed impartially to all her unfortunate children, according to their respective need."[17]

The legislature responded in 1852 by incorporating the Academy for the Blind and appropriating $5,000 for each of the next two years. Paying students, too, attended, but so far as public funds permitted, the school selected and educated indigent blind youths aged twelve to thirty. Having assumed partial responsibility for the academy, the legislature continued its support. Between 1854 and 1859, the state also spent $69,000 to build and furnish a new home for the school.[18]

By the end of the decade, twenty-six students attended the academy. The new building, school principal W. D. Williams reported happily, gave the state ample facilities to educate every blind white youth in Georgia. Like the school for the deaf and dumb, the Academy for the Blind was not designed merely as a warehouse for handicapped children. In the "literary department," students received instruction in all "the various branches usually taught in the common academies for the seeing, with the exception of ancient and modern languages"; they also learned to read "raised print." [19]

The academy also attempted to train each student for a vocation. Indeed, the school derived small amounts of revenue from the sale of "articles of sewing, plain and fancy knitting[,] and ornamental beadwork" that its female pupils made. Though the school desired to train its male students in the trades, it had to abandon an early effort to teach handicrafts because of a shortage of funds. At the end of the decade, with the primary goal of obtaining a large fireproof building approaching attainment, the school requested funds for a "work department." The academy described broom-making as the most remunerative business available to the blind. An extra $1,000 appropriation would allow the school to start such a department, which, according to the experience of other institutions, would not only become self-sustaining but would also generate profits for the academy's use. The legislature granted the request. The academy taught all students music, both vocal and instrumental. Such instruction, "with the blind, is not intended as a merely ornamental branch of education, but to fit them for self-maintenance" as professional musicians and teachers of music. The academy provided further vocational training and opportunity, in that the more advanced students helped instruct the younger ones, and most of the teachers at the school were themselves blind. [20]

State Support

Most pupils in the Academy for the Blind and the Asylum for the Deaf and Dumb were beneficiaries of the state. The benefits of both schools, unlike those of higher education, were widely distributed throughout Georgia. Through 1855 the Academy for the Blind admitted twenty-five students—eight boys and seventeen girls. The state supported all thirteen students from North Georgia and seven from the black belt. The plantation counties sent three paying pupils and a partially paying one, and South Carolina sent another paying student. Of forty-four pupils at the Asylum for the Deaf and Dumb in 1856 (twenty male and twenty-four female), the state supported all but ten—six from Alabama and four from Central Georgia black-belt counties. Of the thirty-four state-supported pupils, half came from the black belt and half from predominantly white counties. [21]

The availability of the three institutions provided Georgia's citizens with something of a low-premium, limited-benefit insurance policy. The lunatic asylum greatly relieved many friends and relatives, and in some cases aided the patient's recovery. For the physically handicapped, smaller in number, the state provided schools that took seriously their task of supplying a rudimentary English education and vocational training that could lead to economic self-sufficiency.

Because all three institutions charged all clients who could afford to pay, the arrangement offered greater benefits to the less wealthy. Yet plantation counties gave more support to welfare spending than did poorer districts. For example, the legislature authorized large-scale improvements in the insane asylum in both the 1851–52 and 1853–54 sessions. Black-belt representatives supported the measures 33–21 and 30–16; by contrast, upcountry legislators voted 23–29 and 18–22.[22]

Beginning in 1856, however, when revenue from the Western and Atlantic became available, voting patterns grew more alike. Senators from the black belt voted 29–19 that year to appropriate $110,000 for new construction; those from predominantly white counties voted 25–19.[23] As in the case of higher education, legislators from yeomen constituencies differed little from their planter colleagues in their willingness to spend—provided such spending would not require an increase in taxes.

State support was crucial to the success of all three institutions. Each derived a portion of its revenue from out-of-state or other paying or part-paying pupils or patients. Each, too, supported itself in part by producing food or other goods, either to be consumed at the institution or sold outside. Most revenue, however, came from the state government. As Governor Cobb had suggested, the net income of the Western and Atlantic Railroad provided increasing support for institutions for Georgia's handicapped citizens.

The Penitentiary

One state institution, the penitentiary, failed to benefit much from the Western and Atlantic's growing profits. Georgians believed it should support itself. During the 1850s, it received little more than 1 percent of all state spending—$44,315 in the years 1851–55 and $59,714 in 1856–60. The penitentiary housed an occasional free black or Indian man, and even a white woman or two at times, but most of the inmates—whose numbers grew from 92 in 1852 to 245 by 1860—were white men. Controversy during the last antebellum decade over the financing of the penitentiary nonetheless foreshadowed the post–Civil War convict lease system.[24]

Early in the nineteenth century, Georgia reformed its penal code regarding white felony convicts by ending corporal punishment, such as public whippings, and establishing a state penitentiary at Milledgeville. Between 1804, when Governor John Milledge first broached the idea of a state prison, and 1817, when the penitentiary opened, two considerations—one financial, one ideological—encouraged those changes. When the legislature made an initial appropriation of $10,000 in 1811 to begin construction of the penitentiary, Georgians were anticipating the proceeds from the 1802 cession of western territory. Moreover, as the legislature declared, "sanguinary and cruel punishments are only suited to despotic and arbitrary governments, and are totally incompatible with the principle of leniency and moderation which should distinguish" republican institutions from all others. The penitentiary system, by contrast, had been "proved by experience to be, the most moral, efficacious and merciful plan of punishment." In 1817 Governor William Rabun anticipated that the new institution would "become a formidable engine, in the hands of a well-regulated government, for the suppression of vice and the encouragement of virtue." [25]

Georgians expected the penitentiary not only to reform convicts but also to support itself—something it never did. Convicts were fed and clothed at public expense. Opponents of the penitentiary system persisted throughout the prewar period, but only once did they take control of public policy. After a destructive fire at the penitentiary in May 1831, the legislature voted to abolish the institution and return to the pre-1817 system of corporal punishment for all new convicts. Inmates already in the penitentiary would serve out their sentences, but in the future many whites, like blacks, would face a punishment of thirty-nine lashes. Governor Wilson Lumpkin, an opponent of the new law, voiced wishful thinking when he promoted the penitentiary system as "by far, the most economical mode of punishment for crime." [26]

Like Lumpkin, many Georgians viewed the penitentiary, despite its shortcomings, as better than the alternative the legislature had adopted. The grand jury of the Wilkes County superior court offered the strongest case for restoring the penitentiary: "We are satisfied that the people of our County are not yet willing to return to the barbarous punishments of cropping branding and whipping, that rather than subject their unfortunate criminal fellow citizens to this kind of punishment they would suffer the guilty to escape. They find many [reasons] to excuse for crimes rather than subject a neighbor or a fellow citizen to such ignominious punishment. The Penitentiary is already built and must be kept up many years for the fulfillment of the punishment of those now in a course of sentence there. The expense will not be materially increased by continuing it in full operation." [27]

If Georgians could view their convicted neighbors as "fellow citizens," and if they saw the state treasury flush and taxes dropping, then they could reconsider their decision to abandon the penitentiary. Thus the 1832 legislature reversed its predecessor's action and gave the system another chance. But unless administration at the penitentiary improved, legislators recognized, Georgians would suffer once again from disappointed expectations that, under the institution's "benign influence, crimes should decrease in number and enormity[,] reformation should speedily work its curing effect upon the guilty, and . . . a handsome revenue should directly flow in upon the State." [28]

A decade later, the fiscal climate had turned bleak, and the penitentiary came under renewed pressure. In 1843 the senate passed a bill "to farm out the Penitentiary . . . and hire out the convicts." The house, however, postponed the measure indefinitely.[29]

At the time of the 1831 fire, prison inmates worked in blacksmith, wagon, carriage, cabinet, coopering, harness, shoe, and other shops. In subsequent years, the legislature authorized the use of convicts in construction at the insane asylum and in grading land for extending the Milledgeville and Gordon Railroad to the penitentiary. Seeing the good work of thirty men employed in a railroad car workshop, a legislative committee noted in 1854 that "properly conducted," such work could "yield a handsome profit to the State"; even if not, proceeds helped cover the costs of maintaining the inmates. But prison authorities and legislative committees recommended discontinuing occupations found to be unprofitable — cabinetmaking and the wheelwright business, because of the difficulty in selling the articles made, and tanning, because materials cost too much.[30]

Reformation, according to the principal keeper, constituted "one of the great ends" of the penitentiary system. The hope was to prepare convicts for productive work and a relatively painless reintegration into society. The purpose of labor, in addition to the paramount financial consideration, was to provide each convict with a trade with which to support himself upon his release. The penitentiary also sought to supply illiterate convicts with an elementary education.[31]

Because the penitentiary required frequent appropriations to pay debts, purchase provisions, and make repairs, many legislators were receptive when the principal keeper offered in 1853 to lease the institution (to himself) for six years without cost to the state — on condition that the state first put it in proper condition. A majority of the Joint Standing Committee on the Penitentiary reported unfavorably, not only because of the large appropriations that would be necessary for repairing dilapidated buildings and erecting additional workshops, but because "the personal interest of the lessee to make convict labor as profitable as possible, would conflict with that of the State." The house, however, was more in accord with the minority report, which recommended leasing in the "interest of taxpayers," and passed the bill. But the senate defeated it.[32]

Rejection of leasing did not indicate satisfaction with the current arrangement. At the following legislative session, the penitentiary committee called for establishment of a new institution and recommended the purchase of Stone Mountain for the purpose. The committee noted that apprentices were worth their board and clothing the first year and became profitable thereafter. Moreover, given that slaves performed their work satisfactorily, convicts, "being naturally so far their superiors," should provide labor at least as remunerative. The committee expressed certainty that quarrying at Stone Mountain, which could last for eternity, might, in combination with other pursuits, at last make the penal system self-sustaining. Like the leasing bill the previous session, however, the Stone Mountain bill to appropriate $70,000 passed only one house.[33]

In addition to efforts at leasing and removal, there were murmurs in the late 1850s of a return to corporal punishment. Recommending in 1858 that the state abolish the penitentiary system, the state senator from Ware County in South Georgia, W. A. McDonald, objected principally to the institution's separation of husbands from their wives and conceded that he supported whipping, but not cropping or other mutilation. He recommended as an alternative that, given that the state owned a huge but currently useless land area in South Georgia, "the best use that could be made of the convicts would be to take them to the Okefenokee Swamp, and let them drain it." [34] He no doubt had in mind a bucket brigade to the Atlantic.

A Milledgeville paper offered more vigorous support for corporal punishment as a substitute for the costly penitentiary if leasing could not be accomplished: "The best thing that could be done for the interest of the State is to lease it out for a term of years, as it never will pay under its present organization. And if not leased out, then burn it down, and try what whipping, branding and hanging will do to diminish crime in the State, provided, honest and intelligent men sit upon criminal cases, and not vagabonds, as is too often the case now." [35]

Nontax Revenue and Social Spending

Because the quest for a tax-free system of public finance was so central a feature of Georgia's history between the War of 1812 and the Civil War, the availability of nontax revenue provides the key to shifts in state spending through those decades. Other explanations prove less satisfying in accounting for Georgia's fiscal behavior. Milton Sydney Heath discerned cycles of public policy, as periods of heightened government activity alternated with periods of relative inaction.[36] No doubt the dominant ideology regarding the appropriate behavior of the state government underwent some changes during those years. Nonetheless the means available were not a function of the vagaries of public thought, or of varying propensities to tax, as fiscal conservatives and liberals alternated in office.

Nor were those means directly tied to prosperity in the private economy, as Dorothy Orr, historian of education in Georgia, suggests. Public revenues and expenditures did not rise and fall with the price of cotton.[37] Increases in tax revenue during times of prosperity cannot account for the timing of Georgia's funding for schools or railroads. The common school fund of 1837, like the Western and Atlantic bill of 1836, was enacted at a time when the state's general tax revenue had dropped to zero, and the increased state spending of the 1850s came at a time when tax revenue showed no change and tax rates were actually dropping.

Legislators' votes on fiscal matters reveal the significance of nontax revenue to spending patterns. Legislators from the upcountry and the black belt differed in their commitment to low taxes and in their willingness to spend money that depended on taxes. In the 1840s and early 1850s, representatives from the black belt and the towns, not those from yeomen districts, provided most of the votes to raise spending and, if necessary, to increase taxes. On questions of social spending, as on railroads, Whig delegates from the more commercial areas were more willing to spend than were Democrats representing yeomen constituencies. In the mid-1850s, the tax consideration receded. As nontax revenue took pressure off taxpayers, the two groups' differences grew less pronounced. Upcountry representatives became more willing than before to vote higher expenditures.

State Power

The growth of state power in Jacksonian America, like the economic development that it promoted, was facilitated by a combination of federal policy, public enterprise, and Indian lands. Land, the basic resource in an agricultural society, also provided the foundation for the growth of state power in Georgia and for that state's efforts to create a tax-free system of public finance. Revenue from land sales, invested in banking, financed much of the Western and Atlantic Railroad. Later, in turn, earnings from the railroad were directed toward social welfare. Without the nontax revenue that Georgia gained from Indian lands and public enterprise, state spending on transportation and education would have stuck at much lower levels, and "the discovery of the asylum" would have had less impact on public policy. The average tax rate in 1860 hardly differed from that of 1820, or even 1800. Yet public policy on the eve of the Civil War contrasted sharply with that at the end of the eighteenth century. The state budgets of the late 1850s clearly displayed Georgia's active promotion of economic growth and social welfare.

In the last few years before secession, the state of Georgia began to realize the fruits of its quest for a tax-free system of public revenue. As revenue patterns changed, so could spending. Though tax revenue remained constant, and rates declined as the tax base grew, the state had increasing amounts of revenue to spend. Money from the Western and Atlantic Railroad enabled the state both to begin financing a new trunk line railroad and to develop significantly the social services that it provided its citizens. During the 1850s, as a consequence of Western and Atlantic revenue, average annual expenditures doubled for welfare institutions, quintupled for elementary schooling, and sextupled for higher education.

Public finance in Georgia in 1860 had arrived at a halfway house on the road to the twentieth century. Far more than in the early years of statehood—more even than in the years of Jackson's presidency—Georgia's citizens favored substantial public expenditures, not only for the promotion of economic growth, but, increasingly, for social welfare purposes as well. Yet antebellum Georgians were unprepared to step into a world that required much direct taxation to finance schooling or public welfare institutions. Rather, social spending still depended on nontax revenue. If public investments or the national government provided adequate funds, then the state promoted social programs. In the 1850s, however, unlike the 1810s and the 1830s, a rise in peacetime public expenditures depended primarily on income to the state treasury generated by developments within Georgia and not in the nation's capital. The fiscal pump was now primed.

The theme of tax-free public finance reveals a significant though little-noticed facet of "the significance of the frontier in American history." Frederick Jackson Turner's frontier fostered the economic and social well-being of many more Americans than those who migrated West. Those who remained East also benefited from western lands.[38] Scenes from Georgia in the late 1850s—a shipper or passenger on the Western and Atlantic Railroad, a student or teacher in a Georgia common school—reflected benefits that white Americans derived from the West.

But the Civil War destroyed Georgia's incipient tax-free system of public finance. To Frederick Jackson Turner, the 1890 census signaled the end of the frontier. From the perspective of a public revenue bonanza, however, the frontier had faded by the time of Civil War and Reconstruction. Dorothy Orr's thesis about social expenditures may not explain beginnings, but it can readily account for endings. In the absence of nontax revenue, prosperity proved insufficient to induce much new spending. But once tax-free sources led to higher expenditures, the continuation of that spending depended on the continuation of prosperity. The depression of the late 1830s contributed mightily to the demise of Georgia's Central Bank, to repeal of the common school act, and to reinstatement of full taxation. The revived Jacksonian pattern of the late 1850s could endure only if peace and prosperity did.

8 DEPRIVING A WHOLE RACE

EVEN BEFORE the growth of state power and the development of new institutions, American voters relied on public authority to shape their social system. Much of antebellum intervention in social relations simply perpetuated traditional patterns of regulating the status of various groups of residents. The criteria for intervention in these traditional ways were not physical handicaps or social behavior but sex and, above all, race.

Speaking for the Georgia Supreme Court in 1857, Justice Henry L. Benning cataloged types of laws that Georgia's legislature could enact—had, in fact, already enacted—limiting the rights of white women, blacks, and convicted criminals. The state enjoyed virtually unlimited power, Benning declared, to enact a law "for the creation, or the destruction, of *any* right" so long as the legislators deemed such laws to be for "the good of the State." On Georgia's statute books were laws "depriving married women of liberty and of the right of property" and "depriving all women of political rights"; laws "depriving men of property, of liberty, of life, for crime"; and laws "depriving a whole race, of every right, except the right to life." Georgians subjected to these laws derived no benefits aside from "good done to the public."[1] Before the Civil War and Reconstruction, neither state nor federal constitution limited Georgia's authority to enact and enforce all such laws.

Paternalism = Protection + Coercion

In defining the highly variable rights and responsibilities of nineteenth-century Americans, public authorities formulated strikingly different social policies for various groups. Paternalism, rather than liberty, provides the key to understanding the social experience of most antebellum Georgians. Liberty in the competitive, anomic world of late antebellum Georgia, as elsewhere in America, was generally reserved for white men. Only they, the perception went (and the justification), could absorb the stresses of life in a world of social insecurity—the burdens of responsibility for success or failure in a disorderly society, absence of unemployment insurance in a market economy, vanishing fixity of status and place.

Paternalistic policies governed white women and children, slaves, and Indians. Paternalism connotes coercion as well as protection, power as well as nurture. For some groups, paternalism was perpetual; for white male children, it was temporary. White women, for example, were largely shielded from economic competition, and they found themselves barred from participating in it. A dependent, whether as daughter or wife, each typically moved from her father's protection and control to her husband's, in the manner that Justice Benning's description suggests.[2] Both the coercion and the protection of paternalism also operated on Afro-Americans and Native Americans. Whites justified their race policies, in part, on the basis that nonwhites could not boast the qualifications to survive in competition with white men. As in the case of white men who functioned in a particularly inept or antisocial manner, special environments were created or maintained for nonwhites. Blacks were perennial children, white Georgians said; slavery supplied blacks' needs and disciplined their excesses.

Above all, whites wanted Indians' land and blacks' labor. As state and federal authorities expelled Indians from Georgia and other states, an Indian Territory west of the Mississippi River segregated one group. Slavery and the plantation system largely enveloped the other, as in Georgia, and Georgia's few "free persons of color" were legally "wards" with white "guardians." White Georgians relied on slavery to provide a labor supply, a means of controlling blacks, and a social floor; and they defended the institution because it represented much of Georgia's wealth.[3]

Slavery aside, most whites wanted no nonwhites in America except slaves— no Indians and no free blacks. In the North, whites sought to create an all-white America; in the South, slaveowners' ideal required that all residents be either free whites or black slaves. The thrust toward an America where only whites were free was primarily coercive; it was based on the exclusion of nonwhites from economic competition and political participation. Never at ease with the notion of large numbers of free blacks, whites sought to restrict their number—Southerners through slavery, Northerners through "colonization," the emigration of free blacks elsewhere.[4]

The conjunction of liberty and paternalism comprised perhaps the major contradiction of culture and policy in antebellum America. The "rise of the common man" occurred in the face of a continuance, even a strengthening, of the slave plantation, and it accompanied the creation of Indian reservations and the promotion of black colonization, in addition to the development of the penitentiary and the insane asylum. Slaveowners defended the plantation as a school for barbarians, but it contrasted sharply with the era's common schools. Few scholars were permitted to graduate from slavery, and the law prohibited their being taught to read or write.

As a rule, only white men had the power to enter into contracts, and only they had the right to cast ballots. In dealing with the legal and political worlds, white men represented both themselves and their dependents. The political universe separated those who experienced liberty from those who experienced paternalism. Public authority interacted directly with white men and, for the most part, acted only indirectly—through them—on their dependents. The franchise represented more than the right to vote for government leaders and thereby help shape public policy; it symbolized the prerogatives of white men. The vote identified all full participants in Jacksonian America, who were permitted, and required, to compete. Like children, no women, blacks, or Indians had the right to vote in antebellum Georgia. For Georgia's white men, the doors to the penitentiary and the insane asylum separated the worlds of liberty and paternalism. Inmates of neither institution had the right to vote.

Black Slavery, Black Freedom

The dual policy of liberty and paternalism prevailed throughout antebellum America, but it displayed its most dramatic form in the Slave South. In the years between Revolution and Civil War, North and South diverged, as both regions experienced economic growth but the North saw more development. Although North and South proved similar in many matters of state policy, they differed fundamentally with regard to slavery. Moreover, slavery evoked regional differences that rippled through all public policy.

In 1827 New York ended slavery, and free blacks there had voting rights. In neither Georgia nor New York were blacks, by law or custom, the equals of whites, but in New York blacks were no longer slaves.[5] In Georgia, by contrast, nearly half the people comprised property, and only whites enjoyed political rights. A New York abolitionist proposed in 1853 that slavery be included in "the list of the exact sciences. From a single fundamental axiom [that slaves were property]," he said, "all the parts of the system are logically and scientifically deduced."[6]

In matters of social welfare, public authorities in Georgia concerned themselves with whites and left slaves to their owners. Until emancipation in the 1860s, the South's state and local governments reinforced the private authority of individual slaveowners and only rarely acted directly on blacks.

Slavery involved both the coercive and the protective features of a paternalistic system of social relations. As a social welfare system, slavery provided blacks with something of a guaranteed subsistence. In the patriarchal world of the plantation South, planters had invested the bulk of their wealth in human property, and to secure productive labor they had to maintain both the morale and the physical health of their slaves.[7] Slaveholders, not public authorities, undertook the care of aged, ill, insane, or otherwise disabled slaves; as a rule, they, not public authorities, also disciplined slaves and sought to control their behavior. Slaves were to be found in neither Georgia's insane asylum nor the penitentiary, nor in the schools for the blind or the deaf.

Slavery provided no guarantee that blacks would accept the roles that whites had assigned them to play. In buttressing the private authority of slaveowners over their slaves, public authority occasionally took direct action to control slaves. The slave patrol operated to secure planters against having their most valuable property run away, and to secure all whites against slave uprisings. When a slave was convicted of a crime, only corporal punishment—whipping, in the main, or execution—appeared an appropriate sentence; fine or imprisonment would punish only the owner, because slaves, it seemed, had neither liberty nor property to lose.[8]

As for insane blacks, a county's inferior court could order any black person, slave or free, confined in the county jail if it considered the person to be a public nuisance or a danger to the community. The owner of an insane slave could, if he wished, maintain custody by posting a bond of $500 to guarantee proper control.[9]

In 1853 Governor Howell Cobb suggested providing space for blacks at the state insane asylum. In response, the institution offered to end its policy of exclusion, but only on a segregated basis, as "it would be essential that entirely separate buildings and enclosures should be erected, at a proper distance from those now occupied." Though the superintendent was more intent on enlarging the facilities for whites, he requested a $10,000 building appropriation for black inmates and suggested that "a very trivial tax upon each slave" could supply sufficient funds for both construction and care.[10] The legislature remained unmoved. Such an insurance scheme would have cost most slaveholders more than it was worth to them. Only after emancipation, when slavery no longer controlled blacks, would Georgia make space for them in the asylum.

Only free whites and black slaves could inhabit the slaveholder's utopia. Therefore, public policy operated to restrict the number of free blacks in Georgia. Free blacks, whatever their behavior, embodied the seditious notion that blacks could be something other than slaves. Seditious propensities must be curbed, and free blacks must not be so free as to endanger the social order by providing autonomous role models that other blacks might emulate. As Justice Joseph H. Lumpkin put it, slavery required "unceasing vigilance and firmness [of whites], as well as uniform kindness, justice and humanity. Everything must be interdicted which is calculated to render the slave discontented with his condition, or which would tend to increase his capacity for mischief."[11]

To limit the possibility of "exciting false hopes of liberty," Georgia enacted laws to prevent an influx of free blacks through migration. And it permitted manumission only on condition that it be "foreign"—that slaves be removed from Georgia before they were freed. Thus, in 1850 Georgia's population of free blacks numbered only 2,931, while the number of slaves had reached 381,682. Following John Brown's raid at Harpers Ferry in 1859, Georgia directed that any free black who subsequently entered the state would be sold into slavery, with the proceeds of the sale to be shared equally by the county treasury and the informer.[12]

An occasional slaveholder wished to free his slaves in his will. Disenchanted heirs challenged those bequests. In one such case that reached Georgia's highest court, Justice Lumpkin denounced the manifest views of some slaveholders "that they will peril their souls if they do not disinherit their offspring by emancipating their slaves!" If the court construed a contested will as seeking to confer freedom on slaves while they were still in Georgia, they remained slaves despite their deceased owner's intention. Not all such wills, however, went unhonored; when Thomas J. Waters desired freedom for forty of his slaves—some of them his own children and grandchildren—the court had to perfect the will but refused to invalidate it. In 1859, however, the general assembly voided all wills that would manumit slaves, whether "within or without the State."[13]

When Pennsylvania embarked on a program of gradual emancipation in 1780, it mandated that all slaves currently residing in the state be registered and that no new slaves be allowed. By contrast, Georgia's laws mandated that all free blacks be registered and that no new ones arrive except by birth to free black mothers. Each year, free black men and women had to pay a fifty-cent registration fee to the clerk of the inferior court. The clerk then advertised their applications in local newspapers, lest they actually be someone's slaves.[14]

Conviction for violating Georgia's registration laws subjected the offender to a fine of $100. In lieu of paying the fine, a free black might be hired out as a laborer. Thirty days after working off the fine, he could again be convicted and fined. In 1850 Bryant Oxendine, unable to pay his $100 fine in Forsyth County, was hired out for eighteen months; the inferior court sold him into temporary slavery to a citizen who paid the fine.[15]

Nor was Oxendine an isolated example. Some cases from Bibb County in the 1850s demonstrate one jurisdiction's enforcement of the registration laws. In November 1851, Bibb County's inferior court convicted William Brewer of failure to register in the county and fined him $100 and costs. The record does not show what then happened, but Brewer was convicted again in August 1854. Unable to pay the fine, he was hired out at public auction to William Darwell, whose bid of forty-two months was the shortest time offered. In February 1858, Brewer's time was up, but he does not appear again in the record. Instead, in that very month Junius Jacobs, son of a free black woman in South Carolina, was convicted and fined $50. In his case, the lowest bidder, E. A. Wilcox, paid the fine and costs in return for thirty-six months' service. Later that year, fined $100, Martin Pollard found himself hired out to Granville Wood for eleven months.[16]

Not content to prevent any increase in the number of free blacks in Georgia through migration or manumission, policymakers sought to reduce the number already there. Neither white nor slave, free blacks inhabited a twilight zone that offered neither liberty nor paternalism. Free blacks, who were not citizens, could not enjoy the same rights as whites. Yet because they were not slaves, whites could not assume sufficient control over them, and because they were not property, whites had little interest in safeguarding them. In the view of many slaveholders, paternalism toward slaves "imperiously require[d]" that public policy take an exceedingly harsh approach to free blacks, else slaves would become restless and require greater repression. Thus some Georgians sought to expel free blacks from the state much as Georgia had previously expelled the Creeks and Cherokees. The inferior courts held the discretionary power of refusing to register any free black person "of bad character." Moreover, any free black who left Georgia, if he entered any but an adjoining state—certainly if he visited a free state—lost his right to register and reside in Georgia.[17]

Given the perceived threat to slavery that free blacks constituted, the legislators who sought the harshest anti-free-black laws typically represented Georgia's black belt. Only if blacks kept their assigned place might planters be paternalists. At the 1849–50 legislative session, for example, a black-belt Whig proposed a bill that called for an annual tax of $100 on every adult free black; the bill went to "the Committee on the subject of removing free persons of color from this State." Most of his support came from other black-belt Whigs.[18]

The same logic that led whites to limit the numbers of free blacks in Georgia also led them to repress those who remained. In many respects, state law made no distinction between free blacks and slaves. Fearing free blacks' anomalous standing in a society based on racial slavery, whites sought to resolve the anomaly by conforming their legal status to race rather than freedom. All blacks, whether free or slave, might be whipped for using "insolent or improper language to a white person." Given the presumption that all blacks were slaves, all were subject to the state's patrol laws, and a free black away from home without his registration certificate might be summarily whipped. Unlike whites, who enjoyed unrestricted ownership of weapons, free blacks were denied the right to "own, use, or carry firearms."[19]

Immediately after David Walker, a free black in the North, justified slave rebellion in his revolutionary *Appeal* (1829), Georgia outlawed the diffusion of literacy among free blacks and thus applied yet another portion of the slave code to "free" blacks as well. If the offending teacher was white, the penalty for teaching blacks to read or write could be a $500 fine and imprisonment; if black, a fine (thus a possible term of slavery for a free black) and/or whipping.[20]

"Like the *slave*, the *free* person of color is incompetent to testify against a free white person," observed Justice Lumpkin as he began to catalog the equation of black slavery and black freedom. "He has neither vote nor voice in forming the laws by which he is governed." Restricted in these and other ways, free blacks in antebellum Georgia experienced only what historian John Hope Franklin has labeled "quasi-free" status. Lumpkin went so far as to disparage free blacks' "fancied freedom" as "all a delusion." [21]

Neither Slave nor Free

Though Georgia's laws often failed to distinguish between black freedom and black slavery, free blacks could sometimes discern significant differences. Antebellum Georgia whites' definition of slavery—the right to life but the negation of liberty and property—implies the distance that separated black freedom from black slavery. In degree, at least, free blacks controlled their own time, and they secured the proceeds of their own labor. Lumpkin meant to narrow the meaning of freedom for free black Georgians, but his definition offered a measure of freedom: "Slavery is the dominion of the master over the slave—the entire subjection of one person to the will of another. Manumission is the withdrawal or renunciation of that dominion." [22]

Despite a broad range of restrictions, then, Georgia's free blacks enjoyed a measure of both liberty and property. Because some whites took advantage of free blacks' precarious status and potential sale value, the legislature enacted a law in 1837 to protect their "right to freedom." From the perspective of public authority, free blacks' guardians functioned as surrogate masters. From the perspective of free blacks themselves, guardians might serve them in a patron-client relationship; for example, though free blacks could not testify against whites, their "next friends" or guardians could act in property disputes for them. An 1818 act, in effect until the end of slavery, declared it illegal for free blacks in Georgia to acquire slaves except by inheritance, as descendants of owners. In Savannah and Augusta, where one in three of Georgia's free blacks resided, the law similarly restricted their acquisition of real estate. Thus, up to a point, free blacks and slaves were equals in their legal incapacity to own or acquire property. Yet free blacks who owned such restricted property before 1818 could retain it and pass it on to their children. Moreover, the law did not limit the ownership of real estate in the rest of Georgia or any forms of personal property other than slaves. Lumpkin had occasion to conclude in 1858: "While . . . I exceedingly doubt the policy of allowing free negroes to acquire and hold real estate, and that too without limitation as to quantity, still the correction of the evil, if it be one, is with the Legislature and not with the Courts." [23]

Lumpkin might pontificate, "All practical men must admit, that the slave who receives the care and protection of a tolerable master, is superior in comfort to the free negro." Free blacks, for their part, might wish to define "comfort" for themselves, and they might observe that not every master, if any, qualified as "tolerable." [24]

Although slaves had neither liberty nor property to lose, free blacks did, so public authorities could make demands on them. Road duty and the poll tax, like the registration laws, could threaten free blacks' liberty and could supply involuntary labor for private citizens and public authorities. Most counties required as many as fifteen days of road duty each year from slave men and white men aged sixteen to forty-five. But they could require up to twenty days of "public work" from "all registered free persons of color" between the ages of fifteen and sixty.[25] Road duty was required of men of all three groups—white, slave, and free black—but among women, only free blacks were subject to it.

Antebellum Georgia's tax system greatly discriminated against free blacks. In the 1850s, the state levied annual poll taxes of $0.25 on white men and $5.00 on free black adults of both sexes. At 1860 rates, a white man's poll tax equaled the tax on only $385 worth of property. A free black couple, by contrast, paid forty times as much in poll taxes, or the equivalent of a tax on $15,384 in property.[26]

Any free black who failed to pay his state poll tax, and who owned no property for the sheriff to seize, might be hired out as a temporary slave "for such price as will produce the amount due the State." Losing freedom for a time, he or she would be auctioned to the bidder who paid the tax and, as compensation, required the shortest amount of time to work off the resulting debt. Authorities published notices in local newspapers warning free blacks that, if they had failed to pay their taxes by the first Tuesday in January, they would be "hired out as the law directs."[27] Had the legislature enacted state poll taxes of $50 or $100, as proposed, free blacks would have faced a choice between leaving the state and chancing successive lengthy terms as slaves.

Because county and town poll taxes resembled the state tax in disparity, size, and enforcement, taxes could pose a serious obstacle to a Georgia free black's continuous liberty. County taxes, levied as a percentage of state taxes, replicated the differential in state taxes. And local poll taxes, though varying from town to town, similarly discriminated. Savannah's were typical—$1.00 on white men, $10.00 on free black men with a trade, and $6.25 on other free black men and on all free black women. Any propertyless free black in Savannah who failed to pay the city poll tax was obliged to work it off "on the streets, or elsewhere for the benefit of the city," at the rate of $1.00 per day for men, $0.50 for women. Milledgeville, the state capital, taxed white men $1.50 in 1856; payment of the tax served as commutation of road and patrol duty; the city taxed free black men $15.00 and free black women $7.50.[28]

All this taxation without representation took place in a political culture that justified poll taxes on the grounds that people should pay something for the right to vote and toward a public education fund. Georgia's state and local governments extracted much heavier taxes from free blacks than from whites, while supplying markedly limited benefits.

Noting that some free blacks owned slaves, historians have advanced three explanations. Some nonwhite slaveowners, particularly those owning sugar plantations in Louisiana, operated as much from commercial motives as their white counterparts. Others had purchased family members, for example, but could not free them because the law barred slaves' manumission or permitted it only if they left the state. Finally, a few kept family members enslaved in order to maintain greater power over them.[29]

To these three explanations might be added a fourth, fiscal explanation. Given the enormous differential between the public obligations of adult blacks as slaves and as free persons, perhaps some free blacks held relatives or friends in nominal bondage in order that the group would carry only the lesser burden of property taxes on them. The state tax on an average slave, $0.39 in 1850 and $0.44 in 1860, amounted to less than one-tenth the $5.00 tax on adult free blacks.[30] Additional burdens on free blacks included the discriminatory county and town taxes, the registration fees, and the extra road duty. This fiscal explanation for black slaveowners might be traced through much of the Slave South.[31] Anthony Odinsells, a free black who inherited slaves from his white father, a planter on an island near Savannah, offers a possible example of such slave ownership in Georgia.[32]

In the 1850s, the Georgia Supreme Court tended to narrow the definition of black freedom by explicitly rejecting the notion that free blacks, "unless restricted by Statute," might claim all the privileges and duties that whites enjoyed. In an 1853 decision that prefigured the Dred Scott decision of 1857, Justice Lumpkin argued that liberty for black Georgians "signifies nothing but exemption from involuntary service." Rather, "to become a citizen of the body politic, capable of contracting, of marrying, of voting, requires something more than the mere act of [manumission]." In short, the court declared, "the status of the African in Georgia, whether bond or free, is such that he has no civil, social or political rights or capacity, whatever, except such as are bestowed on him by Statute."[33]

In the waning years of the Slave South, black freedom grew harder to get, harder to keep, and harder to distinguish from black slavery.

No doubt the law provides an imprecise index to the daily lives of antebellum Georgians—black or white, slave or free, male or female. In practice, free blacks may have enjoyed much more, or even less, freedom than the laws would indicate. The case of a free black teacher from Savannah illustrates the possibilities. In late 1865, soon after emancipation came to Georgia, the Freedmen's Bureau distributed questionnaires to teachers of former slaves. To the question, "How long has your school been organized?" most replies, as expected, were of the order of "three months." By contrast Jane A. Deveaux answered, "30 years." To the question, "Is public sentiment more favorable now, to the education of colored people, than when your school was first organized?" she responded simply, "Yes."[34]

But if Jane Deveaux escaped prosecution through all those years—and that is by no means certain—many free blacks did not. The whims of fortune, at least as much as industry, determined the paths that individual free blacks found in a harsh world. Few blacks obtained their freedom; some, having once obtained it, lost it, at least for a time, for reasons that related solely to race.

Liberty and Power

White Georgians found themselves divided by class but united by race. Merchants and planters dominated the private economy and largely shaped public policy; they paid the bulk of the taxes that financed their state and local governments, but they also benefited much more than did farmers or poor whites from public expenditures. Nevertheless yeomen and poor whites, like planters and merchants, enjoyed white skins and political rights. They too had some say in creating public policy and obtained some of its benefits.

Unlike the benefits, the burdens of public authority in antebellum Georgia fell primarily on social groups outside the political system. Indians, with their lands, and blacks, with their labor, provided the bulk of the resources that supported governmental operations. Race, then—even more than class—provides the key to the distribution of the costs and benefits of government in pre-Civil War Georgia.

For each group of whites—regardless of wealth—benefits outweighed costs. For nonwhites—people outside the political system but not beyond the reach of public authority—costs outweighed benefits.

Blacks and Indians contributed mightily to the liberty and property that white Georgians enjoyed. Slave labor generated much of the wealth in Georgia, and taxation absorbed a portion of that wealth, yet slaves received no discernible benefits from public spending. Rather, public authority buttressed the private power of slaveowners in controlling slaves as property. Free blacks paid poll taxes much greater than those paid by whites, but they obtained neither the educational benefits nor the political rights that provided the contemporary justification for poll taxes. Moreover, through road duty and hiring out—either in lieu of cash taxes or for violation of the registration laws—whites extracted significant amounts of labor from free blacks. Indians paid no poll or property taxes and received little protection of life or property. On the contrary, public authority operated to deprive them of their property and drive them from their land.

No phenomenon better captures the fundamental race bias of public policy in Georgia than the most important undertaking of the state government during its first half-century under the U.S. Constitution: the transfer of land from Indians to whites, land that was in turn, much of it, worked by slaves. Without the seizure of Indian lands and their subsequent sale to white farmers and planters, the state would have obtained neither its income from land sales in Georgia, nor the $1,250,000 from the Cession of 1802, nor the $1,051,000 it received as its share of the federal treasury surplus distribution in 1837. Blacks, too, were crucial to public revenue. Their labor gave value to the land, as public domain was converted to private farms and public funds. Moreover, taxes on slaves constituted nearly half of all the tax revenue of antebellum Georgia's state and local governments, and much of the rest of tax revenue came from land recently acquired from Indians.

Citizens of antebellum America did not equate liberty with the absence of government. Rather, liberty was the freedom to act, the capacity to accomplish their ends, and government served as a tool, gave them leverage. Implementing their instrumental conception of public authority, Georgia's citizens successfully used their state and local governments to promote their social and economic well-being. By employing public authority to deny blacks their freedom and Indians their land, whites enhanced their own liberty and property.

Part 2

REBEL FINANCE

9 RICH MAN'S WAR

CIVIL WAR came to America soon after Georgia and ten other states left the Union and formed the Confederacy. In November 1863, the war was in its third year as Governor Joseph E. Brown addressed the general assembly in Milledgeville. "I have heard it remarked," Brown observed, "that this is the rich man's quarrel and the poor man's fight, and that the abolition of slavery would not injure the poor, who are not slaveholders."[1]

One "poor man" from North Georgia spoke for thousands when he wrote Governor Brown in the spring of 1864. Not quite fifty years old and thus subject, under the recently extended military ages, to be called into action, Harlan Fuller wrote, "I am liable at any time to be taken away from my little crops leaving my family almost without provisions & no hope of making any crop atal. I have sent six sons to the war & now the 7th enrolled he being the last I have no help left atal." Though Fuller described his poor health, he concluded, "I dont mind the battle field but how can any man be there & hear both at the same time." In an attempt to demonstrate that he was no shirker in the cause, he showed how his dilemma applied to state and Confederate taxes as well as to the draft. "I have paid all Tythe & Tax held against me with the acception of 25 lb of bacon which is out of my power to pay til I can make another crop for I have not got that amount in the world."[2]

Yeoman discontent in Georgia and throughout the Confederacy led to cries of "a rich man's war and a poor man's fight." Like Harlan Fuller, a majority of white families owned no slaves and thus had no direct economic interest in protecting slave property. In a "rich man's war" fought to safeguard slavery through political independence, planters had the most to gain from victory, yet nonslaveholders often felt that they carried the burden of battle. The cry of "poor man's fight" resulted primarily from a provision in Confederate draft legislation that exempted one white male for each twenty slaves on a plantation. The law's objective had been to keep slaves under control so as to prevent slave uprisings and to maintain production, but many people perceived the draft exemption as an escape hatch for the wealthy, who also had the option of hiring substitutes to fight in their stead.[3]

Of the war's characterization as "the rich man's quarrel," Governor Brown declared: "A greater error has never been conceived." Brown explained why, in his view, all white Georgians shared a compelling interest in a Confederate victory. He stressed the loss in station that all whites, especially the nonslaveholding majority, would suffer in the event the Union won. A northern triumph would bring "despotism" and "bondage" to Georgia whites—not restoration of prewar conditions but "abolition, subjugation, and confiscation."[4] Blacks would no longer be slaves; as the equals of whites, they would enjoy equal access to schoolroom and ballot box. Georgians' nonslave property would be confiscated to pay the Union war debt, and whites would likely lose political rights while the Union army and former slaves ruled Georgia. Worst of all, Brown told his fellow citizens, propertyless whites would have to compete with blacks for employment and would see their wages bid steadily down. Employers would lose their interest in keeping up the value of labor and their concern with the welfare of their workers. In later years, Brown would have occasion to reflect that portions of his prophecy had come true. Certainly in 1863 he outlined the script that one writer later called "The Tragic Era."[5]

Though insisting that the war was by no means simply "the rich man's quarrel," Brown did not challenge the other half of the equation. Precisely because it was a poor man's fight in military terms, in fiscal terms it must be a rich man's fight. According to Brown, Georgia's slaveholders "are dependent upon our white laborers in the field of battle, for the protection of their property; and in turn, this army of white laborers and their families are dependent upon the slave owners for a support while thus engaged."[6]

The governor returned to these themes throughout the war. All whites needed a Confederate victory, so the poor must fight on. Because nonslaveholders provided the bulk of Confederate manpower, the wealthy must support them and their families. "As the poor have generally paid their part of the cost of this war in military service, exposure, fatigue and blood, the rich, who have been in a much greater degree exempt from these, should meet the money demands of the Government." In fact, Brown declared, "the wealth and property of the State must be taxed to any extent necessary to prevent suffering among the families of our brave defenders."[7] Georgia's fiscal behavior demonstrated that legislators tended to agree with the governor.

State Finance and the Battlefront

Similar as pre-Civil War North and South may have been in their fiscal and other public policies, the leading role that slavery played in Georgia's tax system foreshadowed the role it played in sectional confrontation. Even before Abraham Lincoln's victory in the 1860 presidential election, the threat of war began to affect fiscal policy in the South. Georgia responded to John Brown's raid at Harpers Ferry in 1859 with a legislative appropriation of $75,000 for military preparations. Shortly after Lincoln's election, but before secession, the general assembly voted a military fund for 1861 of $1,000,000, a figure that almost matched the entire state budget for

1860.[8] Even larger appropriations followed, as the fury of war began rapidly to tear down the fiscal structure that antebellum Georgians had built up.

In fiscal terms, Georgia fought the war on both the battlefront and the home front. The procurement of arms and clothing for soldiers absorbed roughly half of all war-related spending; the other half was nonmilitary. The bulk of state expenditures in the first year of the war went toward creating an army, but by 1864 the Confederate government had assumed the major responsibility for military spending. The support of civilians—in general, all indigent whites; in particular, the families of soldiers—took an increasing share of state spending. By spending millions of dollars to purchase and distribute corn, particularly in North Georgia, the state sought to make food available to all needy white Georgians, and not only to soldiers' families, according to need and the ability to pay.[9]

The Georgia Relief and Hospital Association, though it began as a volunteer organization, received a total of $1,280,000 from the state. It attempted to coordinate local efforts in sending physicians, nurses, and hospital supplies to Virginia, where nearly all of Georgia's soldiers were fighting. South Carolina and Louisiana, recognizing that the Confederate government could not immediately provide adequate medical services for their soldiers, organized state hospitals near the battlefront. Following their lead, and collecting both money and medical supplies, the Georgia association established three hospitals in Richmond in September and October 1861 and another the following May. Even in late 1862, a military correspondent disparaged the Confederate medical service in a comparison with the work of the Georgia association. "A planter who would take as little care of the health of his slaves as the government does of its soldiers," he concluded, "would soon have none to care for, while he would be driven out of the community by his indignant neighbors."[10]

The association collected $32,229 in voluntary cash contributions in 1861, but it soon sought public assistance. Its agents, it reported to the legislature that year, "have everywhere been met with the remark that such an organization could only be justly and equitably carried on by appropriations from the State." To support the association solely "by the voluntary contributions of the people, would make the burden fall upon a few which ought to be borne by all." At the governor's urging, the legislature responded with the first of several large annual appropriations. Voluntary contributions of cash and provisions diminished, the dimensions of the task grew ever greater, and the association became increasingly dependent on government funds.[11]

Even if the Confederacy provided full army rations, medical supplies, and attendants for the sick and wounded, the association desired more for the sons of Georgia. From its origins in 1861, the association aspired to provide clothing to the needy as well as care for the disabled. The legislature gradually broadened the association's authority with state funds. The $200,000 appropriation for 1862 was to be used only in caring for sick and wounded Georgia soldiers (or other soldiers wounded in defense of Georgia). As the association reported, however, "a cry of distress was heard from the army of the Potomac. Georgia soldiers were without clothing, shoes, and blankets; and though not sick or wounded, were in great physical suffering." When the legislature appropriated $400,000 for 1863, it included among the association's broader purposes the relief of destitute Georgia soldiers.[12]

Through most of the war, the Georgia Relief and Hospital Association proved a useful adjunct to the Confederacy's and the state's own service agencies. An "Agent of the State in disbursing its noble charity," the association combined a number of advantages that the state itself could not sustain: private contributions, volunteer labor, and "the liberality of those who have sold to us below the market price." These, together with free transportation on railroads, tripled what the association could do with the money it received from the state. Moreover, many hospital supplies, including blankets, "cannot be purchased with money; the ladies from their own private stores alone can furnish them." The association's "wayside homes," established near railroad stations in Georgia, provided medical care, food, clothing, and lodging to disabled soldiers on their way home. In 1863, after the Confederate government began to absorb the costs of hospitals and wayside homes, the legislature directed the association to use state funds to supply clothing and shoes only "to the sick, wounded, and such destitute Georgia soldiers as cannot reasonably obtain these articles from the Confederate Government, or from the clothing Bureau of the State of Georgia." Restricted to soldiers, the association's charity did not extend to civilians, even after Appomattox; at the end of 1865, $300,000 of the $500,000 appropriation for that year remained unexpended.[13]

Home Front

Soldiers might obtain food, clothing, and medical care, but who would look after their families? To assist families of soldiers in service, children and wives of deceased soldiers, and disabled veterans, the general assembly appropriated $2.5 million for 1863, $6 million for 1864, and $8 million for 1865. Agents handling the fund were directed "to see that no person shall receive any aid or assistance . . . who has sufficient property, or means of support, or . . . who might have a sufficiency, by using proper industry and labor." Funds were to be apportioned to the counties according to the number of beneficiaries reported. The 1863 act defined the "indigent" as children under the age of twelve and "Wives, Mothers, Grand Mothers, and all who have to leave their ordinary business in the house, and to labor in the fields to support themselves and children, and who are not able to make a sufficient support for themselves and families." It also directed, if supplies were adequate, that provisions be sold, for cost and transportation, to the "partly self-sustaining."[14]

Not only soldiers and their dependents were threatened with destitution. Corn (to make bread) and salt (to preserve meat) grew increasingly scarce; so did cotton and woolen cards (to prepare fibers for making clothing). As they did so, the state made increasingly urgent efforts to procure the "necessaries of life" and distribute them at cost to the people of Georgia. To obtain these and other commodities, the state established its own factories and its own import trade. Responding to civilian as well as military needs common to all the Confederate states, Georgia's broad actions paralleled those followed elsewhere in the South.[15]

Before the war, Georgians had produced little of the salt they consumed, and with the federal blockade threatening to close off imports, the legislature sought to assure a sufficient supply. In 1861 it made $50,000 available without interest to encourage private Georgia companies to manufacture salt. When that effort proved ineffective, the state took matters more directly into its own hands. In 1862 and again in 1863, it appropriated $500,000 to produce and distribute salt. After saltworks along the Georgia coast fell to federal troops early in the war, Georgia depended for its salt primarily upon producers in Virginia. The state determined to break even on its salt operations; after giving salt (or selling it at a nominal price) to soldiers' dependents, the state sold what remained at a price sufficient to reimburse itself for the entire cost. As the governor reported, "By the adoption of this plan, all who purchase are taxed something for the assistance of the soldiers' families and widows." Despite the disruption of transportation as East Tennessee and other parts of the South fell to the Union, the state was able to continue supplying soldiers' families through late 1864.[16]

To augment the supply of cotton cards, the legislature appropriated $100,000 in 1862, $200,000 in 1863, and $1,000,000 in 1864. The cards—large brushes constructed of wire bristles and a leather and wood backing—constituted both a military and a civilian need. The funds were intended either to encourage private manufacturing or to provide the state itself with the necessary machinery and materials. Georgia established a cotton card factory at the penitentiary. It also imported cotton cards, even through the blockade. The governor was directed to apportion some of the resulting cards among the counties for distribution to "the poor" and to sell the remainder to citizens at prices that would reimburse the state.[17]

In addition to the appropriations to assist soldiers' families, the Georgia legislature passed three acts directed specifically at the needs of North Georgia. "Whereas," it explained in the first one, "owing to the depredations of the enemy, and the presence and necessities of our own army foraging upon the country, and also the extreme droughth and early frost, the people of North Georgia are in great need of breadstuffs; and whereas, nearly the entire laboring population of said section is now in the army, and the people must inevitably suffer unless aided by the generosity of the State," the general assembly authorized a total of $1,890,000 to provide corn in that region. The first act, in November 1863, provided for the purchase of between 3,000 and 10,000 bushels of corn to be distributed in each of sixteen North Georgia counties. The indigent poor in general, as well as the families of soldiers either in service or deceased, were to be given "a sufficient quantity of corn for their bread, and no more, free of charge." Other people, "destitute of corn" but not indigent, might purchase it. In March 1864, the legislature authorized the governor to procure as much as 10,000 bushels each for Habersham County (North Georgia) and any other counties "alike destitute." Finally, in November 1864, the legislature appropriated $800,000 for corn for the indigent poor "in the counties . . . overrun by the enemy, and such other counties as may be destitute," to be distributed free to people unable to pay and sold to others.[18]

The Georgia legislature passed other types of extraordinary welfare measures during the war. Toward the end of the first year of war, a disastrous fire swept Charleston, South Carolina. Upon Governor Brown's request for emergency assistance to a sister city, "threatened by sea and land by . . . [our] powerful and relentless enemy," the legislature appropriated $100,000 "for the relief of the unfortunate sufferers." [19]

In 1862 the governor brought to legislators' attention the danger that returning soldiers might infest their counties with smallpox. The general assembly responded by authorizing special quarantine hospitals, at state expense, for each county's smallpox victims. The governor, subsequently angered by what he considered the exorbitant bills submitted by some doctors, recommended firm guidelines for payments—and compensation at all only for the expenses of people "unable to pay." Overreacting again, the legislature repealed the act. Accounts that arose while the act was still in force, from nearly half the counties in Georgia, cost the state more than $140,000.[20]

By 1862, when the state began to shoulder the burden of assisting soldiers' families, a grain shortage threatened Georgia. In 1863 Governor Brown declared that "the great question in this revolution is now a question of *bread*." Because the blockade prevented exports, Georgians had little need for more cotton, and with Kentucky and Tennessee in Union hands, Georgia had to supply its own food. Moreover, given that whites at the battlefront could not be working in the corn fields, grain production had to come from the black belt; if distilled into alcohol, grain could not become bread. The legislature threatened unauthorized stills with impressment for the military value of the copper they contained, and it limited cotton cultivation to three acres per hand (though Brown repeatedly sought a limit of a quarter-acre).[21]

During the Civil War, the state of Georgia demonstrated an active solicitude for the welfare of its citizens. It attempted to regulate crop productions to assure an adequate food supply. To greater effect, it distributed the "necessaries of life" to people according to their need and their ability to pay. Though these extraordinary welfare measures took the larger share of the state budget in the last two years of the war, total spending for civilian welfare amounted to slightly less than aggregate wartime military expenditures.

Peacetime Spending in Wartime

The state budget ballooned to unprecedented proportions in Georgia during the Civil War, yet, even in the face of enormous inflation, normal expenditures shrank (see table 3.) Though the state continued to finance most of its prewar activities, it obtained some funds for war by cutting normal expenses. The principal of the Academy for the Blind set the tone in the first year of war: "We are in the midst of a war, which taxes very greatly the resources of the State and of the people. It is a time for general retrenchment and the practice of the most rigid economy. Generous and patriotic citizens everywhere are vying with each other in acts of self-denial, sacrifice and devotion to the cause of the country's defence and of Southern Independence." [22]

The state curtailed its support for railroad construction. After spending $500,000 for stock in the Atlantic and Gulf Railroad in the late prewar years, the state invested only $200,000 more. An 1856 act had authorized the governor to purchase, at the rate of $5 in state subscriptions to $6 in private ones, as much as $1,000,000 in stock of the Atlantic and Gulf. After 1862 the state made no further payments during the war. It invested its final $300,000 in the railroad in 1866–67. [23]

Only in part did the state continue to pay principal and interest on its prewar debt, a category of expenditure that continued to dominate the peacetime portion of the budget. That debt, most of it originally incurred to accelerate construction of the state railroad, had been steadily reduced in recent years. Now the debt, which amounted to $2.7 million in 1860, accumulated through failure to keep up interest payments. Many investors, particularly those in Britain and the North, declined to request payment, because they would have received Confederate or Georgia treasury notes. [24] Moreover, the peacetime debt grew by $150,000 when the governor issued that amount in bonds to pay most of the $200,000 invested in the Atlantic and Gulf during the war. Thus each postwar regime, whether Democratic or Republican, would inherit a legacy of heavy public indebtedness from the prewar years, compounded by nonpayment during the war.

In cutting legislative expenses, Georgia resorted to a traditional retrenchment measure. In the early 1840s, to reduce public spending in the face of severe fiscal difficulties, the state had reduced the size of both house and senate, and it had switched from annual to biennial legislative sessions. In the 1850s, as the fiscal squeeze relaxed its grip, the reductions were reversed and the legislature resumed annual sessions. With Georgia facing unknown dangers and costs, however, the secession convention rewrote the state constitution to

TABLE 3. *Annual State Treasury Disbursements, 1859–1864*

	1859		1860		1861	
	($)	(%)	($)	(%)	($)	(%)
Peacetime	874	100.0	1,136	96.4	819	41.9
Military	—	—	43	3.6	1,137	58.1
Wartime welfare	—	—	—	—	—	—
Total	874	100.0	1,179.	100.0	1,956	100.0

Source: Annual Reports of the Comptroller General.
Notes: The fiscal year ended 15 October.
  Dollar amounts are rounded to the nearest $1,000.
  "Peacetime" expenditures included the administrative costs of government, normal social spending (not wartime civilian welfare), investment in the Atlantic and Gulf Railroad, and payments on prewar debt. Exception: The 1862 and 1863 figures for spending on state debt, though counted here as peacetime expenditures, in fact included some unspecified amounts due on wartime indebtedness.

economize again. By grouping counties into senatorial districts, as had been done in the 1840s, the new constitution reduced the size of the senate by two-thirds.[25]

That action held the administrative costs of government to a modest increase, from an annual average of $187,000 in the fiscal years 1856–60 to an average of $212,000 in 1861–64. The general assembly met only once a year through 1862 but, under wartime necessity, it held extra, early sessions in 1863, 1864, and 1865. Expenditures for the legislature, the largest item among the costs of government, nevertheless showed little change before the final year of war. Legislators were paid $6 per day, plus an allowance for mileage as late as 1864, but in early 1865 inflation finally led to a per diem of $30. The regular 1864 and special 1865 legislatures together cost $229,000 in fiscal 1865, compared with only $116,000 for the 1860 session.[26]

As budgetary surpluses rapidly vanished, Georgia reversed the 1850s trend toward greater spending on social welfare. The connection between nontax revenue and social spending continued through the 1860s, but nontax revenue plummeted. Though the state continued to distribute the school fund throughout the war, the amount declined slightly from $150,000 in 1860 to $137,000 in 1864, then sharply to $79,787 in 1865. But that money could educate far fewer students after it paid inflation's toll. An 1863 act stipulated that teachers of poor students should receive the same remuneration as those of paying

1862		1863		1864	
($)	(%)	($)	(%)	($)	(%)
713	9.0	806	11.0	831	6.3
7,202	90.9	4,537	61.6	5,727	43.1
10	0.1	2,009	27.3	6,730	50.6
7,925	100.0	7,352	100.0	13,288	100.0

The military spending figure given here for 1862 includes $2.5 million for the Confederate tax of that year, which the state assumed for its citizens.

Wartime welfare figures include only civilian expenditures—spending on soldiers' families, for example, but not on the Relief and Hospital Association.

students, up to $0.16 per student in attendance each day. A similar act in February 1865 raised the limit to $0.75 per student per day.[27]

Successive statements by Governor Brown demonstrate changing attitudes toward education. In November 1861, he advised the legislature, "While our financial embarrassments growing out of the war may be very considerable," it would be better to levy additional taxes than to use the education fund for other purposes. A year later he recommended that the entire revenue of the Western and Atlantic Railroad—the chief source of education funds—be appropriated for the needy families of soldiers. Toward the end of the war, with General William Tecumseh Sherman driving through Georgia, Brown's priorities had shifted still further: "As our schools cannot be conducted with success, till we have a change in the condition of the country, I recommend that the school fund, for the future, be applied to the support of the widows and orphans of our soldiers, till we can again revive our educational interests."[28]

Georgia's nascent public elementary school system, like its great proponent Governor Brown, bowed to the realities of war. Even aside from inflation's effects, war curtailed the educational and employment opportunities that had flourished with late antebellum public spending on schools. A number of counties diverted education funds to the support of soldiers' families. In 1861, when the legislature empowered counties to use any funds except school funds to clothe soldiers and support their families, it also legitimized prior appropriations made of "any funds." Two years later, it authorized counties to use any "surplus" education funds for the relief of indigent soldiers' families. Only a few counties continued to levy school taxes—and thus to supplement their shares of the state fund—as late as 1863.[29] Not until 1873 would public funding of schools in Georgia again attain the 1860 level.

Appropriations for the insane asylum, even in the face of inflation, remained roughly constant. Patients continued to produce $3,000 to $6,000 worth of garden produce, milk, meat, poultry, eggs, lard, soap, and clothing each year. Revenue from paying patients, $14,000 in 1860, continued in similar amounts, but in depreciating Confederate currency. The 1850s building program ended, but the cost of provisions, the most expensive item in the institution's wartime budget, climbed rapidly. The number of inmates declined by 10 percent during the war, from 322 in 1861 to 290 in late 1864, but appropriations for the support of pauper patients grew from $17,000 to $92,000. The superintendent of the asylum expressed the urgent need to keep it operating: "There never has been a period in which, to the poorer classes of our people, the existence of the Institution, and the provision in it for the care of their unfortunate friends, must have been felt so [great a] blessing. When burdened by [the] cares and anxieties [of] war, and . . . struggling themselves for the means of subsistence, to have had imposed upon them the grievous burden in addition of providing for and taking proper care of one of those hapless ones, would indeed have been a calamity." [30]

The school for the deaf received $10,000 in 1861, its last full year of operations before Reconstruction. After the two principal teachers left to enter the military, the board of trustees sent most pupils home and closed the school in March 1862. As late as 1864, however, the legislature appropriated $1,200 to support two orphan girls "who are left there, and who have no homes nor relatives to take care of them." To look after the two girls and the institution's property, the trustees selected a family to occupy the premises.[31]

The Georgia Academy for the Blind had to struggle, but, like the insane asylum, it maintained operations through the Civil War. In December 1863, when the Confederate army required suitable accommodations for a military hospital near Macon, the academy relinquished its home and moved thirty miles southwest to Fort Valley. The number of students at the school, after reaching a prewar maximum of thirty-one in 1860, ranged in the twenties during the war. "In view of the probable pressure upon the State Treasury, and the necessity of economizing in all branches of the public service," the academy, after receiving $7,000 to pay salaries and maintain pupils in 1861, requested only $6,000 for each of the next two years. As provisions grew more costly, however, the school found it necessary to double its request for 1864 and 1865; rather than see the academy shut down, the legislature granted each request. Funds or no funds, educational and building materials became unavailable, but, though the academy had to economize and change location, it remained open. The principal could write in late 1864 that, though "war, with all its horrors and desolating influences, afflicts the land, this Institution is quietly maintaining its way in the career of beneficence for which it was designed." [32]

Even without taking inflation into account, state spending on higher education dropped after 1860. In an epilogue to the state aid to medical schools in the 1850s, the 1860 legislature appropriated $10,000 for the Medical College of Georgia at Augusta. The only other school to receive state support in the early 1860s was the Georgia Military Institute at Marietta. GMI received $44,000 for what turned out to be not peacetime but wartime purposes. While the stampede of students to the battlefront forced most men's colleges to close, the Georgia Military Institute stayed open to prepare young men for war. Cadets drilled Georgia recruits; graduates became military officers. The school finally closed in spring 1864 when Governor Brown called the cadets to active duty as part of the state militia. The buildings of GMI, like those of other schools that closed down during the war, became military hospitals—first for the Confederate army, then for the Union. Later, the institute's buildings were among those torched by Sherman's army. The school never reopened.[33]

The state penitentiary, having absorbed an annual average of nearly $20,000 in the four years before the war, received only $10,000 in 1861 and nothing further by way of direct appropriation until after the war. The institution's ability to assist the war effort, and its receipt of sums from the state military fund, enabled it to appear self-sustaining. Early in the war, the legislature authorized the use of the penitentiary as both an armory and a card factory. "The prospect of making Guns by convict labor is not very flattering," observed the master armorer in late 1862, though the governor reported more confidently that the armory was prepared to "turn out an excellent arm at the rate of about 125 per month." Citing "the great and pressing need of clothing for our soldiers, and the people," the adjutant general diverted the workers at the armory to constructing machines for a card factory. "Consequently," he reported in 1863, "but little has been done in the manufacture of arms."[34] Despite gloomy assessments, the convicts accomplished both tasks.

In addition to performing such traditional tasks as repairing state buildings, penitentiary inmates produced salt sacks, shoes, cotton cards, guns, tents, furniture, and knapsacks. War conditions blunted the force of normal prison discipline, such as the requirement of silence while at work, when, as the principal keeper observed, "free and convict labor are brought together and employed in the same shop" and even "at the same work-bench or forge." By the last year of the war, the penitentiary's contributions to the war effort diminished. The cost of provisions for men and mules escalated; raw materials became unavailable for manufacturing; and the number of workers declined, though as late as October 1864, inmates still numbered 151 men and 6 women. As General Sherman approached Milledgeville that month, Governor Brown pardoned all convicts except "the worst class," provided they would enter the military. Sherman had ample reason to destroy the penitentiary as a military facility, though the remaining convicts may have set it ablaze before Union troops could do so.[35]

10 RICH MAN'S FIGHT

HOLD THE LINE as it might on normal expenditures, Georgia had to find extraordinary means to finance its wartime endeavors. The state financed its spending with railroad earnings, massive borrowing, and increased taxation. Shifts in the relative importance of these sources reflected significant changes in the ways the state financed operations before, during, and after the war (see table 4). In particular, the wealthy paid a much larger share of taxes in war than in peacetime.

State Revenue

The Western and Atlantic Railroad continued to contribute to the state treasury. It also proved useful in transporting corn from Southwest Georgia to soldiers' families and the other poor in North Georgia. Governor Brown, as he explained, ordered the state railroad's freight rates "raised from time to time, so as to keep them nearly as high as the freights on other Roads. This enables the State to raise, by the use of the Road, a considerable amount of revenue in a manner less burdensome to the people of this State than it could be done in any other way, and to transport freights necessary for the support of the poor without charge." In late 1863, Brown ordered rates doubled on Confederate freight: "With the heavy increase of expenses, it will not be possible to make the Road a source of much revenue and charge less." As the war continued, however, the Western and Atlantic produced less revenue, and other sources supplied much more.[1]

Borrowing proved especially important in the middle years of the war. Indeed, half of the state government's total revenue in the years 1861–65 resulted from the creation of various forms of public indebtedness, particularly state bonds and state treasury notes. After the war, as one of the conditions of readmission to the Union, Georgia repudiated its wartime indebtedness, and thus the value of those bonds and treasury notes vanished. Georgia's wealthier wartime citizens lost all the funds they had gambled on the war effort through loans to the state and Confederate governments.

Georgia issued state bonds for the 1861 military appropriation ($867,000) and the state's assumption of the Confederate war tax for the same year ($2,441,000), for a total of $3,308,500. After 1861, as Governor Brown explained, the state favored "Treasury notes, bearing no interest, in place of

bonds bearing interest." Treasury notes became more readily acceptable because — being generally of smaller denominations than bonds and not intended
primarily for investment purposes — they circulated more easily. Their issue
provided one-fourth of the state's entire revenue in 1862 and two-thirds in
1863 and 1864. Redeemable in taxes, treasury notes were issued for revenue
pending receipt of annual taxes.[2]

Because silver change disappeared from circulation after the banks suspended specie payment in December 1860, the state sought to replace silver
with paper change bills of small denominations. The treasury issued nearly
$1.5 million worth of change bills, and the Western and Atlantic was autho-
rized to issue $200,000, a ceiling later lifted. Secured by the value of the state
railroad, those bills were receivable in payment of any obligations due the
state, including taxes, or to the railroad.[3]

As the war continued, taxation became increasingly important as a source
of state revenue. The gradual decline in property tax rates through the 1850s
was abruptly and radically reversed (see fig. 3). Rates multiplied by fifteen
between 1860 and 1864. In contrast to the late prewar time of nontax bounty,
moreover, taxation remained the major source of state revenue in most postwar years. Until the mid-twentieth century, when Georgia abandoned the state
property tax in favor of a general sales tax, rates remained much higher than
prewar levels. The highest general property tax rate of the 1850s, $1.00 per
$1,000 valuation, was only one-tenth the 1864 rate, $10.00; rates from 1867
through the end of the century ranged from a low of $2.50 to a high of $6.21.[4]

Though the state borrowed most of its budget in the first half of the war, the
property tax rate nearly tripled in that period. At the time of Lincoln's election, the 1860 legislature increased the tax levy for 1861 by half, from $400,000
to $600,000. For 1862, Governor Brown advised that the state not tax the full
amount of revenue it needed that year. As he explained: "The war tax imposed
by the Confederate Government, together with the expenses assumed by different counties for supplies needed by their Companies in the service, will
greatly increase the burdens of taxation." To avoid "too onerous" a burden, he
suggested a tax of $1,000,000 for state purposes, which the legislature autho-
rized. From $0.65 per $1,000 in 1860, the rate rose to $1.05 in 1861 and $1.85
in 1862.[5]

After tax time in April 1862, property values rose sharply as the value of
currency shrank. Because people professed uncertainty whether to report their
holdings in gold or currency values, the state required that, beginning in 1863,
property values be reported in Confederate currency. The total increase in
valuation permitted a slight reduction in the tax rate to $1.70, even though tax
revenue for 1863 was established at $1,500,000, or half again that for the
previous year.[6]

For 1864 the general assembly authorized a state property tax rate of up to 1
percent ($10.00 per $1,000), and that is the figure eventually established. The

TABLE 4. *Annual State Treasury Receipts, 1859–1864*

	1859		1860		1861	
	($)	(%)	($)	(%)	($)	(%)
Borrowing	151	14.6	201	17.3	1,018	50.8
Taxation	425	41.2	431	37.0	483	24.1
Earnings	447	43.3	487	41.8	471	23.5
Miscellaneous	9	0.9	46	3.9	33	1.6
Total	1,033	100.0	1,165	100.0	2,005	100.0

Source: Annual Reports of the Comptroller General.
Notes: The fiscal year ended 15 October.
  Dollar amounts are rounded to the nearest $1,000.

1864 rate, at six times the 1863 rate and fifteen times that of 1860, was the highest state property tax in Georgia's history. For 1865 the legislature at first set a rate of $5.00 per $1,000, and later increased it to $9.00.[7] By such standards, the Reconstruction levies under Democrats and Republicans alike proved modest indeed, even though rates were substantially higher every year after the war than in any year before it.

By 1863, the midpoint of the war, Georgia's tax system had already become less proportional and more progressive than in the past. Not only had inflation driven up assessed property valuation, but tax rates had been increased against those higher values. Poll taxes, by contrast, had not increased and were declining in real terms. For tax purposes the average value of a Georgia slave in 1860 had been $673; by 1863 it was $913. On those values, as the rate rose from $0.65 to $1.70 per $1,000, the average tax paid on a slave jumped from $0.44 to $1.55. At the same time, the value of the $0.25 poll tax, in terms of taxable property, shrank from $385 to $147. By 1864, with the average slave valued at $1,761 (and carrying a state tax of $17.61), the property-value equivalent of the poll tax had dropped to $40.[8]

Because the wholesale price index has been computed as being forty times as high in mid-1864 as in early 1861,[9] the question arises: Did inflation so increase property values relative to their assessed valuation as to render the tax increases only nominal? The nineteenth-century property tax was an effort to tax income indirectly according to wealth, and wholesale prices during the war cannot offer an adequate guide to income. Precisely because commodity production declined, as well as because the state and Confederate governments printed bushels of treasury notes, prices went up and up.

1862		1863		1864	
($)	(%)	($)	(%)	($)	(%)
6,600	79.6	5,742	65.6	9,833	73.7
743	9.0	1,262	14.4	3,055	22.9
476	5.6	1,711	19.5	329	2.5
474	5.7	44	0.5	118	0.9
8,294	100.0	8,758	100.0	13,335	100.0

The 1863 figure for earnings from investments includes a substantial but unspecified sum due the previous year from the Confederate government for its use of the Western and Atlantic Railroad.

In real terms, in fact, most people's wealth and income declined. Real estate values did not keep pace with the cost of bacon or corn, for example, when reductions in manpower led to smaller crops, and then heavy Confederate taxation—particularly impressment and the tax-in-kind—diverted portions of those crops from producers' hands. As the *Milledgeville Southern Recorder* commented in 1864, "The amount already called for by the State and Confederate governments encroaches upon the principal of capital in most cases, as no planter within our knowledge is now making money." [10]

Rising taxes in the face of declining income forced Georgia legislators to reconsider the tax system. Seeking to make it both more productive and more equitable, the legislature renovated the system by combining the principles of the income tax and the ad valorem tax. A legislative resolution called for measures "casting the burdens of the war mainly on those who make a profit out of it." [11] The exigencies of war and the politics of financing it brought about tax changes that went beyond the higher ad valorem rates.

In December 1862 a tax was levied on cotton and other agricultural products held as merchandise. As usual in times of severe shortage, speculators were blamed for high prices. Little cotton left Georgia in 1861 and 1862; much of it was bought by speculators, who failed to report their holdings as taxable property. To clarify the tax status of such property, the new measure declared that all agricultural produce "held for barter or sale" each April 1 beginning in 1863, and "not belonging to the original producer," would be considered merchandise and thus taxable like other property. Thus legislators sought to tap the property of speculators and to encourage the production of food crops instead of cotton. [12]

In April 1863 the general assembly enacted a measure intended both to reach more untaxed wealth and to redistribute that wealth downward in the social structure. A progressive income tax was levied on the net profits from manufacturing or sales (including speculators' sales of agricultural products). Its proceeds were to be used to support disabled soldiers and the indigent families of soldiers either in service or deceased.[13]

Other measures offered direct tax relief to holders of little or no property. "In consideration of the hardships and privations endured by our soldiers in service, and the necessities of the families of many of them," as Governor Brown put it, Georgia reduced its soldiers' tax burdens. For 1863 the legislature exempted from both poll and property taxes any soldier owning less than $1,000 worth of property. For 1864 it doubled the exemption to $2,000 for citizens whose total property was worth no more than $10,000 in the increasingly inflated currency, and it applied the exemption not only to soldiers in service but also to the growing numbers of wives and children of deceased soldiers and to soldiers who returned home disabled.[14]

County Finance

The fiscal behavior of county governments in Civil War Georgia matched that of the state. County governments issued certificates of indebtedness to create purchasing power, and they increased their taxes both to redeem such short-term debt and to spread the wartime costs of government more or less evenly among their taxpayers according to the prewar standard of equity. As the 1861 legislature declared of county finances: "The burdens of common defence . . . against our common enemy, should be borne equally by all, in proportion to the value of their property." [15]

Like the state, counties modified the prewar standard of equity by deriving larger shares of their revenue from wealthier residents. Georgia's tax-relief measures, along with the new tax on speculators' cotton, applied to county as well as state taxes. Each county continued, as before the war, to levy its annual tax as a percentage of each of its taxpayers' state poll and property taxes. Therefore, changes in the state tax system automatically resulted in changes in each county's tax structure.[16]

County taxes also resembled state taxes in that rates rose sharply to new highs. Because the state property tax rate nearly tripled by mid-war, even a constant percentage of the state tax could produce substantially higher county revenue. Most counties, however, increased the percentage itself in the first years of the war. Thus, through 1863 the county tax burden rose even faster than did the state burden.

The tax rates of Early County in the cotton belt offer a good example of the wartime pattern. Early County levied taxes of 75 percent of state rates in

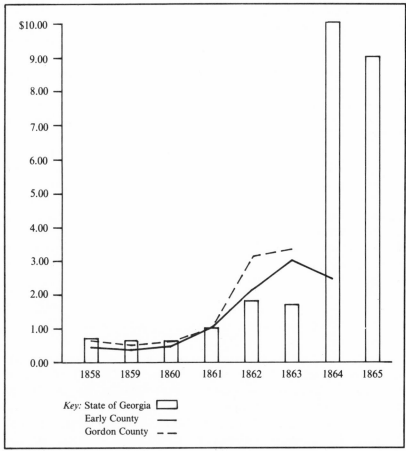

FIGURE 3. *State and County Property Tax Rates, 1858–1865*

Sources: ICM, Early and Gordon counties (mfm, GDAH).
Notes: Rates displayed are per $1,000 valuation. See chapter 10, notes 7, 17.

1860, 100 percent the next year, 115 percent in 1862, and 175 percent in 1863. The sharp rise in the state rate in 1864 permitted the county to lower its rate to 25 percent of state taxes, which brought the effective rate for that year down slightly from the 1863 peak. Effective county rates on property in Early County from 1860 through 1864 amounted to $0.49 per $1,000 in 1860 and, in the four following years, $1.05, $2.13, $2.98, and $2.50 per $1,000. Rates in North Georgia's Gordon County resembled those in black-belt Early County (see fig. 3).[17]

While the state divided its wartime funds almost evenly between military and wartime welfare expenditures, counties spent a larger share on welfare.

Even more than the state, many counties taxed the wealthy to alleviate hardships among families whose menfolk were off at war.[18] At first, volunteers supplied their own equipment, but it soon became clear that many could neither equip themselves nor support their families while away. Throughout the state, citizens voluntarily contributed money, clothing, and provisions for one or both purposes. Like many counties, Early County equalized the burden by levying taxes and using the proceeds to reimburse contributors; thus each resident was required to share such wartime costs "in proportion to his tax." Early County issued certificates, payable for county taxes, to citizens in the amounts they had contributed for the support of soldiers and their families.[19]

The 1861 legislature authorized all counties to issue bonds and impose extra taxes to equip volunteers and, where necessary, support their families. Taxes levied for the support of soldiers' families were payable either in cash or in articles of food and clothing. Beyond such general legislation, special acts authorized specific counties to levy extra taxes. Stewart and Sumter counties, for example, were authorized to levy an extra tax up to three times the state tax to support soldiers' indigent families; soldiers whose property was worth less than $2,000 were to be exempt from this additional tax.[20]

Centralizing Authority

The county governments initiated financial assistance for soldiers' families, but, as Governor Brown repeatedly advised the legislature, the problem required a state solution rather than a local one. Georgia's soldiers "from every part of the State," he noted, "fight for the protection of the liberties of the whole people, and the wealth of the whole State." To combat desertion, Georgians must provide for soldiers' families. "Let our soldiers know that their loved ones at home are provided for," the governor urged. Should the army become "demoralized, " he warned, "our liberties and property are all lost."[21] Many of Georgia's volunteers were "almost destitute of property," and "their families should be supplied, if need be, at the public expense, with such of the necessaries of life as their labor will not afford them, cost the State what it may." Counties varied widely in wealth. Those populated mostly with small farmers, rather than with planters and their slaves, had proportionally less wealth to tax, yet more needy families to support. "Some of the wealthier counties . . . are providing amply for the wants of the soldiers' families, while others are not able, without an oppressive tax, to render the large number within their limits much assistance."[22]

To provide adequate support for soldiers' families and to distribute the cost fairly among Georgia's taxpayers, the governor concluded, both justice and necessity mandated massive state taxes and appropriations. Let planters in the wealthier counties help nonslaveholders in poorer districts. Governor Brown's messages to the general assembly captured the essence of fiscal politics in Civil War Georgia.

Government responsibility grew increasingly concentrated as the war continued, and as responsibilities shifted so did costs. Military spending was absorbed in successive (and overlapping) waves by the volunteers, their county governments, the state government, and, increasingly, the Confederate government. Wartime welfare spending, on the other hand, passed only through the overlapping stages of private, county, and state responsibility. At first, while the state focused its attention on military spending, the counties exerted themselves to support soldiers' families. As the Confederate government absorbed a growing share of military spending, the state took on a larger share of the responsibility for wartime welfare. In nearly every case, county taxes peaked by 1863, while state taxes showed their sharpest rise in 1864, as the state expanded operations and took over functions that, in the first years of war, the counties had managed. That takeover shifted the burden, first of military expenditures and then of wartime welfare, toward those Georgians most able to bear it.

Comprised of many more men from nonslaveholding families than from slaveowning families, the Confederate armies reflected white southern society. Slaveholders and nonslaveholders alike fought for political independence and resisted what they saw as aggression from without. Though nonslaveholders may have perceived no direct economic interest in maintaining slavery, both groups shared a central belief that they must fight to maintain the white supremacy that slavery symbolized and guaranteed. Prodding his constituents to continue their exertions, Governor Brown urged: "Let it never be said that . . . [the poor man] is disinterested, when the momentous decision is to be made, whether he is in future to be the superior, or only the equal of the negro." [23]

Yet as the war ground on, more of the soldiers from the ranks of nonslaveholders grumbled about a "rich man's war and a poor man's fight." When they heard that in their absence their families were suffering deprivation, many deserted the battlefront to return home. The central objective of massive public spending, at state and county levels alike, was to lessen that cause of desertion. [24] And the funds for such expenditures could be extracted only from people who had a surplus.

Robin Hood

Not only did total state and local taxes rise sharply during the war, but Georgia's wealthier citizens carried larger shares of the burden after 1862. An income tax, a tax on cotton, and enormously increased property tax rates were coupled with property-tax reductions for yeomen soldiers and poll taxes that were left unchanged or even suspended entirely. All these measures represented efforts to fend off disaffection on the part of poorer whites as well as a realistic assessment of the limited sources from which additional tax revenue could be derived. Moreover, by levying sharply higher state property taxes in 1864 in order to supply extraordinary welfare needs that the counties had serviced in the first half of the war, Georgia further redistributed the costs of wartime welfare.

The Civil War forced a modification of the prewar principle that taxation should be proportional to the amount of property owned. Even more than the repelling of invasion or the securing of political independence, slavery was the fundamental issue of the war. Prewar attitudes and policy mandated that planters pay the bulk of state and county taxes, but now slavery itself was at stake. In financing a war to secure slave ownership, planters had both the ability and the obligation to pay even more of the taxes. "As the war is now prosecuted by the Lincoln Government, for the avowed purpose of abolishing slavery," Governor Brown warned the legislature soon after the Emancipation Proclamation, "no class of our people has so much at stake as our slaveholders, ... our chief planters." [25]

When social and economic survival replaced economic growth and nontax revenue as the overriding objectives of fiscal policy, public authority in Georgia took on a new role. The prewar program of promoting economic growth and welfare for the entire citizenry, while maintaining the uneven distribution of wealth, gave way to a wartime objective of preserving the social and economic benefits that white Georgians derived from slavery. At the same time that the less wealthy paid proportionally less of Georgia's state and county taxes, they gained larger shares of the benefits from public spending. By shifting costs upward and benefits downward in the white social structure, Georgia's state and local governments used their fiscal powers to reallocate purchasing power. Before the war, public authority had operated to transfer wealth across race lines by expropriating Indian lands and by buttressing slavery. A war to maintain racial domination produced redistribution across class lines.

The Robin Hood pattern of taking from the rich to give to the poor resulted largely from actions taken by the wealthy themselves. North Georgia yeomen and black-belt planters differed less on spending policy than on the means of payment. As before the war, delegates from planter districts tended to advocate higher state taxes than North Georgians were willing to enact. Differences on tax policy clearly emerged halfway through the war when, like Governor Brown, many Georgians became convinced that greatly increased taxation constituted an essential way station on the road to independence. Tax rate proposals for 1864 ranged from $5 to $15 per $1,000. Representative James F. Dever of North Georgia's Polk County (61 percent white in 1860) sought to reduce a proposed $15 tax to $5; only partially successful, he then tried to cut a proposed $10 tax to $7.50. Unsuccessful in that second effort, he initiated a protest against "oppressive taxation." Led by B. H. Bigham of Troup County (only 38 percent white), the cotton belt presented a counterprotest.[26]

The theme of wartime stringency evoked varying renditions among planters and yeomen. In 1864 Judge Iverson L. Harris recited the black belt's version to the Baldwin County grand jury: "No man has performed his whole duty who allows the families of our veteran soldiers to be neglected." In a typical statement from the upcountry, the *Rome Tri-Weekly Courier* observed that "in some sections of the State, the enemy and our own troops have so exhausted the usual resources of the people, that it will be impossible for them to realize anything like their usual income," and therefore a state tax of $10 or $15 per $1,000, in addition to Confederate taxes, would produce "great distress." [27]

Though planters' representatives approved greater reliance on taxation than farmers found acceptable, planters did not welcome higher taxes on themselves. Before final passage of the tax measure for 1864, planters opposed farmers over the question of property tax exemptions. Representing the cotton-belt county of Hancock (32 percent white), Linton Stephens proposed raising the standard exemption from $200 worth of property to $3,500. When Stephens's motion failed, J. D. Matthews of Oglethorpe County (35 percent white) proposed an increase to $1,000. L. N. Trammell, from North Georgia's Catoosa County (86 percent white), countered with a motion to table Matthews's proposal in favor of a higher exemption of $2,000 that would apply only to soldiers' families. Predictably, the black belt demonstrated less support for Trammell's motion than did the upcountry, but on this issue North Georgia had its way.[28]

By March 1863 there could be little question that, as Governor Brown pointed out, "the country and the army are mainly dependent upon slave labor for support." Slaves produced much of the food that supported the white population, military and civilian, upcountry and black belt. If whites could be conscripted, blacks could be impressed, and slaves not only continued to run railroads but also built fortifications. Many planters reluctantly agreed with a Georgia judge's admonition that "everything beyond a mere support should be devoted to the cause." But if planters permitted their slaves to be impressed, how could they, at the same time, supply the cash taxes that would purchase food supplies and the food supplies to be purchased? [29]

Impressment revealed the lineaments of class and race in a slave society at war. White Georgians continued in war to convert to their own uses the labor of blacks, both slave and free. The state impressed free blacks as well as slaves to construct coastal defenses near Savannah. Free blacks suffered hardships when breadwinners were impressed to work for the Confederacy but their families could not qualify for the state and county aid furnished to whites.

Yeomen, meantime, hearing rumors that planters obstructed efforts to impress their slaves, became disenchanted and criticized the war as "a poor man's fight." [30]

Conclusion

Citizens of Georgia argued with each other while they fought the Yankees, but rebel finance failed when resources proved too meager. Like Harlan Fuller, Georgia blacks could not "be there & hear both at the same time." Slaves could not simultaneously build battlements and cultivate corn. In terms of state and county finance, a rich man's war proved to be a rich man's fight, yet the taxes that slaveholders paid to secure the value of their property they paid to no avail.

11 CONFEDERATE CONTEXT

STATE FINANCE in Civil War Georgia must be viewed in the context of Confederate national finance. As in state and county finance, Southerners voiced the prevalent values and ideas regarding the extractive role of government. Taxation, as Confederate Secretary of the Treasury George A. Trenholm observed, provided "the machinery by which the general contribution is distributed and equalized."[1]

The Confederacy, like Georgia, found it increasingly essential to levy taxes. Taxation absorbed funds from the wealthy, who could most afford to have a portion of their purchasing power diverted. It enabled governments at all levels to control the supply of money, and with it the rate of inflation, at least a bit, by taking in some of the currency they distributed to purchase goods and services.

Like the states, however, the Confederacy obtained its funds less by levying taxes than by creating various forms of public indebtedness. Though it imposed a war tax in 1861, not until April 1863, halfway through the war, did it enact a comprehensive tax law. During its four years, the Confederate government derived from taxes only 7 percent of its total revenue.[2]

In fact, much more than Georgia, the Confederacy violated Secretary Trenholm's justification of taxes. Georgia's state and county governments more closely approximated the ideal of taxing citizens "in proportion to the value of their property." In contrast to the Confederacy, Georgia derived half its wartime revenue from either taxation or public investments.[3]

Because the Confederate government did not tax more heavily, it had to borrow funds or seize supplies. Sales of bonds, particularly in the first years of the war, produced one-fourth of total Confederate revenue. Another half came from the issue of treasury notes. When the Confederacy levied taxes insufficient to retrieve the treasury notes from circulation, it created an enormous inflation, and it turned to impressment to obtain provisions and other supplies for the military. Impressment contributed 17 percent of total Confederate receipts—and it often resulted in the war's being a poor man's fight in financial as well as military terms.[4]

Confederate Finance

Before the summer of 1861, the Provisional Congress of the Confederate States levied no direct taxes. Members anticipated no war, or only a short one, and respected what they sensed to be a widespread aversion to direct taxation by a national government. The Congress therefore enacted import and export duties and, through a loan, absorbed the larger portion of the specie held by southern banks. After Fort Sumter, the Confederate Congress authorized the issue of treasury notes and more bonds and made preparations to establish a system of internal revenue.[5]

It may have been possible to believe, in the early months of 1861, that loans backed by revenue from import and export duties would be sufficient to finance a short war. As the war went on, however, expenditures grew, while the federal blockade of southern ports minimized receipts from duties. In finally resorting to internal taxes, and making such taxes payable in treasury notes, Congress hoped to absorb surplus currency and raise funds adequate to redeem portions of the various loans. In August 1861, Congress levied a war tax, at 0.5 percent of the assessed value of property, that ultimately produced $17.4 million. Any head of family whose taxable property was valued at less than $500 was exempt from this tax. The larger items of taxable property were slaves (35 percent of the Confederate aggregate) and real estate (33 percent). Georgia's assessed value accounted for 13.4 percent of the Confederate total.[6]

In the nineteenth century, on the infrequent occasions that a national government levied direct taxes, it was not unusual for a state to assume and pay its citizens' share. In the War of 1812, Georgia had assumed its citizens' direct U.S. tax and paid it by remitting funds, intended to reimburse the state for western territory, still (or already) in the federal treasury. Governor Brown proposed a $1,000,000 state tax for 1862 with the expectation that Georgia taxpayers would also be paying the Confederate war tax. Yet he also advised the legislature to take advantage of a provision of the act authorizing each state to pay its citizens' share of the tax by 1 April 1862—in Confederate treasury notes or specie—at a 10 percent discount.[7]

Following part of Brown's advice, the Georgia legislature authorized the sale of state bonds to pay Georgia's portion of the tax by the April deadline. But it levied no additional tax to redeem those bonds. It thereby chose to relieve Georgians of immediate payment of their share—a total of $2,494,112 —of the burden of the 1861 Confederate war tax. Like most other southern states, Georgia transformed the tax into a loan and in no way helped to diminish the aggregate indebtedness of the Confederacy and the states.[8]

Though the general assembly chose to borrow the funds to pay Georgians' share of the Confederate war tax of 1861, most leaders came gradually to recognize the need for more stringent tax measures. In the second half of the war, Georgia greatly increased its tax rates. Many Georgians were perturbed that the Confederacy, by refusing to do likewise, was deranging everyone's economic affairs. Because the only remedy for "high prices and redundant paper currency" was national taxation, Governor Brown scolded the Confederate Congress for not even "collecting taxes sufficient to pay interest" on the soaring debt. "And as our ports are blockaded, so that we cannot raise money by indirect taxation upon imports, we have no alternative left but direct taxation."[9]

Brown promoted a policy of paying full value in currency, then taxing heavily to retrieve that currency from circulation. Seeking to obtain a doubling of soldiers' pay, he protested: "Let all be affected equally by the increase of prices, and if the volume of the currency is too largely increased, let it be absorbed by taxation, which acts equally upon all. But do not single out our brave defenders and compel them to bear all the burthens of the depreciation without receiving any of the benefits of increased compensation which are allowed to all other classes."[10]

Responding to the need for revenue and to nationwide cries to deflate the currency, Congress levied higher taxes in the second half of the war. In April 1863, it enacted new taxes on occupations, income, produce, and property. The 1863 measure placed license taxes ranging from $50 to $500 on many occupations, levied a graduated tax on net annual incomes of more than $500, and taxed at 8 percent all naval stores, money, and agricultural products "not necessary for family consumption." In addition, it imposed a tax-in-kind of 10 percent of annual agricultural productions beyond an allowance for subsistence. Subsequent measures, in February and June 1864 and March 1865, raised these rates. Like Georgia's tax laws, however, they also allowed larger exemptions, particularly for soldiers' families and for small farmers. As in 1861, there were proponents—in Georgia and throughout the South—of borrowing to assume citizens' Confederate taxes, but this time they were not heeded. Governor Brown firmly opposed such a move, and beginning in 1863 Georgia citizens paid their own Confederate taxes.[11]

In a desperate effort to contract the currency without increasing taxes still further, the Confederate Congress disrupted Georgia state finance by imposing forced loans. A February 1864 law served notice that any treasury notes not funded into bonds, and thereby taken out of circulation, would be taxed at one-third their value. After thus reducing the currency, it authorized a new issue of treasury notes. "The country expected the imposition of a heavy tax," squawked Brown, "but repudiation and bad faith were not expected." Georgia had to adjust its financial policy to fit the Confederacy's vagaries; the state must "receive and pay out only such issues of Confederate notes, as under the acts of Congress pass at par, without the deduction of 33 1/3 or any other per cent." To pay state appropriations (and provide the people with a more reliable currency), Georgia issued state treasury notes in 1864 and 1865, redeemable on Christmas each year in *new*-issue Confederate treasury notes.[12]

Only if the Confederacy levied very heavy taxes could it continue to pay cash to provision its army. It could issue treasury notes to pay for supplies, but in the absence of sufficient taxes to take up that currency, the resulting inflation would force up prices for everyone. The other way to obtain goods was to pay for them in certificates of indebtedness—bonds, for example—that did not circulate readily and would therefore not heighten inflation. Aside from treasury notes, which were used generally in 1861 and 1862, the Confederacy resorted to two methods of obtaining provisions. It made "produce loans" early in the war and, particularly in the second half of the war, it impressed supplies.

Produce loans—Confederate bonds issued in 1861—were intended for subscription by planters and farmers as much as by banks. The bonds were to be sold not only for specie or treasury notes but also for military stores and "for the proceeds of the sale of raw produce, or manufactured articles." By accepting in kind various articles that the army could use directly, such as corn, flour, bacon, pork, and beef, the Confederacy gained supplies for the military. In addition, the Treasury Department desired cotton and tobacco as a basis for credit at home and for foreign exchange. Cotton was not purchased; rather, in exchange for Confederate bonds, a planter agreed that at the time of sale he would loan the government a certain portion of the proceeds of the sale. Finally, the sale of bonds, besides obtaining needed supplies without the issue of currency, would absorb some surplus treasury notes.[13]

The produce loans enabled the Confederacy to improve its credit rating, but they did little for farmers who needed currency. Citizens who could afford to invest in the future of the Confederacy welcomed the bond issues. Writing from Savannah in May 1861, Thomas R. R. Cobb wrote: "The cotton scheme takes well. We shall have large subscriptions. Everybody is willing, and some [are] clamorous for a direct tax." Citizens who needed cash, however, rejected the produce loans and sought treasury notes. A bank president from North Georgia wrote concerning the bonds: "but little can be done with them here. They will do well enough for cotton-growing districts, but this is more of a grain-growing country, and being newly settled, our farmers are generally men of small means." Given "convertible bonds or treasury notes of small denominations," however, "I could buy large amounts of Army supplies. All that is raised in this region for sale could be brought into immediate use for the Army, and almost every one of our farmers are willing to sell to the Confederacy and take such bonds or notes as I have mentioned."[14]

Spring turned to fall, and even planters became pressed for cash. "The people of [black-belt Washington] county, in convention assembled," inquired of Jefferson Davis "if the Government has devised any plan by which the planter can realize money or its equivalent for cotton" and proposed their own plan: "Let the Government condemn for its own use the entire cotton crop, paying the planter a fair price, say ten cents per pound, one-fourth now in Treasury notes, one-fourth the 1st day of January next (also in Treasury notes), the remaining one-half to be paid for in Confederate bonds, as proposed in the produce loan."[15]

Rejecting the cotton planters' pleas, Secretary of the Treasury Christopher G. Memminger replied that he had no power "to lend money for the relief of any interest." Such schemes, he wrote, required that "the Government [pay] out money which is needful to its very existence, and [receive] in exchange planters' notes or produce, which it does not need and cannot in any way make use of." Rather, "it is the duty of the Government to limit . . . [the issue of treasury notes], as far as practicable, to that amount which is the limit of its currency."[16]

Ironically, the more cash there was, the less anyone could do with it. As supplies grew scarce and as the Confederacy suffered military defeats from 1863 on, public confidence in Confederate money grew so weak that open market purchasing was virtually abandoned. Before that time, the army purchased most of its provisions with treasury notes. But as prices soared, few people willingly sold their produce on any terms. Then the supply agencies — particularly the commissary and quartermaster corps — had to resort to impressment, the only remaining method of obtaining supplies.[17]

Impressment, which proved more important than taxation in financing the Confederate cause, was much more onerous to many property owners. All Confederate taxes totaled only two-fifths of the amount ($500 million) of unpaid certificates of indebtedness arising from the impressment of Southerners' property; by 1863 and 1864, the army relied "almost exclusively" upon it. But impressment, as the secretary of war himself described it, was "a harsh, unequal, and odious mode of supply" and, "perhaps, the sorest test of [Southerners'] patriotism and self-sacrificing spirit afforded by the war." The Confederate Congress determined that "current prices constituted no criterion of just compensation required by the Constitution to be allowed for the appropriation of private property to public uses." Though the act regulating impressment expressly exempted "the property necessary for the support of the owner and his family, and to carry on his ordinary agricultural and mechanical business," some people found themselves almost entirely without subsistence. Moreover, as historian Frank E. Vandiver has written, "owners were often paid in the abominable certificates of indebtedness, which carried not even the dignity of a promissory note."[18]

By the middle of the war, Lee's army relied, for months at a time, almost entirely upon corn from Georgia and South Carolina. Impressment pulled much of the surplus from black-belt Georgia, where slave labor continued production through the war, but it worked its greatest burden on North Georgia. There, where few people other than women, children, and old men were available to work the fields, and where the weather during the war years allowed only poor crops, Confederate impressment agents, according to Governor Brown, "have gone among them, and taken from them part of their scanty supply." Impressment of horses for the army's cavalry and artillery, and of oxen for the artillery and for beef, deprived much of Georgia — again particularly the northern counties — of either traction or transportation.[19] How were farmers to plow their fields, or transport their produce to market?

Long before Sherman's troops marched in, impressment brought the war to North Georgia and made it a society of refugees. A Floyd County man, Reuben S. Norton, observed people "leaving good farms and moving to a more secure place." He attributed their actions both to nearby military activity and to "the very arbitrary manner in which their property is taken from them by the army under the plea of military necessity. They say 'tis no use to plant here, to be robbed by soldiers." [20]

Many Georgia citizens sought the heavier taxes that would, they suggested, allow full payment in currency for all property impressed. Former Governor Herschel V. Johnson wrote from black-belt Jefferson County: "How are the farmers to pay their taxes? Why not pay something like market value for supplies? The taxing power enables the Government to reimburse itself amply and fully. Why persist in a policy that produces such deep and wide-spread dissatisfaction?" Worse, "the Government is not paying for what it gets; it is simply giving the planters a receipt for the produce containing a promise to pay, which promise may be redeemed in a reasonable time, or in a year, or never. This is all wrong, suicidal in policy. The Government should pay cash for what it impresses, and pay fair prices." [21]

Governor Brown also castigated what he called "legalized robbery" and again supported higher taxes: "We must abandon the policy of supporting the armies by impressment or forcible seizures of property, and must adopt the policy of purchasing what we need, except in extreme cases which justify impressment, and then we must pay as the Constitution requires, *just compensation* for the property taken. This equalizes the burdens by dividing the whole [amount] among the entire number of taxpayers, in proportion to the amount of property owned by each." [22]

Impressment and the tax-in-kind—particularly in combination with wartime destruction, labor shortages, and bad growing seasons—worked severe hardships in many Georgia counties. Seeking to persuade the Confederate government to ease the situation, Georgians proposed several methods of reimbursing citizens for impressed property; only one of these was full payment in currency. The legislature sought an order from the secretary of war that would allow county officers to commute and purchase, for the use of soldiers' families and other poor people, corn and other provisions collected as tax-in-kind in their counties. It also sought to have all certificates of Confederate indebtedness made receivable in payment of all Confederate taxes. After all, the legislature argued, "the property taken by the Government from the citizen, is the means with which the citizen must pay his tax." [23]

Robin Hood Undone

Georgia citizens paid roughly $32 million in cash (current dollars) in Confederate taxes.[24] In addition, they paid perhaps $11 million in tax-in-kind, as well as $90 million through impressment, and the aggregate of these three figures exceeds $130 million.[25] By contrast, Georgia's state tax revenue from 1861 through 1865 totaled only $19.6 million, a figure which, if increased to roughly $30 million, would include all local taxes.[26] State and local taxes, heavy as they were, accounted for less than one-fifth of Georgians' aggregate wartime tax burden. That one-fifth was levied according to proportional, even progressive, criteria. But the same cannot be said of Confederate impressment, which took more than half of all the material resources demanded of Georgians by their national, state, and local governments during the Civil War.

Countering the Robin Hood pattern that prevailed in state and local finance, the Confederacy's reliance on impressment in the second half of the war converted gains into losses for many upcountry Georgians. Governor Brown observed as early as November 1863: "These impressments have been ruinous to the people of the northeastern part of the State, where . . . probably not half a supply of provisions [is] made for the support of the women and children. One man in fifty may have a surplus, and forty out of the fifty may not have half enough. If the impressing officer is permitted to seize and carry off the little surplus in the hands of the few, those who have not enough have nowhere to look for a supply." Nowhere, that is, except the state. "Every pound of meat and every bushel of grain, carried out of that part of the State by impressing officers, must be replaced by the State at public expense or the wives and children of soldiers in the army must starve for food."[27]

War transformed the role of national government in Georgia finance. At earlier times, the U.S. government had acted as an important source of state revenue. In the 1810s and 1830s, for example, it provided the funds that permitted Georgia to embark on an investment program in banking and then railroads in quest of both economic growth and a permanent source of nontax revenue. The Confederate government, by contrast, seemed to Georgians to have forsaken the role of disbursing agent for that of a voracious extractive agent. Georgians constantly received demands from their new national government for cash, provisions, and manpower. Public benefits, when they came — in terms of wartime welfare on the home front — seemed to emanate exclusively from Georgia's state and local governments. Such disparity did nothing to build loyalty toward a new nation in the making, particularly among yeomen farmers and poor whites.[28]

All Is Gone

Southerners with the most to lose from an antislavery national administration led the struggle to break away from its power and form the Confederate States of America. That power, however, compounded by war weariness on the home front, thwarted their effort. In absolute terms, by 1865 those with the most to lose had lost most. The northern army had just passed through one planter's world, bringing the war home, when, suddenly impoverished but still defiant, he counted his losses and renewed his resolve. Union soldiers, he wrote, "kept 84 of my negroes, 28 horses and mules and 4 waggons, took about 300 bales of my cotton and destroyed my crops, stock, tools, fowls, etc. With what they took and our Army burned, I lost 1000 bales. They have ruined my son, took most of my son in law's property. But if we gain our independence and lose all our property we will be better off than to remain [in the Union]."[29]

The costs of being crushed between warring governments and their armies —taxes, impressment, destruction, and, at the end, abolition and repudiation, not to mention the carnage—took an enormous toll. By war's end, most white Georgians had lost not only their "property" but their "independence" as well. Roughly thirty thousand—some having owned much property and some none at all—lost their lives, and many more were permanently crippled.[30] Speaking in economic terms, a Savannah factor exclaimed at the close of the war, "I staked all on the Confederacy and all is gone."[31]

Part 3

AFTER WAR AND
EMANCIPATION

12 POWER AND POLICY

PUBLIC POLICY in postwar Georgia, like light shining out of the past, was refracted through the prism of 1865. Rays veered off in new directions. Three changes proved central features of the postwar southern experience. The war brought immense poverty, emancipation ended slavery, and federal power directed still further change. As before the war, Georgia resembled Alabama more than it did New York. Even through the trauma of war and Reconstruction, however, North and South continued to share common patterns in many matters of public policy.[1]

After Slavery

Whitelaw Reid, a northern journalist writing from Savannah in the summer of 1865, observed that life in Georgia's largest city had changed little since before Sherman arrived. "Save that the schools were filled with negroes," he wrote, "and the rebel newspapers had been succeeded by loyal ones, and guards in blue, instead of gray, stood here and there, it was the rebel Savannah unchanged."[2] Like Reid, black Georgians had ample reason to feel that too little had changed. In churches and schools and in politics, they worked to create a broader definition of black freedom.

White Georgians, for their part, felt that too much had changed already, and they directed their best efforts toward containing further change. No rebel would have mistaken the Savannah of Reid's description as anything but a world turned upside down—the South no longer Confederate, the Union salvaged, slavery abolished. The War for Southern Independence had failed, and southern life had begun its transformation from prewar patterns. No one yet knew how much change the act of emancipation, in itself, might effect, or how much more the Union, in its triumph, might demand. On the other hand, no one yet knew how resourceful the white South, even in defeat, would prove in resistance.

Beginning with emancipation, the federal government launched a new career of shaping behavior previously left within the jurisdiction of state governments and private individuals. Policy mandates from the national government began by 1865 to channel social welfare and social control in Georgia in new directions. The most consequential shift in federal policy occurred when President

Lincoln issued his Emancipation Proclamation and Union victory gave it force. Enactment of the Civil Rights Act of 1866 and the Reconstruction Acts of 1867 made further demands on southern whites and southern governments.

The removal from southern life of so central an institution as slavery created a fundamentally different policy environment for postwar policymakers of both parties. Slavery's effects had rippled through all public policy in antebellum and wartime Georgia, from black freedom to taxation; so did its removal in 1865. As state and local authorities wrestled with new social and political conditions, they had to try out new policies. The prewar experience of Georgia's free blacks offered one model for postwar public policy toward freedmen. Yet much of that experience had been determined by slavery's dictates, which lost much of their force with abolition. Moreover, prewar policy flowed unobstructed from white Georgians' initiatives, but federal directives framed the structure of public authority in the postwar South. Former slaves and former free blacks alike, Georgia's black residents moved into new legal territory in 1865, and they kept moving, as the federal government forced new changes and, for a time, granted blacks increasing leverage over their lives.

Starting Over: Repudiating the War Debt

From the very beginning, postwar Georgia's political leaders acted under the scrutiny of federal authorities. In mid-1865 President Andrew Johnson appointed as provisional governor James Johnson, who in 1861 had opposed secession. The governor carried out his main responsibility when he called a convention of the citizens of Georgia, whose delegates gathered in the state capital, Milledgeville, from 25 October to 8 November 1865, with the task of reestablishing civil government. Acting in part as a legislature, the convention tended to such housekeeping matters as authorization of a bond issue for repairing the Western and Atlantic Railroad. More important, the session acted as a constitutional convention to restore Georgia as one of the United States.

President Johnson's restoration program required positive actions against slavery, secession, and the state's war debt. Thus the delegates set out, by passing ordinances and rewriting Georgia's fundamental law, to recognize new conditions arising out of the war. With little delay, but less grace, convention members acted on the questions of secession and slavery. Rather than declare —as Joshua Hill, a Unionist in 1861, proposed—that the ordinances to secede and to adopt the Confederate Constitution "are now, and always have been, null and void," members simply repealed them. Expressly attributing slavery's demise to a federal "war measure," they consigned blacks to a status somewhere between slave and citizen.[3] Those actions left the matter of public indebtedness, an issue that aroused much debate.

Georgia emerged from the Civil War with a staggering debt. The 1860 debt of $2.7 million looked tiny next to the $21 million the state owed five years later. Of that amount, $3.3 million was in state bonds issued in support of the war: $0.9 million under a November 1860 act to establish a defense fund just after Lincoln's election; and $2.4 million to fund the state's payment of Georgians' 1861 Confederate tax. Another $8.6 million consisted of treasury notes (convertible into bonds) that had been issued to pay appropriations for such purposes as supporting the Georgia Relief and Hospital Association and the families of Georgia's soldiers. In addition, $5.2 million in treasury notes and $1.0 million in change bills remained in circulation. Not convertible into state bonds, those items were redeemable only in Confederate treasury notes (now worthless) or in payment of taxes.[4]

Comptroller General Peterson Thweatt launched an impassioned defense of the state's credit and earnestly fought any repudiation. But Thweatt did note that the $6.2 million in treasury notes and change bills might justly be redeemed at their value at the time of issue, which was much less than face value. Thweatt estimated that, given that a large portion of the 1864 state tax had not yet arrived in Milledgeville, up to $1 million in those notes and bills might already be in the hands of tax collectors. But even by allowing $1 million there and by scaling the other $5.2 million of inconvertible debt down by 95 percent, Thweatt could not produce a figure for Georgia's war debt smaller than $12 million.[5] At from 6 to 8 percent interest, even that amount would add to postwar state expenditures each year an amount as great as the entire state budget had averaged in the 1840s or 1850s.

The convention had to decide whether to honor Georgia's entire war debt, scale it down, or repudiate it all. At first, proponents of outright repudiation numbered no more than one-fourth of the delegates. Sidney Andrews, a northern newspaper correspondent and close observer of the convention's proceedings, estimated that at least one-third of the delegates were determined to see the debt assumed in full. The remaining members, a large and strategic minority, favored reducing the debt but rejected an outright repudiation of the entire amount.[6]

Seeing the convention's inclination toward recognizing the debt, together with many delegates' uncertainty about just what was required of them, Provisional Governor James Johnson wired President Andrew Johnson for a definite statement. Secretary of State William E. Seward replied that the president's view of southern loyalty to the Union left no room for any state's continued recognition of public debts created to promote rebellion. The president himself wrote: "The people of Georgia should not hesitate one single moment in repudiating every single dollar of debt created for the purpose of aiding the Rebellion. . . . [N]o debt contracted for the purpose of dissolving the Union of the States can or will be paid by taxes levied on the people."[7]

In addition to fiscal considerations, three powerful cross-currents characterized debates on the debt—one pecuniary, one sentimental, and one political. Bondholders, together with people in possession of large quantities of state treasury notes, shuddered at the thought of repudiation, even more than many taxpayers, who held neither bonds nor treasury notes, shuddered at the tax bills they faced in the absence of repudiation. Concern for state honor—and, more important, retrospective valuations of secession and the war for independence—colored many delegates' attitudes. Political considerations became increasingly important throughout the convention's proceedings. Delegates could not ignore the federal conditions for reseating Georgia's representatives in Congress. Though one delegate advised, "Don't let us do more than is required of us," another declared it the convention's responsibility to do whatever was necessary to rid the state of "military despotism."[8]

Two men's arguments exemplified those made by Georgians favoring recognition of the entire debt. Peterson Thweatt, comptroller general since 1855, wrote in his final report in the fall of 1865: "How could the State refuse to make provision for [its soldiers] and their families? And how can the State now drive away from the door of her Treasury the public creditors who enabled her to discharge so sacred a duty?" Solomon Cohen, delegate from Savannah, directed his attention more toward the federal government and postwar race relations. Cohen applauded Andrew Johnson's "endeavoring to stay the waves of Northern fanaticism," but he could not support the president on the question of state debt. The fanatics, he exclaimed, "would not be satisfied with repudiation, unless joined with negro evidence [testimony in court], negro suffrage, negro equality, social and political." Defeat, emancipation, and repeal of the secession ordinance were surely enough to concede.[9]

Seeking to avert early repudiation, some members advocated either referring the whole matter to the legislature soon to be elected or taking no action until Congress met and clearly demanded that Georgia repudiate the debt. At least two delegates went so far as to suggest that, should the debt be repudiated in order to placate federal demands, once Georgia's Congressmen and Senators had been readmitted to Congress, the state should reverse the decision and assume the debt after all.[10]

Members who sought repudiation were equally vehement in expressing their thoughts and feelings. In an early message to the convention, the provisional governor noted: "Our burdens are already great, and our strength greatly diminished." Retaining the war debt would surely "add to our weakness" and "increase our taxes." "No one expected payment if finally defeated in our efforts to secure independence," he explained. "The currency and the cause flourished together while in life," but upon Union victory "all Confederate debts became extinct," and surely Georgia's war debt deserved no better fate.[11]

J. R. Parrott, a North Georgia delegate who would soon become a Republican and then serve as president of the 1867–68 constitutional convention, had harsher words. He distinguished between the many who had served in the "bullet department" of the Confederate forces and the few who had operated in the "speculating or stay-at-home department." His cry was "no preferred debt." People had lost the value of their slaves, of much other property, and of all Confederate money, he noted. Why should the state debt be paid? Rejecting the notion of "throwing the burden of the war" on thousands of hard-pressed taxpayers, he declared that the debt "should pass away with the unfortunate war just ended." [12]

Those who sought at least partial recognition of the war debt formulated various proposals regarding how much debt should be paid and how the state should finance any payment. To skirt the president's ban against using tax revenue to pay the debt, some proposed to obtain the funds by selling the Western and Atlantic Railroad. Others, accepting the prohibition against paying debts incurred to prosecute the war, offered to divide the debt by function, paying some portions in full and others not at all; this method would disallow debts incurred for direct military expenditures but would recognize debts undertaken to pay costs of administration and of support for soldiers' families. Still others called for scaling back the entire debt; recognizing that changes in currency had grossly distorted values of debt instruments, these delegates favored redemption according to the value in gold at the time the debt was contracted.

Eventually—grudgingly, conditionally, and by only a narrow margin—the convention voided Georgia's entire war debt. Supporters of repudiation came mostly from the white counties of North and South Georgia, while major opposition came from the relatively wealthy constituencies of the cities and the black belt. Delegates from Georgia's four larger cities unanimously cast eleven votes against the ordinance. Opponents of total repudiation, though a large majority in the beginning, proved unable to agree on a compromise between full payment and none at all. Moreover, their ranks lost members who capitulated to President Johnson's demands. But the final vote was only 135–117. [13]

The ordinance repudiated all debts that Georgia had contracted in support of the war. Because peacetime revenue had been adequate to pay peacetime expenditures, according to the ordinance, all wartime debts must have been incurred for war purposes. But it left a loophole—"through which speculators may drive a chariot and four," in Sidney Andrews's judgment—for any claims that the legislature might judge to have been incurred for purposes unconnected with the war. Of the entire debt from the war years, however, the only portion ever recognized was $150,000 in bonds issued to purchase stock in the Atlantic and Gulf Railroad. The debt shrank by $18 million. [14]

Change or Continuity: Two Distinct Periods

The seven years after Appomattox saw a variety of state administrations, civilian and military, Conservative and Republican. Georgia's first election under the Constitution of 1865 gave the governorship to Charles J. Jenkins, an old-Whig patrician who served from December 1865 until January 1868. During that time, federal troops remained stationed in Georgia, but the state was under civilian control.[15] The legislature, after its first postwar session in 1865–66, met again only at the end of 1866. By its scheduled meeting time in 1867, Congress had enacted new legislation remanding most of the former Confederate states to military government. Georgia became a part of the Third Military District, which also contained Alabama and Florida. During the first half of 1868, after the commanding general of the Third District removed Jenkins from office for failure to follow orders, Brigadier General Thomas H. Ruger acted as provisional governor.

In April 1868, under the watchful eyes of federal troops, an electorate that included men of both races gave Republicans the governorship and a majority in both houses of the Georgia General Assembly. Though no new state elections took place for two and a half years, and Governor Rufus B. Bullock retained his office until late 1871, politics in Georgia continued turbulent. Both houses of the legislature expelled their black members in September 1868; their places were taken by Democratic runners-up in the previous spring's elections. For the last six weeks of the 1868 session and for the entire 1869 legislative session, Democrats controlled the house of representatives, although Republicans retained their majority in the senate even after the expulsion.[16]

In late 1869, Georgia underwent its "third Reconstruction." The military was once again briefly in control, though Bullock continued as governor. More important, the black legislators replaced their Democratic usurpers. Throughout the 1870 session, therefore, Republicans enjoyed considerable majorities in both houses, and they still held the governorship.[17]

After elections in the autumn of 1870, Democrats regained the governorship and control of the legislature. By early 1872, Georgia's Congressmen and Senators had resumed their seats in Washington, and local control had returned to the Conservatives. Georgia's journey through Reconstruction had ended. The state had been "redeemed."

This zigzag in postwar politics continues to shape the prevailing ideas of Reconstruction. In the dominant view of southern history, great shifts occurred in public policy during the postwar years, with the most significant break coming between Presidential Restoration and Congressional Reconstruction. Congress intervened in southern affairs and introduced black suffrage; new men and new social groups wrested political power, for a time, from the traditional elite. A second major break followed Reconstruction, as newly triumphant southern-born white Democrats vigorously turned their energies to eliminating Republican programs and reviving as much as possible of the Old South.

In fact, war and emancipation forced greater changes in Georgia than did

Congress's Reconstruction Acts of 1867. The drama of postwar state politics has diverted Americans in general, and historians in particular, from scrutinizing the differences that separated the postwar period from the prewar years. Important changes certainly took place during and after Republican rule, but to focus directly on postwar developments excludes from one's frame of vision the enormous differences between antebellum and postbellum Georgia. The traditional emphasis on discontinuity *within* the postwar years has deflected attention from the more radical differences that separated prewar from postwar patterns. In sum, the year 1866 resembled 1870 more than it did 1860.

The great dividing line in nineteenth-century southern history falls across the year 1865, when the effort to establish a southern republic finally failed — and with it the antebellum society that rested, fiscally as in so many other ways, on racial slavery. The greatest postwar changes in Georgia's budgetary affairs, in social policy and taxation alike, took place in the immediate aftermath of war, not during Congressional Reconstruction. Even when major new changes in state policy developed under Republican control, Redemption failed to erase the changes. When black children began attending public schools, for example, black votes, federal power, and southern whites' notions of social control combined to support that behavior as the new norm.

One son of an antebellum planter in Georgia, writing his memoirs in the 1920s, looked back on the Civil War as the event that shattered one world and inaugurated another. Edward J. Thomas spoke for many: "My young manhood having been spent in the South just before, during and after the War of Secession, I may say I lived in two distinct periods of our Southern history, for this war completely severed the grand old plantation life, with all its peculiar interests and demands, from the stirring and striving conditions that followed." [18]

A Case Study: Extraordinary Welfare

Working within a framework furnished by the federal government, Georgia's postwar regimes all resembled each other more than any looked like its prewar predecessors. Still, they were hardly identical. In part, state policy depended on which party, and what social groups, held power. Conservatives and Republicans courted differing constituencies and promoted differing policies. The chapters that follow detail developments in education, taxes, and other matters, but the example of extraordinary welfare spending (especially by the state) illustrates those differences.

Destitution mandated that extraordinary welfare measures not end abruptly in 1865. Taking over where Georgia's wartime efforts left off, the Freedmen's Bureau and the U.S. Army moved to prevent starvation. Many Georgians in Savannah and other cities, in the black belt, and in North Georgia received emergency food supplies from the federal government. In contrast to the state's wartime and postwar policy, however, close to three-fourths of these rations went to blacks. Much as such efforts helped in 1865 and 1866, Governor Jenkins wrote General Davis Tillson, "I have no doubt at all that 1867 will be a year of greater suffering in this state than 1866." The Freedmen's Bureau continued to distribute food through the summer of 1867, but by 1868 counties had been prodded into taking over pauper support, even for blacks.[19]

Nor did the state's welfare measures end with Appomattox. During Presidential Restoration, Georgia continued to supply soldiers' families and other destitute Georgians "unable by their own labor to obtain bread." As the 1865 constitutional convention urged, the legislature appropriated $200,000 in early 1866 to purchase corn for deceased soldiers' children and widows, disabled veterans, and other "aged or infirm white persons." Otherwise, Governor Jenkins advised the general assembly, suffering among such people would be "most intense," particularly before the next harvest in areas "overrun by both armies" during the war. Counties receiving the larger amounts of corn were either urban or North Georgian.[20]

The legislature proved somewhat less generous in late 1866 than it had been the previous winter. It authorized $20,000 to pay the freight on supplies donated by people in Kentucky and other states. And it appropriated $100,000, solely for disabled soldiers and the families of Confederate dead, provided that "a sufficiency of corn will not be contributed from voluntary sources."[21]

Aside from the emergency distribution of food in 1865 and 1866, in which federal, state, and local governments all participated, the state directed its extraordinary welfare efforts of the postwar generation entirely toward Confederate veterans and their families. The Restoration sessions of 1865–66 and fall 1866 provided $50,000 to furnish artificial limbs to maimed Confederate veterans. By contrast, the Republican session of 1868 appropriated only a final $143 to repay the Georgia Railroad for transporting beneficiaries to the artificial limbs factory.[22] For the reburial of Confederate dead, the 1866 session appropriated $6,000, the 1868 legislature a modest $2,000, and the Redemption legislatures of 1872 and 1873 a further $7,800.[23] In addition, the 1866 session inaugurated a program that paid more than $100,000 to assist Confederate veterans to attend college.[24]

The Redeemers' Constitution of 1877 carries a reputation for retrenchment, but it specifically authorized the state government to appropriate money to procure artificial limbs for Confederate veterans. In the first year after an 1879 act implemented that provision, Georgia spent $70,000 to provide legs or arms (and in five cases both a leg and an arm) for hundreds of men. Beginning in 1886, moreover, several constitutional amendments empowered the legislature to provide pensions, first to disabled Confederate veterans, then to widows of Confederate soldiers, and finally to all indigent Confederate veterans.[25]

Republicans curtailed the programs to assist disabled Confederate veterans in obtaining artificial limbs and college educations. After returning to power, the Democrats resumed the Restoration program of paying for artificial limbs. They subsequently inaugurated a vast new program of pensions for Confederate veterans and their widows. The prevailing notion of postwar finance — one of parsimonious Conservative administrations bracketing a Republican spending spree — is curiously inverted as regards extraordinary social welfare spending.

Conclusion

Two constraints influenced public policy in postwar Georgia. Pervasive poverty and federal power each limited what policymakers could do, one by limiting their resources, the other by restraining their discretion. Still, within those limits, it mattered a great deal whether Democrats or Republicans were in charge. Aside from the brief Republican interlude, Democrats dominated Georgia politics in the postwar years. Most of the time, then, Democrats had the power to shape policy and allocate resources.

13 FREEDMEN AND CITIZENS

Though He Attain to the Age of Methuselah

In 1853 the chief justice of Georgia's supreme court, Joseph H. Lumpkin, declared that, unlike a white child, "a free person of color never ceases to be a ward, though he attain to the age of Methuselah. His legal existence is forever merged in that of his [white] guardian." A free black in pre–Civil War Georgia differed from a slave only in that he lived "without a domestic master to control his movements; but to be civilly and politically free, to be the peer and equal of the white man—to enjoy the offices, trusts, and privileges our institutions confer upon the white man—is not now, never has been, and never will be the condition of this degraded race." [1]

Ten years later, in the midst of the Civil War, President Abraham Lincoln proclaimed the emancipation of slaves to be one of his government's central war aims. When General Robert E. Lee surrendered at Appomattox Courthouse, it became inevitable that Methuselah would know a different life in his later years. How different remained to be discovered. As federal mandates transformed social policy in the South, differences in state treatment of blacks and whites grew less pronounced; differences in policy toward former slaves and former free blacks vanished.

Nearly one-half million Georgians journeyed from slavery to citizenship in the 1860s. Changes in social policy evolved as the federal government first decreed black freedom and then black citizenship. Immediately following the war, whites responded to emancipation by creating institutional substitutes for the social control features of slavery; they made space for blacks in the insane asylum and the penitentiary, and they instituted the chain gang. A second generation of changes, focusing on social welfare, followed the advent of Congressional Reconstruction, as citizenship brought blacks certain social and political rights, particularly education and the vote. By the mid-1870s, the state was regularly supplying public funds for elementary and higher education for blacks. By the mid-1880s, both races could also be found in the schools for the deaf and blind.

Slavery Is with the Days beyond the Flood

By transforming slaves into freedmen, emancipation loosened both the coercive and the protective features of slavery's paternalism.

Slavery had been a system of social control, in that it secured whites against racial upheavals, and a system of social welfare, in that it provided blacks with a measure of economic security. Emancipation released planters from their traditional responsibilities for either controlling blacks' behavior or providing their subsistence.

With emancipation, planters lost much of their property, and blacks gained a measure of liberty. Neither blacks nor whites could forget the social world they left behind, but as slavery receded into the recent past, both races sought to create viable new patterns for their daily lives. Public policy inevitably would shape those private efforts as well as reflect them. For former slaves and former slaveowners alike, emancipation was only the threshold of a new world.

In August 1865 John M. McCrary, a Meriwether County planter, entered into a contract with "his former Slaves now Freedmen" to secure their labor for his plantation. That contract provides a measure of how much, and how little, had changed for former slaves. The planter's responsibilities were "to furnish said Freedmen good and wholesome food, usual clothing and medical attention." In return, his former slaves agreed "to work faithfully . . . and to be respectful and obedient to the said John M. McCrary and his family at all times." A postscript to the contract manifested whites' distaste for the new arrangement: "This was a yankey humbug to harrass the Southern people." [2]

Nominally free to seek employment wherever and on whatever terms they could find it, freedmen, who had labor but no property, confronted planters, who had land but little cash. Former slaves now faced the coercion of the marketplace; they found that their new legal capacity to make contracts offered little to people who enjoyed liberty but not property. The obstacles they met were the greater in view of whites' continued perception of them as bondservants and—by custom, law, and nature—social inferiors. Class *and* race militated against the benefits that freedmen could hope to realize from their newfound contractual equality. And yet freedmen were not slaves.[3]

Under the auspices of federal authority, emancipation inaugurated a transformation in the legal status and the social conditions of black Georgians. Never again would Georgia law state that having one black great-grandparent sufficed "to disable a person from contracting." [4] Aside from the legal capacity to enter work contracts, blacks could also contract marriage—in fact, were expected to do so. When slavery vanished, so did Georgia's criminal penalties for teaching blacks to read or write, and the law no longer excluded blacks from occupations requiring the ability to read and write. The advent of legal literacy by no means required the use of public funds for blacks' schooling, but it left blacks more or less free to pursue the "three R's" on their own initiative, an opportunity that many freedmen quickly exploited.

None of these changes resulted from any alterations in Georgia's statute books. Rather, each reflected policies undertaken by the Freedmen's Bureau and its Siamese twin, the U.S. Army, as they supervised civil relations in

Georgia in the months after the war. Well before the end of 1865, black Georgians were marrying, making labor contracts, and teaching and attending schools.[5]

Federal actions also affected freedmen in ways that substituted for major social welfare and social control functions displaced at slavery's demise. The federal government distributed about 800,000 rations in Georgia in the fourteen months between September 1865 and October 1866, of which blacks received three-quarters. Coercion accompanied benevolence. According to an October 1865 order, which banned rations for able-bodied people who refused to support themselves, freedmen remaining in cities without employment would "be compelled, if necessary, to go to the country and accept places of labor found by themselves or for them by officers or agents of the bureau."[6]

Freedmen were no longer slaves, but they were not yet citizens. As President Andrew Johnson directed, Georgia's constitutional convention of October and November 1865 declared slavery to be abolished. Besides leaving open the question of subsequent federal compensation, however, the convention retained an exclusively white suffrage. Moreover, the constitution instructed the general assembly to consider restricting the immigration of free blacks from other states and, in any case, to enact legislation regulating relations between "citizens" and "free persons of color."[7]

The constitution directed the legislature to create a new system of social control and social welfare for freedmen, to provide for their "government" and "protection" so as to guard "them and the State against any evil that may arise from their sudden emancipation." First, the legislature amended the law regarding court testimony. A December 1865 statute conferred on all "free persons of color" the right to testify in all civil or criminal cases involving other blacks (but not those involving only whites). The state sought to regularize marital and other familial relations among freedmen by declaring those living together to be husband and wife and by legitimating their children. (Such extension of the law over blacks meant that they, like whites, could now be charged with fornication and adultery.) It imposed on black parents and their children, if economically capable, the same legal obligation imposed on whites to provide for each other's support. In March 1866, the state conformed its pauper and apprentice laws to the new conditions by providing that children, unless they had parents living in the same county who were capable of looking after them, might be bound out to "any respectable person"—who in practice usually turned out to be the former owner.[8]

In short, emancipation brought new liabilities as well as new opportunities. When Georgia amended the vagrancy laws, blacks remained a potential source of unpaid labor for both private citizens and public authorities. Before 1866, whites convicted of vagrancy could be confined at hard labor in the penitentiary for two to four years, or they might post a maximum bond of $400 for their "good behavior and future industry for one year." A March 1866 statute reduced the maximum bond to $200 and established possible penalties of a fine, a jail sentence, or a maximum one-year term either working on public works and roads or hired out to a private individual.[9]

Formal distinctions among "slaves," "free persons of color," and "citizens" progressively disappeared from Georgia's laws in the years following emancipation. During that time, the relations between public authority and black Georgians remained fluid. Though the greatest adjustment to emancipation had occurred by the summer of 1865, the status of blacks continued to change. Nomenclature suggests the changes. Emancipation moved a half million Georgians from the legal category of "slaves" to that of "free persons of color," where they joined a few thousand people already occupying that status. In November 1865, the constitutional convention referred to freedmen as "free persons of color," as did the legislature the following month. White Georgians recognized that they had to make some concessions to war, emancipation, and federal authority, but so far as possible they sought to conform postwar black freedom to its prewar standard. In March 1866, however, Georgia enacted a civil rights act virtually identical to that enacted by Congress the following month. Both acts provided full property rights and declared blacks to be competent witnesses in all judicial cases—"just as if they were white," in the words of Justice Dawson A. Walker of Georgia's supreme court.[10]

The two acts, state and federal, differed significantly in only one respect. The federal civil rights act defined freedmen as U.S. citizens. Georgia's, by contrast, created a new class of noncitizens—"persons of color"—defined as residents with at least "one-eighth negro, or African blood," the same criterion as before. It simultaneously repealed all legislation concerning "slaves" and "free persons of color" that conflicted with the new law.[11] All persons of color being "free," the adjective had become redundant; the law now granted identical rights and privileges to all blacks, whatever their prewar status.

Both groups—former slaves and antebellum free blacks—were moving into a new status. Chief Justice Joseph H. Lumpkin, dwelling now in a legal world very different from the one he had inhabited in the 1850s, decided a case in December 1866 that coupled "the abolition of slavery" with the black code's "establishment of equal rights." "Persons of color," Lumpkin noted, now enjoyed much greater liberty than had "free persons of color" under the old dispensation. "Free persons of color were restrained by the law, as it formerly stood, from doing many things which freedmen can now do without let or hindrance."[12] In short, two emancipations had occurred. For freedmen, and for former "free persons of color" too, the rights to which they could lay claim had grown significantly.

Whites continued, often with success, to attempt to coerce blacks, but blacks had gained rights that white men need sometimes respect. Local courts often operated to maintain the private authority of former slaveowners, but the Georgia Supreme Court, beginning at its December 1866 session, over-

ruled a number of lower court decisions and decided in favor of black peti-
tioners. Under the March 1866 apprentice act, in particular, many black children found themselves bound out to whites, in most cases their former owners.
Some whites abused the law by kidnapping young black men from their
parents, or from other white employers with whom the children had contracted, and obtaining indentures from complaisant local officials. Such actions could threaten the integrity of black families much as slavery and the
slave trade had.[13]

Georgia's highest court heard its first such case in December 1866, when
Jacob Comas sought to secure custody of his son, Henry. At the end of the
war, Comas and his twelve-year-old son lived with two different whites in
Appling County. Henry continued to live with his former owner until September 1865, when he left to live with his father, who took him in and provided
for him. In May 1866, Henry was bound out to his former owner. His father
challenged that action in superior court and then, tenacious, appealed an adverse decision to the Georgia Supreme Court.[14]

Many months before the Republican party came to power in Georgia, Justice Iverson L. Harris handed down a decision that would have done honor to
any Radical Republican. He declared that the act applied to white and black
alike "without discrimination," assigned the boy to his father's custody, and
issued a stern lecture to local members of Georgia's judiciary. Local officials,
he warned, "should be vigilant in preventing any one, under the name of
master [under the apprentice law], from getting the control of the labor and
services of such minor apprentice, as if he were still a slave. It should be borne
always in mind, and at all times should regulate the conduct of the white man,
that slavery is with the days beyond the flood; that it is prohibited by the
Constitution of the State of Georgia, and by that paramount authority, the
Constitution of the United States; and that its continuance will not by any
honest public functionary be tolerated, under the forms of law or otherwise,
directly or indirectly." [15]

Schoolhouse and Ballot Box

Although the legal equality of Georgia's "citizens" and "persons of color" had advanced by April 1866, only with ratification of a new state
constitution in April 1868 did black Georgians become citizens of their state.
Besides defining Georgia citizenship so as to include freedmen, the new constitution obliterated three major remaining distinctions between the races. First,
the Constitution of 1868 outlawed whipping as a punishment for crime. A
means of punishment used exclusively on blacks in the later days of slavery,
whipping was one of the ways in which public authorities had refused to distinguish between slaves and free blacks.[16]

The other major innovations of the new constitution related to political and educational rights. In the nineteenth century, three phenomena—the poll tax, public schools, and the franchise—defined the basic rights and responsibilities of free men, and in 1868 Georgia began to apply that trinity to blacks as well as whites. Educational and voting rights would no longer be the exclusive attributes of whites. Though no state system of public schools yet existed, the constitution directed the legislature to establish one that would be open to both blacks and whites, "all children of the State," and allocated all poll tax revenue to such a system. It also tied the franchise to the payment of all taxes due by black men as well as white.[17]

The early postwar history of the state poll tax provides a guide to the major changes taking place in Georgia society and politics, to the transformed relations between public authority and black Georgians, and, indeed, to general questions concerning change and continuity across the entire Civil War–Reconstruction period. The tax law already treated blacks and whites equally in 1866 and 1867.[18] That equality was related not to the state's delivery of services, however, but only to its extractive role. The difference between the state poll tax of 1867 and that of 1868, after the Republicans had come to power, lay not in the amount levied but in its linkage to other attributes of public authority. A major break in the development of social and political rights came in 1868, when the new state constitution transformed public policy by allocating the poll tax to schools—schools for blacks as well as whites— and by establishing voting rights for both races.

Let Out to the Lowest Bidder

Pauper support, like poverty, proved color-blind in postwar Georgia. Local governments had traditionally supported white people who were too poor to provide for themselves, particularly aged widows. Before the Civil War, perhaps a third of Georgia's counties established poorhouses, generally termed "asylums for the invalid poor," where paupers produced a portion of their support; other counties established poorhouses soon after the war. Well over half the counties continued to engage in noninstitutional relief; they provided cash or supplies of food, clothing, or medicine to needy individuals.[19]

The war greatly magnified the problem of poor relief and called forth extraordinary efforts. During the war, roughly half of all spending by Georgia's state and local governments went to the support of Confederate soldiers' families and other destitute whites. Immediately after the war, the Freedmen's Bureau supplied emergency rations to thousands of people, particularly freedmen, and Georgia's first postwar legislature appropriated $200,000 to purchase corn for disabled Confederate veterans, deceased soldiers' wives and children, and other "aged or infirm white persons."[20]

When traditional functions were returned to the counties, a major difference between prewar and postwar policy related to the inclusion of former slaves among those receiving public relief. With the end of slavery, planters no longer supported the very old and other black dependents, and thus such people had to look elsewhere for their support. At first, the Freedmen's Bureau looked after them, but by about 1868 the counties took over the responsibility. Beginning in 1869, for example, Gordon County supplied Ben Knight, "colored and blind," $4.00 per month in cash or provisions.[21]

Appling County auctioned off its paupers, both black and white, to anyone willing to provide minimal care. At such auctions, the winning bid came from the person willing to charge the county the least amount. In 1872 Asa Middleton, for example, a white man in his eighties, being "put on the County, as a pauper," and "let out to the lowest bidder, at the Court house door, was knocked off to Lumpkins Beacher" for $150 for the year. The next year, Joseph Patterson offered the low bid of $96. Similarly, Grace Sellers, "a Blind African Negro Woman, over One hundred years old," on becoming a county charge, was "let out, before the Court-house-door, and knocked off to Samuel Sellers," a black farmer, at rates of $75 for 1871, $99 for 1872, and $150 for 1873.[22]

Reconstructing the Welfare Institutions

After war and emancipation, Georgia's institutions for the insane, blind, and deaf faced two challenges. Wartime destruction and postwar poverty combined to diminish the resources, yet increase the needs, of all three institutions, even for whites. In addition, emancipation and equal rights mandates led—though not all at once—to provision of similar, though segregated, facilities for blacks. As the state established facilities for blacks, it reflected the displacement, from slaveowners to public authorities, of slavery's social welfare and social control functions. Moreover, it revealed the relative importance of welfare and control to policymakers.

Having entered the Civil War with three welfare institutions, Georgia exited with two. In the spring of 1865, the school for the deaf had already been closed for three years, and it did not reopen for another two years. As for the Academy for the Blind, the Confederate army used its building as a military hospital from December 1863 until the spring of 1865, and then the federal army took charge and used it as a hospital until late July. After nearly two years in Fort Valley, the school returned to its Macon home and attempted to refurnish its equipment. In addition to suffering damage from a leaky roof, the school's principal reported, the academy lost much of its furniture and many of its musical instruments and other possessions to souvenir-seeking Union soldiers.[23] The insane asylum, never closed down and never moved, was in the best condition at war's end.

The year 1865 was the hardest year of all for the academy and the asylum. Without negotiable currency, they depended on credit and the federal army for provisions. When the legislature met at the end of the year, it passed a resolution advancing $2,500 to the Academy for the Blind and $20,000 to the Lunatic Asylum.[24]

Georgia's welfare institutions began to rebuild, quickly returned to their prewar size, and then resumed the gradual expansion that had characterized their prewar history. For 1866 the legislature appropriated as much to support the schools for the deaf ($8,000) and the blind ($7,000) as it had for 1860. It authorized $14,500 for salaries and $50,000 (up from $15,000 before the war) to support pauper patients at the insane asylum. To repair and improve buildings and to replace furnishings and educational supplies, the state also spent $2,500 on the school for the deaf and $7,500 on that for the blind in 1866 and 1867. Citing the state's "fiscal embarrassments," however, Governor Charles J. Jenkins declined to approve expenditures to reopen the school for the deaf until February 1867.[25]

Though no legislature met in 1867 to make appropriations for 1868, expenditures for all three institutions continued with hardly a ripple. In October 1867 General John Pope, commanding the Third Military District, ordered the state treasurer to continue making quarterly payments to state officers, the penitentiary, and the three welfare institutions. In turn Governor Jenkins, before he was removed from his post, ordered the Western and Atlantic Railroad's superintendent to supply the quarterly funds that each institution would have received if the 1867 session had met and roughly duplicated the 1866 appropriations act. Provisional Governor Thomas H. Ruger perpetuated this plan when he took office. The Western and Atlantic's net earnings, about $25,000 per month, sufficed to support all three welfare institutions at their authorized spending levels. The Academy for the Blind received $4,500 in the eight months between the lapse of its 1867 appropriation and the convening of the 1868 legislature; the school for the deaf received $6,000; the insane asylum, $42,800.[26]

All three institutions, never having had black students or patients before emancipation, had yet to face the question of supplying black Georgians' needs. The school for the deaf noted in its 1868 report the need for segregated state facilities for blacks, and it estimated that these would cost $3,000 or $4,000 to build and furnish. But the school did not insist, and the legislature did not respond. The Academy for the Blind did not even raise the subject until its 1875 report. Not until the early 1880s did either school provide facilities for blacks.[27]

As early as 17 August 1865, by contrast, the insane asylum reluctantly received its first black patient, a fifty-eight-year-old man, and the superintendent, Dr. Thomas F. Green, feared the arrival of many more. He observed in his 1865 report that, under slavery, blacks "enjoyed entire freedom from cares and anxieties, and in the rare instances in which an insane negro could be found, there was an owner who could and did take care of the poor creature. Now . . . they are undoubtedly under the influence of almost every exciting cause of disorder of the brain. . . . The dictates of humanity and the welfare of society," he concluded, required "proper arrangements" in "separate quarters." A joint legislative committee similarly reported in 1866 that, with the end of slavery but not of "unbridled lust," Georgia might anticipate "insanity in the negro much more common under this new dispensation than it was under the old and better code." [28]

The state felt compelled to provide adequate facilities for insane blacks. The 1866 legislative committee's majority report suggested an appropriation of $20,000, and the minority report $10,000, to provide accommodations for "the most unfortunate class of that unfortunate race." Responding to "the dictates of humanity and the welfare of society," the legislature appropriated $10,000 in 1866 to provide a building for about fifty black inmates. Because the building became full within months of its completion in August 1867, the institution sought a similar appropriation for a second building. In addition, it urgently needed funds to supply black inmates with furniture, bedding, clothing, food, and medicine. In the absence of state money for these items in 1867 and 1868, the Freedmen's Bureau supplied monthly rations. Subsequent legislatures, completing the task begun in 1866, authorized funds for support (without reference to race) as well as construction.[29] "Radical Reconstruction" in Georgia, which did nothing to provide facilities for deaf or blind blacks, did little more than continue what was already being done with insane freedmen.

The asylum soon ran out of space for more residents, either black or white, and had to seek more funds for construction and support. In October 1865, the institution held 275 inmates; by mid-1868, it held 336 whites and 52 blacks and could accept new applicants only as vacancies opened. Struggling with the cost of provisions, feeding more patients yet receiving less money from paying ones, the institution relied on the state for ever-larger appropriations. It also needed building funds to cope with overcrowding and a growing backlog of applications. For substantial spending on construction, the institution had to await actions by the last Republican legislature, which authorized $68,000 ($18,000 for accommodations for 50 more black patients and $50,000 for 150 more whites), and the first Redeemer session, which appropriated $54,855. An 1877 act ended the policy of charging Georgia residents who could afford to pay for their own support, and by the 1880s annual appropriations for support exceeded $100,000.[30]

The Georgia Institution for the Education of the Deaf and Dumb reopened in February 1867, and by 1869 it had more than fifty students. It required annual appropriations larger than those before the war, its board of directors explained to the governor, because it had more students, all of them state-supported; it had to pay high salaries for qualified teachers and much higher prices for provisions; and it had to subsidize the mechanical department, which, with more advanced students and lower prices for materials, had been self-sustaining before the war. Opening the school without charge to all qualified applicants, the legislature ended distinctions between paying and state-supported students in 1868. In addition to free tuition, the institution was to provide shoes for all its pupils and clothing for students whose parents were unable to pay for it. During Reconstruction the school depended entirely on the state for its revenue, and it suffered financial difficulties in 1869, when the more conservative legislature that year slashed its funding. But beginning the next year, annual appropriations moved to higher levels and never dropped below $12,500. In 1880, a $15,000 appropriation supported sixty-four white students, thirty-two of each sex.[31]

Enrollment at the Academy for the Blind, which had held in the low twenties in the late 1850s and through the war, exceeded fifty by the mid-1870s. In 1866 it inaugurated its mechanical department, for which it had waited a decade. In addition to teaching music and academic courses, the school could now teach its male students to make brooms and other items, while the females continued their instruction "in plain sewing and other branches of domestic employment." Throughout the late 1860s, the school continued to derive about 5 percent of its income from paying students. As the school grew, it needed more revenue; each Reconstruction legislature, beginning in 1866, gave the academy an $11,000 annual appropriation for support. In 1877 the academy's appropriation of $13,500 provided schooling for sixty-two white students, thirty-four male and twenty-eight female. As late as 1876 and 1877, students from the black-belt counties of Wilkes and Houston paid tuition, but in 1883 the legislature established free tuition for all Georgia residents admitted to the school.[32]

In 1875, for the first time, the Academy for the Blind raised the question of accommodations for blacks. Former owners and county authorities had notified the school of several blind freedmen, "too old to derive benefit from the school department, but not too old to receive industrial training." Beginning in 1878 two young black men from Macon, living at home, received day school instruction "in a room in the workshop." Finally, in 1880, the school began a campaign for funds to open a segregated branch and requested an appropriation of $10,000 to obtain buildings and begin a program. The principal, W. D. Williams, reported statistics showing fully as many blind black children as whites and noted that he had had to reject applications by several on account of their race. Not only had North Carolina and Maryland supplied facilities for blind and deaf blacks, he observed, but Georgia had undertaken the responsibility of providing public funds for blacks in common schools, a university, and a mental institution. Surely it was time to expand that responsibility.[33]

The legislature responded favorably to this strong argument and specific request by authorizing the $10,000. By 1882 the academy had bought a nearby site and had erected a brick building to house perhaps forty students. Black students were first admitted in November 1882, and by the next year six black students attended classes in literature and music in addition to the workshop. Growing slowly, the "colored department" reported eleven students, all male, in 1885.[34]

The school for the deaf, like that for the blind, eventually turned its attention to the needs of black Georgians. After the first mention in its 1868 report, the school made no further reference to the question until 1873, when officers reported having turned away black applicants because state law prevented their being educated "in the same house together" with whites. Noting that "humanity, charity, and the Civil Rights bill" all favored action, the president of the school's board of trustees suggested that to ignore blacks' undeniable needs much longer might be seen as "intentional neglect." He requested $4,000 to erect a building and $2,000 as an annual support fund. Repeating its request in 1875, the school sought an additional $2,000 to buy a suitable building three hundred yards from the school for whites, $1,000 to provide a separate dining room and kitchen, and $500 for furnishings. The legislature gave the school the authority to admit blacks and granted an initial $2,000 appropriation. Requesting money for repairs and support, the school promised that the branches would be kept "as distinctly separate as though the two Institutions were in different towns." In 1882, at last, twenty black students—twelve male, eight female—began classes.[35]

After the military, financial, and political disruption of the Civil War and Reconstruction, Georgia's state-supported institutions resumed their prewar growth. Operations in the 1880s, even for whites, greatly exceeded those of the 1850s. By 1883, moreover, the state had terminated the previous distinctions between paying and nonpaying patients and students at all three institutions. In a more dramatic change, by the end of 1882 blacks as well as whites were routinely admitted, on a segregated basis, to the mental institution and the schools for the blind and the deaf.

Conclusion

Emancipation alone, even before Congressional Reconstruction and black enfranchisement, promoted Georgia's blacks to a very different status by 1866. Though "persons of color" differed greatly from "citizens," the differences that separated postwar "persons of color" from both prewar "free persons of color" and "slaves" were even more distinct. The act of emancipation transformed both prewar groups.

In the first postwar years, Georgia's state and local governments focused their attention and resources on the welfare of whites and the control of both races. For social welfare, blacks at first relied upon themselves or on northern societies or the Freedmen's Bureau. Soon local authorities began to include black paupers on their relief rolls. Only later did the state assume responsibility for black welfare.

Federal authority provided the framework for postwar policy, but Republican rule in Georgia had little specific impact on social policy. The Republican-controlled legislative sessions did little more than continue what was already being done with the insane, and they continued their predecessors' neglect of blind or deaf blacks. The Restoration administration, not its Republican successor, opened the mental institution to blacks. Republican rule ended in Georgia a decade before either the Academy for the Blind or the Asylum for the Deaf made room for blacks. The story was much the same regarding elementary and higher education.

14 ALL THE CHILDREN OF THE STATE

IN THE 1870s, Joseph E. Brown presided over the Atlanta Board of Education. Though the former governor's jurisdiction had shrunk, his concept of public education had grown. In 1858 Brown had called for common schools for "every free white child in the State" and had asserted, "Let there be no aristocracy there but an aristocracy of color and of conduct." In his new position, Brown declared that schools were designed for "all the children of the city, both rich and poor, white and colored." [1]

New currents in postwar Georgia, as elsewhere in the South, reshaped elementary schooling and higher education. After serious disruption throughout the years of war and Reconstruction, educational services expanded until, by the late 1880s, they had far outstripped their prewar dimensions, even for whites. As in the case of the welfare institutions, however, even more striking changes took place as blacks entered Georgia's schools both as students and as teachers, albeit on a segregated basis. All these changes came in the face of a serious decline in the nontax public revenue that had facilitated the prewar rise in Georgia's social spending.

The Reconstruction of Elementary Education

No smooth development of a new, biracial public school system occurred. In 1865, the system of public schools white Georgians had enjoyed at the beginning of the war lay in shambles, and whites did not anticipate that blacks would be included when schools were restored. How to provide schools even for whites was not at all clear, but economic devastation had contradictory effects. Financial support for any school system became more difficult to secure, yet many parents could no longer afford to send their children to private schools. Thus a broader base of support for public spending on education developed.

Congressional legislation declared blacks to be citizens and gave black men the vote. Traditional arguments regarding the necessity for educating voters now applied to blacks as well as whites, and the votes blacks now enjoyed gave them purchasing power in the political marketplace. Moreover, the Civil

Rights Act of 1866 and the Fourteenth Amendment made it improbable that Georgia could supply schools for whites and deny them to blacks.

People who established or maintained schools in Georgia during Reconstruction had to rely on financial resources other than the state government. Children who could paid tuition. Several cities and even a few county governments levied school taxes. The Freedmen's Bureau supplied school buildings, and various northern groups sent teachers and money. A survey of those various actions provides more than a narrative of education in Georgia at a time when state support had lapsed. It also reveals the array of forces working to provide the schools that served as a foundation on which the state eventually built a public school system.

During Reconstruction, state spending for elementary education depended, as it always had, on the availability of a large surplus of nontax revenue, and after 1865 there was no surplus. The state contributed no money to elementary education after the Civil War until 1871, and not before 1873 did it resume substantial school spending. The 1865–66 legislative session required only that county governments issue certificates of indebtedness to pay amounts owed teachers of poor children for 1865. The 1866 legislature passed a bill to create a full-fledged school system, complete with state superintendent, for the tuition-free education of all white children. That act authorized a heavy county school tax—as high as 100 percent of the state tax—but was otherwise vague about finances. The act was scheduled to take effect in 1868, but Congressional Reconstruction intervened before it could be implemented.[2]

The Republican-authored Constitution of 1868 promised significant changes in public schooling in Georgia. Seeking to make room for black children in a public school system, the convention directed the legislature, at its first session after ratification, to "provide a thorough system of general education, to be forever free to all children of the State." To support that system, the constitution authorized a $1.00 poll tax, some minor revenue sources, and even, if necessary, a state property tax for schools. Thus, schools "free to all children" were to replace the old system in which teachers received both tuition from paying students and state money for poor children. The constitution did not merely authorize the general assembly to establish and maintain elementary schools; it mandated such action. These education rights were to apply not only to whites, but also, on a segregated basis, to blacks. And if revenue from poll taxes (for the first time allocated specifically to schools) and nontax sources proved insufficient, the state had the option of resorting to a school tax on property.[3]

The legislature took no action on education in 1868 or 1869, but in 1870 it enacted a new school law. Prohibiting integration, it declared that "the children of the white and colored races shall not be taught together." Not for many years would Georgia levy a state property tax for schools, but the 1870 act allocated to the new education fund half the state's annual income from the

Western and Atlantic Railroad. That income did not amount to anything in 1870, as the railroad ran up a large deficit, but under a leasing arrangement established that year the schools would receive $150,000 annually. The state collected some poll tax revenue due during the Republican years, but at election time (in 1868 and again in 1870) Governor Bullock ordered collection suspended so as to allow poor whites and blacks to vote, and even the sums collected did not go to education.[4] Thus it remained for Democratic administrations after Redemption to create a school system for Georgia.

Before the war, the state education fund had three sources of revenue, and all three disappeared when the war ended. Bank dividends failed when Georgia's banks collapsed, their capital tied up in now-worthless Confederate and state war bonds and treasury notes. Another vanished resource was $100,000 from the Western and Atlantic Railroad's net annual income; repairs absorbed any income at first, and when the 1865–66 legislature authorized the issue of $3 million worth of mortgage bonds, it diverted the Western and Atlantic's earnings to pay the interest. And schools received nothing after the war from the third source, the annual interest ($23,355 in 1865) on an amount equal to however much state debt had been redeemed since 1858.[5]

Evaporation of the school fund exemplified postwar Georgia's complete break with the past and forced a reconsideration of the public's role in financing education in Georgia. The antebellum public school system, such as it was, had relied on neither state property taxes nor poll taxes, but on nontax revenue —payments by the United States for Georgia's western lands early in the century, distribution of a U.S. Treasury surplus in the 1830s, and finally, beginning in the late 1850s, the Western and Atlantic Railroad's earnings. Income from bank dividends and the state railroad represented Georgia's antebellum search for a tax-free method of paying for public expenditures, and the third source of the education fund symbolized Georgia's late antebellum switch from economic investments to social spending. The war collapsed both efforts. Nonetheless, growing support for public education in the late 1860s made it more difficult than it had been a generation earlier simply to retrench when sources of nontax income vanished.

White Georgians believed that, if there were to be school taxes at all, taxes on whites should pay only for schools for whites. As one observed soon after the war: "I think it would be well to have the negro educated, but I do not think the people of this State would tax themselves for such a purpose. The people are too poor and have too many other things to take care of. We have to look for that to the people of the North. The North having freed the negroes, ought to see to it that they be elevated."[6] In fact, Northerners did much to assist blacks to secure an education, and whites declined even to tax themselves for white schools.

Compared with the 1850s, elementary schools were scarce throughout the Reconstruction era. The end of slavery, together with population growth, could have doubled the number of students in elementary schools between 1860 and 1870. What happened instead was a sharp decline in the total numbers of schools, teachers, and students—in educational opportunities for children and in occupational opportunities for adults.[7]

Learning to Read

A major change in southern schooling began by summer 1865. Teaching blacks to read or write had long been an offense that could bring a white a hefty fine and imprisonment, and a black a fine and/or whipping. But apprenticeship provisions of the postwar Black Code required masters to see that their apprentices were taught to read English. In that private relationship, the law of Georgia swung from prohibiting the promotion of black literacy to mandating it. With some assistance, particularly from Northerners, many blacks in Georgia took advantage of the new dispensation. No state-supported schools were yet open to blacks, but as a freedman in Macon exclaimed, "Now we are no longer slaves, and we are learning to read." In Savannah, the Colored Education Association established the Bryan Free School in the old Bryan Slave Mart.[8]

Schools for freedmen opened around the state in summer 1865. An average of eighty students attended a school established in Griffin in July. None had previously been to school, but two could read. One of the teachers wrote the Freedmen's Bureau that "our School employs three Teachers all colored men, we were Slaves untell made free by the goodness of God and by President Lincoln Emancipation Proclamation." Among their difficulties, he reported, "our Education is Limited, our means amount to allmost nothing with but little prospect of improvement. . . . If we had one White Teacher of experience to aid us, we would be greatly benefited but we are not able to pay him any thing."[9]

A middle-aged southern white woman, Mrs. E. A. Christian, organized a school for freedmen in Americus in July 1865. As many as sixty-five students attended her school, which she held at her home. Tuition was the usual dollar a month, but after three months, she reported in October, fewer than half had been able to pay her. Writing to the Freedmen's Bureau, she described the motivations behind her new role and the difficulties she was meeting. "I have had to struggle against obstacles almost insurmountable, and have established my School against the opposition of the whole [white] community." But her "condition in life—being widowed, very poor, and having two daughters to support"—forced her to find work. So she began her school for freedmen, "and although as yet my school has not supported me," she wrote, "I am in hopes, that with your assistance, I may be enabled to render it useful, as well as profitable."[10] The bureau helped, and the school prospered.

The federal government and northern citizens paid some of the costs of schooling in early postwar Georgia. The Freedmen's Bureau and various northern aid societies cooperated in establishing and maintaining schools; the bureau was primarily responsible for providing school buildings and the societies for procuring teachers. In the first three postwar years, the Freedmen's Bureau spent about $100,000 on education in Georgia. The aid societies spent about $20,000 in 1865–66, $42,000 to support 80 teachers the following year, and $50,000 to support 123 teachers in 1867–68. The American Missionary Association, much the largest of the aid societies, also spent $30,000 for school land and buildings. Most, although not all, of these schools were for blacks. Edmund Asa Ware, superintendent of education for the Freedmen's Bureau in Georgia, reported in July 1868 that the largest number of students in all these schools in any one month had been 13,000, but that a total of perhaps 30,000 had learned at least to read.[11]

Free Schools for the Whole People: The Peabody Fund

George Peabody, a Georgia-born philanthropist living in the North, established an educational fund in 1867 that was to have a broad impact on public schooling in Georgia. The Peabody Education Fund's objective— "free schools for the whole people"—called for establishing a system of public schools in every southern state. The fund's general agent, the Rev. Dr. Barnas Sears, brought four decades of experience in teaching and educational administration to his new position. He had succeeded Horace Mann as secretary of the Massachusetts Board of Education and then served as president of Brown University. As general agent, he traveled through the South to generate enthusiasm for public school systems.[12]

In language intended to secure support from influential southern educators and politicians, Sears articulated his concerns and objectives. In utilitarian terms, Sears announced that the fund was "seeking the greatest good of the greatest number." In language reminiscent of Jefferson's, he declared that "the aristocracy of talent does not correspond with the aristocracy of wealth or rank." Combining the economic and social control arguments of Jacksonian days, Sears contended that schooled workers were more productive workers; that schools, like railroads, drove up property values; that education routed out poverty, ignorance, and crime; that money put into schools was a better bargain than money put into penitentiaries; and that money put into public schools was much more efficient than the same money pumped into private schools.[13]

Beyond economic and social considerations were political ones. Sears urged upon his listeners that "one-half of the white children in all these States are growing up in ignorance, and have been doing so for eight years; . . . unless something is speedily done to prevent it, a semi-barbarous generation will in the last quarter of the nineteenth century control the destinies" of the South. Sears related a Virginian's story of Noah and the great flood: "If the building of the ark had been proposed to me, I should have objected. It was altogether too big. I should have said that putting all those animals into it was too much of an undertaking. But the flood has come. The ark is beginning to float; and lest I be engulfed, . . . *I go for universal education.*"[14] Sears seemed concerned at first only with white society, but that changed when blacks obtained the vote.

City taxes combined with the Peabody Education Fund to establish the first postwar public school systems in Georgia. Cities had greater financial resources and more compact populations than their rural hinterlands and thus could more easily overcome two of the major obstacles to school progress. As the Freedmen's Bureau and the American Missionary Association made schools available to blacks, cities moved to provide schools for whites. The Freedmen's Bureau and the A.M.A. were most active in financing schools in the immediate postwar years; city taxes and the Peabody Fund became more important after 1868. The Peabody Fund generally followed Sears's advice to "limit ourselves to rendering aid to schools where larger numbers can be gathered, and where a model system of schools can be organized." Thus a city property tax of one-fifth of 1 percent of value, together with a substantial grant from the Peabody Fund, enabled Columbus to launch its public elementary schools for whites in 1867–68. By 1870, the cities of Savannah, Columbus, Atlanta, and Augusta were all receiving between $1,000 and $2,000 from the Peabody Fund each year as they developed "model" school systems that could survive without such assistance. A few smaller systems also received funds.[15]

In the fall of 1868, Sears and the Peabody Education Fund began to turn their attention to the educational needs of black Georgians. At first the fund contributed money to independent black schools, but Sears sought to persuade city authorities to make room in their model systems for black students. In October 1868, the fund provided $170 to 18 black schools in Georgia with a total of 782 students, and for the year 1870 it supplied $7,000 to such schools. By 1872 city school systems that the Peabody Fund had helped launch were establishing (or incorporating into their systems) black schools as well as white. In that year, Brunswick reported 210 blacks and 307 whites in its public schools. Augusta reported 934 whites enrolled and, in schoolhouses originally erected by the Freedmen's Bureau, 683 blacks. The president of Savannah's board of education reported that, because no state funds had yet arrived, no public schools for blacks had opened; but by spring 1873 such schools were in operation there as well.[16]

In 1872 Columbus, which no longer required Peabody Fund assistance for its white schools, received $600 to open black schools. Average attendance in the Columbus public schools included 375 blacks and 480 whites, numbers that reflected the racial makeup of the city's population. When the black school opened, the principal and two assistants were black men; but when the assistants resigned, four black women replaced them. Annual costs per student at Columbus schools (based on average attendance) were $15.91 for whites, $4.73 for blacks. The city superintendent of public schools observed that, given the Peabody money, together with blacks' share of state funds, black schools "cost the city nothing." [17]

Atlanta

Atlanta had a representative experience in establishing public schools for both blacks and whites. Between 1869, when the city council appointed a committee to investigate the feasibility of creating a public school system, and February 1872, when the first schools in the infant system opened their doors, the city examined alternatives and made decisions that provided the broad outlines of public education in Atlanta for the rest of the century and beyond. Despite differences over details in the proposed system, a large majority of the citizens of Atlanta—black and white, Democratic and Republican—came to favor public schools. City leaders showed less concern for schooling black children than for whites; as the committee report observed in 1869, the needs of white children were "more immediate and pressing." In part, blacks were expendable; some people objected to raising money "to educate colored children, when the white people had the burthen of the taxes to bear." In part, as the committee noted, between the Freedmen's Bureau and the aid societies, "the facilities for the [free] education of the colored children are more extensive" than those for whites.[18]

Still, the Atlanta public school system opened with schools for blacks as well as for whites. In the first year, the system had nine schools—two high schools for whites (one for boys, another for girls) and seven elementary schools, two of them for blacks. Roughly 30 percent of Atlanta's school-age children were black; 27 percent of those attending the public schools in 1872 were black. Missionary societies provided the two black school buildings. The American Missionary Association rented the Storrs School to the board of education free of charge, provided the A.M.A. be permitted to nominate the teachers, who were subject to approval by the board. In an arrangement with the Freedman's Aid Society of the Methodist Episcopal church, the city rented the Summer Hill School free of charge, maintained its buildings and grounds, and appointed the teachers. Money for Atlanta's schools came from the Peabody Fund, from a city property tax of one-third of 1 percent, and from Atlanta's share of the Fulton County portion of the state school fund.[19]

At first, all the teachers in Atlanta's public school system, even those in the "colored schools," were white. Succumbing to pressure from the black community, and responding also to evidence that black teachers had worked out well in the black schools of other Georgia cities, Atlanta appointed its first black public school teachers in 1877. Within a decade, the board of education reported with satisfaction that it had changed completely to black personnel at the black schools. Politics and economics pointed in the same direction; just as women teachers would work for lower pay than men, black teachers could be be hired at lower pay than whites.[20]

Retrospectives

Two retrospectives on what might have been point up elementary schooling's development in the years after secession. In the 1920s Edgar W. Knight, historian of education, sought to deny that there existed anything like what W. E. B. DuBois termed the "benefits" of Reconstruction. Emphasizing progress if it was prewar, and ignoring it if postwar, Knight wrote: "But for the inauguration of the congressional plan of restoring the South, the educational needs of both white and colored children would have been more properly cared for during the years following the war." [21] Cheerfully revising the past, Knight neglected the white-only provision of the 1866 education act as well as the absence of financing.

Emphasizing the Civil War rather than Reconstruction, a state official expressed regret that the war had killed the antebellum dream of a common school system funded by the Western and Atlantic. Writing in the 1870s, Thomas P. Janes recalled the education act of 1858, with its creation of a school fund from a part of the railroad's earnings, as well as its provision that the state would increase its spending on schools as payments on the debt diminished. Janes wrote: "These measures contemplated at no distant day a fund sufficient to establish free schools throughout the State; and it would undoubtedly have so resulted long since, but for the war." [22]

But for the war. The inclusion of blacks among school children radically distinguished the postwar dispensation. New, too, was enactment of the occasional prewar call for a higher poll tax allocated to schools. Unchanged, however, was the reliance on sources other than a state property tax for schools. Even the county "poor school" tax had gone; almost nowhere in Georgia, outside the cities, did any property-tax revenue support schools in 1875 or 1880. A regressive poll tax had replaced a redistributive property tax in the counties. Yet the $150,000 fund of 1860, financed largely by the Western and Atlantic Railroad, found its echo in the 1870s in a reconstituted school fund, supplied in large part by half the proceeds from the railroad's rental.

15 HIGHER EDUCATION FOR A NEW SOUTH

CONSTITUTIONAL CHANGES during the Civil War and Reconstruction dramatically reshaped higher education as well as elementary schooling in the South. The advent of legal literacy for blacks led to new questions: Should blacks have access to institutions more advanced than common schools? Where were teachers for black elementary schools to come from? What roles should the state take in supporting higher education for blacks and in training black teachers?

Emancipation and the Fourteenth Amendment were not the only manifestations of changed relations between the federal government and the states. During the war, the federal government began to offer the states financial support for higher education. Like the Homestead Act, which Congress passed in the 1850s but the president vetoed, the Morrill Land Grant Act of 1862 became law soon after the Republican party secured the White House.[1] Under a second Morrill Act, passed in 1890, the federal purse would help sustain colleges for whites only if blacks gained a share in that support.

Barriers to higher education on grounds of class, sex, or race declined after the Civil War. State funds enabled Confederate veterans to attend five Georgia colleges free of charge for a short time after the war. Several branches of the University of Georgia developed in the 1870s and 1880s; each offered tuition-free education, and some admitted women as well as men.

The University of Georgia

The University of Georgia emerged from the Civil War with its operations suspended, its endowment from the state ($100,000 in bank stock) totally lost, and its buildings the barracks of federal troops. The constitutional convention of 1865 directed the legislature to "provide for the early resumption of the regular exercises of the University of Georgia, by the adequate endowment of the same." Anticipating state aid, the university reopened in January 1866 with seventy-eight students. The following month the state house of representatives indefinitely postponed consideration of a bill to appropriate money to the school. But because the Code of Georgia already provided the university a guaranteed annual income, neither new constitutional nor statutory authority was necessary except to enlarge that income. The code perpetuated an 1821 act requiring the state to make up the difference whenever annual bank dividends fell below $8,000. Beginning in 1866, therefore, the state treasury provided the full $8,000 each year.[2]

If the legislature declined to use tax funds beyond the annual $8,000 figure, it could, as Governor Jenkins observed, tap an alternative source of funding "without imposing any burden on our impoverished people." The Morrill Act, passed by the U.S. Congress while Georgia was in the Confederacy, offered the state 270,000 acres of public land in the West, to be converted into an education fund for an agricultural college. Jenkins advised the general assembly to establish such an institution as a department of the state university. The legislature authorized acceptance of the federal offer in 1866, though Georgia failed to make use of the funds until 1872.[3]

To meet three of Georgia's needs, the 1866 legislature enacted a law designed to assist the state's institutions of higher education; produce "native educated teachers"; and help support Georgia's "many indigent maimed soldiers, . . . who, by reason of loss of limbs, are deprived of the ability to perform physical labor." Any such person under age thirty could attend any of five Georgia schools—the University of Georgia, Emory College, Mercer University, Oglethorpe University, or Bowdon Collegiate Institute—with no charge for tuition or other expenses, up to a $300 limit per year, until graduation. His obligation in return was to teach in the state's schools for as many years as he benefited from the act's provisions. One beneficiary, Samuel J. Brown, survived the war with only one arm. He enrolled at Bowdon when it reopened in 1867, graduated in 1871, and taught school in Carroll County for the next four years before becoming county school commissioner.[4]

Though the program survived for barely two years, the state spent more than $100,000 on it. That money was more important to some of the schools than to others, but it helped all five through the difficult early postwar years. Emory College's president recognized that, by supplying more students and more income, the soldiers' appropriation "greatly benefitted" his institution. Emory received more income from the state than from paying students during the time the 1866 law was in effect. Official figures, though incomplete, show that total grants under the soldiers' appropriation exceeded $50,000 to the state university, $27,000 to Emory, and $27,000 to the other schools combined. The Republican-dominated 1868 legislature appropriated $44,000 for amounts then due but provided that no new students were to be admitted under the program. Despite a collective effort by recipient schools to have the appropriation extended, the 1869 session repealed the act outright and appropriated only sufficient funds to pay for obligations incurred through the end of 1868.[5]

The University of Georgia proved more vulnerable than usual to outside pressures during Reconstruction. Benjamin H. Hill, a university trustee, led the opposition in Georgia to the "Military Bills" passed by Congress in 1867. Particularly effective and well publicized were his "Davis Hall speech," given in Atlanta on 16 July, and his "Notes on the Situation," published in the *Augusta Chronicle and Sentinel* between 19 June and 1 August and widely reprinted. At the university's commencement exercises in early August, a student speaker named Albert H. Cox vigorously attacked Republicans and Radical Reconstruction. His impassioned speech found an enthusiastic audience that included Hill, who had just been offered a law professorship. News of the incident outraged General John Pope, commander of the Third Military District. Believing Hill to have inspired both the speaker and the speech, Pope ordered that the university close, the state treasury halt payments to it, and troops again occupy its buildings.[6]

Friends of the university were frantic. One trustee, Iverson L. Harris, could see no solution short of Hill's immediately declining the professorship and, better still, resigning his trusteeship. Governor Jenkins, also a trustee, warned university treasurer William L. Mitchell that suspension of state support might freeze not only the $8,000 annuity but also the soldiers' appropriation. (And Emory College's president, understanding that the soldiers' appropriation was imperiled for all recipient schools, went to work to secure revocation of Pope's order suspending payments.) Chancellor Andrew A. Lipscomb sought to mollify Pope, who rescinded only his order converting college classrooms into army barracks. Lipscomb wrote Mitchell: "I think that the state payment will not be restored. . . . But I believe that we shall be permitted to open the University." The school did reopen, though Pope refused to restore state support and sought Hill's resignation as trustee. In time, the trustees persuaded General Ulysses S. Grant to order payments resumed, and Hill continued on the faculty and the board of trustees.[7]

Though neither the Jenkins nor the Bullock administrations launched an agricultural school under the Morrill Act, their successors did. Governor Benjamin Conley, during his brief tenure, sold Georgia's land scrip in January 1872 for $242,202. The university's board of trustees quickly established a new institution at Athens and applied for the fund. To the disappointment of several other towns and institutions, Governor James M. Smith granted the application. Sharing facilities and teachers with Franklin College (as the regular undergraduate school was generally called), the State College of Agriculture and Mechanic Arts opened at Athens in May 1872. In addition to the state's $8,000 annuity, therefore, the university received roughly $17,000 annually through the Morrill Act.[8]

Considerations of Policy: Atlanta University

In a sharp break from prewar policy, the Georgia General Assembly in 1870 appropriated $8,000 for a school for blacks. Atlanta University had opened the year before, funded largely by the Freedmen's Bureau and the American Missionary Association. Its immediate purposes were to offer elementary, secondary, and (before very long) higher education to black men and women (though whites were always admitted as well) and to train black teachers. Those teachers would supply leadership to black communities and schooling for black children. Calling for "the true reconstruction of the States lately in rebellion, a reconstruction founded upon the education of all the people," General Rufus Saxton viewed the combination of elementary schools and normal schools for blacks as "a most powerful means for the Elevation of a people which is in its present condition through no agency of its own, and under Providence made free by the act of the U.S. Government. It is plain that the advancement of the race is an Essential Element of the future peace and prosperity of the Nation." Saxton commended Edmund Asa Ware, president of Atlanta University, for seeking "aid to build side by side with the future capital of Georgia, an edifice for the Education of a people who have just been admitted to a share in its government." [9]

In an early example of a separate-but-equal policy, the state made identical appropriations of $8,000 each to the Athens school for whites and to the Atlanta school for blacks. William McKinley, a white Democratic state senator, described a legislative struggle among the "negro power," the "Planter Race," and the "Mountain party," in which Bainbridge, Milledgeville, Dahlonega, and various other towns, including Atlanta and Athens, vied for state money. From McKinley's perspective, the major objective was "to buy off the negroes and Radicals, from Athens, by donating liberally to the Negro college in Atlanta," and thus "forever to protect the University against Negro students." Athens might have to share the Morrill Act proceeds, he wrote a university trustee, but "a little, far off, wild land will be no pay to Athens for negro classes in your College" in another year or two. In the end, as Henry M. Turner, a black state representative, later reported, black Republicans and white Democrats came to an agreement that "we would never bother Franklin University if the State would make an equal appropriation to our University" each year. Atlanta University collected $8,000 in 1870 and again in 1871, but by 1872 Democrats had regained control of the legislature. [10] With few black constituents to court, Redeemer legislators neglected to reenact the appropriation.

Spokesmen for black Georgia refused to permit the matter to end there. Supporters of A.U., already among the opponents of Governor Smith's action granting the entire proceeds of the Morrill Act to the University of Georgia, challenged what they viewed as yet another outrage. Henry M. Turner, for example, no longer in the legislature, published a powerful letter in a black newspaper, the *Savannah Morning News*. Edmund Asa Ware wrote both the governor and the university's board of trustees inquiring about the reception of black applicants to the agricultural college at Athens. To Governor Smith,

Ware pointed out that "about one half of the Industrial Classes of Georgia, for whose benefit Congress made the grant, are colored people." To a member of the faculty at Athens, he wrote: "If you call to mind the conversations which you and Mr. Lumpkin had with me during the session of the Legislature concerning the disposition of the 'Agricultural College Scrip' you will not wonder that I was surprised when I heard that the Governor of Georgia had appropriated, and that the Trustees . . . had consented to receive, the whole of the income of the said scrip. I can only explain their action, and rid my mind of a feeling that there has been unfair dealing somewhere, by supposing that . . . [you] have decided to admit all students, regardless of color, to the benefits of this grant." [11]

The board of trustees at Athens pondered "the negro interest in the land scrip fund." The university's supporters were primarily interested in retaining the entire fund, and they had something to offer friends of Atlanta University for support against other competitors. If Athens retained the land scrip fund, the black school might regain its annual $8,000. So the 1873 legislature revived the appropriation for A.U. and appointed a special joint committee to investigate the matter and make recommendations for a permanent settlement. [12]

When the joint committee reported at the 1874 session, it gave strong support to making the appropriation permanent. Federal relations ("considerations of policy") and state politics (a "compromise . . . absolutely binding") pointed in the same direction. "It is not for a moment pretended that this scrip was given solely for the white race," the committee declared. Moreover, a new civil rights bill was bobbing around in Congress, and if it should pass, and apply to educational institutions, then "the State's protection of this college for the education of the colored people, would be a safeguard thrown around the University, and the other [white] Colleges of Georgia." Finally, a division of the land scrip fund would "seriously impair the usefulness of the State Agricultural College, and of its branch at Dahlonega." Thus an annual appropriation of $8,000 to the Atlanta school offered protection all around. The University of Georgia could enjoy the entire land scrip fund; white colleges might be better protected against integration under a new civil rights bill; and angry black legislators and constituents would be placated. Such an appropriation could also protect black Georgians "against the whims and feelings of changing Legislatures." The committee urged passage of a bill establishing the appropriation on a permanent basis so as to "finally settle this complicated trouble." [13]

Thus it was that Bourbon Georgia continued to provide annual support for a black university. Republicans had made an inexpensive gesture toward their largely black constituency; Democrats expressly provided that the annual appropriation be "in lieu of any claim of the colored population" on the Morrill Act proceeds. The legislature established a further requirement similar to that made of colleges that received financial assistance before the war. The 1874 act required Atlanta University to admit, free of tuition charge, "as many colored pupils from each county" as there were members in the state house of representatives from that county, to be nominated by the respective legislators. A board of visitors would ascertain each year, as did the boards of state institutions, whether the money was being spent appropriately.[14]

Tree of Knowledge

In the dozen years after Redemption, Georgia established branches of the state university at Dahlonega, Milledgeville, Thomasville, Cuthbert, and Hamilton. An 1871 act of Congress donated ten acres of land and the U.S. Branch Mint building in Dahlonega, where the North Georgia Agricultural College (today's North Georgia College) opened in 1873.[15] Later, the state laid the foundations for the other schools. When still other towns expressed interest in becoming locations for new university branches, the board of trustees agreed to accept such branches as member institutions on condition that the legislature incorporate and support them. Members of the university's board of trustees had several objectives. They sought to enlarge the university's power and to assert that power over life in Georgia.[16] They hoped that branch schools, offering what would today be called a junior college curriculum, would funnel upper-division students to the Athens campus. By geographically dispersing some operations, they might generate greater public support for the university. Moreover, organizers of the North Georgia school had hoped to obtain the land scrip fund for their institution, and the university trustees compromised by funneling a portion of the proceeds to Dahlonega.

Branch colleges deviated from what university trustees expected of them. All five branches were allowed to charge annual matriculation fees of $10.00 but, if they wanted state support, no tuition. Like the State College of Agriculture and Mechanic Arts, they posted only nominal entrance requirements and thus had to offer secondary as well as college-level courses. For example, North Georgia's student population included sub-freshman classes until 1927, by which time Georgia had established public high schools adequate to permit termination of colleges' preparatory departments. North Georgia's officers fleshed out their charter by admitting women students, establishing a "Normal Department," offering courses in mining engineering, and successfully petitioning in a local court for the power to grant degrees and thus offer a four-year undergraduate program. From the beginning, the schools at Dahlonega and Milledgeville were coeducational, and in 1889 the legislature granted white women equal privileges at other branches as well.[17]

Student populations at Athens and the branch colleges varied in composition. In the academic year 1884–85, 171 students attended Franklin College or the A & M school at Athens. All were male, and all took college-level classes.

All students at the Thomasville and Cuthbert campuses were also male, but most were in preparatory classes; only 2 of 117 students at Thomasville and 22 of 92 at Cuthbert were graded as college-level. The Dahlonega school had 143 students, including 21 women; 54 took college courses. The largest school, and the most fully coeducational, was the Milledgeville campus, where 113 of 401 students were college undergraduates, and women were in a small majority in both the preparatory and college departments.[18]

The university at Athens was disappointed to see the branch campuses develop more as competitors than as feeders. One reason students did not advance from the new institutions to the main campus was Dahlonega's aggressive leadership. More important, nearly half the college students at the branch schools were young women, and Franklin College admitted no women before World War I.

University trustees speculated that lower tuition might attract more students. For decades the board had proposed reduced tuition charges for undergraduates. In the 1850s, Governors Herschel V. Johnson and Joseph E. Brown recommended legislation to endow the university with funds to provide scholarships. Though the legislature took no such action, in 1856 the board of trustees began to offer scholarships to as many as ten young men each year. After the war, when annual charges had doubled to $100, the university increased the number of potential beneficiaries to fifty, with no more than one at a time from any county. In 1868 the university reported twenty-seven students on full scholarships and fourteen others on partial scholarships. "As a remuneration to the State," they were obliged to teach at a public or private school in Georgia for as many years as they studied tuition-free at the university.[19]

Beginning in 1871, the trustees discussed more earnestly the possibilities of offering free tuition to "all the children of the State" (provided they were not black or female). Proceeds of the Morrill Act already made tuition-free education available to scores of white Georgians at the agricultural colleges at Athens and Dahlonega. In the mid-1870s, the university reduced tuition from $100 to $75 but initiated a separate annual library fee of $5. Later, the university proposed to offer free tuition for all undergraduates at Athens in exchange for an appropriation of $2,000, which the legislature granted in 1881. In the 1880s, therefore, all undergraduates in Athens and at the various university branches paid only matriculation and library fees. Annual charges of $10 and $15 were much lower than the tuition charges they replaced. Only medical and law students continued to pay tuition.[20]

Despite the advent of several new schools, state appropriations for higher education showed little change into the 1880s. The state authorized funds for improvements at the agricultural college at Athens ($15,000) and for repairs after a fire at the Dahlonega school ($25,000). In the fifteen years after the end of the soldiers' appropriation, the only other extra spending was the $2,000 appropriation that permitted Franklin College to begin offering free tuition.

Thus the only public money for the annual support of higher education in Georgia came from the twin $8,000 annuities and the land scrip fund. The latter provided roughly half the state university's annual income for most of the 1870s and 1880s, though by the 1880s close to half that money went to the support of branch campuses. The university granted Dahlonega at least $2,000 annually and generally made funds available to other branches as well. In 1882–83, for example, the land scrip fund provided $17,914 of the university's total income of $30,259, but $8,625 went to branch institutions: $2,625 to Dahlonega and $2,000 each to Cuthbert, Thomasville, and Milledgeville. Fractions of the Morrill Act's land scrip fund provided the sole public support for the university branches, and any money from the fund going to those branches meant less for the Athens campus. In 1889, however, branch colleges began to receive direct state appropriations, and the university then distributed only the annual $2,000 to Dahlonega.[21]

Between 1885 and 1895, direct state appropriations launched three new university branches for white Georgians. An 1885 act appropriated $65,000 to establish a School of Technology (today the Georgia Institute of Technology) and support it for a year. Tech opened in Atlanta in 1888. In the early 1890s, Georgia sought to establish "a first-class college for the education of white girls," the Georgia Normal and Industrial College (today's Georgia College), in the old state buildings in Milledgeville. At the same time, the State Normal School (now the University of Georgia's Department of Education) began operations in Athens. At first, only men were to be admitted there, but an 1893 act opened the school to women as well, and for the first time a department of the University of Georgia at Athens accepted female students. Annual appropriations to support the School of Technology started at $18,000 for 1890 but then rose to $22,500, and similar appropriations went to the two other new schools. Thus, beginning in the late 1880s Georgia greatly increased its spending on higher education. White colleges received only $8,000 from the state treasury most years in the two decades after the war, but in 1897 they received more than $100,000.[22]

Outpost in a Hostile Country

Despite continuing challenges, Atlanta University continued to receive state aid into the 1880s, and soon after Georgia terminated support for one black institution it established another. Articulating the feelings of many white Georgians, state school commissioner Gustavus Orr attacked the state's resumption in 1874 of its support for Atlanta University. He was particularly critical of interracial fraternizing at the school, where "white teachers and their colored pupils sit together at the same table at their meals." The appropriation was unconstitutional, he argued, because it went to a sectarian (American Missionary Association, or Congregationalist) school; unwise, he was certain, because the school was not subject to state control and its board of trustees included several Northerners; and impractical, he contended, because the state's greatest need was for teachers in black schools, but Atlanta University offered (among its programs) a classical curriculum. He also charged that the teachers the school sent out would infect their students with impolitic attitudes. The appropriation, he concluded, should be diverted to the support of a state-controlled normal school to train black teachers for black elementary schools. But the general assembly, unwilling to unsettle the arrangement of 1874, spurned Orr's advice.[23]

Yet, like the University of Georgia in 1867, Atlanta University proved vulnerable to outside pressures two decades later. Like the Athens school, the Atlanta one survived. But it lost its state support. Despite what Governor John B. Gordon termed "the settled policy of the state against the co-education of the races," a few children of white faculty members had attended classes. When state officials chose to give official recognition to that fact, the 1887 legislature made the $8,000 annuity contingent on the exclusion of white students. Atlanta University replied that it had no intention of discriminating among its applicants on grounds of race.[24]

After receiving a total of $136,000 between 1870 and 1887, Atlanta University received no further state support. The *Macon Telegraph* expressed the dominant attitude in white Georgia when it declared in 1890 that "the University can recover its income of $8,000 whenever it will agree to conform to the state's law. . . . But if its managers prefer to consider this institution an outpost in a hostile country, they should not complain if the enemy refuses to voluntarily furnish supplies for its garrison. It is enough that they do not abolish it."[25]

In a move to tighten the state's race laws, the 1890 legislature prohibited black students from attending the University of Georgia and white students from attending a state-supported school for blacks. It also repealed the 1874 act that had granted an annual appropriation of $8,000 to Atlanta University. One of Orr's wishes had come true. No black school received the annuity for 1888, 1889, or 1890.[26]

In 1890 Congress enacted a second Morrill Land Grant Act and thus spurred new changes in Georgia's higher education. According to that act, each state would receive annual amounts, beginning at $15,000 in 1890 and rising gradually to $25,000 a decade later. Unlike the first Morrill Act in 1862, which was silent on race, the 1890 act offered annual payments only on condition that they go to blacks as well as whites. And yet it did not require integrated facilities. Segregation was acceptable so long as a state's fund was "equitably divided" between "a college for white students" and an "institution for colored students."[27] The statute thus embodied the separate-but-equal doctrine to which the U.S. Supreme Court would give broader currency six years later in *Plessy* v. *Ferguson*.

Governor John B. Gordon admonished the general assembly to apportion blacks' share of the second Morrill Act proceeds to a "non-sectarian" institution to be "taught and patronized exclusively by colored people." To fulfill those conditions, Georgia established a coeducational school for blacks as a new branch of the University of Georgia. The Georgia State Industrial College (now Savannah State College) opened in 1891 with free tuition to black residents of Georgia. The new school received both the old $8,000 annuity (in lieu of any claim on the 1862 fund) and one-third of the 1890 fund. All faculty members of the Savannah school were black men, including the president, Richard R. Wright. Born a slave in 1853, Wright entered Atlanta University at its founding in 1869 and graduated with its first college class in 1876. In Augusta in 1880, he established the first black public high school in Georgia, which he headed until his new appointment. Like Atlanta University before it, the college began operations with no college-level students, but the president's son became its first college graduate in 1898 and stayed on as a teacher.[28]

Conclusion

Public aid to higher education in Georgia was a very different matter in the 1890s from what it had been in the 1850s. Before the Civil War, aid was much more limited in amount, in sources, and in recipients. In the last prewar decade, the state had never had to make up a deficit in the University of Georgia's income from bank dividends. The only public aid had reflected deteriorating federal relations or the elitist nature of higher education, as when the state supported and then purchased the Georgia Military Institute, or when it granted each of four medical schools lump sums of $5,000 to $15,000. Only white men benefited directly from any of these expenditures, and most of them came from comfortable backgrounds in the towns or black belt. By the end of the century, *federal* aid to Georgia's institutions of higher education amounted to more than $40,000 annually; *state* aid, more than $100,000.

Gone was the basis of Governor Wilson Lumpkin's prewar complaint of a "general impression . . . that the almost exclusive object of a college education is to multiply doctors and lawyers."[29] State funds now supported schools for black men, black women, and white women, three groups excluded before 1870. A common school system, growing numbers of public secondary schools, and free tuition—both at Franklin College and at the university's many new branches—made higher education available to large numbers of white men who would have had no such opportunity a generation earlier. A liberal arts education was still valued and available, but most institutions directed their curricula more toward training teachers, farmers, and engineers. Higher education had become more practical and more accessible.

16 RAILROADS, DEBT, AND RECONSTRUCTION

PUBLIC DEBT posed a central concern throughout the postwar era. In the prosperous 1850s, payments on the debt had taken the largest portion of each year's budget, but the burden was not onerous. When the war ended, Georgia was much poorer and the debt much larger. In view of the widespread poverty and disrupted economy, moreover, the state at first borrowed funds for its operations rather than levy taxes.

Many Georgians, like other Southerners, looked to the railroads to alleviate their poverty and bring prosperity. With private resources scant and in disarray, many saw state aid as imperative. Although efforts to secure such aid involved both Republicans and Democrats, some members in both parties thought it beyond Georgia's means and sought to restrict it. Regardless, aid to railroads led to even greater state debt.

Presidential Reconstruction and the State Debt

Though the legislature levied property and poll taxes for 1866 and again for 1867, the state borrowed most of its money in both years. Meeting shortly before the legislature, the 1865 constitutional convention authorized the issue of $500,000 in five-year bonds to finance normal expenditures "until by the collection of taxes the State may dispense with loans," and an additional $100,000 to repair the Western and Atlantic Railroad. As the comptroller general had advised, the railroad's income was responsible for paying interest and principal on those bonds.[1] The legislature soon approved a much larger bond issue.

Together, the convention and the first postwar legislature authorized the issue of bonds amounting to $3.6 million, a figure one-third greater than the state's entire prewar bonded indebtedness ($2.7 million in 1860). Although the convention repudiated the Civil War debt, it continued to recognize the prewar debt and overdue interest left unpaid during the war. New debt from the years 1865–67 meant that, when Republicans came to power in Georgia in 1868, the state debt was approximately $6 million.[2]

The Western and Atlantic

The Western and Atlantic Railroad, keystone of the state's financial system in the late 1850s, produced little revenue during the early postwar years. Repairs consumed much of the railroad's earnings, as the Jenkins administration spent $800,000 on equipment and construction, and then mismanagement dissipated profits. At first the line was in capable hands. Both Major Campbell Wallace (under Jenkins) and Ed Hulbert (under Bullock) were fairly worthy successors to the men who had superintended the state railroad in the 1850s. But at the beginning of 1870 Foster Blodgett assumed control, and the previous year's quarter-million-dollar profit became a half-million-dollar loss. Later that year, hoping for improved administration and revived revenue, legislators authorized a lease of the property.[3]

The governor leased the line for $300,000 a year to a group that included former governor Joseph E. Brown. Beginning in 1871, the railroad again provided substantial revenue on a regular basis, but at only two-thirds the 1860 amount. Because public expenditures had increased, the Western and Atlantic was contributing only about one-fifth of state revenue, merely half its share in the late 1850s. Georgia citizens' antebellum hopes of obtaining increasing services tax-free became a casualty of the war.

The Interest of Cities

As in the prewar years, railroads were the central force in Georgia's postwar system of public finance. But public debt, railroads, and taxation interrelated in new ways after the war. The Western and Atlantic Railroad occupied center stage in the generation before the war. Servicing the debt that the state contracted to build the Western and Atlantic absorbed the lion's share of prewar state spending, and on the eve of the war the state railroad became the largest source of state income. After the war, the Western and Atlantic required massive repairs before it could recover its late antebellum role in generating public revenue. And new actors now crowded the stage. The state had to respond to dozens of requests from private railroads for public assistance. The nature of its responses shaped the fate of railroads, regions, entrepreneurs, and the state treasury.

Prewar aspirations combined with postwar devastation to make railroads appear the only route to salvation. Robert Somers, a northern reporter touring the South, perceived that "Georgians had come to believe in railways at a crisis when faith in any other material interest had almost departed." A Carroll County man was extremely anxious that the Savannah, Griffin, and North Alabama Railroad run near Bowdon: "My lot here without the road is worth $500, with the road it is worth $1000."[4]

Like other newspapers scattered through the state, the *Milledgeville Southern Recorder* forecast glowing results from new railroad construction. "Look to-day at North-East and North-West Georgia—one without a railroad, the other with one through its very center; the price of land alone and the building up of towns along the Road, have repaid the state in taxation; while North-East Georgia, is comparatively unknown; its resources undeveloped though great, and a burthen upon the State rather than a profit." In short, the paper implied, if the state would help put a railroad through Northeast Georgia, not only would the railroad bring the region prosperity, but the region's taxpayers would benefit the state treasury. New railroads in regions already served by a line would also bring good fortune. The same paper welcomed the competition new railroads might provide: "It is to the interest of cities at least that Railroad fares should be low."[5]

On the surface, there appears to be great discontinuity in Georgia's state aid to railroads between the Restoration administration and its Republican successor. In the first two legislative sessions after the war, only one bill to assist railroads was enacted. Between 1868 and 1870, by contrast, dozens of such bills became law, and successive governors endorsed railroad bonds amounting to a figure considerably larger than the entire prewar state debt.

But that apparent break is misleading. Rather, one major break separated the political economy of railroad finance before the war from that after the war, when the state forged a policy dramatically different from its earlier one. Another separated the late 1860s from the 1870s, when the state gradually disentangled itself from obligations that originated in railroad-aid laws both from 1866 and from 1868–70.

Before Georgia embarked on its postwar ventures in aiding railroads, it completed its support for a line to which it had previously pledged its aid. In 1866 and 1867, in an epilogue to its prewar policy of aid to major trunk line railroads, the state fulfilled its obligation to the Atlantic and Gulf by subscribing to $300,000 worth of that railroad's stock. That action, under Governor Charles J. Jenkins, brought total state investment in the railroad to the $1 million figure authorized by an 1856 act. For the most part, it also brought to an end the supply of state funds to build railroads.[6]

Georgia's prewar railroad policy, it should be recalled, had had two major objectives—to promote economic growth and to find a substitute for taxation. Building up the private economy would create new wealth from which to collect taxes, and a growing tax base might permit lower tax rates; a twin object was the creation of a tax-free source of state revenue. Through a combination of private and public resources, Georgia had sought to establish a system of railroads. The state itself had built the Western and Atlantic Railroad connecting Atlanta and Chattanooga. The Georgia Railroad and the Central of Georgia Railroad, with substantial government backing from Augusta and Savannah, had built lines connecting those cities with Atlanta. This arrangement gave the state railroad two outlets to the sea, and it gave the other two railroads a guaranteed source of freight from the Tennessee and Mississippi River valleys. Moreover, it provided a skeletal framework that began to fill out in the 1850s. The policy worked. The Western and Atlantic began to pay its own way and provided large profits to the state treasury. Other railroads in Georgia prospered, as did farmers and merchants throughout the state.

Even before the Western and Atlantic began to make substantial contributions to the state treasury in the mid-1850s, other railroads sought state aid. Until the Western and Atlantic was at least paying its own way, however, the state declined to begin new ventures. Even afterwards, only the Atlantic and Gulf, a trunk line penetrating South Georgia from the coast, obtained significant state aid; other railroads had to depend on private or local capital. In the railroad politics of the 1850s, the city of Savannah and the Central of Georgia Railroad tried to block state aid to new lines that might divert traffic from both the city and the railroad; merchants sought to protect their shares of trade, and the city acted to protect its major taxpayers and its own investment in the Central Railroad.

Opponents of Savannah and the Central included the towns of Brunswick and Macon. Brunswick, which historian Ulrich B. Phillips has characterized as not a city but "an aspiration," offered excellent harbor facilities but, with neither a river nor a railroad to tap its hinterland, could not compete effectively with Savannah. Macon, a prosperous fall line town in the Central Georgia cotton belt, sought an alternative route to the sea, one that would compete directly with the Central. Savannah and the Central prevailed through the 1850s; the legislature refused state aid to build a line between Macon and Brunswick. In the case of the Atlantic and Gulf, Savannah and Brunswick played to a draw; the authorized route represented a compromise that could bring traffic to both ports.[7]

After the War

After the war, the various proposals surfaced again, together with many new ones. This time the floodgates opened, and the state made public assistance available to dozens of lines. The old arrangement, dating from the 1830s, was discarded. The shift in legislative attitudes portended a spate of new railway construction, new threats to the stability of the established Georgia and Central railroads, and a huge potential increase in the public debt. Gone was the old method of helping to create only the outlines of a railroad system. Aid was offered to a great many lines, many of them of only local consequence, and some designed to compete with established lines. In perhaps the greatest break with the past, Georgia displayed no concern that the embryo railroads eventually produce nontax revenue for the state treasury. Georgia's new method of assisting railroads called for no direct outlays of capital and anticipated no subsequent earnings from public investments.

Contending forces in the wars of the railroads in Reconstruction Georgia made up complex, shifting alliances. The Georgia Railroad, like the Central, opposed threats of publicly financed competition from new lines. Yet the Georgia line—together with the cities of Macon, Milledgeville, and Augusta—sought assistance to build a connection to Macon.[8] Democrats and Republicans often displayed party differences, but in no consistent manner; the pattern was not one of Republicans fostering the notion of public activity and Democrats working to limit governmental assistance to railroads.

The roles of a few of the men and the cities involved in postwar railroad finance suggest some of the forces at work in Reconstruction Georgia. The new capital, Atlanta, played a leading role. The *Atlanta Daily Intelligencer*, a Democratic paper, published a strong editorial in 1869, entitled "Railroad Monopolies," in support of state aid and against the Central Railroad. Besides seeking support to build a line northeast from the city (the Georgia Air Line Railroad), Atlanta spokesmen gave enthusiastic support to the Macon and Brunswick Railroad.[9] Savannah, Georgia's largest city, and the Central Railroad, the dominant private corporation before the war, found themselves displaced as shapers of state railroad policy. The postwar president of the Central, William M. Wadley, energetically opposed construction of lines that would compete with his. The city of Savannah, although interested in the fate of the Central, was more concerned that it not lose trade to such rival cities as Brunswick and Augusta. Augusta, however, and the Georgia Railroad that terminated there, wished to divert trade from Savannah and the Central and thus promoted the Macon and Augusta Railroad.

Macon, also seeking new outlets, backed the Macon and Augusta line to the northeast and the Macon and Brunswick to the southeast. Macon's George H. Hazlehurst served as president of both lines. Savannah and the Central saw the likelihood that their trade would be diverted at Macon to both Brunswick and Augusta. But Brunswick had ambitions beyond tapping the trade at Macon. Having promoted the Macon and Brunswick and the Atlantic and Gulf railroads, Brunswick now worked to create the Brunswick and Albany line, which was designed to cut off Savannah, bypass Macon, and tap the rich black-belt region of Southwest Georgia. The driving force behind the Brunswick and Albany was Governor Bullock's alter ego, Hannibal I. Kimball.[10]

General Aid

The 1866 Restoration legislature passed four bills to endorse the bonds of private railroad corporations. One was the Air Line Railroad, a line eventually extending from Atlanta to Richmond that had obtained its charter a decade earlier but had yet to complete any construction. The legislature's bill pledged future aid from the state, to be granted when fifty miles had been completed in Georgia. Two other bills promised aid to the Muscogee Railroad and the Savannah, Griffin, and North Alabama Railroad.

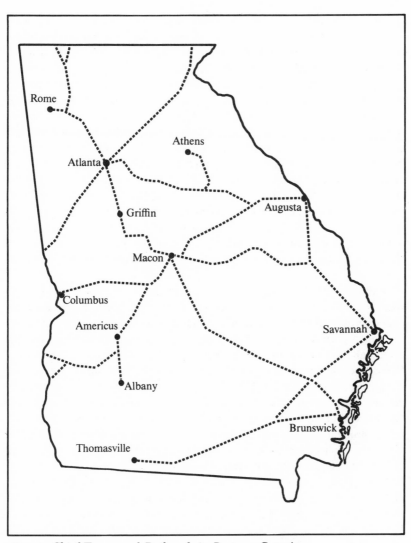

MAP 4. *Chief Towns and Railroads in Postwar Georgia*

The fourth measure provided assistance to the Macon and Brunswick. Stretching east toward the Atlantic coast from Macon, the Macon and Brunswick had already finished construction of fifty miles of road, which it had completely equipped and on which it was running daily trains. Another seventy miles were graded and ready for the ties and rails. Among the railroad's qualifications for assistance, the bill cited two considerations that became a familiar litany in other railroad legislation during Reconstruction: "Its completion . . . [would do much to promote the development of Georgia's] agricultural, commercial and manufacturing interests"; and "by reason of the financial embarrassments resulting from the late war, the stockholders of said railroad are unable to supply the capital necessary to the completion of this great work." According to the act, the state would endorse bonds of the company up to $10,000 per mile then completed and the same amount per mile as subsequent ten-mile sections were completed. If—and this, too, became part of the litany—the company failed to pay interest on the bonds, then the state would make the payments and, in return, take control of all the company's assets.[11]

Of these four bills, Governor Jenkins approved only the Macon and Brunswick bill. In carefully worded messages to the legislature, he reviewed the history of state aid to railroads in Georgia. Applauding the state's prewar role in financing trunk lines, he nevertheless urged the state to be "chary of her credit" and extend aid to no railroads. "Crippled as she now is," he warned, "Georgia could not make a greater mistake, at this time, than to venture upon a large expansion of her credit." After scrutinizing the merits of each bill, he decided that, in view of the general utility of the Macon and Brunswick, and "the Capital actually invested in construction, the security offered, and the strong probability, that the aid there sought, would complete the work," he could sign that one bill. To avoid setting a "precedent for general aid," he vetoed the others. Efforts to override his vetoes failed.[12]

The Republican-dominated convention of 1867–68 gave constitutional sanction to the change the Democratic legislature had initiated in financing railroads. No longer would the state completely finance a railroad, as it had the Western and Atlantic, or invest in a joint public-private enterprise, as in the case of the Atlantic and Gulf. Instead it would endorse railroad corporations' bonds. Policy inaugurated with respect to the Macon and Brunswick now applied to all state-aided railroads.

Seeking to protect the state's credit, the new constitution prohibited aid to railroads in the absence of two conditions. An amount equal to that endorsed by the state must first have been invested by private persons. If the railroad defaulted on its interest payments, the state became responsible for making those payments and ultimately for the principal as well, but in turn it took possession of the delinquent company's assets. It was expected that any recipient railroad would stand a reasonable chance of proving profitable. And if a railroad did default on its payments, its assets should compensate the state for the resulting costs.[13]

Even with these safeguards, Republicans in the 1868 legislature voiced concern that the state's credit was not yet sturdy enough to sustain any significant endorsement of railroad bonds. A majority on the Committee on Internal Improvement, unwilling to report against passage of several state aid bills and satisfied that at least some of the requests were "meritorious," nevertheless advised that all such bills "be laid over until the next session." A minority report made an exception of an Air Line Railroad bill and urged its passage.[14]

Despite the committee report, the 1868 legislature proved unable to restrain itself. The 1866 legislature had passed four bills to grant state aid to railroads, and later sessions followed suit. The 1868 session enacted three aid bills, the 1869 session five, and the more prodigal 1870 session thirty. All three offers of aid that the governor rejected in 1866 were enacted later. Two approved in 1868 were a line to connect Macon and Augusta, which now offered considerable security, and the Georgia Air Line Railroad. The Savannah, Griffin, and North Alabama, rejected by the legislature in 1866, had by 1870 completed 36 miles on which it ran daily trains, had partially graded much more, and received an endorsement of $12,000 per mile. Most of the other acts passed by the legislature both incorporated a railroad and offered to endorse its bonds, at $8,000 to $15,000 per mile, after completion of a certain amount of track. The state thus realized the fruits, foreseen by Jenkins, of establishing "a precedent for general aid." [15]

From one legislative session to another between 1866 and 1870, the main difference in state aid to railroads lay not so much in the willingness of the legislature to authorize extension of the state's credit, but in the alacrity with which the governor approved it. The legislature had no need to change direction in 1868 or 1870. In 1866 it already supported massive state aid and had already broken with the prewar tradition of contributing only to trunk lines. The 1866 legislative session was distinguished mainly by the governor's firm defense of the public credit. Bullock himself vetoed a railroad aid bill in 1869, but in 1870 he ignored even constitutional and legislative guidelines designed to protect the state's credit.[16]

Railroads in Alaska

Many Reconstruction legislators promoted railroads as the most promising cure for the poverty that prevailed after the war. Edwin Belcher, on the other hand, a black representative from Wilkes County, as fervently hoped for a cure for the railroad disease. In 1870 he proposed a resolution for his colleagues to consider: "Whereas this Legislature is characterized by fanaticism on railroad matters; and, whereas, there is no more territory [in

Georgia] for the construction of railroads; therefore be it Resolved, That we ask the United States Government for permission to construct railroads in Alaska, and that we be allowed to extend State aid in the same." [17]

When Democrats returned to power at the end of Congressional Reconstruction in Georgia, railroad endorsements under the acts of 1866–70 already amounted to about $8 million, and many more railroad companies had authorization to receive state endorsement as soon as they qualified. One of the first actions taken by the new administration was to scale down the contingent debt. Two of Hannibal I. Kimball's enterprises—the Brunswick and Albany Railroad and the Bainbridge, Cuthbert, and Columbus line—defaulted in 1872, and the state repudiated its endorsements the same year. Obligations to another Kimball enterprise were quickly disposed of when endorsements of the Cherokee Railroad's bonds were voided. The Cartersville and Van Wert Railroad had received the offer of bond endorsement in 1869; it reincorporated as the Cherokee the following year and again received authorization in its latest incarnation. Although it had barely begun construction, it received endorsement by Bullock under both names. Given that one set of bonds was supposed to have replaced another, certainly no more than one could be valid; because neither set merited endorsement, both were voided. Of all the bonds endorsed before 1872, the only ones that survived repudiation were $1,950,000 in Macon and Brunswick bonds under the 1866 act and $464,000 in the South Georgia and Florida (a Kimball company) under acts of 1868 and 1870. Not another endorsement survived. Among the proponents of wholesale repudiation was none other than William M. Wadley, president of the Central Railroad. [18]

The state gradually freed itself from the commitments of the early postwar years. After 1870 the legislature authorized no further bond endorsements by the state, though it continued to authorize some county governments to endorse railroad bonds. After a decisive first round of repudiations in 1872, the legislature went further. With authorizations from 1868–70 still pending, it repealed provisions for some endorsements. In 1877 two new actions emphatically brought the Reconstruction policy to a close. An amendment to the Constitution of 1868, ratified in 1877, prohibited subsequent changes of heart by the general assembly regarding those bonds whose endorsements had been recently repudiated. And the Constitution of 1877 prohibited new offers of aid by either the state or local governments. [19]

Decades to Disentangle

Debt repudiation and constitutional amendments still left in place various state obligations. Some companies received state endorsement after Reconstruction and then proved unable to make regular interest payments. For example, the North and South Railroad, whose projected route reached from Columbus to Rome, received the promise of endorsement in 1870, and three years later Governor James M. Smith endorsed $240,000 of its bonds. When the company failed to pay interest on those bonds in April 1874, Smith took possession of the line, and in 1877 Governor Alfred H. Colquitt sold it for $40,500. But the buyers had no cash; the state loaned them the money at 7 percent interest and finally recovered the purchase price in 1881.[20]

The Macon and Brunswick Railroad had a representatively rocky experience with the politics and economics of the 1870s. Among the railroads that the 1866 legislature sought to assist, the Macon and Brunswick was the sole survivor of Jenkins's vetoes. Bonds endorsed under the 1866 act, at $10,000 a mile, amounted to $1,950,000. Bonds endorsed under a supplemental 1870 act added $3,000 per mile, or $600,000, and brought the total of endorsed bonds to $2,550,000. In July 1873 the line defaulted in payment of interest on the state-endorsed bonds, and in accordance with the law, Governor James M. Smith took possession of the railroad. He subsequently bought it for the state at an auction for $1,000,000. Meanwhile the legislature repudiated the bonds endorsed under the 1870 act, and Governor Smith thought that an additional $1 million—half the amount endorsed under the 1866 act—should go as well. The state continued to run the Macon and Brunswick through the 1870s, earning about $230,000 for the treasury. In 1878, however, Governor Alfred H. Colquitt, though impressed with the line's importance, advised that it be sold, and that the state get out of the railroad business. In 1880 Georgia leased out the Macon and Brunswick for $194,000 a year and soon afterwards sold it outright for $1,125,000. Thus the state earned a small amount from operating income and took a thumping loss on bonds endorsed under the 1866 act.[21]

The Memphis Branch Railroad (a line projected west from Rome) and the Marietta and North Georgia Railroad provide examples of state involvement with other corporations in the 1870s. Under an 1870 act, Governor Smith endorsed $34,000 in Memphis Branch bonds in 1874. The company defaulted in payment of interest, and Smith seized the line in 1876. His successor, Governor Colquitt, sold the Memphis Branch the following year for $9,000 to William Phillips, president of the Marietta and North Georgia Railroad. That line, unconnected to the Memphis Branch, was being built north from Marietta by convict labor. An 1870 act had authorized endorsement of its bonds, but a subsequent act had rescinded the offer. To assist the Marietta and North Georgia, the state loaned it the next five years' net earnings from convict labor, or roughly $70,000. The railroad secured that loan with twenty-year first mortgage bonds paying 7 percent interest. When it bought the Memphis Branch Railroad, it borrowed the purchase price from the state—to be repaid by letting the state retain the 1880 proceeds from convict labor.[22]

By the mid-1880s, the state of Georgia was less active in promoting railroads than at any time since the inception of work on the Western and Atlantic half a century before. Of all the lines involved in state endorsements under legislation enacted between 1866 and 1870, only the Northeastern and the South Georgia and Florida railroads still represented state obligations. The major concern was once again the Western and Atlantic, and that line was in the middle of a twenty-year lease. With the creation in 1879 of a railroad commission, the state became much more involved in regulating freight rates. In the 1880s, too, revenue from railroad taxes rose rapidly.[23]

In a sense, Georgia had taken a new route to an old destination. The desire for lower freight rates had powered the postwar state-aid bills, which were designed to promote railroad construction as an indirect method of securing lower rates through competition. But state-supported competition proved costly to taxpayers. A surer method lay in directly regulating freight rates. This the railroad commission accomplished as it forced rates down.[24]

One railroad's connection with state finances had a particularly long and occasionally turbulent history, but a happy ending. The Northeastern Railroad, which was the subject of aid legislation in 1870 and had its bonds endorsed in 1878, figured in state politics and finances until the eve of World War I. Extending into North Georgia from Athens, the line first opened in 1876. After satisfying the law's requirements, the Northeastern secured Governor Colquitt's reluctant endorsement of $240,000 of its bonds in early 1878.[25] Political opposition flared, and a legislative investigation ensued, but otherwise matters unfolded uneventfully until 1893. Then, shortly before its endorsed bonds were to mature, the line defaulted on payment of interest.

Governor William J. Northen immediately took possession of the Northeastern and began operating it for the state. The line's net earnings were sufficient to make current interest payments and provide a small surplus for the state treasury. To redeem the Northeastern's maturing bonds, state bonds were sold in 1895. Governor William Y. Atkinson advertised the railroad for sale, but when no suitable bid resulted he bought it for the state for $100,000. Pursuant to new instructions from the legislature, he leased it in 1896 for $18,600 a year. But the lessee defaulted on payments. The governor repossessed the railroad and, though continuing to recommend sale, noted that the state's earnings from the line were easily paying the interest on the bonds and were also providing a fair return on the $100,000 purchase price. An 1897 auction produced no acceptable bid (the state required a minimum of $287,000 to cover the bonds). But in 1899 Governor Allen D. Candler's administration accepted a bid of $307,000, part of which was deferred until 1914, when the bonds would become due. When the Southern Railway made the final payment on schedule, the story of Reconstruction endorsements concluded.[26] The state had shaken free of its railroad obligations.

Georgia's postwar policy of endorsing the bonds of private railway companies did not prove felicitous. The idea was not a new or particularly weak one; Georgia's last two prewar governors, including Joseph E. Brown, had supported such a policy while in office.[27] Its implementation, however, failed to meet expectations. In virtually every case that the governor endorsed railroad bonds under authority granted in legislation of 1866 through 1870, either the state legislature subsequently repudiated its obligations or the state treasury took losses.

Only one railroad caused the state no difficulties. The South Georgia and Florida, a Kimball enterprise, was a beneficiary of legislation in 1868 and 1870 and received Governor Bullock's endorsement. It managed not only to keep the trains running and the semiannual interest checks going out, it also did the other things trains were expected to do.[28] It moved people and things, built up trade and property values, and paid taxes.

Three railroads received bond endorsement by Bullock's Democratic successors. All three—the North and South, the Memphis Branch, and the Northeastern—defaulted on interest payments and were seized and sold, two of them at losses. Their fate suggests that, although Bullock may have ignored the law's stringent requirements for state support, carefully following those requirements was no guarantor of good fortune.

Debt in the Saddle

To those who had controlled antebellum Georgia, Rufus B. Bullock's presence in the governor's chair represented all the reasons that they should still rule—and the reasons they no longer did. James M. Smith said in 1872, when he became the first post-Republican governor, "I come in response to the call of the people of my native State . . . after a long and cheerless night of misrule." Some Georgians, like Charles J. Jenkins, never accepted Bullock's legitimacy. After Jenkins's removal from office in early 1868, as he wrote Governor Smith four years later, he completely "refrained from communicating with the *de facto* government of the State." Others adapted to the realities of the situation and, for a season, accepted Congressional Reconstruction because they saw no alternative. Joseph E. Brown exemplified such adaptation.[29]

Bullock's predecessors and successors alike surely agreed that he violated the cardinal rules of Georgia politics. With former slaves in his constituency and in his legislative party, he symbolized "negro equality" and "military despotism." In addition, under his governorship the carefully tooled source of so much nontax revenue, the Western and Atlantic Railroad, became a liability. Blodgett's mismanagement of the railroad in 1870 did nothing to enhance Bullock's survival chances. In 1869 the legislature contacted several eminent Georgians for advice on the future of the state railroad. In reply, Joseph E.

Brown declared his belief, grounded in his own experience, that nothing a governor could do would do him more damage or more good than how he handled the state railroad.[30]

When the railroad ran up a huge debt in 1870, it deprived the state of income and helped force the state itself into debt. That year, the Western and Atlantic's operations absorbed state funds rather than producing them; moreover, Bullock became casual about signing both railroad bills and railroad bonds. Bullock never was firmly in control of political Georgia; events of 1870 guaranteed that he never would be.

Debt service weighed heavily on Georgia's post-Reconstruction administrations, but interest payments did not finance Republican extravagance. The state continued to recognize, and struggled to pay, indebtedness that derived, in almost equal amounts, from railroad aid before the war and from general appropriations in 1866–67. Bonds from 1870, however, like those from the Civil War, were voided, each under the dispensation that followed their issue.

Georgians in the 1880s, and many observers since that time, thought that the Republicans left the state saddled with a debt when they lost power. That was true, but the debt had accumulated before the advent of Republican rule. In 1866, before Congress inaugurated what is known as Radical Reconstruction, the Georgia debt had already taken on its postwar contours. So had the tax system.

17 A TAX BASE WITHOUT SLAVES

IN February 1866, a member of the Georgia General Assembly observed of his colleagues' search for public revenue: "Somebody has got to pay something soon for there is not a dollar in the Treasury. I wish you could see the members walking about the streets with their heads down—I inquired of Judge Thomas what their heads were down for and he said he supposed they were looking for money." [1]

When legislators at that first postwar session returned to work, their pensive walks in the streets of Milledgeville finished, they enacted laws to help a state government "looking for money." They authorized bond issues greater than the state's entire prewar debt. And they passed a tax law that, compared with those of the 1850s, introduced changes far more dramatic than any produced in subsequent sessions.

After War and Emancipation

War and emancipation transformed public revenue in Georgia. They created new conditions that Democrats and Republicans alike had to contend with in shaping public policy. Tax policy showed fundamental changes between the prewar and postwar periods, but only comparatively minor changes from Presidential Restoration to Congressional Reconstruction or after Bourbon Redemption.

For decades Georgia had sought, occasionally with success, to avoid relying on taxes to finance state spending. In the late 1850s, state tax rates in Georgia were low and declining, even as expenditures rose. And in 1860, the state government derived more income from the Western and Atlantic Railroad than from all taxes combined. With its treasury amply supplied each year, the state had no need for temporary loans. It contracted bonded indebtedness only to invest in the Atlantic and Gulf Railroad, which, lawmakers confidently expected, would soon begin to emulate the Western and Atlantic in reducing the necessity for state taxes.

The Civil War changed all that. The prewar expectation of continuing declines in Georgia's state property tax rate assumed three conditions: that state properties would generate increasing public revenue; that public expenditures would increase no more than did nontax revenue; and that property in slaves would remain the backbone of the tax system. None of these conditions survived the war. Not for some time could the state rely on income from the Western and Atlantic, because most of its meager earnings were needed for repairing wartime damage and depreciation. The two main sources of prewar public revenue—slavery and proceeds from the state railroad—vanished at the same time that demands on the treasury multiplied. After the war, therefore, enlarged expenditures and diminished nontax income mandated greater reliance on either taxes or borrowing. Borrowing created more debt; servicing that debt required more taxes.

Higher Rates

When the first postwar state legislature met, the treasury was empty. Virtually all the state's revenue in fiscal 1865 came early in the year as citizens paid their 1864 taxes. Paid in Confederate or state treasury notes, that money's value died with the war that spawned it. By the middle of April (when Georgians normally reported to tax receivers the value of their taxable property), the Confederacy had disintegrated. When Union troops took possession of Georgia, the military prohibited execution of any laws enacted since 1861, and thus the state never collected the property tax, $9.00 per $1,000 valuation, authorized for 1865.[2] In any case, ruins of war now marked the landscape, and people were much too exhausted to tolerate high taxes right away. Yet the state had to find funds to service its debt, support its welfare institutions, and finance its other operations.

Peterson Thweatt's duties as state comptroller general included forecasting the next year's expenditures and proposing means to pay them. Shortly before the 1865 convention voided Georgia's war debt, he anticipated total expenditures in 1866 of $2.1 million, two-thirds of which would go for debt service. He suggested two means of meeting those expenditures. A property tax of $2.50 to $5.00 per $1,000, he thought, would produce a large portion of the needed revenue, though the state would have to take out temporary loans while waiting for the taxes to come in. Alternatively, by pledging the Western and Atlantic's future revenue to pay principal and interest, Georgia could issue state bonds.[3] Either way would be onerous, and Thweatt's forecasts proved optimistic. His figure for probable expenditures became realistic only after repudiation of the war debt. His proposed tax would have produced a maximum of $0.9 to $1.8 million on a property valuation equal to the 1860 aggregate (excluding slaves), and postwar valuations ran much lower than that figure.

The first postwar legislature levied a property tax of $350,000 for 1866.

Though the amount to be collected was no greater than in the 1850s, the rate had to be much higher. With property valued at less than one-third the prewar figure, even tripling the 1860 rate would fail to produce as much revenue.[4]

The state property tax for 1866, at $1.67 per $1,000, was much too low to be continued indefinitely, and it proved by far the lowest postwar rate.[5] The 1866 legislature, the last one before Congressional Reconstruction, increased the annual amount to be obtained from state property taxes from $350,000 to $500,000, which required a rate of $3.00 per $1,000 valuation in 1867.[6] That figure, nearly five times the 1860 rate, fell within the range that Peterson Thweatt had recommended for the previous year.

By the following session, the Republicans had come to power. They retained the $500,000 figure, yet still the rate rose. When the first county tax reports for 1868 showed a decline in valuation, the *Milledgeville Southern Recorder*, always on the alert for extravagance, warned: "If the other counties fall off in the same proportion the whole property of the state will not be valued at much over $175,000,000. If this be the case, an assessment for the State purposes will have to be made of 35 to 40 cents on the value of $100." Sure enough, the basic rate became $4.00 per $1,000 for 1868, and it remained at that level, under Republican and Democratic regimes, for a decade.[7]

In addition to the regular property tax, the state levied an extra tax of $1.00 per $1,000 in 1868, again in 1872, and in each of the years 1874–80. The constitutional convention of 1867–68 ordered the tax to pay convention expenses. The 1872 tax went to pay public school teachers for their work the previous year. In 1873 a massive new bond issue was passed to bring the public debt under control, and the state levied an additional tax each year through the rest of the decade. Nor was that an end to supplemental taxes. Between 1885 and 1889, one series of taxes paid for a new state capitol building in Atlanta. Beginning in 1887, still another was imposed to reduce the state debt.[8]

Wolf at the Door

War and emancipation had consequences for public revenue and spending in Georgia far greater than any postwar legislation. While major revenue sources lapsed, the state needed more income than before the war. With the end of slavery, Georgia began—sooner or later—to make space for blacks in schools, the insane asylum, and other facilities, as public authorities, not private slaveowners, became responsible for social control of, and social services for, blacks as well as whites.

It was the public debt, however, and not the near doubling of Georgia's civil population, that forced the growth in the state's budget. Even before the war,

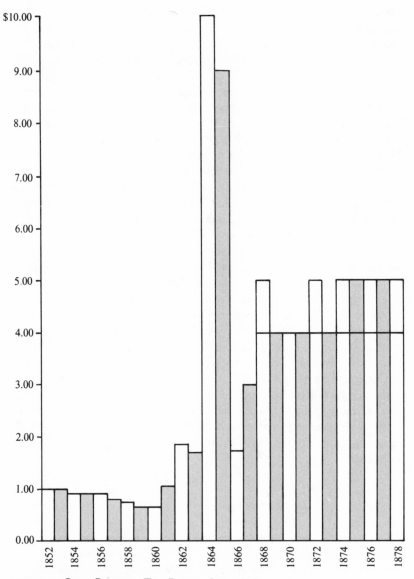

FIGURE 4. *State Property Tax Rates, 1852–1878*

Sources: Executive Minutes (mfm, GDAH); Annual Reports of the Comptroller General.
Notes:
Rates displayed were levied per $1,000 valuation.
Federal authorities prevented implementation of an act that called for a $9.00 tax for 1865.
Extra taxes of $1.00 (above the $4.00 base rate) were levied in 1868 (to pay convention expenses); in 1872 (to pay for the previous year's costs of elementary education); and beginning in 1874 (to fund state debt).

debt service had taken the largest part of state expenditures. Before Republicans gained control of the state government in 1868, the debt had grown to $6 million, and annual interest payments had more than doubled since 1860.[9]

Conservatives and Republicans alike had difficulty managing Georgia and its unprecedented peacetime budgetary problems. Democrats spent the 1870s bringing those problems under control. In particular, they cut outlays for public debt and for the administrative costs of government. Although they did not reduce the size of the legislature, they switched from annual to biennial legislative sessions, and they cut government officers' pay.[10]

Property tax rates never returned to their prewar levels. After remaining at $4.00 or $5.00 per $1,000 every year from 1868 through 1880, the rates dipped to $3.00 in 1881 and 1882, then to a low of $2.50 in 1883. But the $2.50 rate proved inadequate to pay all appropriations, and it offers the only instance of a state tax lower than $3.00 after 1866. The rate then gradually rose to $6.20 before a constitutional amendment in 1904 clamped a lid of $5.00 per $1,000 on state taxes, leaving them where they had generally been for almost four decades.[11]

In the 1880s, two changes occurred in Georgia's tax system. The legislature required more tax revenue from corporations, particularly railroads. As a revenue producer, corporate taxation overtook neither the general property tax nor the rental of the Western and Atlantic Railroad, but it amounted to more than $200,000 annually by the 1890s. In addition, as the state recovered from war, its tax base gradually grew.[12] Thus even a constant rate generated increasing revenue. But that growth, too, remained small until long after Reconstruction had ended in Georgia.

Redistributing the Burden

Besides leading to higher tax rates, the abolition of slavery had major consequences for Georgia's fiscal system. Before 1865 slaves accounted for nearly half of the total assessed property valuation. After war and emancipation, the property that remained had to carry the full burden of state and local property taxes. Just as a tax base without slaves necessitated much higher rates, it forced a redistribution of the burden. Rural real estate, which comprised only 24 percent of the assessed valuation in 1860, climbed to 46 percent of the 1866 total (see table 5).[13]

Town real estate, which amounted to only 5 percent of Georgia's property valuation in 1860, rose to more than 20 percent by 1868. By the early 1870s, the cities had already regained their prewar levels of aggregate taxable wealth, something that the state as a whole would be unable to do until the twentieth century. Fulton County (Atlanta) offered an extreme example of urban growth. Its urban real estate nearly doubled in value between 1860 and 1866

TABLE 5. *The State Property Tax Burden, Selected Years*

	1860		1866	
Property	($)	(%)	($)	(%)
Rural real estate	162	24.1	103	46.4
Urban real estate	35	5.2	39	17.7
Slaves	303	45.0	—	—
Misc. personal property	45	6.7	30	13.5
Merchandise	16	2.3	11	4.9
Capital	112	16.7	39	17.5
Railroads	—	—	—	—
Aggregate value	672	100.0	222	100.0
Taxable value	NA	NA	207	NA

Source: Annual Reports of the Comptroller General.
Notes: Dollar amounts are rounded to the nearest $1,000,000.
The category "miscellaneous personal property" includes household furniture, farm tools, and livestock.

(from $2.8 million to $5.3) and doubled again by 1872 (to $11.3 million). Merchandise, another form of urban property, also took up some of the slack in public revenue left by the death of slavery.[14]

In terms of class and section, therefore, emancipation forced a redistribution of the tax burden. Most rural black-belt counties paid a much smaller share of state property taxes during Reconstruction than before. The predominantly white counties of North and South Georgia, by contrast, paid a sharply higher percentage. And urban counties, whose wealth grew not only relative to that of most rural counties but even (in the case of Atlanta) in absolute terms, paid a much greater share of state property taxes after the war.

The abolition of slavery destroyed the economic foundation of rural wealth in the South. Emancipation diminished the credit base of former slaveowners and much of the property tax base. In dollar amounts, plantation owners suffered most from war and emancipation—"they who had most, had most to lose." None of Georgia's 132 counties reported as high a property valuation in 1866 as in 1860. Only 16 counties reported even half as much assessed value. Four of those contained Georgia's largest cities—Atlanta, Augusta, Savannah, and Macon; among the other 12, 11 had populations more than 80 percent white, and most families had had few slaves to lose with emancipation.[15]

	1870		1879		1888	
	($)	(%)	($)	(%)	($)	(%)
	96	42.3	90	38.5	111	31.0
	48	21.2	49	20.9	85	23.8
	—	—	—	—	—	—
	33	14.4	34	14.5	54	15.0
	13	5.7	13	5.5	19	5.2
	37	16.4	39	16.6	60	16.8
	—	—	9	4.0	29	8.2
	226	100.0	235	100.0	357	100.0
	211	NA	235	100.0	357	100.0

Deductions (from 1852 until repeal in the 1870s) included a $200 standard exemption as well as certain amounts of such other types of property as farm tools and household furniture.

The railroad tax listed here is on property and is in addition to the corporation tax on stock.

Because the black-belt share of Georgia's wealth was much smaller after the war, North Georgia paid a larger share of state property taxes. The nonslave-holding landowners of 1860 carried the greatest proportional increases in tax burdens. Some planters' tax bills actually declined because they no longer paid property taxes on their laborers. The smaller the proportion of wealth a taxpayer had invested in slaves in 1860, the more he paid in 1866 or 1870. Thus yeomen as well as planters had reason to participate in postwar southern taxpayers' revolts.

A few individual cases will illustrate the changes in tax burdens resulting from the emancipation of slaves and increases in tax rates. It must be stressed that former slaveholders did not see themselves as lightly taxed under either Conservatives or Republicans. In 1860 Harris Musgrove, a Columbia County planter, owned twenty-two slaves worth $11,000—or half his total holdings—and paid a state property tax of $14.08; in 1866 the amount dropped to $6.35. A neighbor, John Savage, owned only four slaves in 1860, worth $1,400 or one-third his holdings, and about four hundred acres of land. Rather than declining after the war, his taxes rose from $2.63 in 1860 to $3.23 in 1866; his tax on nonslave property nearly doubled. Because rates climbed even higher in 1867 and again in 1868—in the 1870s they stuck at triple the 1866 rates—

nearly everyone paid higher taxes than before the war, but the disparity in increases remained.[16]

Like other southern states, Georgia adopted a much higher poll tax immediately after the war. The postwar state poll tax, at $1.00 on each man, accentuated the changes effected by the redistribution of the property tax burden. The postwar poll tax placed a much greater burden on white men, who had paid only $0.25 a year since 1850, and a much lower burden on free black women and men, who had been paying $5.00 each.[17] In this respect, Georgia's first postwar tax law inaugurated equal treatment of blacks and whites.

North Georgia, where substantial numbers of white men held little or no property but nonetheless paid poll taxes, became subject to much higher taxes. The postwar poll tax on black men had less impact on the regional distribution of state taxes. The average value of a slave in 1860 was $673, and at the 1860 rate it would have taken a slave valued at $1,538 to produce $1.00 in state revenue. The postwar poll tax was higher than the prewar tax on an average slave, but it applied only to men, whereas the prewar tax had applied to slave children and women, too. The postwar poll tax on blacks produced much less revenue than the prewar property tax on slaves.[18]

Power and Policy

Though the greatest changes in the tax system occurred in 1866, others were made during and after the Republican interlude. In the most significant tax change introduced by the Republicans, the Constitution of 1868 limited annual poll taxes to a maximum of $1.00 and prohibited their assessment for any purpose other than education.[19] Republicans left in place the postwar figure for state poll taxes, but the rate ceiling meant that counties could no longer levy additional taxes. Thus the Constitution of 1868 cut most men's poll taxes by about one-half from 1867 to 1868. Whether collected by the state (as in the first postwar years) or by the counties (as it was after 1873), poll tax revenue was constitutionally allocated to the support of public schools.

The poll tax remained caught up in the currents of the postwar political economy. In 1866 and 1867 Georgia, like other southern states, engaged planters as fiscal agents, directed by law to pay their hands' poll taxes and then withhold the appropriate amounts from their pay. This usage vanished when the poll tax became connected to freedmen's right to vote. In 1868 and again in 1870, precisely because of that connection, Republicans suspended collection of the poll tax. Because the education system that was to be funded by the poll tax had not yet been established, they claimed, the tax could not be justified, and election time seemed a propitious time to suspend the requirement that constituents pay their poll tax before voting.[20]

Democrats made no subsequent changes in the amount or fiscal purpose of the poll tax. But the Constitution of 1877 effected a major political change when it tightened suffrage requirements. To satisfy one of Georgia's traditional voting requirements for any election, men had to pay their taxes for that year. After 1877 voters had to have paid all taxes due under the new constitution, and thus the poll tax became cumulative. Where early-nineteenth-century changes had brought the political "rise of the common man" for whites, and Republicans had extended democracy to blacks during Reconstruction, now the Bourbons reversed such changes and restricted the suffrage. The only exceptions to the new rule were the many disabled Confederate veterans, whom an 1883 act exempted from the poll tax.[21]

Further changes in the property tax laws in the 1870s heightened the more dramatic changes that had followed emancipation. In the years immediately following Redemption, the legislature reduced the property tax exemptions that were established along with uniform ad valorem taxation in 1852, thus requiring from the lower reaches of the social structure still more public revenue. Between 1872 and 1875, the legislature slashed the exemption on tools from unlimited value to $25 per taxpayer and that on furniture from $300 to $50 value for each family head. More important, it completely eliminated the standard property exemption of $200 value.[22]

Reducing exemptions raised the amounts of taxable property for all property owners, but the smaller the property holding, the greater the proportional increase in taxable property. This change hit the most modest holdings among blacks and whites. In the nineteenth century blacks never held as much as 4 percent of Georgia's assessed property valuation. As holders, in the main, of only small amounts of property, most of which would have been covered by the $200 exemption, blacks were among those most affected by the curtailment.[23]

As wealth in Georgia took new forms, the state's system of taxation, so promising in the 1850s, grew less and less satisfactory. When emancipation eliminated nearly half the prewar tax base, it removed a form of tangible property. Wealth invested in stocks and bonds, which could have taken up more of the slack than it did, easily escaped notice by tax officers. A legislative committee, illustrating "the evils of the present system of levying and assessing taxes," observed that property values reported for city purposes in Atlanta were considerably higher than those reported for state purposes in all of Fulton County, and surely much wealth also escaped city taxation. Thus the system failed "to distribute [tax] burdens equally upon all classes of citizens according to the amount of property owned by them."[24]

A Georgia farmer was less abstract in his denunciation: "The moneylender often escapes from bearing his just proportion of the burdens of government, but the poor farmer is made to pay tax upon his rocky knolls and gaping gullies. His every inch of land is taxed. He cannot hide [his land]; he cannot escape [paying taxes on] it. Though his wife and children cry for bread, the tax gatherer walks his rounds."[25]

County Finance

Three major developments forced an expansion of county operations in the late 1860s. First, some expenditures that the state had covered earlier in the decade were now shifted to the counties. Second, as one consequence of war and emancipation, the costs of supporting paupers grew. Third, local governments in the first postwar decade spent tremendous sums for capital construction—bridges, roads, courthouses, jails, even railroads.

All counties supported paupers before, during, and after the Civil War. In the early postwar years, however, many more whites were unable to support themselves—maimed soldiers; children and old people who had been dependents of now-deceased soldiers; and people whose property holdings had been obliterated by impressment, military destruction, repudiation, or emancipation. In addition, with the end of slavery came the end of a primitive social security system for blacks. Planters no longer supported the very old and young and other dependents through a portion of the surplus their workers produced, and thus such people looked to their county's pauper fund as their only means of support.

Immediately after the war, the state retreated from its wartime role and forced the counties to resume financing extraordinary welfare expenditures. When the state ended its support for soldiers and their families, it empowered the counties to levy taxes to take over that function. An 1866 act authorized each county to levy an annual tax as high as the state tax to provide the basic needs of disabled Confederate veterans and the indigent families of deceased Confederate soldiers. Citizens could pay the tax in kind, as during the war, and thereby directly supply items necessary for recipients' support. Few counties actually sold bonds or levied taxes specifically to support former soldiers or their families. Early County, one of the few that did, levied a tax equal to half the state tax in 1866. Dooly County required one-tenth the state rate in 1866 and 1867. Most counties simply added the intended beneficiaries of the 1866 act to their pauper lists and supported them all together out of the pauper funds. Most county taxes for support of the poor ranged from 10 to 25 percent of the state tax, though Franklin County's pauper tax climbed to 75 percent in 1870.[26]

In early 1866, the legislature authorized the establishment of county and municipal hospitals to provide medical attention and quarantine for all small-pox victims. As in the similar 1862 act, no people were to be forced into public hospitals "when they are properly provided for and guarded at their own expense." Unlike the earlier act, the 1866 law left local governments to shoulder the financial burden of these hospitals; counties received authority to levy whatever tax was necessary to pay smallpox expenses. Meriwether County levied smallpox taxes of 40 percent of the state tax in 1867 and 7 percent in 1868. To pay smallpox expenses in 1866, Early County ordered an extra tax of

300 percent of the state property tax (and one-fourth the poll and professional taxes).[27]

Education was another item of expenditure that the state thrust upon the counties. Because the state provided no school funds during Reconstruction, only local governments supplied public aid. Many teachers of poor children received none or only part of their pay in 1865, so the following winter the legislature empowered counties to give those teachers certificates of indebtedness, redeemable through taxation. Although some counties levied taxes to pay their 1865 accounts, most county records indicate no spending at all for schools. Among the few counties to levy school taxes specifically in accordance with the 1866 act were Franklin and Meriwether.[28]

For eight or ten years beginning during the war, teachers in many counties received no state or county funds for educating children unable to pay tuition. The Jones County authorities, for example, found "no necessity" for an education tax in 1869. Referring to "the vacuum in the Treasury" and "the claims of the destitute," Hancock County determined in 1866 that "there be no assessment made for the Poor School Fund," particularly in view of the state's failure to supply funds.[29] A few counties, however, levied education taxes in the late 1860s. In addition to the smallpox tax, Early County levied school taxes averaging 15 percent of the state tax between 1866 and 1870, and Columbia County assessed a 15 percent school tax in 1867.[30]

In the early postwar years, dozens of counties levied taxes or issued bonds to finance the construction of roads, bridges, courthouses, and jails. To build a bridge, South Georgia's Echols County levied a tax at twice the state rate in 1866. North Georgia's Whitfield County, finding "the public buildings, bridges and roads . . . all in a dilapidated condition, requiring large expenditures to repair," levied a tax of half the state tax in 1866 and again in 1867 just for repairs.[31]

County tax rates in Georgia were much higher after the Civil War than before it. In the 1850s they typically ran at about half the level of state taxes, but after the war they were roughly equal to the much higher state rates. Though local taxes in some counties were occasionally two to five times as high as state taxes, the Reconstruction years—unlike the Civil War years— produced no general pattern of that sort. County rates depended largely on the development of the local tax base; the more property valuation declined in the 1860s, the more local rates had to increase to produce constant revenue. But regardless of the rate increase necessary to bring revenues up to their antebellum levels, most counties demanded more.

Whereas the state property tax rate multiplied by six between 1860 and 1870, county rates rose to anywhere from three to twenty times as high. After 1867, however, taxes in most counties remained stable throughout the 1870s and 1880s. As in the case of state property taxes, changes were much more pronounced between 1860 and 1867 than in the years that followed. The tax that stunned Scarlett O'Hara, threatened her with the loss of Tara, and drove her to turn drapes into a dress, came in 1866.[32]

Black and White

At the first postwar legislative session, Governor Charles J. Jenkins suggested that the counties levy "a moderate capitation tax . . . upon each adult person of color, capable of earning wages," the revenue to be "devoted exclusively to the support" of pauper freedmen. The legislature declined to follow the governor's advice. It did adopt a poll tax for 1866, and again for 1867, but did not allocate the revenue to the support of freedmen. In those years, blacks had reason to think that their poll tax payments served instead to subsidize spending for whites. Efforts to segregate taxes and spending by race persisted for decades. When whites called for such a policy, they hoped, as Jenkins had, to supply services for blacks without requiring any subsidy of blacks by whites. But fiscal segregation could cut either way.[33]

Under Republicans and Redeemers, state property taxes, county property taxes, and poll taxes had different consequences. Unlike postwar state property rates, county levies went toward current expenditures, not debt service. Thus the ratio of current benefits to current costs appeared much more favorable. In the 1870s and 1880s, to the extent that blacks' poll taxes financed black schools and whites' poll taxes paid for white schools, the tax resulted in little transfer of benefits from one race, region, or class to another.[34] Property taxes at the county level did not finance schools, but they did contribute to the support of paupers. Though there was less transfer from middle-class whites to poor whites than before or especially during the war, still there was some. And property owners, most of them white, paid a small portion of their county taxes to support black paupers, too.

Conclusion

In Georgians' prewar experience, state taxes paid legislators' per diem, other government costs, and the state debt; earnings from public investments paid for schools. The war doubled the size of the state debt, yet emancipation halved the tax base. The ravages of war diminished the tax base still further but drove up the demands for public funds. Though tax rates were much higher in 1867 and 1870 than they were before the war, benefits were smaller—especially before a new education fund began to operate in the 1870s. Thus it was that yeomen failed to see greater benefits accompany their higher taxes. Postwar rates reflected the swollen costs of debt service and the eviscerated tax base, not an increase in social spending.

By the time the Republicans came to power, emancipation had shifted much of the property tax burden onto real estate, and legislation had increased the poll tax. It is not clear what alternative tax program Republicans might have embraced; as long as property taxation remained a major revenue source, change could take the form only of a switch from uniform ad valorem taxes or an adjustment in deductions. Three things are clear. First, Republicans inherited the essentials of the tax structure they left behind. Second, they in effect raised deductions when they halved the poll tax burden. Finally, they left the standard $200 property exemption in place; the Redeemers eliminated it. During Presidential Restoration and again after Redemption, Conservatives added to the taxes on the poor, though they and Republicans alike left in place the outlines of an ad valorem system that had lost its largest component.

18 CONSCRIPTS, CONVICTS, AND GOOD ROADS

THE Thirteenth Amendment had been a part of the U.S. Constitution for half a century when Jake Butler went to court to challenge his "involuntary servitude." Under Florida law, local authorities had called Butler out for his six days' annual labor on the county roads. Convicted of a misdemeanor when he failed to appear for the work, he appealed his conviction all the way to the U.S. Supreme Court.

The Supreme Court rebuffed his appeal. "From Colonial days to the present time," Justice James C. McReynolds wrote in the unanimous opinion, "conscripted labor has been relied on for the construction and maintenance of roads." The Northwest Ordinance of 1787—the source of the wording adopted in the Thirteenth Amendment—outlawed involuntary servitude except as punishment for crime, he noted, yet the territorial legislature established road duty requirements. So did the states that subsequently arose out of the Territory. Constitutional changes of the 1860s had in no way curtailed the "essential powers" of "effective government," including the capacity to demand jury duty, military service, or road duty.[1]

Toward Repeal of Statute Labor

Transportation improvements included roads as well as railroads. Although court cases like Butler's in both North and South demonstrated opposition to what McReynolds termed "conscripted labor" (more often called "statute labor"), many states continued to make use of the labor tax into the twentieth century.[2] At the dawn of the new century, a survey of Georgia's counties revealed that Murray County required an annual average of six days' "statute labor," as did Rabun, Habersham, Madison, and Fayette counties. Lincoln County, which required only two days' annual labor, suffered from poor roads; Polk, with ten days, and Randolph, with fifteen, sported good ones. Not until 1935 did Georgia terminate road duty as an obligation due the counties. And only in 1951 did the state repeal an Atlanta city charter provision requiring residents to work on the city streets each year or pay a commutation tax.[3]

Road duty produced results, though they were neither systematic nor elegant. In 1893 William L. Coleman, Jr., was appointed "overseer on the public road" in his district of Hancock County. He was assigned "the hands on his place" and on four nearby ones and was advised: "There are only a few places on said road that you can do any good. The plank bridge near the Crawford school house of the colored people between Devereux & the Sally Hall place . . . [needs repair]. Please attend to it and other bad places on said road this week. Make your hands cut a tree down & split it open & patch up the broken places in said bridge."[4]

As the quest for better roads in Georgia picked up momentum in the closing years of the nineteenth century, casual labor continued to prove neither disciplined nor skilled. Lumpkin County, for example, obtained about seven days' statute labor from its residents, but "much of this time is idled away." Clarke County's superintendent of public roads complained, "It is well nigh impossible to have farm-hands do good work, because they are untrained; and the overseers, as a rule, allow them to kill time." A Baldwin County official denigrated the traditional system as "a farce."[5] How could authorities heighten discipline and increase effectiveness?

Public Works and Private Interests

Increasingly, Georgia's local governments found a new labor force to build and maintain the roads that supplied transportation and promoted economic growth. But they did not turn directly to paid labor. Rather, Georgia moved from one nonmarket labor supply to another—from conscripts to convicts. Counties that no longer relied on road duty from their residents typically depended instead on chain gang labor. Road duty shifted from a civic obligation to a method of criminal punishment.

Only beginning in the 1890s, however, did the chain gang became a dominant feature of public policy. Even before the chain gang supplanted road duty, postwar penal slavery followed the abolition of plantation slavery. The chronic failure of the penitentiary either to pay for itself or to rehabilitate inmates made it relatively easy for lawmakers to abandon, all the more so as the number of convicts grew and the proportion of whites among them diminished. Forging a new penal policy, Georgia subjected freedmen and whites to the same criminal code.

At both state and local levels, the new system supplied labor for private interests or public works. Almost immediately after emancipation, Georgia abandoned the penitentiary system in favor of leasing felony convicts to private authorities, particularly railroad corporations. For misdemeanor convicts, public authorities adopted either a local counterpart to convict leasing or, increasingly, the chain gang. For many years Clarke County leased prisoners out to local citizens, for example, but in 1899 it established a chain gang on the county roads.[6] When the state finally abolished convict leasing, it supplied felony convicts to the counties for use in their chain gangs.

From Whipping Post to Chain Gang

Towns, like counties, relied on conscript labor. Town residents were subject to town rather than county authorities. In Macon, for example, men between the ages of sixteen and forty-five might be levied a street tax of up to $5.00, which they could pay by working the streets for ten days. Brunswick could require up to fifteen days per year "on the streets, public squares, and drains."[7]

In fact, emancipation led to a striking increase in the towns' street tax on white men. Before the war, towns had encouraged white residents to pay a cash tax, while their rural kin either paid in labor or sent a substitute. As commutation for road and patrol duty, for example, Milledgeville in 1860 levied a poll tax of $1.00 on each white male resident aged sixteen to sixty. (At the same time, the city's taxes on free blacks amounted to $10.00 on men and $5.00 on women.) In 1865, by contrast, Milledgeville levied a $5.00 tax on "all male persons" aged sixteen to sixty "as a commutation of Street Service" or, alternatively, ten days' work on the streets.[8]

The years 1865–68 constituted a transition period in the punishment of Georgia blacks. The incidence of whipping by public authorities in Georgia had largely ended by early 1867, and the 1868 constitution outlawed it "as a punishment for crime." The switch could be from whipping post to chain gang.[9] In May 1864, for example, the mayor's court of Milledgeville sentenced Viney, a slave convicted of using "impudent language to a white person," to thirty-nine lashes on her bare back. In August 1865, soon after emancipation, the same court convicted Charles Harris, a freedman, of malicious mischief. Rather than order Harris whipped, the court fined him $25.00 plus costs. In default of payment, his sentence was "commuted to wearing Ball and Chain and working on the streets" for fifteen days.[10]

Harris's sentence foreshadowed things to come. The general assembly amended Georgia's criminal code in 1866. Henceforth, at the judge's discretion, misdemeanors were punishable by any combination of a fine up to $1,000, imprisonment for as long as six months, a whipping not to exceed the traditional thirty-nine lashes, or working in a chain gang on the public works for up to twelve months. In addition, "all persons leading an idle, immoral or profligate life, who have no property to support them, and are able to work, and do not work," might be convicted of vagrancy and, among possible punishments, be sentenced to work on public works and roads for up to a year.[11]

Street tax and chain gang tended to merge—as did, more generally, all public obligations. Like the property tax, the road tax would be collected. An owner of property might have a portion seized to pay the road tax commutation. Failing either to work or to pay, residents could be put to work at "compulsory labor." The city of Atlanta, for example, might "enforce the payment of fines, for a violation of the city ordinances, . . . and enforce the payment of street taxes [alike], by compelling parties, who fail, or refuse, to pay such fines, or taxes, to work on the streets, or public works." [12] Like the poll tax, moreover, the street tax comprised an obstacle to voting. [13]

Cash Taxes and Convict Labor

During more than a half century after the Civil War, various counties, like towns, established chain gangs to work the roads. Urban counties acted first. County authorities began to consider the virtues of the chain gang as early as 1866, when the Fulton County grand jury observed: "Owing to the limited number of hands liable to road duty, we find the roads in the county in bad order. We would therefore recommend that . . . [misdemeanor convicts be] organized in chain gangs and put to work on our public roads." [14]

An 1891 statute fostered the changeover from road duty—sometimes to free hired labor, more often to the chain gang. That act authorized counties to levy a property tax as high as $2.00 per $1,000 for the roads. Together with a commutation tax from residents subject to road duty—up to $0.50 per day for up to ten days—the new property tax would supply a "Public Road Fund" to buy mules and machinery and to employ wage labor or to support misdemeanor convicts. Failure to fulfill the road duty requirement, by either labor or commutation tax, carried any of three penalties: fine, imprisonment, or work in the chain gang for up to ninety days. [15]

One after another, counties replaced primary reliance on "statute labor" with the chain gang and a property tax. Putnam County, for example, switched in 1892 from road duty to free hired labor, for which it paid $0.50 per day plus rations. In 1898, in what was called "another step forward in . . . highway improvement," the county adopted convict labor. Putnam collected $1.75 as a commutation tax, and it levied a road tax of $1.75 per $1,000 valuation. [16]

Counties relied on various combinations of road duty, hired labor, and chain gang. Spalding County started using convict labor in 1890. A decade later, the county was levying a property tax of $1.00 per $1,000 and a commutation tax of $1.50 in lieu of six days' labor. Some residents continued to work the tax out, but the county reported, "The result of the low price placed upon statute labor is that nearly all persons pay the commutation-tax." Chattooga County, on the other hand, also levied a $1.00 road tax on property, but charged $3.00 as commutation tax for six days' labor, and most residents paid in labor because of its "high-rated money value." The cash proceeds paid for "team-hire for road-working, building and repairing bridges," and free hired labor, but no chain gang. Wilkes County collected a $2.00 road tax per $1,000 property value as well as a $2.00 commutation tax for six days' labor. The proceeds covered the costs of seventy-one convicts (at an average $0.44 per day) as well as hired free labor (at $0.75 per day).[17]

The transition from road duty to convict or wage labor proved neither immediate nor uniform. Ten years after enactment of the 1891 road law, counties were still experimenting. Bartow County had used a chain gang for a few years, then abandoned it as too expensive and reverted to statute labor, but the wish for better roads evoked support for reestablishing the chain gang. Authorities in Fayette County, where statute labor had been found "unsatisfactory," were about to begin hiring free labor with the proceeds of a property tax of $2.00 per $1,000. Hall and Warren counties planned to levy a road tax on property to pay for either convict or hired free labor, while an Irwin County official complained: "We use only statute labor, and our roads are poorly worked. I am satisfied, that we can never have good roads, until they are worked by direct taxation, and the use of the chain-gang."[18]

Despite the shift by most counties, a few retained the traditional road duty system for some time. In a survey of county practices in 1901, Colquitt County reported an average annual levy of five days' labor and "no desire to change." Pickens and Worth counties expressed similar satisfaction, and Telfair County characterized statute labor as the "best" available system. By 1910, 107 of Georgia's 146 counties had opted for the chain gang; only 39 depended on either statute or hired labor, and the number continued to drop. The predominantly white counties provided most of the holdouts.[19]

The commercial significance of good roads was readily apparent to merchants, planters, and urban and black-belt county officials, who believed that convict labor offered the best means of securing good roads. Proponents of "good roads" contrasted normal loads of twelve bales of cotton on improved roads with loads of only three bales over the bumps and through the mud of unimproved roads. Chagrined that Stewart County continued to rely on ten to fifteen days of statute labor, an official discounted it as a poor system; noting that improved roads would lead to higher real estate values, he favored using misdemeanor convicts and machinery. DeKalb County worked thirty-five convicts full-time on the main roads and allocated statute labor to the less important roads. Chatham County also used convict labor on the main roads and statute labor on the others, and it reported that chain gang members cost only $0.26 a day.[20]

Black-belt and urban counties were generally the first to adopt convict labor for the roads. There the "leading citizens" most needed the improved transportation that the new system would facilitate.[21] Moreover, they could more easily pay the cash taxes required to maintain convicts and purchase road-building equipment. And such counties contained more black candidates for the chain gang.

From Penitentiary to Convict Lease

Three circumstances in Georgia in the 1860s combined to encourage adoption of some alternative to the penitentiary system. First, the burning of the penitentiary at Milledgeville in November 1864 necessitated some action. Second, emancipation meant that, at least in one respect, blacks approached equality with whites; with their former masters no longer responsible for controlling their behavior, they became liable to public prosecution for a broader range of criminal offenses. Finally, the state had long sought an economically self-sustaining arrangement for convicts. After the war, it could ill afford the annual costs of security and subsistence for even the prewar number of prisoners, much less the increased postwar convict population.

Given these circumstances, alternatives that echoed from the 1850s and even earlier again gained adherents in Georgia. Move the penitentiary to Stone Mountain, one view suggested, and let the convicts earn their keep by quarrying granite. Others argued that it would be better to lease them out— the state might make a profit; certainly whoever hired the convicts should be able to support them. Finally, as Governor Brown urged in February 1865, abolish the penitentiary system completely and, rather than leasing out convicts to hard labor for some contractor, subject them to corporal punishment —branding, cropping, whipping, and hanging. Anyway, Brown asserted, the penitentiary was "certainly not a place of reformation." Hard labor and solitary confinement had failed, for the half century since inauguration of the penitentiary, either to induce perceptible penitence or to pay for the prisoners' provisions. One newspaper's remedy was "Hang, hang quick." [22]

Despite the popularity of Governor Brown's approach, both the general assembly and the 1865 constitutional convention deferred a final decision. Though the house of representatives agreed with the governor and passed a resolution in February 1865 to abolish the penitentiary and revert to corporal punishment, the senate blocked the action. As a compromise judgment, the legislature directed the governor to sell what could be salvaged from the Civil War card factory and armory and to make whatever repairs were needed to provide accommodations and workshops for the small number of convicts. The constitutional convention that year took no action on motions to abolish the penitentiary or move it to Stone Mountain.[23]

To confront the problem of criminal punishment after war and emancipation, Georgia at first simply shuffled the legal code. In 1866 the legislature increased the penalty for several crimes (rape, burglary at night, stealing a horse or mule) from imprisonment to death. It reduced other crimes (stabbing, receiving stolen goods, hog stealing, simple larceny) from felonies to misdemeanors—punishable by a combination of fine, imprisonment, whipping, or the chain gang.[24] Such changes would curtail the need for a penitentiary, yet they would maintain the control of convicts by public authorities.

When the state authorized local courts to bind out vagrants to private parties, however, it pointed in a new direction. Private parties, willing to take on slave labor for the price of a fine, could now appropriate the labor of Georgians convicted of misdemeanors; as historian E. Merton Coulter observed of these convicts, "courts sold them to the highest bidders." If the state decided to turn over felony convicts, too, to private contractors, it could do so either by hiring out the convicts or by leasing out the entire penitentiary.[25]

By 1868 the Georgia courts were overcrowding the penitentiary with an increasingly black population. One newspaper facetiously observed that it would "take a small county" to accommodate all the black convicts. The same paper declared: "We cannot conceive how the negro can be worked to an advantage in the Penitentiary. It will not pay to make a mechanic of him, and the small space within the walls will soon be filled. . . . The best thing that can be done with him is to put him on a plantation, and his legs so chained, as to allow him to walk with ease and follow a plow." [26]

As early as 1866, the legislature initiated arrangements for leasing. One act authorized the state to lease out the penitentiary for up to five years, provided an arrangement could "be made relieving the State from all further expenses, during the term of the lease." Another act at the same session incorporated the Cartersville and Van Wert Railroad, intended as a feeder line to the state railroad; it directed the penitentiary keeper to detail convicts "to work on the grading" of the new railroad, "without any expense to the State for their subsistence, clothing and custody." If the lease act failed to specify where convicts would be worked, the railroad act left no doubt that it would be outside the penitentiary; and in either case they would be working for private parties instead of for the state.[27]

Though the legislature had authorized leasing the penitentiary, Governor Charles J. Jenkins disliked the policy, and not until May 1868 was a lease made. Provisional Governor Thomas H. Ruger contracted with William A. Fort, a railroad builder, to supply 100 "able bodied and healthy Negro Convicts, now confined in the State-Penitentiary," to work for one year on the Georgia portion of the Georgia and Alabama Railroad. The state would provide transportation over the Western and Atlantic Railroad; Fort would pay the state $2,500 and would provide an adequate guard and all food, clothing, and medical attention. Soon afterward, the state leased another 100 convicts (no race specified) for one year to the Selma, Rome, and Dalton Railroad for $1,000 and their support. Finally, in November 1868, the state contracted with

Grant, Alexander, and Company to provide 100 to 500 able-bodied convicts. The *Milledgeville Southern Recorder* approved of this method as "the practical solution of the whole penitentiary question."[28]

The contracts of 1868 largely emptied the overcrowded penitentiary, supported a large number of convicts at no cost to the state, and even provided the penitentiary with a nominal revenue. But the institution remained a drain on the state treasury. The legislature appropriated $20,000 for the penitentiary's support and repairs in 1868 and again in 1869, as well as salaries for officers and guards. In June 1869, Governor Rufus B. Bullock leased the entire penitentiary to Grant, Alexander, and Company for two years. That company absorbed all expenses except the salary of the principal keeper, who was retained to inspect the conditions under which convicts were kept and to report contract violations to the governor.[29]

As the *Milledgeville Southern Recorder* observed of the 1869 contract with Grant, Alexander, and Company, "If the State can be saved the annual expense of its support, that much is gained if nothing more, though we believe it could be made a paying institution to the State, besides being self-sustaining." The first post-Reconstruction legislature, recognizing the success of the experiment, again authorized the governor to farm out the entire penitentiary, but it required contractors to pay at least $25.00 per convict each year. Beginning in 1872, the state earned a small net annual income from leasing convicts.[30]

Penal Slavery

Georgians retained a tenuous commitment to the penitentiary system from its inauguration in 1817 until the buildings burned in November 1864, except for a brief time in the early 1830s after another fire. Efforts to do away with what had become the customary system of punishment began in earnest in the legislative session of February 1865, in the closing weeks of the war. The state lurched toward its new policy through the next several years, with little to distinguish one administration from another. The leasing of convicts to private contractors became an established policy—in Georgia as elsewhere in the South—that lasted into the twentieth century. While the state disposed of felony convicts in this manner, people convicted of misdemeanors were handled by county officials in much the same way.

Republicans did little to alter the course of postwar penal policy. Legislative majorities from 1866 on worked to replace the penitentiary with convict leasing. Ironically, it was a military governor, not a Bourbon, who let the first contract for convict labor, and Rufus B. Bullock who turned the remainder of the inmates over to lessees. The major break in policy, however, predated Congressional Reconstruction, as a new penal system—one that would flourish into the twentieth century—came to replace a system half a century old. Like the penitentiary, the new system would remain a center of controversy but, also like its predecessor, it would survive for decades.

The Thirteenth Amendment may have declared the death of slavery, but the recent past reverberated into the postemancipation world. Across the dividing line of 1865, several related shifts occurred—from whipping post to chain gang, from road duty to chain gang, and from prewar chattel slavery to postwar penal slavery. Blacks no longer belonged to individual whites whose economic interests prevented the confiscation of their labor by anyone else. Both before and after the Civil War, free black defendants could be sold to private parties who paid their fines and thereby bought their labor.[31]

Like prewar slavery, the penal systems of the postwar South were designed and maintained to secure race control and a labor supply. As Gunnar Myrdal wrote, vagrancy laws permitted "employers to let the police act as labor agents." A person charged with vagrancy could not choose whether to engage in forced labor, though he or she might get to choose whether to be bound out to a private employer or to the chain gang. Some of the captives worked for public authorities, some for private interests; in the 1870s, private control dominated, but by around 1900, throughout much of the South, public authorities had retrieved control and put convicts to work on the roads.[32] The court system supplied private interests with a *means* of obtaining labor, but the chain gang also operated as an *end* in itself to secure a disciplined work force for the roads.

Among the convicts were representatives of each sex, each race, and every age from early teens to septuagenarians. Among the twenty-nine chain gang members in Worth County in May 1900, for example, were four black women with twelve-month sentences: a twenty-five-year-old convicted of vagrancy, a seventeen-year-old sentenced for adultery and fornication, and a sixteen-year-old and her seventeen-year-old friend, caught along with their boyfriends in the act of "gaming." There was also one white man. In the typical pattern, however, almost all of the convicts were black, most were male, and all but two of the twenty-nine were between the ages of sixteen and thirty-five.[33]

Like their prewar plantation counterparts, postwar penal slaves were perceived as chronically idle and disobedient. Despite the standard twelve-month sentence on the chain gang, some misdemeanor convicts found themselves consigned to private contractors; in view of the high death rates, many served what turned out to be life sentences. Some carried multiple terms of twenty-four, thirty-six, or even forty-eight months. In Baker County in May 1900, for example, where all the convicts were black men except two thirty-five-year-old women (one white and one black), one man serving a twenty-four-month term was "bought by Sharp" and thus continued his servitude elsewhere, and a seventy-five-year-old man died in the fourth month of his term. Without exception, all the convicts had exhibited "bad" conduct, mostly "laseness," for which each had been whipped at least once during the month.[34]

Georgia's penal system in 1900 constituted something other than (as Governor George R. Gilmer had phrased the antebellum attitude) "the best means of preserving the reputation, lives, property and personal liberty of every member of the community, from the lawless attacks of the vicious and the violent." Postwar policy reflected the abandonment of reform in favor of retribution, and of rehabilitative objectives in favor of speculative, as state and local governments sought to ensure that the penal system not only paid its way but also produced a profit, whether for private interests or on public works.[35]

In 1908 Georgia outlawed one major facet of its postwar penal system. With convict leases soon to expire, Governor Hoke Smith called a special session of the legislature to consider the matter. Smith voiced extravagant plans to extend the Western and Atlantic Railroad to the ocean, an enterprise that would "yield a handsome net profit to the State." The state, the governor thought, should resume control of felony convicts, and the convicts would do the work. Like the convict lease system, the new system would pay its own way. Legislators did not buy Smith's entire plan, but they did act to terminate the leasing system. Henceforth felony convicts, like misdemeanor convicts, were organized into chain gangs and worked Georgia's roads.[36]

Georgia's road and penal policies, whether of the Bourbon era or the Progressive period, had roots deep in the past. No longer, as they had before the war, did public authorities sell for a term free blacks who failed to register their names or pay their poll tax. Under the new dispensation, however, remnants of the old regime lived on. Where the state and some counties had once purchased "public hands" to work on roads and riverways, now public authorities convicted citizens of gaming, vagrancy, fornication, and petty larceny to appropriate their labor. Whipping no longer served as a punishment for crime, yet once they were convicted and sentenced to serve time, Georgians were routinely whipped to maintain discipline and productivity.

Two slave narratives offer a striking comparison of antebellum slavery and the twentieth-century chain gang. At point after point, John Brown's *Slave Life in Georgia*, written by a fugitive from slavery in the 1850s, finds an echo in its counterpart from the 1930s, *I Am a Fugitive from a Georgia Chain Gang!* by Robert E. Burns. The narratives are separated by more than three-quarters of a century in time, and Brown was black, and Burns white, as postwar penal slavery captured people of both races. But the narratives are companion pieces in their themes of the arbitrariness of power and powerlessness, the harshness of living and working conditions, and the intricacies of plotting and implementing an escape.[37]

Georgians who operated mines, built railroads, or ran plantations had a substitute for the old slavery, a new means to secure labor. So did county politicians and their leading constituents who wished to improve the local roads. They more or less scrupulously followed the injunction of the Thirteenth Amendment that "neither slavery nor involuntary servitude, except as a punishment for crime whereof the party shall have been duly convicted, shall exist within the United States."

North, South, and the Twentieth Century

In 1890 Georgia's system of road duty had its counterparts throughout the nation, in both North and South. During the next generation, the ancient system everywhere swiftly diminished in significance, but North and South followed divergent paths into the twentieth century. In 1908, for example, New York investigated the relative merits of the "labor system" and the "money system" and found that at least three-fourths of the towns in that state had abandoned road duty in favor of free hired labor. When the state outlawed road duty that year, it sought to force all local governments to adopt a cash tax instead of a labor levy, and to shift from conscript labor to hired workers.[38] That same year, when Georgia outlawed the practice of leasing felony convicts to private contractors, it, too, was moving from road duty to property taxation, but its newly prevalent practice was to work prisoners, not hired hands—to shift from conscript labor to convicts.

Road duty, like various proposals for its replacement, persisted in Georgia from the eighteenth century to the twentieth. In the 1790s, Judge George Walton, in his charge to the Liberty County grand jury, advised that, among possible methods of opening a road, "a small Company of Negroes employed for a term equal to the Object, and properly directed would be best." At about the same time, the Jefferson County grand jury recommended "the levying of moderate taxes which will reach every person now liable to work on the Roads, in lieu of the present mode."[39] Those components—a cash tax and black labor, whether Old South chattel slaves or New South penal slaves—characterized both the proposed alternative of the 1790s and the state's new policies of the 1890s and 1910s.

The year 1916 brought a culmination of developments in road building in America. In that year, the U.S. Supreme Court gave its unanimous endorsement of road duty as a legitimate means for governments to supply roads. Yet, by that time, a number of southern states had come to rely primarily on property taxation rather than a labor levy, and they had largely replaced road duty with the chain gang; most northern states had turned to free hired labor.[40] Nor were changes in state law the only evidence of the success of the "Good Roads" movement.

That same year, Congress enacted a National Highway Act. In response, Georgia organized a Highway Department to qualify for federal matching funds and to oversee improvements on major transportation routes. Subsequent federal legislation expanded the role of state and federal governments in supplying transportation needs previously the responsibility of local governments. And in the 1930s, in legislation designed to generate jobs and combat the Great Depression, Congress prohibited the use of chain gangs on roads financed with federal funds. The Emergency Relief and Construction Act of 1932 and the National Industrial Recovery Act of 1933 supplied precedents for a provision in the Appropriations Act of 1935 that "none of the money herein appropriated shall be paid to any State on account of any project on which convict labor shall be employed."[41] The chain gang went the way of the labor tax.

In the Third American Revolution in the 1930s, like the Second in the 1860s, actions of the national government forced changes in traditional southern ways. In the emergency of the Great Depression, public works constituted a means more than an end. The national administration acted to relieve unemployment and get wages into the pockets of free workers. Such objectives took precedence over saving public funds through convict labor. The funds came from Washington, not from county or state taxes, and the jobs went to whites.

The system of road duty, a labor levy on all able-bodied men, was clearly in decline by the end of the nineteenth century—in Georgia and throughout America—and had virtually vanished by the 1930s. Vermont, for example, outlawed the labor tax in 1892, New York in 1908, and Utah in 1919. North Carolina finally ended road duty as a county obligation in 1931, Georgia in 1935.[42] Convict labor proved the favored southern replacement for statute labor. Southern governments tended, in the first generation after 1865, to turn over their convicts to private interests; in the second, to retain them for work on the roads. By the third generation, that policy, too, was in decline.

In America, the career of *corvée*, or conscript labor, lasted from the seventeenth century into the twentieth. Convict labor, although it had precursors before the Civil War and could be found in the North as well as the South, found its typical time and place in the New South between the 1890s and the 1930s.[43] In contrast to the conscript system, which reflected a lack of cash, convict labor depended on cash taxes to finance subsistence and equipment. The new system hinged on a combination of developments: the Thirteenth Amendment, the legacy of slavery, and the needs of commercial agriculture; the growth of towns and the advent of the automobile; and the use of the court system as a means to secure a labor force to construct and maintain roads. Convict labor appeared more disciplined and more productive than its predecessor, statute labor, and preferable, too, in its advocates' view, to free labor.

EPILOGUE:
FROM
EIGHTEENTH
CENTURY TO
TWENTIETH

A Weak, Parsimonious Government

Leading historians of late-nineteenth-century Georgia have expressed no doubts about its social policies, especially programs that took funds from the state treasury. They have characterized those policies as miserly and the progenitors of unfortunate twentieth-century patterns. In a general statement on the post-Reconstruction South, C. Vann Woodward wrote of "the Redeemers' policy of retrenchment" that "Measured in terms of ignorance and suffering the results of the Redeemers' neglect of social responsibilities were grave." Focusing on Georgia in the Bourbon years 1872 through 1890, Judson C. Ward, Jr., echoed that assessment: "Perhaps the greatest condemnation of the advocates of the New Departure," Ward wrote in the 1950s, "is the heritage they left Georgia of . . . a weak, parsimonious government unwilling to support in adequate fashion the state's public services. Georgia suffers from this heritage to the present day."[1] Yet the Bourbons themselves inherited whatever legacy of neglect that they passed on to the twentieth century.

Measured by mid- or late-twentieth-century standards, Georgia's state government may not have accomplished much in the 1880s; but it did much more, not less, than ever before regarding elementary schooling, higher education, and other social welfare functions. At several earlier times—in 1817–21, 1835–37, and 1856–59—the state had assumed new responsibilities, and expenditures for social welfare soared. In the sweep of an entire century, from 1815 to 1915, the Bourbon period takes on a new look. Reconstruction fades as a watershed in state spending on education and welfare functions, and the years of the late 1880s take their place among those earlier times of growth in state responsibility and spending. Initiatives of the late 1880s launched the changes that are associated with the Progressive period.

In the decades before the Civil War, citizens of Georgia wanted such public services as elementary schooling. They wanted those services very much. Yet one thing they wanted even more was freedom from the taxes that might have paid for them. A summary of that antebellum experience offers an essential backdrop for assessing the changes of the 1880s. Elementary education can serve as a proxy for social spending in general because of similarities in timing with other programs. After decades of failure to provide financial support for public education, in 1817 the Georgia legislature set aside a fund, which it doubled four years later, for schools. In 1837, it merged that earlier money in a new, much larger, common school fund. And in 1858 it created another, still larger fund for common schools.

The key in each case was a windfall of nontax revenue that enabled the state to increase spending without raising taxes. The major source for the first fund consisted of payments from the U.S. government for Georgia's western lands. Other nontax sources—profits from state investments in banking, revenue from public land distributed in Georgia, or Georgia's share of the federal treasury surplus—made the new social spending of the 1830s possible at a time when the state property tax had been suspended entirely. The earnings of Georgia's exercise in public enterprise, the Western and Atlantic Railroad, made possible the sharp increase in social spending in the late 1850s. Each of these three efforts depended on surges in nontax state revenue. Despite ambitious new spending programs, state tax rates on the eve of the Civil War differed little from those of a half-century earlier.

After the Civil War, Georgia faced a grim fiscal situation. A tax base less than one-third its prewar size meant that taxes had to more than triple just to bring in the same amount of revenue. Georgia repudiated its Civil War debt, but new bond issues during Presidential Restoration, together with unpaid interest during the war on the prewar debt, required more than twice the previous outlays each year for debt service. And the Western and Atlantic's annual contributions to the state treasury stuck at a lower level than on the eve of the war. All three factors limited social spending by both Republicans and Bourbons.

Aside from fiscal considerations, Civil War and Reconstruction transformed the social policy environment. As a consequence of emancipation and the Fourteenth Amendment, Georgia's citizens nearly doubled in number. Though the 1866 legislature reconstituted a school fund for white Georgians only, the ban against teaching blacks to read or write had vanished with slavery, and new mandates from the federal government required that space be made in any public school system for blacks as well as whites. In the 1870s and 1880s, Georgia's education fund helped support segregated schools for both races. Republican rule in Georgia had only a limited impact on social policy, but the federal government had placed new demands on any regime, Republican or Democratic, and the Bourbons showed that they knew it.

In the aftermath of emancipation, public authorities throughout the South had to respond to the end of both the social welfare and the social control features of slavery. In 1865 and 1866, public authorities at state and local levels in Georgia focused on control by pressing blacks into penal and mental institutions, and they left responsibility for social welfare to the Freedmen's Bureau. When Republicans came to power in 1868, the state had already financed construction of a black wing at the lunatic asylum, made the switch from whipping post to chain gang as a means of dealing with misdemeanors and extracting black labor for public works, and authorized the lease of felony convicts and the sale of misdemeanor convicts.

Only later, after those initial changes of Presidential Restoration, did state and local authorities undertake responsibility for black residents' social welfare —providing funds for elementary schooling and higher education, according black paupers treatment similar to white paupers, and admitting blacks to schools for the deaf and the blind. In Georgia the years of Republican rule during Reconstruction brought little change in most of these matters. The Restoration regime began routinely placing black Georgians in the penal system and the mental institution, and not until well into the Bourbon years did the schools for the deaf or blind open their doors, on a segregated basis, to black students. Though Republicans made gestures toward including blacks among the beneficiaries of state spending on elementary and higher education, the Bourbon regime took positive actions either to implement or at least to maintain such policies.

At no time before Reconstruction did any tax money go to Georgia's state education fund. The Constitution of 1868 allocated the poll tax to schools, and as a rule that money was left with the counties in which it was collected. The Republican legislature of 1870 provided for the establishment of a school system, but the state neglected to provide the funds for 1871, the first year of operations. Thus the irony that the Democratic legislature of 1872 called for a supplementary, one-year state property tax for education to pay for the previous year. That exception aside, Georgia's school fund continued until the late 1880s to depend on sources of revenue other than a general property tax. Its largest component was the half rental of the Western and Atlantic Railroad, amounting to $150,000.

Prelude to Southern Progressivism

The state school fund more than held its own through the Bourbon era. Growing slowly at first, it reached a new level in 1884 of $300,000 (even aside from the poll tax), or twice the largest pre–Civil War appropriation. Already the state was spending more total dollars on public schools than at any previous time, but in 1888, a biennial session of the Georgia legislature enacted a state property tax for schools. First levied in 1889, the tax collected was $0.50 per $1,000 assessed valuation, an amount increased for 1890 to $1.00 per $1,000. Thus by 1890 the fund exceeded $600,000, and the next year it reached $900,000. The average school fund of the 1880s doubled by 1890, tripled by 1891, and continued to grow.[2] The Progressive pattern in public school finance had its origins in the 1888 act.

Before the Civil War, Georgia supplied its institutions of higher education with little public money. The state supplied funds for medical schools in the 1830s and 1850s and for Georgia Military Institute in the 1850s, but otherwise it made only one commitment to higher education. Early in the century Georgia endowed the state university with $100,000 in bank stock, and it pledged in 1821 that it would make up the difference any year that the school's income from the bank dividends fell below $8,000, something that happened occasionally even before Reconstruction. Because the bank stock was worthless after the war, each year beginning in 1866 the state supplied the $8,000.

New factors affected state policy after the war. The Morrill Act, passed by Congress in 1862, supplied land scrip that was converted to an annual $17,914 and allocated, in 1872, to an agricultural and mechanical school connected with the state university at Athens. In the 1870s and 1880s, new branches of the university were organized, and each, at times, received a share of that fund. Despite the new schools, state appropriations for higher education remained nearly constant until an 1885 act appropriated $65,000 to launch the Georgia Institute of Technology. Annual appropriations for Tech, at $18,000 in 1890, drifted upwards. The state began to supply other funds, too; an 1888 act, for example, inaugurated direct appropriations for annual support to the various branch colleges, which left more Morrill Act money for the university at Athens. By the late 1890s, annual state funds for higher education exceeded $100,000.[3]

In a dramatic break from the Slave South, the general assembly in 1870 appropriated an annual $8,000 for Atlanta University, a school for blacks. After a brief interruption, Bourbon Georgia continued to provide annual support for the school. Viewed as a twin to the state university's $8,000, Atlanta University's appropriation constituted an equivalent outlay of state funds. Viewed, however, as black Georgians' share of the land scrip fund, it was federal money, and the state contributed nothing to higher education for blacks. In this limited sense, Atlanta University continued to receive state aid until 1887.

At just the time the state increased its support for higher education for whites, it halted its only contribution to higher education for blacks. Three years later, however, after Congress enacted a second Morrill Act, which granted more money but required that some of it go to a black school, Georgia established what is now Savannah State College. The new school received shares of both federal monies—the old $8,000 annuity and one-third of the 1890 fund.

One obstacle on "the road to reunion" after the Civil War—an obstacle almost completely overlooked by historians—was the amount paid in pensions to Civil War veterans. In the decades after the war, the U.S. Congress (often controlled by Republicans) raised tariff rates and used much of the resulting revenue to increase both the size of pensions and the number of their beneficiaries.[4] The South, however, traditionally low-tariff in sentiment and economic interest, obtained few of those pensions. United States pensions were for Yankee veterans only. Confederate veterans, who lived in the nation's poorest region, could look only to private charity or their state or local governments for support.

But while the Grand Army of the Republic captured so many supporters in northern and Republican politics, the mystique of the Lost Cause was a potent force in the late-nineteenth-century South. So were the men who had *fought* for the Lost Cause; particularly after introduction of the cumulative poll tax, and exemption of maimed Confederate veterans from paying it, former soldiers had great influence in Georgia politics. Reflecting both mystique and constituency, the legislature appropriated ever-greater amounts to support Confederate veterans and their dependents. The first such spending benefited amputees and other disabled Confederate veterans. Later the state extended aid to the widows of Confederate soldiers and finally to all indigent Confederate veterans.

A series of constitutional changes during the Bourbon years—the 1877 constitution and then, beginning in 1886, amendments to it—authorized these new expenditures. Such spending had its origins just after the Civil War, when the legislature, in 1865 and 1866, appropriated funds for artificial limbs and inaugurated a G.I. bill to pay educational expenses. Republicans curtailed both programs, but the Redeemers began anew. Beginning in 1879, the state paid out an annual average of about $60,000 to "maimed soldiers," an amount that tripled to more than $180,000 beginning in 1890. In 1896 the state spent $310,000 for maimed or indigent veterans and another $241,000 for widows of Confederate troops. By 1911 these pensions took $1.2 million, or 22 percent of the state's total budget.[5]

A medley of changes in Georgia's fiscal affairs began about 1885, a generation after the Civil War, when Georgia launched a new beginning in social spending. As the tax base increased by about 60 percent in the 1880s, taking pressure off the state budget, Georgians found it easier to spend more money on higher education and Confederate veterans.[6] Just as important was the declining role of debt service in the budget.[7] Nonetheless, an annual state property tax specifically for elementary schools—something few Georgians proposed before the 1880s, let alone before the Civil War—was strikingly new. For the first time, Georgia resorted to substantial taxation to finance social spending. Georgia ended the nineteenth century with larger school budgets and higher (peacetime) tax rates than ever before. State taxes and public responsibilities had attained greater dimensions, and they had become more closely linked.

In the 1890s, Georgia's governors acknowledged the heavy tax burden but

spoke glowingly of "the position which the State has taken respecting its treatment of the old soldiers and the education of its children."[8] By the early 1910s,
state spending on education alone amounted to more than an entire annual
budget from the 1880s. But schools for black children received only one-sixth
of the money spent on school construction and teachers' salaries. Moreover, all
state spending on higher education, and all that on soldiers' pensions, went to
whites only. Roughly half of Georgia's annual budgets in the Progressive years
went to Confederate pensions or schools for whites. Meanwhile, segregation
and disfranchisement tightened their grip on black Georgians.

The flurry of activity in Georgia in the decade before World War I represented, as C. Vann Woodward has characterized it, progressivism "for whites
only."[9] The Bourbon era—in particular the shift in the years beginning in
1885—was also for whites only. Woodward and Ward perceived Bourbon
social policy as miserly, and they bemoaned its unhappy implications for the
twentieth century. Their descriptions of that policy, though misleading with
regard to spending on white Georgians, are more apt with regard to spending
on blacks. While the changes of the Bourbon period constituted a prelude to
Progressivism, they just as surely heralded a southern variant of Progressivism.

Public Schools and Public Roads

The 1920s capped a century of growth in state power. In
Georgia, that development originated in the decade after the War of 1812,
when the state began to supply funds for elementary education and improved
transportation. In the decade after World War I, Georgia built on generations
of experience, a new infusion of federal funds, and voters' continuing demands
that public authority supply schools and roads. According to the prevailing
conception, property taxes, not private tuition, should pay teachers' salaries. A
tax on motor fuels, not tolls on private turnpikes, should pay for highway
construction. Public schools and public roads should absorb the bulk of state
spending. Most federal money available to states should go to the improvement of public highways.

Americans had long expected their governments to provide access to education and transportation. In the 1920s they could not imagine a time, though it
had been only a hundred years, that governments had not done so. Rhetoric
about limited government found no audience among people who thought of
government—state and local—as an extension of their private wills. Citizens'
instrumental conception of public authority had burst the bounds that, before
the Second American Revolution, had largely limited social spending to what
tax-free sources of revenue could finance.

In the 1920s, America was on the eve of an enormous expansion of national power. The Third American Revolution was about to free social spending from the limits imposed by state and local taxes. In Americans' minds in the next half-century, government, or "the government," would come to mean the federal government, as it took on vast new powers and shaped in new contours the behavior of private individuals and of state and local governments.

ESSAY ON
PRIMARY
SOURCES

MY SOURCES can be found in my notes, and I have supplied a bibliography. Here I offer a tour guide through the maze of primary sources — mostly state and local public records — on which this study so heavily depends.

Three major reference works track Georgia's legislative and constitutional history of the period. Under such headings as "Tax" and "Penitentiary," Thomas R. R. Cobb compiled all legislation still in force in Georgia as of the end of the 1849–50 legislative session (*Digest of the Statute Laws of the State of Georgia*). Francis Newton Thorpe (comp., *The Federal and State Constitutions*) follows Benjamin Perley Poore (comp., *The Federal and State Constitutions*) in neglecting important constitutional amendments in Georgia in the 1850s. The authoritative constitutional history of Georgia is Walter McElreath's *Treatise on the Constitution of Georgia*. McElreath succinctly outlines nineteenth-century changes in the Georgia constitution — those regarding legislative apportionment and Confederate veterans' pensions, for example. He also reprints every state constitution (including that of 1861, which Thorpe and Poore exclude) and its amendments until the time of his publication (1912).

Essential sources for legislative history include the *Acts of the General Assembly of the State of Georgia*, the *Journal of the House of Representatives*, and the *Journal of the Senate*. Each legislative session produced a volume of each. Because the journals contain roll-call votes, as well as procedural information regarding the progress of bills through the legislature, they permit one to trace parliamentary maneuvering. But given that they never contain legislators' speeches and only rarely give the full wording of a bill under discussion, the precise content of contending measures frequently remains uncertain, as does the rationale for each member's vote.

The Executive Minutes are the basic source for governors' actions. In them are recorded such routine activities of the governor as action on legislation and the establishment of annual state property tax rates; these minutes can be consulted on microfilm in the Georgia Department of Archives and History in Atlanta. At the convening of each annual (or biennial or semi-annual) session of the legislature, the governor gave an address to a joint session of the general assembly. Sometimes he droned on about such topics as a boundary dispute with Florida. Still, when the state's chief executives were urging enactment of a new tax system, castigating the Confederate government for ill-advised financial actions, or reporting on the results of pension legislation benefiting Confederate veterans, their messages provide an excellent introduction to social and economic as well as political and administrative developments. Like frequent shorter messages, these addresses are generally most accessible in the journals of the house and senate; they are also available in the Executive Minutes and in many cases were published separately or reprinted in newspapers.

The *Annual Reports of the Comptroller General of the State of Georgia* provide the most indispensable single source of information for a study of public revenue and spending. For some years before 1850, the reports of the comptroller general were printed in the house or senate journals or the *Acts of the General Assembly*. After 1850 they were published separately, though in 1867 the comptroller general made no annual report; figures for an extended year "1867" can be found in the legislative journals of 1868. Before 1857 the reports gave only limited information other than state treasury receipts and disbursements (available with much less detail in the *Annual Reports of the Treasurer of the State of Georgia*, which are also useful regarding state debt) and total state taxes levied in each county. After that, they listed the valuation of each category of property (slaves, rural real estate, etc.) for each county. Beginning in the mid-1870s, the reports also listed county tax rates and gave separate figures for black taxpayers' property holdings by category and county.

To ascertain the operations of state institutions—the Academy for the Blind, the Institution for the Education of the Deaf and Dumb, the Lunatic Asylum, the penitentiary—it is necessary to study their annual reports to the governor. Because the essential purpose of these reports was to inform the governor and legislature of how the institutions were functioning, they tend to be quite full and contain much specific information regarding the outlays of expenditures, the numbers of students or inmates, and so on. Because they were presented with the hope of maintaining existing levels of funding, or even of eliciting greater appropriations, favorable assessments of institutions' performances must be viewed with some skepticism. Many of these reports are located at the Library of Congress or the Georgia State Library; some are compiled in John C. Butler, *Origin and History of the Georgia Academy for the Blind*; most are available on microfilm from the Library of Congress.[1]

Some of the state's Confederate records are easier to track down. Many have been published in Allen D. Candler, comp., *Confederate Records of the State of Georgia*. The location of a variety of Georgia's Civil War public documents can be determined from several checklists of Confederate imprints compiled by Marjorie Lyle Crandall or Richard Harwell.[2] Yet not all available items are mentioned in these guides; the 1863 and 1864 reports of the Georgia Relief and Hospital Association, for example, are in the Georgia State Library. And, because the Library of Congress microfilmed chiefly the Georgia documents available at the Georgia Department of Archives and History and the Georgia State Library, it neglected other documents, among them the 1863 and 1864 reports of the penitentiary, which can be consulted at Duke University and the Boston Athenaeum, respectively.

I used newspapers both to supplement the legislative journals and to ascertain public attitudes. During the struggle for ad valorem taxation, for example, newspapers often identified contending tax bills and editorialized on their respective merits. Similarly, on occasion they discussed public investments in railroads, bills to increase state expenditures for education and welfare institutions, and the fate of the penitentiary and convict lease systems. The *Augusta Daily Chronicle and Sentinel*, the *Savannah Daily Republican*, the *Georgia Messenger and Journal* (Macon), and other newspapers have provided helpful material. But the most valuable single Georgia newspaper for the period of this study is the *Milledgeville Southern Recorder*; the Georgia State Library has a virtually complete file of volumes 10–51 (1829–70). Otherwise, the best place to find Georgia newspapers (on microfilm) is the University of Georgia.

Among the manuscript returns of the U.S. census are "Free Inhabitants" (Schedule 1 in 1850 and 1860), "Slave Inhabitants" (Schedule 2 in 1850 and 1860), "Inhabitants" (Schedule 1 in 1870), "Productions of Agriculture" (Schedule 4), and "Social Statistics" (Schedule 6 in 1850, Schedule 5 in 1860 and 1870).[3] Historians have used Schedules 1 and 2 ever since Frank L. Owsley made a convincing case for their utility. Yet "Social Statistics," which gives a variety of social and financial data, much of it unavailable elsewhere, is a schedule rarely used. For a majority of Georgia counties, the social statistics schedule lists the amounts of state taxes (generally available also in the *Annual Reports of the Comptroller*) as well as county taxes (frequently according to purpose); in some cases, it also gives town taxes. The social statistics schedule also provides data on such other topics as local schooling, churches, pauper support, and average wages. (The manuscript schedule contains no tax data for a number of counties; thus the published volumes for 1850 and 1860, which give only aggregate tax data by states, give incomplete totals.)

Tax lists (called "tax digests" in Georgia) are available on microfilm at the Georgia Department of Archives and History. Some counties boast a virtually complete series for the entire nineteenth century; others appear to have no surviving tax lists. Where available, these lists provide detailed information about individual property holdings and tax burdens. Taxpayers are listed, as a rule alphabetically within each militia district (county subdivision), together with the number and value of slaves or of acres of different qualities of land, and the values of other types of property. As indexes of property holding, besides being more precise—as well as possibly more reliable—than are the manuscript U.S. census returns, tax lists have the advantage of being annual rather than decennial.[4]

The county legislative body, called the inferior court in Georgia until Reconstruction, determined tax rates and expenditures (within levels authorized by the state legislature). The minutes of the county inferior courts, therefore, can provide the local equivalent of the *Acts* of the state legislature. They are particularly important as a source of information regarding county tax rates (a percentage of the state tax for each taxpayer) and the distribution of county spending among such items as education, public support of the poor, and (during the Civil War) military or extraordinary welfare expenditures. By no means have all inferior court minutes survived; like the tax lists, those that have can be consulted on microfilm at the Georgia Department of Archives and History.

The reports of Georgia's appellate courts provide a rich source for a study of social attitudes and public policy. A behavioral analysis of the legislative process can contribute a firm sense of the priorities of political leaders and their constituents, but little in the way of legislative debates has survived. In the *Georgia Reports*, by contrast, the historian can see the actual implementation of Georgia's laws in their application to specific situations. There, for example, Joseph Henry Lumpkin, a justice on the Georgia Supreme Court from its creation in 1845 to his death in 1867, expounded at length on the reasoning behind the court's decisions. Dry statutes and flesh-and-blood Georgians tangled, laws shaped lives, and an eloquent judge described how and explained why.

NOTES

ABBREVIATIONS USED IN NOTES

Acts	*Acts of the General Assembly*
ADD	Georgia Asylum for the Deaf and Dumb, *Annual Report*
AU	Trevor Arnett Library, Atlanta University Center, Atlanta
BTM	Board of Trustees' Minutes
CG	Comptroller General, *Annual Report*
CRSG	Candler, *Confederate Records of the State of Georgia*
EU	Robert W. Woodruff Library, Emory University, Atlanta
"FSSTNS"	Wallenstein, "From Slave South to New South"
GAB	Georgia Academy for the Blind, *Annual Report*
GDAH	Georgia Department of Archives and History, Atlanta
GR	*Georgia Reports*
GSL	Georgia State Library, Atlanta
ICM	Inferior Court Minutes
JHR	*Journal of the House of Representatives*
JS	*Journal of the Senate*
LA	Lunatic Asylum of the State of Georgia, *Annual Report*
mfm	microfilm
MSR	*Milledgeville Southern Recorder*
NA	National Archives
PEN	Penitentiary, *Report*
SCM	Superior Court Minutes
SCS	State Commissioner of Schools, *Report*
Treas.	Treasurer, *Report*
UGA	University of Georgia

NOTES ON STATE RECORDS:

When the *Acts, JHR,* or *JS* are cited, the date(s) in parentheses denote the legislative session.

In the reports of state officers and institutions — ADD, CG, GAB, LA, PEN, and *Treas.* — the date(s) in parentheses indicate the fiscal year(s) covered in the report. Some reports are numbered; in those cases, the number precedes the date.

References are to Georgia unless another state is specified.

NOTES ON FEDERAL RECORDS:

Volumes of U.S. *Statutes at Large* are cited by title and volume number.

Published census materials are cited by volume title, but they appear in the bibliography under U.S. Census Bureau.

Manuscript schedules of the U.S. census for Georgia are cited by title and year ("Social Statistics" [1850, 1860, 1870]; "Slave Inhabitants" [1850]; and "Inhabitants" [1870]); they are available on microfilm at the National Archives (see discussion in the Essay on Primary Sources).

CHAPTER I. SOCIETY AND POLITICS

1. On Georgia's first half century, see Coleman, *History of Georgia*, 3–88 and bibliography, and Wood, *Slavery in Colonial Georgia*.

2. *Compendium of the Ninth Census*, 11, 17. For maps depicting Georgia's growth, see Phillips, *Georgia and State Rights* (the 1902 edition, not a reprint).

3. Bonner, *History of Georgia Agriculture*, 2–8.

4. Ibid., 17–21, 24–25, 47–50.

5. Ibid., 50–56; Gray, *History of Agriculture*, 2:673–90.

6. *Compendium of the Ninth Census*, 12–19.

7. Coleman, *History of Georgia*, 89–104.

8. Abernethy, *South in the New Nation*, 136–54. For vigorous grand jury present-ments against the Yazoo sale, see the *Georgia Gazette* (Savannah), 5 Mar. (Screven County), 19 Mar. (Effingham County), and 27 Aug. (Chatham County) 1795.

9. Carter and Bloom, *Territorial Papers of the United States*, 5:142–46.

10. Jefferson to Milledge, 22 Nov. 1802, in Salley, *Correspondence of John Milledge*, 82 (commas added).

11. *Statutes at Large*, 4:411–12, 7:36–40, 366–68, 478–89 (*Indian Treaties*); Vipperman, "'Particular Mission' of Wilson Lumpkin"; Hudson, *Southeastern Indians*, 427–73; Foreman, *Indian Removal*.

12. Heath, *Constructive Liberalism*, ch. 7.

13. *Compendium of the Seventh Census*, 114, 116–17.

14. Ibid., 63, 114–18.

15. Ibid., 398–99. See Haunton, "Savannah in the 1850's," ch. 2; Reidy, "Masters and Slaves," 106–24 (for Macon); and Wade, *Slavery in the Cities*, ch. 9.

16. *Compendium of the Seventh Census*, 338–93; *Population in 1860*, 74. For a study of the merchant community in Savannah, see Haunton, ch. 3.

17. *Population in 1860*, 73.

18. Friedman, *History of American Law*, 184–86; Boatwright, "Women in Georgia."

19. *Compendium of the Seventh Census*, 95, 99; Gray, *History of Agriculture*, 1:530.

20. Manuscript tax digest, Columbia County, District no. 1, 1851 (mfm 61-10, GDAH). See Wright, *Political Economy of the Cotton South*, ch. 2; Owsley, *Plain Folk of the Old South*, 170–81; Linden, "Economic Democracy in the Slave South"; North, *Growth and Welfare*, ch. 7. In the Owsley tradition, James Oakes emphasizes the more numerous owners of small holdings rather than the planters (*Ruling Race*). Owsley's comparisons of social structures in 1850 and 1860 are misleading, in that some of his counties (e.g., Franklin and Forsyth) lost considerable territory to neighboring counties formed in the 1850s; in some cases, it was the county lines, and not the farmers, that migrated.

21. Georgia's 2,166 overseers in 1850 comprised one of every sixty occupied adult free white males; the census does not provide the number of farm laborers. *Seventh Census*, 376. See Bonner, "Profile of a Late Ante-Bellum Community"; Buck, "Poor Whites"; Terrill, "Eager Hands"; Hahn, *Roots of Southern Populism*, 64–69; Reidy, "Masters and Slaves," 56–74; Harris, *Plain Folk and Gentry*, 86–93.

22. I use the term "black belt" in reference to demography, not soil type.

23. Population and crop production figures can be found in *Seventh Census*, 364–65, 378–81; *Population in 1860*, 72–73; *Agriculture in 1860*, 22–29. See Harris, *Plain Folk and Gentry*, 11–122, and Reidy, "Masters and Slaves," 10–94.

24. *Compendium of the Ninth Census*, 34.

25. Hahn, *Roots of Southern Populism*, 20–27, 40–49; Green, "Georgia's Forgotten Industry"; *Agriculture in 1860*, 27.

26. *Agriculture in 1860*, 26–27, 29; McDonald and McWhiney, "Antebellum Southern Herdsman," 154.

27. Cooper, *South and the Politics of Slavery*.

28. Phillips, *Georgia and State Rights*, 53–65. The episode can be followed in Fortune, "George M. Troup," ch.8; and Ames, *State Documents on Federal Relations*, 113–30.

29. Hughes, *County Government in Georgia*, 11–17; Hahn, *Roots of Southern Populism*, 91–97.

30. Thorpe, *Federal and State Constitutions*, 2:779–809.

31. For a discussion of the continuing struggle between predominantly white, subsistence-farming North Georgia and the black belt over the basis of apportionment—e.g., by white population, total population, federal population, or county—see Roberts, "Sectional Factors."

32. Before 1843 a federal population of 3,000 permitted two representatives; 7,000 allowed three; and 12,000 (e.g., Chatham County) the maximum four. Thorpe, *Federal and State Constitutions*, 2:791–92, 808.

33. *Compendium of the Ninth Census*, 34–35.

34. *The Tribune Almanac for the Years 1838 to 1868*, 2 vols. (New York: New York Tribune, 1868); Shryock, *Georgia and the Union in 1850*; Murray, "Party Organization in Georgia Politics"; Montgomery, *Cracker Politics*; McCormick, *Second American Party System*, 236–46; DeBats, "Elites and Masses." For a list of Georgia's governors and their political affiliations, see Coleman, *History of Georgia*, Appendix A.

35. Election returns by county are available in *The Tribune Almanac*. The sectional and class basis of antebellum politics in Georgia constitutes a recurring theme in Phillips (*Georgia and State Rights*, 87, 96, 103–7, 140) and elsewhere.

36. I am indebted to Professor Ralph A. Wooster of Lamar University for the use of his manuscript notes, based on "Slave Inhabitants" (1850).

37. Where evidence of slave ownership did not emerge from Ralph A. Wooster's survey (or my own) of the manuscript census returns, I checked the appropriate county tax lists, where available (see "FSSTNS," tables 6–7). I discovered more planters and fewer nonslaveholders than Wooster's less complete findings indicate (*People in Power*, 133). I failed to find slaveholdings for only 10 of 47 senators (2 of 22 Whigs, 8 of 25 Democrats) and for 25 of 130 representatives (7 of 63 Whigs, 18 of 67 Democrats).

38. *Savannah Georgian*, quoted in *MSR*, 23 Nov. 1841.

CHAPTER 2. STATE POWER AND TAX-FREE FINANCE

1. For surveys of the literature, see Edwin A. Miles, "The Jacksonian Era," in Link and Patrick, *Writing Southern History*, 125–46; Wilentz, "On Class and Politics."

2. Lively, "American System." Among surveys of subsequent literature see Scheiber, *Ohio Canal Era*, 411–22.

3. McMaster, *People of the United States*, 4:347–48.

4. Rothman, *Discovery of the Asylum*.

5. *JS* (1830), 17. Georgians' hopes of nontax bounty echoed others'. For an example, see a report of the Maryland House Ways and Means Committee in the *Maryland Gazette and Political Intelligencer* (Annapolis), 1 Feb. 1819.

6. Wallenstein, "Maine, Massachusetts, and the Missouri Compromise"; Turner, *United States, 1830–1850*, 436. Harry N. Scheiber describes the states at that time as "the significant locus . . . of real power, vigorously exercised" ("Federalism and the American Economic Order," 96); see Wiebe, *Opening of American Society*, ch. 10.

7. Scheiber, "Federalism and the American Economic Order," 96; Horwitz, *Transformation of American Law*, 99–101; Scheiber, "Government and the Economy." See below, ch. 3.

8. Report of George F. Pierce, Samuel K. Talmadge, and Leonidas B. Mercer, in Lewis, *Report on Public Education*, 12.

9. See above, ch. 1.

10. Heath, *Constructive Liberalism*, ch. 7. See the address of Governor John Milledge to the general assembly, 18 Apr. 1803, in Executive Minutes (1802–1805), 123–25 (mfm 50-45, GDAH); manuscript "JHR" for the Apr.–May 1803 session (GDAH).

11. Heath, *Constructive Liberalism*, 157.

12. *Statutes at Large*, 3:53–72, 164–80, 255–56; *JS* (1813), 12; (1814), 5–6; (1815), 5. Such behavior did not mean that Georgians made only the same tax payments as in peacetime. To reimburse the state, at least in part, the general assembly enacted an extra state tax, equal to one-half the regular tax, for each year from 1813 through 1816. (See fig. 1.) It used the additional revenue to pay for such wartime costs as the defense of Savannah. Lamar, *Compilation*, 877–87.

13. Georgia's Wilson Lumpkin, like Calhoun, moved from a committed nationalism in the 1810s, voting for the Bank Act and the Tariff Act of 1816, to increasing disaffection in later years, as sectional tensions over slavery grew. Writing in the 1850s, Lumpkin declared he had "long since repudiated" those actions. Lumpkin, *Removal of the Cherokee Indians*, 1:24–25; *Annals of Congress*, 14th Cong., 2d sess., 191, 296–97, 933–34, 1059–62. See below, ch. 3, note 2.

14. Heath, *Constructive Liberalism*, 175–80, 237–38, 345; annual reports of Georgia's state treasurer can be found appended to *JS* (1817 and 1818); see also Green, "Georgia's Board of Public Works." Governor David B. Mitchell offered a pragmatic rationale for investing in bank stock: "The collection of the revenue arising from funds of this description is both safe and easy, whilst that arising from taxation is attended with considerable expense and loss" (*JHR* [1817], 5, 8). In 1819, neighboring North Carolina established an internal improvements fund consisting of public revenue from two nontax sources—dividends from state-owned bank stock and proceeds from the

sale of lands recently acquired from Cherokee Indians (Sydnor, *Development of Southern Sectionalism*, 80–82).

15. Georgia's tax legislation can be traced in Cobb, *Digest*. Because Cobb depicted the statutory situation at midcentury, however, and did not attempt a complete history, one must also consult the legislative acts of the annual or biennial sessions.

16. Govan, "Banking and the Credit System"; Heath, *Constructive Liberalism*, 190–201.

17. *JS* (1823), 15–16; (1829), 13–15.

18. Tax collectors continued to gather poll and property taxes for county governments, but no longer for the state. Figure 1 portrays annual state tax rates, but in addition it depicts some "county" taxes for 1824–40. In 1824, for example, tax collectors sought the same amounts as in previous years, but only half the amount went to the state, while the other half remained with the county in which it was collected. In this manner, additional county taxes became unnecessary. On the other hand, the tax statutes now essentially established county tax rates equal to half the former state rates, whereas, previously, counties were permitted to levy at no more than half rates.

19. CG (1859), 29–30; (1830), 16 (appended to *JS* [1830]); *Acts* (1834), 27, 281–85, 307.

20. Turner, *United States*, 173–76, 435–37; Bourne, *Surplus Revenue of 1837*, 1–20, 56. For a detailed account of nineteenth-century federal transfer payments to the states see Elazar, *American Partnership*. For a conceptual rebuttal see Scheiber, *Condition of American Federalism*.

21. *Acts* (1837), 33–35, 94–99; Bourne, *Surplus Revenue of 1837*, 44–124; Knight, *Public Education in the South*, 160–89.

22. Heath, *Constructive Liberalism*, 254–74; ch. 3, below.

23. "Documents Accompanying the Report of the Commissioners on the State Finances" (1839), 32 (GSL); *JHR* (1842), 9–12; Heath, *Constructive Liberalism*, 199–201, 211–20.

24. See fig. 1 and ch. 5, below.

25. Thornton, *Politics and Power in a Slave Society*, 104, 113; Jewett, *Financial History of Maine*, 30–32; Sowers, *Financial History of New York State*, 333; Bullock, "Financial Policy of Massachusetts," ch. 4.

26. *JS* (1829), 353–57; Heath, *Constructive Liberalism*, 190–201; Charlotte A. Ford, "Tomlinson Fort," in Coleman and Gurr, *Dictionary of Georgia Biography*, 1:318–20; Fort, *Fort and Fannin Families*, 133–44.

27. See below, chs. 6–7.

CHAPTER 3. THE ACCOMMODATION OF THE PUBLIC

1. 4 *GR* 326–28 (1866).

2. White, *The Jeffersonians*, 484–88; McMaster, *People of the United States*, 4:407–29; Julius Rubin, "An Innovating Public Improvement: The Erie Canal," in Goodrich, *Canals and American Economic Development*, 15–66.

3. Quoted in Horwitz, *Transformation of American Law*, 65. In 23 *GR* 65, 73 (1857), the Georgia court relied on the authority of a U.S. Supreme Court decision, *Barron* v. *Baltimore*, 7 Pet. 243.

4. Heath, *Constructive Liberalism*, 287–89. I have made one adjustment in Heath's figures; he includes in his figures for public investment the entire $1,000,000 stock subscription in the Atlantic and Gulf Railroad authorized by an 1856 act, but the state actually invested only half that amount before 1861.

5. Ibid., 289.

6. Ibid.

7. White, *The Jeffersonians*, 360–62; "Laws of the United States Relating to the Improvement of Rivers and Harbors from August 11, 1790 to March 4, 1913," H. Doc. 1491, 62d Cong., 3d sess., 1:33, 129; Heath, "Public Co-operation in Railroad Construction," 87–98. For an overview of the American partnership—private and public, federal and state, state and local—see Bruchey, *Roots of American Economic Growth*, 122–36.

8. *Acts* (1835), 226–27. See also Scheiber, "Property Law"; Horwitz, *Transformation of American Law*, ch. 3.

9. Heath, *Constructive Liberalism*, 286–88.

10. Henry, *Digest*, 429; *Acts* (1847), 285–86.

11. See Phillips, *Transportation in the Eastern Cotton Belt*, esp. ch. 7, and Heath, *Constructive Liberalism*, ch. 11.

12. Western and Atlantic Railroad, *Report* (1846), 5; (1847), 9.

13. *Acts* (1843), 139; Western and Atlantic Railroad, *Report* (1847), 1; (1846), 5.

14. *Reports of the Chief Engineers, Presidents and Superintendents of the South-Western R.R. Co., of Georgia, from No. 1 to No. 22* (Macon, 1869), 126–27, 145.

15. Western and Atlantic Railroad, *Report* (1855), 8–9. See also *JS* (1855–56), 606–9.

16. For a similar example of the behavior of public authorities, see Salsbury, *The State, the Investor, and the Railroad*. For the later disputes, see Benson, *Merchants, Farmers, and Railroads*, and Kolko, *Railroads and Regulation*.

17. *Georgia Messenger and Journal* (Macon), 21 Feb. 1849.

18. The view presented elsewhere—that the social benefits of public (or private) spending on railroads and other modes of transportation in nineteenth-century America were widely shared—appears to apply only with serious reservation to the Slave South. The aggregate social benefits may well have been immense, but the distribution of rewards proved highly uneven. See Goodrich, *Canals and American Economic Development*, 216–55, and Fogel, *Union Pacific Railroad*, 91–103.

19. Western and Atlantic Railroad, *Report* (1849), 13; *Reports of the Presidents, Engineers-in-Chief and Superintendents, of the Central Rail-road and Banking Company of Georgia, from No. 1 to No. 19 Inclusive* (Savannah, 1854), 34, 44, 200, 208; *Georgia Messenger and Journal* (Macon), 14 Feb. 1849, 1 Oct. 1851. See also *MSR*, 9 Jan. 1849; South-Western R.R. Company, *Reports*, 241; Starobin, *Industrial Slavery in the Old South*.

20. Slaves, however, not land, constituted the bulk of most planters' wealth, and, unlike land, did not respond in market value to the coming of a railroad through any particular area. Wright makes this point in *Political Economy of the Cotton South*, 117, 125; he elaborates it in *Old South, New South*, ch. 2 (esp. pp. 17–23). Despite his distinction between "laborlords" and "landlords," railroad promoters before the war, too, employed the language of land values.

21. Small farmers elsewhere in Georgia, too, often benefited from railroad con-

struction, most of which, although promoted by no direct aid from the state, received assistance directly from local governments and/or indirectly by the state's efforts to encourage the entire system. CG (1857), 40; (1860), 43; Western and Atlantic Railroad, *Report* (1850), table 1; (1860), 17. See Hahn, *Roots of Southern Populism*, 34–37, 45–49. For a table showing annual down freight figures on the state railroad in the 1850s, see Russell, "Atlanta," 26.

CHAPTER 4. TAX UPON THE TIME AND LABOR OF OUR CITIZENS

1. Cobb, *Digest*, 1040–81. For a change to ad valorem taxation in 1852, see below, ch. 5.

2. "Taxes in Georgia," compiled from the tax lists of 1849 in the comptroller general's office and published by *MSR*, 18 Nov. 1851. Merchandise was valued on tax day (1 Apr.).

3. The rate on bank stock was the same as that on town lots and merchandise, or $3.91 per $1,000 at midcentury. Separately administered, the bank stock tax differed somewhat from the poll, professional, and general property taxes. Bank officials bypassed local tax officers and paid the tax directly into the state treasury. That method of collection meant, first, that collection entailed no tax officers' commissions and, second, that when the counties levied their taxes (as percentages of the state tax collected in their counties) they could not levy taxes against bank stock. Cobb, *Digest*, 1062–64. Only in 1850 did the state begin to tax railroads.

4. Brooks, *Financing Government in Georgia*, 12. For similar statements that "the chief burden of taxation" in antebellum Georgia fell on land, see Orr, *History of Education*, 177, and Simpson, *Howell Cobb*, 89. For surveys of the role of slave property in antebellum southern public finance, see Thornton, "Fiscal Policy," 352–60, and Woolfolk, "Taxes and Slavery."

5. Tax rates can be traced in Cobb, *Digest*, 1041–44, 1055, 1072–80. The average value per slave reported in Georgia in 1857, the first year for which the comptroller general reported such information, was $525 (CG [1857], 18).

6. By midcentury, changes in land values had distorted their 1804 relation to taxes. Rich cotton lands in Central and Southwest Georgia had grown more valuable, and therefore undertaxed, while land along the coast now appeared overtaxed. *Seventh Census*, 378; Cobb, *Digest*, 1043–44; Heath, *Constructive Liberalism*, 374–75.

7. Cobb, *Digest*, 1044, 1055, 1074, 1080. For a more detailed treatment of free blacks' taxes (and other obligations), see below, ch. 8.

8. "Per capita" figures given here are based on total population, black and white.

9. CG (1850), 5; *Seventh Census*, 364–65. Map 7 in "FSSTNS" displays counties' per capita state taxes for 1850.

10. The ratio of tax to valuation correlated only imperfectly with counties' wealth or racial composition. Because real estate was generally taxed at higher rates relative to its value on the coast as well as in many white counties, the coastal rice counties, like the cities and North Georgia, paid higher-than-average tax-to-property rates. County totals for real and personal property can be found in "Social Statistics" (1850); they were published in *MSR*, 18 Nov. 1851. See "FSSTNS," 31n and map 8.

11. Viewing tax burdens in per capita terms rather than relative to wealth, Thornton arrives at a contrary conclusion (*Politics and Power in a Slave Society*, 100–105); see also Thornton, "Fiscal Policy," 352–59.

12. For example, Alabama levied a state tax of $2.00 per $1,000 valuation on land and slaves alike. Slaves were classified by age to establish approximate values and to standardize them for tax purposes—from $100 to $550 in most cases. No doubt the market value of land normally exceeded its reported value for tax purposes, yet a tax on slaves that valued most of them at between $100 and $550 does not appear invidious. As in Georgia, the most productive objects of state property taxation in late antebellum Alabama were slaves (47.6 percent of the total in 1850) and agricultural land (22.6 percent). Alabama, *Acts* (1847–48), 24, 36; (1849–50), 6–7; Alabama, Comptroller of Public Accounts, *Biennial Report* (1850–51), 43.

Thornton's argument, that Alabama's heavy reliance on slave taxation demonstrates a Jacksonian fear of power and a consequent effort to rein in the wealthy, appears to assume that the occasional colonial practice of taxing all free families equally regardless of their wealth offers the most appropriate standard of fiscal fairness. South Carolina, however—the state most sensitive to attacks in any form, real or imagined, against slavery—derived 63.1 percent of all state property tax revenue at midcentury from taxes on slaves. Yet its tax on slaves, $0.56 "per head on all slaves," when calculated at the rate levied on land ($3.50 per $1,000 valuation), amounted to a value for tax purposes of only $160 per slave. South Carolina property holders, even more than those of Georgia or Alabama, had invested the bulk of their wealth in slaves, and that wealth carried no more than its share of the burden. South Carolina, *Acts* (1849), 550; "Report of the Comptroller General," in South Carolina, *Reports and Resolutions* (1850), 9–10; Becker, "Revolution and Reform."

13. According to the *Compendium of the Seventh Census*, 190, state taxes comprised 56 percent of all state, county, and town tax revenue in Georgia at midcentury. The published figures were derived from the manuscript returns of "Social Statistics" (1850). That schedule, however, lists neither the local taxes of most towns nor any county taxes for seven of Georgia's ninety-five counties for 1850; if the missing figures were included in the aggregate, the proportion of state taxes would drop to nearer one-half.

14. The county inferior court (on recommendation by the grand jury of the superior court) levied the county's annual taxes. Tax receivers and tax collectors, elected annually in each county, simultaneously received returns or collected taxes for state and county. After deducting commissions (which absorbed more than a tenth of all tax money paid), the collector turned over county taxes to the county treasurer and state taxes to the state comptroller general. Cobb, *Digest*, 200, 1022–34, 1045–47, 1073–77; *Acts* (1851–52), 290–91.

15. Cobb, *Digest*, 184; "Social Statistics" (1850).

16. Liberty County residents paid a county tax of only 17.5 percent, and those in Glynn County paid only 25 percent; both were coastal rice counties—wealthy and, relative to that wealth, overtaxed. "Social Statistics" (1850). Of eighteen counties reporting county tax rates of less than 50 percent of state taxes in 1850, eight were in the quartile of counties paying the highest state taxes relative to property valuation. See "FSSTNS," table 10, for tax rates in various counties, 1852–74.

17. *Acts* (1841), 55–56; (1843), 95, 106–7.

18. See Cobb, *Digest*, 545–54. County creditors, like jurors and teachers, often met with long delays in obtaining even partial payment for their services.

19. See Cobb, *Digest*, 736–73; Hancock County, Ordinary, Regimental Court of Inquiry, 14th Regiment Militia, Minutes (1804–62), 2 (mfm 142-51, GDAH); Greene, *First One Hundred Years*, 16. An 1839 act declared it no longer lawful to fine a militia private for failure to supply his own arms and equipment—providing he was "not able to own such equipage, without disposing of property actually necessary for the support of himself or his family" (Cobb, *Digest*, 765). The militia persisted as a fossil, with Georgia's local jurisdictions termed "militia districts."

20. SCM, Liberty County (1794–1800), 51 (mfm 30-45, GDAH).

21. According to an 1854 law, fines—up to $5.00 for failing to report on assignment—went to the county's education fund. Cobb, *Compilation*, ch. 33.

22. The term "statute labor" stems from the system in England which, under an act of Parliament, as amended, endured from 1555 to 1835. Jackman, *Transportation in Modern England*, 231–60; Webb and Webb, *Story of the King's Highway*; Wallenstein, "Conscripts and Convicts"; contract dated 14 Dec. 1857, John S. Dobbins Papers (mfm 322-2, EU).

23. *Acts* (1855–56), 506–8; *MSR*, 30 Mar. 1852.

24. Commutation was available, in that residents' failure to fulfill their obligations, when called, resulted in fines of from $1.00 to $3.00 per day, and citizens could hire substitutes to work in their stead. Cobb, *Compilation*, 500–533, 613–14; Heath, *Constructive Liberalism*, ch. 10; see below, ch. 18. A town resident was subject to road and patrol duty in his town but escaped additional obligations to his county. Labor service in the towns could be commuted to a cash tax; Milledgeville's local poll tax, $1.00 on white males aged sixteen to sixty in 1860 (though it ranged from $0.50 to $2.00 in the 1850s), served "as a commutation for road and patroll duty." City of Milledgeville, Mayor and Aldermen, Minutes (1855–76), 20, 84–85, 121–22, 157 (mfm 270-28, GDAH). For a striking account of road (and militia) duty in neighboring North Carolina in an earlier period, see Kay and Price, " 'To Ride the Wood Mare.' "

25. *JHR* (1847), 525.

26. *Report of the Commissioners . . . on the Subject of the State Finances* (Milledgeville, 1839), 39–40. Like many of the other state records cited here, the *Report* is available on microfilm; see Jenkins, *Guide to the Microfilm Collection of Early State Records*.

27. *Report of the Commissioners*, 8; *JS* (1849–50), 14–17; "An Old Tax Payer," letter "To the Members of the Legislature," *MSR*, 16 Dec. 1851.

28. Local authorities might "remit" the poll tax in "all cases of extreme indigence or infirmity." I have found only one such instance. On the grounds that "John Duff is in indigent circumstances having no taxable property + suffering considerable from bodily infirmity," the Telfair County inferior court exempted him in 1844 from paying a poll tax. Cobb, *Digest*, 1044; ICM, Telfair County (1832–69), 1 July 1844 (mfm 172-47, GDAH).

29. Property in towns was also subject to town taxes. The smaller towns' local property taxes—as in the cases of Griffin, Albany, and Cassville (see note 17)—were normally a fraction of state or county taxes. Much less discriminatory than state taxes

or rates based on them, the larger cities' local taxes as a rule greatly overshadowed state and county rates (for Savannah, see Henry, *Digest*, 420, 434, 438–40). Local taxes, of course, were spent at home.

While state and county taxes on merchandise were relatively high in terms of assessed value, they may not have been so high in terms of income. Merchandise may well have brought a somewhat higher rate of return on investment than did a slave plantation. In any case, merchants could no doubt shift much of the tax on merchandise—pass it along to customers—more successfully than planters or farmers could shift the actual incidence of the taxes on their land and other property. Such considerations leave intact, however, the difference in tax rates on urban and rural residences.

30. *Savannah Republican*, quoted in Greene, "Politics in Georgia," 14. For a study of fiscal politics in Georgia in the 1840s and early 1850s, see below, ch. 5.

31. *Compendium of the Seventh Census*, 339, 381; *Population in 1860*, 74.

32. "Social Statistics" (1850).

33. *Acts* (1847), 185–88.

34. "Social Statistics" (1850); Cobb, *Digest*, 346–47; Klebaner, "Public Poor Relief in America," 95–96; *Compendium of the Seventh Census*, 163.

CHAPTER 5. CREATING A NEW REVENUE SYSTEM

1. The outlines of Georgia's early tax legislation can be traced in Cobb, *Digest*, 1065–71.

2. Heath, *Constructive Liberalism*, 139–223, 254–76, 368–77.

3. *Augusta Constitutionalist*, quoted in *Milledgeville Federal Union*, 19 Nov. 1839; "Governor's Message," in *Milledgeville Federal Union*, 5 Nov. 1839.

4. Ely, *Taxation*, 131–39; Becker, *Politics of American Taxation*; Woolfolk, "Taxes and Slavery," 197.

5. I use the term "black belt" with reference to demography, not soil type. To be precise, I consider the Georgia black belt to be that half of the state's counties with the highest percentage black population at each census.

6. Though Whigs consistently voted for higher levels of taxes and spending than did Democrats, Milton S. Heath characterizes Whigs as the fiscal "conservatives" (*Constructive Liberalism*, 273), and Paul Murray emphasizes the Whigs' commitment to reductions in taxes and spending (*Whig Party in Georgia*, 120). For valuable comments that relate these questions to other states, see Benson, *Concept of Jacksonian Democracy*, 86–109; Ershkowitz and Shade, "Consensus or Conflict?" On the basis of developments in Georgia, however, I would emphasize the role that tax considerations played in the Democrats' greater reluctance to spend public money, and I see less difference between North and South than do Ershkowitz and Shade.

7. *Report of the Commissioners . . . on the Subject of the State Finances* (Milledgeville, 1839), 3–4. The commissioners were John MacPherson Berrien, a once and future U.S. senator; William W. Holt, for many years a judge of the middle district; and Absalom H. Chappell.

8. Ibid., 3, 5, 7, 43–44, 55–59. For a discussion of the incidence of the 1804 tax act, as amended, see above, ch. 4.

9. *Report of the Commissioners*, 8–10, 44–45, 58.

10. Given that taxes at the time had been suspended, my statements regarding reductions compare the proposed rates with an assumed resumption of the 1804 rates.

11. *Report of the Commissioners*, 57–59.

12. *MSR*, 29 Dec. 1840; "The Taxes," *Milledgeville Federal Union*, 14, 28 Sept. 1841. For more detail on legislative maneuvers of the 1840s, see "FSSTNS," tables 14 and 15, which give roll-call voting patterns by party and constituency (black-belt and predominantly white), and Wallenstein, "Origins of Georgia's Ad Valorem Tax System."

13. Reconsidered after rejection, the tax increase of 1842 would have failed but for the nearly unanimous support of urban legislators. As a money-saving measure, Georgia reduced the size of the legislature and switched from annual to biennial sessions. Roberts, "Sectional Factors," 120–22.

14. *JHR* (1847), 368–73, 385–92; *JS* (1849–50), 14–17.

15. *JS* (1849–50), 14–15.

16. Ibid., 16.

17. *Georgia Messenger and Journal* (Macon), 7 Feb. 1849; "The Legislature," *MSR*, 16 Oct. 1849.

18. *JHR* (1849–50), 525–30, 562–64, 757, 778–82; *MSR*, 4 Dec. 1849.

19. *JHR* (1849–50), 424–26, 440–72, 531–51; *Acts* (1849–50), 378–79.

20. "An Old Tax Payer," letter "To the Members of the Legislature," *MSR*, 16 Dec. 1851 (italics in original).

21. Georgia Finance Committee, "Report" (18 Dec. 1848), 6–7 (GSL); *JHR* (1851–52), 469–79; *JS* (1851–52), 441–44.

22. *JHR* (1851–52), 426–32.

23. *JHR* (1851–52), 436, 450–51; *Augusta Daily Chronicle and Sentinel*, 27 Dec. 1851; *Savannah Republican*, 27 Dec. 1851.

24. *JHR* (1851–52), 453–54. The "index of dissimilarity" was 45. That index offers a comparison of the two parties' voting patterns in the legislature. It is obtained by subtracting one party's percentage of "yea" votes from the other's; the higher the difference, or index, the greater the disagreement. If, for example, one party votes 4–0, and the other 0–4, the index is 100; if 3–1 and 1–3, it is 50; if both the same, 0. See Holt, *Political Crisis of the 1850s*, 27.

25. *JS* (1851–52), 367–78; *Savannah Republican*, 1 Jan. 1852.

26. *JHR* (1851–52), 694–97.

27. The index of dissimilarity was 30. *JS* (1851–52), 594, 602–3, 616; *JHR* (1851–52), 796–97, 816–22.

28. *JHR* (1853–54), 16. Although the legislature stipulated a return of $375,000, some previous writers on the tax change of 1852 have been impressed, either that revenue increased so much under the new tax law or, alternatively, that it grew so little. Either way, they confuse the switch to ad valorem with the simultaneous, but separate, increase in total taxes. Simpson, *Howell Cobb*, 89; Thornton, "Fiscal Policy," 358–59.

29. *Compendium of the Seventh Census*, 338–93; *JHR* (1851–52), 453–54; see also Sellers, "Who Were the Southern Whigs?" Aside from the crucial support of urban interests, two other factors contributed to the enactment of Georgia's new tax system. Given the narrow margin in favor of passage—four votes of forty in the senate, nine of ninety-one in the house—passage may be attributed in part to the antebellum system of apportionment in the house, which was based on the federal ratio and gave the black

belt a perennial advantage over the upcountry, and in part to the 1851–52 legislative session's unusual party alignment.

30. *Savannah Republican*, 27 Dec. 1851 (italics in original).

31. Characterizing the ad valorem tax as antiplanter, some writers invert the politics of Georgia taxation and reverse the consequences of the new system for planters and yeomen: Woolfolk, "Taxes and Slavery," 197–98; Siegel, "Artisans and Immigrants," 224n. Regarding Georgia planters' tax burdens and slavery, see above, ch. 4. In Virginia and North Carolina, however, the switch to ad valorem shifted a portion of the tax burden to planters and comprised a concession to yeomen at the time of secession. See Shanks, "Conservative Constitutional Tendencies," and Butts, "'Irrepressible Conflict.'"

32. No statewide totals are available for years between 1849 and 1857. My figures for both years differ from those in Heath (*Constructive Liberalism*, 376) for reasons I explain in "FSSTNS," 363. And my percentages for 1857, though precise for categories of property, must be approximate for tax shares because of the $200 exemption.

33. The uneven distribution of wealth helps explain how so many rural property holders could pay so much more than the average tax increase.

34. CG (1850), 5; (1860), 50–55. For fuller evidence regarding changes in the distribution of the state property tax burden, including tabular statements of groups' and individuals' taxes, see "FSSTNS," tables 18–21 and maps 7–9 and 14–15. Per capita figures here, as elsewhere, are for white and black populations combined.

35. CG (1854), 6; (1855), 4; (1856), 8; (1857), 22; (1858), 42; (1859), 38; (1860), 36; Avery, *History of Georgia*, 71–72; Johnston, *Western and Atlantic Railroad*, 43–53, and table giving a financial summary of the Western and Atlantic, 1836–70, pp. 106–7. For a fuller description of state finance in late antebellum Georgia, see Wallenstein, "Rich Man's War," 18–23.

36. Governor Howell Cobb promised the legislature in 1853, "As soon as the public debt shall have been extinguished, we can with propriety reduce our taxes one half." *JS* (1853–54), 19.

37. "FSSTNS," 123–24; *Acts* (1853–54), 109–10. The 1854 act also made general the provisions of the 1850 and 1852 acts taxing the net annual income of only certain specified railroads.

38. *Compendium of the Seventh Census*, 190; *JHR* (1853–54), 16; CG (1857), 13; (1858), 6; (1859), 9; (1860), 8, 55. See fig. 4.

39. Others included Peterson Thweatt, who served as comptroller general beginning in 1855. Part of the large increase in Georgia's property valuation reflected tighter administration of the tax laws by local tax officers, largely a result of Thweatt's supervision. Avery, *History of Georgia*, 71; Parks, *Joseph E. Brown*, 53–89; CG (1857), 9–17; (1859), 6–17; (1860), 4–5, 12–20.

40. Parks, *Joseph E. Brown*, 83–84; Andrews, *South since the War*, 243.

CHAPTER 6. WHAT DISPOSITION SHALL BE MADE OF THE MONEY?

1. Fairlie, *Administration in New York State*, 27, 83. For a comparison of North and South, see Kaestle, *Pillars of the Republic*, ch. 8.

2. *JHR* (1858), 19.

3. The difference between total state revenue during the half-decade 1851–55 ($3,001,845) and the total for 1856–60 ($4,059,493) was $1,057,648. The difference between state treasury receipts from the Western and Atlantic Railroad for 1851–55 ($150,000) and 1856–60 ($1,213,500) was slightly larger, $1,063,500. Figures here, as elsewhere, are derived from the annual reports of the comptroller general.

4. Of the $500,000 investment in the Atlantic and Gulf, $50,000 was in cash instead of bonds. Heath, *Constructive Liberalism*, 276–92; *Acts* (1855–56), 158–61; CG (1860), 9–10.

5. CG (1859), 5; (1860), 9, 11.

6. Ibid. (1850), 7; (1860), 8–9.

7. Between 1840 and 1850, the reported number of illiterate whites over the age of twenty increased from 30,717 to 41,200; the percentage slipped from 19.1 to 18.9. Two-fifths of the illiterates were men. *Sixth Census: Compendium*, 48–51; *Seventh Census*, 355–58, 376; Constitution of 1777, art. 54, in Thorpe, *Federal and State Constitutions*, 2:784. For the regional distribution of white illiteracy, see Shryock, *Georgia and the Union in 1850*, map 4.

8. *Acts* (1821), 113–14; (1822), 4–5; Orr, *History of Education*, 69–81.

9. "Report of the Joint Select Committee of the Legislature of Georgia, of 1836, on Common School Education," in *MSR*, 27 Feb. 1838 (italics in original); see Mathews, "Politics of Education," 88–116.

10. *Acts* (1837), 94–99; (1838), 96–98.

11. Ibid. (1840), 61–65; (1843), 43–45; Orr, *History of Education*, 97–101.

12. *JS* (1847), 22–23, 66, 179; (1849–50), 217–18; *JHR* (1847), 519–20; *Savannah Daily Republican*, 12 Nov. 1853.

13. Report of George F. Pierce, Samuel K. Talmadge, and Leonidas B. Mercer (all leaders of higher education in Georgia), in Lewis, *Report on Public Education*, 11–23 (quotation, p. 12). For details regarding educational efforts of the 1850s, see Orr, *History of Education*, ch. 8.

14. *Acts* (1851–52), 3; David A. Reese, Alonzo Church, and George F. Pierce, "To the People of Georgia," in Lewis, *Report on Public Education*, 25–33 (quotations, pp. 26, 27).

15. Reese et al., "To the People of Georgia," in Lewis, *Report on Public Education*, 32.

16. Ibid., 32, 17–18.

17. A memorial to the legislature from "the friends of Public Education" in 1858 asked about the state railroad's profits: "Shall this fund be given to the people in the way of education, or by reducing the taxes?" By comparing average state taxes and annual costs of tuition, it demonstrated that "three-fourths of the voters of Georgia will derive more direct pecuniary benefit by devoting it to Free Education, than by relieving them entirely of taxation." Ibid., 35–39.

18. *Cassville Standard*, 29 Nov. 1855. See *JHR* (1855–56), 226–27.

19. *JHR* (1857), 23–26; (1858), 20–21; see McCash, *Thomas R. R. Cobb*, 112–13.

20. Mathews, "Politics of Education," 196–203.

21. *Acts* (1858), 49–51; (1859), 28–30. In 1860, 93 of Georgia's 132 counties levied school taxes. School tax rates ranged from 5 to 100 percent of the state tax, though only 8 of the counties levied school taxes as high as 50 percent of the state rate. Lewis,

Report on Public Education, 186–89. It is not clear that these figures represented a substantial increase in local support for schools. Gordon County, for example, which had levied a tax of 20 or 25 percent of the state rate in the preceding years, levied no school tax at all in 1859 or succeeding years. ICM, Gordon County (1850–72; mfm 135-60, GDAH).

22. *JHR* (1858), 386–87; *JS* (1858), 423–24.

23. CG (1859), 5; (1860), 8.

24. *JHR* (1834), 20.

25. UGA, *Catalogue* (1859–60), 5–8, 20; Coulter, *College Life*, 171, and map showing attendance by counties, facing p. 172.

26. Cobb, *Digest*, 1085; *Acts* (1849–50), 379–80; (1851–52), 288–92; (1855–56), 279–80 (quotation).

27. CG (1859), 23–26.

28. *Acts* (1830) 4–6; (1831), 6–7; (1841), 84; see Dyer, *University of Georgia*, 34–98. For a table showing the university's spendable income each year from 1799 to 1955, see Brooks, *University of Georgia*, 237–39.

29. *JS* (1855–56), 493–95; Coulter, *College Life*, 83.

30. *Acts* (1851–52), 300; (1855–56), 279; (1857), 22, 128; (1860), 66; CG (1859), 29–30.

31. In 1855, before state aid required scholarships, every one of the thirty-six Georgia students at the Savannah Medical College came from a black-belt county. *Acts* (1860), 66; Savannah Medical College, *Circular and Catalogue, of the Trustees, Faculty & Students* (Savannah, 1855), 3–4, 7.

32. Knight, *Documentary History*, 4:149–243; Franklin, *Militant South*, ch. 8.

33. *Acts* (1851–52), 6–8, 298–99.

34. In 1858, 129 cadets attended the school, 80 from Georgia, including 10 state cadets. All but 3 of the 80 came from Georgia's black belt or from Cobb County (where the institute was located) or Richmond County (Augusta). Even state cadets had to provide their own clothing, and the uniform alone cost more than $60. *Acts* (1851–52), 6–7; *Official Register of the Officers and Cadets of the Georgia Military Institute, Marietta, July, 1858* (Atlanta, 1858), 9–14, 19–21; Holland, "Georgia Military Institute," 225–47. The *Register* does not indicate which students were state cadets.

35. *JS* (1855–56), 100, 296; *Acts* (1855–56), 9–10.

36. *Acts* (1857), 63–64. See also *JS* (1851–52), 32–33; (1857), 21–22; (1860), 15–17.

37. *JHR* (1851–52), 830–31; (1857), 268–69, 373; see "FSSTNS," 157–58n.

38. *JHR* (1857), 26–27.

39. Ibid. (1858), 21–25; see also ibid. (1860), 10–13.

40. See below, ch. 15.

41. *JHR* (1858), 20; *Acts* (1858), 51.

CHAPTER 7. GREAT OBJECTS OF THE STATE'S CHARITY

1. Cobb, lecturing before the Milledgeville Lyceum in 1852, as quoted in Butler, *Georgia Academy for the Blind*, 15. Spending figures here, as elsewhere, are taken from annual reports of the comptroller general.

2. Best, *Deafness and the Deaf*, ch. 22; Best, *Blindness and the Blind*, ch. 21; Weiner, "Blind Man"; Dain, *Concepts of Insanity*, ch. 1; Grob, *Mental Institutions in America*, chs. 1–3.

3. Best, *Deafness and the Deaf*, 385–432.

4. Best, *Blindness and the Blind*, 306–33; Schwartz, *Samuel Gridley Howe*, 40–66.

5. Coulter, *John Jacobus Flournoy*, 40–42; *JS* (1834), 23–24; *Acts* (1834), 281–85; (1835), 23–24; Cochrane, "Early Treatment"; Bonner, *Milledgeville*, 81–82.

6. The 1850 census enumerated 294 insane whites. The asylum was also intended for white idiots—of whom 515 were reported—and epileptics. *Acts* (1837), 33–35; (1839), 21–22; (1840), 18; (1841), 153–57; (1842), 22–24; (1843), 9–10; (1845), 4; (1847), 4; (1849–50), 4; *Seventh Census*, 368. See also Hurd, *Institutional Care of the Insane*, 2:158–67, 4:417–18; Committee Reports in *Acts* (1838), 284–85; *JS* (1847), 226–30; (1849–50), 257–60.

7. LA (1859), 21–22, 26; (1862), 8; *Acts* (1853–54), 81; (1860), 13–14; CG (1859), 22–23.

8. Not every state had such an institution, and some paid Georgia to provide care for their citizens; one-third of the revenue from paying patients came from out-of-state. LA (1859), 20–23; (1860), 5.

9. Dix to [?], 16 Mar. 1850 (on the Mississippi River), in Dorothea L. Dix Letters, Houghton Library, Harvard Univ. (by permission of the Houghton Library); Marshall, *Dorothea Dix*, 112.

10. Dix to [?], 18 Feb. 1850 (from Jackson, Miss.); LA (1858–59), 10; Green to Dix, 25 Jan., 25 July 1859, in Dorothea Lynde Dix Papers, Houghton Library.

11. *Acts* (1834), 281–85; (1835), 330–32; (1838), 92–93; *JHR* (1838), 17–18; ADD, 34 (1899), 35–43. See also Cathy, "Georgia School for the Deaf."

12. ADD, 35 (1899), 35–43; *Acts* (1845), 25–26; (1847), 94–96; (1849–50), 18–19. The *Seventh Census* (p. 368) counted 208 "deaf and dumb" white Georgians and another 41 "deaf."

13. *Acts* (1851–52), 80–81; (1853–54), 30–31; ADD 2 (1851), 16; 6 (1855), 6–7; 7 (1856), 9–10, 15–16; *MSR*, 17 Nov. 1855.

14. ADD (1851), 7–8, 12–15; (1855), 7, 17; (1856), 6; *Acts* (1855–56), 139.

15. ADD (1851), 21; *Acts* (1853–54), 30–31.

16. *Seventh Census*, 368; Butler, *Georgia Academy for the Blind*, 5–9.

17. Butler, *Georgia Academy for the Blind*, 5–14, 44; "The Blind of Georgia," *Georgia Citizen* (Macon), 5 Apr. 1851, quoted in Butler, 6. The memorial is reprinted in full, ibid., 11–14.

18. Earlier the legislature had authorized the school for the deaf to admit blind students as well. *Acts* (1845), 26; (1851–52), 4–6; (1859), 16; CG (1859), 27–28; *JHR* (1855–56), 452–53; Butler, *Georgia Academy for the Blind*, 86.

19. Butler, *Georgia Academy for the Blind*, 89, 104, 114, 126.

20. Ibid., 44–132 (quotations from p. 48 and from GAB 3 [1854], 3); *Acts* (1860), 35. Most of the music and trade teachers were graduates and former teachers at the Pennsylvania or New York institutes for the blind.

21. Butler, *Georgia Academy for the Blind*, 67; ADD (1856), 15–16. Black and white populations are determined from the 1860 census.

22. *JHR* (1851–52), 720–21; (1853–54), 837.

23. *JS* (1855–56), 624–25.

24. PEN (1852–53), 9; (1860), 3. For brief histories see PEN (1872–73), 9–21, and Bonner, "Georgia Penitentiary." For an analysis of the penitentiary and of crime and punishment in three counties in antebellum Georgia—one urban, one black-belt, and one upcountry—see Ayers, *Vengeance and Justice*, 34–137.

25. Lamar, *Compilation*, 48, 564; *JHR* (1817), 6. See also McKelvey, *American Prisons*, chs. 1–2; Rothman, *Discovery of the Asylum*, chs. 3–4, 10.

Corporal punishment of whites largely ended with inauguration of the penitentiary in 1817, but it continued for blacks for another half century. Even before 1817, whipping had diminished as a punishment for whites. As early as 1806, for example, a statute barred the town of Watkinsville from imposing "corporal punishment (except [on] people of color)." Clayton, *Laws of the State of Georgia*, 305–6. Official treatment of wayward slaves changed, too; authorities' gradual abandonment of such physical mutilations as branding slaves or cropping their ears left the death penalty and whipping as the prevailing methods of corporal punishment. See below, ch. 8, and Flanders, *Plantation Slavery in Georgia*, 261.

26. Lamar, *Compilation*, 662; *Acts* (1831), 169–70; *JS* (1832), 14–15.

27. Presentments of grand jury, July 1832, SCM, Wilkes County (1826–39), 28 (mfm 42-70, GDAH).

28. *Acts* (1832), 140–41, 218–20, 323–28.

29. *JHR* (1843), 415–16, 490–91.

30. *Acts* (1832), 302; (1849–50), 403; (1851–52), 254; PEN (1852–53), 4–5; *JHR* (1853–54), 729. A portion of the 1816 act that inaugurated the penitentiary is identical to its New Jersey counterpart. Lamar, *Compilation*, 662; Rothman, *Discovery of the Asylum*, 93.

31. PEN (1852–53), 3, 19; (1854–55), 5.

32. *JHR* (1853–54), 244, 410, 727–34; *JS* (1853–54), 720, 839–40.

33. *JHR* (1855–56), 17–19, 168–72; *MSR*, 4 Mar. 1856.

34. *MSR*, 14 Dec. 1858.

35. Ibid., 1 Nov. 1859.

36. Heath, *Constructive Liberalism*, 9.

37. Orr, *History of Education*, 177–78.

38. Turner, *Frontier in American History*, 1–38; Webb, *Great Frontier*, 393–405.

CHAPTER 8. DEPRIVING A WHOLE RACE

1. 23 *GR* 65, 76, 80 (1857).

2. Single women and widows faced fewer restrictions, but their status was viewed as anomalous and presumably temporary. For a singular statement of the burdens that accompanied white men's prerogatives, see Barker-Benfield, "Spermatic Economy." See also Wyatt-Brown, *Southern Honor*, ch. 10; Boatwright, "Women in Georgia"; Friedman, *Inventors of the Promised Land*, chs. 4–5; Bloomfield, *American Lawyers in a Changing Society*, ch. 4.

3. For an analysis of Indian-white relations from twin market and paternalist perspectives, see Rogin, *Fathers and Children*. Eugene D. Genovese, in *Roll, Jordan, Roll*, analyzes slavery from a paternalist perspective.

4. Antebellum whites advocated "removal" of Indians in much the same terms used to promote the "colonization" of blacks. Thomas Jefferson, for example, advocated an Indian Territory in part as a sanctuary. Robert Goodloe Harper, one of the prime movers behind the American Colonization Society, articulated a similar rationale (he also offered others) for colonization. See Harper, letter [to the A.C.S.], 20 Aug. 1817, in Pease and Pease, *Antislavery Argument*, 18–32; Friedman, *Inventors of the Promised Land*, chs. 6–7; Jordan, *White over Black*, ch. 15.

From a paternalist perspective, whites established areas where Indians might have time to prepare for eventual entry into the competition and—a more prevalent conception—areas where Indians and blacks would be free of the disabilities that whites imposed, while whites would shake off the inconvenience of a nonwhite presence. In practice, colonization proved less coercive than either slavery or removal. Unlike slaves and Indians, free blacks had some choice in the matter, and colonization was attempted primarily in the private sector, much less so through public authority. See Gifford, "African Colonization Movement," 170, for an upward revision (to 1,149) of the number of black Georgians, most of them slaves, who left for Liberia before the Civil War.

5. McManus, *Negro Slavery in New York*, 174–96.

6. William Goodell, quoted in Friedman, *History of American Law*, 197.

7. Public policy and private practice supply ambiguous evidence on the physical treatment of slaves. Such treatment no doubt improved in the antebellum years, if for no other reason than slaveholders' material interests, given the rising demand for slaves together with the end of slave imports. To curtail cases of neglect, however, the general assembly directed owners to look after their slaves, particularly superannuated ones, to provide adequate food and clothing, and to desist from extreme overwork or barbarous attacks. See Cobb, *Compilation*, 610, 635–36; see also Rose, *Slavery and Freedom*, ch. 2.

8. Flanders, *Plantation Slavery in Georgia*, 22–32, 233–79; see also Wyatt-Brown, *Southern Honor*, ch. 15. At the close of the prewar period, Georgia law still stipulated that, for a slave convicted of manslaughter, "part of the punishment shall be branding in a conspicuous place with the letter 'M.'" Clark et al., *Code of Georgia* (1861), art. 919.

9. There was a charge of $4.00 per month for food during confinement: in the case of a slave, the owner paid; in the case of a free black, he paid his own fee if he owned property, and if not the county paid. Cobb, *Compilation*, 636.

10. *JS* (1853–54), 28; LA (1859), 15; (1860), 7.

11. 14 *GR* 185, 203 (1853).

12. An 1828 resolution of the Georgia legislature, quoted in 16 *GR* 496, 516 (1854); *Acts* (1859), 68–69; 4 *GR* 445, 458–60 (1848); *Compendium of the Seventh Census*, 63, 82. For other accounts of free blacks in antebellum Georgia, see Rogers, "Free Negro Legislation"; Flanders, "Free Negro in Ante-Bellum Georgia"; and Sweat, "Free Negro in Ante-Bellum Georgia." The 1859 act put the burden of proof on the free black defendant to demonstrate legitimate residence.

13. 23 *GR* 448, 465 (1857; source of quotation); 4 *GR* 75, 90–95 (1848); 6 *GR* 539, 546–49 (1849); 16 *GR* 496 (1854); 25 *GR* 109 (1857); *Acts* (1859), 68; see also Tushnet, *American Law of Slavery*, 218–28.

14. Zilversmit, *First Emancipation*, 124–37; Cobb, *Digest*, 990–93, 1008.

15. Cobb, *Digest*, 1008–9; *Acts* (1853–54), 533–34; Berlin, *Slaves Without Masters*, 316–40.

16. ICM, Bibb County, 1851–64 (mfm 88-68, GDAH), 42, 168, 400, 470. Pyle, "Free Negro in Bibb County," 20–21, drew my attention to these cases.

17. Cobb, *Digest*, 990, 1009–10; *JHR* (1858), 112–13.

18. Two other bills considered at the 1849–50 session provided for the "removal or sale" of free blacks under certain conditions and proposed "to banish and expel all free negroes, mulattoes, mustizoes, over and under certain ages, from and beyond the limits of the State." As with the votes on levying higher taxes on free blacks, black-belt counties tended more than white counties to support this anti–free black legislation. For example, Democrats from white counties voted 33–9 to table the banishment bill; black-belt Whigs voted 15–24 against the motion. *JHR* (1849–50), 71, 107, 147, 550–54, 583–84.

19. Clark et al. *Code of Georgia* (1861), arts. 4512, 4715; Cobb, *Compilation*, 589–90, 625; 14 *GR* 185, 202–3; see also Tushnet, *American Law of Slavery*, 139–56. T. R. R. Cobb grouped together the laws regarding "slaves, patrols and free persons of color" (*Digest*, 964–1021); Howell Cobb did the same with "Slaves and Free Persons of Color" (*Compilation*, ch. 34).

20. Cobb, *Digest*, 981, 1001. Savannah had a similar law; any person convicted of teaching a slave or free black to read or write might be fined $100 and, if black (slave or free), might be given up to thirty-nine lashes. Henry, *Digest*, 345.

21. 14 *GR* 185, 202, 205; Franklin, *From Slavery to Freedom*, ch. 11.

22. 16 *GR* 496, 505 (1854).

23. Dudley, *Reports*, 42–58; Cobb, *Digest*, 985–99, 1007, 1010–12; 14 *GR* 185, 204–6 (1853); 25 *GR* 430, 441 (1858); *Population in 1860*, 73–74.

In 1830, according to Carter G. Woodson, 61 free blacks in Georgia owned a total of 207 slaves (*Free Negro Owners of Slaves*, 3–4). For a warning, however, that some of Woodson's black-owned slaves may in fact have been owned by whites, see Jackson, *Free Negro*, 201–2n.

The definition of a "free person of color"—a free person at least one-eighth black, that is, one of whose great-grandparents had been an African—sometimes necessitated an exercise in genealogy to determine an individual's rights. All agreed, for example, that Joseph Nunez's mother had been white; his legal right to have sold some of his slaves turned on whether his father had been a Portuguese immigrant, an Indian, or a free black. 14 *GR* 185.

24. 14 *GR* 185, 205–6.

25. Cobb, *Digest*, 947, 993.

26. *Acts* (1849–50), 376; CG (1860), 8. The amount of taxable property required to generate the same amount of revenue as one poll is readily calculated as the poll tax, divided by the property tax per $1,000 ($0.65 in 1860), multiplied by $1,000.

27. Such lists from Chatham County contained 67 names in 1855, 113 in 1858. Cobb, *Digest*, 1062; *Savannah Daily Morning News*, 15 Dec. 1855, 25 Dec. 1858. White men, by contrast, if they owned no property and failed to pay their poll taxes, were simply listed as "insolvents"; they lost the right to vote in that year's elections, but they were not bound out to labor.

28. Henry, *Digest*, 420, 426; City of Milledgeville, Mayor and Aldermen, Minutes, 1855–76 (mfm 270-28, GDAH), 8 Oct. 1856.

29. Woodson, *Free Negro Owners of Slaves*, v–viii. See also Koger, *Black Slaveowners*, ch. 6; Halliburton, "Free Black Owners of Slaves."

30. The $0.44 figure for 1860 reflects a tax rate of $0.65 per $1,000 on an average reported slave value of $673. CG (1860), 7–8.

31. For examples from Alabama and South Carolina, see Wallenstein, "Rich Man's War," 21n.

32. See Parsons, "Anthony Odinsells."

33. 14 *GR* 185, 197–203.

34. A similar reply came from Lucinda Jackson, whose school, she said, had opened in Savannah seven years before. Bureau of Refugees, Freedmen, and Abandoned Lands, Records of the Superintendent of Education for the State of Georgia (mfm M799-20, NA).

CHAPTER 9. RICH MAN'S WAR

1. *CRSG*, 2:483. The governor's wartime messages to the Georgia legislature are quoted generously and placed in context in Parks, *Joseph E. Brown*.

2. Harlan Fuller to Joseph E. Brown, 1 May 1864, in Incoming Correspondence of Governor Joseph E. Brown (GDAH).

3. Ramsdell, *Behind the Lines*, 51–52; Ambrose, "Yeoman Discontent in the Confederacy"; Escott, "Southern Yeomen and the Confederacy"; Lonn, *Desertion during the Civil War*, 14; Wiley, *Life of Johnny Reb*, 337; Wiley, *Plain People of the Confederacy*, 65; *CRSG*, 2:488–92.

4. *CRSG*, 2:130, 483–84, 487–88.

5. Ibid., 1:56, 2:118–24, 483–88; Bowers, *Tragic Era*.

6. *CRSG*, 2:369. Given Georgia's social structure, even if every white male of military age had fought, and nearly all did, the war would inevitably be fought largely by nonslaveholders. See Wallenstein, "Rich Man's War," 17n.

7. *CRSG*, 2:761, 765.

8. *Acts* (1859), 11–12; (1860), 49.

9. My conclusions are based on appropriations acts of the legislature and reports of the comptroller general. For discussions of similar actions by other states in both South and North, see Ramsdell, *Behind the Lines*, 61–74; Bremner, *Public Good*, 74–78; Schneider, *Public Welfare in New York State*, 281–86.

10. *Report of the Executive Committee of the Georgia Relief and Hospital Association to the Board of Superintendents, With the Proceedings of the Board Convened at Augusta, Ga., October 29, 1862* (Augusta, 1862), 3–6, 26, 29; P. W. A., writing from Winchester, Va., in the *Savannah Republican*, 21, 22 Oct. 1862. See also Coddington, "Soldiers' Relief"; Bryan, *Confederate Georgia*, 29–31; Corley, *Confederate City*, 63–69.

11. *Report of Rev. J. O. A. Clark, One of the Executive Committee of the Georgia Relief and Hospital Association, to the Committee on Military Affairs of the House of Representatives of the Georgia Legislature* (Milledgeville, 1861), 5–7, 14; *JHR* (1861),

28–29; *Acts* (1861), 13; *Report of the Board of Superintendents of the Georgia Relief & Hospital Association to the Governor and General Assembly of Georgia, with the Proceedings of the Board, Convened at Augusta, Ga., October 5, 1864* (Augusta, 1864), 37.

12. Henry F. Campbell, Medical Director of Georgia Hospitals in Richmond, to Rev. Joseph R. Wilson, Chairman of Executive Committee of Georgia Relief and Hospital Association, "Report" (1 Nov. 1861), 3 (GSL); *Report of Rev. J. O. A. Clark*, 8–9; *Report* (1862), 6, 20–21; *Report of the Board of Superintendents of the Georgia Relief & Hospital Association . . . , October 28, 1863* (Augusta, 1863), 35–36, 46; *Acts* (1861), 36–38; (1862), 31–33.

13. *Report* (1862), 27–28, 37–39; (1863), 16, 45; (1864), 37–38, 43; *Acts* (1863–64), 75–76; (1864–65), 8; CG (1865), 79.

14. *Acts* (1862), 49–52; (1863–64), 69–74; (1864–65), 8, 62–65; *CRSG*, 2:398–406, 450–53; see also Coddington, "Social and Economic History," ch. 3.

15. For surveys of the actions of other Confederate states, see Ringold, *Role of the State Legislatures*, chs. 4, 6; Coulter, *Confederate States of America*, 424–35.

16. The governor directed the Commissary General in 1862 to provide one-half bushel free to each deceased soldier's widow and each widow who had lost a son in service, and to sell to the county inferior courts a half bushel for $1.00 for each family of a soldier in service (or widow with a son in service). At that time he estimated that it would be necessary to charge about $5.00 per bushel for the remainder. By late 1864, the cost to families who could afford to pay had more than doubled to $6.00 per half bushel plus costs of delivery. Counties purchased salt for soldiers' families out of their allocation of the state appropriation for those families. *Acts* (1861), 7–8; (1862), 6–8, 52; (1863–64), 8; *CRSG*, 2:223–31, 237–38, 277–82, 321, 413–31, 477–78, 519–20, 546–50, 692–97, 728–32, 3:246–48; CG (1862), 7–9; (1863), pt. 1, 7–9; (1864), pt. 1, 7–8; see Lonn, *Salt as a Factor*.

17. *Acts* (1862), 8–9; (1863–64), 8, 123; *CRSG*, 2:360–64, 395–98, 520–21, 666–67, 784–85, 856–57, 872.

18. The state spent $575,000, $515,000, and $105,000 (of $800,000), respectively, on the three appropriations. The counties refunded $200,000 of the cost of executing the second act. Because the Confederate army drew heavily on the surplus productions of Southwest Georgia, the state obtained much of the corn for its civilians from Central Alabama. And as the quartermaster general of Georgia explained in late 1864, the retreat of the Army of Tennessee prevented carrying out the full requisition even of the first act, "for by it many of the counties mentioned were left within the lines of the enemy. Fearing this, the counties farthest north were supplied first." *Acts* (1863–64), 66–68, 133; (1864–65), 8–9; CG (1864), pt. 1, 83; (1865), 7, 76; Quartermaster General, *Report* (Milledgeville, 1864), 18–21; *CRSG*, 2:503–4, 862–67, 873, 3:501–2.

19. *CRSG*, 2:170–71; *Acts* (1861), 14–15.

20. *CRSG*, 2:276, 374–75; *Acts* (1862–63), 33–34, 162; CG (1863), pt. 1, 86–89; (1864), pt. 1, 97–101; (1865), 66–67. Claims continued to come in after the war; see *JS* (1866), 164–66.

21. *CRSG*, 2:259–61, 267–69, 367–72, 504–7, 591–92; *Acts* (1862–63), 5–6, 25–28, 141–42.

22. Butler, *Georgia Academy for the Blind*, 141–42.

23. *Acts* (1855–56), 158–61; Atlantic and Gulf Rail Road Company, *Tenth Report* (1864).

24. CG (1865), 14.

25. To forestall further increases in the size of the house (to which each county elected at least one representative), the new constitution also made it more difficult for the legislature to create new counties. No "second revolution" moving Georgia "toward a patriarchal republic" is necessary to explain such changes. In 1859, in fact, Governor Brown, usually perceived as a spokesman for the upcountry, had proposed an even sharper reduction to 33 members in the senate, as well as a reduction to 152 in the house, in the interests of efficiency and economy. Moreover, the changes introduced in 1861 endured virtually intact through the constitutions of 1865, 1868, and 1877. McElreath, *Treatise on the Constitution of Georgia*, 276–80; Johnson, *Toward a Patriarchal Republic*, 168–72; *JS* (1859), 13–14; see the preamble to resolution no. 5 in *Acts* (1861), 132.

26. *Acts* (1859), 11, 14; (1863–64), 5–6, 121–22; (1864–65), 41–42.

27. CG (1865), 41–44; *Acts* (1863–64), 24–25; (1864–65), 50; "FSSTNS," 211n.

28. *CRSG*, 2:263, 769; *JHR* (1861), 32 (passage deleted in *CRSG*).

29. *Acts* (1861), 77; (1863–64), 25. For examples of county school taxes see "FSSTNS," 211–12n.

30. CG (1860), 9; (1864), pt. 1, 7; LA (1860), 11–13; (1862), 5 (quotation), 7–9; (1865), 11–14.

31. CG (1861), 108; (1862), 104; (1863), pt. 1, 69; (1865), 68; ADD 34 (1899), 47–51; *Acts* (1863–64), 123.

32. Butler, *Georgia Academy for the Blind*, 132–98 passim.

33. *Acts* (1860), 66; (1870), 455–56; *CRSG*, 2:773–74; Bryan, *Confederate Georgia*, 216–21; Temple, *First Hundred Years*, 197, 323, 339, 354–56; Holland, "Georgia Military Institute," 242–47.

34. CG (1863), pt. 1, 7; (1865), 40; *Acts* (1861), 65; (1862), 8; *CRSG*, 2:252–53, 395–98; Adjutant General, *Report* (Milledgeville, 1862), 18; Adjutant and Inspector General, *Report* (Milledgeville, 1863), 9, 29–30; Bonner, "Georgia Penitentiary," 316–17; PEN (1862), 3, 28; (1863), 3–6, 26; (1864), 3, 6, 27, 30; Avery, *History of Georgia*, 308–9; CG (1861), 115–34; (1862), 110–25; (1863), pt. 1, 75–79, 122.

35. *CRSG*, 2:830–32.

CHAPTER 10. RICH MAN'S FIGHT

1. *CRSG*, 2:372, 522–23 (amended to conform to *JS* [Nov. 1863], 31), 4:556.

2. *CRSG*, 2:99–100, 243–45; *Acts* (1861), 13; (1862), 14–15; (1863–64), 161.

3. Parks, *Joseph E. Brown*, 121–23. 226; *CRSG*, 2:254–56; *Acts* (1861), 18–19, 25–28; (1862–63), 136–37.

4. See below, ch. 17 and fig. 4.

5. *Acts* (1860), 13; (1861), 80; *CRSG*, 2:95; CG (1861), 7; (1863), pt. 1, 4–5.

6. *Acts* (1862–63), 56–57, 179–80.

7. *Acts* (1863–64), 79; (1864–65), 18, 69. Because the war ended before the tax measures for 1865 could be implemented, and federal authorities prohibited subsequent

execution of wartime laws, the next Georgia tax collected after 1864 was that of 1866. CG (1865), 26.

According to the literature on Georgia's Civil War finance, no annual property-tax rate exceeded one-quarter of 1 percent ($2.50 per $1,000 valuation). Bass began the tradition ("Civil War Finance in Georgia," 220). Relying on Bass, largely verbatim and without citation, Bryan made it a twice-told tale (*Confederate Georgia*, 56). Ringold perpetuated the error (*Role of the State Legislatures*, 90). According to Coleman, "The state's ad valorem taxes were raised only a little" (*History of Georgia*, 192). In fact, however, the source that Bass cites for his $2.50 figure (*MSR*, 23 Aug. 1864), gives the correct rate ($10.00) in a tax notice from the comptroller general and again in an editorial comment.

8. CG (1860), 7; (1864), pt. 2, 5. Previous accounts to the contrary, Georgia's state poll tax on free blacks did not rise to $25.00 during the war (Nelson, "Legislative Control," 34; Bryan, *Confederate Georgia*, 56). The measure that both authors cite (*Acts* [1861], 88) related not to state taxes but only to municipal taxes in the tiny town of Americus.

9. Lerner, "Money, Prices, and Wages in the Confederacy," 24.

10. Coulter, *Confederate States of America*, 219–26; "Appropriations," in *MSR*, 8 Nov. 1864. Public authorities took special pains during the war to increase tax valuations by seeing that taxpayers returned their property at sufficient values (Wallenstein, "Rich Man's War," 29n).

11. *Acts* (1863–64), 110–11.

12. CG (1862), 32–33; *Acts* (1862–63), 59–60. See also Foner, *Tom Paine*, ch. 5.

13. The income-tax act exempted profits of less than 20 percent. Rates ranged from one-half of 1 percent on profits of 20 percent to 5 percent on profits of 90 percent. Subsequent acts lowered the exemption to 8 percent, then raised it to 10, and levied rates ranging from 5 to 25 percent. *Acts* (1862–63), 176–78; (1863–64), 80–81; (1864–65), 65–67.

14. *CRSG*, 2:265; *Acts* (1862–63), 179 (see also p. 61); (1863–64), 79; see Wallenstein, "Rich Man's War," 30n.

15. *Acts* (1861), 127.

16. Ibid., 76–78, 123–29. The income tax was exclusively a state tax, as were taxes on railroads and banks.

17. ICM, Early County (mfm 31-49) and Gordon County (mfm 135-60), both in GDAH. Because the 1865 state tax act could not be implemented, no county levied a tax that year. Occupied by Union forces, Gordon County levied no tax in 1864 either; state taxes could not be collected in nineteen North Georgia counties that year. CG (1864), pt. 1, 5.

18. Many normal county expenditures were delayed until after the war. For example, the legislature repealed an 1859 act authorizing Ware County to levy an extra tax for a new courthouse. The tax was suspended for the duration of the war, and money already collected under the act was instead to "be applied to the support of indigent families of soldiers." *Acts* (1861), 128.

19. ICM, Early County, 21 July 1861. For greater detail on wartime county finance, see "FSSTNS," 228–34, table 10.

20. *Acts* (1861), 30, 76–78, 123–29.

21. *CRSG*, 2:503, 765.

22. Ibid., 503, 263–64 (amended as in *JS* [1862], 20). For a strikingly similar statement from Alabama, see the joint resolution in Alabama, *Acts* (called session, 1863), 50–51.

23. *CRSG*, 2:485–86.

24. Ibid., 769–72; Lonn, *Desertion during the Civil War*, 12–14, 114–17; Wiley, *Life of Johnny Reb*, 135, 210, 376; Wiley, *Plain People of the Confederacy*, 30–67.

25. *CRSG*, 2:369.

26. Representatives from the black belt voted 19–50 against cutting the tax to $7.50; those from predominantly white counties were divided almost evenly (30–33); and three others from unidentified counties voted 1–2. (For purposes of roll-call analysis, Georgia's counties are divided evenly here). Indicating the various undercurrents of dissatisfaction with the tax bill for 1864, the counterprotest endorsed the increased exemptions the measure provided; observed that, unlike previous tax measures, this one established a maximum tax rate; and argued that the poor should not have to fight and then after the war also pay heavy taxes to redeem the war debt. *JHR* (Nov. 1863), 198, 236–37, 245–47 (quotation, p. 245).

27. "Baldwin Grand Jury," in *MSR*, 8 Mar. 1864; *Rome Tri-Weekly Courier*, 5 Dec. 1863.

28. Delegates from predominantly white counties voted 46–20 in favor of raising the exemption only for soldiers' families; less enthusiastic, those from the black belt voted 37–27 (and two from unidentified counties voted 2–0). Other measures elicited patterns that proved variations on the theme of black belt versus upcountry. A protest of fifteen against passage of an income-tax act received most of its support from urban counties and the black belt. A North Georgia creation, the income tax passed by a margin of 69–51. *JHR* (Nov. 1863), 237, 243–44, 274; see also Wallenstein, "Rich Man's War," 36n.

29. On a procedural roll call, representatives of predominantly white counties voted 41–17 for the cotton acreage measure, while black belt delegates voted against it 27–47 (and legislators from unidentified counties voted 1–2). *JHR* (Nov. 1863), 218–19; *CRSG*, 2:368; *MSR*, 8 Mar. 1864; *Rome Tri-Weekly Courier*, 8 Dec. 1863.

30. *CRSG*, 2:375–76; Trexler, "Opposition of Planters"; Mohr, *On the Threshold of Freedom*, 120–89.

CHAPTER II. CONFEDERATE CONTEXT

1. George A. Trenholm to T. S. Bocock, Speaker of the House of Representatives, 9 Jan. 1865, in Thian, *Reports*, 425 (mfm, NA).

2. Percentages are based on current (not constant) dollars. Todd, *Confederate Finance*, 84, 120, 130–40, 156, 174.

3. *Acts* (1861), 127; see above, ch. 10.

4. Todd, *Confederate Finance*, 84, 120, 174. See also Schwab, *Confederate States of America*, esp. ch. 13.

5. Todd, *Confederate Finance*, 25–42, 121–25. See Jefferson Davis, Message to Congress, 7 Dec. 1863, in *War of the Rebellion*, 4th ser., 2:1035.

6. Todd, *Confederate Finance*, 130–36; Report of the Commissioner of Taxes, Nov. 1863, in Thian, *Reports*, 212–13.

7. *CRSG*, 2:113–15. See above, ch. 2.

8. Georgia derived its tax payment from the sale of bonds ($2,441,000), the issue of state treasury notes ($33,974), and interest from investing the proceeds awaiting the April deadline. *Acts* (1861), 79; *CRSG*, 2:245–48. For similar actions by other states in both the South and the North, see Todd, *Confederate Finance*, 133–36, and Smith, *United States Federal Internal Tax History*, 28–29, 38–40.

9. *CRSG*, 2:387, 390, 391 (corrected to conform to *JS* [Mar. 1863], 21).

10. *CRSG*, 2:498–500.

11. James M. Matthews, ed., *Public Laws of the Confederate States of America, Passed at the Third Session of the First Congress, 1863* (Richmond, 1863), 115–26; Todd, *Confederate Finance*, 136–56; *CRSG*, 2:378–95.

For an example of the exemptions, the February 1864 law exempted from all taxes, including the tax-in-kind, $500 worth of property of any head of family, plus $100 for each minor child, and $500 for each minor son in service or disabled (regarding the tax-in-kind) or for each son who died in the military (the other taxes). Every soldier in service or disabled, or the widow or minor children of a soldier who died in the military, received a $1,000 property exemption. James M. Matthews, ed., *Public Laws of the Confederate States of America, Passed at the Fourth Session of the First Congress, 1863–64* (Richmond, 1864), 209–11, 215–27.

12. As Brown explained his proposal: "The Act should provide that all taxes hereafter due the State for this year, shall be payable in Confederate Treasury Notes of the new issue, . . . to redeem the State notes payable in them. . . . As the State tax is not due till next fall, there will be an abundant supply of the new Confederate notes in circulation by that time to obviate all difficulty in obtaining them by our people to pay the tax." Todd, *Confederate Finance*, 109–14; *CRSG*, 2:595–600; see also *Acts* (1864–65), 23–24. Of Confederate treasury notes in circulation, the state accepted the "new issue only" in payment of state taxes in 1864. Executive Department, "Circular for 1864.— No. 3" (22 Aug. 1864), 8 (Keith M. Read Confederate Collection, EU).

13. Todd, *Confederate Finance*, 31–42; Christopher G. Memminger, "Instructions for the Agents for Collecting Subscriptions to the Produce Loan" (3 Jan. 1862), 1–3 (Keith M. Read Confederate Collection, EU).

14. Cobb to Christopher G. Memminger, Secretary of the Treasury, 29 May 1861, in Thian, *Correspondence*, 1861–62, 120 (mfm, NA); L. Fullilove, President of Bank of Whitfield, Dalton, Georgia, to Memminger, 27 June 1861, ibid., 168.

15. Thomas M. Harris et al., Committee, Sandersville, Georgia, to Jefferson Davis, 3 Oct. 1861, ibid., 359.

16. Memminger to "The Commissioners Appointed to Receive Subscriptions to the Produce Loan" (15 Oct. 1861), 1–4 (EU). See also Bryan, *Confederate Georgia*, 50–53.

Memminger insisted on paying the Confederacy's debts to the Western and Atlantic in Confederate bonds, but the governor refused to accept payment except in treasury notes, for "there is no law of the State authorizing the Superintendent to receive bonds and pay them into the Treasury; and . . . it is not the policy of the State, while she is in debt, to invest in the bonds of any other State or government." *CRSG*, 2:270.

If the Confederate government refused to help the planters, Governor Brown proposed that the Georgia state government provide them with relief. He advised a plan whereby the state would store cotton in warehouses and advance to its owners two-thirds of its value in treasury notes. The legislature instead authorized a private bank, the Cotton Planters Bank of Georgia. See *CRSG*, 2:100-102; *Acts* (1861), 18-20; Wallenstein, "Rich Man's War," 36n.

17. Vandiver, *Rebel Brass*, 89-96.

18. Todd, *Confederate Finance*, 156, 174; James A. Seddon, Secretary of War, to Jefferson Davis, 26 Nov. 1863, in *War of the Rebellion*, 4th ser., 2:1008-10; Matthews, *Public Laws Passed at the Third Session* (1863), 102-4; Vandiver, *Rebel Brass*, 93.

19. *War of the Rebellion*, 4th ser., 2:1008; *CRSG*, 2:505 (quotation), 514-16, 588-89.

20. Reuben S. Norton (Rome, Floyd County), Diary (mfm 2-23, GDAH), 8 Dec. 1863 entry; see Thomas, *Memoirs of a Southerner*, 43-48.

21. Johnson to G. A. Trenholm, Secretary of the Treasury, 16 Aug. 1864, in Thian, *Correspondence* (1863-65), 459-63 (mfm, NA). See also Bryan, *Confederate Georgia*, 90-93, 142; Christian, "Georgia and the Confederate Policy of Impressing Supplies."

22. *CRSG*, 2:840, 850 (italics in original).

23. *Acts* (1864-65), 32-34, 88-89. See also *Acts* (1863-64), 105-6, 109; P. A. Lawson, Griffin, Ga., to Jefferson Davis, 27 Dec. 1864, in *War of the Rebellion*, 4th ser., 3:967-68; *CRSG*, 2:850.

24. Georgia citizens paid $29.4 million under the tax acts of 1863 and 1864 (Thompson Allan, Commissioner of Taxes, to Trenholm, 28 Oct. 1864, in Thian, *Reports*, 384). They did not pay the War Tax of 1861—$2.5 million for Georgia—directly; the state sold state bonds, most of which were purchased by banks. But at the end of the war these bonds, as all other forms of public indebtedness contracted to prosecute the war, were worthless. The purchasing power absorbed through sale of the bonds was gone as irretrievably as it would have been had it been exchanged for tax receipts; the burden in Georgia was as large, but fell differently.

25. Todd gives aggregate Confederate figures of $62 million for the tax-in-kind and $500 million for unpaid certificates of indebtedness received for impressed property (*Confederate Finance*, 156, 174). His sources do not apportion individual states' shares. I have allocated 18 percent of these figures to Georgia. A minimal percentage would seem to be 13.4 percent, Georgia citizens' portion of the total assessed value for the War Tax of 1861. It would seem just as reasonable, though, to take 22 percent (Georgia's share of total assessed taxes in 1863 and 1864) or even 25 percent (the portion of total Confederate taxes that Georgia citizens actually paid in those two years). Ibid., 153. The 13.4 percent figure produces an aggregate of $107.3 million in Confederate taxes; the 25 percent figure, $172.5 million.

26. Bass doubles the state figure, but he includes private donations and, more important, underestimates the ratio of state to local taxes ("Civil War Finance in Georgia," 222). But even his estimate would leave Georgia's state and local taxes at less than one-fourth of the aggregate.

27. *CRSG*, 2:515-16 (adjusted to conform to *JS* [Nov. 1863], 27-28).

28. Escott, "Problem of Poverty" and *After Secession*.

29. Extract of letter from Isaac Winston, in Reuben S. Norton, Diary (mfm 2-23, GDAH), June 1863 entry (commas added).

30. Wallenstein, "Rich Man's War," 38n.

31. Quoted in Woodman, *King Cotton and His Retainers*, 258.

CHAPTER 12. POWER AND POLICY

1. Keller, *Affairs of State*, ch. 6. For detailed treatments of postwar Georgia, see Thompson, *Reconstruction in Georgia*; Nathans, *Losing the Peace*; Busbee, "Presidential Reconstruction"; Ward, "Georgia under the Bourbon Democrats."

2. Reid, *After the War*, 137.

3. Andrews, *South since the War*, 243–47; *CRSG*, 4:8–10, 38–45, 404–5, 414–15; Constitution of 1865, art. 1, par. 20, and art. 5, par. 1. See Perman, *Reunion without Compromise*, 68–81.

4. Thompson, *Reconstruction in Georgia*, 29; CG (1865), 11–18; *CRSG*, 4:85–95.

5. CG (1865), 13–14, 18–23.

6. Andrews, *South since the War*, 260–80. See also Busbee, "Presidential Reconstruction," 147–58; Carter, *When the War Was Over*, 70–82.

7. *CRSG*, 4:50–51; Perman, *Reunion without Compromise*, 76–77.

8. Andrews, *South since the War*, 267, 265.

9. Ibid., 261, 269.

10. Ibid., 266–68, 284.

11. *CRSG*, 4:42–44.

12. Andrews, *South since the War*, 272–74.

13. *CRSG*, 4:335–39, 402–4; Andrews, *South since the War*, 279–80, 377; Busbee, "Presidential Reconstruction," 158; *Augusta Daily Constitutionalist*, 15 Nov. 1865.

14. Andrews, *South since the War*, 286–87.

15. Jenkins, for his part, urged that federal troops remain to restrain white marauders. Jenkins to Maj. Gen. J. G. Brannan, 12 Apr. 1866, Jenkins Papers, Manuscripts Division, William R. Perkins Library, Duke Univ.

16. Bloom, "Georgia Election"; Nathans, *Losing the Peace*, ch. 5.

17. Ibid., ch. 9 and Epilogue; Gillette, *Retreat from Reconstruction*, 85–90; see also Drago, *Black Politicians*, 42–65.

18. I realize I am flying in the face of a generation's interpretation of Reconstruction. As Eric Foner has observed, "Recent studies . . . have been united by a single theme — continuity between the Old and New South." Foner, "Reconstruction Revisited," 84; Thomas, *Memoirs of a Southerner*, 5; see also the full title to Avery, *History of Georgia*.

19. "Freedmen's Affairs," *Sen. Ex. Doc.* no. 6, 39th Cong., 2d sess. (ser. 1276), 57–58; Jenkins to Tillson, Governor's Letter Book (GDAH); Report of Gen. O. O. Howard to the Secretary of War, 24 Oct. 1868, in *House Exec. Docs.*, 40th Cong., 3d sess. (ser. 1367), 1027, 1044; Busbee, "Presidential Reconstruction," 35–38, 47–53, 345–53; Cimbala, "Terms of Freedom," 460–90.

20. Eleven of the thirteen counties reporting more than 600 beneficiaries each were in North Georgia. Peterson Thweatt to Governor Jenkins, 30 Oct. 1866, Thweatt Papers (GDAH); *Acts* (1865–66), 12–13; *CRSG*, 4:284–85, 398–99, 495–97.

21. *Acts* (1866), 10–11; Busbee, "Presidential Reconstruction," 171–80.

22. In 1872 the Central Railroad received another $1,429. *Acts* (1865–66), 14, 320; (1866), 10, 12, 144–46, 217–18; (1868), 11–14; CG (1872), 19.

23. *Acts* (1866), 12; (1868), 13–14; (1872), 487; (1873), 13.

24. See below, ch. 15.

25. Constitution of 1877, art. 7, sec. 1; *Acts* (1879), 41–42; CG (1880), 50–80; see also below, Epilogue.

CHAPTER 13. FREEDMEN AND CITIZENS

1. 14 *GR* 185, 202, 205 (1853).

2. John M. McCrary Collection, Atlanta Historical Society, Atlanta, Ga. For a portrait of planters as their property rights in slaves vanished and their private authority over their laborers weakened, see Roark, *Masters without Slaves*.

3. Robert Higgs analyzes the conjunction of "a competitive economic system" and "a coercive racial system" (*Competition and Coercion*, 13). What economic security slavery had provided, as I see it, largely died with slavery, while much of the economic control lived on. See also Harris, "Plantations and Power"; Flynn, *White Land, Black Labor*, 1–114; Woodman, "Sequel to Slavery"; Cimbala, "Terms of Freedom," 126–91, 339–99; Engerrand, " 'Now Scratch or Die' "; Litwack, *Been in the Storm So Long*, chs. 7–8; Carter, *When the War Was Over*, ch. 5.

4. 20 *GR* 488, 512 (1856).

5. Cimbala, "Terms of Freedom," chs. 3, 8.

6. "Freedmen's Affairs," *Sen. Exec. Doc.* no. 6, 39th Cong., 2d sess. (ser. 1276), 57.

7. Constitution of 1865, art. 2, sec. 5, par. 5, in Thorpe, *Federal and State Constitutions*, 2:815.

8. Ibid.; *Acts* (1865–66), 6–8, 234–35, 239–40; Nieman, *To Set the Law in Motion*, 94–96; Cimbala, "Terms of Freedom," 513–56.

9. Clark et al., *Code of Georgia* (1861), arts. 716, 725, 4419, 4435, 4698; *Acts* (1865–66), 6–8, 234–35, 239–40.

10. 35 *GR* 75, 80 (1866). See Carter, *When the War Was Over*, ch. 6.

11. *Statutes at Large*, 14:27; *Acts* (1865–66), 239–40, 253–54. Before emancipation, the one-eighth rule had relevance only to free people; regardless of the fraction white, if mother were a slave, child was a slave.

12. 35 *GR* 145, 148 (1866). By no means did all southern free people of color feel they had benefited from the end of slavery; see Rankin, "Impact of the Civil War."

13. Cimbala, "Terms of Freedom," 556–73; Reidy, "Masters and Slaves," 213–18; Engerrand, " 'Now Scratch or Die,' " 215–21. See also Gutman, *Black Family in Slavery and Freedom*, 402–12; Alexander, *North Carolina Faces the Freedmen*, 112–19.

14. 35 *GR* 236–38 (1866).

15. Ibid.

16. Constitution of 1868, art. 1, sec. 22. For more extended treatments of the law of freedom, see Hyman, *A More Perfect Union*, 414–515; Fairman, *Reconstruction and Reunion*.

17. Constitution of 1868, art. 2, sec. 2; art. 6, secs. 1, 3.

18. See above, ch. 8, and below, ch. 17.

19. See above, ch. 4.

20. *Acts* (1865–66), 12; see above, ch. 9.

21. Cimbala, "Terms of Freedom," 481–90; ICM, Gordon County (1855–72), 211,

321 (mfm 135-60, GDAH). County support for black paupers did not end when Reconstruction did. According to census figures, white paupers numbered 1,036 in 1850; 1,196 in 1860; and 1,309 in 1870, when black paupers numbered 507. The total dropped from 1,816 in 1870 to 1,278 in 1880, of whom 550 (385 whites, 165 blacks) lived in almshouses and another 728 obtained "outdoor" relief. If the 728 displayed the same proportions as the 550, then most of the decade's decline occurred among whites (from 1,309 to 895 since the first postwar census, contrasted with a decline of only 14 to 483 among blacks), though blacks as a group continued to get proportionally less in relief funds (even if members of both races received similar stipends). *Compendium of the Ninth Census*, 531–35; *Compendium of the Tenth Census*, part 2, 1675.

22. ICM, Appling County (1857–82), 273, 328, 344, 367 (mfm 50-77, GDAH); "Inhabitants" (1870).

23. Butler, *Georgia Academy for the Blind*, 193–94.

24. Ibid., 192–93; *Acts* (1865–66), 56; LA (1865), 4–5.

25. *Acts* (1860), 14, 18, 35; (1865–66), 12–15; (1866), 8–9; *JS* (1866), 22.

26. Headquarters, Third Military District, Atlanta, to John Jones, state treasurer, Milledgeville, 26 Oct. 1867, in "Reconstruction File" (GDAH); *CRSG*, 4:598–99; Butler, *Georgia Academy for the Blind*, 224–31; ADD 12 (1868), 26; LA (1867), 35, 38 (supplemental report for fiscal 1868 appended to previous year's report); *JHR* (1868), 71, 85.

27. ADD (1868), 14–15. But see this text, 149. See also Rabinowitz, "From Exclusion to Segregation: Health and Welfare Services."

28. LA (1867), 8, 23; (1865), 8–9; "Report of the Majority and Minority of the Committee on the Lunatic Asylum" (1866), 7 (GSL).

29. Committee "Report," 8, 12; LA (1867), 7–9; (1868), 31–32, 35–36; *Acts* (1866), 8; (1868), 10; (1869), 10; (1870), 7–8.

30. *Acts* (1870), 8; (1871–72), 10; (1877), 113. For a table showing the numbers of black paupers, white paupers, and paying (or partially paying) patients admitted in various postwar years, see "FSSTNS," 273n.

31. ADD 12 (1867–68), 8–18, 26; 13 (1869), 14–15, 22; 14 (1870–71), 7–8, 25–28, 45; 21 (1879–80), 18, 23; *Acts* (1868), 12–13; (1869), 9; (1870), 8; (1871–72), 11; *JHR* (1870), pt. 1, 421.

32. Butler, *Georgia Academy for the Blind*, 191–264; GAB 24 (1875), 9; 25 (1876), 8, 13; 26 (1877), 5, 23–24 (reprinted ibid.); *Acts* (1866), 8; (1868), 10; (1869), 9; (1870), 8, 494; (1871–72), 10; (1883), 61.

33. GAB 24 (1875), 6–7; 26 (1877), 5, 23–24; 27 (1878), 9; 29 (1880), 4–5, 13–18; see below, chs. 14, 15.

34. *Acts* (1880–81), 16; GAB 31 (1882), 4–5; 32 (1883), 11–12; 34 (1885), 8.

35. ADD 16 (1873), 8–9; 18 (1875), 7–8; 19 (1876), 6; 22 (1881–82), 20; *Acts* (1876), 117–18; (1877), 7, 9; (1880–81), 10, 14.

CHAPTER 14. ALL THE CHILDREN OF THE STATE

1. *JS* (1858), 21–22; Atlanta Board of Education, *Report* 2 (1873), 12.

2. *Acts* (1865–66), 77–78; (1866), 58–64. For accounts of public education in postwar Georgia, see Orr, *History of Education*, chs. 9–10; Ward, "Georgia Under the

Bourbon Democrats," 435–65; Hollingsworth, "Education and Reconstruction in Georgia."

3. Constitution of 1868, art. 6.

4. *Acts* (1870), 49–61; Nathans, *Losing the Peace*, 141, 202.

5. CG (1865), 23–24; *Acts* (1865–66), 18–20; *JS* (1866), 17–18.

6. William King, conversation with Carl Schurz, 31 July 1865, in "Condition of the South," *Sen. Ex. Doc.* no. 2, 39th Cong., 1st sess. (ser. 1237), 83.

7. *Ninth Census*, vol. 1, *Population*, 450–53; "Social Statistics" (1870); Lewis, *Report on Public Education*, 186.

8. "Freedmen's Affairs," *Sen. Exec. Doc.* no. 6, 39th Cong., 2d sess. (ser. 1276), 180; Conway, *Reconstruction of Georgia*, 86; see above, ch. 8.

9. Bureau of Refugees, Freedmen, and Abandoned Lands, Records of the Superintendent of Education for the State of Georgia (mfm M799-20, NA).

10. Ibid.; see Wolfe, "Women Who Dared," 119–23. See also Wallenstein, "Rich Man's War," 24n.

11. *JS* (1868), 78–79; see Jones, *Soldiers of Light and Love*.

12. Peabody Education Fund, *Proceedings*, 5 vols. (Boston: Press of John Wilson and Son, 1875–1900), 1:61.

13. Peabody Education Fund, *Proceedings*, 1:61–83. Brown used similar arguments (Atlanta Board of Education, *Report* 1 [1872], 25; 2 [1873], 11–12). So did Orr (SCS 3 [1874], 12–17, 19–20, 24).

14. Peabody Education Fund, *Proceedings*, 1:86, 80.

15. Ibid., 1:56, 203–5; *Reports of the Superintendent of the Public Schools, of Columbus, Georgia, for Years 1868 to 1874* (Columbus, 1874), 3, 19.

16. Peabody Education Fund, *Proceedings*, 1:137, 205, 305; Bowden, *Two Hundred Years of Education*, 251–65.

17. *Public Schools of Columbus*, 62–65, 87.

18. "Report of the Committee on Public Schools to the City Council of Atlanta, Georgia" (1869), 11.

19. Thornbery, "Development of Black Atlanta," ch. 3; Racine, "Atlanta's Schools," chs. 1–3; Taylor, "From the Ashes," ch. 5.

20. Atlanta Board of Education, *Report* 1 (1872), 6–8, 18, 22–23; 2 (1873), 28, 34–36; see Rabinowitz, "Half a Loaf."

21. DuBois, "Reconstruction and its Benefits"; Knight, *Public Education in the South*, 317.

22. Janes, *Hand-Book*, 179.

CHAPTER 15. HIGHER EDUCATION
FOR A NEW SOUTH

1. Curry, *Blueprint for Modern America*, 108–15.

2. In 1870 the university received an extra $8,000 for 1865. UGA, BTM (1858–71), 103 (typescript, UGA); *JS* (1865–66), 93–95; *CRSG*, 4:268, 376; *JHR* (1865–66), 268; *Acts* (1821), 69–70; Clark et al., *Code of Georgia* (1861), art. 1134; (1867), art. 1215; CG (1866), pt. 2, 80; (1869), 131; (1870), 129.

3. *JHR* (1866), 17–18; *Acts* (1865–66), 5; (1866), 64–65; *Statutes at Large*,

12:503–5. For a partial explanation of the delay, see Le Duc, "Agricultural College Land Scrip."

4. Most students under the act, academically unprepared for college courses, entered preparatory classes at the schools they attended. *Acts* (1866), 143–44; Caswell, "Bowdon College," 84.

5. *Acts* (1868), 12; (1869), 11, 22; *JHR* (1868), 72, 265; CG (1868), n.p.; (1869), 99, 113, 116–18; Emory College, BTM (1836–71), 330–73 (Ms., EU; quotation, p. 332). See also Lide, "Five Georgia Colleges," 93–101; Bullock, *Emory University*, 150–52; Tankersley, *Old Oglethorpe*, 117–21; Dowell, *Mercer University*, 116–17 (a negative assessment); Caswell, "Bowdon College," 82–90; Roberts, "Georgia's Civil War G.I. Bill."

6. Benjamin C. Yancey to David C. Barrow, 12 Aug. 1867, UGA Trustees' Correspondence (UGA); UGA, BTM (1836–71), 136; Pearce, *Benjamin H. Hill*, 142–60; Hull, *Historical Sketch*, 89–90, appendix; Coulter, *College Life*, 261–64. For texts of Hill's speech and "Notes," see Hill, *Senator Benjamin H. Hill*, 294–307, 730–811.

7. Suggesting that the university seek independence from both the military and "unfriendly legislatures," Trustee Joel A. Billups advised Mitchell that large private donations might be "the most favorable . . . general advertisement a Northern merchant could have among Southern merchants." Harris to Barrow, 24 Aug. 1867; Jenkins to Mitchell, 16 Aug. 1867; Lipscomb to Mitchell, 18 Aug. 1867; Billups to Mitchell, 27 Aug. 1867, in UGA Trustees' Corr. (UGA); UGA, BTM (1858–71), 151, 167; Emory College, BTM (1836–71), 344.

8. The university received $96,000 in state 8 percent bonds, $56,000 in Georgia 7 percent bonds, and credit for $90,202.14 left "uninvested" in the state treasury, from which it received annual appropriations of $6,314.14 as interest. Contemporary sources give figures with minor discrepancies. *JHR* (1872), 23, 125–26; (1873), 18–19; (1897), 209–19, 228–46; UGA, BTM (1858–77), 350, 387–411; Governor's Letterbooks (1872), 10–13, 24–38, 201–17; Brooks, *University of Georgia*, ch. 5.

9. Saxton "to all the friends of the true reconstruction . . . ," 3 May 1868 (Edmund Asa Ware Papers, AU).

10. *Acts* (1870), 8; CG (1870), 138; (1871), 111; William McKinley to David C. Barrow, 10, 13 Oct. 1870, in David C. Barrow Papers, UGA; H. M. Turner, "The Agricultural Land Scrip and the Colored People," *Savannah Morning News*, 6 Jan. 1874; see "The State House," *MSR*, 1 Nov. 1870. See also Range, *Negro Colleges*, 21–22, 35–36; Bacote, *Atlanta University*, chs. 1–2.

11. *Savannah Morning News*, 6 Jan. 1874; Ware to Smith, 9 Apr. 1872; Ware to Prof. W. L. Brown, 9 Apr. 1872 (Edmund Asa Ware Papers, AU).

12. UGA, BTM (1858–77), 449 (22 Oct. 1872); *Acts* (1873), 10; *JHR* (1874), 395; Bacote, *Atlanta University*, 70–75.

13. *JHR* (1874), 395–99.

14. *Acts* (1874), 32–33.

15. *Statutes at Large*, 17:19.

16. See UGA, BTM (1858–77), 343–51, 421–23.

17. *Acts* (1875), 11–12; (1878–79), 91–92, 97–98; (1880–81), 100–101; (1888–89), 2:123–24; Dismukes, "North Georgia College"; UGA, BTM (1878–86), 414, 452–53, 484, 578–80; (1887–1914), 282–87. See also Hull, *Historical Sketch*, 96–98; Ward, "Georgia under the Bourbon Democrats," 466–78.

18. UGA, BTM (1878–86), 578–80.

19. *JHR* (1857), 26–27; *JS* (1858), 22–24; UGA, *Catalogue* (1858–59), 20; (1866–68), 46 (GSL).

20. UGA, BTM (1858–71), 154, 262, 291–92, 306–32; (1872–77), 373–74, 450–51, 458; *Acts* (1880–81), 16.

21. *Acts* (1875), 11–12; (1880–81), 18; (1882–83), 16; (1886–87), 10; (1888), 11; UGA, BTM (1878–86), 452–58; Brooks, *University of Georgia*, ch. 6.

22. *Acts* (1884–85), 69–72; (1888), 11; (1888–89), 2:10–14; (1890–91), 1:13, 126–27; (1892), 12–13; (1893), 67; (1894), 11–12; (1896), 13–14. See also Orr, *History of Education*, 346–54; McMath et al., *Engineering the New South*, chs. 1–2.

23. SCS 3 (1874), 30–31 (a nearly identical observation, probably Orr's source, appears in "Report of Visitors," 1874 [AU]); 4 (1875), 24–26; 5 (1876), 9–13; Bacote, *Atlanta University*, 75–78.

24. *Acts* (1886–87), 2:901; *JHR* (1887), 17–20; (1888), 33–36.

25. CG (1887), 99; (1888), 93; Bacote, *Atlanta University*, chs. 3–4 (*Telegraph* quotation, p. 109).

26. *Acts* (1890–91), 1:117.

27. *Statutes at Large*, 26:417–19.

28. *JHR* (1890–91), 52–56; (1892), 43–44; (1895), 64–65; *Acts* (1890–91), 1:114–17; *Announcement and Catalogue of the Georgia State Industrial College, 1898–1899* (Atlanta, 1899), 59; Range, *Negro Colleges*, 59–65;

29. *JS* (1834), 20. For prewar background, see above, ch. 6.

CHAPTER 16. RAILROADS, DEBT, AND RECONSTRUCTION

1. *CRSG*, 4:396–97, 404–5.

2. Of the total $3.6 million, $200,000 was to procure corn for the destitute, $600,000 to pay Georgians' share of the Civil War federal land tax, $830,550 to fund past-due bonds and interest, and $2,000,000 to repair the Western and Atlantic and pay for other appropriations. Not all the new bond issue represented increased public debt (a small portion was used to take up past-due prewar bonds), but most of the amount for debt service went for interest payments that had accumulated through the war. No bonds, Governor Charles J. Jenkins reported at the end of 1866, were sold at a greater discount than 10 percent, but most were sold at below par. The state issued $3.0 million in bonds during the Jenkins administration and, when Congress suspended collection of the federal land tax, used the remainder to fund prewar bonds and interest that came due. *Acts* (1865–66), 12–13, 18–20; *JS* (1866), 11–13; CG (1866), pt. 1, 8–9; "FSSTNS," 309n.

3. For discussions of railroads and the state in Reconstruction Georgia, see Thompson, *Reconstruction*, 238–54; Nathans, *Losing the Peace*, 206–21; Conway, *Reconstruction of Georgia*, 202–15.

4. Somers, *Southern States since the War*, 87; James Barrow to Col. David C. Barrow, 21 May 1872, Col. David C. Barrow Papers (UGA). Summers emphasizes this theme in his South-wide *Gospel of Prosperity*.

5. *MSR*, 12 Jan. 1869.

6. CG (1866), pt. 1, 9–10; (1868), 7–8; *JS* (1868), 301.

7. See Phillips, *Transportation in the Eastern Cotton Belt*, 356–59; Heath, *Constructive Liberalism*, 276–88; Dixon, "Central Railroad," ch. 6.

8. Klein, "Southern Railroad Leaders."

9. *Atlanta Daily Intelligencer*, 27 Jan. 1869. Horace Mann Bond pioneered this kind of approach ("Social and Economic Factors in Alabama Reconstruction").

10. Governor Rufus B. Bullock, himself from Augusta, served as president of the Macon and Augusta before his elevation to the governorship. Dixon, "Central Railroad," ch. 9; Henry V. Poor, *Manual of the Railroads of the United States, for 1868–69* (New York: H. V. and H. W. Poor, 1868), 222.

11. *Acts* (1866), 127–28.

12. Had the governor vetoed the Macon and Brunswick bill, the legislature might conceivably have overridden his veto; the vote for passage was 93–56 in the house (there was no roll call in the senate). Before passing bills to assist the other three railroads (by margins of 72–54, 72–43, and 76–56), the house had first rejected them and then voted to reconsider them. Two other bills, to assist the Macon and Augusta and the Wills Valley Railroads, failed to pass the house. The senate voted 12–11 in an effort to obtain the two-thirds majority necessary to overcome Jenkins's veto of the Savannah, Griffin, and North Alabama bill; the house voted 47–41 in a similar effort concerning the Muscogee bill. *JHR* (1866), 108–9, 156–61, 181–87, 244–46, 263–66, 333, 380–84, 404, 417–18; *JS* (1866), 163, 264, 445–49.

13. Constitution of 1868, art. 3, sec. 6, par. 5.

14. *JS* (1868), 248–49, 259–60.

15. *Acts* (1868), 141–47; (1869), 147–57; (1870), 274–367; "Acts . . . Passed in . . . 1870, but Omitted in the Compilation Published by Authority," appended to *Acts* (1870), 5–12. Goodrich treats every southern state ("Public Aid to Railroads" [pp. 417–20 on Georgia]); and see Summers, *Gospel of Prosperity*, esp. 75–77.

16. Returning a bill to aid the Memphis Branch Railroad, Bullock warned a Democratic house of representatives against state endorsement of the bonds of redundant railroads, and he explained his veto on the grounds that the Memphis Branch threatened the profits of the state's own Western and Atlantic Railroad. *JHR* (1869), 522–24. The legislature passed, and Bullock approved, a similar bill to aid that line the following year.

17. "House of Representatives," *Atlanta Constitution*, 1 Sept. 1870.

18. *Acts* (1869), 152–53; (1870), 310–12; Thompson, *Reconstruction*, 229–38.

19. Scott, *Repudiation of State Debts*, 97–107; Constitution of 1877, art. 7, secs. 5, 6, 11. Many railroads, though they received authorization, failed to secure endorsement of their bonds; two others, though they qualified for assistance, declined the offer. Thompson, *Reconstruction*, 318–19.

20. *Acts* (1870), 347–50; (1876), 11, 123–24; Janes, *Hand-Book*, 175; *JHR* (1878–79), pt. 1, 30–31; CG (1876), 15; (1881), 9.

21. Janes, *Hand-Book*, 174; *Acts* (1866), 127–28; (1870), 336–37; (1875), 371–72; *JHR* (1877), 29–30; (1878–79), 28–30; (1880–81), pt. 1, 25–28.

22. *Acts* (1877), 29–31; *JHR* (1878–79), 31–32.

23. Ward, "Georgia under the Bourbon Democrats," 324–26; CG (1890), 4.

24. Brock, *Investigation and Responsibility*, 203–6; Ward, "Georgia Under the

Bourbon Democrats," 358–70; Cherry, "Georgia Railroad Commission"; Ferguson, *State Regulation of Railroads*, 95–107.

25. *JHR* (1878), 32–35.

26. *JHR* (1894), 25–27; (1895), 50–55; (1899), 42–46; (1900), 51–52; CG (1914), 48. See also McGuire, "Athens and the Railroads."

27. *JHR* (1855–56), 19–22; (1857), 15–17; (1858), 26.

28. *Acts* (1868), 145–47; (1870), 366–67; CG (1876), 15; *Treas.* (1899), 21.

29. *JHR* (1872), 31, 405; Parks, *Joseph E. Brown*, ch. 18.

30. *JS* (1869), 470–73. The quotations are from ch. 12, above.

CHAPTER 17. A TAX BASE WITHOUT SLAVES

1. "An Account of the Proceedings of the Legislature by a Member," *MSR*, 27 Feb. 1866.

2. *Acts* (1864–65), 18–19, 69; CG (1865), 5, 7.

3. CG (1865), 9–12.

4. *Acts* (1865–66), 253–54. See also "FSSTNS," 308n.

5. After allowing for the standard $200 and other property exemptions, together with tax officers' commissions, the $1.67 tax rate could not generate $350,000; a $2.00 rate might have sufficed. (In constant dollars, the 1866 valuation was less than one-fourth the 1860 figure.) CG (1866), pt. 1, 27.

6. *Acts* (1866), 164–69; Executive Minutes (1866–70), 98, 256. Executive Minutes (as well as tax lists and inferior court minutes) cited in this chapter are available on microfilm at GDAH.

7. *Acts* (1868), 152–55; (1869), 159–63; (1870), 431–33; *MSR*, 12 Jan., 2 Feb. 1869; Executive Minutes (1866–70), 400, 558; (1870–74), 397, 679.

8. Levied on the property listed in the 1867 tax digests, the convention tax was to be collected by 1 May 1868. Executive Minutes (1866–70), 116; (1874–77), 130, 413, 723; (1877–81), 234, 389, 554, 728; *Acts* (1872), 62–64; (1873), 16–17; (1887), 19–20; SCS, 3 (1874), 6–9; Ward, "Georgia under the Bourbon Democrats," 316.

9. The other major item of expenditure in peacetime, administrative costs of government, remained fairly constant, with various years in the late 1850s, the late 1860s, and the early 1870s not greatly different. But there was one exception. The legislative session of 1870, at $9.00 per day per member, ground on with occasional breaks from January to October and cost two to three times what the 1868 and 1869 sessions each had. Republicans were praying that elections might be postponed. CG (1868), 11; (1869), 13; (1870), 13.

10. Legislators' per diem at each session from 1865–66 through 1870 was $9.00, an amount reduced to $7.00 in 1871 and, finally, to $4.00 according to the Constitution of 1877 (art. 3, secs. 4, 9), which also established biennial sessions. *Acts* (1865–66), 11; (1870), 6; (1871–72), 8.

11. CG (1875), 7; (1890), 8–9; (1920), 15; McElreath, *Treatise on the Constitution*, 408.

12. CG (1900), 4.

13. The theme of displacement of the tax burden, a direct consequence of emancipa-

tion and a central feature of the political economy of Reconstruction, has received little attention, at least until recently, but see Brandfon, *Cotton Kingdom of the New South*, 40–45; "FSSTNS," 303–33 (esp. 314–21), 380–83; and Thornton, "Fiscal Policy" (esp. 366–71). For another statement of the model offered here, see Wallenstein, "Rich Man's War," 39n.

14. CG (1860), 49; (1866), pt. 2, 10; (1872), 36.

15. Sellers, "Economic Incidence," 191; CG (1860), 50–55; (1866), pt. 1, 20–25. See "FSSTNS," map 17.

16. Tax digests, Columbia County, 1860 and 1866 (mfm 91–210).

17. *Acts* (1865–66), 253–54; for prewar rates, see above, ch. 4.

18. Wallenstein, "Rich Man's War," 39.

19. Constitution of 1868, art. 1, sec. 29. But see below, ch. 18, for street taxes.

20. Kousser, *Shaping of Southern Politics*, 210. The David C.Barrow Papers (UGA) contain letters from tax collector to planter demanding payment of freedmen's poll taxes for 1866–67.

21. Ibid., 65–68, 209–23; Constitution of 1877, art. 7, sec. 2, par. 3; *Acts* (1882–83), 120.

22. *Acts* (1871–72), 277; (1874), 104; (1875), 117–18.

23. CG (1914), 13, 15. See also DuBois, "Negro Landholder of Georgia," 665, 676, 682.

24. *JS* (1884), 23–25.

25. Ward, "Georgia under the Bourbon Democrats," 320–26.

26. ICM, Dooly County (1863–74), Oct. 1866, Nov. 1867 (mfm 182–46); Early County (1851–82), 17 Oct. 1866 (mfm 31–49); *Acts* (1865–66), 230, 257–58; ICM, Franklin County (1864–75), 82, 119–20, 164–65, 199, 241; "FSSTNS," 326–27n.

27. *Acts* (1865–66), 88–89; ICM, Meriwether County (1860–77), 7 Sept. 1867, 22 Jan. 1869 (mfm 13-26); Early County, 17 Oct. 1866.

28. ICM, Franklin County, 31 Oct. 1867, 30 Oct. 1869; Meriwether County, Oct. 1866, 7 Sept. 1867.

29. ICM, Jones County, 1 Feb. 1869; SCM, Hancock County (1858–1868), 478 (mfm 107-29). For similar refusals by Fulton and DeKalb counties, see Garrett, *Atlanta and Environs*, 1:708–9.

30. ICM, Early County, 17 Oct. 1866, 7 Oct. 1867, 4 Oct. 1869, 20 Oct. 1870; Columbia County, 3 Sept. 1867.

31. ICM, Whitfield County, 1 Oct. 1866, 3 Sept. 1867; *Acts* (1866), 27–30, 51–52; (1868), 162–63; (1869), 171–81; (1870), 438–59; (1871–72), 215–19.

Some counties sought and received legislative sanction to invest in local railroads. Provided the citizens of each county first consented in a referendum, the legislature in 1866 authorized Thomas and Mitchell counties to issue bonds and take stock in the South Georgia and Florida Railroad, a line the state later aided. Four years later, the accepted method of publicly promoting railroad construction called for endorsing a company's bonds (see above, ch. 16). In 1870 the legislature authorized Houston County to endorse up to $150,000 of the bonds of the Fort Valley and Hawkinsville Railroad, a company that the state also offered to assist (though it never did so). *Acts* (1866), 31–32; (1870), 453–54.

32. Mitchell, *Gone with the Wind*, 519–24, 536–47. For county tax revenue figures as well as state aggregates for state, county, and municipal taxes in 1880 and 1890, see

Compendium of the Tenth Census, pt. 2, 1524–26; *Wealth, Debt, and Taxation: 1890*, pt. 2, 125–28. For greater documentation regarding county taxes during Reconstruction, see "FSSTNS," tables 10 and 29.

33. *JS* (1865–66), 96–97. See Alexander, *North Carolina Faces the Freedmen*, 51–52.

34. Beginning in 1874, the poll tax remained in the counties in which it was collected (*Acts* [1874], 32). Allocation of the proceeds between black schools and white ones depended on the actions of local authorities. The largest portion of the state education fund derived from the rental of the Western and Atlantic. Blacks had reason to feel that they had contributed their collective share to the costs of constructing the state railroad (see above, chs. 4, 8).

CHAPTER 18. CONSCRIPTS, CONVICTS, AND GOOD ROADS

1. *Butler v. Perry, Sheriff of Columbia County, Florida*, 67 Fla. 405 (1914); 240 U.S. 328, 331, 333 (1916).

2. For antebellum road duty, see above, ch. 4. For surveys of state policy, see Jenks, "Road Legislation," 26 and app. 2, and Brindley, *Road Legislation*, 265–350. For examples of court cases, see *In re Dassler*, 35 *Kansas Reports* 678 (1886); *Dennis v. Simon*, 51 *Ohio State Reports* 233 (1894); *State v. F. M. Sharp*, 125 *North Carolina Reports* 628 (1899); and *State v. Wheeler*, 141 *North Carolina Reports* 589/773 (1906).

3. Atlanta had required male residents aged twenty-one to fifty to work five days or pay three dollars. McCallie, *Preliminary Report*, 115, 130–32, 143–44, 177, 172, 123, 239; *Acts* (1935), 159–60; (1951), 3022–24; *Code of the City of Atlanta of 1942* (Atlanta: Harrison, 1942), art. 87–110.

4. M. Arnold, Road Commissioner, to William L. Coleman, Jr., 30 Jan. 1893, in Coleman Family Papers, UGA. Robert C. McMath, Jr., brought this item to my attention.

5. McCallie, *Preliminary Report*, 135, 167, 212.

6. Schinkel, "Negro in Athens and Clarke County," 83. Given the plantation elite's political domination, at state and local levels alike, the boundaries between private and public proved blurred. One plantation diary includes entries in 1879 of "picking cotton," "gathering corn," and "working the road," with no explicit indication whether the latter entry related to a public obligation (official road duty) or private maintenance (just another plantation chore)—though on successive days, hands "Got timber for bridge abutment," were "at work on bridge abutment," and "worked road": 1879 Diary, 29 July, 16–18 Oct. 1879, David C. Barrow Papers (UGA).

7. *Acts* (1865–66), 283–84, 273.

8. City of Milledgeville, Mayor and Alderman, Minutes (1855–76), 157–58, 262–63 (mfm 270-28, GDAH).

9. Engerrand, "'Now Scratch or Die,'" 197–99, 213; Constitution of 1868, art. 1, sec. 22; but see "FSSTNS," 290n.

10. Milledgeville, Mayor's Court, Minutes (1854–70), 14 May 1864, 17 Aug. 1865 (mfm 200-6, GDAH).

11. Busbee, "Presidential Reconstruction," 341–45; *Acts* (1865–66), 233–34.

12. For another example, Americus could impose a jail sentence of up to twenty days for violating a local law, and inmates usually worked the streets. Any resident of Americus who failed to pay his city taxes could be required to work his tax off on the streets, at $0.50 per day if the city provided his rations, at $1.00 if he supplied his own. *Acts* (1865–66), 268; (1866), 179.

13. The city of Tifton provides a turn-of-the-century example of the connections among street tax, chain gang, and political rights. Male inhabitants might be required to work fifteen days or pay a commutation tax of $5.00. Refusal either to pay the tax or to work it off carried any one of three penalties—a $25.00 fine, thirty days in the guardhouse, or thirty days in the city's chain gang. To vote in a municipal election required that, in addition to qualifying to vote for members of the general assembly, one have paid all state and city taxes, "including street tax." *Acts* (1902), 646, 650–51. This $5.00 tax was much heftier than the $1.00 poll tax levied under state law, the only one to appear in most accounts of postwar developments.

14. Garrett, *Atlanta and Environs*, 1:720.

15. The act stipulated that the two categories of workers—residents who did not pay the commutation tax and convicts in the chain gang—be worked separately. *Acts* (1890–91), 1:135–38; McCallie, *Preliminary Report*, 20–22. Residents of cities and towns would pay the new property tax, if their county imposed it, and they would continue to satisfy their town's street tax requirements, but they would continue to be exempt from working the roads outside their town or paying the county's commutation tax.

16. McCallie, *Preliminary Report*, 200–201.

17. Ibid., 193, 117, 171.

18. Ibid., 121–22, 177, 138 (quotation), 204, 235 (quotation).

19. Ibid., 246 (quotation), 127, 236, 234 (quotation); McCallie, *Second Report*, 11.

20. McCallie, *Preliminary Report*, photo facing p. 256 (quotation), 225, 160, 256–57.

21. Ibid., 193.

22. *JS* (Feb. 1865), 14–15; "The Governor's Message," *MSR*, 16 Jan. 1866.

23. *JHR* (Feb. 1865), 37; *Acts* (1864–65), 90; *CRSG*, 4:287.

24. The gravity of stealing a horse or mule, unlike a cow or pig, indicated the serious shortage of motive power for farming and transportation after the war. *Acts* (1865–66), 232–33; (1866), 151.

25. See *Acts* (1865–66), 37–38, 234–35; (1866), 26; *JS* (1866), 24–27; *CRSG*, 4:592–93; Coulter, *James Monroe Smith*, 64–92 (quotation, p. 66).

26. The newspaper made no effort to square its pejorative comments with the testimony of the penitentiary's principal keeper, who said, it reported, "he never saw better hands to work than negroes." *MSR*, 23 Jan., 22 May, 3 July 1866.

In the penitentiary's manuscript records (GDAH), the pages for the first few postwar years have been torn out, so a precise breakdown of inmates by race is not possible. See "FSSTNS," 289n, for a table giving the numbers of inmates, by race and sex, received each year and still imprisoned in 1869. At the beginning of 1870, the penitentiary contained (or had leased out) 394 convicts; the highest prewar number had been 245 in 1860.

27. *Acts* (1866), 121–23, 155–56.

28. Because the contract of 5 November does not appear in the Executive Minutes,

it must be surmised that the terms resembled those in the first two contracts. Grant, Alexander took 200 convicts from the penitentiary in November to work on the Macon and Brunswick Railroad. Executive Minutes (1866–70), 124–25, 131, 372–73 (mfm 171-41, GDAH); *MSR*, 17 Nov. 1868.

29. *Acts* (1868), 11; (1869), 9–10. The governor could have acted under the 1866 act, but the terms of the contract followed those specified in an 1869 bill, though that bill does not appear in *Acts* (1869); see "FSSTNS," 292n.

30. *MSR*, 6 July 1869; *Acts* (1871–72), 24–26. On the convict leasing system after about 1869, see Taylor, "Origin and Development," and Ayers, *Vengeance and Justice*, ch. 6. For surveys of developments throughout the South, see Ayers; McKelvey, "Penal Slavery"; and Green, "Convict Lease System."

31. See above, ch. 8.

32. Myrdal, *American Dilemma*, 1:227–29; 2:551–52, 1192–93; Dittmer, *Black Georgia*, 72–89; Rabinowitz, *Race Relations*, 47–51; Engerrand, "'Now Scratch or Die'"; Cohen, "Negro Involuntary Servitude," 47–52; Harris, *Political Power in Birmingham*, 123, 198–202; Novak, *Wheel of Servitude*, 2–35; Woodman, "Sequel to Slavery"; Zimmerman, "Penal Reform Movement," 465–71; Steiner and Brown, *North Carolina Chain Gang*, 3–4, 14, 28–41.

The American South's post–Civil War trajectory can be placed in the context of other societies' postemancipation experiences. In Brazil, too, for example, vagrancy statutes provided a means for landholders to appropriate freedmen's labor. See Daniel, "Metamorphosis of Slavery"; Foner, *Nothing But Freedom*, 1–54; Huggins, *From Slavery to Vagrancy in Brazil*, 71–76.

In the literature on unfree labor in world history, one insight, not yet brought into the study of postemancipation New World societies, emphasizes the use of such labor for public works. Until recent times, public works were widely prosecuted through some kind of unfree labor. See Lasker, *Human Bondage in Southeast Asia*, 168–206; Wittfogel, *Oriental Despotism*.

33. "Monthly Reports of Misdemeanor Chain Gangs, 1898–1901," Worth County, May 1900 (GDAH); see Dittmer, *Black Georgia*, 72–89.

34. "Monthly Reports of Misdemeanor Chain Gangs, 1898–1901," Baker County, May 1900 (GDAH).

35. *JHR* (1831), 17. The change constitutes a postwar reversal of some of the themes traced in Rothman, *Discovery of the Asylum*.

36. *Acts* (1908), 1049–55, 1119–30; Grantham, *Southern Progressivism*, 127–42.

37. Boney, *Slave Life in Georgia*, 18–77; Burns, *I Am a Fugitive*, 47–61, 141–65; Wallenstein, "Rich Man's War," 41–42.

38. "Report of the Joint Committee on Highways," 5–6, in New York, *Documents of the Senate* (1908), vol. 3; New York, *Acts* (1908), 980.

39. SCM, Liberty County (1794–1800), 51 (mfm 30-45, GDAH); Jefferson County (1796–1819), 160 (mfm 72-36, GDAH; commas added).

40. By the 1910s, all eleven former Confederate states had authorized convict labor on the roads, and all had authorized a property tax for roads, though among them only one (Virginia) no longer permitted counties to require road duty or commutation. See Brindley, *Road Legislation*, 293–350; "Federal Aid to Good Roads," Report of the Joint Committee on Federal Aid in the Construction of Post Roads, 63d Cong., 3d sess. (25 Nov. 1914), 119–74.

41. "A Short History of Highway Development in Georgia," in State Highway Board, *Thirteenth Report* (1931), 8–13; *Statutes at Large* 47, pt. 1, 724; 48, pt. 1, 204; 49, pt. 1, 272. See also Dearing, *American Highway Policy*, 86–98; Foster, "Georgia State Highway Department."

42. Wood, *Taxation in Vermont*, 22–23, 108–11; Utah, *Acts* (1919), 270; North Carolina, *Acts* (1931), 210.

43. Wallenstein, "Conscripts and Convicts."

EPILOGUE

1. Woodward, *Origins of the New South*, 61; Ward, "New Departure Democrats of Georgia," 236. Such statements persist; a recent example is Dyer, *University of Georgia*, 118–19.

2. Harlan, *Separate and Unequal*, 235; *Acts* (1888), 19–20. Alabama, like Georgia, displayed a notable increase in education and other social spending beginning in the mid-1880s. Going, *Bourbon Democracy in Alabama*, chs. 10, 12.

3. *Acts* (1884–85), 69–72; (1888), 11; (1890–91), 1:19, 21–22; CG (1898), 10–11.

4. Glasson, *Federal Military Pensions*, pt. 2.

5. McElreath, *Treatise on the Constitution*, 403–7, 417; CG (1888), 7; (1890), 8; (1896), 6–7; (1911), 26–27.

6. CG (1890), 4.

7. That explanation has application outside the South, too, as northern states and communities paid off their enormous Civil War debts, which—unlike the South—they had never repudiated.

8. *JHR* (1892), 51–52; (1898), 54 (quotation).

9. Woodward, *Origins of the New South*, ch. 14. See also Dittmer, *Black Georgia*; Harlan, *Separate and Unequal*; Grantham, *Southern Progressivism*; Jones, "Progressivism in Georgia."

ESSAY ON PRIMARY SOURCES

1. See Jenkins, *Guide to the Microfilm Collection of Early State Records*.

2. Marjorie Lyle Crandall, *Confederate Imprints: A Check List Based Principally on the Collection of the Boston Athenaeum*, 2 vols. (Boston: Boston Athenaeum, 1955); Richard Harwell, *Confederate Imprints in the University of Georgia Libraries* (Athens: University of Georgia Press, 1964); Richard Harwell, *More Confederate Imprints*, 2 vols. (Richmond: Virginia State Library, 1957); Richard Harwell, "A Short-Title List of Books, Pamphlets, Newspapers, and Periodicals Comprising the Keith M. Read Confederate Collection of the Emory University Library, 1941" (EU).

3. Lathrop, "History from the Census Returns."

4. Wallenstein, "History from the Tax Returns." Regarding the relative reliability of tax lists, see Jackson, introduction to *Free Negro Labor*.

BIBLIOGRAPHY

This is a select bibliography. It includes few sources that do not appear in the notes. And it excludes most state and local records cited in the Essay on Primary Sources, as well as a number of primary sources—published collections of railroad reports, for example—whose full citations appear in the notes.

Abernethy, Thomas Perkins. *The South in the New Nation, 1789-1819*. Baton Rouge: Louisiana State University Press, 1961.

Alexander, Roberta Sue. *North Carolina Faces the Freedmen: Race Relations during Presidential Reconstruction, 1865-67*. Durham, N.C.: Duke University Press, 1985.

Ambrose, Stephen E. "Yeoman Discontent in the Confederacy." *Civil War History* 8 (September 1962): 259-68.

Ames, Herman V., ed. *State Documents on Federal Relations: The States and the United States*. Philadelphia: n.p., 1911.

Andrews, Sidney. *The South since the War*. Boston: Ticknor and Fields, 1866.

Avery, Isaac W. *The History of Georgia from 1850 to 1881, Embracing the Three Important Epochs: The Decade Before the War of 1861-5; the War; the Period of Reconstruction*. New York: Brown and Derby, 1881.

Ayers, Edward L. *Vengeance and Justice: Crime and Punishment in the Nineteenth-Century American South*. New York: Oxford University Press, 1984.

Bacote, Clarence A. *The Story of Atlanta University: A Century of Service, 1865-1965*. Atlanta: Atlanta University, 1969.

Barker-Benfield, Ben. "The Spermatic Economy: A Nineteenth-Century View of Sexuality." *Feminist Studies* 1 (Summer 1972): 45-74.

Bartley, Numan V. *The Creation of Modern Georgia*. Athens: University of Georgia Press, 1983.

Bass, J. Horace. "Civil War Finance in Georgia." *Georgia Historical Quarterly* 26 (September–December 1942): 213-24.

Becker, Robert A. "Revolution and Reform: An Interpretation of Southern Taxation, 1763 to 1783." *William and Mary Quarterly* 3d ser., 23 (July 1975): 417-42.

———. *Revolution, Reform, and the Politics of American Taxation, 1763-1783*. Baton Rouge: Louisiana State University Press, 1980.

Benson, Lee. *The Concept of Jacksonian Democracy: New York as a Test Case*. Princeton: Princeton University Press, 1961.

———. *Merchants, Farmers, and Railroads: Railroad Regulation and New York Politics, 1850-1887*. Cambridge: Harvard University Press, 1955.

Berlin, Ira. *Slaves without Masters: The Free Negro in the Antebellum South*. New York: Pantheon, 1974.

Best, Harry. *Blindness and the Blind in the United States*. New York: Macmillan, 1934.

———. *Deafness and the Deaf in the United States*. New York: Macmillan, 1943.

Bloom, Charles G. "The Georgia Election of April, 1868: A Re-examination of the Politics of Georgia Reconstruction." M.A. thesis, University of Chicago, 1963.

Bloomfield, Maxwell. *American Lawyers in a Changing Society, 1776–1876*. Cambridge: Harvard University Press, 1976.

Boatwright, Eleanor M. "The Political and Civil Status of Women in Georgia, 1783–1860." *Georgia Historical Quarterly* 25 (December 1941): 301–24.

Bodenhamer, David J., and James W. Ely, Jr., eds. *Ambivalent Legacy: A Legal History of the South*. Jackson: University of Mississippi Press, 1984.

Bond, Horace Mann. *Negro Education in Alabama: A Study in Cotton and Steel*. 1939. Reprint. New York: Atheneum, 1969.

————. "Social and Economic Factors in Alabama Reconstruction." *Journal of Negro History* 23 (July 1938): 290–348.

Boney, F. Nash, ed. *Slave Life in Georgia: A Narrative of the Life, Sufferings, and Escape of John Brown, a Fugitive Slave*. Savannah: Beehive Press, 1972.

Bonner, James C. "The Georgia Penitentiary at Milledgeville, 1817–1874." *Georgia Historical Quarterly* 60 (Fall 1971): 303–28.

————. *A History of Georgia Agriculture, 1732–1860*. Athens: University of Georgia Press, 1964.

————. *Milledgeville, Georgia's Ante-Bellum Capital*. Athens: University of Georgia Press, 1978.

————. "Profile of a Late Ante-Bellum Community [Hancock County, Georgia]." *American Historical Review* 49 (July 1944): 663–80.

Bourne, Edward G. *The History of the Surplus Revenue of 1837*. New York: G. P. Putnam's Sons, 1885.

Bowden, Haygood S. *Two Hundred Years of Education, Bicentennial 1733–1933: Savannah, Chatham County, Georgia*. Richmond, Va.: Dietz, 1932.

Bowers, Claude G. *The Tragic Era: The Revolution After Lincoln*. Cambridge, Mass.: Houghton Mifflin, 1929.

Brandfon, Robert L. *Cotton Kingdom of the New South: A History of the Yazoo Mississippi Delta from Reconstruction to the Twentieth Century*. Cambridge: Harvard University Press, 1967.

Bremner, Robert H. *The Public Good: Philanthropy and Welfare in the Civil War Era*. New York: Knopf, 1980.

Brindley, John E. *History of Road Legislation in Iowa*. Iowa City: State Historical Society of Iowa, 1912.

Brock, William R. *Investigation and Responsibility: Public Responsibility in the United States, 1865–1900*. Cambridge: Cambridge University Press, 1984.

Brooks, Robert Preston. *Financing Government in Georgia, 1850–1944*. Institute for the Study of Georgia Problems, Bulletin of the University of Georgia, vol. 46, no. 5 (May 1946).

————. *The University of Georgia under Sixteen Administrations, 1785–1955*. Athens: University of Georgia Press, 1956.

Bruchey, Stuart. *The Roots of American Economic Growth, 1607–1860: An Essay in Social Causation*. New York: Harper and Row, 1965.

Bryan, T. Conn. *Confederate Georgia*. Athens: University of Georgia Press, 1953.

Buck, Paul H. "The Poor Whites of the Ante-Bellum South." *American Historical Review* 31 (October 1925): 41–54.

Bullock, Charles J. "Historical Sketch of the Finances and Financial Policy of

Massachusetts, from 1780 to 1905." *American Economic Association Publications* 3d ser. 8 (May 1907): 269–412.

Bullock, Henry Morton. *A History of Emory University*. Nashville, Tenn.: Parthenon Press, 1936.

Burns, Robert E. *I Am a Fugitive from a Georgia Chain Gang!* New York: Grossett and Dunlap, 1932.

Busbee, Westley Floyd, Jr. "Presidential Reconstruction in Georgia, 1865–1867." Ph.D. diss., University of Alabama, 1972.

Butler, John C., comp. *Origin and History of the Georgia Academy for the Blind, with Documents from the Beginning, 1851, to 1887*. Macon: J. W. Burke, 1887.

Butts, Donald C. "The 'Irrepressible Conflict': Slave Taxation and North Carolina's Gubernatorial Election of 1860." *North Carolina Historical Review* 58 (January 1981): 44–66.

Candler, Allen D., comp. *The Confederate Records of the State of Georgia*. 6 vols. (vol. 5 never published). Atlanta: Charles P. Byrd, 1909–11.

Carter, Clarence Edwin, and John Porter Bloom, comps. *The Territorial Papers of the United States*. 28 vols. to date. Washington, D.C.: Government Printing Office, 1934–.

Carter, Dan T. *When the War Was Over: The Failure of Self-Reconstruction in the South, 1865–1867*. Baton Rouge: Louisiana State University Press, 1985.

Caswell, Render R. "The History of Bowdon College." M.S. thesis, University of Georgia, 1952.

Cathy, Esther. "A History of the Georgia School for the Deaf." M.A. thesis, Emory University, 1939.

Cherry, Jim David. "The Georgia Railroad Commission, 1879–1888." M.A. thesis, University of North Carolina, 1941.

Christian, Rebecca. "Georgia and the Confederate Policy of Impressing Supplies." *Georgia Historical Quarterly* 28 (March 1944): 1–33.

Cimbala, Paul A. "The Terms of Freedom: The Freedmen's Bureau and Reconstruction in Georgia, 1865–1870." Ph.D. diss., Emory University, 1983.

Clark, Richard H., Thomas R. R. Cobb, and David Irwin, comps. *The Code of the State of Georgia*. Atlanta: John H. Seals, 1861.

———. *The Code of the State of Georgia*. Atlanta: Franklin Steam Printing House, 1867.

Clayton, Augustin Smith, comp. *A Compilation of the Laws of the State of Georgia*. Augusta: Adams and Duyckinck, 1812.

Cobb, Howell, comp. *A Compilation of the General and Public Statutes of the State of Georgia*. New York: Edward O. Jenkins, 1859.

Cobb, Thomas R. R., comp. *A Digest of the Statute Laws of the State of Georgia*. Athens: Christy, Kelsea and Burke, 1851.

Cochrane, Hortense S. "Early Treatment of the Mentally Ill in Georgia." *Georgia Historical Quarterly* 32 (June 1948): 105–118.

Coddington, Edwin Broughton. "A Social and Economic History of the Seaboard States of the Southern Confederacy." Ph.D. diss., Clark University, 1939.

———. "Soldiers' Relief in the Seaboard States of the Southern Confederacy." *Mississippi Valley Historical Review* 37 (June 1950): 17–38.

Cohen, William. "Negro Involuntary Servitude in the South, 1865–1940: A Preliminary Analysis." *Journal of Southern History* 42 (February 1976): 31–60.

Coleman, Kenneth, ed. *A History of Georgia.* Athens: University of Georgia Press, 1977.

Coleman, Kenneth, and Charles Stephen Gurr, eds. *Dictionary of Georgia Biography.* 2 vols. Athens: University of Georgia Press, 1983.

Collins, Bruce. *White Society in the Antebellum South.* London: Longman, 1985.

Conway, Alan. *The Reconstruction of Georgia.* Minneapolis: University of Minnesota Press, 1966.

Cooper, William J., Jr. *The South and the Politics of Slavery, 1828–1856.* Baton Rouge: Louisiana State University Press, 1978.

Corley, Florence Fleming. *Confederate City: Augusta, Georgia, 1860–1865.* Columbia: University of South Carolina Press, 1960.

Coulter, E. Merton. *College Life in the Old South.* 2d ed. Athens: University of Georgia Press, 1951.

———. *The Confederate States of America, 1861–1865.* Baton Rouge: Louisiana State University Press, 1950.

———. *James Monroe Smith, Georgia Planter.* Athens: University of Georgia Press, 1961.

———. *John Jacobus Flournoy: Champion of the Common Man in the Antebellum South.* Savannah: Georgia Historical Society, 1942.

Curry, Leonard P. *Blueprint for Modern America: Nonmilitary Legislation of the First Civil War Congress.* Nashville, Tenn.: Vanderbilt University Press, 1968.

Dain, Norman. *Concepts of Insanity in the United States, 1789–1865.* New Brunswick, N.J.: Rutgers University Press, 1964.

Daniel, Pete. "The Metamorphosis of Slavery, 1865–1900." *Journal of American History* 66 (June 1979): 88–99.

Dearing, Charles L. *American Highway Policy.* Washington, D.C.: Brookings Institution, 1941.

DeBats, Donald A. "Elites and Masses: Political Structure, Communication and Behavior in Ante-Bellum Georgia." Ph.D. diss., University of Wisconsin, 1973.

Dismukes, Camillus J. "North Georgia College under the Trustees." *Georgia Historical Quarterly* 56 (Spring 1972): 92–100.

Dittmer, John. *Black Georgia in the Progressive Era, 1900–1920.* Urbana: University of Illinois Press, 1977.

Dixon, Jefferson Max. "The Central Railroad of Georgia, 1833–1892." Ph.D. diss., George Peabody College for Teachers, 1953.

Dowell, Spright. *A History of Mercer University, 1833–1953.* Macon: Mercer University, 1958.

Drago, Edmund L. *Black Politicians and Reconstruction in Georgia: A Splendid Failure.* Baton Rouge: Louisiana State University Press, 1982.

DuBois, W. E. B. "The Negro Landholder of Georgia." *Bulletin of the Department of Labor,* no. 35. Washington, D.C.: Government Printing Office, 1901.

———. "Reconstruction and its Benefits." *American Historical Review* 15 (July 1910): 781–99.

Dudley, George M., comp. *Reports of Decisions Made by the Judges of the Superior*

Courts of Law and Chancery of the State of Georgia. New York: Collins, Keese, 1837.

Dyer, Thomas G. *The University of Georgia: A Bicentennial History, 1785–1985.* Athens: University of Georgia Press, 1985.

Elazar, Daniel J. *The American Partnership: Intergovernmental Co-operation in the Nineteenth-Century United States.* Chicago: University of Chicago Press, 1962.

Ely, Richard T. *Taxation in American States and Cities.* New York: T. Y. Crowell, 1888.

Engerrand, Steven William. "'Now Scratch or Die': The Genesis of Capitalistic Agricultural Labor in Georgia, 1865–1880." Ph.D. diss., University of Georgia, 1981.

Ershkowitz, Herbert, and William G. Shade. "Consensus or Conflict? Political Behavior in the State Legislatures During the Jacksonian Era." *Journal of American History* 58 (December 1971): 591–621.

Escott, Paul D. *After Secession: Jefferson Davis and the Failure of Confederate Nationalism.* Baton Rouge: Louisiana State University Press, 1978.

———. "Joseph E. Brown, Jefferson Davis, and the Problem of Poverty in the Confederacy." *Georgia Historical Quarterly* 61 (Spring 1977): 59–71.

———. "Southern Yeomen and the Confederacy." *South Atlantic Quarterly* 77 (Spring 1978): 146–58.

Fairlie, John Archibald. *The Centralization of Administration in New York State.* New York: Columbia University Press, 1898.

Fairman, Charles. *Reconstruction and Reunion, 1864–1888, Part One.* Vol. 6 of *The Oliver Wendell Homes Devise: History of the Supreme Court of the United States.* New York: Macmillan, 1971.

Ferguson, E. James. "Currency Finance: An Interpretation of Colonial Monetary Practices." *William and Mary Quarterly* 3d ser., 10 (April 1953): 153–80.

Ferguson, Maxwell. *State Regulation of Railroads in the South.* New York: Columbia University Press, 1916.

Fields, Barbara Jeanne. *Slavery and Freedom on the Middle Ground: Maryland during the Nineteenth Century.* New Haven: Yale University Press, 1985.

Flanders, Ralph B. "The Free Negro in Ante-Bellum Georgia." *North Carolina Historical Review* 9 (July 1932): 250–72.

———. *Plantation Slavery in Georgia.* Chapel Hill: University of North Carolina Press, 1933.

Flynn, Charles L., Jr. *White Land, Black Labor: Caste and Class in Late Nineteenth-Century Georgia.* Baton Rouge: Louisiana State University Press, 1983.

Fogel, Robert William. *The Union Pacific Railroad: A Case Study in Premature Enterprise.* Baltimore: Johns Hopkins University Press, 1960.

Foner, Eric. *Nothing but Freedom: Emancipation and Its Legacy.* Baton Rouge: Louisiana State University Press, 1983.

———. "Reconstruction Revisited." *Reviews in American History* 10 (December 1982): 82–100.

———. *Tom Paine and Revolutionary America.* New York: Oxford University Press, 1976.

Foreman, Grant. *Indian Removal: The Emigration of the Five Civilized Tribes of Indians.* Norman: University of Oklahoma Press, 1932.

Fort, Kate Haynes, comp. *Memoirs of the Fort and Fannin Families*. Chattanooga, Tenn.: Press of MacGowan and Cooke, 1903.

Fortune, Porter L., Jr. "George M. Troup: Leading State Rights Advocate." Ph.D. diss., University of North Carolina, 1949.

Foster, Albert Pafford. "The Georgia State Highway Department—Its Origin, Development, and Administration." M.A. thesis, Emory University, 1949.

Franklin, John Hope. *From Slavery to Freedom: A History of Negro Americans*. 5th ed. New York: Knopf, 1980.

———. *The Militant South, 1800–1861*. Cambridge: Harvard University Press, 1956.

Friedman, Lawrence J. *Inventors of the Promised Land*. New York: Knopf, 1975.

Friedman, Lawrence M. *A History of American Law*. New York: Simon and Schuster, 1973.

Garrett, Franklin M. *Atlanta and Environs: A Chronicle of Its Events and People*. 2 vols. New York: Lewis Historical Publishing Company, 1954.

Genovese, Eugene D. *Roll, Jordan, Roll: The World the Slaves Made*. New York: Pantheon, 1974.

Gifford, James M. "The African Colonization Movement in Georgia, 1817–1860." Ph.D. diss., University of Georgia, 1977.

Gillette, William. *Retreat from Reconstruction, 1869–1879*. Baton Rouge: Louisiana State University Press, 1979.

Glasson, William H. *Federal Military Pensions in the United States*. New York: Oxford University Press, 1918.

Going, Allen Johnston. *Bourbon Democracy in Alabama, 1874–1890*. University: University of Alabama Press, 1951.

Goodrich, Carter. "Public Aid to Railroads in the Reconstruction South." *Political Science Quarterly* 71 (September 1956): 407–42.

———, ed. *Canals and American Economic Development*. New York: Columbia University Press, 1961.

Govan, Thomas P. "Banking and the Credit System in Georgia, 1810–1860." *Journal of Southern History* 4 (May 1938): 164–84.

Grantham, Dewey W. *Southern Progressivism: The Reconciliation of Progress and Tradition*. Knoxville: University of Tennessee Press, 1983.

Gray, Lewis Cecil. *History of Agriculture in the Southern United States to 1860*. 2 vols. Washington, D.C.: Carnegie Institute of Washington, 1933.

Green, Fletcher M. "Georgia's Board of Public Works, 1817–1826." *Georgia Historical Quarterly* 22 (June 1938): 117–37.

———. "Georgia's Forgotten Industry: Gold Mining." *Georgia Historical Quarterly* 19 (1935): 93–111, 210–28.

———. "Some Aspects of the Convict Lease System in the Southern States." In *Essays in Southern History Presented to Joseph Gregoire de Roulhac Hamilton . . .*, edited by Fletcher M. Green, 112–23. Chapel Hill: University of North Carolina Press, 1949.

Greene, Frances. *The First One Hundred Years [of Tallapoosa, Georgia]*. N.p., 1972.

Greene, Helen Ione. "Politics in Georgia, 1830–1854." Ph.D. diss., University of Chicago, 1945.

Grob, Gerald N. *Mental Institutions in America: Social Policy to 1875*. New York: Free Press, 1973.

Gutman, Herbert G. *The Black Family in Slavery and Freedom, 1750-1925*. New York: Pantheon, 1976.

Hahn, Steven. *The Roots of Southern Populism: Yeoman Farmers and the Transformation of the Georgia Upcountry, 1850-1890*. New York: Oxford University Press, 1983.

Halliburton, R., Jr. "Free Black Owners of Slaves: A Reappraisal of the Woodson Thesis." *South Carolina Historical Magazine* 76 (July 1975): 129-42.

Harlan, Louis R. *Separate and Unequal: Public School Campaigns and Racism in the Southern Seaboard States, 1901-1915*. Chapel Hill: University of North Carolina Press, 1958.

Harris, Carl V. *Political Power in Birmingham, 1871-1921*. Knoxville: University of Tennessee Press, 1978.

Harris, J. William. *Plain Folk and Gentry in a Slave Society: White Liberty and Black Slavery in Augusta's Hinterlands*. Middletown, Conn.: Wesleyan University Press, 1985.

————. "Plantations and Power: Emancipation on the David Barrow Plantation." In *Toward a New South? Studies in Post-Civil War Southern Communities*, edited by Orville Vernon Burton and Robert C. McMath, Jr., 246-64. Westport, Conn.: Greenwood Press, 1982.

Haunton, Richard H. "Savannah in the 1850s." Ph.D. diss., Emory University, 1968.

Heath, Milton Sydney. *Constructive Liberalism: The Role of the State in Economic Development in Georgia to 1860*. Cambridge: Harvard University Press, 1954.

————. "Public Co-operation in Railroad Construction in the Southern United States to 1861." Ph.D. diss., Harvard University, 1937.

Henry, Charles S., comp. *A Digest of all the Ordinances of the City of Savannah*. Savannah: Purse's Print, 1854.

Higgs, Robert. *Competition and Coercion: Blacks in the American Economy, 1865-1914*. Cambridge: Cambridge University Press, 1977.

Hill, Benjamin H., Jr. *Senator Benjamin H. Hill of Georgia: His Life, Speeches and Writings*. Atlanta: H. C. Hudgins, 1891.

Holland, Lynwood M. "Georgia Military Institute, the West Point of Georgia: 1851-1864." *Georgia Historical Quarterly* 43 (September 1959): 225-47.

Hollander, Jacob H., ed. *Studies in State Taxation, with Particular Reference to the Southern States*. Baltimore: Johns Hopkins Press, 1900.

Hollingsworth, R. R. "Education and Reconstruction in Georgia." *Georgia Historical Quarterly* 19 (1935): 112-33, 229-50.

Holt, Michael F. *The Political Crisis of the 1850s*. New York: Wiley, 1978.

Horwitz, Morton J. *The Transformation of American Law, 1780-1860*. Cambridge: Harvard University Press, 1977.

Hudson, Charles. *The Southeastern Indians*. Knoxville: University of Tennessee Press, 1976.

Huggins, Martha Knisely. *From Slavery to Vagrancy in Brazil: Crime and Social Control in the Third World*. New Brunswick: Rutgers University Press, 1985.

Hughes, Melvin Clyde. *County Government in Georgia*. Athens: University of Georgia Press, 1944.

Hull, Augustus L. *A Historical Sketch of the University of Georgia*. Atlanta: Foote and Davies, 1894.

Hurd, Henry M., ed. *The Institutional Care of the Insane in the United States and Canada.* 4 vols. Baltimore: Johns Hopkins University Press, 1916–17.

Hyman, Harold M. *A More Perfect Union: The Impact of the Civil War and Reconstruction on the Constitution.* New York: Knopf, 1973.

Jackman, William T. *The Development of Transportation in Modern England.* 3d ed. New York: Augustus M. Kelley, 1968.

Jackson, Luther Porter. *Free Negro Labor and Property Holding in Virginia, 1830–1860.* 1942. Reprint. New York: Atheneum, 1969.

Janes, Thomas P. *Hand-Book of the State of Georgia.* Atlanta: n.p., 1876.

Jenkins, William Sumner, comp. *A Guide to the Microfilm Collection of Early State Records.* Washington, D.C.: Library of Congress, 1950.

Jenks, Jeremiah W. "Road Legislation for the American State." *American Economic Association Publications* 1st ser., no. 4 (May 1889): 145–227.

Jewett, Fred Eugene. *A Financial History of Maine.* New York: Columbia University Press, 1937.

Johnson, Michael P. *Toward a Patriarchal Republic: The Secession of Georgia.* Baton Rouge: Louisiana State University Press, 1977.

Johnston, James Houstoun. *Western and Atlantic Railroad of the State of Georgia.* Atlanta: Stein Printing Company, 1932.

Jones, Alton DuMar. "Progressivism in Georgia, 1898–1918." Ph.D. diss., Emory University, 1963.

Jones, Jacqueline. *Soldiers of Light and Love: Northern Teachers and Georgia Blacks, 1865–1873.* Chapel Hill: University of North Carolina Press, 1980.

Jordan, Winthrop D. *White over Black: American Attitudes Toward the Negro, 1550–1812.* Chapel Hill: University of North Carolina Press, 1968.

Kaestle, Carl F. *Pillars of the Republic: Common Schools and American Society, 1780–1860.* New York: Hill and Wang, 1983.

Kay, Michael L. Marvin, and William S. Price, Jr. "'To Ride the Wood Mare': Road Building and Militia Service in Colonial North Carolina, 1740–1775." *North Carolina Historical Review* 57 (Autumn 1980): 361–409.

Keller, Morton. *Affairs of State: Public Life in Late Nineteenth Century America.* Cambridge: Harvard University Press, 1977.

Klebaner, Joseph Benjamin. "Public Poor Relief in America, 1790–1860." Ph.D. diss., Columbia University, 1952.

Klein, Maury. "Southern Railroad Leaders, 1865–1893: Identities and Ideologies." *Business History Review* 42 (Autumn 1968): 288–310.

Knight, Edgar W. *Public Education in the South.* Boston: Ginn, 1922.

———, ed. *A Documentary History of Education in the South Before 1860.* 5 vols. Chapel Hill: University of North Carolina Press, 1949–53.

Koger, Larry. *Black Slaveowners: Free Black Slave Masters in South Carolina, 1790–1860.* Jefferson, N.C.: McFarland, 1985.

Kolko, Gabriel. *Railroads and Regulation, 1877–1916.* Princeton: Princeton University Press, 1965.

Kousser, J. Morgan. "Progressivism—for Middle Class Whites Only: North Carolina Education, 1880–1910." *Journal of Southern History* 46 (May 1980): 169–94.

———. *The Shaping of Southern Politics: Suffrage Restriction and the Establishment of the One-Party South, 1880–1910.* New Haven: Yale University Press, 1974.

Lamar, Lucius Q. C., comp. *A Compilation of the Laws of the State of Georgia, 1810–19*. Augusta: T. S. Hannon, 1821.

Lasker, Bruno. *Human Bondage in Southeast Asia*. 1950. Reprint. Greenwood, Conn.: Greenwood Press, 1972.

Lathrop, Barnes F. "History from the Census Returns." *Southwestern Historical Quarterly* 51 (April 1948): 293–312.

Le Duc, Thomas. "State Disposal of the Agricultural College Land Scrip." *Agricultural History* 28 (July 1954): 99–107.

Lerner, Eugene M. "Money, Prices, and Wages in the Confederacy, 1861–65." *Journal of Political Economy* 63 (February 1955): 20–40.

Lewis, David W., comp. *Report on Public Education*. Milledgeville: Boughton, Nisbet and Barnes, 1860.

Lide, Anne. "Five Georgia Colleges from 1850 to 1875." M.A. thesis, Emory University, 1957.

Linden, Fabian. "Economic Democracy in the Slave South: An Appraisal of Some Recent Views." *Journal of Negro History* 31 (April 1946): 140–89.

Link, Arthur S., and Rembert W. Patrick, eds. *Writing Southern History: Essays in Honor of Fletcher M. Green*. Baton Rouge: Louisiana State University Press, 1965.

Litwack, Leon F. *Been in the Storm So Long: The Aftermath of Slavery*. New York: Knopf, 1979.

Lively, Robert A. "The American System: A Review Article." *Business History Review* 29 (March 1955): 81–96.

Lonn, Ella. *Desertion during the Civil War*. New York: Century, 1928.

———. *Salt as a Factor in the Confederacy*. New York: Walter Neale, 1933.

Lumpkin, Wilson. *The Removal of the Cherokee Indians from Georgia*. 2 vols. New York: Dodd, Mead, 1907.

McCallie, Samuel W. *A Preliminary Report on the Roads and Road-Building Materials of Georgia*. Bulletin no. 8, Geological Survey of Georgia. Atlanta: George W. Harrison, 1901.

———. *A Second Report on the Public Roads of Georgia*. Bulletin no. 24, Geological Survey of Georgia. Atlanta: Charles P. Byrd, 1910.

McCash, William B. *Thomas R. R. Cobb (1823–1862): The Making of a Southern Nationalist*. Macon: Mercer University Press, 1983.

McCormick, Richard P. *The Second American Party System: Party Formation in the Jacksonian Era*. Chapel Hill: University of North Carolina Press, 1966.

McDonald, Forrest, and Grady McWhiney. "The Antebellum Southern Herdsman: A Reinterpretation." *Journal of Southern History* 41 (May 1975): 147–66.

McElreath, Walter. *A Treatise on the Constitution of Georgia*. Atlanta: Harrison, 1912.

McGuire, Peter S. "Athens and the Railroads." *Georgia Historical Quarterly* 18 (1934): 1–26, 118–44.

McKelvey, Blake. *American Prisons: A Study in American Social History Prior to 1915*. Chicago: University of Chicago Press, 1936.

———. "Penal Slavery and Southern Reconstruction." *Journal of Negro History* 20 (April 1935): 153–79.

McManus, Edgar J. *A History of Negro Slavery in New York*. Syracuse, N.Y.: Syracuse University Press, 1966.

McMaster, John Bach. *A History of the People of the United States, from the Revolu-*

tion to the Civil War. 8 vols. New York: D. Appleton, 1883–1913.

McMath, Robert C., Jr., Ronald H. Bayor, James E. Brittain, Lawrence Foster, August W. Giebelhaus, and Germaine M. Reed. *Engineering the New South: Georgia Tech, 1885–1985.* Athens: University of Georgia Press, 1985.

Marshall, Helen E. *Dorothea Dix, Forgotten Samaritan.* Chapel Hill: University of North Carolina Press, 1937.

Mathews, Forrest David. "The Politics of Education in the Deep South: Georgia and Alabama, 1830–1860." Ph.D. diss., Columbia University, 1965.

Mitchell, Margaret. *Gone with the Wind.* New York: Macmillan, 1936.

Mohr, Clarence L. *On the Threshold of Freedom: Masters and Slaves in Civil War Georgia.* Athens: University of Georgia Press, 1986.

Montgomery, Horace. *Cracker Politics.* Baton Rouge: Louisiana State University Press, 1950.

Murray, Paul. "Party Organization in Georgia Politics, 1825–1853." *Georgia Historical Quarterly* 29 (December 1945): 195–210.

———. *The Whig Party in Georgia, 1825–1853.* Chapel Hill: University of North Carolina Press, 1948.

Myrdal, Gunnar. *An American Dilemma.* 2 vols. 1944. Reprint. New York: McGraw-Hill, 1964.

Nathans, Elizabeth Studley. *Losing the Peace: Georgia Republicans and Reconstruction, 1865–1871.* Baton Rouge: Louisiana State University Press, 1968.

Nelson, Bernard H. "Legislative Control of the Southern Free Negro, 1861–1865." *Catholic Historical Review* 32 (April 1946): 28–46.

Nieman, Donald G. *To Set the Law in Motion: The Freedmen's Bureau and the Legal Rights of Blacks, 1865–1868.* Millwood, N.Y.: KTO Press, 1979.

North, Douglass C. *Growth and Welfare in the American Past: A New Economic History.* Englewood Cliffs, N.J.: Prentice-Hall, 1966.

Novak, Daniel A. *The Wheel of Servitude: Black Forced Labor After Slavery.* Lexington: University Press of Kentucky, 1978.

Oakes, James. "The Present Becomes the Past: The Planter Class in the Postbellum South." In *New Perspectives on Race and Slavery in America: Essays in Honor of Kenneth M. Stampp,* edited by Robert H. Abzug and Stephen E. Maizlish, 149–63. Lexington, University Press of Kentucky, 1986.

———. *The Ruling Race: A History of American Slaveholders.* New York: Knopf, 1982.

Orr, Dorothy. *A History of Education in Georgia.* Chapel Hill: University of North Carolina Press, 1950.

Owsley, Frank L. *Plain Folk of the Old South.* Baton Rouge: Louisiana State University Press, 1949.

Parks, Joseph H. *Joseph E. Brown of Georgia.* Baton Rouge: Louisiana State University Press, 1977.

Parsons, Joseph. "Anthony Odinsells: A Romance of Little Wassaw." *Georgia Historical Quarterly* 55 (Summer 1971): 208–21.

Pearce, Haywood J., Jr. *Benjamin H. Hill: Secession and Reconstruction.* Chicago: University of Chicago Press, 1928.

Pease, William H., and Jane H. Pease, eds. *The Antislavery Argument.* Indianapolis: Bobbs-Merrill, 1965.

Perman, Michael. *Reunion without Compromise: The South and Reconstruction, 1865–1868*. Cambridge: Cambridge University Press, 1973.

———. *The Road to Redemption: Southern Politics, 1869–1879*. Chapel Hill: University of North Carolina Press, 1984.

Phillips, Ulrich Bonnell. *Georgia and State Rights: A Study of the Political History of Georgia from the Revolution to the Civil War, with Particular Regard to Federal Relations*. Washington, D.C.: Government Printing Office, 1902.

———. *A History of Transportation in the Eastern Cotton Belt to 1860*. New York: Columbia University Press, 1908.

Poore, Benjamin Perley, comp. *The Federal and State Constitutions, Colonial Charters, and Other Organic Laws of the United States*. 2 vols. Washington, D.C.: Government Printing Office, 1877.

Pyle, Barbara C. "The Free Negro in Bibb County, Georgia, 1850–1860." B.A. honors thesis, Emory University, 1974.

Rabinowitz, Howard N. "From Exclusion to Segregation: Health and Welfare Services for Southern Blacks, 1865–1890." *Social Service Review* 48 (September 1974): 327–54.

———. "Half a Loaf: The Shift from White to Black Teachers in the Negro Schools of the Urban South, 1865–1890." *Journal of Southern History* 40 (November 1974): 565–94.

———. *Race Relations in the Urban South, 1865–1890*. New York: Oxford University Press, 1978.

Racine, Philip Noel. "Atlanta's Schools: A History of the Public School System, 1869–1955." Ph.D. diss., Emory University, 1969.

Ramsdell, Charles W. *Behind the Lines in the Southern Confederacy*. Edited by Wendell H. Stephenson. Baton Rouge: Louisiana State University Press, 1944.

Range, Willard. *The Rise and Progress of Negro Colleges in Georgia, 1865–1949*. Athens: University of Georgia Press, 1951.

Rankin, David C. "The Impact of the Civil War on the Free Colored Community of New Orleans." *Perspectives in American History* 11 (1977–78): 379–416.

Reid, Whitelaw. *After the War: A Southern Tour. May 1, 1865, to May 1, 1866*. New York: Moore, Wilstach and Baldwin, 1866.

Reidy, Joseph Patrick. "Masters and Slaves, Planters and Freedmen: The Transition from Slavery to Freedom in Central Georgia, 1820–1880." Ph.D. diss., Northern Illinois University, 1982.

Ringold, May Spencer. *The Role of the State Legislatures in the Confederacy*. Athens: University of Georgia Press, 1966.

Roark, James A. *Masters without Slaves: Southern Planters in the Civil War and Reconstruction*. New York: Norton, 1977.

Roberts, Derrell. "The University of Georgia and Georgia's Civil War G.I. Bill." *Georgia Historical Quarterly* 49 (December 1965): 418–23.

Roberts, Lucien E. "Sectional Factors in the Movements for Legislative Reapportionment and Reduction in Georgia, 1777–1860." In *Studies in Georgia History and Government*, edited by James C. Bonner and Lucien E. Roberts, 94–122. Athens: University of Georgia Press, 1940.

Rogers, W. McDowell. "Free Negro Legislation in Georgia before 1865." *Georgia Historical Quarterly* 16 (March 1932): 27–37.

Rogin, Michael Paul. *Fathers and Children: Andrew Jackson and the Subjugation of the American Indian.* New York: Knopf, 1975.

Rose, Willie Lee. *Slavery and Freedom.* Edited by William W. Freehling. New York: Oxford University Press, 1982.

Rothman, David J. *The Discovery of the Asylum: Social Order and Disorder in the New Republic.* Boston: Little, Brown, 1971.

Russell, James Michael. "Atlanta, Gate City of the South, 1845 to 1885." Ph.D. diss., Princeton University, 1972.

Salley, Harriet Milledge, ed. *Correspondence of John Milledge, Governor of Georgia, 1802-1806.* Columbia, S.C.: State Commercial Printing Company, 1949.

Salsbury, Stephen. *The State, the Investor, and the Railroad: The Boston and Albany, 1825-1867.* Cambridge: Harvard University Press, 1967.

Scheiber, Harry N. *The Condition of American Federalism: An Historian's View.* Washington, D.C.: Government Printing Office, 1966.

——. "Federalism and the American Economic Order, 1789-1910." *Law and Society Review* 10 (Fall 1975): 57-117.

——. "Government and the Economy: Studies of the 'Commonwealth' Policy in Nineteenth-Century America." *Journal of Interdisciplinary History* 3 (Summer 1972): 135-51.

——. *Ohio Canal Era: A Case Study of Government and the Economy, 1820-1861.* Athens: Ohio University Press, 1969.

——. "Property Law, Expropriation, and Resource Allocation by Government: The United States, 1789-1910." *Journal of Economic History* 33 (March 1973): 232-51.

Schinkel, Peter Evans. "The Negro in Athens and Clarke County, 1872-1900." M.A. thesis, University of Georgia, 1971.

Schneider, David M. *The History of Public Welfare in New York State, 1609-1866.* 1938. Reprint. Montclair, N.J.: Patterson Smith, 1969.

Schwab, John Christopher. *The Confederate States of America, 1861-1865: A Financial and Industrial History of the South during the Civil War.* New York: Charles Scribner's Sons, 1901.

Schwartz, Harold. *Samuel Gridley Howe, Social Reformer, 1801-1876.* Cambridge: Harvard University Press, 1956.

Scott, Anne Firor. *The Southern Lady: From Pedestal to Politics, 1830-1930.* Chicago: University of Chicago Press, 1970.

Scott, William A. *The Repudiation of State Debts.* New York: Thomas Y. Crowell, 1893.

Sellers, Charles Grier, Jr. "Who Were the Southern Whigs?" *American Historical Review* 59 (January 1954): 335-46.

Sellers, James L. "The Economic Incidence of the Civil War in the South." *Mississippi Valley Historical Review* 14 (September 1927): 179-91.

Shanks, Henry Thomas. "Conservative Constitutional Tendencies of the Virginia Secession Convention." In *Essays in Southern History: Presented to Joseph Gregoire de Roulhac Hamilton...,* edited by Fletcher M. Green, 28-48. Chapel Hill: University of North Carolina Press, 1949.

Shryock, Richard Harrison. *Georgia and the Union in 1850.* Durham, N.C.: Duke University Press, 1926.

Siegel, Fred. "Artisans and Immigrants in the Politics of Late Antebellum Georgia." *Civil War History* 27 (September 1981): 221–30.

Simpson, John Eddins. *Howell Cobb: The Politics of Ambition*. Chicago: Adams Press, 1973.

Smith, Harry Edwin. *The United States Federal Internal Tax History from 1861 to 1871*. Cambridge, Mass.: Riverside Press, 1914.

Smith, Julia Floyd. *Slavery and Rice Culture in Low Country Georgia, 1750–1860*. Knoxville: University of Tennessee Press, 1985.

Somers, Robert. *The Southern States since the War*. New York: Macmillan, 1871.

Sowers, Don C. *The Financial History of New York State from 1789 to 1912*. New York: Columbia University Press, 1914.

Starobin, Robert S. *Industrial Slavery in the Old South*. New York: Oxford University Press, 1970.

Steiner, Jesse F., and Roy M. Brown. *North Carolina Chain Gang: A Study of County Convict Road Work*. 1927. Reprint. Westport, Conn.: Negro Universities Press, 1970.

Summers, Mark W. *Railroads, Reconstruction, and the Gospel of Prosperity: Aid under the Radical Republicans*. Princeton: Princeton University Press, 1984.

Sweat, Edward F. "The Free Negro in Ante-Bellum Georgia." Ph.D. diss., Indiana University, 1957.

Sydnor, Charles S. *The Development of Southern Sectionalism, 1819–1848*. Baton Rouge: Louisiana State University Press, 1948.

Tankersley, Allen P. *College Life at Old Oglethorpe*. Athens: University of Georgia Press, 1951.

Taylor, A. Elizabeth. "The Origin and Development of the Convict Lease System in Georgia." *Georgia Historical Quarterly* 26 (June 1942): 113–28.

Taylor, Arthur Reed. "From the Ashes: Atlanta during Reconstruction, 1865–1876." Ph.D. diss., Emory University, 1973.

Temple, Sarah Blackwell Gober. *The First Hundred Years: A Short History of Cobb County, in Georgia*. Atlanta: Walter W. Brown, 1935.

Terrill, Tom E. "Eager Hands: Labor for Southern Textiles, 1850–1860." *Journal of Economic History* 36 (March 1976): 84–99.

Thian, Raphael P., comp. *Correspondence with the Treasury Department of the Confederate States of America, 1861–'65*, Appendix, pt. 5. Washington, D.C.: n.p., 1880.

———. *Reports of the Secretary of the Treasury of the Confederate States of America, 1861–'65*, Appendix, pt. 3. Washington, D.C.: n.p., 1878.

Thomas, Edward J. *Memoirs of a Southerner, 1840–1923*. Savannah: n.p., 1923.

Thompson, C. Mildred. *Reconstruction in Georgia: Economic, Social, Political, 1865–1872*. Columbia University Press, 1915.

Thornbery, Jerry John. "The Development of Black Atlanta, 1865–1885." Ph.D. diss., University of Maryland, 1977.

Thornton, J. Mills, III. "Fiscal Policy and the Failure of Radical Reconstruction in the Lower South." In *Region, Race, and Reconstruction: Essays in Honor of C. Vann Woodward*, edited by J. Morgan Kousser and James M. McPherson, 349–94. New York: Oxford University Press, 1982.

————. *Politics and Power in a Slave Society: Alabama, 1800–1860*. Baton Rouge: Louisiana State University Press, 1978.

Thorpe, Francis Newton, ed. *The Federal and State Constitutions, Colonial Charters, and Other Organic Laws of the States, Territories, and Colonies*. 7 vols. Washington, D.C.: Government Printing Office, 1909.

Tilly, Charles, ed. *The Formation of the National States in Western Europe*. Princeton: Princeton University Press, 1975.

Todd, Richard Cecil. *Confederate Finance*. Athens: University of Georgia Press, 1954.

Trexler, Harrison A. "The Opposition of Planters to the Employment of Slaves as Laborers by the Confederacy." *Mississippi Valley Historical Review* 27 (September 1940): 211–24.

Turner, Frederick Jackson. *The Frontier in American History*. New York: Henry Holt, 1920.

————. *The United States, 1830–1850*. 1935. Reprint. New York: Norton, 1965.

Tushnet, Mark V. *The American Law of Slavery, 1810–1860: Considerations of Humanity and Interest*. Princeton: Princeton University Press, 1981.

U.S. Census Bureau. *Agriculture of the United States in 1860*. Washington, D.C.: Government Printing Office, 1864.

————. *Compendium of the Ninth Census*. Washington, D.C.: Government Printing Office, 1872.

————. *Compendium of the Seventh Census*. Washington, D.C.: Beverley Tucker, 1854.

————. *Compendium of the Tenth Census, Part 2*. Rev. ed. Washington, D.C.: Government Printing Office, 1888.

————. *Ninth Census*. Vol. 1. *The Statistics of the Population of the United States*. Washington, D.C.: Government Printing Office, 1872.

————. *Population of the United States in 1860*. Washington, D.C.: Government Printing Office, 1864.

————. *Seventh Census of the United States: 1850*. Washington, D.C.: Robert Armstrong, 1853.

————. *Sixth Census: Compendium*. Washington, D.C.: Thomas Allen, 1841.

————. *Wealth, Debt, and Taxation: 1890, Part 2*. Washington, D.C.: Government Printing Office, 1895.

U.S. Department of War. *The War of the Rebellion: A Compilation of the Official Records of the Union and Confederate Armies*. 128 vols. Washington, D.C.: Government Printing Office, 1880–1901.

Vandiver, Frank E. *Rebel Brass: The Confederate Command System*. Baton Rouge: Louisiana State University Press, 1956.

Vipperman, Carl J. "The 'Particular Mission' of Wilson Lumpkin." *Georgia Historical Quarterly* 66 (Fall 1982): 295–316.

Wade, Richard C. *Slavery in the Cities: The South, 1820–1860*. New York: Oxford University Press, 1964.

Wallenstein, Peter. "Conscripts and Convicts: From Road Duty to Chain Gang." Paper presented at the annual meeting of the Organization of American Historians, New York, N.Y., April 1986.

————. "From Slave South to New South: Taxes and Spending in Georgia from 1850 through Reconstruction." Ph.D. diss., Johns Hopkins University, 1973.

―――. "History from the Tax Returns." Paper given at the Workshop on Community Studies in the Nineteenth-Century South, annual meeting of the American Historical Association, Washington, D.C., December 1976.

―――. "Maine, Massachusetts, and the Missouri Compromise: Public Lands in the Political Economy of the Early Republic." Paper given at the annual meeting of the Society for Historians of the Early American Republic, Waltham, Mass., July 1983.

―――. "'More Unequally Taxed than any People in the Civilized World': The Origins of Georgia's Ad Valorem Tax System." *Georgia Historical Quarterly* 69 (Winter 1985): 459–87.

―――. "Rich Man's War, Rich Man's Fight: Civil War and the Transformation of Public Finance in Georgia." *Journal of Southern History* 50 (February 1984): 15–42.

Ward, Judson Clements, Jr. "Georgia Under the Bourbon Democrats, 1872–1890." Ph.D. diss., University of North Carolina, 1947.

―――. "The New Departure Democrats of Georgia: An Interpretation." *Georgia Historical Quarterly* 41 (September 1957): 227–36.

Webb, Sidney, and Beatrice Webb. *The Story of the King's Highway.* Vol. 5 of *English Local Government.* 1906. Reprint. Hamden, Conn.: Archon, 1963.

Webb, Walter Prescott. *The Great Frontier.* Boston: Houghton Mifflin, 1952.

Weiner, Dora B. "The Blind Man and the French Revolution." *Bulletin of the History of Medicine* 48 (Spring 1974): 60–89.

Wetherington, Mark Vickers. "The New South Comes to Wiregrass Georgia, 1865–1910." Ph.D. diss., University of Tennessee, 1985.

White, Leonard D. *The Jeffersonians: A Study in Administrative History, 1801–1829.* New York: Macmillan, 1951.

Wiebe, Robert H. *The Opening of American Society: From the Adoption of the Constitution to the Eve of Disunion.* New York: Knopf, 1984.

Wilentz, Sean. "On Class and Politics in Jacksonian America." *Reviews in American History* 10 (December 1982): 45–63.

Wiley, Bell I. *The Life of Johnny Reb: The Common Soldier of the Confederacy.* Indianapolis: Bobbs-Merrill, 1943.

―――. *The Plain People of the Confederacy.* Baton Rouge: Louisiana State University Press, 1944.

Wittfogel, Karl A. *Oriental Despotism: A Comparative Study of Total Power.* New Haven: Yale University Press, 1957.

Wolfe, Allis. "Women Who Dared: Northern Teachers of the Southern Freedmen." Ph.D. diss., City University of New York, 1982.

Wood, Betty. *Slavery in Colonial Georgia, 1730–1775.* Athens: University of Georgia Press, 1984.

Wood, Frederick A. *History of Taxation in Vermont.* 1894. Reprint. New York: AMS Press, 1968.

Woodman, Harold D. *King Cotton and His Retainers: Financing and Marketing the Cotton Crop of the South, 1800–1925.* Lexington: University Press of Kentucky, 1968.

―――. "Sequel to Slavery: The New History Views the Postbellum South." *Journal of Southern History* 43 (November 1977): 523–54.

Woodson, Carter G., comp. *Free Negro Owners of Slaves in the United States in 1830.*

1924. Reprint. New York: Negro Universities Press, 1968.

Woodward, C. Vann. *Origins of the New South, 1877–1913.* Baton Rouge: Louisiana State University Press, 1951.

Woolfolk, George Ruble. "Taxes and Slavery in the Ante-Bellum South." *Journal of Southern History* 26 (May 1960): 180–200.

Wooster, Ralph A. *The People in Power: Courthouse and Statehouse in the Lower South, 1850–1860.* Knoxville: University of Tennessee Press, 1969.

Wright, Gavin. *Old South, New South: Revolutions in the Southern Economy since the Civil War.* New York: Basic Books, 1986.

———. *The Political Economy of the Cotton South: Households, Markets, and Wealth in the Nineteenth Century.* New York: Norton, 1978.

Wyatt-Brown, Bertram. *Southern Honor: Ethics and Behavior in the Old South.* New York: Oxford University Press, 1982.

Yearns, W. Buck, ed. *The Confederate Governors.* Athens: University of Georgia Press, 1985.

Zilversmit, Arthur. *The First Emancipation: The Abolition of Slavery in the North.* Chicago: University of Chicago Press, 1967.

Zimmerman, Hilda Jane. "The Penal Reform Movement in the South during the Progressive Period, 1890–1917." *Journal of Southern History* 17 (November 1951): 462–92.

INDEX

The
Inflammation
Syndrome

*The Complete Nutritional Program
to Prevent and Reverse Heart Disease,
Arthritis, Diabetes, Allergies, and Asthma*

Jack Challem

WILEY

John Wiley & Sons, Inc.

The Inflammation Syndrome™ and Anti-Inflammation Syndrome™ are trademarks of Jack Challem.

Table on page 42 is from S. B. Eaton and S. B. Eaton II, "Paleolithic vs. Modern Diets—Selected Pathophysical Implications," *European Journal of Nutrition* 39, no. 2 (2000): 67–70. Reprinted with permission.

Quick Chicken or Turkey Rice Soup recipe on page 94 was adapted with permission from Helen Smith and Melissa Diane Smith.

For general information about our other products and services, please contact our Customer Care Department within the United States at (800) 762-2974, outside the United States at (317) 572-3993 or fax (317) 572-4002.

Wiley also publishes its books in a variety of electronic formats. Some content that appears in print may not be available in electronic books. For additional information about Wiley products, visit our website at www.wiley.com.

Library of Congress Cataloging-in-Publication Data:
Challem, Jack.
   The inflammation syndrome : the complete nutritional program to prevent and reverse heart disease, arthritis, diabetes, allergies, and asthma / Jack Challem.
       p. ; cm.
Includes bibliographical references and index.
   ISBN 0-471-20271-1 (cloth)
   1. Inflammation—Diet therapy.   2. Inflammation—Alternative treatment.
3. Chronic diseases—Etiology.
   [DNLM: 1. Inflammation—diet therapy—Popular Works.   2. Anti-Inflammatory Agents—Popular Works.   3. Autoimmune Diseases—diet therapy—Popular Works.
QW 700 C437i 2003]   I. Title.
   RB131 .C475   2003
   616'.0473—dc21   2002014015

10 9 8 7 6 5 4 3 2 1

In memory of Harold G. Miller,
teacher, mentor, and friend.

CONTENTS

FOREWORD

Occasional injuries are part of the human experience, and healing is the body's self-repair process. Healing begins with inflammation, which nature meant to clean up damaged tissues and protect against infection. So if inflammation is beneficial, why are so many modern diseases characterized by chronic and unhealthy inflammation?

The Inflammation Syndrome answers a big part of this important question. Chronic inflammation underscores and promotes virtually every disease, affecting millions of people, and yet inflammation also is a symptom rather than the fundamental cause of these diseases. When we dig deeper, we find that chronic inflammation is the consequence of an injury to the body combined with nutritional imbalances or deficiencies. To properly treat inflammatory diseases, it is essential to correct the underlying dietary problems.

We speak from experience. At the Center for the Improvement of Human Functioning International, physicians, nurses, and other staff members have focused on these objectives for more than twenty-seven years. We use careful clinical and laboratory workups—what is now termed evidence-based medicine—to assess the health, nutritional reserves, and biochemical uniqueness of each patient. We have successfully treated people from around the country and around the world, many of whom were considered untreatable or incurable by conventional medicine.

Through these detailed individual workups, we have gained an understanding of chronic, or sustained, inflammation. More often than not, individuals with chronic inflammation, such as with arthritis and asthma, have low levels of anti-inflammatory antioxidants (such as vitamins E and C), omega-3 fatty acids, and many other important nutrients. Many patients also have previously undetected adverse food reactions, abnormal gut permeability, yeast overgrowth, and hormonal imbalances. All of these factors can impair normal functioning of the immune system, sustaining inflammation well beyond its biological usefulness.

The pharmaceutical perspective of inflammation focuses on relieving symptoms through over-the-counter analgesics and far more powerful prescription drugs. Inflammation does not result from a deficiency of aspirin, cortisone, or Cox-2 inhibitors. Rather, as *The Inflammation Syndrome* so well documents, there is a desperate need to address the basic nutritional influences on chronic inflammation. After all, no drug can ever make up for a nutritional deficiency. Under these circumstances, it becomes paramount to feed a person's biochemistry with the best nutrition.

This is where measuring a patient's nutrient levels proves to be so helpful in confirming the underlying nutritional and biochemical causes of inflammation and motivating patients to action. It would be easy to lecture a patient on the anti-inflammatory effects of good nutrition, omega-3 fatty acids (which include fish oils), or vitamin E. But a far more powerful motivator is testing and demonstrating the patient's low levels.

By doing so, we have found time and again that such hard evidence is extremely persuasive. This meaningful individual information, combined with the ease of dietary improvements and supplementation, empowers patients with knowledge and motivates them toward self-healing. Patients develop the attitude, "I want my levels to be optimal," and then they work toward achieving them. Furthermore, from our medical perspective, laboratory testing enables us to later recheck nutrient values to confirm proper absorption and utilization.

Through testing, we have realized that no one can ever assume that a person's diet is adequate. For example, a cardiac surgeon would never simply hope his patient's potassium level is sufficient to prevent fatal arrhythmias during heart surgery; he ensures that it is. The same approach applies to the treatment of chronic inflammation. To achieve optimal levels of many nutrients, one must often consume levels of vitamins, minerals, and other nutrients above those "officially" recommended for health. There is nothing wrong in doing so, especially when tests have shown patients to be low in these nutrients. At the very least, erring on the side of modest excess provides a margin of safety, a dose of nutritional insurance.

Jack Challem, the author of *The Inflammation Syndrome,* is a gifted health writer with a profound understanding of the role good nutrition plays in health. He has written a sound and practical book of benefit to anyone with chronic inflammation. As we read and discussed his book, we visualized Jack working in a huge lighthouse. The light being emitted is the cumulative scientific evidence so deftly organized and clearly presented here. The danger is the jagged rocks of chronic, sustained inflammation, which underlie almost every serious health issue facing modern society—and the reason for the lighthouse. All of us—readers, patients, and physicians alike—are piloting our own boats and, as a society, we are heading for the rocks. Will we see the light? Can we avoid the forces making us drift in the dark? To survive, we must rediscover the great Hippocratic ideal: Let food be thy medicine.

—Ronald E. Hunninghake, M.D.
Medical Director
The Olive W. Garvey Center for Healing Arts
Wichita, Kansas

—Hugh D. Riordan, M.D.
President
The Center for the Improvement of
Human Functioning International, Inc.
Wichita, Kansas

ACKNOWLEDGMENTS

Many individuals made major and minor contributions to this book. I thank Melissa Diane Smith, who helped renew my interest in wholesome foods and coached me in the kitchen before I began this book. The chapters relating to diet and recipes would not have been possible without her influence.

My sincere appreciation and thanks go to my agent, the late Michael Cohn, and my editor at John Wiley & Sons, Tom Miller, for their commitment to this book's message. I also thank Kimberly Monroe-Hill and William Drennan for their careful copyediting of this book, especially Kimberly's editing of my recipes.

I thank Hugh D. Riordan, M.D., and Ronald E. Hunninghake, M.D., for their encouragement, advice, and kindness.

I thank Hunter Yost, M.D., Malcolm Riley, D.D.S., and Bill Thomson for their reading of the initial manuscript and their excellent suggestions for improvement.

I thank Mary Larsen for her careful reading of the finished manuscript.

I also thank Burt Berkson, M.D., Ph.D., Ashton Embry, Matt Embry, Victor A. Feddersen, Abram Hoffer, M.D., Ph.D., Richard P. Huemer, M.D., Judy Hutt, N.D., Robert Ivker, D.O., Richard Kunin, M.D., Shari Lieberman, Ph.D., Soren Mavrogenis, and the others who kindly contributed case histories.

Special thanks go to Claus Gehringer, Ph.D., Björn Falck Madsen, and Eddie Vos for sharing ideas and pointing out research that I would otherwise have missed.

Introduction

One condition explains your stiff fingers, aching muscles, and arthritic joints. One condition lies at the root of your troublesome allergies and asthma. And one condition describes the underlying cause of heart disease, Alzheimer's disease, and some types of cancer.

It is *inflammation*.

As you read this, medicine is rapidly redefining coronary artery (heart) disease, the leading cause of death among people in the United States and most other Westernized nations, as an inflammatory disease of the blood vessels. Physicians are quickly adopting a new and inexpensive blood test—high-sensitivity C-reactive protein—to measure their patients' level of inflammation and risk of suffering a heart attack. And as the evidence mounts, physicians and medical researchers are recognizing that other major chronic diseases are fueled by inflammation as well.

Most of us understand inflammation as something that causes redness, tenderness, stiffness, and pain. It is the core of inflammatory "-itis" disease, and it also is intertwined in every disease, including obesity, diabetes, and multiple sclerosis.

Inflammation is why professional athletes and weekend warriors often development muscle aches. It is why some people's gums bleed whenever they brush their teeth. And it is why some people develop stomach ulcers.

Despite their different symptoms, all of these health problems are united by the same thread: they have runaway inflammation in common.

And as you may well realize, many people suffer from more than one inflammatory disorder. This constellation of related diseases, such as the combination of heart disease, arthritis, and periodontitis, can best be described as the Inflammation Syndrome.

—⁄⁄⁄—

Estimated Number of North Americans with Some Inflammatory Diseases

Millions of North Americans suffer from inflammatory disorders, some of which have only recently been recognized as inflammatory in nature:

Allergic and nonallergic rhinitis	39 million
Asthma	17 million
Cardiovascular diseases	60 million
Arthritis (all types combined)	70 million
Osteoarthritis	21 million
Rheumatoid arthritis	2 million

—⁄⁄⁄—

Everyone experiences inflammation at one time or another, and we actually need it to survive. But *chronic inflammation* is a sign that something has gone seriously awry with your health. Instead of protecting and healing, chronic inflammation breaks down your body and makes you older and more frail.

Most people treat inflammation with one or more over-the-counter or prescription drugs. At best these drugs temporarily mask the symptoms of inflammation, not treat its underlying causes. Worse, the side effects of these drugs can often be extraordinarily dangerous, causing weight gain, severe stomach pain, bone deformities, and heart failure.

Unfortunately, a physician's diagnosis of many -itis diseases, such as dermatitis or gastritis, is often meaningless. The doctor might feel proud of his diagnosis, but it is merely a description of the symptoms, not of its cause.

To understand the cause of the modern epidemic of inflammatory diseases, we have to look at how the average person's diet has deteriorated over the past two or three generations. The bottom line is that the foods you eat have a powerful bearing on your health and, specifically, inflammation.

How does food influence your inflammation, your aches and pains?

Your body is a remarkable biological machine, designed to make an assortment of pro- and anti-inflammatory substances. What you eat—proteins, carbohydrates, fats, vitamins and vitaminlike nutrients, and minerals—provides the nutritional building blocks of these substances. Some nutrients help form your body's inflammation-promoting compounds, which normally help fight infections. Others help produce your body's anti-inflammatory substances, which moderate and turn off inflammation.

Until recently, people ate a relative balance of pro- and anti-inflammatory nutrients. Today, because of extensive food processing, our diet has become seriously unbalanced. The typical Western diet now contains at least thirty times more of pro-inflammatory nutrients than just a century ago. As a result, people have become nutritionally and biochemically primed for powerful, out-of-control inflammatory reactions. An injury, infection, or sometimes nothing more than age-related wear and tear create the spark that, in a manner of speaking, sets your body on fire.

The Inflammation Syndrome reveals many of the hidden dangers in foods that set the stage for inflammation, worsen aches and pains, and increase the long-term risk of debilitating and life-threatening diseases. This book explains how and why inflammation eats away at your health.

For example:

- Common cooking oils, such as corn, safflower, and soy oils, can make arthritis and asthma worse.
- Fries and other deep-fried foods, breakfast bars, and cookies can interfere with your body's innate ability to control inflammation.
- Corn-fed beef, promoted as healthy, is far worse than grass-fed beef and can aggravate your inflammation.
- Not eating your vegetables or taking your vitamins can increase breathing problems in people with asthma.
- Being overweight increases your body's production of inflammation-causing substances.
- Taking common anti-inflammatory drugs will actually make your osteoarthritis far worse.
- If you have one inflammatory disease, you are likely to develop others in the coming years, because the inflammation will eventually spread and affect other parts of your body.

I have had my own experience with inflammation and how I have avoided chronic pain. Several years ago, while in the British Museum in London, I paid careful attention to a sign reading "Mind the Step." Unfortunately for me, the area was not well lit and the sign failed to warn me of a second step. I tripped and seriously injured my right foot. The pain was so excruciating that I almost passed out. I sat down while my head cleared and, I had hoped, for the pain to ease.

It didn't. By the next morning, my entire foot was literally turning black and blue. Although no bones were broken, I did give myself one of the most serious types of muscle strain. A couple of days later, on the next leg of my trip, in France, I hobbled around at a scientific conference on antioxidant vitamins. Climbing into the shower was an ordeal, as was putting on my socks and shoes. My foot had swelled, its color was awful, and I was taking aspirin several times daily to reduce the inflammation, swelling, and pain.

Weeks later, at home, my foot had regained its normal color and, by all outward signs, had healed. However, I still felt a sharp pain in the foot whenever I walked. I realized that this injury, if it did not heal soon and properly, could lead to a lifetime of chronic inflammation and pain. Frustratingly, all of the vitamin supplements I had been taking for years didn't seem to help. And then it dawned on me. That scientific meeting in France was about a well-known herbal antioxidant made from French maritime pine bark (called Pycnogenol), and the scientific literature showed it to have powerful anti-inflammatory effects. I started taking it, and within days the pain went away. To rule out the power of suggestion, I stopped taking the supplement for a few days, and the pain returned. I started taking the supplement again and the inflammation and pain went away and have never returned. I walk and hike long distances without any discomfort in the foot.

The Inflammation Syndrome does not simply dwell on the problem of inflammation. Most of this book coaches you on how to avoid the foods that make you more susceptible to information and to instead select foods that can reduce inflammation and your risk of many diseases. *The Inflammation Syndrome* describes a new way of viewing inflammatory disorders as a consequence of eating an unbalanced diet.

You will learn plenty of practical information about how to prevent and reverse inflammation. The book's Anti-Inflammation Syndrome Diet Plan describes

- the dietary imbalances that lead to chronic inflammation;
- a balanced, nutritious diet plan to reduce inflammation;
- tasty recipes and guidelines for making your own anti-inflammatory meals;

- the best natural anti-inflammation supplements, such as fish oils, vitamin E, herbs, and many others;
- case histories of patients treated by nutritionally oriented practitioners.

You may wonder why you should trust the advice of someone who is not a physician.

The reason is simple, though it may surprise you: while I believe the majority of physicians are sincere and well-meaning, most do not understand the fundamental role of nutrition in health. Medical schools teach virtually nothing about the practical, preventive, and therapeutic uses of nutrition and supplements. The doctors I write about in this book are notable exceptions to this rule in that they are both sincere *and* have an understanding of nutrition.

For more than twenty-five years, I have been reading scientific and medical journals; talking with nutritionally oriented biologists, biochemists, and physicians; and writing about how vitamins, minerals, and other aspects of nutrition can greatly improve health. I have also published original research articles in medical journals, something rare for nutrition writers. Though I am not a medical scientist, I have a solid understanding of the science behind the health benefits of nutrition and supplements.

In many ways, *The Inflammation Syndrome* expands on the concepts described in my previous book *Syndrome X: The Complete Nutritional Program to Prevent and Reverse Insulin Resistance.* Far more than genes, poor eating habits are at the core of most modern degenerative disorders, including chronic inflammation. *The Inflammation Syndrome* is supported by hundreds of scientific studies and by successful clinical experiences, many of which you will read. Some of my scientific references are at the back of this book, and I encourage you to share all of them with your physician.

Ultimately, you alone are responsible for your own health. You cannot ignore your personal responsibility and simply turn your body over to a doctor the way you might ask a mechanic to fix your car. This book provides a plan for you to empower yourself to safely prevent and overcome inflammatory disorders. You will discover how easy it is to take charge of your diet and your health—and to feel better than you ever imagined.

PART I

The Inflammation-
Disease Connection

CHAPTER 1

Meet the Inflammation Syndrome

Hank and Debra: The Deadly Effects of the Inflammation Syndrome

For Hank and Debra, what they didn't know came back to hurt them.

In college they were athletic, trim, and attractive. Hank was the star of the college football team, and Debra was an avid tennis player. Youth was on their side, and they quickly recovered from the inevitable athletic injuries.

After they graduated and married Hank pursued a career in sales, enjoying its competitive nature but not immediately recognizing how it kept him from exercising. Meanwhile, Debra juggled motherhood and periodic jobs to earn extra money. Like many people, they learned to save time by eating mostly ready-to-heat convenience foods and fast-food restaurant meals, which tended to be high in fat and carbohydrates and low in vegetables.

Hank regularly suffered from heartburn and indigestion, but he never figured out that his poor food choices were the source of his stomach upsets. Debra had developed asthma and mild rheumatoid arthritis. Both were prescribed medications by their physicians, but diet was never even considered a potential factor in their deteriorating health.

By middle age their trim athletic figures were little more than a memory. Hank had gone from a lean 180 to 250 pounds, and Debra's weight had ballooned from 110 to 180 pounds. Hank's blood cholesterol was elevated and, combined with his weight, significantly increased his risk for heart disease. He had also developed chronic aches and pains in his shoulders and hips, a result of old football injuries. Meanwhile, Debra's asthma and arthritis had gotten worse, and she was taking prednisone and other medications to control her symptoms.

In their fifties Hank developed adult-onset (type 2) diabetes and Debra was diagnosed with breast cancer. Hank was prescribed a glucose-lowering drug, and Debra underwent surgery and chemotherapy.

Having gone through all that, their health seemed relatively stable for several years. But retirement saw no relief for their health problems. Hank was taking eight prescription medications and Debra was taking six. At age sixty-two Debra's breast cancer reappeared, and treatment failed. She died at age sixty-three. Hank, who was largely confined to home (and had hot meals and groceries delivered by a local social service organization) had a heart attack and died at sixty-five.

All of Hank and Debra's health problems were treated according to the prevailing medical standards of care. But their doctors failed to see that poor food choices and chronic inflammation were intertwined in many of their health problems. As a result the doctors treated only symptoms, not the causes of Hank and Debra's problems.

Every disease, every ache, and every pain you suffer revolves around inflammation.

Inflammation is what causes the pain of arthritis, the discomfort of allergies, the wheezing of asthma, and the stiffness from overusing your muscles. Inflammation also underlies the most devastating and catastrophic of all diseases: heart disease, Alzheimer's disease, and many forms of cancer.

If that seems hard to believe, consider that over-the-counter anti-inflammatory drugs reduce the risk of heart attacks and Alzheimer's disease. But this book is not going to recommend that you take drugs to reduce inflammation. Their side effects all too often outweigh their benefits, especially when natural and safe anti-inflammatory foods and nutrients abound.

Even if you seem to be pretty healthy today, odds are that inflammation is simmering in your body, quietly damaging your heart, your mind, your organs. Such inflammation may be stirred up by physical injuries,

frequent colds and flus, allergies, eating the wrong types of fats and carbohydrates, and by having a "spare tire" around your middle. At a certain point your inflammation will boil over into painful and debilitating
symptoms.

Inflammation is a normal process that can go dreadfully wrong. It is
supposed to protect us from infections and promote healing when we are
injured.

Chronic inflammation does just the opposite: it breaks down our bodies and makes us more susceptible to disease. Inflammation forces millions of people with arthritis to alter their daily lives, and it adds caution
to the millions of people with asthma who do not know when their next
suffocating attack will occur. Millions of other people—with multiple
sclerosis, lupus, diabetes, and other disorders—also suffer from chronic
inflammation.

The Inflammation Syndrome

Individual inflammatory disorders such as asthma or rheumatoid arthritis
are bad enough. Far more insidious is the Inflammation Syndrome, the
significance of which is only now being recognized in medical circles.

A syndrome is a group of symptoms that characterizes a particular
disorder. For example, in my previous book *Syndrome X: The Complete
Nutritional Program to Prevent and Reverse Insulin Resistance*, Syndrome X was defined as the clustering of abdominal fat, insulin resistance, hypertension, and elevated cholesterol—all of which significantly
increase the risk of diabetes and coronary artery disease.

Similarly, the Inflammation Syndrome reflects the coexistence of at
least two inflammatory disorders that significantly increase the risk of
more serious inflammatory diseases. What causes this ongoing buildup in
inflammation? Although an inflammatory response may primarily affect
specific tissues, such as the knees, it commonly radiates through the body
and randomly attacks other tissues. Over a number of years this systemic
(bodywide) inflammation can contribute to diseases that might appear unrelated but that do share a common thread of chronic inflammation.

Some examples of the inflammation syndrome are in order. Let's start
with being overweight, a condition that affects two-thirds of Americans
and growing numbers of people in most other developed countries.

Excess weight contributes to inflammation because fat cells secrete
chemicals, such as C-reactive protein and interleukin-6, that promote inflammation. Being overweight increases the risk of many other diseases,

and part of the reason is related to inflammation. If you are overweight, you have a greater risk of developing adult-onset diabetes, which also has a strong inflammatory component. Inflammation in diabetes is related to being overweight, to having elevated blood sugar and insulin levels, and to consuming too many refined carbohydrates (such as white bread and sugary breakfast cereals).

The Inflammation Syndrome does not stop here. Having diabetes also increases the risk of periodontitis, a type of dental inflammation. Each of these disorders—overweight, diabetes, and periodontitis—is serious by itself. But as the inflammation in these disorders simmers year after year, it also increases the risk of coronary artery disease, which medicine has recently recognized as an inflammatory disease of the blood vessels. In a nutshell each inflammatory disorder has an additive effect, increasing the body's overall level of inflammation and the risk of very serious diseases.

Many other examples of the Inflammation Syndrome abound. Allergies stir up the inflammatory response, increasing the risk of rheumatoid arthritis, an autoimmune (self-allergic) disease. Infections also trigger an immune response, and chronic infections and inflammation account for an estimated 30 percent of cancers. Joint injuries frequently set an inflammatory response into motion, setting the stage for osteoarthritis. Serious head injuries and their resultant brain inflammation increase the long-term risk of Alzheimer's disease, which is also being viewed by doctors as an inflammatory process affecting brain cells.

This is serious and scary stuff, and the stakes for your health are very high. But the point of this book is that chronic inflammation and the inflammation syndrome can be prevented and reversed. This book shows you how.

What Is Chronic Inflammation?

Inflammation assumes many different forms, and everyone experiences it at one time or another. Perhaps the most common type of inflammation is sudden and acute, such as when you burn yourself in the kitchen, overuse muscles when moving furniture, or injure tendons when playing sports. The injured area swells, turns red, and becomes tender to touch.

Under normal circumstances inflammation helps you heal, and it can even save your life. For example, if you accidentally cut your finger with a knife, bacteria from the knife, air, or surface of your skin immediately penetrate the breach. Unchecked, these bacteria would quickly spread through your bloodstream and kill you.

However, your body's immune system almost immediately recognizes these bacteria as foreign and unleashes a coordinated attack to contain and stop the infection. Inflammation encourages tiny blood vessels in your finger to dilate, allowing a variety of white blood cells to leak out, track, and engulf bacteria. Some of these white blood cells also pick up and destroy cells damaged by the cut. In addition, inflammation signals the body to grow new cells to seal the cut. Within a day or two your cut finger becomes less inflamed, and a few days later it is completely healed.

Your body responds in similar fashion if you strain a muscle, such as by lifting too heavy a box, or by overexerting yourself during sports. The resulting inflammation, characterized by swelling, pain, and stiffness, is designed to remove damaged muscle cells and help initiate the healing process to replace those cells. Again, within a few days the inflammation decreases and you are well on the road to recovery.

Chronic inflammation, however, is very different. It does not go away, at least not quickly, and many people believe from their own experience that it will never go away. It results in persistent swelling, stiffness, or pain. Furthermore, you become more susceptible to inflammation as you age, but that, too, may be reversible.

—ɷ—

QUIZ 1

How Is Your Current Health?

Have you been diagnosed with one of the following conditions, regardless of whether you are taking medications for treatment:

AIDS or HIV infection	*Add 2 points* _____
Asthma	*Add 2 points* _____
Bronchitis	*Add 1 point* _____
Celiac disease or gluten intolerance	*Add 2 points* _____
Coronary artery (heart) disease	*Add 2 points* _____
Diabetes or elevated blood sugar	*Add 2 points* _____
Gingivitis or periodontitis	*Add 1 point* _____
Hepatitis	*Add 2 points* _____
Inflammatory bowel disease	*Add 2 points* _____

Rheumatoid arthritis	*Add 2 points*	_____
Osteoarthritis	*Add 2 points*	_____
Eczema, psoriasis, or frequent sunburn	*Add 1 point*	_____
Stomach ulcers	*Add 1 point*	_____
Ulcerated varicose veins	*Add 2 points*	_____
A recent physical injury—by accident, or through sports/athletics, or via a severe sunburn	*Add 1 point*	_____

Do you have any consistently stiff or aching joints, such as those in your fingers or knees?

Add 1 point _____

Does your body feel stiff when you get out of bed in the morning?

Add 1 point _____

If you are overweight by ten pounds or less, do you carry all or most of the extra fat around your abdomen?

Add 1 point _____

If you are obese (more than twenty pounds over your ideal weight), do you carry all or most of the extra fat around your abdomen?

Add 2 points _____

Is your nose stuffed up or runny a lot of the time?

Add 1 point _____

Do you get injured (anything from serious bruises to broken bones several or more times a year) because of accidents, the nature of your work, or athletic activities?

Add 1 point _____

Have you been hospitalized for surgery during the past twelve months?

Add 1 point _____

Do you smoke or chew tobacco products?

Add 2 points _____

Do you get frequent colds or flus?

Add 1 point _____

Do you have any seasonal allergies, such as to pollens or molds?

Add 1 point _____

Do you have any skin sores or rashes that don't seem to go away?

Add 1 point _____

Your score on quiz 1: _____

Interpretation and ranking:

0–1 Low. You have a low level of inflammation, which is healthy.
2–6 Moderate. You have a moderate level of inflammation that affects your current health and poses risks to your long-term health, and you should work to reverse it.
7–20 High. You have a high level of inflammation, which is very harmful and requires immediate attention to reverse.
21+ Very high. Although rare, your level of inflammation is extremely high and should be reversed without delay.

Can Your Doctor Measure Inflammation?

For many disorders inflammation is so obvious it does not have to be measured. For example, the pain of arthritis is a clear enough sign of inflammation. Swelling, redness, and tenderness to the touch also are obvious signs of inflammation in muscle injuries, gingivitis, and many other disorders. These are typically localized forms of inflammation, though they burden the entire body with a variety of inflammation-promoting substances. Tests to confirm inflammation in these situations may be an unnecessary expense.

More general systemic, or bodywide, inflammation is not always apparent. Inflammation of blood vessel walls increases the risk of a heart attack, and inflammation of the stomach wall (gastritis) greatly increases the risk of ulcers and gastric cancer.

A common blood test measures the sedimentation rate (or "sed rate"), reflecting how fast red blood cells settle and form a sediment. Inflammation makes blood cells settle faster. The drawback to the sedimentation rate is that it is an extremely general indicator of inflammation.

Another test, called the high-sensitivity C-reactive protein (hs CRP) test, is a better indicator of systemic inflammation, though it still has the drawback of being a general indicator rather than pointing to a specific type of inflammation. Elevated CRP levels are associated with a 4.5 greater risk of having a heart attack, making it a far more accurate predictor than elevated cholesterol. Elevated CRP levels also are found in people with Alzheimer's disease, cancer, arthritis, acute infection, and physical trauma.

Recognizing Inflammatory Disorders

Physicians often speak in their own language, but it is actually very easy to identify most inflammatory diseases when you hear them in conversation or read about them. Most inflammatory diseases end with the suffix "-itis." For example, gastritis means inflammation of the stomach, tendinitis refers to inflammation of the tendons, and gingivitis means inflammation of the gingiva (gums).

At one time a physician's diagnosis typically included both the symptoms and the apparent cause of a disease. Unfortunately, that has changed, and the diagnosis of an -itis disease (and most other diseases as well) is now often nothing more than a description of symptoms. Dermatitis, an inflammation of the skin, can have many causes, including allergies, infections, a toxic reaction to a chemical, or abrasion. As good as you or your doctor might feel after a diagnosis, it is not likely that he or she will actually identify the underlying cause.

In the case of coronary artery disease something inflames blood vessel walls, triggering a cascade of events. That "something" might be a corrosive protein by-product called homocysteine, a low-grade infection, or oxidized cholesterol, all of which increase the risk of heart disease. (This relationship between inflammatory and cardiovascular disease will be discussed in depth in chapters 9 and 12.) In response, white blood cells migrate to artery walls, where they release free radicals, fuel inflammation, and exacerbate the damage. The most accurate predictor of whether you will have a heart attack is not your cholesterol, triglyceride, or blood sugar level. Rather, it is a high blood level of C-reactive protein, an indicator of your body's overall inflammation.

Common Inflammatory Diseases and Disorders

Inflammation is a symptom of virtually every disease process, and it often makes the condition worse. These are some examples of common disorders that involve inflammation:

Arthritis
   Osteoarthritis
   Rheumatoid arthritis
Injuries
   Athletic: tendinitis, bursitis, muscle strains, and bruises
   Cuts, broken bones, bruises, surgery

Infections
   Colds, flus, otitis media, hepatitis C, HIV, parasites, vague low-grade infections
Allergies/autoimmune
   Pollen and other inhalant allergies (rhinitis, nonallergic rhinitis)
   Food allergies
   Celiac disease (gluten intolerance)
   Lupus erythematosus
Pulmonary
   Asthma
   Chronic obstructive pulmonary disease
   Bronchitis
Cardiovascular
   Coronary artery disease, myocarditis, hypertension
   Phlebitis, varicose veins
Cancer
   Various types, including gastric, lung, breast, and prostate
Neurological
   Alzheimer's disease
Skin
   Sunburn (erythema)
   Eczema and dermatitis
   Psoriasis
Dental
   Gingivitis
   Periodontitis
Eye
   Conjunctivitis
   Uveitis
Digestive tract
   Gastritis, ulcers
   Crohn's disease
   Ulcerative colitis
   Diverticulitis
Miscellaneous
   Sinusitis
   Multiple sclerosis
   Obesity
   Diabetes

The Prevalence of Inflammation

One way to look at the prevalence of inflammatory diseases is to track sales (and, by implication, the use) of anti-inflammatory drugs such as aspirin, ibuprofen, naproxen sodium, and Cox-2 inhibitors. Each year more than 30 billion tablets of nonsteroidal anti-inflammatory drugs (NSAIDs) are sold over the counter in the United States—more than one hundred for every man, woman, and child. In addition, doctors write 70 million prescriptions for even stronger NSAIDs. Although some NSAIDs are often used to treat headaches (which may be caused by inflammation), these numbers reflect an enormous dependency on anti-inflammatory drugs.

Indeed, one of the pieces of evidence that coronary artery disease and Alzheimer's disease are inflammatory diseases is the fact that both may be prevented with some anti-inflammatory drugs. Aspirin reduces the risk of a heart attack, and ibuprofen (the active ingredient in Advil) appears to reduce the risk of Alzheimer's disease. Unfortunately, serious and sometimes life-threatening side effects are common from both drugs, which makes them undesirable approaches to prevention or treatment.

None of these drugs treats the underlying causes of inflammation. At best, they provide short-term relief. Worse, some NSAIDs hasten the breakdown of joint cartilage, increasing the damage and the progression of osteoarthritis. You will learn more about the dangers of anti-inflammatory drugs in chapter 5.

CHAPTER 2

Your Inflammation Triggers

Georgia: Allergies and Sinusitis

Georgia had suffered from chronic sinusitis, an inflammation or infection of the air spaces near the nose, since she was twelve, and developed asthma at age forty-one. She was also allergic to dust, grasses, smoke, perfumes, wool, and some cosmetics. Within a few years of her asthma diagnosis, Georgia was taking a variety of prescription drugs: oral and nasal, a bronchodilator, antibiotics, and other medications. She started to feel addicted to her asthma drugs and was afraid to be without them.

Her asthma was aggravated by the sinus problems, and Georgia found herself taking increasingly stronger medications. She also was having frequent and severe headaches. At age fifty-two, she consulted holistic physician Robert S. Ivker, D.O., of Denver, Colorado, author of several books, including *Sinus Survival, Asthma Survival,* and *Headache Survival.*

Ivker recommended a number of nutritional supplements, including vitamins E and C, beta-carotene, selenium, zinc, and an overall multivitamin, as well as a herbal echinacea and goldenseal combination. He also treated Georgia for candida infection and recommended that she purchase a negative-ion generator to improve the air quality in her home. These changes were combined with a tapering off of some of her medications and the beginning of a gradual exercise program, with walking and riding a stationary bicycle.

Two months after Georgia's first visit to Ivker, she had a new vitality and higher energy levels. She also had lost five pounds. Over the next year or so she was able to stop using all of her medications. Recognizing the role of emotion in illness, Ivker asked Georgia to focus on strengthening her family relationships. Today, with her newfound health, Georgia and her husband are planning for an active retirement.

Inflammation Triggers

Physicians and patients alike routinely confuse the *causes* of inflammation with its *triggers*. The causes of inflammation are often related to dietary imbalances or deficiencies, which prime the immune system for a powerful and chronic inflammatory reaction.

In contrast, inflammation triggers are the events that precipitate a specific inflammatory response *after* the body is already primed for an overreaction. Although it is not the same as correcting the causes of inflammation, it is very important to avoid events that trigger inflammation. Doing so helps settle down an easily agitated immune system.

First, try to reduce your exposure to inflammation triggers. For example, if you have food allergies, make a point of avoiding troublesome foods. Similarly, if you are a weekend-warrior athlete who frequently gets injured, it might be good to take up a more moderate and regular physical activity, such as swimming or walking. Repeated injuries keep revving up the body's inflammatory response.

Second, it is important to dampen the immune response to unavoidable triggers (e.g., seasonal pollen allergies). And third, it would be ideal to normalize the immune response to inflammation triggers. The second and third approaches rely chiefly on dietary changes and nutritional supplements, and these approaches are discussed in depth in later chapters.

For now, there are six general categories of inflammatory triggers to understand.

1. Age-Related Wear and Tear: What Is Your *Biological* Age?

Every living creature ages, and age is characterized by less biological efficiency and an accelerated breakdown of tissue and normal biochemical processes. When tissues break down white blood cells are mobilized to clean up, in a manner of speaking, the biological dust. The aging process occurs at individual rates of speed and is influenced by a variety of factors, including genetics, diet, frequency of infections, stress, and overall lifestyle. Of particular interest, levels of the body's key pro-inflammatory substances generally increase with age. This rise may be due to age-related tissue breakdown—and the immune system's response to it—or perhaps to the long-term effect of eating a pro-inflammatory diet.

Although most of us think of our age chronologically, our biological age is actually far more important. Chronological age refers to how many years old a person is, whereas biological age assesses age in terms of physical and mental performance. Many people in their seventies and eighties have more vigor and better health than do people half their age. Some researchers have noted that healthy centenarians are not simply healthy old people. They are often healthier than younger seniors and in many ways on a par with people in their forties.

One way to maintain a lower biological age is to reduce tissue breakdown and the inflammation it stimulates. In a general way diets rich in vegetables and fruits provide large quantities of antioxidants, such as vitamin C, carotenoids, and flavonoids. These antioxidants neutralize damaging free radicals. For example, people who eat large amounts of antioxidant-rich vegetables develop fewer wrinkles and look younger. In a more specific example, many people take glucosamine sulfate supplements, which help maintain "younger" joints and reduce the pain of osteoarthritis.

2. Physical Injuries

Physical injuries can accelerate the aging of specific tissues, such as joints, muscles, and bone. Many such injuries, such as falling and breaking a bone, or musculoskeletal athletic injuries, can become the source of painful and debilitating lifelong health problems. Former heavyweight boxing champion Muhammed Ali, who was physically and mentally agile as a young man, developed Parkinson's disease as a consequence of cumulative brain damage in the ring. These injuries become sources of chronic inflammation and pain because they are initially serious, repeated, do not heal properly, or promote sustained low-grade inflammation in the damaged tissues.

To minimize your chances of suffering a physical injury, you have to be careful of reckless behavior. For example, it's smart to drive defensively and to watch where you step, so you reduce the risk of tripping. As you reach middle age it may be better to adopt low-impact activities, such as swimming or walking.

3. Infections

In January 2002 researchers reported in the journal *Circulation* that repeated infections greatly increased a person's risk of dying from coronary artery disease. Literally, the more infections people experienced, the more likely they were to develop and die from heart disease. It wasn't that the bacteria and viruses were directly infecting the heart. More likely, repeated infections maintained a heightened activity of immune cells, which unleashed part of their damage on blood vessel walls.

Infections turn on the body's most powerful inflammatory responses, and sometimes the body ends up fighting itself. For example, a person who catches one cold after another suffers through a state of chronic inflammation with periodic peaks of inflammation, which slowly but surely attack and break down the entire body.

It is possible, nutritionally, to boost the *efficiency* of the immune system's response to infections. Vitamins C and E and a nutritional supplement called N-acetylcysteine (NAC) can greatly reduce the inflammatory symptoms of infections.

—⟋⟍—

Common Inflammation Triggers

Triggers prompt an inflammatory response when the body is already primed for such a reaction. These triggers do not cause an abnormal inflammatory reaction when the body is not primed for an overreaction.

Age-related wear and tear
    Lifelong breakdown of tissues
    Accelerated aging from poor dietary and lifestyle decisions
Physical injuries
    Repeated or severe athletic injuries
    Broken bones, cuts, wounds, burns, temporomandibular disease
Infections
    Frequent or chronic low-grade (e.g., colds and flus)
    Hepatitis or HIV
    Sepsis
    Chronic parasitic
Environmental stresses
    Sunburn, sunlight (ultraviolet rays)
    Tobacco, air pollution, lung irritants

Ionizing radiation
Cold air, exercise (asthma triggers)
Allergies and food sensitivities
   Pollen, mold, and other inhalant allergies
   Food sensitivities (may lead to ear infections), nightshades
   Cerebral allergies (affecting behavior and cognition)
   Celiac disease, gluten intolerance, lectin intolerance
Dietary imbalances and deficiencies
   Obesity (increases pro-inflammatory substances)
   Diabetes (elevates blood sugar)
   Inadequate vitamin C (increases blood vessel leakage)
   Inadequate B-complex vitamins (elevates homocysteine)
   Inadequate dietary antioxidants (stimulates inflammation)
   Imbalance in dietary fats (stimulates inflammation)

4. Environmental Stresses

Many common environmental stresses also can stimulate acute and chronic inflammatory responses. For example, tobacco smoke and other forms of air pollution irritate the lungs and activate large numbers of white blood cells, which contribute to further damage.

Cold air and exercise trigger severe asthma attacks in many people. The immune system of a person with asthma misreads the physiological changes triggered by cold air and exercise and overreacts to them. People with asthma are known to have abnormally high levels of free radicals, which prolong inflammation, but they can be reduced with such antioxidants as vitamin C and beta-carotene.

5. Allergies and Food Sensitivities

Pollen allergies, such as to ragweed, are common and have been increasing in prevalence. The most common allergenic pollens are from grasses, trees, and weeds, with sensitive people reacting when these plants release pollen into the air. Many people are also allergic to molds and dust. Their symptoms are collectively referred to as allergic rhinitis. About 15 percent of the North American population suffers from seasonal allergic rhinitis, and millions more people experience nonallergic rhinitis—basically nasal congestion or a runny nose unrelated to inhaled allergens.

Food sensitivities are allergiclike reactions. Some common allergies, such as to peanuts or shrimp, raise levels of IgE (immunoglobulin E), the conventional marker of an allergy. Beyond this, the topic of food allergies has often been charged with controversy because it has been difficult to identify a specific immune sign of a reaction. However, in recent years some physicians have found that many food allergies raise levels of IgG, which, like IgE, triggers a cascade of events that alter physical and mental health. Because blood tests may not always identify a specific immune reaction, you may have to rely on symptoms related to specific foods.

Nutritionally oriented physicians recommend strict avoidance of food allergens, and they often suggest that patients follow a "rotation diet" to reduce the likelihood of new food allergies developing. A rotation diet prohibits eating the same food or food from the same family (such as dairy) more often than once every four days. Sometimes allergic reactivity will diminish after several months of avoiding problematic foods.

Abnormal gut permeability may be created by an imbalance in various species of intestinal bacteria and the overgrowth of undesirable bacteria or yeasts such as *Candida albicans.* A "yeast infection," whatever the cause, can aggravate gut permeability, allergies, and inflammatory symptoms.

Maureen: Drugs Didn't Work

Maureen, a fifty-seven-year-old woman, had chronic but mild and manageable muscle and joint pains. She rarely ate tomatoes until her neighbor shared a bumper crop of tomatoes and eggplants, foods that are members of the nightshade plant family.

She soon began experiencing a significant increase in her joint pain, which was not relieved by anti-inflammatory medications. When Maureen related her health history to Hunter Yost, M.D., of Tucson, Arizona, he immediately recognized the likely cause of her increased pain: she is one of those people who is nightshade-sensitive.

Dr. Yost asked her to immediately stop eating all nightshades, which also include red and green peppers and potatoes. Within one week of eliminating all of these foods, Maureen had a significant decrease in joint pain, though her muscle pain did persist.

6. Dietary Imbalances and Deficiencies

Many dietary factors besides food allergies can lead to chronic inflammation. Being overweight—most often a consequence of either too many calories or too many carbohydrates—is a risk factor for many diseases, such as heart disease, cancer, diabetes, and osteoarthritis. The type of fat cells that develop around the abdomen generate large amounts of powerful inflammatory substances, such as C-reactive protein. Yes, obesity is an inflammatory disease.

An imbalance of dietary fats is a major promoter of inflammation. Many of the inflammation-sustaining fats are found in common cooking oils and packaged foods. When a balance of dietary fats is restored, through diet and supplements, the body regains its natural ability to both turn on and turn off inflammation.

Elevated blood sugar (glucose) levels, stemming from a diet with too many refined carbohydrates and sugars, also can increase inflammation in the body. People with insulin resistance commonly have high levels of C-reactive protein, a sign of inflammation. Insulin resistance is at the heart of Syndrome X and type 2 diabetes. Syndrome X, which increases the risk of both diabetes and heart disease, is also marked by fat around the waist, high blood pressure, and high cholesterol and triglycerides. For more information on Syndrome X see my earlier book *Syndrome X*.

The next chapter explains what happens during an inflammatory reaction, how the body makes powerful inflammation-producing substances from foods, and why many foods make us overreact to inflammation triggers.

CHAPTER 3

The Dietary Causes
of Inflammation

If injuries, infections, pollens, and other physical insults merely trigger inflammatory reactions, the obvious question is: What makes a normal process go out of control?

The answer lies in the foods we eat. If you eat the typical North American (or Western) diet, with abundant convenience and fast foods, you likely consume an unbalanced intake of the nutrients that promote inflammation. This imbalance results in large part from massive changes to our food supply over the past half century or so. During this time highly processed pro-inflammatory foods have largely replaced anti-inflammatory fresh and natural foods. The consequence has primed our bodies for chronic, excessive, and self-destructive levels of inflammation.

How do foods affect inflammation? The foods you eat provide the building blocks of your body and, of particular importance, your immune system, which regulates inflammation. Your immune system consists of dozens of specialized types of cells and molecules that constantly monitor your body for anything "foreign" or unusual. To envision this, it might help to picture how a taut, silken web alerts its resident spider to the presence of an insect. When a fly touches some threads in the web the resulting vibrations are transmitted and amplified throughout the web. These vibrations alert the spider, which moves in for the kill.

The cells of the immune system operate much like the interlocking filaments of the spider web. An immune cell senses the presence of an intruder (such as infectious bacteria or some other material, such as a damaged or dead cell) that does not belong in the body. An immune cell shares information about the peculiarity with other immune cells. Together they coordinate a response and, if the immune system is working properly, dispose of the foreign material.

You might wonder whether a powerful immune response is really necessary, but there is a biological rationale for it. Historically, infections have been the leading cause of human deaths. Even today, infections remain the third leading cause of death in the United States and the leading cause worldwide. A strong immune response gave us a fighting chance against infections. However, intense inflammatory responses are inappropriate when they target healthy tissues or harmless pollens, or when the body lacks normal switches to turn off inflammation.

Barbara: Inflammation, Rheumatoid Arthritis, and Asthma

At age forty-one, Barbara had suffered with rheumatoid arthritis and asthma for years and was taking half a dozen prescription drugs, which barely kept her symptoms in check. Then Barbara's physician started her on the hormone prednisone. After seven months on the drug she had gained 100 pounds—she was carrying 251 pounds on her 5'2" frame—and also developed the "moon face" characteristic of prednisone users. The cure was worse than the disease.

As a last-ditch effort, she went to a nutritionally oriented medical center in Wichita, Kansas. There, Hugh D. Riordan, M.D., and Ronald E. Hunninghake, M.D., found Barbara low in two essential "good" fats that are natural anti-inflammatory nutrients, as well as low in vitamins C and E and other nutrients. Lab tests also determined that Barbara had several allergylike food and chemical sensitivities, which helped fuel her overactive immune system and runaway inflammation.

The prescription was remarkably simple. Drs. Riordan and Hunninghake recommended that Barbara eat a more wholesome diet, avoid the foods and chemicals she was sensitive to, and take fish oil supplements (which contain the good fats) and vitamins. Nine months later, her asthma was completely gone, her arthritic symptoms were so mild that she reduced her prednisone to less than one-thousandth of the dose she had been taking—from 40 mg daily to 1 mg per month—and she was able to stop taking all the other medications. Barbara also had lost seventy pounds, and her outlook toward life changed as well. She was now energetic, upbeat, and outgoing.

Pro- and Anti-Inflammatory Counterbalances

With all the bad news we hear about fats, it may surprise you to read that some types of fats form the foundation of the body's pro- and anti-inflammatory compounds. Contrary to what you may have heard, fats (also known as fatty acids) are not inherently bad for health. Many fats are as essential for health as proteins, carbohydrates, vitamins, and minerals. Pro- and anti-inflammatory fats should serve as counterbalances to each other. Chronic inflammation can develop when there is a sharp imbalance in the types of fats consumed.

To understand how some fats increase or decrease inflammation, it helps to see them (and other pro- and anti-inflammatory substances) in simple terms, such as "matches" or "firefighters." Chronic inflammation often results from too many dietary matches. However, by making greater use of dietary firefighters you can restore a balance that prevents or even reverses chronic inflammation.

Pro-Inflammatory Matches

Two specific types of fats, as well as free radicals, prime our bodies for inflammation. Here is a brief description of them.

- The *omega-6* family of fatty acids supplies the building blocks of a variety of powerful pro-inflammatory substances. The omega-6 fatty acids are commonly found as *linoleic acid,* most often in vegetable oils such as corn, safflower, peanut, cottonseed, and soy oils, as well as in processed and packaged foods containing these oils. The omega-6 fatty acids stimulate the body's production of many other inflammation-causing chemicals, such as prostaglandin E_2.
- *Trans fatty acids* are hidden in products containing "partially hydrogenated vegetable oils," including salad dressings, breakfast bars, shortening, nondairy creamers, stick margarines, and many baked items such as cakes and cookies. Omega-6 vegetable oils are bad enough in themselves, but hydrogenation gives them many of the characteristics of saturated fats. Trans fatty acids do much of their damage by interfering with the body's handling of anti-inflammatory fats, specifically the omega-3 fatty acids.
- *Free radicals* are hazardous molecules that damage the body's cells, increase the risk of many diseases, and accelerate the aging process. They also stimulate and prolong inflammatory reactions.

Anti-Inflammatory Firefighters

Three specific types of fats, as well as antioxidant nutrients, help control inflammation. Here is a brief overview of them.

- The *omega-3* family of fatty acids supplies the building blocks of a variety of powerful anti-inflammatory substances. The parent fat of the omega-3s, *alpha-linolenic acid,* is found in dark green leafy vegetables and flaxseed. More potent omega-3s, especially EPA (eicosapentaenoic acid), are found in coldwater fish such as salmon and herring. Basically, the omega-3s encourage the body's production of inflammation-suppressing compounds. They help remind the body to turn inflammatory reactions off when they are no longer needed.
- *GLA (gamma-linolenic acid)* is technically an omega-6 fatty acid, but it behaves more like an anti-inflammatory omega-3. It enhances the inflammation-suppressing effect of omega-3s.
- The *omega-9* family of fatty acids works with the omega-3s as anti-inflammatory compounds. They are found in olive oil, avocados, macadamia nuts, and macadamia nut oil.
- *Antioxidants* such as vitamins E and C are particular types of nutrients that neutralize free radicals and help quell inflammatory reactions.

The Pro-Inflammatory Pathway

Linoleic acid, the basis of all the other omega-6 fatty acids, is essential for health. However, the modern diet provides far too much of it, shifting our bodies toward chronic inflammation. The widespread use of vegetable cooking oils—in kitchens, restaurants, and packaged foods—is a principal reason for the prevalence of inflammatory disorders. As but one illustration, a study in the January 2002 *American Journal of Clinical Nutrition* showed that the omega-6 fats in vegetable oils increased inflammation in heart cells.

The body converts linoleic acid to a series of more powerful compounds. Chief among them is *arachidonic acid,* which is subsequently converted into a variety of very powerful inflammation-causing compounds known as *eicosanoids.* Eicosanoids include such substances as prostaglandin E_2.

The conversion of arachidonic acid to more powerful inflammation-causing substances such as prostaglandin E_2 is strongly influenced by a

—✕—

Pro- and Anti-Inflammatory Pathways

OMEGA-6 FATTY ACIDS	OMEGA-3 FATTY ACIDS
Linoleic Acid	Alpha-Linolenic Acid
Found in margarine, shortening, and vegetable oils	Found in leafy vegetables, flaxseed, and fish
↓	↓
Production of pro-inflammatory compounds	Production of anti-inflammatory compounds

—✕—

group of proteins called *cytokines*. Some of these cytokines, such as interleukin-6 (IL-6) and C-reactive protein (CRP), prompt cells to unleash a variety of pro-inflammatory compounds.

The Anti-Inflammatory Pathway

In parallel with linoleic acid, alpha-linolenic acid is the parent molecule of many of the body's anti-inflammatory firefighters. However, the omega-3 fatty acids are less active biologically, which places them at an immediate disadvantage against the omega-6 fatty acids. A person has to make an extra effort to consume foods or supplements rich in omega-3 fatty acids to compensate for their weaker activity.

The body uses various enzymes to convert alpha-linolenic acid to more active substances, particularly eicosapentaenoic acid (EPA). EPA is ultimately converted to a group of eicosanoids that are either anti-inflammatory or "less inflammatory" than those in the omega-6 family. The advantage of coldwater fish such as salmon or mackerel over other foods is that they contain large amounts of preformed EPA and docosahexaenoic acid (DHA), thus saving your body the time and effort needed to make them from alpha-linolenic acid.

If the diet is dominated by linoleic acid, as is the case with the typical modern Western diet, the body will make abnormally large amounts of inflammation-causing compounds. However, increased intake of alpha-linolenic acid or EPA will exert an anti-inflammatory effect.

Although GLA is technically a member of the omega-6 family, it behaves more like an anti-inflammatory omega-3 fatty acid. GLA increases the body's levels of the anti-inflammatory substance called prostaglandin E_1. It is among the body's checks and balances designed to prevent the omega-6s from getting completely out of control.

Considerable research has shown that people eating diets rich in alpha-linolenic acid, EPA, and DHA—think fish and vegetables—are less prone to inflammatory diseases. Research has similarly shown that supplements containing EPA, DHA, and GLA have striking anti-inflammatory properties in arthritis, allergies, asthma, and many other -itis diseases. This is why these fatty acids are the first-line supplements for preventing and reversing inflammation.

More Firefighters: Omega-9 Fatty Acids

Another group of fatty acids, known as the omega-9 family, also possesses impressive anti-inflammatory properties. Your body can make omega-9 fatty acids from other fats, assuming that things work the way they should, but some foods provide a direct source of them. The basic building block of the omega-9 fatty acids is oleic acid, a monounsaturated fat found abundantly in olive oil, macadamia nuts, and avocados.

Many studies have found that diets rich in olive oil reduce the risk or severity of inflammatory diseases such as coronary artery disease and rheumatoid arthritis. In general the omega-9 family is synergistic with the anti-inflammatory omega-3 family.

Skewing the Balance with Trans Fatty Acids

In human diets the ratio of omega-6 to omega-3 fatty acids has historically been in the range of 1:1 to 2:1. Today, omega-6 fatty acids dominate omega-3 fatty acids by ratios estimated between 20:1 and 30:1 in the typical Western diet. This lopsided intake of omega-6 fatty acids smothers the minuscule amounts of alpha-linolenic acid, EPA, and DHA found in most modern diets. The huge quantity of omega-6 fatty acids in the diet encourages chronic inflammation, without any effective means of turning it off.

Trans fatty acids add significantly to this problem. They naturally occur in very small quantities in beef (being produced in the guts of ruminants), and have traditionally played only a minor role in human diets. Over the past several decades, however, the quantity of trans fatty acids in Western diets has skyrocketed.

Partially Hydrogenated Hazards

Beginning in the 1960s and 1970s, public health officials began urging people to consume more polyunsaturated fats, particularly the omega-6 variety, and fewer saturated fats as a step toward reducing the incidence of coronary heart disease. To expand the use of omega-6 oils, food makers began hydrogenating them. Hydrogenation adds many of the qualities of saturated fat, such as butter, and also increases the amount of trans fatty acids. Until very recently, trans fatty acids were considered safe.

This is no longer the case. Scientists have learned that trans fatty acids are far more hazardous to health than are the saturated fats in butter and fatty meats. Trans fatty acids inhibit many of the enzymes needed to convert linoleic acid and alpha-linolenic acid to pro- and anti-inflammatory compounds. In essence, trans fatty acids gum up the body's processing of other fatty acids at several stages.

If all things were equal, trans fatty acids would dampen production of both the body's pro- and anti-inflammatory compounds. However, it appears that trans fatty acids inhibit more of the enzymes needed by the anti-inflammatory omega-3 fatty acids than those involved with the omega-6 fatty acids. The consequence is that trans fatty acids interfere to a greater extent with the body's anti-inflammatory compounds.

It should come as no surprise that recent studies have found trans fatty acids to significantly increase the risk of heart disease, diabetes, and other diseases. For example, a major study by Harvard University researchers found that a high intake of trans fatty acids was strongly associated with the risk of coronary heart disease. In contrast, saturated fats (commonly thought of as the culprits) were only weakly associated with heart disease.

—⁕—

Key Inflammation Matches and Firefighters

PRO-INFLAMMATORY MATCHES	ANTI-INFLAMMATORY FIREFIGHTERS
Linoleic acid	Alpha-linolenic acid
Vegetable oils (e.g., corn and safflower)	Gamma-linolenic acid
Arachidonic acid	Eicosapentaenoic acid (EPA)
Partially hydrogenated oils	Oleic acid (in olive oil)
Free radicals	Vitamins E and C

—⁕—

Free Radicals, Antioxidants, and Inflammation

Hazardous molecules known as free radicals damage cells and accelerate the aging process, as well as cause such age-related diseases as coronary artery disease and cancer. In simple terms free radicals lack a subatomic particle called an electron. Typically, electrons come in pairs, and to restore the pair, a free radical steals one from another molecule. That theft damages what had been a healthy cell.

Free radicals are found in virtually all dangerous chemicals, including air pollutants and cigarette smoke, and are generated when your body is exposed to radiation (even from sunlight). They are also created when your body burns food for energy, breaks down harmful chemicals in the liver, or fights infections. Indeed, your body's white blood cells generate large quantities of free radicals to destroy bacteria and virus-infected cells.

Free radicals also stimulate inflammation in several ways. They increase the activity of genes involved in making pro-inflammatory compounds such as IL-6. Free radicals also activate several different types of *adhesion molecules,* which enable various types of white blood cells to stick to other cells. Adhesion molecules should only stick to infectious microbes and damaged cells marked for cleanup. But in chronic inflammation, they can adhere to normal cells, including those in arteries and joints.

Antioxidants Are Anti-Inflammatory

The natural antidotes for free radicals are antioxidants, which include vitamins E and C and many other nutrients, particularly the many flavonoids found in vegetables, fruits, and herbs. Many antioxidants directly counteract the pro-inflammatory effects of free radicals. For example, vitamin E helps turn off genes involved in inflammation, as well as some types of adhesion molecules.

In the next chapter we will see how specific dietary changes have increased our intake of pro-inflammatory omega-6 fatty acids and decreased our consumption of anti-inflammatory omega-3 fatty acids.

CHAPTER 4

Balancing a Diet That's Out of Balance

Although imbalances in fatty acids cause much of a body's overactive inflammatory response, we need to know *why* imbalances occur. The answer is that most people no longer eat many health-promoting and anti-inflammatory foods. Instead, they eat foods that actually stoke the fires of inflammation.

Matt: Treating Multiple Sclerosis with the Original Balanced Diet

In 1995, when Matt was eighteen years old, he suddenly developed severe leg twitches, problems with balance, and an extreme sensitivity to temperature on his left side. One month later, a magnetic resonance imaging scan identified a dozen lesions in his brain and spinal column. The diagnosis was unmistakably multiple sclerosis (MS). Matt envisioned life in a wheelchair—and "almost shut down and gave up," he says.

Matt's dad, Ashton, a scientist, started reading everything about MS he could get hold of—in books, in medical journals, on the Internet. He quickly realized that few researchers and physicians had seriously considered the roles of diet and alternative treatments in controlling MS. Yet such treatments appeared to hold far more promise than drug treatments ridden with side effects.

Ashton suggested two therapies to Matt, who was initially skeptical. First came acupuncture. After ten acupuncture treatments, many of Matt's MS symptoms cleared, along with his headaches, night sweats, and allergies. Next came diet. Ashton asked Matt to follow a "Paleolithic," or caveman, diet consisting of simple and unprocessed foods such as fruits, vegetables, fish, skinless chicken breasts, and a little rice, and avoiding all dairy, gluten, legumes, fried foods, and yeast. In addition, Matt began taking a variety of supplements, including vitamins, minerals, omega-3 fatty acids, and GLA.

Since making these changes, Matt has remained completely free of MS symptoms, even while working toward his college degree and then getting a stress-filled job as a television producer. "I stick with the diet religiously," he says. "It was rough for the first six months, but then it became easy. Sure, the foods aren't real exciting, but I would rather use my hand to bring these foods to my mouth than not to be able to use my hand at all. It changed my whole perspective. I don't take as many things for granted."

Nutrients as the Building Blocks of Health

The vital role of nutrition in health is hardly a new idea. Hippocrates, who lived twenty-four hundred years ago and was the father of Western medicine, is remembered by modern physicians for the Hippocratic Oath: first, do no harm (to patients). But Hippocrates' belief that food is our best medicine is considered nothing more than quaint by many physicians familiar with it.

For many years, Western medicine has believed that therapeutic advancements are made only through science and, more recently, through technology—essentially that doctors can become masters of nature. Today, genes are considered medicine's Rosetta stone, the key to understanding why people become ill and the source of future pharmaceutical treatments. But the emphasis on genetic research and gene therapy has placed invention and technology over basic nutritional science.

There may be no better example of this folly than in genetics itself. Genes, built from molecules of deoxyribonucleic acid (DNA), certainly do contain the instructions for life. Damaged, they can and often do lead to disease. But genes do not function in a vacuum. To work the right way, genes depend on a person's consumption of the right nutrients. When genes receive inadequate nutrition or antinutrients (substances that interfere with or deplete needed nutrients), they tend to malfunction. It would be like putting water instead of gasoline in your car's fuel system.

Your body requires a variety of protein building blocks (amino acids) and some of the B-complex vitamins to make and repair DNA. In addition, many nutrients, such as vitamins C and E, protect DNA and genes from free-radical damage. Nutrients also can turn on and turn off genes, spurring them to action and calming them down. Genes may be fundamental to life, but nutrition is fundamental to genes—and all aspects of life and health.

It is essential to remember that nutrients—chiefly vitamins, minerals, proteins, and fats—are the building blocks of your entire body. They form not just your skeleton, skin, and organs, but are also the basis of your hormones and the thousands of biochemicals involved in forming new cells and tissue, healing injuries, and creating energy. Chronically low levels of nutrients or imbalances among nutrients can inhibit essential biochemical reactions and plant the seeds for degenerative diseases later in life. Yet as fundamental as nutrition is in health—and even in genetics—physicians routinely take the diets of their patients for granted. They assume that their patients are adequately nourished unless they display outright symptoms of now-rare classic vitamin deficiency diseases.

Rediscovering Our Original Diet

The huge amount of biomedical information generated in recent years has left many people confused about which diet might best enable them to thrive. How can you determine which one is the ideal—and anti-inflammatory—diet for you?

The soundest approach, in my opinion, is to study what our ancient ancestors ate and, just as importantly, what they did *not* eat. The basic idea behind the "evolutionary" diet of human beings is relatively simple. Over millions of years, humans evolved in a biological milieu that provided them certain nutrients, which became necessary for life and health. This nutritional environment helped shape our present-day genes and the rest of our biochemistry and biology.

Despite stunning cultural, scientific, and technological achievements, our genes are identical to those of Paleolithic, or Stone Age, people who lived roughly 10,000 to 40,000 years ago. Indeed, our genes have changed relatively little—only about 0.5 percent—over the 2 million previous years. We are, biologically, cavemen and cavewomen, but most of us now eat food products that did not exist until very recently.

Evolutionary vs. Modern Diets

Until relatively recently, understanding the Paleolithic diet was largely the province of anthropologists and archeologists, scientists who worked in obscurity at museums and universities. In 1985 S. Boyd Eaton, M.D., of Emory University, Atlanta, and his anthropologist colleagues published a watershed article in the *New England Journal of Medicine* that gave medical credibility to ancient nutrition.

Since that time, Eaton and his colleagues, as well as Loren Cordain, Ph.D., of Colorado State University, author of *The Paleo Diet,* have greatly expanded our understanding of the Paleolithic diet and how it differs from our modern diets. These scientists have based their ideas on a vast body of archaeological evidence, including bones, coprolites, and food remains at prehistoric sites, as well as detailed ethnographic records of 229 "hunter-gatherer" cultures that existed through the nineteenth or twentieth centuries.

Paleolithic people lived before the advent of agriculture, the intentional growing of crops. For sustenance, they hunted large and small game animals and foraged a variety of plant foods, including leaves, roots, fruits seeds, and nuts. As you might imagine, living without modern conveniences was hard and life expectancies were short, with injuries and infections being the leading causes of death. However, the archaeological record indicates that these primitive people were generally healthier than people today, and they rarely experienced our modern diseases.

It is important to note that the "typical" Paleolithic diet is a composite of many different diets, just as the average American (Western) diet also is a composite. In addition, while Paleolithic food choices varied by geography and season, they were often consistent in macronutrient (protein, carbohydrate, fat) and micronutrient (vitamin and mineral) levels, as well as in the foods *not* eaten. Despite the differences in geography, Paleolithic peoples were sophisticated hunters and gatherers, and they consumed an extraordinarily diverse selection of meats, fish (if they lived near oceans or lakes), and vegetables.

Humans Need Protein

Protein forms the foundation of our physical structure—that is, our muscle, organs, glands, and to a great extent, our bones and teeth. The components of protein are also needed by the body to synthesize DNA, hormones, neurochemicals, and other biochemicals, including those involved in pro- and anti-inflammatory reactions.

There is no evidence of an entirely vegetarian or even mostly vegetarian hunter-gatherer society. Paleolithic and hunter-gatherer societies preferred animal foods, including fish, over plant foods, according to the latest research by Cordain. Nearly three-fourths (73 percent) of hunter-gatherer societies worldwide obtained more than half of their food from animals. In contrast, only about one-eighth (14 percent) of societies obtained more than half of their food from plants. Indeed, many anthropologists believe that the development of agriculture became a necessity because human populations had overhunted large game.

The typical Paleolithic intake of protein ranged from 19 to 35 percent of calories and sometimes as much as 50 percent of calories. In general, the amount of animal foods increased and plant foods decreased in people living farther from the equator. (Long-term intake of a diet containing more than 50 percent protein can be toxic, and Cordain believes that hunter-gatherers balanced a very high protein intake by increasing their consumption of animal fat.) In contrast, the typical American adult obtains about 15 percent of his or her calories from protein, substantially less than Paleolithic peoples and hunter-gatherer societies.

Humans Need Fats

Like protein, fats have multiple roles. They help form the walls of cells and regulate what enters and exits those cells, and they also are an integral part of most all body tissues and many biochemicals. As you know, fats form the building blocks of the body's pro- and anti-inflammatory compounds.

Paleolithic people and hunter-gatherer societies consumed 28 to 58 percent of their calories in the form of fat, a quantity that is for the most part higher than the average intake of 34 percent today. Despite the large amount of fat, the specific types of fat were very different in Paleolithic times—and far more balanced in terms of inflammation-promoting or inflammation-suppressing fats. The ratio of omega-6 (inflammation-promoting) to omega-3 (inflammation-suppressing) fatty acids in the diet ranged from about 1:1 to 2:1.

Meat from wild game, the mainstay of most Paleolithic peoples and hunter-gatherer societies, is considerably leaner than meat from modern domesticated cattle. For example, grass-fed cattle (whose diet would be similar to that of wild game) have six to eight times less fat than do grain-fed cattle. In addition, beef from grass-fed cattle has two to six times more omega-3 fatty acids, compared with meat from grain-fed cattle. A similar pattern occurs in other types of livestock. Grass-fed bison have seven times more omega-3 fatty acids than do grain-fed bison. The grasses and leaves eaten by animals contain substantial amounts of omega-3 fatty acids, which are eventually deposited in the animals' muscle and fat. When people eat such meats, as they did in the past, they consume these anti-inflammatory omega-3 fatty acids.

Today's domesticated livestock are typically fed cereal grains (such as corn) for several months before slaughter, increasing their overall fat, saturated fat, and pro-inflammatory omega-6 fatty acids. Such meat contains low levels of omega-6 fatty acids and even less omega-3 fatty acids, leading to a high ratio of omega-6 to omega-3 fatty acids. For example, about 3 percent of the fat in wild game consists of omega-3 fatty acids, but only 0.4 percent (less than one-seventh the amount) of the fat in grain-fed beef does. So when people consume meat from grain-fed domesticated animals, the lopsided omega-6 to omega-3 ratio further contributes to their pro-inflammatory profile.

Perhaps surprisingly, cholesterol consumption has not changed significantly since Paleolithic times, but people now consume more of the specific saturated fats that boost the body's production of cholesterol. Elevated cholesterol levels per se are not necessarily problematic, but they can become pro-inflammatory when combined with a low intake of antioxidants, such as in a diet with few vegetables and fruit.

Based on an analysis of 829 plants, wild plant foods contain an average of 24 percent fat, a surprisingly large amount. Such plants, as well as modern leafy green vegetables (kale, spinach, dark green lettuces, greens), contain substantial amounts of alpha-linolenic acid, the building block of the omega-3 fatty acids. During our evolutionary development this mix of natural, uncultivated plant foods and wild game meat led to a balanced intake of omega-6 and omega-3 fatty acids, which tempered abnormal inflammatory responses.

Especially significant, Paleolithic peoples and later hunter-gatherer societies did not consume *any* oils or fats unless they were part of meat or vegetables. Our ancestors *never* consumed pressed or refined oils. This contrasts sharply with today, with corn, soy, and safflower oil—all rich in pro-inflammatory omega-6 fatty acids—being ubiquitous in kitchens and foods. These oils, often manipulated to mimic saturated fats and to form trans fatty acids, are used to lubricate fry pans; to deep-fry potatoes, chicken, and fish; and are added to the vast majority of processed (packaged) foods, such as salad dressings, microwave meals, meat extenders, baked goods, and chocolate bars.

Switching from a diet high in saturated fat to one high in omega-6 fatty acids—the very change that public health authorities have recommended to Americans over the past thirty years—actually decreases the body's production of anti-inflammatory omega-3 compounds (specifically, EPA and DHA) by 40 to 50 percent. In addition, many foods, such as fried potatoes and fried chicken, are cooked in oxidized vegetable oils, increasing their content of free radicals and adding to the pro-inflammatory burden.

Humans Need Carbohydrates and Fiber

Carbohydrates, made up of starches and sugars, provide most of the body's energy—that is, they are burned for fuel or stored as fat. In Paleolithic times and in hunter-gatherer societies, carbohydrates came almost entirely from uncultivated low-starch vegetables (leaves, shoots, buds, roots), fruit, seeds, and nuts. The carbohydrates in uncultivated and unprocessed vegetables are complex, meaning that they are digested slowly, in contrast to simple sugars, which are absorbed rapidly. Complex carbohydrates are part of the plant's matrix, which includes substantial amounts of protein, vitamins, minerals, and indigestible fiber. In other words, Paleolithic peoples and hunter-gatherer societies ate relatively low-carbohydrate diets, and the carbohydrates were not readily absorbed.

Today, only a minority of people regularly consume substantive amounts of vegetables and fruit daily. Instead, the vast majority of dietary carbohydrates and calories come from highly refined grains (chiefly wheat but also corn and rye), sugars (sucrose and high-fructose corn syrup, particularly in soft drinks and other beverages), and fried potatoes (which contain trans fatty acids and oxidized omega-6 fatty acids).

One excellent marker of vegetable intake is dietary fiber content. In Paleolithic times, people ate an average of 100 grams of fiber daily, almost entirely from vegetables and fruit. Today, the typical Westerner eats only 20 grams daily, mostly from grains. Although whole grains, such as whole-wheat bread, provide some vitamins, minerals, and fiber, they still fall far short of vegetables in vitamins, minerals, and fiber. And as grain consumption has increased over the years, vegetable and fruit consumption has decreased.

The impact of refined grains and sugars on inflammation is significant, though not as obvious as with oils and fats. Consumption of refined grains and sugars typically raises blood sugar levels and, over the long term, increases the risk of diabetes. Recently, researchers have reported that very modest chronic increases in blood sugar, even when in the normal range, significantly increase the risk of developing diabetes or heart disease within just a few years. Both diseases have inflammatory undercurrents, and elevations in blood sugar spontaneously generate free radicals, which can stimulate inflammation.

Humans Need Vitamins, Minerals, and Phytonutrients

Over the course of a year Paleolithic peoples and hunter-gatherer societies typically consumed more than a hundred different types of plants. These were very different foods from what most people consume today. Ancient uncultivated vegetables were more akin to nutrient-packed kale than to iceberg lettuce, and uncultivated fruit looked more like crabapples and rose hips than supersweet pears and bananas.

Only 9 to 32 percent of North Americans consume the five daily servings of vegetables and fruit recommended by the federal government, meaning that 68 to 91 percent of Americans do not eat a particularly rich dietary source of vitamins and other micronutrients. Of those people who do eat vegetables and fruit, most choose from a limited selection, such as potatoes, which are often fried; corn; peas; carrots; and iceberg lettuce. As a consequence, most people today fall far short of the greater quantity and diversity of vitamins, minerals, and phytonutrients consumed by Paleolithic peoples and hunter-gatherers.

Based on the calculations by Eaton and Cordain, Paleolithic peoples consumed an average of two to ten times more vitamins and minerals than people do today. These levels range from three to six times the federal government's Recommended Dietary Allowance (or Daily Value) for vitamins and minerals. For example, a Paleolithic person likely ate about 600 mg of vitamin C daily, compared with an RDA of 60 mg, and a typical North American daily intake of 45 mg or less daily.

In addition, vegetables and fruit contain large amounts of vitaminlike antioxidant nutrients, particularly flavonoids and carotenoids. A diet containing a diverse selection of vegetables and fruit would likely provide hundreds of flavonoids and dozens of carotenoids. Researchers estimate that people nowadays consume between 23 and 170 mg of flavonoids daily, but that they may have consumed five to twenty-four times more (115 to 4,080 mg daily) in the past. Such a huge dietary intake of antioxidants—now missing from most people's diets—would moderate inflammatory reactions.

—⚮—

Past and Present Intake of Vitamins and Minerals

VITAMINS	PALEOLITHIC* (MG/DAY)	CURRENT U.S.† (MG/DAY)	RATIO
Vitamin C	604	93	6.5
Vitamin E	32.8	8.5	3.9
Vitamin B$_2$	6.49	1.71	3.8
Vitamin B$_1$	3.91	1.42	2.8
Vitamin A	17.2	7.8	2.2
Folic acid	0.36	0.18	2

MINERALS	PALEOLITHIC* (MG/DAY)	CURRENT U.S.† (MG/DAY)	RATIO
Copper	12.2	1.2	10.2
Iron	87.4	10.5	8.3
Manganese	13.3	3	4.4
Potassium	10,500	2,500	4.2
Magnesium	1,223	320	3.8
Zinc	43.4	12.5	3.5
Phosphorus	3,223	1,510	2.1
Calcium	1,622	920	1.8
Sodium	768	4,000	0.2

* Based on 3,000 calories daily, 35 percent animal and 65 percent plant subsistence.
† Average of U.S. men and women; Food and Nutrition Board, 1989.

—⚮—

The Turning Points in Our Diet

Americans, and increasingly Canadians and Europeans, certainly do enjoy full stomachs. The latest statistics show that 65 percent of Americans (two of every three) are overweight and 31 percent (almost one in three) are clinically obese—at least thirty pounds over their ideal weight. Being overweight is not a sign of good nutrition; rather, it is a sign of excessive calorie and carbohydrate intake, usually at the expense of more nutrient-dense and wholesome foods.

There are many ways to look at the history of dietary changes and to analyze how these changes have affected people's health. Because this book is about inflammation, the emphasis in our brief examination of food history will be on how the diet has shifted from relatively balanced to clearly pro-inflammatory. Three major periods of dietary change have occurred: the agricultural revolution, the industrial revolution, and the convenience/fast-food revolution. All of these changes have been characterized by two basic trends: (1) through a variety of processing and refining methods, the modern diet less and less resembles our evolutionary diet, and (2) the majority of foods sold in supermarkets less and less resemble their original appearance in nature.

—∽—

How the Diet Has Changed

PALEOLITHIC DIET

Highly diverse diet, consisting of lean meats, fish, and vegetable matter

Balanced intake (1:1 ratio) of pro- and anti-inflammatory fats and very high intake of anti-inflammatory vitamins and minerals

AGRICULTURAL REVOLUTION

Greatly increased intake of grains, lower intake of vegetables and meat

Displacement of nutrient-dense vegetables and meat with moderate shift toward pro-inflammatory diet

INDUSTRIAL REVOLUTION

Extensive refining and processing of grains and sugar, enabling large segments of the population to afford and consume such foods

Further displacement of nutrient-dense foods and greater risk of elevated pro-inflammatory blood sugar levels

CONVENIENCE/FAST-FOOD REVOLUTION

Refining, processing, and industrial manipulation of foods widespread, creating a typical diet high in carbohydrates, unbalanced fat intake, and very low intake of vegetables

Diet contains twenty to thirty times more pro-inflammatory than anti-inflammatory fats and substantially fewer anti-inflammatory vitamins and minerals

—∽—

The Agricultural Revolution

The first major changes to the diet—that is, departures from lean meat, fish, and plant foods—occurred approximately ten thousand years ago with the development of agriculture, the domestication of livestock, and the use of milk and other dairy products. Agriculture stabilized the movement of hunter-gatherer societies, which eventually led to the growth of cities and the development of complex cultures. But the use of grains also led to health problems that were not immediately evident.

The cultivation and consumption of grains introduced the protein gluten to the diet of humans. Gluten is an umbrella term for forty related proteins in a handful of grains, particularly wheat, rye, and barley. You might think that a new vegetarian source of protein would be good, but gluten has been a mixed blessing.

Many people—approximately one in every hundred—are allergic to gluten, causing what is known as celiac disease. In these people, eating gluten triggers an immune (inflammatory) response, which primarily attacks the gastrointestinal tract and interferes with vitamin and mineral absorption. Archeologists have noted that the health of humans, based largely on analysis of ancient bones, took a turn for the worse after gluten-containing grains became popular foods. Osteoporosis, arthritis, and even birth defects became more common after people began eating grains.

The health effects of gluten proteins in grains may be problematic for many people who do not have an inborn sensitivity to gluten. According to Melissa Diane Smith, a nutritionist and author of *Going Against the Grain,* half of Westerners may be sensitive to gluten without exhibiting any of the traditional symptoms of celiac disease. Instead, gluten sensitivity may appear as immunological reactions affecting the nervous system, balance, and behavior, as well as a person's overall sense of well-being. According to Smith, a second family of grain (and legume) proteins, called lectins, may also damage the gut and interfere with nutrient absorption. Meanwhile, Loren Cordain's research has shown that lectins play a role in rheumatoid arthritis and possibly other inflammatory autoimmune diseases. The bottom line is that most grains are neither the much-heralded staff of life nor the breakfast of champions.

Ten millennia ago—too short of a time for genetic evolution—people also began domesticating livestock for meat and, in the case of cows and goats, for milk and other dairy products. As long as livestock were exclusively grass-fed, their meat and milk yielded a balance of pro- and anti-inflammatory fatty acids. This changed when animals were fed corn,

Some Differences between Paleolithic and Modern Diets

	PALEOLITHIC	MODERN
FOOD GROUP		
Protein	Very lean	Fatty
Carbohydrates	From vegetables	From grains and refined sugars
Fats	Balanced intake	Pro-inflammatory
FOOD TYPES		
Animal/fish foods*	65 percent of diet	15 percent of diet
Vegetables/fruit	About 100 different plants	Very narrow selection
Fiber	100 grams daily	20 grams daily
Vitamins/minerals	Substantially more	Substantially less
Grains	None	Substantial intake
Dairy	None	Substantial intake
Pressed oils	None	Substantial intake
Trans fatty acids	Negligible	Substantial intake
Alcohol	None	3 percent of calories

* Animal and fish foods were not exclusively protein. These foods also supplied fat and bone.

which, as previously noted, increases the animals' overall fat and saturated fat and reduces anti-inflammatory omega-3 fatty acids.

Many people have questioned the health benefits of cow's milk, but a couple of points are especially relevant in the context of our evolutionary diet. One is that no species, other than humans over the past ten thousand years, has ever consumed milk beyond infancy. Another is that no species other than humans has ever consumed the milk of another mammal. Like grains, cow's milk appears to be a mismatch for our genetic heritage. The situation is made worse today because milk products from grain-fed cows contain no appreciable amounts of omega-3 fatty acids.

The Industrial Revolution

Many dietary changes occurred over the next ten millennia, including greater cultivation of vegetables and fruit, which increased the sugar content and reduced the bitterness of produce. But perhaps the most significant changes relate to the refining of wheat, which has become a staple food. The use of new technologies to refine grains as well as sugars foreshadowed many other changes.

In the nineteenth century metal rollers replaced stone grinding wheels (grindstones), enabling millers to achieve a more mechanized and efficient means of processing grains into flour. Grains could be processed faster, yielding much finer flour, without bits of stone being eroded and ending up in the flour. In addition, the new technologies enabled easier separation of the grain's germ and bran from the endosperm, which was mostly carbohydrate. The nutrient-lacking endosperm was used for baking bread and other products, whereas the germ and bran were often fed to livestock. In addition, the endosperm-based flour used in baking was bleached chemically to make it white, increasing its consumer appeal.

The industrialization of the grain-refining process yielded "white bread" for the masses instead of only for a limited number of wealthy people. Nutritionally, the difference between whole-grain and white bread was disastrous. During the 1930s increasing consumption of white bread contributed to deficiencies of several B vitamins in North America and Europe. The situation led to government-mandated "enrichment" of flours to replace a handful of the many nutrients removed during grain refining.

The Convenience/Fast-Food Revolution

After the end of World War II, technologists helped guide unprecedented prosperity in the United States. The first Swanson brand TV dinner, a frozen meal on a metal tray, was introduced in 1953, heralding the start of the convenience/fast-food revolution. It was a commercial success. Several years later, in southern California, automobiles and food intersected, giving birth to McDonald's and the fast-food industry. The trade-off for fast, convenient food was lower nutritional value and fewer anti-inflammatory nutrients.

Meanwhile, more women entered the workforce and had less time than before to prepare large home-cooked meals—with most men not helping. The need to reduce time in the kitchen fueled the popularity of the microwave oven in the 1970s. TV dinners that baked in the oven for forty minutes were quickly replaced by microwave meals ready in fewer than five minutes. For the first time in history, large numbers of people did not have to wait very long, or expend much effort, before sitting down and eating. This was a major change from when people spent their entire days hunting and gathering food.

The economic climate of the 1990s reinforced the demand for convenience and fast—and faster—food. The entire pace of business quickened with the pressures of international competition, overnight deliveries, and e-mail. People who had once comfortably ended their workday at 5:00 P.M. are now connected to their offices 24/7 via e-mail, pagers, and cell phones. More and more, fast and convenience foods have become the way to sandwich meals into hectic schedules.

For the most part, these meals are made with ingredients high in refined carbohydrates and pro-inflammatory omega-6 and trans fatty acids and very low in vitamins, minerals, fiber, and protein. A recent study published in the *Journal of the American Dietetic Association* found that two-thirds of the carbohydrates consumed by American adults come from bread, soft drinks, cakes and cookies, refined cereal, pasta, cooked grains, and ice cream. These refined carbohydrates raise blood sugar levels, creating a prediabetic or diabeticlike blood profile, which generates pro-inflammatory free radicals. Recent research by Simin Liu, M.D., Ph.D., of Harvard Medical School has found that diets high in refined carbohydrates and high-glycemic foods (which rapidly raise blood sugar levels) increase inflammation. In Liu's study, women eating large amounts of potatoes, breakfast cereals, white bread, muffins, and white rice had elevated C-reactive protein levels, indicating high levels of inflammation and an increased risk of heart disease. Overweight women who ate a lot of these foods had the highest and most dangerous CRP levels. All of these carbohydrates (and the fat they are often combined with) displace far healthier foods, such as anti-inflammatory vegetables, fruit, and fish.

In addition, research published in November 2002 showed that yet another inflammation-causing substance forms when foods are cooked at high temperatures. Advanced glycation end products (AGEs) are created when sugars bind in a particular way to proteins. As the acronym suggests, AGEs accelerate the aging process. However, AGEs also increase levels of C-reactive protein, a powerful promoter of inflammation. In a study with diabetic patients, those who consumed foods cooked at high temperatures had a 65 percent increase in AGEs after just two weeks. However, people eating the same foods cooked at low temperatures had a 30 percent decrease in AGEs. The AGE-lowering foods were cooked by boiling or steaming—or were quickly sautéed with a small amount of oil. Baking foods for hours, such as how the typical Thanksgiving turkey is prepared, generates large amounts of AGEs. In addition, coffee, cola drinks, chocolate drinks, and fried foods are very high in AGEs.

—⁓—

A New Definition of Hot and Cold Foods

It helps to look at foods as either "hot" pro-inflammatory or "cold" anti-inflammatory. Hot foods set the stage for the burning pain of inflammation, whereas cold foods reduce inflammation.

"HOT" PRO-INFLAMMATORY FOODS	"COLD" ANTI-INFLAMMATORY FOODS
Most vegetable oils	Olive oil
French fries	Fish, particularly cold-water species
Fried chicken and fish	
Margarine	Fresh vegetables
Most salad dressings	Low-sugar fruits (e.g., berries)
Breads and other bakery products	Free-range beef and chicken
Many packaged microwave foods	Game meats (not corn-fed)
Fast-food meals	Mineral water
Beverages with sugars	

—⁓—

What is the bottom line with all of these refined, processed foods? First, they displace many important nutrients, such as anti-inflammatory vitamins, minerals, protein, and omega-3 fatty acids. Second, many grains contain antinutrients, which actually interfere with normal nutrient absorption. Third, highly refined sugars and carbohydrates draw nutrients such as vitamins and minerals from the body's reserves to aid the metabolic processes that normally burn these foods for energy. Fourth, the sheer quantity of calories and carbohydrates in refined sugars and carbohydrates promotes obesity, and fat cells generate large quantities of interleukin-6 and C-reactive protein, two of the most powerful pro-inflammatory compounds made by the body.

The end result is a diet high in pro-inflammatory fats, devoid of anti-inflammatory fats, and nearly empty of anti-inflammatory antioxidants.

And anti-inflammatory drugs don't really help, as we'll see in the next chapter.

CHAPTER 5

What's Wrong with Anti-Inflammatory Drugs

Melinda: When the Cure Is Worse Than the Disease

You might think that "iatrogenic disease" is some sort of rare condition. But the term actually refers to any illness caused by a physician or treatment. And it's surprisingly common. In a typical year, more than a hundred thousand hospitalized patients die from medications they had been prescribed, and more than 2 million others suffer severe side effects. Incredibly, no one knows the number of serious adverse reactions and deaths from drugs related to over-the-counter medications.

When Melinda was in her midthirties, she sought more aggressive medical treatment of her allergies and asthma, as well as of her increasingly stiff joints. Up to this point, she had used either over-the-counter or prescription antihistamines for her allergies, nasal corticosteroid hormones for her asthma, and ibuprofen (an NSAID, or nonsteroidal anti-inflammatory drug) for her rheumatoid arthritis.

Melinda's physician put her on prednisone, a hormone treatment for allergies and arthritis, and a potent prescription-strength NSAID. Side effects from the prednisone included a seventy-pound weight gain, weakened bones, and increased susceptibility to colds and flus, which left

Melinda feeling tired much of the time. The NSAID caused a painful gastric ulcer, which was treated by a drug to reduce stomach acid.

The medications and Melinda's weight gain substantially increased her risk of heart disease and, particularly, heart failure (a catastrophic weakening of the heart muscle). Melinda's physician tried to head off the damage, but he relied solely on pharmaceutical treatment and never discussed nutrition or an anti-inflammatory diet with her. Two years later, after a battery of laboratory tests, he noted that her C-reactive protein levels were elevated, a sign of serious inflammation, so he prescribed a cholesterol-lowering "statin" drug to reduce her risk of heart disease.

The statin drug lowered Melinda's cholesterol, but it also reduced her body's production of coenzyme Q_{10}, a vitaminlike substance needed for normal heart function. Both the statin and the NSAID increased her risk of heart failure. As Melinda's heart function declined, her physician prescribed one more drug to stimulate the heart.

Sadly, her downward spiral could not be stopped. Melinda died of heart failure at age thirty-nine, even though her symptoms could have been reversed by diet and safe nutritional supplements.

With dozens of over-the-counter and prescription anti-inflammatory drugs on the market, you might think that the cure for your aches and pains is as near as the corner pharmacy. Many of these drugs, such as aspirin and ibuprofen, provide relief to millions of people around the world. But these and other drugs have a dark side that, perhaps in the majority of cases, outweighs their benefits. In this chapter we will look at the hazards of several classes of anti-inflammatory drugs.

Anti-Inflammatory Drugs and Their Hazards

Pharmaceutical drugs, used appropriately and for short periods of time, can quickly relieve pain and inflammation. However, they are anything but magic bullets. The longer such drugs are used, and this is the case with chronic inflammatory diseases, the greater the risk of serious side effects.

Drug companies market more than 30 different types of NSAIDs, the most widely used class of drugs. Many other drugs also are used to treat inflammation, and 250 are sold for the treatment of arthritis alone. Each year, pharmacists in the United States fill more than 70 million prescriptions for NSAIDs, and consumers buy about 30 billion over-the-counter

NSAID products. According to an article in the *New England Journal of Medicine,* NSAID complications lead to 7,500 bleeding ulcers, 103,000 hospitalizations, and 16,500 deaths annually (about the same number of deaths caused by AIDS), costing more than $2 billion in medical expenses.

Three classes of medications are used to treat inflammatory diseases, and a fourth is rapidly emerging. These medications are corticosteroids, conventional over-the-counter and prescription NSAIDs, the first generation of selective Cox-2 inhibiting NSAIDs, and the relatively new use of "statin" drugs to reduce C-reactive protein levels.

Corticosteroids

Introduced in the 1950s, cortisonelike drugs called corticosteroids or glucocorticoids became—and still are—extraordinarily popular. These drugs are synthetic mimics of stress-response hormones produced in the adrenal glands. Physicians can choose among dozens of corticosteroids to treat inflammation, but perhaps the best-known corticosteroid is prednisone, which is sold under a variety of brand names.

Corticosteroids are frequently the first treatment physicians prescribe to patients diagnosed with autoimmune diseases such as rheumatoid arthritis, asthma, lupus erythematosus, or multiple sclerosis. They rapidly and dramatically dampen the body's overactive immune response and sometimes are necessary as a *brief* intervention. That's the good news. The bad news about prednisone and other corticosteroids reads like a chamber of medical horrors. Over several weeks or months, oral or injected corticosteroids affect almost every organ and lead to serious side effects while the drugs are being taken, as well as permanent damage.

Among the most common side effects is a rounded "moon face," which is considered characteristic of prednisone use. An increase in abdominal obesity also is common. Because prednisone and other corticosteroids dampen the immune response, they increase susceptibility to infection, often masking symptoms of active infections, and they interfere with the normal healing of wounds. As a consequence, people taking corticosteroids for many weeks or months are more susceptible to infections; and cuts, scrapes, and more serious injuries are slow to heal.

Corticosteroids also interfere with the metabolism of key nutrients, including folic acid, vitamins B_6 and B_{12}, potassium, and zinc. Because *these drugs also reduce vitamin D and calcium levels,* they prevent normal bone development in young people. In adults, long-term use of corticosteroids leads to decreased bone density and osteoporosis. Some corticosteroids can be injected directly into the joints of people with arthritis, but repeated injections accelerate joint damage.

Other common side effects of corticosteroids include a thinning of the skin and bruising, high blood pressure, elevated blood sugar levels (which increase the risk of diabetes and coronary artery disease), cataracts and glaucoma, male infertility, menstrual irregularities, and loss of muscle mass.

Conventional NSAIDs

Aspirin, ibuprofen (Advil, Motrin, and generic brands), naproxen sodium, (Aleve and others) are the most popular over-the-counter non-steroidal anti-inflammatory drugs, and many higher-potency NSAIDs are available by prescription. The term NSAID means that these drugs are anti-inflammatory but not based on steroid hormones. NSAIDs are very effective in relieving headaches, controlling inflammation, easing pain, and reducing fevers. But like other anti-inflammatory drugs, they pose considerable dangers, particularly when used regularly.

Aspirin, which has been widely used since about 1900, is the oldest pharmaceutical NSAID. Before aspirin was synthesized, people often used willow bark, which contains a compound very similar to synthetic aspirin. For many years, researchers believed that NSAIDs worked by inhibiting the activity of cyclooxygenase, an enzyme critical to the conversion of fatty acids to pro- and anti-inflammatory compounds. In the early 1990s researchers discovered a second form of cyclooxygenase, so the two compounds are now referred to as Cox-1 and Cox-2. The prevailing view in medicine has been that Cox-1, whose levels are generally steady, performs normal cell functions. In contrast, doctors have believed that Cox-2 levels rise as part of the body's inflammatory response.

In the course of research scientists quickly realized that most NSAIDs interfere with both Cox-1 and Cox-2, causing a variety of side effects in many people. The most common side effect of NSAIDs is an upset stomach, which affects at least 10 to 20 percent of people taking these drugs, but according to some studies may affect up to 50 percent. In 10 to 25 percent of people regularly taking NSAIDs, the stomach wall erodes, leading to gastritis (inflammation of the stomach wall) and the formation of gastric ulcers. Ironically, as physicians have successfully treated *Helicobacter pylori* infections, a major cause of stomach ulcers, NSAIDs have become the leading cause of ulcers. The reason is NSAIDs' suppression of Cox-1, which is essential for maintaining the integrity of stomach and duodenal (upper part of the intestine, just below the stomach) walls.

NSAID-induced damage to the gut wall can lead to leaky-gut syndrome. A leaky gut increases the permeability of the stomach wall and permits incompletely digested proteins to enter the bloodstream, where they can trigger inflammatory immune reactions. Allergylike food sensitivities, whether inborn or caused by a leaky gut, can worsen pollen allergies, and they have been shown to increase symptoms of rheumatoid arthritis. Indeed, the "feel better one day, feel worse another day" nature of osteoarthritis and rheumatoid arthritis may reflect sporadic exposure to food allergens.

Aspirin, specifically, also is a potent anticoagulant, largely because it interferes with chemicals involved in blood clotting. Many physicians recommend a very small amount of aspirin daily to reduce the long-term risk of coronary artery disease. But aspirin's blood-thinning effect also increases the tendency toward bleeding (such as in nosebleeds) and bleeding time, making wounds slower to close and heal.

Two lines of research indicate that NSAIDs can be even more dangerous. A recent study published in *Archives of Internal Medicine* found that the regular use of NSAIDs (other than aspirin) doubles a person's risk of being hospitalized for heart failure. Physicians John Page, M.B.B.S., and David Henry M.B.ChB., of the University of Newcastle, Newcastle, Australia, found that NSAID use among seniors with a history of heart disease increased the risk of hospitalization for heart failure by ten times. Seniors are the biggest users of NSAIDs, chiefly for rheumatoid arthritis, osteoarthritis, and other aches and pains. Page and Henry calculated that NSAID use might account for 19 percent (almost one-fifth) of all hospital admissions for heart failure, one of the most serious of all heart diseases.

The other, truly mind-boggling feature of regular NSAID use is that some of these drugs, particularly aspirin and ibuprofen, have been to shown to *accelerate* the breakdown of cartilage in joints. This is especially ironic among people who take NSAIDs to relieve the pain of osteoarthritis, a disease characterized by the destruction of cartilage padding in the joints. Although this breakdown of joint cartilage is very well documented, few patients are ever told of it. In a perverse irony the use of NSAIDs to relieve osteoarthritic pain actually speeds up the underlying disease process. (Although acetaminophen is not an NSAID, it appears to have a similar effect on promoting osteoarthritis.)

Cox-2 Inhibitors

With the discovery of two forms of cyclooxygenase, and the belief that only Cox-2 was involved in inflammation, several pharmaceutical companies began massive research projects to develop a new generation of Cox-2 inhibitors. In theory, these drugs would stop inflammation by suppressing Cox-2 activity, but avoid gastrointestinal side effects associated with inhibition of Cox-1.

Celebrex and Vioxx were the first "selective" Cox-2 inhibitors. But the new generation of Cox-2 inhibitors (often referred to as "coxibs") was only 20 percent selective for Cox-2. In other words they were 80 percent, just like traditional NSAIDs. Coxibs were no more effective therapeutically and no safer than earlier NSAIDs.

One study, testing Vioxx against naproxen, found that the Cox-2 inhibitor increased the incidence of heart attack by four times, compared with the older NSAID. A recent analysis of four studies of Cox-2 inhibitors confirmed that this new class of drugs increases the risk of heart attack and stroke, according to an article in the *Journal of the American Medical Association*.

The problems run even deeper. The drug companies assumed that only Cox-2, not Cox-1, was involved in inflammatory reactions. It now appears that both Cox-1 and Cox-2 play fundamental housekeeping roles in cells and normal health, and both also have roles in inflammation. In other words the very theory behind the development of selective coxibs may well have been wrong.

Researchers have recently discovered that Cox-2 has diverse fundamental roles in human biology, aside from its place in eicosanoid production. Like Cox-1, Cox-2 is involved in maintaining the integrity of the stomach wall, as well as in normal kidney and blood platelet function. Cox-2 also appears to be active in brain development, activity, and memory. It also is involved in ovulation and implantation of the egg into the womb. So it should come as no surprise that suppression of Cox-2 leads to undesirable side effects. It is likely that other undesirable side effects will emerge after the second generation of Cox-2 inhibitors reach the marketplace.

CRP-Lowering Agents

C-reactive protein (CRP) has long been recognized as an indicator of intense, systemic (bodywide) inflammation. Slowly, experts have come to see CRP as a promoter of inflammation, instead of simply as a marker.

In the late 1990s Paul M. Ridker, M.D., of Harvard Medical School, found that elevated blood levels of CRP increased the risk of heart attack by 4.5 times, a relationship far stronger than that between cholesterol or homocysteine and heart disease. Other research teams have found that elevated CRP levels are associated with Alzheimer's, arthritis, cancer, diabetes, overweight, asthma, and many other inflammatory diseases. The body makes CRP from interleukin-6, one of the most pro-inflammatory of all cytokines. Although some CRP is made in the liver, an organ best described as the body's chemical processing factor, large amounts also are made by abdominal fat cells.

Although many studies have found that vitamin E and other nutrients significantly reduce CRP levels, several major pharmaceutical trials have begun positioning "statin" drugs as the therapy of choice for lowering CRP levels. The statin drugs, which include Lipitor (atorvastatin), Mevacor (lovastatin), Pravachol (pravastatin), Zocor (simvastatin), Baycol (cerivastatin), and the more recent Bextra (valdecoxib), have been the most common medical treatments for lowering cholesterol.

Despite their popularity and a common perception of safety, statins pose serious risks. They reduce the body's production of cholesterol by inhibiting an enzyme known as HMG-CoA-reductase. This enzyme is active early in a series of biochemical reactions that eventually leads to the production of cholesterol (which, by the way, is the core molecule in all of the body's steroid hormones, including estrogen, testosterone, and corticosteroids). The problem is that statins also turn off the body's production of all the other compounds that depend on HMG-CoA-reductase.

One of these downstream compounds is coenzyme Q_{10} (CoQ_{10}). CoQ_{10} is a vitaminlike substance that plays a pivotal role in how the body's cells produce energy. CoQ_{10} is so crucial to health that research on it formed the basis of the 1978 Nobel Prize in chemistry. A small number of cardiologists in the United States and Europe, and far more in Japan, have successfully used large amounts (approximately 400 mg daily) of supplemental CoQ_{10} to treat cardiomyopathy and heart failure, diseases characterized by a catastrophic loss of energy in heart cells.

All of these findings should raise red flags about the use of statins in lowering cholesterol and, now, in lowering CRP levels. One common side effect of statins is muscle weakness, significant because muscle cells (particularly the heart) contain the largest amounts of CoQ_{10}. In August 2001 Bayer A.G., a giant German pharmaceutical company, withdrew its Baycol statin drug from the marketplace. Thirty-one patients had died while taking the drug, all because of a rare condition in which muscle tissue broke down.

Although anti-inflammatory drugs can be therapeutically useful at times, they treat symptoms and not the causes of disease, and some even speed the progression of inflammatory diseases. The side effects of anti-inflammatory drugs derive from the fact that they are biochemical inter-lopers that disrupt, rather than enhance, the normal functions of the body.

In the next chapter and the remainder of this book we will focus on safe dietary changes and supplements to boost the body's production of natural anti-inflammatory substances.

PART II

The Anti-Inflammation Syndrome Diet Plan

.

CHAPTER 6

Fifteen Steps to Fight the Inflammation Syndrome

—⚏—

What Are Your Current Eating Habits?

Rationale: Highly processed foods—those most commonly eaten—contain many pro-inflammatory substances. If you are not very careful about what you eat, you likely consume large amounts of pro-inflammatory foods.

Eating Habits at Home

Do you or your significant other cook with corn, peanut, sunflower, safflower, or soy oil (as opposed to olive or grapeseed oil)?

Add 3 points _____

Do you eat a prepackaged microwave meal that provides a full meal (as opposed to only frozen vegetables) more than once a week?

Add 1 point _____

Do you eat any foods packaged in boxes, such as ready-to-eat cereals, flavored rices, meat extenders, and other boxed foods, more than once a week?

Add 1 point _____

When you eat at home, do you use bottled salad dressings that contain soy or safflower oil or partially hydrogenated fats (as opposed to olive oil)? Check the label.

Add 2 points _____

Do you eat pasta, bread, or pizza (one, some, or all three) daily?

Add 2 points _____

Do you eat baked goods, such as cookies, coffee cakes, other cakes, doughnuts, packaged brownies, cakes, or similar food products at least once a week?

Add 2 points _____

Do you use margarine instead of butter?

Add 2 points _____

Do you eat a lot of hamburgers?

Add 1 point _____

Do you dislike eating fish?

Add 1 point _____

Do you drink regular (sweetened) soft drinks or add sugar to your coffee or tea?

Add 1 point _____

Eating Habits in Restaurants

Do you eat at fast-food restaurants such as McDonald's, Burger King, KFC, Taco Bell, or others at least once a week?

Add 2 points _____

Do you eat at a Chinese restaurant more than once a week?

Add 2 points _____

Do you eat pasta or pizza in a restaurant at least once a week?

Add 2 points _____

Do you eat breaded and fried fish or deep-fried shrimp more than once every week or two?

Add 2 points _____

Do you eat French fries?

Add 2 points _____

Do you eat mostly beef?

Add 1 point _____

If you eat beef, is hamburger your favorite type?

Add 1 point _____

Do you order soft drinks when you eat out?

Add 1 point _____

Your score on quiz 2: _____

Interpretation and ranking:

- **0–2** **Low.** You are eating a low-inflammation diet, which is the best way to protect yourself from chronic inflammation.
- **3–5** **Moderate.** You are eating a moderate-inflammation diet, which may set the stage for chronic inflammation.
- **6–19** **High.** You are eating a high-inflammation diet, which substantially increases your risk of inflammatory diseases.
- **20+** **Very high.** You are eating a very high inflammation diet, which greatly increases your risk of disease.

High or very high on quiz 2 but not quiz 1 (page 14): You are at risk for developing inflammatory diseases in the coming years. This would be a good time to bolster your long-term health.

High or very high on both *quiz 1 and quiz 2:* You likely have a high level of inflammation. The reason is probably that you are eating too many pro-inflammatory foods. You would do well to go on the Anti-Inflammation Syndrome Diet Plan and take steps to improve your long-term health.

High or very high on quiz 1 but not quiz 2: You have probably adopted a very good diet but may have to further fine-tune your diet and supplement program.

Now that you understand how the modern diet sets the stage for abnormally strong inflammatory reactions, you can focus on eating anti-inflammatory and neutral foods. The best anti-inflammatory foods are fish, especially cold-water varieties such as salmon, and a diverse selection of vegetables. The old adage "Eat a lot of color" definitely applies here because, to a great extent, bright and deep colors often indicate the presence of natural anti-inflammatory nutrients.

In this chapter you will read about fifteen anti-inflammation dietary steps to follow while cooking at home or eating out. These steps form the foundation of the Anti-Inflammation Syndrome Diet Plan. Don't worry about trying to remember all fifteen of the steps. If you adhere strictly to step 1, you won't have to remember most of the remaining ones, and following just some of the steps will likely be a major improvement over your current diet. The fifteenth step adapts the Anti-Inflammation Syndrome Diet Plan for losing weight, so it may or may not apply to you. Maintaining a normal weight is important because fat increases the amount of inflammation-causing substances made by the body.

Although the steps are remarkably simple, some may seem difficult to follow at the beginning, because you will have to break some bad eating habits and learn some good ones. It is important to remember that your previous eating habits created health problems for you, and that fact should help motivate you to stick with your new eating habits. If you still dread making these changes, give them a try for just one week. You will likely start to feel noticeably better during this time.

The goals of the Anti-Inflammation Syndrome Diet Plan are twofold: one, offsetting the damage of a pro-inflammatory diet, and two, restoring and maintaining a diet that reduces your risk of chronic inflammatory diseases and symptoms. By emphasizing anti-inflammatory foods, at least for several months, you can establish a more normal balance between pro- and anti-inflammatory compounds in your body. Once you have achieved such a balance, you may be able to eat more "neutral" foods and even tolerate an occasional pro-inflammatory food.

You will be pleased to know that the Anti-Inflammation Syndrome Diet Plan does not ask that you eat like a caveman or a cavewoman—but it does encourage you to take the best of the past and current knowledge of nutrition science. As you will discover when trying the recipes in the following chapter, the diet is relatively easy and tasty.

—⁓—

The Anti-Inflammation Syndrome Diet Steps

1. Eat a variety of fresh and whole foods.
2. Eat more fish, especially cold-water varieties.
3. Eat lean meats (not corn-fed) from free-range chicken and turkey, grass-fed cattle and buffalo, and game meats such as duck and ostrich.
4. Eat a lot of vegetables, the more colorful the better.
5. Use spices and herbs to flavor foods, and limit your use of salt and pepper.
6. Use olive oil as your primary cooking oil.

7. Avoid conventional cooking oils such as corn, safflower, sunflower, and soybean oil, as well as vegetable shortening, margarine, and partially hydrogenated oils.
8. Identify and avoid food allergens.
9. Avoid or strictly limit your intake of food products that contain sugars, such as sucrose or high-fructose corn syrup.
10. Avoid or limit your intake of refined grains.
11. Limit your intake of dairy products.
12. Snack on nuts and seeds.
13. When thirsty, drink water.
14. Whenever possible, buy and eat organically raised foods.
15. To lose weight, reduce both carbohydrates and calories.

The Anti-Inflammation Syndrome Step 1: Eat a Variety of Fresh and Whole Foods

Most of the following steps are more specific versions of this first one: eat a variety of fresh and whole foods. These are foods that are in or close to their original state. They have not been processed or altered beyond refrigeration, kitchen preparation, and cooking. In other words such foods look pretty much the way they did in nature (which is not how processed foods look). A couple of examples should help clarify the meaning of fresh and whole foods.

A freshly broiled piece of fish *looks, smells,* and *tastes* like a piece of fish. It is very different from breaded and deep-fried fish, which is coated in refined flour and then cooked in a mix of vegetable and partially hydrogenated vegetable oils.

A piece of baked chicken still looks like a part of a chicken, which breaded and deep-fried chicken nuggets do not.

A carrot looks like a carrot, which carrot juice (devoid of fiber) does not.

An apple looks like an apple, which applesauce and apple juice do not.

A baked potato looks like a potato, which French fries (boiled in hydrogenated or oxidized oils) do not.

In practice, avoid any food that does not resemble what it looked like as it was growing or being raised. (The exceptions are foods that have just been cut up or prepared in a food processor or blender.) Following this principle means that you will have to strictly limit foods sold in boxes, cans, jars, and bottles—often, even those sold in health and natural-food stores. The reason is that boxing, canning, and bottling usually indicate some sort of processing or alteration from the food's original state, plus the addition of unwanted ingredients such as sugars, refined grains, most oils, flavor enhancers, texturizers, and more. Canned vegetables may or may not have added sugar; regardless, they are less nutritious than frozen, and frozen vegetables are usually less nutritious than fresh.

So as you stare into your cupboard, you must be wondering what you will eat. It's simple: fresh (or frozen) fish, lean meats, spices and herbs for seasoning, lots of vegetables, and some fruit. Such foods are straightforward, uncomplicated, and easy to prepare and vary.

The Anti-Inflammation Syndrome Step 2: Eat More Fish, Especially Cold-Water Varieties

Cold-water fish contain the largest amounts of the most biologically active, "preformed" omega-3 fatty acids. Preformed means that the fatty acids exist as eicosapentaenoic acid (EPA) and docosahexaenoic acid (DHA), and the body does not have to make them from alpha-linolenic acid. This shortcut enables your body to put the anti-inflammatory properties of EPA and DHA to work right away.

An ideal amount of dietary omega-3 fatty acids is about 7 grams a week, which you can obtain in two to three servings of fish. Of course, eating fish more often is even better, particularly during the first couple months of the Anti-Inflammation Syndrome Diet Plan. (Fish oil supplements, which will be discussed in chapter 8, also can rapidly boost your intake of EPA and DHA.)

The fish with the highest concentrations of omega-3 fatty acids are mackerel, Pacific herring, anchovy, lake trout, king salmon, and Atlantic salmon. Tuna, halibut, cod, sole, snapper, crab, and shrimp contain smaller quantities of omega-3 fatty acids, but they are still healthy. Wild salmon contains a higher portion of anti-inflammatory omega-3 fatty acids compared with farmed salmon. All types of Alaskan salmon—including king, coho, and sokeye—are always wild. By 2004, labeling laws will require distributors to identify whether the salmon was wild or farmed.

Although fresh fish is always better (and smells less fishy) than frozen, most fish is delivered frozen to supermarkets. You may be broil, bake, poach, grill, or pan fry the fish in olive oil (and you should specify one of these when ordering in restaurants). Never eat breaded and deep-fried fish. The breading adds empty calories, and the frying saturates the breading and fish with highly processed, pro-inflammatory omega-6 and trans fatty acids. At home, you can also stir fry a dense fish in olive oil.

If you do not like the taste of fish (or are a vegetarian), you can increase your intake of EPA and DHA in other ways. Freshly ground flaxseed sprinkled on a salad or vegetables, or flaxseed oil drizzled on them, contains large amounts of alpha-linolenic acid. Of course, your body will have to convert it to EPA and DHA. In addition, you can eat eggs enriched with omega-3 fatty acids or one of the growing number of products containing deodorized fish oils, such as some types of Millina's Finest tomato sauces.

—⚂—

The Issue of Mercury in Fish

Some types of fish absorb mercury, a toxic metal. So how do you address this issue when eating anti-inflammatory fish?

One way is to avoid fish that you know are from polluted waters. Farm-raised fish are likely free of mercury, though they have the disadvantage of having slightly more omega-6 fatty acids compared with wild fish (because farm-raised fish are fed grains). A second way to deal with this problem is to take selenium supplements. Garry F. Gordon, M.D., of Payson, Arizona, an expert on heavy metal toxicity, points out that selenium binds with mercury and blocks its toxicity.

Taking selenium supplements might not be a bad idea in general, because this essential mineral boosts antioxidant levels in the body, which will have an anti-inflammatory effect. A daily supplement containing 200 mcg of selenium supplements (preferably the high-selenium yeast form, which will be identified on the label) makes good sense.

Mercury, however, is not an issue with fish-oil supplements. A ConsumerLab.com analysis of different brands of fish-oil capsules found no detectable amounts of mercury.

—⚂—

The Anti-Inflammation Syndrome Step 3: Eat Meat from Free-Range or Grass-Fed Animals

The animals that provided meat to Paleolithic peoples ate grass and leaves, which are rich sources of alpha-linolenic acid. For this reason, game meat contains large amounts of anti-inflammatory omega-3 fatty acids. Today, when farm animals are fed corn and other grains, their muscles contain almost no omega-3 fatty acids and substantial amounts of saturated fats.

It is important to avoid, or strictly limit your intake of, meat from corn-fed animals. This caution often applies to meat or eggs from "vegetarian-fed" animals, which may be corn-fed. Many natural foods stores, such as the Wild Oats and Whole Foods chains, have full-service meat departments, and many of their meats are from grass-fed or free-range animals. Similarly, chicken, turkey, and duck should come from animals that were allowed to peck around for their natural diet, not fed corn and other grains. Always ask your butcher to be sure. See appendix B for sources of meat from grass-fed animals.

The Anti-Inflammation Syndrome Step 4: Eat a Lot of Vegetables, the More Colorful the Better

Vegetables and many fruits are the best dietary sources of antioxidants, which help dampen overactive immune responses. Contrary to popular opinion, most of these antioxidants are not vitamins. The lion's share are a large family of vitaminlike nutrients known as polphenolic flavonoids.

More than five thousand flavonoids (one subfamily among polyphenols) have been identified in plants. Quercetin, one particular anti-inflammatory flavonoid, is found in apples and onions. A small apple (about 3.5 oz) contains approximately 5.7 mg of vitamin C, but more than 500 mg of antioxidant polyphenols and flavonoids, which together are equivalent to 1,500 mg of vitamin C.

In addition, vegetables and fruit are also rich sources of carotenoids, another class of powerful antioxidants. Although more than six hundred carotenoids have been found in nature, only a handful appear important for humans. These include alpha-carotene, beta-carotene, lutein, and lycopene.

The rule to follow is diversity. Eat at least five servings of vegetables or fruit daily, and make a point of eating different types. Try to eat one large salad daily, made with dark leafy green lettuces (not iceberg lettuce, which was created in 1903 to withstand damage in shipping) or spinach, tomatoes, scallions, shredded carrots, and other vegetables. You can certainly add some grilled chicken, fish, or shrimp to the salad.

With another meal, steam, sauté, or grill vegetables as a side dish to fish or meat. On one day, you might want to steam broccoli and cauliflower. On another, you can pan fry baby asparagus and green beans in olive oil and garlic. To keep things interesting, on still another day, you might grill or broil slices of squash, eggplant, and fennel, brushing them with olive oil and garlic powder. A little garlic, olive oil, and lemon will enhance the flavor of almost any vegetable.

The Anti-Inflammation Syndrome Step 5: Use Spices and Herbs to Flavor Foods

For many people salt (sodium chloride) and black pepper are the usual flavor enhancers sprinkled onto foods. The Paleolithic diet contained large amounts of potassium and small amounts of naturally occurring sodium. With large amounts of salt added during the manufacture of food products (once again, carefully read package labels) and still more at the table, today's diets typically contain far more sodium than potassium. Excess intake of sodium can raise blood pressure and interfere with the body's use of calcium.

A variety of spices and herbs adds a palette of flavors to foods. But the benefits of basil, oregano, garlic, and other spices and herbs go beyond taste. Culinary herbs are rich in antioxidant flavonoids and natural Cox-2 inhibitors. While the amounts of spices and herbs in a single meal may not have a substantial anti-inflammatory effect, they enhance an anti-inflammatory dietary regimen.

If you enjoy a pungent kick with some of your foods, substitute a little cayenne powder for black pepper (unless you are allergic to night-shades—see step 8). Cayenne contains substances that block the transmission of pain between nerve cells.

The Anti-Inflammation Syndrome Step 6: Use Olive Oil as Your Primary Cooking Oil

Extra-virgin olive oil should be your main cooking oil. It is rich in anti-inflammatory oleic acid (an omega-9 fatty acid), vitamin E, and polyphenolic flavonoids. Different brands of olive oil, and olive oil derived from different types of olives, have different flavors, so it is good to try different ones. Always use extra-virgin olive oil, an indicator of high quality, and look for a date on the bottle. The olive oil is best used within a year of picking and bottling, but it can be used for cooking for two to three years.

Although olive oil is a pressed oil, which was not consumed during our Paleolithic development, it is an acceptable compromise for our modern times. The omega-9 fatty acids in olive oil help offset years of excessive omega-6 intake. Olive oil, like fish oil, is also valuable for its potent anti-inflammatory properties. Consider it a "supplement" with an exceptional flavor.

As an alternative to olive oil if you want a cooking oil with a different taste, cold pressed macadamia nut oil is a good substitute. Macadamia nut oil is rich in anti-inflammatory oleic acid, the same omega-9 fat found in olive oil. Australian Mac Nut oil is an excellent product. (See appendix B.) It has a high smoke point, so you can cook with it at higher temperatures than you could with olive oil.

Several other oils or fats in small amounts can be used as well. A little butter adds a nice flavor to many meals, and its saturated fat should not pose a problem as long as you are consuming large amounts of omega-3 fatty acids. Grapeseed oil and canola oil also contain omega-9 and omega-3 fatty acids, and they withstand high cooking temperatures very well. However, most grapeseed and canola oils are obtained through chemical extraction (in contrast to mechanical pressing), which may leave trace amounts of solvents in the oils. Look more carefully in grocery stores and you will likely find mechanically pressed grapeseed and canola oils—although olive oil is still preferable to them.

Do not heat flaxseed or fish oils, and do not use them to cook foods. High temperatures rapidly oxidize and break them down, leading to the formation of pro-inflammatory free radicals. It is all right, of course, to cook fish because its mass resists those high temperatures unless, of course, you happen to overcook or burn it.

The Anti-Inflammation Syndrome Step 7: Avoid Conventional Cooking Oils

Conventional cooking oils, such as corn, peanut, safflower, soybean, sunflower, and cottonseed oils, are high in pro-inflammatory omega-6 fatty acids and contain virtually no anti-inflammatory omega-3 or omega-9 fatty acids. These oils are commonly used in an enormous number of processed and packaged foods, including microwave meals, breakfast bars, salad dressings, and in many restaurants. The extensive use of these cooking oils is largely why the modern diet contains twenty to thirty times more pro-inflammatory than anti-inflammatory oils.

The worst oils are partially hydrogenated vegetable oils. All partially hydrogenated oils contain trans fatty acids, which are considerably more dangerous than saturated fats. Vegetable shortenings and hard margarines are among the worst of such products, but you will find partially hydrogenated oils in salad dressings, nondairy creamers, bakery products, and many processed foods.

It is always wise to carefully read the label of a food package. You are most likely to run into all of these pro-inflammatory oils in fast-food restaurants (McDonald's, Burger King, KFC), Chinese restaurants, and "low end" chain restaurants (Denny's and Carrow's), which rely heavily on processed, ready-to-heat foods.

—⚬⚬—

Navigating Restaurant Food

If you are hoping to follow the Anti-Inflammation Syndrome Diet Plan while eating at fast-food restaurants, the advice is simple: forget it. All of these chains rely on mass-produced food products, which are highly processed and loaded with pro-inflammatory nutrients, such as omega-6 fatty acids, trans fatty acids, sugars, and refined grains.

Family-run ethnic and upscale nouvelle cuisine restaurants often use fresh ingredients, more anti-inflammatory nutrients, and are generally more accommodating when diners ask for modifications to meals. For example, restaurants will usually serve, when asked, a sandwich without bread and substitute some sort of steamed vegetable or a salad for French fries.

Your best bets when eating out are Greek, Italian, and Middle Eastern restaurants. These cuisines typically use olive oil and tasty spices. Most meat and vegetable dishes are safe on the Anti-Inflammation Syndrome Diet Plan, but watch out for the occasional breaded meat or vegetable, as well as for pita bread, falafel, or couscous.

Japanese food also is a good choice, as long as you stick with simple fish dishes or sushi and sashimi. Teriyaki sauces usually contain some sugar, and tempuras are deep fried, though quickly.

Mexican foods tend to include a lot of grains and dairy—common allergens and abundant calories. However, fajitas are generally all right if you avoid the tortillas. Chinese foods are typically stir fried in soybean oil, which is high in pro-inflammatory fats.

—⚬⚬—

The Anti-Inflammation Syndrome Step 8: Identify and Avoid Food Allergens

Food allergies or allergylike food sensitivities can rev up the immune system and contribute to chronic inflammation. It is relatively easy and inexpensive to obtain a "food allergy panel" using a simple blood test. Indeed, the health mobiles that occasionally visit supermarkets can perform allergy panel tests for about $30.

It may be easier to assess your likelihood of being allergic to certain foods when you don't already have an obvious reaction after eating a particular food. The reason is that people often become allergic to the foods they eat most often, for biochemical reasons too involved to discuss here. In addition, food allergies often take the form of a food addiction—such as a food you crave or cannot imagine living without. If you avoid a suspect food and all related foods (such as all foods with dairy) for a week, and you are in fact allergic to it, you will feel better. However, you also might not notice any difference in how you feel until you add that food back to your diet, when you suddenly feel worse.

In *Going Against the Grain,* nutritionist Melissa Diane Smith writes that as many as half of Americans have some degree of gluten intolerance. The gut damage from gluten can predispose people to numerous other food allergies. A damaged, or leaky, gut can allow undigested food proteins to enter the bloodstream, where they trigger an immune response. The most common sources of gluten are wheat, rye, barley, and oats.

Nightshades are another problematic group of foods for many people with rheumatoid arthritis. These foods include tomatoes, potatoes, eggplants, and peppers. Although tobacco is not a food, it is a member of the nightshade family. Before Columbus discovered Native Americans eating tomatoes and peppers, Europeans considered nightshades to be poisonous. Nightshades do contain a variety of mildly toxic compounds and, by some estimates, one of every five arthritics has allergiclike sensitivities to nightshades. Given the prevalence of tomatoes and potatoes (such as ketchup on fries), as well as their inclusion in many processed foods, it is advisable for arthritics to stop eating these foods for several weeks to see if symptoms lessen.

The Anti-Inflammation Syndrome Step 9: Avoid or Strictly Limit Sugars

Refined sugars are the ultimate in empty calories. They provide carbohydrates and calories but no vitamins, minerals, or protein. And sugars appear on labels by a variety of names: sucrose, high-fructose corn syrup, dextrose, glucose, and other names, which reflect slightly different chemical structures or food sources. Even boxes of salt contain a little sugar, and many popular sugar substitutes (NutraSweet, Equal) contain some sugar in the form of maltodextrose.

With two-thirds of all Americans now overweight, there is no justification for people to consume such empty calories. High-sugar and highly refined carbohydrate diets in general elevate levels of pro-inflammatory C-reactive protein (CRP), even in thin people.

For an occasional sweetener, a small amount of honey might suffice; it is far too sweet to consume excessively. Stevia, a noncaloric herbal sweetener available at health food stores, is three hundred times sweeter than sugar and is an excellent sugar substitute. "Raw sugar" is merely dirty white sugar; it contains almost undetectable amounts of a few minerals (which can be better obtained in other, more nutritious foods).

Soft drinks may be the worst single source of sugar and high-fructose corn syrup (a blend of two sugars, sucrose and fructose). Fifty years ago, most soft drinks were sold in tiny 6-ounce bottles. Today, 1-liter cups and 2-liter bottles are common. A 2-liter bottle of Coca-Cola contains almost 0.5 cup of sugars in the form of high-fructose corn syrup. Even worse, a 2-liter bottle of Sunkist orange soda contains considerably more than 0.5 cup of sugars. The Center for Science in the Public Interest, a consumer organization, has accurately described soft drinks as "liquid candy." The *average* American consumes 53 gallons of soft drinks a year, and a total of about 150 pounds of refined sugars, thus heavily contributing to this pro-inflammatory profile. Because these amounts are averages, many people consume far greater amounts of soft drinks and sugars.

The Anti-Inflammation Syndrome Step 10: Avoid or Limit Refined Grains

Like sugars, refined grains provide mostly empty calories, even though many grain products have been "enriched" with a few vitamins. The most common grain in the Western diet is wheat, used to make bread, pasta, muffins, bagels, cookies, and a near-infinite variety of pastries. Many processed foods contain a combination of refined grains, sugars, and partially hydrogenated vegetable oils.

Some people might argue that whole-wheat bread is far superior to refined white bread. While whole-wheat bread does contain more fiber and a few more vitamins and minerals, it also contains more antinutrients, such as lectins. Lectins, a family of proteins, interfere with the absorption of vitamins and minerals and, in some people, stimulate unneeded immune cell activity. According to Loren Cordain, Ph.D., of Colorado State University at Fort Collins and author of *The Paleo Diet,* lectins may exacerbate the abnormal immune response at the heart of rheumatoid arthritis.

Overall, grains are a poor substitute for the greater nutritional value of vegetables.

White rice is similar to refined white bread in that most of its important nutrients have been refined out and mostly carbohydrate is left. Brown rice is far superior, although it, too, contains some lectins. Although relatively high in carbohydrate, it also contains vitamins, minerals, protein, and fiber, and no gluten.

It is not necessary to eliminate all grains when on the Anti-Inflammation Syndrome Diet Plan, unless you are sensitive to gluten. However, it is wise to greatly reduce their intake so they are only an occasional treat. If nothing else, large quantities of grains, such as in the form of breads and pastas, displace far more nutritious foods.

—⚂—

Navigating the Supermarket

In *Syndrome X: The Complete Nutritional Program to Prevent and Reverse Insulin Resistance,* my coauthors and I provided detailed instructions for shopping at supermarkets and natural foods markets. The best way to navigate supermarkets is simple: shop along the perimeter.

Nearly all supermarkets follow a similar floor plan, with refrigerated foods (produce, meat, and dairy) on the perimeter, and heavily processed foods in the center of the store. Fresh foods generally require refrigeration, and you will want to do most of your food shopping in the produce, meat, and fish departments.

As you move toward the center of the store, you will find entire aisles dedicated to soft drinks, cookies, breads, and cereals. All of these foods are incompatible with the Anti-Inflammation Syndrome Diet Plan. The same is true for the frozen-food aisles, typically located right in the middle. The freezers usually are filled with variations of ice cream, high-sugar juices, and highly processed microwave meals.

—⚂—

The Anti-Inflammation Syndrome Step 11: Limit Your Intake of Dairy Products

Dairy products, with the exception of mother's milk during infancy, is another recent addition to the human diet. Many people, particularly Asians and Africans, lose the ability to digest milk after childhood. In addition, no species on Earth naturally consumes the milk of another species, with the exception of people. In terms of chemical composition, cow's milk is intended to nurture calves, not humans of any age.

Cow's milk also is a common allergen. It provides considerable saturated fat, and some people have argued that homogenization alters the size and metabolism of milk fat, making it more likely to promote heart disease. As beverages, milk and milk shakes provide a large quantity of calories, when the body really requires only water.

Small amounts of cheeses may be all right for many people, unless they are allergic to dairy. Cheeses do provide concentrated protein, but most of their fat is saturated because cows are fed grains rather than simply allowed to feed on grass. However, given the evolutionary implications of dairy consumption, it is best to limit your intake of milk and other dairy products.

The Anti-Inflammation Syndrome Step 12:
Snack on Nuts and Seeds

So what do you do with your sweet tooth? Try eating more nuts, such as almonds, cashews, filberts, macadamias, and pistachios, as well as seeds, such as pumpkin seeds. Nuts and seeds are relatively high in fat, a mix of both linoleic and alpha-linolenic acids, and their fat content provides a sweet taste. In particular, almond butter tastes very sweet and is less allergenic than peanuts (although people sensitive to peanuts must make sure that there is no trace of peanuts in almond butter).

Studies have found that regularly eating nuts (preferably raw or dry roasted) reduces the risk of heart disease. One reason for this may be that nuts are very filling and can displace foods with saturated fat. Also, nuts and seeds are also rich in many minerals such as magnesium that are necessary for a healthy heart.

The Anti-Inflammation Syndrome Step 13:
When Thirsty, Drink Water

Water is the beverage virtually all animals—again, except for people—consume for life. If you live in an urban area and the quality or taste of tap water leaves a lot to be desired, drink filtered water. Both the Brita and Pur systems filter out chlorine, heavy metals, and, unfortunately, even some of the dietary minerals (such as calcium and magnesium). Buy a brand of sparkling mineral water with a particularly high mineral content, such as Gerolsteiner. Scientists have found that drinking high-mineral water immediately triggers a series of bone-building biochemical reactions. A wedge of lime or lemon adds a citrus flavor to the water, whether sparkling or still.

While water should be your main drink, another beverage option is tea. Various teas—black, green, and herbal—provide antioxidant polyphenol flavonoids, which have been shown to reduce the risk of heart disease and cancer. Some research has also found that the topical application of green tea (cooled down, of course) can reverse some types of dermatitis. It is easy to make iced tea simply by refrigerating warm tea or sun tea.

And what of coffee, the beverage consumed each day by the majority of Westerners? Although the research is contradictory, the risk of health problems does seem to increase when more than a couple of cups of coffee are consumed daily. Some research indicates that the caffeine in coffee and many teas may stimulate inflammation, so it might be worthwhile eliminating caffeinated beverages for a week or two and seeing how you feel.

Some research has shown that red wines, because of their high antioxidant content, may reduce the risk of coronary artery disease. Other alcoholic beverages, such as spirits, have a deleterious effect on health, largely because they are liver toxins and provide no nutritional value. Moderate amounts of red wine, such as a couple of glasses per week, should be fine on the Anti-Inflammation Syndrome Diet Plan.

The best guidance is to drink mostly water and a little tea. And, as noted in step 9, avoid all soft drinks and other beverages (including energy drinks and so-called quick thirst quenchers) that contain sugar, high-fructose corn syrup, or other caloric sweeteners.

—⚅—

Smoking and Inflammation

Virtually everyone who smokes (or chews) tobacco products knows that they are hazardous to health. In addition to increasing the risk of lung cancer, tobacco smoke boosts the risk of many other types of cancer, emphysema, and coronary artery disease. Smoking significantly elevates levels of C-reactive protein (CRP), a powerful promoter of inflammation. Even after a person stops smoking, his or her CRP levels remain higher than normal for years. If you don't smoke, don't start. And if you do, try to break the habit.

—⚅—

The Anti-Inflammation Syndrome Step 14:
Buy and Eat Organically Raised Foods

Organic foods are produced without any synthetic pesticides in an environmentally sustainable fashion. That means, essentially, that the soil quality is preserved and enhanced, which is in sharp contrast to conventional farming practices. Organic foods are generally a little more expensive than conventional foods. Consider organics as a desirable option when you can afford them.

There are two justifications for considering organics. One is that they are free of pesticides and genetically engineered material. Many pesticides are estrogen mimics, meaning that they simulate the effect of estrogen and may disrupt the actions of our own hormones. Although pesticides may or may not influence inflammation, it may be best to act conservatively and avoid exposure to them.

The second justification is that several small research studies have found that organic vegetables and fruit tend to have higher vitamin and mineral levels, compared with conventional produce. And, although this is a subjective judgment, many people feel that organics taste better than conventional vegetables and fruit.

Finally, if you eat meat from free-range or grass-fed animals, it is likely to be free of pesticides. Often, corn and other grains intended for farm animals are not organic, and they are also treated with pesticides to prevent destruction by insects. So, for many reasons, it is best to opt for organic foods when obtainable and affordable.

The Anti-Inflammation Syndrome Step 15:
To Lose Weight, Reduce Both Carbohydrates and Calories

Sixty-five percent—two-thirds—of Americans are now overweight. In addition, 31 percent—more than one-fourth—of Americans also are obese, that is, more than thirty pounds over their ideal weight. In 2002 scientists reported that overweight is increasing worldwide, largely the result of Americans exporting their unhealthy food habits to other nations.

Fat cells, particularly the type that form around the abdomen, produce large amounts of two powerful inflammation-causing substances, interleukin-6 and C-reactive protein. These high levels of inflammatory compounds are a big part of the reason why being overweight greatly increases a person's risk of diabetes, heart disease, osteoarthritis, and other inflammatory disorders.

Eating according to the Anti-Inflammation Syndrome Diet Plan will likely lead to some weight loss. This is because the diet discourages the use of convenience and fast foods, which contain large amounts of calories and carbohydrates relative to protein, vitamins, minerals, good fats, and fiber. Another reason is that calories from anti-inflammatory omega-3 and omega-9 fatty acids are not converted to body fat as readily as calories from omega-6 fatty acids and saturated fats.

Still, you may wish to further reduce your weight on the Anti-Inflammation Syndrome Diet Plan. You can accomplish this by modifying the diet plan so it is a little more consistent with the weight-loss recommendations in my previous book *Syndrome X: The Complete Nutritional Program to Prevent and Reverse Insulin Resistance.* Some compelling research suggests that the worst possible diet (in terms of Syndrome X, diabetes, and weight gain) is one high in both refined carbohydrates and saturated fats—that is, the typical American diet. So the reasonable alternative is an anti-inflammatory diet that further restricts carbohydrates and saturated fats.

To put these ideas into practice and to lose weight, you will need to eliminate all or nearly all grain-based foods, including whole grains, since these foods (as well as foods with refined sugars) are the principal source of dietary calories and carbohydrates. (This is easier than you might think. I lost twenty pounds and four inches from my waist after giving up pasta.) In addition, you might curtail your intake of legumes, because they also contain substantial amounts of carbohydrates.

Although these recommendations have similarities to the Atkins diet, they are very different. It is important to replace these grain- and legume-based carbohydrates with ample quantities of nonstarchy or low-starch vegetables and fruit. Such foods include spinach, broccoli, cauliflower, lettuces, tomatoes, cucumbers, apples, and berries. Basically, one large salad daily (with an olive oil dressing) and sides of vegetables or fruit with lunch and dinner should provide modest amounts of carbohydrates and respectable quantities of fiber. To lower your intake of saturated fat, eat less beef, pork, and lamb, but increase your consumption of fish, chicken, and turkey.

Physical activity is important as well. Numerous studies have found that going for a walk each day improves insulin function and lowers blood sugar levels, which also contribute to maintaining normal weight. Going for a thirty-minute walk each day is sufficient, though longer walks and more vigorous exercise will yield greater benefits. If you engage in regular exercise, bear in mind that muscle weighs more than fat.

Therefore, you may gain a little weight, even though you are trimmer or more muscular.

If you happen to lose more weight than you wish, you can increase your intake of nutritious unrefined carbohydrates, such as those in brown rice, sweet potatoes, yams, and squash. As with any diet, you will have to make individual adjustments. Your guideposts are how you feel and how you look.

The following pyramid illustrates the points made in this chapter.

The Anti-Inflammation Syndrome Food Pyramid

Avoid or Restrict
Alcohol, Partially Hydrogenated Oils, Refined Sugars, Refined Grains, and Saturated Fats

1 Daily Serving or Less from Any Food in this Group
Dairy, Whole Grains, Brown Rice, Starchy Fruits, and Starchy Vegetables

Nuts and Seeds
1 Daily Serving

Olive Oil
2 Daily Servings

Nonstarchy or Low-Starch Fruits
Examples: Berries, Apples, Kiwi
1 to 2 Daily Servings

Lean Meats or Game Meats
Examples: Chicken, Turkey, Duck, Grass-Fed Beef
1 to 2 Daily Servings

Fish
Examples: Coldwater varieties, such as Salmon and Mackerel
1 to 3 Daily Servings

Nonstarchy or Low-Starch Vegetables
Examples: Broccoli, Cauliflower, Green Beans, Salad Greens, Tomatoes, Onions
6 to 10 Daily Servings

Because of the widespread use of the U.S. Department of Agriculture's food pyramid, this drawing might help some people visualize the Anti-Inflammation Syndrome Food Pyramid. Foods toward the top are those you would eat the least of, whereas those toward the bottom are those you would eat the most of.

CHAPTER 7

Anti-Inflammation Syndrome Menu Plans and Recipes

By following most or all of the anti-inflammation dietary steps, you will find that it is relatively easy to order healthy meals in many restaurants. However, you may be wondering about what to cook at home. This chapter offers a number of recipes for breakfast, lunch, and dinner, as well as a sample seven-day menu plan. This menu plan is merely a guideline and is not meant as a strict rule for what you must eat on any given day. Overall, this chapter takes a very positive approach to food selection, emphasizing what you should eat instead of what you should not.

Unlike many diet plans that are extremely rigid, the Anti-Inflammation Syndrome Diet Plan encourages flexibility and creativity in cooking and food choices. Inflexible dietary regimens can, for many people, become difficult to follow, and such plans often beg to be violated. So, in following the recipes in this chapter, please feel comfortable adjusting quantities, particularly of spices, to suit your personal tastes.

It is worthwhile keeping several guidelines in mind when preparing anti-inflammatory meals at home.

1. You will have to plan some of your major meals generally one to two days in advance. Poor meal planning has become very common and, combined with hunger pangs, often leads to picking the fastest meal

obtainable—a pizza, burger and fries, or microwave lunch or dinner—which are typically rich in pro-inflammatory ingredients. Making a fresh, anti-inflammatory dinner will not take a long time if you have done a modicum of planning. You can do this planning with a pen and pad of paper during television commercials, during a break at work, and perhaps while commuting. You can also stimulate your culinary creativity by thumbing through cookbooks in bookstores.

2. Keep your meals simple if you have time constraints. Many diet books and cookbooks contain extraordinarily complex recipes, with five or ten different spices and intricate preparation. Relatively few of us have the time to prepare such meals, except perhaps on a weekend or for a special occasion. With this situation in mind, the recipes in this chapter contain relatively few ingredients and are easy to prepare. Still, some people may complain that the following recipes—as simple as they are—take too much time. They certainly do take more time than a microwave meal or driving through a fast-food restaurant. But as with everything else in life, you are faced with choices: Do you want to continue living the way that made you sick, or do you want to take the steps needed to be healthy?

3. With the time you invest in making a major meal, such as dinner, it is efficient to scale up (i.e., to double) the quantities so you have great-tasting leftovers. Leftovers have gotten a bad reputation—often deserved—because reheated junk foods often taste much worse than when originally heated. However, leftovers from tasty meals usually remain tasty the second time around. They can be quickly spruced up, reheated, or used in still other recipes—what one friend refers to as "planovers." For example, leftovers from a chicken or turkey dinner can be used in a quick-to-prepare breakfast or a brown-bag lunch at the office. In addition, some recipes, such as the Tomato-Free Ratatouille, are meant as both a side dish with dinner and as part of breakfast.

4. It is worthwhile experimenting and trying to be creative in the kitchen, modifying recipes as you go. Methodically measuring out every single ingredient—3 tablespoons or this and ½ teaspoon of that—may be a good method while learning the basics of cooking, but sometimes being a little less precise can make cooking more *fun*. I say this as a man who did not learn how to cook until age forty-nine. After learning some of the basics and also making some mistakes, I discovered that cooking is enjoyable and creative. If I can do this, you can also, regardless of your circumstances.

As with any creative pursuit, set aside some time, and approach cooking as a personally rewarding activity, not a stressful chore. It helps to envision all of your ingredients—meat or fish, vegetables, condiments, and spices—as comparable to the palette of paints used by an artist. Of course, some foods (like colors) work better together than others. If you are not used to cooking, it may take several months to develop this level of comfort, but along the way you will gain a sense of accomplishment and greater confidence from the tasty meals you create.

5. To stimulate your interest in culinary experiments, read other recipe books for ideas, and watch the Food Network (www.foodtv.com) on television to learn new cooking techniques and recipes. It is relatively easy to experiment and modify many conventional recipes to the principles of the Anti-Inflammation Syndrome Diet Plan. For example, you can substitute olive oil for nearly any other cooking oil, and often you can use rice flour instead of wheat flour for dredging chicken and fish.

6. Many of the dinner recipes emphasize fish because of their rich reservoir of anti-inflammatory compounds. If you hate the taste of fish, don't give up. Follow the other dietary principles and be sure to take fish oil capsules to obtain the necessary eicosapentaenoic acid (EPA) and docosahexaenoic acid (DHA). You might also try just one fish recipe, such as fresh tuna, to determine whether you genuinely dislike fish or whether you have simply had bad experiences with fish. Fresh fish does not have a strong fishy odor.

Anti-Inflammation Syndrome Diet Plan Meals

The recipes are organized counterintuitively, with dinner first, followed by dinner side dishes, and then by lunch and breakfast. There is a reason for this type of flow. Dinner leftovers, used creatively, can be used in making lunches and breakfasts, thus saving considerable time preparing other meals. All of these recipes can be easily doubled, so you have plenty of tasty leftovers.

—⁓—

Quick Tip: Natural Flavor Enhancers

To enhance the flavor of almost any fish or fowl, add some olive oil, garlic, or fresh-squeezed lemon juice. Oregano and basil also add a lot of flavor, as long as they do not compete with other spices and herbs (such as herbes de Provence or dill).

—ᗰ—

Dinner Main Courses

Baked Salmon *(Serves 2)*

> olive oil
> 2 salmon fillets, about 4 to 6 ounces each
> basil, to taste
> oregano, to taste
> 1 to 3 teaspoons basalmic vinaigrette, to taste

Preheat the oven to 350 degrees.

Coat the bottom of a baking dish with olive oil. Rinse and pat excess water off the salmon, and place them in the baking dish. Apply a thin coat of olive oil on top of the fillets (to add flavor and to prevent burning). Sprinkle basil and oregano to taste on the fillets. Drizzle the balsamic vinaigrette on the fillets. Bake for approximately 10 minutes. The cooking time may vary by a couple of minutes, depending on the oven and thickness of the fillets, so examine after 8 minutes to ensure that they are not burning or undercooked. The baked salmon goes well with Spinach and Leek Sauté (page 89) and Flavorful Brown Rice (page 89).

Pumpkin Seed Crusted Halibut *(Serves 2)*

> ½ teaspoon coriander
> ¼ cup raw pumpkin seeds, chopped
> ¼ cup olive oil
> 1 pound halibut, cut into two pieces
> 2 pats butter
> 1 lemon
> 1 tablespoon parsley

Preheat the oven to 350 degrees.

Add the coriander to the pumpkin seeds, then chop the seeds in a food processor, being careful to avoid a flourlike texture. Meanwhile, spread the olive oil over the bottom of baking dish. Dredge the halibut through the olive oil so all sides of the fish are lightly coated. With one hand, spoon the chopped pumpkin seeds onto all sides of the fish, while using the fingers of your other hand to pat the seeds onto the fish. Add one pat of butter to the top of each piece of fish. Bake the fish 10 minutes per inch of thickness. When done, squeeze lemon juice on each piece of fish, and sprinkle with parsley.

—✺—

Quick Tip: Sanitary Gloves

Preparing food can often get a little messy. To avoid having to repeatedly wash your hands (such as after handling fish or rubbing olive oil into fish or meats), wear disposable, sanitary plastic gloves. Large quantities of these gloves are available inexpensively at Price-Costco and many other stores. Using these gloves also reduces possible bacterial contamination of your hands and the food.

—✺—

Pan Fried Swordfish with Citrus Marinade *(Serves 2)*

2 swordfish steaks, approximately 1 pound total
2 tablespoons olive oil

Marinade
1 tablespoon olive oil
2 scallions, diced
1 large lemon, juiced
1 lime, juiced
½ orange, juiced (optional)
4 cloves garlic
1 teaspoon ground coriander
⅛ teaspoon cumin

Prepare the marinade by mixing the marinade ingredients.

Trim the skin from the swordfish and soak in the marinade, refrigerating for 1 to 2 hours. When ready to cook, drain off as much liquid as possible from the marinade. Heat a frypan on medium heat with olive oil, then add the swordfish, with the remainder of the marinade next to the fish. Cook approximately 3 minutes per side. Serve with vegetables and rice.

Simple Poached Salmon *(Serves 4)*

    1 quart water
    1 cup vermouth
    1 onion, sliced
    1 carrot, sliced
    1 stalk celery, sliced
    1 bay leaf
    1 teaspoon RealSalt or sea salt
    1 pinch of ground black pepper
    1 large fillet of salmon with skin on one side
    1 lemon

Fill a large, low-profile pot with water. Add the vermouth, onion, carrot, celery, bay leaf, salt, and pepper. Bring to a boil, then simmer for 20 minutes. Meanwhile, completely wrap the salmon in a strip of cheesecloth. Fold the cheesecloth so you can unwrap it slightly to check the fish, and leave the ends long enough to drape over the sides of the pan.

Insert the fish into the simmering broth, ideally with 1 inch or 2 inches of water above it. Be careful to keep the ends of the cheesecloth away from the flame or heating element. Bring the water to a boil again, then simmer. Allow 8 minutes per pound for the fish to cook. Unwrap the fish to test with a fork whether it is flaky and done. If it is not done, simmer for a couple more minutes and check again.

When the fish is cooked, lift it out of the pot by grabbing it with the two ends of the cheesecloth. Place the fish on a platter and remove the cheesecloth. Squeeze lemon juice on fish for additional flavor. The fish can be eaten with a Greek-style Tzatziki cucumber-yogurt sauce (available at many supermarkets or ethnic grocers) or a mayonnaise-based sauce (find one at a natural foods grocer), along with vegetables and rice.

Baked Shrimp and Scallops *(Serves 2)*

    olive oil
    4 to 6 garlic cloves, diced

2 scallions, diced
12 large shrimp, peeled and cleaned
8 large scallops, sliced in half
1 teaspoon each Deliciously Dill spice mix (sold under The Spice
    Hunter label) or oregano and basil
1 lemon, juiced

Coat a large nonstick frypan or wok with olive oil. Sauté garlic and scallions. When the scallions soften, add the shrimp, scallops, and spices. (The scallops should be sliced in half so they cook at the same rate as the shrimp.) Add lemon juice to create a flavorful sauce. The shrimp are cooked when they turn pink on all sides. Serve with rice and vegetables, or toss with a baked spaghetti squash.

Wonderful Baked Chicken Breasts *(Serves 2)*

1 whole or 2 half chicken breasts, boneless
    and skinless
1 cup chicken broth
½ cup olive oil
1 lemon
3 large or 6 small garlic cloves, diced
1 shallot, diced
1 heaping tablespoon of capers
2 tablespoons dried oregano
1 tablespoon dried basil

Preheat oven to 350 degrees.

Trim excess fat and gristle from the chicken. It's all right if the chicken pieces vary in size. If the breasts are thick, carefully slice them laterally, so they end up about half as thick (about ¼ inch each). Spread out the chicken slices and pieces in a baking pan. Next, add the chicken broth, then drizzle the olive oil over the chicken. Cut the lemon, and squeeze the juice over the chicken. Add the garlic, shallots, capers, oregano, and basil. Bake for 30 to 35 minutes. This is an easy-to-prepare and very flavorful dinner and can be served with Pan Fried Veggies (page 90) and Flavorful Brown Rice (page 89).

—⋙—

Quick Tip: Using a Natural Salt

It is important for many people to reduce their intake of salt (sodium chloride). Unfortunately, most salt is added to foods during their manufacture, long before they reach the dining table. In Paleolithic times people consumed far more potassium than sodium, but today people tend to consume far more sodium than potassium. The biggest step in reducing your salt intake is to avoid processed and prepackaged foods, convenience foods, and fast foods. Unprocessed foods—fish, fowl, and vegetables—generally provide more potassium than sodium.

Still, if you would like to use a little salt—just a little—with your meals, try RealSalt. This product, which is extracted from an ancient seabed in southern Utah, contains trace amounts of many minerals. It is available at nearly all health and natural food stores. For more information go to www.realsalt.com.

—⋙—

Evan's Chicken Schnitzel *(Serves 2–3)*

This meal is similar to a chicken fried steak. However, instead of using wheat flour or bread crumbs, you should use Lotus Foods' Bhutanese Red Rice Flour, or order it directly from www.lotusfoods.com. The rice flour is much lighter than wheat; browns nicely; and adds a wonderful, rich flavor.

    1 to 1½ pounds chicken breasts, boneless and skinless
    1 egg, beaten in a bowl
    ¼ cup Bhutanese Red Rice Flour (potato flour can be substituted)
    olive oil
    pat of butter (optional)

Trim excess fat and gristle from the chicken. Slice into thin pieces, running the length of each chicken breast so the pieces are no more than about ¼ inch thick. Dip each piece into the egg, then dredge through the flour. When all of the chicken pieces are prepared (you can prepare very small pieces of chicken similarly to minimize waste), heat the olive oil (and butter, if you choose) in a nonstick frypan. Place the chicken in the pan, cooking about 2 minutes or less per side. Serve with rice and your choice of vegetables.

Saffron Chicken Stir-Fry *(Serves 2–3)*

¼ to ½ teaspoon saffron, ground
¼ cup water
olive oil
pat of butter (optional)
1 to 1½ pounds chicken breast meat, skinless and boneless
6 cloves garlic, diced
1 to 1½ lemons, juiced

To grind the saffron: grind the strands between your fingers in a small bowl. Adding a pinch of salt will help you grind the saffron into a powder. Add water (room temperature or warm) to the bowl with the saffron. Set aside.

Slice or cube the chicken, removing unwanted fat and gristle. Coat a nonstick wok with olive oil (and butter if you wish) over medium heat. Add the chicken and begin stir-frying. When the chicken turns white, add the garlic and saffron mixture and continue to stir-fry for a couple more minutes. Add the lemon juice and stir-fry for another 1 or 2 minutes. The saffron mixture and lemon juice will prevent the chicken from drying out. Serve with rice and vegetables.

Spaghetti Squash Toss *(Serves 1–2)*

This makes for a nice dinner for one or two people, plus leftovers that can be reheated in the microwave for lunch the next day.

1 medium-size spaghetti squash (2 to 2 ½ pounds)
1 boneless, skinless chicken breast or 10 to 20 shrimp and scallops
olive oil
4 to 6 garlic cloves, diced
1 teaspoon basil
1 teaspoon oregano

2 to 3 ounces fresh baby spinach leaves
1 to 2 lemons, juiced
1 lime, juiced
½ orange, juiced
RealSalt (or sea salt) and black pepper, to taste

Bake the spaghetti squash for 1 hour or so, at 350 to 375 degrees, until the skin is soft to the touch. (Use a pot holder or fork to touch it.) Remove the squash from the oven, cut in half lengthwise, and use a spoon to scoop out the seeds. Run a fork along the fruit so you create spaghettilike strands. While the squash is baking, stir-fry the chicken or shrimp and scallops in olive oil along with the garlic, basil, and oregano in a frypan over medium heat. Add the spinach and continue to stir-fry. Add the lemon, lime, and orange juices when the meat is almost cooked. Serve on top of the spaghetti squash. Add RealSalt and black pepper to taste. The stir-frying should take no more than 5 to 10 minutes, so you can time it for when the squash will be ready.

Quick Tip: Quality Chicken Broths

When using packaged chicken broth in a recipe, quality makes a big difference. Health Valley and Pacific organic free-range chicken broths are simple and tasty, without thickeners and excessive amounts of salt. Both brands are available at natural foods grocery stores.

Baked Turkey Breast Provençal *(Serves 4)*

1 turkey breast, on bone or boneless (2 ½ to 3 pounds)
herbes de Provence
rubbed or finely ground dried sage
chicken broth
2 bay leaves
2 tablespoons olive oil, plus additional as needed
1 lemon, juiced
water

Preheat the oven to 350 degrees.

Place the turkey breast in a deep roasting pot, and use your hands to separate but not completely detach the skin from the top of the turkey. Rub a little olive oil on the turkey to keep it from burning or drying out. Sprinkle on herbes de Provence and sage, then place the skin over the spices. You may add a little more olive oil and spices to the skin if you wish. Add about ½ an inch high-quality chicken broth (such as Health Valley or Pacific organic free-range chicken broth) to the bottom of the pot. Add a little more of the spices, plus the bay leaves, 2 tablespoons olive oil, and lemon juice. Bake uncovered for 30 to 40 minutes per pound, approximately 90 minutes to 2 hours total. Add water every 30 minutes or so to maintain the level of the broth, which will become your au jus. During the final 30 minutes, cover the pot. Save leftover turkey and au jus for other meals or recipes, such as Turkey Rice Soup (page 94).

Saffron Seafood Soup *(Serves 4)*

1 small onion, finely diced
1 leek, very thinly sliced (white part only)
1 carrot, thinly sliced
2 teaspoons butter
½ cup dry vermouth or dry white wine
3 to 4 cups fish stock
1 cup short-grain brown rice, already cooked
0.01 ounce saffron, ground
½ teaspoon dried dill or Deliciously Dill seasoning
½ to 1 cup heavy cream
4 ounces salmon filet, cut into small pieces
6 to 8 large shrimp, cut into small pieces
1 to 2 oysters, shucked and rinsed
½ teaspoon RealSalt or sea salt

Sauté the onion, leek, and carrot in butter in a large saucepan over medium heat. When they soften (3 to 5 minutes), add the vermouth, fish stock, rice, and saffron. Bring to a boil, then add the dill and let simmer for 10 to 15 minutes. (If you prefer to have a thick rather than chunky soup, allow to cool slightly and pureé until smooth, then continue simmering.) Stir the cream into the simmering soup, then add the salmon, shrimp, oysters, and RealSalt. Simmer for another 3 to 5 minutes until the fish is cooked and tender.

Side Dishes

Spinach and Leek Sauté *(Serves 1–2)*

1 6-ounce bag fresh spinach
1 leek, white part only
2 pats of butter
water
1 tablespoon pine nuts
garlic powder, to taste

Pinch the stems from the spinach leaves and place the leaves in a large colander. Slice the leek into pieces just over the thickness of a quarter. In a 10-inch nonstick frypan, over medium heat, sauté the leek with a pat of butter until the leek starts to caramelize. Meanwhile, boil a pot of water and pour over the spinach in a colander. This will gently wilt and compress the spinach. Allow the spinach to cool a little, then press out the excess water. When the leek starts to caramelize, add the other pat of butter and then the spinach; you may need to use a fork to separate the clumps of spinach. Sauté and add the pine nuts and garlic powder.

This provides a modest vegetable side dish for two people that goes well with Baked Salmon (page 81). Quantities can easily be doubled.

Flavorful Brown Rice *(Serves 2)*

Short-grain brown rice has a wonderful flavor, and at the table you can add a small amount of RealSalt or sea salt and butter to taste.

1 cup short-grain brown rice
1 cup chicken broth (or plain water)
1 cup bottled or filtered water

Rinse the rice in a strainer, then put in a 2-quart saucepan. Add the broth and water (or simply water if you're not using broth). Use very high heat and boil for 5 minutes, then turn the heat down to simmer. The rice should cook fully in about 40 minutes; you may have to adjust the heat above a simmer to accomplish this.

As a variation, consider frying some finely diced shallots, garlic, and onions in as little olive oil as possible, then mixing them into the rice before you start cooking it.

—ᘯ—

Quick Tip: Nice Rice

Tired of the same old rice? White rice is pretty bland (and nothing more than pure carbohydrate), but brown rice can get a little boring after a while. Lotus Foods (www.lotusfoods.com) markets a selection of rich-tasting rices from Asia that are unlike any other type of rice. The company's Bhutanese Red Rice is a tasty red rice, and Forbidden Rice is a flavorful purple-colored rice. Both types cook faster than brown rice and require less broth (or water), so be careful to follow label directions. Both rices, and others, are also available as flours.

—ᘯ—

Cauliflower and Broccoli *(Serves 2)*

> ½ head cauliflower
> ½ bunch broccoli
> ½ stick (⅛ pound) butter
> 2 to 3 tablespoons pine nuts, sliced almonds, or pecan or hazelnut
>   pieces

Cut the cauliflower and broccoli into florets about ½ to 1 inch in diameter. Steam in a pot for 10 minutes over high heat. While doing this, melt the butter in a pan, then add nuts of your choice. Transfer the cauliflower and broccoli to a bowl, then pour the butter/nut mixture over and toss. Serve immediately.

Pan Fried Veggies *(Serves 2)*

> ¼ cup olive oil
> 1 pat unsalted butter (optional)

1 or 2 small zucchini squashes
1 cup frozen corn kernels
1 large garlic clove, diced
1 scallion, diced
¼ teaspoon garlic powder
½ teaspoon dried oregano
½ teaspoon dried basil
¼ cup pine nuts
1 tablespoon golden raisins

Add olive oil and butter to a 10-inch frypan or wok. Cut the tops and bottoms off the zucchini, quarter them lengthwise, and dice so the pieces are roughly the size of dimes, but a little thicker. Put the zucchini in the pan along with the corn and diced garlic, scallion, garlic powder, oregano, and basil. With a spatula, mix around as you start heating (medium setting) the vegetables. Cover the pan (loosely with a piece of aluminum foil if you don't have a cover). Stir every couple of minutes. After about 5 minutes, add the pine nuts. Cook until the zucchini softens and the corn starts to turn brown and caramelize. After a few minutes more, add the raisins. It should be ready to eat in 10 to 15 minutes. This is an easy side dish and goes great with Wonderful Baked Chicken Breasts (page 84).

—⁂—

Quick Tip: The Secret of
Tomato-Free Ratatouille

Traditional ratatouille consists of sautéed vegetables, including tomatoes. The following recipe avoids tomatoes, a nightshade plant that can aggravate arthritic symptoms in some people. Instead, it uses tomatillos *(Physalis ixocarpa),* also known as Mexican green tomatoes. Tomatillos, which can be bought fresh or canned at supermarkets, are also members of the nightshade family, but they are more closely related to the Cape gooseberry than to tomatoes. If you are very sensitive to nightshades, substitute extra zucchini for the eggplant (another nightshade), and test whether you are sensitive to tomatillos. All of these vegetables cook down, so use a large, covered, nonstick, woklike pan. The amounts below can easily be doubled, allowing the ratatouille to be used as a vegetable side dish and with breakfasts as well. See the Omelette with Tomato-Free

Ratatouille Filling recipe (page 95). Please note: If you react to all nightshade plants, this is not a recipe you should try.

—◇—

Tomato-Free Ratatouille *(Serves 2–3)*

 ¼ to ½ cup olive oil
 2 small or 1 large eggplant, diced
 1 large bell pepper, or the equivalent from several colored
  varieties, diced
 2 zucchinis, each about 10 inches long, diced
 1 medium red or sweet onion, diced
 1 to 2 teaspoons thyme
 1 to 2 teaspoons basil
 1 bay leaf
 4 garlic cloves, finely diced
 3 to 4 ripe tomatillos (should have yellow-green lime color), diced
 RealSalt or sea salt, to taste

Pour about ¼ cup of olive oil into a pan. Turn the heat to medium. When the olive oil is warm, add the eggplant, stirring occasionally. The eggplant will soak up the olive oil, but keep the pan covered to retain moisture. Add the bell pepper, zucchinis, and onion. After a few minutes, add the thyme, basil, bay leaf, garlic, and tomatillos. Stir occasionally to keep the vegetables from burning, and keep covered when not stirring. Add a little more olive oil if necessary. Turn the heat down and allow to simmer for about 40 minutes or until all of the vegetables are very soft. Add RealSalt or sea salt. Dispose of the bay leaf before serving.

Green Bean and Mushroom Stir-Fry *(Serves 2)*

 pat of butter
 2 tablespoons olive oil
 2 handfuls fresh or frozen green beans, ideally French cut
 4 to 5 fresh mushrooms, sliced
 garlic powder, to taste
 ⅛ cup sliced almonds

Heat the butter and olive oil in a nonstick frypan or wok over medium heat. Add the green beans and cook until they start to get soft. Add the mushroom slices and garlic powder. When the green beans and mushrooms are almost cooked, add the sliced almonds.

Mushroom and Spinach Sauté *(Serves 1)*

> olive oil
> 6 to 10 small mushrooms, sliced
> 3 small scallions, diced
> 3 ounces (about ½ bag) fresh spinach
> garlic powder, to taste

Coat a nonstick frypan with olive oil, add the mushrooms and scallions, and sauté over medium heat. Meanwhile, pinch the stems from the spinach leaves (or leave on, if you prefer). When the mushrooms and scallions soften, add the spinach, then add the garlic powder. Stir to thoroughly mix the vegetables together. For variety, use a different type of mushroom, such as shiitake or chanterelle.

Tangy Butternut Squash *(Serves 2)*

> 1 to 2 butternut squashes
> ½ to 1 teaspoon plus additional as needed thyme (dried)
> 1 teaspoon plus additional as needed walnut, hazelnut, or
>   olive oil
> ½ teaspoon balsamic vinegar, plus additional as needed

Preheat oven to 350 degrees.

Cut off the tip of the squash stem, then cut the squash in half lengthwise. Remove the seeds with a spoon (a serrated grapefruit spoon works well). Lightly coat the inside of the squash with olive oil to minimize burning. Place the cut side down (skin side up) on a baking pan, and bake for approximately 1 hour. The squash is cooked when the skin is tender to the touch. (Use a fork or a spoon to touch, not your hand.) Take the squash from the oven, scrape the fruit with a spoon, and place the fruit in a bowl. Add about ½ teaspoon of thyme per squash, plus about 1 teaspoon of walnut or other oil and about ½ teaspoon of basalmic vinegar. Mix together with a fork, adding additional thyme, oil, or vinegar to suit your taste.

Lunch Meals

Wonderful Whatever Salad *(Serves 1)*

> any green leafy lettuce (not iceberg) or spinach
> cucumber
> scallion, diced
> tomato or bell peppers
> sliced almonds
> artichoke hearts (packed in water, not oil)
> hemp nut seed
> chicken or turkey diced, or pieces of poached salmon

No amounts are given because they are purely at your discretion. Prepare ingredients in desired amounts and toss. Avoid dressings with soybean oil or hydrogenated vegetable oil. Two recommended salad dressings are Stonewall Kitchen Roasted Garlic Vinaigrette (www.stonewallkitchen.com) and Zeus Greek Salad Dressing (www.zeusfoods.com).

Quick Chicken or Turkey Rice Soup *(Serves 2)*

This soup is a creative, tasty, and adaptable use of leftover chicken or turkey, regardless of how it was originally prepared.

> ⅛ to ¼ cup leftover meat juice
> 2 cups chicken broth
> 2 ounces turkey or chicken
> ½ cup cooked short-grain brown rice
> 1 diced scallion
> ⅓ cup diced mushrooms
> 1 egg, beaten
> garlic powder, to taste
> salt, to taste
> pepper, to taste

Pour meat juice and chicken broth in a saucepan and begin heating. Cut up the chicken or turkey into pieces about ¼ inch in size. Put into the broth along with the rice, scallions, and mushrooms. Stir occasionally and bring to a light boil. Add the egg, which will thicken the soup like an eggdrop soup, and stir occasionally. Cook until the egg starts to turn white. Serve, adding the garlic powder, salt, and pepper at the table.

Breakfasts

Breakfast Scramble *(Serves 1–2)*

> olive oil or butter
> 1 scallion, diced, per person
> spinach (either fresh with stems removed or defrosted)
> 2 tablespoons cooked brown rice
> 1 to 2 tablespoons leftover chicken or turkey, diced
> 2 eggs, beaten, per person

Heat a frypan with olive oil, and sauté the scallions over medium heat until they soften. Add the spinach, brown rice, and pieces of meat. When the spinach is wilted, pour in the eggs and mix thoroughly with a spatula. Serve when the eggs are cooked. Add fresh fruit as a side dish.

Omelette with Tomato-Free Ratatouille Filling *(Serves 1)*

> pat of butter or olive oil
> 2 to 3 eggs
> 2 tablespoons Tomato-Free Ratatouille (page 92)

Heat a pat of butter or a little olive oil in a frypan. Beat and pour the eggs into the pan and begin cooking as a plain omelette. Meanwhile, heat 2 tablespoons of Tomato-Free Ratatouille on a small plate in a microwave. After you flip the omelette, spoon the ratatouille on one side, then fold over the omelette. Serve with fresh fruit, such as berries or apple slices.

Breakfast Mini Chicken Patties *(Serves 2–3)*

    1 pound ground chicken (turkey alternative)
    4 cloves garlic, diced
    4 pitted olives, finely diced
    1 tablespoon oregano
    1 tablespoon basil

Preheat the oven to 350 degrees.

Put ground chicken in a mixing bowl. (Many natural foods grocers sell ground chicken, frozen, in 1-pound packages.) Add the garlic, olives, oregano, and basil. Mix thoroughly with your hands (wear disposable gloves) and form patties about ¼ inch thick and about the size of an old-fashioned silver dollar (1½ to 2 inches in diameter). One pound of ground chicken should yield about a dozen patties, though you can make them smaller. Place the patties in a baking dish and bake for 20 minutes. When done, soak up extra fat with paper towels.

Tip: Follow the same recipe to make chickenburgers comparable to the size of a hamburger. Use different types of pitted olives (such as green or Kalamata) to vary the flavor. You also can substitute ground turkey for ground chicken.

Breakfast Muesli *(Serves 1)*

This breakfast takes about 5 minutes to prepare the night before and is ready in about 2 minutes in the morning. Use a high-quality muesli, such as the Earth Song Grandpa's Secret Omega-3 Muesli (www. earthsongwholefoods.com). Mix ⅓ cup of muesli with about ½ cup of coconut milk, water, or milk (if you are not allergic to dairy) in a small bowl. Cover the bowl, and leave it in the refrigerator over-night. Meanwhile, defrost a total of 2 to 3 tablespoons of raspberries and blueberries overnight, or be sure to have some fresh fruit on hand for the morning, such as berries, an apple, or a banana. In the morning add the fruit (dice the apple or banana) and mix into the muesli. Add a little cinnamon or a very small amount of nutmeg for flavoring. Eat as a side dish with a few reheated Breakfast Mini Chicken Patties (above).

Baked Sweet Potatoes or Yams *(Serves 1–2)*

> 1 to 2 sweet potatoes or yams
> butter
> 1 tablespoon fresh chives or scallions, finely diced
> salt, to taste

Preheat the oven to 375 degrees.

Place the potatoes on aluminum foil and bake for 1 to 1½ hours, depending on their size. Cut in half and serve as you would a baked potato, with butter and chives, or scallions. Add salt.

Sample Week-Long Meal Plan

This meal plan is *not* intended as a rigid you-must-follow-or-else dietary plan. Rather, it is just what the name says—a sample of what you might choose to cook, reuse as creative leftovers, or order in a restaurant. The key is following, at every meal, the dietary principles discussed in chapter 6. An asterisk indicates that the recipe is included in this chapter.

Day 1

Breakfast   Breakfast Scramble,* fresh fruit, and a wheat-free waffle with almond butter.

Lunch   In a restaurant, order a grilled chicken breast, minus the bun, and a side of vegetables instead of fries. Sparkling water to drink.

Dinner   Baked Salmon,* Spinach and Leek Sauté,* and rice.

Day 2

Breakfast   Breakfast Mini Chicken Patties,* fresh fruit, and sliced gluten-free bread toasted with almond butter.

Lunch   Wonderful Whatever Salad,* with leftover pieces of salmon from last evening's dinner.

Dinner   Baked Turkey Breast Provençal,* Mushroom and Spinach Sauté,* and rice or baked squash.

Day 3

Breakfast   Leftover Breakfast Mini Chicken Patties,* and Breakfast Musili* with fruit.

| Lunch | Reheated turkey with au jus, Spinach and Leek Sauté,* and rice. |
| Dinner | Pumpkin Seed Crusted Halibut,* Green Bean and Mushroom Stir-Fry,* and Forbidden Rice spinach salad on the side. |

Day 4

Breakfast	Omelette with Tomato-Free Ratatouille Filling,* and fresh fruit.
Lunch	Quick Chicken or Turkey Rice Soup* and a side salad with butter lettuce.
Dinner	In a restaurant, order baked or broiled fish with vegetables and a small green salad.

Day 5

Breakfast	Omelette with baby shrimp and sautéed scallions and spinach.
Lunch	Salmon or halibut fish patty (see "Specialty Foods" in appendix B), mushroom and green bean sauté, rice, and a small green salad.
Dinner	Pan Fried Swordfish,* steamed cauliflower and broccoli, and rice.

Day 6

Breakfast	Breakfast Scramble* with diced turkey.
Lunch	Wonderful Whatever Salad* with leftover diced turkey.
Dinner	Wonderful Baked Chicken Breasts,* Green Bean and Mushroom Stir-Fry,* rice, and a small green salad.

Day 7

Breakfast	Breakfast Scramble* using diced chicken and small amounts of the Green Bean and Mushroom Stir-Fry,* and rice from last evening's dinner.
Lunch	Tuna salad with salad greens.
Dinner	Baked Shrimp and Scallops,* or your choice of rice or vegetable, stir-fried.

Beverages, Snacks, and Desserts

Often people stray from a diet when choosing beverages, snacks, and desserts. Here are some suggestions to keep things simple, and to keep you on the Anti-Inflammation Syndrome Diet Plan.

For cold beverages, stick with sparkling mineral or still waters and a wedge of lemon, lime, or orange. Many sparkling mineral waters, such as Gerolsteiner, have substantial calcium and magnesium levels—good for your health. For hot beverages, a herbal tea or a green tea is a good choice.

For snacks, it is best to stick with unsalted raw or roasted nuts. You can make your own blend of nuts and seeds that is probably superior to any commercial trail mix. Use almonds, pistachios, pumpkin seeds, macadamias, sunflower seeds, and organic raisins. You can also adapt a Moroccan appetizer by eating a couple of dates or figs with half a dozen raw almonds.

For desserts, one of the issues is not eating too much—a problem when you make or bake a dessert at home. It may be better to buy small amounts of "healthy" dessert items. Some possibilities include small amounts of Earthsong Cranberry-Orange and Apple-Walnut Whole Food Bars (www.earthsongwholefoods.com), Jennie's Coconut Macaroons (www.redmillfarms.com) bars, Nutiva Flax & Raisin bars (www.nutiva.com), and Hadley date rolls with almonds (www.hadley dates.com). Another possibility is a Van's apple-cinnamon toaster waffle, with almond butter or banana slices and powdered cinnamon.

PART III

The Anti-Inflammation Syndrome Supplement Plan

CHAPTER 8

Good Fats That Rev Up Your Body's Natural Anti-Inflammatories

—ⁿⁿⁿ—

QUIZ 3

What Nutritional Supplements Do You Take?

Taking individual supplements indicates that you care about preserving your health, and taking specific anti-inflammatory supplements suggests that you are already trying to prevent or reverse an inflammatory disorder.

Do not include any supplements found in multivitamins or any other type of once-a-day supplement. The questions refer only to stand-alone supplements.

Do you take any supplements identified as fish oil, salmon oil, omega-3, EPA, DHA, or GLA?

Add 2 points _____

Do you take vitamin E supplements?

Add 2 points _____

Do you take vitamin C supplements?

Add 1 point _____

Do you take glucosamine or chondroitin supplements?

Add 1 point _____

Do you take devil's claw, green tea, Pycnogenol, grape seed extract, or quercetin supplements?

Add 1 point _____

Do you take herbal supplements such as St. John's wort, ginseng, ginkgo, or any other?

Add 1 point _____

Your score on quiz 3: _____

Initial interpretation and ranking:

0 **Low.** You do not take any anti-inflammation supplements, either because you do not need them or because you are not aware of them.

1–3 **Moderate.** You take some anti-inflammation supplements, which offer some protection.

4–8 **High.** You take numerous anti-inflammation supplements, suggesting that you are trying to reverse a chronic inflammatory condition.

Please note your quiz 1 score: _____ and ranking _____

Please note your quiz 2 score: _____ and ranking _____

Please note your quiz 3 score: _____ and ranking _____

—⁓—

How to Interpret the Results of all Three Quizzes

High or very high on quiz 1 (page 14): You likely have considerable inflammation. The higher the score, the higher your level of inflammation.

High or very high on quiz 2 (page 61) *but not quiz 1:* You are at risk for developing inflammatory diseases in the coming years. This would be a good time to bolster your long-term health.

High or very high on both *quiz 1 and quiz 2:* You likely have a high level of inflammation. The reason is probably that you are eating too many pro-inflammatory foods. You would do well to go on the Anti-Inflammation Syndrome Diet Plan and take steps to improve your long-term health.

High or very high on quiz 1 but not quiz 2: You probably have adopted a very good diet, but may have to further fine-tune your diet and supplement program.

Factoring In Your Anti-Inflammatory Supplements

High on quiz 3: You are already taking some important supplements that can reduce your risk of inflammation.

High or very high on quizzes 1 and 3: You may need to take different supplements or increase their dosage.

High or very high on quizzes 2 and 3: You will have to work on improving your diet.

High or very high on quizzes 1, 2, and 3: You likely have a high level of inflammation, but you are only taking supplements instead of taking supplements *and* improving your diet. To improve your health, you must focus on *both* diet and supplements.

High or very high on quizzes 1 or 2 but low on quiz 3: You have been or are at high risk of chronic inflammation. You should take anti-inflammatory supplements.

Healthy oils play a pivotal role in controlling and reversing inflammation because they contain highly concentrated amounts of specific anti-inflammatory nutrients. Chief among these highly beneficial nutrients are omega-3 fatty acids found in fish oils; gamma-linolenic acid; and olive oil.

A wholesome diet, such as the one recommended in this book, provides ample quantities of these oils. However, you may want extra amounts of them to either jump-start your body's anti-inflammatory activities or to reverse health problems. You can buy omega-3 fatty acids, and gamma-linolenic acid in capsule form. Even though olive oil is a food product, not a supplement that comes in capsule form, this chapter discusses all three of these oils because they work together in the body to stem inflammation. Using generous amounts of olive oil in your cooking is a way to supplement your diet with extra amounts of it.

Anita: Fish Oil for Lower Blood Pressure

Anita was a widowed single mother who looked much older than her thirty-six years. The pressures of working and mothering three young children forced her to stop making home-cooked meals in favor of burgers, fries, pizzas, and quick-energy foods such as candy bars and soft drinks. At the end of each day she would collapse in bed, exhausted and drained.

Over two years Anita had gained thirty pounds and was now experiencing frequent headaches and suffering joint pain in her hips, shoulders, and hands. Her medical doctor prescribed ibuprofen, and a rheumatologist told her she had some (but not all) of the signs of lupus erythematosus. She was developing stomach pain from the ibuprofen, and medication for the lupuslike symptoms caused double vision. In addition, Anita's blood pressure had risen to 190/100 and her blood sugar was more than 240, clearly in the diabetic range. These clinical findings led to additional prescriptions for hypertensive and glucose-lowering medications.

A friend recommended that Anita consult with Judy A. Hutt, N.D., a naturopathic physician in Tucson, Arizona. After a workup Hutt asked Anita to eat a simple, wholesome diet similar to the Anti-Inflammation Syndrome Diet Plan. Anita began eating more fish, chicken, turkey, and vegetables, while avoiding processed foods, soft drinks, coffee, and dairy products. Hutt also asked her to take several anti-inflammatory supplements, including fish oil capsules (1,000 mg twice daily), as well as ginger, turmeric, and bromelain.

Anita's response was dramatic. After three weeks she had lost ten pounds and her glucose had normalized, enabling her to stop taking the glucose-lowering medications. Her pain, swelling, and stiffness decreased considerably, and her energy levels began increasing. At a six-week follow-up visit Anita had lost a total of eighteen pounds, and her blood pressure was normal, so she was able to stop taking the hypertensive medications. In addition, her joint pain was almost entirely gone, flaring up only when she went off her diet of simple, wholesome foods. Anita no longer had a need to take cortisone drugs for her lupuslike symptoms. Her headaches were gone, her energy levels were better, and she actually looked younger.

Omega-3 Fish Oils

As you read in chapter 3, the omega-3 family of fatty acids forms the building blocks of many of the body's natural anti-inflammatory compounds. Fish oil supplements, which are typically produced from salmon oil, are especially rich in eicosapentaenoic acid (EPA) and docosahexaenoic acid (DHA). Although both fatty acids are essential for health, EPA plays a more important role in the body's defenses against inflammation.

The advantage of taking fish oil or salmon oil capsules is simple: your body does not have to go through the many steps involved in converting alpha-linolenic acid (found in leafy green vegetables and flaxseed) to EPA and DHA. By taking capsules, you can leapfrog these steps and the potential bottlenecks that interfere with the conversion and help your body rapidly convert EPA to inflammation-suppressing eicosanoids.

Although you will read more about rheumatoid arthritis and osteoarthritis in later chapters, these two conditions serve as excellent examples of how fish oils can benefit your health. Numerous studies have documented that diets high in either fish or fish oils improve the balance of fatty acids in tissues, raising levels of anti-inflammatory and lowering amounts of pro-inflammatory substances.

More than two thousand studies on omega-3 fatty acids have been published in medical journals, adding up to a wealth of persuasive data, and many studies have found that supplements and omega-3 rich foods can significantly reduce levels of several inflammation-promoting compounds in people: thromboxane B_2, prostaglandin E_2, interleukin-1, and C-reactive protein. In a very real sense, fish oils snuff out many of the matches of inflammation.

This anti-inflammatory effect of fish oils has been demonstrated over and over again. For example, in a Scottish study, researchers asked sixty-four men and women with rheumatoid arthritis to take daily fish oil capsules, containing a little more than 1.7 grams of EPA and 1 gram of DHA or a placebo (dummy pill) daily. After three months many of the patients taking the fish oil capsules benefited from reduced pain and were able to lower their intake of nonsteroidal anti-inflammatory drugs (NSAIDs). By the end of the year-long study, 40 percent of the patients taking fish oil capsules had been able to lower or eliminate their NSAIDs, reducing their risk of drug-related side effects.

Fish oils actually help rebuild articular cartilage. Bruce Caterson, Ph.D., of Cardiff University, Wales, led a team of molecular biologists who discovered specifically why fish oils reduce inflammation and inhibit the breakdown of cartilage, one of the characteristics of osteoarthritis. Caterson first determined that chondrocytes, one of the key types of cells forming cartilage, readily absorbed alpha-linolenic acid (the parent omega-3 fatty acid) and displaced other fatty acids in the process. The same thing happened when he grew chondrocytes with EPA and DHA. But significantly, all of the omega-3 fatty acids deactivated "aggrecanases," a family of enzymes known to break down cartilage. The omega-3 fatty acids also stopped the genetic programming that increased levels of pro-inflammatory compounds, including interleukin-1 (IL-1), tumor necrosis factor alpha (TNFa), and cyclooxygenase-2 (Cox-2).

—\\\—

Benefits of Omega-3 Fish Oils

- Reduce inflammation
- Natural, mild blood thinner
- Help maintain heart rhythm
- Reduce blood pressure
- Lower triglycerides
- Slow proliferation of cancer cells
- Improve mood disorders

—\\\—

Fish Oils Protect the Heart

Early Arctic explorers made note of the rarity of coronary artery disease in Eskimos, despite their consumption of a high-fat and high-cholesterol diet. It wasn't until 1973 that two Danish researchers compared the diets of Arctic Eskimos to that of Greenland Eskimos, who ate diets similar to other Danes. The Greenland Eskimos, who consumed more saturated fat and cholesterol from meat and dairy products, had a higher rate of heart disease.

Since then, many other studies have confirmed the heart-protective effect of omega-3 fatty acids, especially EPA. For example, a twenty-five-year study of dietary and health data of almost thirteen thousand men in seven countries found that elevated blood cholesterol levels were associated with heart disease only in areas where intake of omega-3 and omega-9 fatty acids were low. A separate study of four hundred people, conducted by Michel de Lorgeril, M.D., of Saint-Étienne, France, found that adoption of a Mediterranean-style diet can greatly lower the likelihood of a second heart attack. Lorgeril and his colleagues asked patients to follow a Mediterranean-style diet, high in fish, vegetables, and olive oil, or to continue eating their usual diet. People eating the Mediterranean-style diet were 50 to 70 percent less likely to have a second heart attack during the four-year study. They also had less than half the risk of developing cancer or dying from any natural cause.

In 2001 Canadian researchers reported that Eskimos who adhere to their traditional diet experience relatively little heart disease. The Nunavik Inuit of Québec eat a diet that includes both a traditional diet, consisting of fish and marine mammals, along with some Western refined foods. They maintain high blood levels of EPA and DHA—and have half the incidence of death from heart disease compared with other residents of Québec.

Fish oils have at least two other cardiovascular benefits: they are mild and natural blood thinners, and they help maintain a normal heart rhythm. Arrhythmias are erratic heartbeats that can go out of control, leading to ventricular tachycardia and cardiac arrest. Experiments by Alexander Leaf, M.D., of Harvard Medical School, found that supplemental EPA and DHA could prevent arrhythmias and ventricular fibrillations. A separate study of more than eight hundred people conducted by David S. Siscovick, M.D., of the University of Washington, found that one fish meal weekly reduced the risk of cardiac arrest by half, compared with people who ate no fish at all. Five ounces of salmon contain about 7.5 grams of omega-3 fatty acids.

Fish Oils May Reduce Cancer Risk

The health benefits of fish oils extend to general protection against cancer. Bruce N. Ames, Ph.D., an eminent cell biologist at the University of California, Berkeley, has pointed out that 30 percent of cancers result from chronic inflammation and chronic infections (and infections cause inflammation).

In fact, large amounts of omega-6 fatty acids, in the form of linoleic acid-rich corn and safflower oils, promote the proliferation of breast and prostate cancers. In contrast, fish oils clearly prevent and slow the growth of cancers. Corn oil has an omega-6 to omega-3 ratio of 60:1, and safflower oil a ratio of 77:1—far from the evolutionary balance of 1:1.

Human studies are consistent with animal studies showing that omega-3 fish oils protect against cancer. Paul Terry, Ph.D., and his colleagues at the Karolinska Institute in Stockholm, tracked the health of more than six thousand male twins who were, on average, in their mid-fifties when the study began. Terry found that men who regularly ate fish had one-half to one-third the risk of prostate cancer, compared with those who ate no fish.

Other Anti-Inflammatory Benefits of Fish Oils

Evidence of the broader anti-inflammatory effects of fish and fish oil supplements comes from other types of medical research, such as on asthma and Crohn's disease, a type of inflammatory bowel disease. For example, an Australian study found that children with asthma were half as likely to consume fish rich in omega-3 fatty acids. As little as one fish meal per week was enough to reduce the likelihood of asthma.

In a separate study, described in the *New England Journal of Medicine,* researchers gave either fish oil supplements or placebos to seventy-eight patients with Crohn's disease. The fish oil capsules provided about 600 mg of EPA and 300 mg of DHA daily. After one year 59 percent of the patients taking fish oil capsules were still in remission, more than twice that of the placebo group.

How to Buy and Use Fish Oil Supplements

There are so many omega-3 fish oil supplements on the market that it is often confusing to choose a brand. If you can, opt for a brand from fish caught in relatively pollution-free waters. Doing so will lower your likelihood of consuming extra mercury or other toxins. Some companies identify the source of their fish oils, such as Norwegian salmon.

Most fish oil supplements contain roughly three-fifths EPA and two-fifths DHA. If you want a high-EPA supplement use Omega-Brite, which contains 90 percent EPA and 10 percent DHA. To enhance the anti-inflammatory effects of omega-3 fish oils take gamma-linolenic acid supplements. (See the following section.) DHA supplements made from algae may not have the anti-inflammatory effect of EPA, but they may provide other health benefits, such as improving memory.

Flaxseed is a rich nonanimal source of alpha-linolenic acid, and flaxseed oil capsules are sometimes recommended as a source of omega-3 fatty acids. While flaxseed is indeed an excellent source of alpha-linolenic acid, many people have difficulty converting it to EPA and DHA, which would limit its usefulness as a supplement.

Dosage: For prevention of inflammatory disorders, take 1 gram of omega-3 fish oil capsules daily. If you have a form of arthritis, take at least 3 grams daily of omega-3 fish oils. If you never eat fish, you may want to take at least 5 grams of fish oils daily. In addition, take 400 IU of natural vitamin E daily, which will protect the fish oils from free-radical damage.

Side effects: Fish oil supplements have been shown to lower blood levels of triglyceride, a fat associated with an increased risk of coronary artery disease, but sometimes to raise cholesterol levels slightly. In addition, the blood-thinning effect of fish oils may be magnified if you take several other blood thinners, including vitamin E, ginkgo, or Coumadin.

Ask your physician to monitor you, especially if you are taking Coumadin, a prescription anticoagulant drug.

Nelda: Fish Oil to Relieve Pain

Back in 1980, at age sixty-three, Nelda was displaying all the signs of rheumatoid arthritis. Her fingers, which hurt all the time, were becoming red and deformed. She was taking prescription pain relievers six to eight times daily, and her family physician was suggesting that it might be better to replace her right knee and left hip joints. Nelda was also taking nitroglycerin for her heart and a blood pressure-lowering medication.

She figured there had to be an alternative, so she visited Hugh D. Riordan, M.D., president of the Center for the Improvement of Human Functioning International in Wichita, Kansas. Laboratory tests showed Nelda sensitive to some of her favorite foods, specifically dairy products and white potatoes, which she immediately stopped eating. She also began taking a number of anti-inflammatory supplements, including fish oils and antioxidant vitamins.

In less than a year Nelda was virtually pain-free and had regained flexibility in her fingers. She stood straight and no longer needed a cane or a walker. For the next twenty years Nelda remained active, healthier in her seventies and eighties than in her sixties.

Gamma-Linolenic Acid

Gamma-linolenic acid, or GLA, is part of the omega-6 family, but it behaves more like an anti-inflammatory omega-3 fatty acid. GLA is found in seeds, and nearly all supplemental forms are derived from borage, evening primrose, or black currant seeds. It constitutes about 20 percent of borage seed oil, 15 to 19 percent of black currant seed oil, and 9 percent of evening primrose seed oil. If you have been consuming vegetable oils such as corn, safflower, or soy, do not assume that your body has been converting its linoleic acid to GLA. Foods high in these oils are often high in trans fatty acids, which interfere with the conversion process.

As with fish oil EPA and DHA supplements, GLA supplements leapfrog several steps and quickly raise blood levels of GLA. GLA boosts production of DGLA, the immediate precursor of prostaglandin E_1, which suppresses inflammation.

Several human trials have found GLA supplements to greatly benefit patients with rheumatoid arthritis; they also seem to help restore more normal immune responses. In one investigation, Robert Zurier, M.D., of the University of Massachusetts at Worcester, treated thirty-seven patients with rheumatoid arthritis and inflamed joints. He gave them either 1.4 grams of GLA or placebos daily. After twenty-four weeks both physicians and patients noted significant reductions in symptoms. The number of tender joints among patients taking GLA was reduced by 36 percent, and the overall score on tests measuring tender joints declined by 45 percent. In addition, the number of swollen joints decreased by 28 percent, and the patients' overall score for swollen joints fell by 41 percent. Some people benefited far more than did others, but that is frequently the case with nutritional supplements. It is likely that better responses would have occurred with a broader supplement regimen, but the study was designed to test GLA only.

In another study Zurier doubled the dosage of GLA, giving fifty-six patients either 2.8 grams daily of the supplement or placebos for six months. This higher dosage resulted in significant improvements—at least a 25 percent improvement in four of eight measures of rheumatoid arthritis severity. For a second six-month period, Zurier gave GLA to all of the patients, and improvements were noted across the board. The group originally given GLA continued to improve over the course of a year, with more than three-fourths of the patients benefiting from improvements in their arthritis symptoms.

How to Buy and Use GLA Supplements

Virtually all supplemental GLA is derived from evening primrose, borage, or black currant seed oils. Many of the GLA supplements sold are actually labeled as "evening primrose," "borage seed oil," or "black currant seed oil," with the actual quantity of GLA listed in fine print on the back of the label. As you might expect, each type of oil has its proponent, often because of financial interests.

Although the concentration of GLA is highest in borage seed oil and lowest in evening primrose oil, it is more important to identify the specific quantity of GLA per capsule (or per several capsules). All of this information is on the label. Once you have identified the quantity of GLA per daily serving, calculate its cost and compare it in similar fashion to other GLA supplements.

Dosage: The dosage of GLA used in arthritis studies ranges from 1.4 to 2.8 grams daily—again, this is the dosage of GLA, not the total weight of oil in the capsules. As always, read supplement labels carefully. For example, a product may contain 1,000 mg of black current seed oil but only 150 mg of GLA per two capsules. Depending on the brand, 2.8 grams of GLA might translate to more than twenty capsules daily! You can likely benefit from lower dosages of GLA if you take them with other supplements, such as fish oils and vitamin E.

Side effects: Rare.

Victor: Olympic Nutrition

Søren Mavrogenis, the physiotherapist for the Danish Olympic team, began recommending a combination of omega-3 fatty acids, gamma-linolenic acid, and antioxidants in 1996. At the time he had been treating the inflamed knee of a female rower but had not been able to help her. Because of the side effects of nonsteroidal anti-inflammatory drugs (NSAIDs), Mavrogenis was reluctant to recommend them for long-term use.

Mavrogenis's conversations with health writer Bjørn Falck Madsen and a researcher at a Scandinavian vitamin company led to a specific supplement regimen. The rower started taking the supplements and was able to resume rowing within a few weeks. One success led to another, and today Mavrogenis routinely uses a combination of omega-3 fatty acids, gamma-linolenic acid, and antioxidants (brand name Bio-Sport), along with deep muscle massage, to treat chronic overuse and inflammatory disorders. About one-third of his clinic's patients are elite athletes.

One of Mavrogenis's patients has been Victor A. Feddersen, a world champion rower and Olympic gold medalist in 1996. During training and competition, Feddersen suffered inflammatory injuries to his elbows. In the past he had to take a break from training and use NSAIDs. But for the past several years Feddersen has taken fatty acid and antioxidant supplements while also undergoing Mavrogenis's deep-muscle massage. It has made a big difference. He responds quickly to the supplements and has been able to continue training while recuperating.

Other Danish Olympic athletes have benefited similarly with a variety of inflammatory injuries, including those of the shoulders, arms, legs, and Achilles' heal. In general, inflammation subsides about a month after starting the supplements, but some people have responded within a week, while others take several months.

Olive Oil

Think of olive oil as one of the tastiest "supplements" you can eat. A common constituent of Greek and Italian diets, olive oil is rich in oleic acid, an omega-9 fatty acid. Many of the heart-healthy benefits of the traditional Mediterranean diet have been attributed to its abundant use of olive oil. Although other aspects of the diet (e.g., fruits, vegetables, and fish) are healthful, scientific studies have found olive oil to possess impressive anti-inflammatory properties in its own right.

Diets high in olive oil appear to reduce the likelihood of developing rheumatoid arthritis. Christos S. Mantzoros, M.D., D.Sc., of Harvard Medical School, and researchers from the Athens Medical School, found that consumption of olive oil was associated with a 61 percent lower risk of having rheumatoid arthritis. In another study, Parveen Yaqoob, Ph.D., a researcher at the University of Southampton, England, asked healthy middle-age men to eat either a conventional diet or one high in olive oil for two months. The men eating extra olive oil had a specific type of "adhesion molecule" that was 20 percent less active. This adhesion molecule, known as ICAM-1, sustains inflammatory and allergic reactions. By reducing the activity of adhesion molecules, olive oil tempers inflammatory reactions.

How to Buy and Use Olive Oil

As was discussed in chapter 6, the best varieties of olive oil are "extra virgin," because they are produced during the first mechanical pressing of olives. Pure or classic olive oil also is made from the first pressing, but it is slightly more acidic and can tolerate higher cooking temperatures. Light olive oil has been filtered to reduce its natural fragrance; it has no fewer calories than the other forms.

You should use olive oil exclusively or nearly exclusively as your cooking oil. Grapeseed oil also is rich in omega-9 fatty acids, but it is often produced through chemical extraction. Some mechanically pressed grapeseed oil is available, but you have to search for it in stores. While grapeseed oil is tolerant of very high temperatures, olive oil is still the preferred oil at home and in restaurants.

Other major food sources of omega-9 fatty acids are avocados and macadamia nuts. Both foods have been shown to reduce blood cholesterol levels, though their health benefits may be partly related to other nutrients.

Dosage: While there is no specific recommended amount, use extra-virgin olive oil liberally when cooking at home.

Side effects: Rare.

In this chapter you have read how "good" fats can help restore a normal inflammatory response and, in doing so, reduce symptoms of rheumatoid arthritis, osteoarthritis, and other inflammatory disorders. These fats also can lower blood pressure and lower your risk of heart disease and cancer. In the following chapter you will learn how vitamin E is now being recognized as the leading anti-inflammatory vitamin.

CHAPTER 9

Vitamin E to Extinguish the Flames of Inflammation

Long known to reduce the risk of coronary artery (heart) disease, vitamin E has recently been shown, in scientific studies with people, to possess significant anti-inflammatory properties. More than any other single nutrient, vitamin E can significantly reduce a variety of key indicators and promoters of inflammation.

For example, vitamin E lowers levels of C-reactive protein and interleukin-6 and reduces the activity of various types of "adhesion molecules" that promote inflammation throughout the body. In fact, vitamin E may be the single most important nutrient for lowering CRP levels. It should therefore not come as a surprise that, in addition to reducing the risk of heart disease, vitamin E is beneficial in Alzheimer's disease, arthritis, allergies, cancer, and many other inflammatory diseases. This chapter will focus on its emerging role as the premier anti-inflammatory vitamin.

Dr. Kunin and Susan: Antioxidants for Health

Years ago, Richard Kunin, M.D., of San Francisco, California, described himself as a "nasal neurotic." He had asthma, was allergic to dogs and cats, and sneezed literally a hundred times a day. He became interested in nutritional medicine, cured himself of all of his nasal and respiratory problems, and has gone on to become one of the most original and eclectic thinkers in "orthomolecular medicine," which focuses on using nutrition to achieve optimal health.

One patient, Susan, had high blood pressure much of her adult life but opted not to treat it medically. By her late sixties she had undergone a triple coronary-artery bypass. She consulted Dr. Kunin after repeated attacks of angina (heart pain), arrhythmias after exercising, muscle aches, postoperative memory loss, bronchitis, and coughing. Memory loss is common after bypass surgery, and Susan had difficulty recalling her recent medical history.

Based on Susan's medical history and laboratory tests, Kunin diagnosed her high prothrombin (blood clotting) activity and that it was likely the result of a genetic propensity toward excessive blood clotting. He also felt that Susan's muscle aches were the result of the statin drug interfering with her body's production of coenzyme Q_{10}, a vitaminlike substance needed for energy production in muscle cells.

Susan also had an acute sense of smell, which Kunin recognized as a likely sign of chemical sensitivity. The most likely culprit was Susan's forced-air gas furnace. Such furnaces, as well as gas stoves, release burned hydrocarbons into the air, and sensitive people react to these compounds. Kunin recommended that she replace the filter and update her heating system.

Kunin then developed an antioxidant and anticoagulant regimen for Susan to follow, based in part on the fact that vitamin antioxidants also have blood-thinning properties. Use of bromelain supplements served as a natural way to reduce blood viscosity (caused by excessive fibrin), as did use of small oral amounts of heparin, an anticoagulant drug. Heparin, Kunin explained, has anticoagulant effects when taken orally (not just by injection) but does not interfere with vitamin K metabolism the way Coumadin does.

Because Susan had large numbers of "activated" blood platelet cells, Kunin also recommended that she take supplements of the herb Ginkgo biloba, which inhibits platelet activity. Among the other supplements were B vitamins, vitamin C, vitamin E, alpha-lipoic acid, and the amino acid arginine.

Susan's health has improved considerably. Her blood pressure has been reduced, and she no longer has arrhythmias or muscle aches.

Vitamin E and Heart Disease

The role of vitamin E in preventing and reversing cardiovascular diseases was first reported by Canadian physicians Evan V. Shute, M.D., Wilfrid Shute, M.D., and their colleagues in the 1940s. At that time no one understood the role of inflammation in cardiovascular diseases, and C-reactive protein had not yet been discovered. Indeed, until the 1990s, the medical establishment was generally skeptical that a single vitamin could play a pivotal role in reversing heart disease.

Today, with a clearer picture of the role of inflammation in heart disease and good documentation for the anti-inflammatory and heart-protective role of vitamin E, the early successes of the Shute brothers are better understood. Certainly, vitamin E has important health roles beyond that of just a mild and safe anti-inflammatory nutrient. It is the body's principal fat-soluble antioxidant and, as such, blocks free-radical oxidation to cholesterol, which stimulates inflammation and is one of the initiators of heart disease. As an anticoagulant, vitamin E helps prevent abnormal blood clots. It also inhibits the proliferation of "smooth muscle" cells in coronary arteries, which contributes to the narrowing of blood vessels.

The striking benefits of vitamin E in preventing and reversing heart disease have been confirmed by several recent human trials. The most impressive study, conducted in England and published in the highly respected journal *Lancet,* involved two thousand patients with heart disease. About half were given either 400 or 800 IU of natural vitamin E, while the others received placebos. After an average of eighteen months the group taking vitamin E had only one-fourth the number of nonfatal heart attacks as did the placebo group. Although the vitamin E group experienced slightly more fatal heart attacks, a subsequent analysis of the data found that almost all of these deaths were among people who failed to take their vitamin E supplements.

It is rare, however, for biomedical studies to be 100 percent consistent in their results, and this is true with vitamin E studies. For example, one recent study found no benefits from taking the vitamin, which has made many physicians reconsider their use of vitamin E. Yet in a recent analysis of the five largest studies of vitamin E and heart disease, Ishwarlal "Kenny" Jialal, M.D., a cardiologist and antioxidant researcher at the University of Texas Southwestern Medical Center, Dallas, noted that four of the largest human trials supported the use of vitamin E and the fifth had troubling design problems.

Roberta: Natural Anti-Inflammatories for Crohn's Disease

Shari Lieberman, Ph.D., who has been a clinical nutritionist for more than twenty years, explains it this way: if you were a child and told your mother that your stomach hurt, she would ask what you had eaten. Lieberman can't understand why many physicians don't do the same when it comes to gastrointestinal disorders such as Crohn's disease.

In 1986 Roberta consulted with Lieberman about a diagnosis of Crohn's disease. She was fourteen years old and previously had seen several gastrointestinal specialists. By this time Roberta was taking two prescription anti-inflammatory drugs, prednisone and sulfasalazine, but was still experiencing vomiting and diarrhea and had lost weight. Her physician had recently suggested surgery to remove the lower portion of her ileum, part of the small intestine.

After an evaluation, Lieberman suspected that gluten intolerance was at the core of Roberta's problems and that dairy was likely a contributing factor. In gluten-sensitive people this protein triggers an autoimmune reaction that often leads to wide-ranging food sensitivities. Roberta was also under considerable stress related to family issues, and Lieberman made a referral to help Roberta cope with these problems.

In terms of diet, Lieberman recommended that Roberta avoid all food containing gluten—chiefly wheat, rye, and barley—as well as dairy. She also suggested a number of supplements. Among them were betonite clay and psyllium supplements, both of which add bulk without being a laxative. This nonlaxative effect was important to avoid further diarrhea. Lieberman also suggested fish oils for their anti-inflammatory properties and a number of antioxidants, including 1,000 mg of vitamin C and 1,200 of natural vitamin E, plus a high-potency multivitamin/multimineral supplement.

Within two weeks Roberta's diarrhea ceased and blood stopped appearing in her stools. After six months her physician saw no further need for the prescription drugs. The only times symptoms of Crohn's disease have reappeared were when Roberta has been under extreme psychological stress. She has been in remission for more than fifteen years.

How Vitamin E Reduces Inflammation

The details of how coronary artery disease begins are complex, and sometimes, like the chicken-and-egg story, it is difficult to discern exactly what step comes before another. It is likely that many events are occurring simultaneously, including inflammation of the arteries.

During the 1990s it became clear that high levels of the low-density lipoprotein (LDL) form of cholesterol increased the risk of heart disease. Basically, the idea is that LDL appears to be neutral until it is oxidized, or damaged by free radicals.

It has become fashionable to describe LDL as the "bad" form of cholesterol, but this is a misnomer because it is not inherently unhealthy. LDL is necessary for transporting vitamin E and other fat-soluble nutrients through the blood. In other words, these antioxidants should normally be present in LDL and prevent its oxidation. LDL oxidation occurs when dietary vitamin E and other antioxidants are insufficient, or when there is a large amount of cholesterol relative to vitamin E.

Free radicals stimulate and amplify inflammatory reactions through a number of mechanisms. For example, free radicals activate some of the genes involved in inflammation. They also turn on a variety of adhesion molecules, which, as the term suggests, encourage white blood cells to stick to normal cells, such as the endothelial cells that line blood vessel walls.

Vitamin E blocks the inflammatory process in a variety of ways:

- As an antioxidant, it quenches free radicals, thus reducing their ability to stimulate abnormal inflammatory responses.
- Vitamin E inhibits at least two transcription factors, preventing the activation of some of the genes involved in inflammation.
- It turns off a variety of adhesion molecules, helping to keep inflammatory reactions from going out of control.
- The vitamin blocks one of the omega-6 pathways (5-lipoxygenase) involved in making inflammation-causing substances.
- Vitamin E prevents the oxidation of LDL cholesterol, thus discouraging white blood cells from migrating toward the arteries.
- It is a mild cyclooxygenase-2 (Cox-2) inhibitor. By quenching peroxynitrite, a type of free radical, vitamin E reduces levels of pro-inflammatory prostaglandin E_2, which subsequently lowers Cox-2 activity.
- Vitamin E supplements can lower CRP levels in many people by 30 to 50 percent.

This remarkable CRP-lowering effect has so far been demonstrated in two well-designed human trials. In one, Jane E. Upritchard, Ph.D., and her colleagues at the University of Otago, New Zealand, tested the effects of three antioxidants on fifty-seven people with adult-onset diabetes. The supplements included 800 IU of natural vitamin E, 500 mg of vitamin C, and tomato juice (rich in lycopene) daily for four weeks. Upritchard reported in *Diabetes Care* that the vitamin E supplements, but not other antioxidants, lowered CRP levels by half!

In the other study Ishwarlal Jialal, M.D., asked seventy-two subjects, including some healthy and others with diabetes or heart disease, to take 1,200 IU of natural vitamin E daily for three months. Each of the three groups had decreases in CRP by an average of 30 percent and IL-6 by 50 percent.

—*m*—

C-Reactive Protein: The Current Standard for Measuring Inflammation

C-reactive protein (CRP), found in trace amounts in healthy people, has quickly emerged as the leading marker of systemic (or bodywide) inflammation. It is easy and inexpensive to test for, and you should ask your physician to measure your levels. You'll be hearing more and more about it: people with elevated CRP levels are 4½ times more likely to have a heart attack, compared with people who have normal levels of the protein. Furthermore, a variety of serious diseases are associated with high blood levels of CRP.

The good news is that natural vitamin E supplements can lower CRP levels by 30 to 50 percent.

Normal high-sensitivity levels are less than 0.11 milligram per deciliter of blood (mg/dL). Moderate CRP levels, of 0.12 to 0.19 mg/dL, are a cause for concern, and high CRP levels are 0.20 to 1.50 mg/dL. However, CRP levels can go up to 400 to 500 mg/dL in seriously ill people.

CRP levels are elevated in many different diseases and conditions.

Heart disease. High CRP levels are a better indicator than total cholesterol, LDL cholesterol, or homocysteine in predicting the risk of a heart attack, as well as of death in the first month after coronary artery bypass surgery. CRP is present in lesions (commonly but incorrectly referred to as cholesterol deposits) that form on blood vessel walls but not on normal blood vessel walls. CRP also is strongly associated with the rupture of these lesions, which can lead to dangerous blood vessel clots.

Blood sugar disorders. Insulin resistance, Syndrome X, and diabetes are all associated with increased levels of CRP. This is significant because each of these conditions increases the risk of coronary artery disease.

Dental disease. People with periodontal disease also have elevated CRP levels. This elevation may be the result of chronic infection or inflammation of the gums. It may also reflect inadequate levels of antioxidants, which would promote healing.

Smoking. Tobacco smoke raises CRP levels, and some researchers have found that they remain elevated in ex-smokers.

Overweight and obesity. Being overweight increases CRP levels. The reason is that adipose cells, particularly those that form around the abdomen (belly), produce large amounts of IL-6 and CRP. The implications are significant: being fat is partly an inflammatory disorder, and body fat promotes inflammation. This may be part of the reason why being overweight increases the risk of diabetes, heart disease, and other disorders. CRP levels are generally elevated in overweight children as well as adults.

Alzheimer's disease. High CRP levels also have been identified in patients with Alzheimer's disease, which researchers increasingly view as an inflammatory brain disorder.

Cancer. Many cancer patients have elevated CRP levels, which reflect an undercurrent of inflammation. This systemic inflammation may contribute to the breakdown of tissues and increase the risk of the cancer spreading.

Arthritis. People with "traditional" inflammatory diseases, such as arthritis and asthma, commonly have elevated levels of CRP or other markers of abnormally high inflammation.

—〜—

Vitamin E and Rheumatoid Arthritis

Consistent with the anti-inflammatory properties of vitamin E are clinical studies showing that it can reduce inflammation and pain in patients with rheumatoid arthritis. The first study, published in *Annals of the Rheumatic Diseases* in 1997, described how a team of British and German researchers treated forty-two patients with either about 1,800 IU (900 IU twice daily) of vitamin E or placebos daily for twelve weeks. The subjects kept a daily diary describing their early-morning stiffness, evening pain, and pain after routine daily activities.

On average, arthritis pain decreased by about half among patients taking vitamin E supplements. Furthermore, more patients taking vitamin E improved compared with those taking placebos—60 percent versus 32 percent. The researchers suggested that vitamin E might work, in part, by quenching nitric oxide, a free radical involved in the sensation of pain.

A second study, published in the German medical journal *Arzneimittel Forschung/Drug Research* in 2001, tested three treatments on a group of thirty patients with rheumatoid arthritis: one entailed pharmaceutical treatment, another was pharmaceutical treatment plus a modest antioxidant supplement, and the other was pharmaceutical treatment plus 600 IU of vitamin E three times daily. Significantly, patients taking the antioxidants or the vitamin E noted tangible improvements during the first month of treatment. Those taking only the drug treatment did not report any benefits until the end of the second month. Patients taking the antioxidants or vitamin E had higher levels of glutathione peroxidase, a powerful antioxidant made by the body, and lower levels of free radicals.

—✺—

Talking Nutrition with Your Physician

If you are like many people, you have been frustrated when trying to discuss diet or supplements with your physician. All too often, doctors quickly and arrogantly dismiss their patients' questions on these subjects.

Why? Nobel laureate and vitamin advocate Linus Pauling, Ph.D., explained it this way: "If a doctor isn't 'up' on something, he's 'down' on it." That is *really* the case.

The truth is that most physicians don't know much about nutrition because medical schools have given the subject a very low priority. Medicine, as the name suggests, places greatest emphasis on pharmaceutical medicines and surgery. It's hard for many people, including physicians, to admit that they don't know much about a particular subject.

Physicians also can be as gullible as the rest of us, swayed by the limitations of their own training, pharmaceutical company advertising, and misleading articles that question the value of diet and vitamin supplements.

Nutritionally oriented physicians have suggested that the best way to talk about nutritional therapies with a skeptical doc is to be firm but nonconfrontational. Physicians don't have a lot of time to keep up with their specialty, let alone delve into another one, such as nutrition. They may also have financial and therapeutic constraints imposed by a health maintenance organization (HMO), insurer, or even the other doctors in his office.

One approach might be to say something like: "Doctor, using vitamins and fatty acids to treat my inflammation appeals to me because they are safe and the evidence seems pretty solid. I would prefer not to treat myself so, as your patient, I would like you to take some time to seriously study some of the research in this area. I'll even loan you this book, which contains medical references at the back. Please do me a favor and take the time to look into this and work with me."

If that fails, you might have to change physicians to find one who is nutritionally oriented. This is easier than it used to be, and the names of several organizations making referrals to nutritionally oriented physicians are listed in appendix B. Most nutritionally oriented physicians are not part of HMOs, and insurers may reimburse for only some of their services. In other words, they work in a traditional fee-for-service arrangement, so you will have to pay by cash, check, or credit card. This may be more expensive, but it will likely lead to a nutritional program, a doctor who takes a little more time with you, and better care.

—⟶⟵—

Vitamin E and Nasal Allergies

Two studies have pointed to benefits from vitamin E in nasal and respiratory allergies. Andrew Fogarty, M.D., of the University of Nottingham, England, analyzed dietary data and blood levels of immunoglobulin E (IgE) from about twenty-five hundred people. IgE is an antibody produced in excessive amounts by people with asthma, rhinitis, and hay fever. Fogarty reported in *Lancet* that higher vitamin E intake was associated with lower levels of IgE. Each 1-mg increase in vitamin E intake, up to 7 mg (about 11 IU), was related to a 5.2 percent reduction in IgE levels.

This finding is consistent with animal research showing that vitamin E can lower IgE levels and, consequently, may lessen the symptoms of some allergies. One of those studies, using laboratory mice, found that supplemental vitamin E lowered blood levels of IgE as well as cytokines.

Based on all of these studies, you might think that vitamin E can suppress immunity and increase the risk of infections. However, the opposite appears to be true, suggesting that vitamin E plays a role in regulating normal immune responses. Simin Nikbin Meydani, D.V.M., Ph.D., of Tufts University, gave seventy-eight healthy seniors various amounts of vitamin E or placebos for eight months. She found that people taking 200 IU of vitamin E daily improved their immune response, measured by a viral or bacterial challenge in the skin, by an average of 65 percent. Levels of prostaglandin E_2 decreased, hinting that high levels of this pro-inflammatory substance interfere with the normal immune response to infection. Although the study was not intended to measure whether vitamin E reduced the number of infections, Meydani did find that patients taking vitamin E reported having 30 percent fewer colds than did the placebo group.

Vitamin E and Alzheimer's Disease

Research has shown that long-term use of anti-inflammatory medications such as nonsteroidal anti-inflammatory drugs (NSAIDs) can lower the risk of Alzheimer's disease and help maintain cognitive function in patients with the disease. However, NSAIDs pose serious side effects and do not address the root of the problem.

Hazardous free radicals, which go out of control when people fail to consume enough antioxidants, were implicated in the aging process back in 1954. Their role in damaging genes and cells is now generally accepted in medicine, and many Alzheimer's disease researchers believe that free radicals play a major role in the cognitive decline and behavioral changes characteristic of this disease.

For example, amyloid beta protein, which strangles brain cells in Alzheimer's disease, releases large numbers of free radicals that injure brain cells, according to research by Ashley I. Bush, M.D., Ph.D., a neurology researcher at Harvard Medical School. In an experiment with brain cells from rats, Allan Butterfield, Ph.D., a professor of chemistry at the University of Kentucky, Lexington, found that vitamin E prevented the formation of free radicals in brain cells and protected them from the toxic effects of amyloid beta protein. The benefits of vitamin E were demonstrated by Mary Sano, Ph.D., of Columbia University College of Physicians and Surgeons, New York, in a study of 342 patients with advanced Alzheimer's disease. Some of the patients received 2,000 IU of vitamin E (a hefty dose, not recommended for healthy people), while others received a drug or placebo for two years. This relatively short period of vitamin E supplementation delayed the onset of end-stage Alzheimer's disease by almost eight months.

At the time of this study, Sano considered only vitamin E's antioxidant effect against free radicals. However, research has shown that a variety of pro-inflammatory compounds congregate in the brain of patients with Alzheimer's disease. It is likely that vitamin E's anti-inflammatory properties also help prevent and slow the disease's progression. Meanwhile, Sano has begun a new study to determine whether large amounts of supplemental vitamin E might slow the progress of Alzheimer's disease in its earlier stages.

Optimizing the "Antioxidant Network"

You may obtain greater benefits by taking multiple antioxidants in addition to vitamin E. According to Lester Packer, Ph.D., of the University of California, Berkeley, antioxidants work best as a team. Antioxidants get used up rapidly fighting free radicals, but a diversity of antioxidants helps them regenerate to full strength. Many different antioxidants also help neutralize many different types of free radicals, with the result often being a faster recovery time.

For example, physicians at Loyola University Medical Center, Chicago, found that a combination of vitamins E and C reduced radiation proctitis—a type of rectal inflammation caused by radiation treatment. As another example, Italian researchers reported that hereditary pancreatitis, a painful recurring inflammation of the pancreas, could be reduced by a combination of vitamins E and C, selenium, and other antioxidants.

How to Take and Use Vitamin E

Vitamin E's impressive anti-inflammatory properties suggest that supplements would be beneficial in most and perhaps all inflammatory diseases, though its effect may be very subtle in some conditions. The food supply—even a diet built around whole foods—does not provide sufficient amounts of vitamin E, and most dietary vitamin E consists of the gamma tocopherol form, which has a limited role in human health.

Various binding and transport molecules select primarily the natural d-alpha tocopherol (or tocopheryl) form of the vitamin over all other natural and synthetic forms. To distinguish natural from synthetic vitamin E, you have to read the fine print on the label: "d-alpha . . ." refers to natural, and "dl-alpha . . ." refers to synthetic vitamin E. These two molecules are different. The natural form is absorbed twice as well in blood and tissues compared with the synthetic form, so do not buy synthetic vitamin E or any product where the source is ambiguous.

Good choices are d-alpha tocopheryl acetate, d-alpha tocopheryl succinate, d-alpha tocopherol with other mixed natural tocopherols, w... would include a little beta and gamma tocopherol, or a mix of natural vitamin E tocopherols and tocotrienols. The mixed tocopherols most closely resemble how the vitamin occurs in nature, and at least gamma tocopherol may provide additional anti-inflammatory properties. Another option would be a supplement containing mixed natural vitamin E tocopherols and tocotrienols (a less well-known group of vitamin E molecules, but one that is gaining more recognition). Health and natural food stores tend to sell natural vitamin E products and generally have many choices, whereas pharmacies tend to sell synthetic vitamin E supplements. There are many excellent brands, but one of the most reliable is produced by J. R. Carlson Laboratories (888-234-5656; more details in appendix B).

Based on the research, a minimum of 200 IU of vitamin E daily is required to gain any significant health benefits; 400 IU (a small capsule) is a more ideal dosage. Some studies have used 800 IU and 1,200 IU daily, but the extra benefits do not appear to be worth the extra cost for most people. However, if you have a very high total cholesterol or LDL cholesterol level, 800 IU may certainly do a better job of preventing your cholesterol from being oxidized. It would also be important to drastically reduce your intake of cooking oils, except for olive oil.

In this chapter you have learned about the impressive anti-inflammatory properties of vitamin E. It lowers levels of CRP and many other pro-inflammatory compounds, and it reduces the risk of coronary artery disease. In addition, vitamin E supplements can, for many people, ease the symptoms of rheumatoid arthritis, allergies, and Alzheimer's disease. In the next chapter you will read about three nutrients that play a central role in maintaining and rebuilding tissues in the body.

CHAPTER 10

Glucosamine, Chondroitin, and Vitamin C to Rebuild Your Tissues

In the 1990s millions of people with osteoarthritis began taking supplements of two obscure dietary supplements, glucosamine and chondroitin. At the time of their initial popularity, glucosamine and chondroitin were supported by tantalizing evidence but limited clinical experience. The groundswell of interest in these supplements prompted physicians to conduct many clinical trials with people, which have confirmed that the supplements are effective in relieving pain *and* in restoring the cartilage pads that protect joints. Many of these studies also included vitamin C, an essential nutrient needed for the formation of cartilage and other tissue proteins.

This chapter will describe the recent research on glucosamine, chondroitin, and vitamin C. It begins with a brief overview of their roles in the formation of cartilage, then shifts to a discussion of the research, which is extraordinarily persuasive, on osteoarthritis. (Chapter 12 will discuss osteoarthritis in greater depth.) In a very real sense, these nutrients help hold us together, and supplements can help reinforce our health, slowing the breakdown of many tissues from age and injury.

The Basics of Cartilage

Your skin, organs, and glands—virtually your entire physical being—consist of a biological matrix woven with threads of proteins, fats, minerals, and vitamins. Cartilage is one of the principal soft structural materials of the body. Your nose, ears, tendons, and ligaments are made of it.

The cartilage forming the pads in your joints, such as your knees and elbows, is denser than other types of cartilage and slightly different in composition from them. These pads are known as "articular cartilage" because they are located where the body articulates, or moves. Articular cartilage in the knees absorbs the impact of walking, thus keeping the interlocking bones of joints from grinding against each other. Similarly, articular cartilage in the elbows, fingers, and mandibular joints of the jaw cushion against impact but also provide a smooth surface that allows joints to swivel and swing. When articular cartilage wears out, the bones themselves rub against one another, leading to excessive wear and tear, inflammation, and pain. Cartilage, in turn, consists largely of collagen, one of the principal proteins of the body.

The best way to think about glucosamine, chondroitin, and vitamin C is as the bricks and mortar of cartilage. Chondroitin typically refers to a group of chemical compounds called glycosaminoglycans, which form cartilage. These compounds are produced by cartilage cells called chondrocytes. Glucosamine stimulates the conversion of glycosaminoglycans to proteoglycans, which give cartilage its resiliency. Vitamin C is involved in some of the chemical reactions that form cartilage. That's about as technical as this chapter will get.

Cartilage breaks down throughout life and is replaced by new cartilage. However, production of new cartilage declines with age, partly because of growing cellular inefficiency and probably because of inadequate nutritional (biochemical) support as well. This is why osteoarthritis is usually but not always age-related. Athletic injuries, particularly to knee joints, accelerate the destruction of articular cartilage and, in effect, speed the aging of joints. Although research shows that glucosamine, chondroitin, and vitamin C supplements help rebuild articular cartilage, bear in mind that they also can help reinforce cartilage throughout the body.

Recent Studies on Glucosamine, Chondroitin, and Vitamin C

Several recent studies, using similar combinations of supplements, clearly convey the benefits of glucosamine, chondroitin, and vitamin C in people with osteoarthritis. In particular, glucosamine and chondroitin help rebuild articular cartilage and also have anti-inflammatory properties, which may explain why they reduce joint pain. These two actions likely reduce the influx of white blood cells into joints, where they would release inflammation-promoting free radicals.

In one study, Alan F. Philippi, M.D., of the U.S. Navy treated thirty-two navy SEALs in their forties who had chronic knee or low-back pain or both. For eight weeks some of the subjects received daily supplements containing 1,500 mg of glucosamine hydrochloride, 1,200 mg of chondroitin sulfate, and 228 mg of manganese ascorbate (a form of vitamin C). Meanwhile, other subjects received placebos, and all the subjects were crossed over to the opposite regimen for another eight weeks.

During the study about half of the patients with osteoarthritis of the knees improved, with reductions of 26 to 43 percent in symptoms, while taking the supplements. However, the supplements did not help with low-back pain.

In a separate clinical trial, Amal K. Das Jr., M.D., of Hendersonville Orthopedics Associates, Hendersonville, N.C., asked ninety-three patients with knee osteoarthritis to take 2,000 mg of glucosamine hydrochloride, 1,600 mg of chondroitin sulfate, and 304 mg of manganese ascorbate or to take placebos daily for six months.

Fifty-two percent of patients with mild or moderate osteoarthritis of the knee benefited from symptom reductions of 25 percent or more after taking the dietary supplements. In contrast, only about half that number of patients improved with the placebo.

Perhaps the most significant recent study was directed by Jean-Yves Reginster, M.D., of the University of Liège, Belgium. He and his fellow Belgian, Italian, and British researchers used digitized X rays to carefully measure the rate of knee cartilage damage in 106 patients with osteoarthritis. The patients then took either 1,500 mg of glucosamine sulfate or a placebo daily for three years.

People taking glucosamine had an average negligible loss of 0.06 millimeter in joint space, and many patients actually gained new cartilage. In contrast, people taking the placebo had a much greater 0.31-millimeter loss in joint space. Reginster reported that people taking glucosamine had a 20 to 25 percent improvement in symptoms, whereas those taking placebos has a slight worsening. In addition, twice as many patients taking placebos had significant degeneration of their joints compared with those taking glucosamine.

Is It the Glucosamine or the Sulfur That Works?

A recent study by L. John Hoffer, M.D., Ph.D., of Jewish General Hospital, Montréal, suggested that the sulfur (sulfate), not the glucosamine, may be why glucosamine sulfate supplements help rebuild articular cartilage. Sulfur is essential for life, although it is not officially regarded as an essential nutrient. The mineral helps form many of the chemical bonds that hold together skin, collagen, cartilage, and other tissues.

In an article in the journal *Metabolism,* Hoffer pointed out that sulfur is needed for glycosaminoglycan synthesis. However, glucosamine sulfate supplements do not raise blood levels of glucosamine, while they do boost blood sulfur levels. The absorption of sulfur suggests that it is the more biologically active part of the compound, so Hoffer gave 1 gram of glucosamine sulfate to seven healthy subjects; three hours later they had a 13 percent increase in blood sulfur levels. These findings did not directly confirm that glucosamine sulfate helps in osteoarthritis, but they did suggest a biological explanation for why it might work. Also, Hoffer found that when the glucosamine sulfate was given along with acetaminophen (Tylenol), blood sulfur levels dropped by almost 11 percent.

A Controversy: Is Glucosamine Safe in Diabetes?

In 1999 a letter to the journal *Lancet* raised questions about whether glucosamine supplements could increase glucose (blood sugar) levels, cause insulin resistance, and lead to or aggravate diabetes. The questions raised in this letter were widely reported in the *University of California Berkeley Wellness Letter,* the *Tufts University Health & Nutrition Letter,* and other publications toward the end of that year (the delay resulting from publication schedules). These newsletters warned that glucosamine supplements could lead to or worsen diabetes.

But just as those newsletters were being mailed to subscribers, *Lancet* published several letters in response to the original one. Unfortunately, it was too late, and the warnings about glucosamine were starting to become a minor urban (i.e., false) legend, to be repeated by health reporters across the country. Follow-up letters to *Lancet* noted that the original statements were speculative and based only on limited animal research. In contrast, clinical experiences with humans indicated that glucosamine supplements had a tendency to slightly lower blood sugar levels, which would reduce the risk of diabetes. One researcher reported that glucosamine supplements improved wound healing, reduced headaches, and eased inflammatory bowel disease in patients. None of these "side benefits" were reported by the above-named Berkeley and Tufts publications.

Joan: Vitamins and Psoriasis

Since her early twenties, Joan had suffered from psoriasis, which was treated with limited success over the years with a variety of medications. At age fifty-six she visited Richard P. Huemer, M.D., a nutritionally oriented physician in Lancaster, California. Huemer confirmed the original diagnosis of psoriasis, based on characteristic skin lesions, measleslike rashing, and scaling.

He also diagnosed Joan with intestinal dysbiosis, which can result in myriad symptoms, including allergylike symptoms and skin disorders. He recommended that Joan take digestive aid supplements as well as vitamin C, vitamin E, and gamma-linolenic acid supplements. Huemer also recommended homeopathic remedies, including graphites (6X). He also suggested that Joan use Dovonex, a cream containing a form of vitamin D, but Joan did not follow up on this.

Joan's psoriasis improved over the next several months. After four months she was pleased to report to Huemer that her friends told her she no longer had any signs of psoriasis.

Vitamin C and Your Health

Although vitamin C became controversial after Nobel laureate Linus Pauling, Ph.D., recommended supplements to treat the common cold and influenza, the vitamin has many varied and essential roles in maintaining health.

Cartilage and virtually all other tissues in the body are built with large amounts of collagen, a protein often described as the body's "tissue cement." Vitamin C plays an essential role in the synthesis of enzymes needed during the manufacture of collagen. In other words, a complete lack of vitamin C would lead to a disintegration of our skin, organs, and glands. Vitamin C also is needed for the body's synthesis of carnitine, which plays a pivotal role in burning fat for energy, so without vitamin C, we would also feel very fatigued. In addition, vitamin C is one of the major water-soluble antioxidants in the body, protecting against dangerous free radicals.

From a biological standpoint, we may need far more than the 90 mg daily officially recommended for men and women. The rationale for higher levels of vitamin C comes from an examination of vitamin C in other animals. Nearly every mammal—and there are four thousand species—makes its own vitamin C, converting blood sugar to the vitamin. The only exceptions are humans, a handful of higher primates, guinea pigs, and one species of bat. The evolutionary evidence indicates that a common ancestor of humans and some primates lost the ability to make vitamin C about 35 million years ago. Humans still carry the gene that programs for vitamin C production, but it is damaged and nonfunctional.

In the animal kingdom vitamin C is produced at a rate equivalent to 1.8 to 13 grams daily in a person weighing about 150 pounds. The official recommended daily intake for vitamin C ranges from less than 1 percent to 5 percent of this range. One view is that people no longer require as much vitamin C. Another view is that while people lost their ability to make vitamin C, they did not lose their requirement for large amounts of it. One of vitamin C's key roles is in maintaining homeostasis—that is, physiological stability. When stressed, animals increase their production of vitamin C. In humans, stress just seems to exacerbate the vitamin C deficit.

Vitamin C and Inflammatory Disorders

The inability to convert blood sugar to vitamin C may very well predispose people to adult-onset diabetes; excess glucose remains in the blood instead of being converted to vitamin C. Indeed, the chemical similarities between blood sugar and vitamin C lead to a competition between them; both molecules enter the cell on the same transporter protein. This competition takes on greater significance when one considers that diabetes has a strong inflammatory component. People with diabetes typically have elevated levels of interleukin-6 and C-reactive protein. Increasing vitamin C consumption can displace some of the abnormally high blood sugar and improve glucose metabolism.

In particular, vitamin C (like many other antioxidants) appears to dampen inflammation by quenching free radicals and reducing the activity of pro-inflammatory adhesion molecules. Conversely, inadequate intake of vitamin E is associated with inflammatory disorders. For example, a report in the journal *Circulation* noted that patients with peripheral arterial disease (affecting the legs) were more likely to have greater inflammation and severe heart disease when their blood levels of vitamin C were low.

Using Glucosamine, Chondroitin, and Vitamin C

In the past people often obtained the building blocks of cartilage by chewing meat down to the bone, eating gristle attached to meat, or by making soups with bones. Boiling the bones in water releases glucosamine and chondroitin, which are consumed as part of the soup. Research has shown that these substances migrate after digestion to cartilage tissues in people.

The two principal forms of glucosamine in supplements are glucosamine sulfate and glucosamine hydrochloride, and both appear to be equally effective. There is evidence suggesting that glucosamine and chondroitin sulfate are synergistic, with glucosamine enhancing the production of new cartilage and chondroitin slowing the breakdown of cartilage. Many supplements contain both, and people with osteoarthritis should consider taking 1,200 to 1,500 mg of glucosamine and 1,200 mg of chondroitin daily. As part of an osteoarthritic regimen, 500 to 1,000 mg of vitamin C should be included. Although some of the described studies used manganese ascorbate, this type of vitamin C is difficult to find. Any form of vitamin C should suffice.

In general, it would be worthwhile for every person to consume a minimum of 500 mg of supplemental vitamin C. The recent recommendation of 90 mg daily was based on studies of young, healthy men and women. Older people and those with medical conditions very likely will require far more. A far better dosage would be 2,000 to 5,000 mg daily. Robert Cathcart III, M.D., a leading expert in the clinical use of vitamin C to fight infections, developed the "bowel tolerance" method of determining the ideal individual dosage. Using this method, divide your total daily vitamin C dosage into three or four doses over the course of a day, such as with each meal and before bed. Then increase each of the dosages until your stools soften. At that point, reduce your dosage slightly. The dosage will vary from person to person, on average between 1,000 mg and 10,000 mg (10 grams) daily, and your tolerance of vitamin C will increase when you are sick.

In this chapter we have explored the roles of glucosamine, chondroitin, and vitamin C in the body's production of cartilage and collagen, proteins that form a large part of our physical structure. While many nutrients are needed for health, these three nutrients stand out for their roles in reversing osteoarthritis and other inflammatory diseases. In the next chapter you will learn about a variety of other nutrients that also have anti-inflammatory properties.

CHAPTER 11

B Vitamins and More to Reduce Inflammation

In a sense, all essential nutrients play roles in the body's management of inflammation, because all such nutrients help maintain overall health. However, a number of additional nutrients, as well as herbs, stand out for their anti-inflammatory or health-regenerating, properties. These nutrients work in a variety of ways. For example, some B vitamins prevent inflammation-triggering damage to artery walls, whereas some antioxidants inhibit specific inflammation-promoting substances. Herbs also work in a number of ways, as antioxidants and as mild Cox-2 inhibitors.

This chapter describes approximately two dozen additional supplements and herbs that can be of benefit in inflammatory disorders. In general, these supplements should be tried after you have followed the Anti-Inflammation Syndrome Diet Plan and principal inflammation-reversing supplements. Some of these supplements, such as Pycnogenol, have powerful anti-inflammatory effects; it may be worthwhile trying it and others one at a time for one or two months each. The culinary herbs can and should be added as flavorings to meals.

Why not take several of these supplements at once? Doing so may very well alleviate some of your inflammatory symptoms, but you would not know whether you were obtaining the benefits from one or most or all of the supplements you decided to take. You might say that that doesn't matter if you feel better quickly, but it could be a more costly approach than identifying the individual supplement or supplements that help you the most. Finally, it is worth pointing out that you probably would not want or need to consume all of the following nutrients, for financial reasons if nothing else.

Dorothy: Nutritional Supplements to Treat Cancer

Abram Hoffer, M.D., Ph.D., one of the pioneers in vitamin therapy, initially began treating cancer patients for depression and anxiety. He soon found that patients taking large dosages of vitamin C and other vitamins and minerals were living longer than those who did not. When his cases were analyzed by Nobel laureate Linus Pauling, Ph.D., it became clear that cancer patients were living several times longer (postdiagnosis) when they took supplements, compared with patients who chose not to take supplements.

Hoffer has treated more than twelve hundred cancer patients since 1977, and some types of cancer (such as breast and prostate) are more responsive to supplements than other types (such as lung). One of his patients is Dorothy of Victoria, British Columbia, Canada.

Dorothy was first diagnosed with breast cancer in 1975, when she was forty-nine years old and going through an emotionally draining divorce. Doctors performed a lumpectomy, gave her radiation therapy, and pronounced her treated and cured.

But conventional medicine didn't cure Dorothy. Her cancer eventually reappeared in one of her breasts and also spread to her lungs. For the past few years, however, she has been healthy and free of cancer. Dorothy credits her long-term survival to "quality" vitamin supplements, a good diet, and a great attitude toward life.

For many years Dorothy took large amounts of vitamin A to reduce the risk of metastasis. However, the cancer did metastasize to her lungs in 1995, but it receded after drug treatment.

In 1997 she consulted with Hoffer, and she has since been taking a high-powered assortment of nutritional supplements, including vitamins A, C, D, and E, beta-carotene, selenium, and the vitaminlike coenzyme Q_{10}. "I do feel I need these extra supplements," Dorothy says. "I think anyone in this situation would need them."

Dorothy emphasizes organic foods in her diet, eating a lot of fish, vegetables, and occasionally game meats (deer, elk). In her midseventies, Dorothy is physically active—much more so than many other seniors who have not battled cancer. She soothes her soul and reduces stress with music, meditation, visualization, long walks, and a positive mental attitude.

The B-Complex Vitamins

Several B vitamins, including folic acid and vitamins B_6 and B_{12}, can lower blood levels of homocysteine, a toxic amino acid that damages blood vessel walls, initiates localized inflammation, and increases the risk of coronary artery disease and stroke.

Homocysteine plays a role in normal biochemistry. It is formed as a by-product of methionine, an essential amino acid found in protein. However, homocysteine should exist relatively briefly in the related chemical reactions, and blood levels should remain low. Folic acid and vitamin B_{12} help convert homocysteine back to methionine, and vitamin B_6 helps convert to cystathionine, another necessary compound in the reactions.

However, when a person has low levels of one or more of these vitamins, homocysteine cannot be converted, and blood levels rise. This imbalance usually occurs for one of several reasons: too much protein, too few B vitamins, or a common genetic defect that partially interferes with how the body uses folic acid. Without sufficient B vitamins, homocysteine injures blood vessel walls, particularly those in the heart and brain. This injury triggers an immune response, attracting white blood cells to the blood vessel wall and damaging it.

It is best to maintain homocysteine levels as low as possible—4 to 6 micromoles (mmoles) per liter of blood is ideal. The risk of heart disease noticeably increases when levels increase. A level of 10 mmoles is abnormally elevated, and 13 or higher is very dangerous. Folic acid supplements by themselves can generally lower homocysteine levels, and health food stores sell several brands of homocysteine-lowering supplements, which generally contain two other B vitamins. However, it might be better to simply take a high-potency B-complex supplement. Look for a B-complex supplement containing 10 to 25 mg of vitamin B_1—this is a clue to the higher potency of other B vitamins in the formula.

The B vitamins exert an analgesic effect as well. A paper published in the German medical journal *Schmerz* (which means "pain") described how vitamins B_1, B_6, and B_{12}, especially when taken in combination, reduce musculoskeletal pain and enhance the effects of nonsteroidal anti-inflammatory drugs (NSAIDs). A separate study, which focused on 303 elderly American veterans, found body pain strongly associated with a deficiency of vitamin B_{12}, which affected more than one-fifth of the subjects.

Flavonoids and Polyphenols

As a family of vitaminlike nutrients, flavonoids and polyphenols possess striking anti-inflammatory properties. More than five thousand flavonoids, sometimes referred to as bioflavonoids, have been identified in plants, and they are part of a larger group of water-soluble chemical antioxidants known as polyphenols. All of these compounds function as light-absorbing plant pigments; as they absorb light, they limit the formation of hazardous free radicals. Flavonoids and polyphenols provide the blue in blueberries and the red in raspberries and strawberries. (Some of the other colors are the result of carotenoids. See "Beta-Carotene" on page 143.) It is likely that in a diet that includes a variety of fresh fruits and vegetables, a person consumes hundreds if not thousands of these antioxidants.

Flavonoids and polyphenols provide the lion's share of antioxidants in fruits and vegetables. For example, 100 g (about 3.5 oz) of a fresh apple provides about 5.7 mg of vitamin C. However, the same apple, including the skin, contains 219 mg of flavonoids and 290 mg of other polyphenols, which together are equivalent to the antioxidant activity of about 1,500 mg of vitamin C. Eating a variety of fruits and vegetables likely provides several hundred different types of flavonoids and/or polyphenols. All of these flavonoids and polyphenols are related and often form new compounds, creating a chemical kaleidoscope of antioxidants. All of these different chemical structures are like thousands of puzzle pieces, matching up to the many different types of inflammation-promoting free radicals.

Quercetin

One of the most popular flavonoid supplements is also one of the most misunderstood. Quercetin (pronounced kwair-sih-tin), found in apples and onions, can inhibit the activity of some types of adhesion molecules, which promote many types of inflammatory reactions. Adhesion molecules enable white blood cells, which secrete pro-inflammatory compounds, to attach to normal cells. In terms of chemical structure, quercetin is similar to both rutin, another naturally occurring flavonoid, and to cromolyn sodium (NasalCrom), a synthetic flavonoid drug used to prevent pollen allergies.

Many physicians have found quercetin supplements, 300 to 500 mg daily, helpful in treating pollen allergies, but there is a catch. Quercetin supplements have failed to pass the Ames test for mutagenicity, which means they cause breaks in genetic material and conceivably could increase the risk of cancer. In practical terms this risk may be remote because fruits and vegetables supply many nutrients that enhance the body's repair mechanisms. But still, there is something troubling about taking a potential carcinogen to treat inflammation or allergies. Only one form of quercetin has passed the Ames test. That is quercetin chalcone, made by Thorne Research (208-263-1337).

Pycnogenol and Grape Seed Extract

Pycnogenol (pronounced pick-noj'-in-nall) is a patented complex of about forty antioxidants, mostly proanthocyanidins (a family of flavonoids) and a variety of other antioxidants, including organic acids (such as cinnamic acids, caffeic acid, and ferulic acid). It is extracted from the bark of French maritime pine trees and sold under the Pycnogenol brand name by many different companies.

The many different antioxidants in Pycnogenol make its sum far greater than any of its individual parts. Studies by Lester Packer, Ph.D., an antioxidant expert and professor emeritus at the University of California, Berkeley, have found that Pycnogenol is a powerful antioxidant. In addition to quenching free radicals, it also turns off some of the genes involved in producing inflammation. One study has found that Pycnogenol supplements reduced inflammation in patients with lupus erythematosus.

Traditionally, Pycnogenol is best known for strengthening blood vessel walls, preventing the leakage of blood and abnormal bruising. It is likely that it achieves these benefits partly by inhibiting inflammation in blood vessel walls. Studies with laboratory animals have determined that it is a powerful anti-inflammatory nutrient. In addition, many physicians have found that Pycnogenol supplements, ranging from 25 to 200 mg daily, can often have dramatic effects in people with rheumatic diseases.

Pycnogenol works in part by inhibiting production of peroxides, which stimulate inflammatory activity in white blood cells. In a laboratory experiment, researchers found that Pycnogenol reduced peroxide formation and increased levels of glutathione, an anti-inflammatory antioxidant.

Grape seed extracts are also rich in proanthocyanidins, though the specific types of antioxidants in this supplement are somewhat different from those in Pycnogenol. Grape seed extracts have a similar effect on blood vessel walls, and they also possess anti-inflammatory properties. Some of the physicians who use both supplements feel that there are subtle differences between the two in patient responses. It may be worthwhile to try one, then the other to see if one is better for you.

Glutathione Boosters

Glutathione is the principal antioxidant made by the body, though it is commonly found in foods with other antioxidants. Glutathione supplements are generally unreliable because the molecule may be broken down during digestion. Taking almost any antioxidant supplement, such as vitamin E or vitamin C, will increase the body's production of glutathione. The following three supplements are particularly good glutathione boosters because they contain precursors of glutathione.

N-acetylcysteine

N-acetylcysteine (NAC) is an exceptionally safe form of the amino acid cysteine. Its safety is important to note because pure cysteine can become neurotoxic at high dosages. Cysteine is a direct precursor to glutathione and the many different glutathione compounds made and used in the body.

NAC is used in every hospital emergency room in the nation to treat overdoses of acetaminophen (Tylenol). Acetaminophen depletes liver levels of glutathione and, in large amounts, can rapidly lead to liver failure. NAC quickly rebuilds normal glutathione levels in the liver, which then helps the organ break down and detoxify the drug. The same glutathione-enhancing effect of NAC has also been found to increase the life expectancy of people with AIDS, which depletes glutathione levels.

The National Cancer Institute has studied NAC as a potential cancer-preventive nutrient, but the most dramatic study published was actually on NAC and flu symptoms. Silvio De Flora, M.D., of the University of Genoa, Italy, gave 262 elderly subjects either 1,200 mg of NAC or placebos daily during the winter flu season. Although NAC did not prevent flu infections, it had a "striking" effect on symptoms. Of the subjects with laboratory-confirmed flus, only 25 percent of those taking NAC developed flu symptoms, and they were generally mild and of short duration. In contrast, 79 percent of the people taking placebos had more severe flu symptoms, according to De Flora's article in the *European Respiratory*

Journal. This symptom-reducing effect is very important in controlling inflammation related to infection.

Alpha-Lipoic Acid

This antioxidant, found in spinach and beef, is approved in Germany for the treatment of diabetic neuropathy (nerve disease). Several studies have found that it can greatly improve insulin function and reduce blood sugar levels by 10 to 30 percent in diabetics. Like NAC, alpha-lipoic acid is a sulfur-containing molecule that may be a more efficient glutathione booster.

Research over the past twenty-five years by Burton M. Berkson, M.D., Ph.D., an adjunct professor at New Mexico State University, Las Cruces, has found alpha-lipoic acid to greatly enhance liver function and liver glutathione levels. This effect is particularly important in controlling chronic hepatitis. Patients with hepatitis C consistently and significantly improve when following his "triple antioxidant" regimen, which included 600 mg of alpha-lipoic acid, 400 mcg of selenium, and 900 mg of silymarin (an extract of the herb milk thistle) daily. This program leads to a near normalization of liver function.

Selenium

Selenium is an essential dietary mineral and an essential part of several glutathione peroxidases, powerful antioxidant and anti-inflammatory enzymes made by the body. Selenium supplements, 200 mcg daily, increase the body's production of glutathione peroxidases. These compounds enhance resistance to infection, which reduces one source of inflammatory reactions and also prevents very dangerous mutations in flu and other viruses. In addition, a human trial at the University of Arizona, Tucson, found that selenium supplements reduced the risk of breast and prostate cancers by about half.

Cynthia: Antioxidants to Treat Hepatitis

At age thirty-three, Cynthia had received a blood transfusion following the birth of her daughter. Several weeks later she developed a general sense of fatigue, along with muscle pains and jaundice. She quickly became too sick to care for her daughter.

Laboratory tests indicated that Cynthia had contracted hepatitis C, and her physician noted that the virus also had damaged her pancreas, resulting in elevated blood sugar levels and diabetes. Her prognosis was poor, but a specialist suggested that she have an injection of interferon and an antiviral drug, which would result in flulike symptoms for about six months. In addition, Cynthia was told that she would eventually need a liver transplant.

Seeking an alternative to interferon therapy and a liver transplant, Cynthia consulted with Burton M. Berkson, M.D., Ph.D., of Las Cruces, New Mexico. At the time she was fatigued and her liver was enlarged and tender. Tests indicated that her liver enzymes were very high and her fasting blood sugar level was 300 mg/dl. (Normal is 75 to 85 mg/dl.)

Berkson started Cynthia on his "triple antioxidant" approach, which included 600 mg of alpha-lipoic acid, 400 mcg of selenium, and 900 mg of silymarin daily. He also asked her to follow a diet similar to the Anti-Inflammation Syndrome Diet Plan, rich in protein and vegetables and low in refined carbohydrates. After two weeks she had an increase in energy and was able to resume many normal activities. By the sixth week of supplementation Cynthia's liver enzymes had fallen to near-normal levels and her fasting glucose was 112 mg/dl. She has been following the diet and supplement regimen for more than five years and reports that she still feels great.

Beta-Carotene

In addition to flavonoids, fruits and vegetables contain large quantities of carotenoids, a family of fat-soluble antioxidants. Several studies suggest that these nutrients—chiefly beta-carotene, lutein, and lycopene—are associated with relatively low levels of C-reactive protein (CRP). This association does not necessarily mean that carotenoids lower CRP levels, though this effect would be consistent with other research on antioxidants. Carotenoid levels might simply reflect fruit and vegetable consumption and the combined anti-inflammatory action of carotenoids, flavonoids, and vitamins.

In one study of several thousand people, researchers found that high levels of all the major dietary carotenoids were associated with low levels of inflammatory markers, including CRP. Another group of researchers found that both CRP and high white blood cell counts, another marker or inflammation, were associated with low beta-carotene levels. All of the major dietary carotenoids neutralize peroxinitrite, a type of free radical that increases inflammation.

Methylsulfonylmethane (MSM)

This supplement consists of about one-third elemental sulfur, a nutrient that exists in nutritional limbo. Sulfur is not considered an essential nutrient, but every indication points to its crucial role in health and life itself. Glutathione, NAC, and alpha-lipoic acid all contain sulfur molecules. So does the B vitamin biotin, the anticoagulant heparin, and the hormone insulin. Sulfur also is an integral part of the biological cement that forms skin, hair, nails, and the cartilage that shapes your nose and pads your joints.

Published, controlled studies on MSM are limited, but more than fifty-five thousand studies have been published on a very similar molecule, dimethyl sulfoxide (DMSO). Stanley Jacob, M.D., of Oregon Health Sciences University, Portland, a pioneer in researching both substances, has found MSM very effective in reducing muscle and joint pain, interstitial cystitis (a type of very painful bladder inflammation), and even pollen allergies in some people.

Dietitians have generally assumed that people obtain sufficient sulfur through dietary methionine and cysteine. However, the extraordinary successes obtained by Jacob suggest that other chemical forms of sulfur (besides those in amino acids) may be readily used in the body. Jacob recommends daily supplementation of 1,000 to 2,000 mg daily, though larger amounts are safe.

S-adenosyl-L-methionine

Usually referred to as SAMe (pronounced "sammy"), this sulfur-containing nutrient donates "methyl groups" to more than forty major chemical reactions in the body. Methyl groups provide carbon and hydrogen and are necessary for creating new cells. SAMe has often been recommended for treating inflammation and arthritis: it donates sulfur molecules to glucosamine and chondroitin sulfate, enabling the body to build new collagen and cartilage.

SAMe also has been found helpful in treating depression, though B-complex vitamins can boost SAMe levels and are less expensive. Its benefit in depression suggests a common biochemical defect with

inflammation. Depression is frequently associated with some inflammatory diseases such as asthma, Alzheimer's, coronary artery disease, and
diabetes.

Herbs and Spices

Medicinal and culinary herbs are rich sources of anti-inflammatory antioxidants, especially flavonoids. They also contain trace amounts of natural Cox-2 inhibitors, such as salicylates. Medicinal herbs can be
especially potent, while culinary herbs are perhaps less potent but more
tasty anti-inflammatory nutrients.

Over the past several years herbal medicines have moved from folk-
medicine status to scientifically supported treatments. Major drug companies routinely fund expeditions to the Amazon and other undeveloped
regions to identify new plants and potentially therapeutic molecules. Almost half of all modern drugs have either been developed from plant compounds or are synthetic replicas of molecules found in plants.

Unlike pharmaceutical drugs, which are usually built around a
single synthetic molecule, herbs may contain hundreds if not thousands of
active principles. The diversity and frequent synergism of these anti-
inflammatory compounds lead to a multifaceted biochemical attack on inflammation, instead of overwhelming a single biochemical pathway and
causing side effects. In fact, many of the substances in herbs are also
found in common fruits and vegetables, which means they have historically played a role in human nutrition and evolution. Indeed, the anti-
inflammatory nutrients in fruits, vegetables, and herbs may have
historically helped control excessive inflammation.

Devil's Claw

Devil's claw *(Harpagophytum procumbens)* is a traditional southern
African herb used to treat pain and upset stomachs. Its name comes from
its clawlike fruit, which resemble the feet of birds. Ten clinical studies
conducted between 1982 and 2000 have found that devil's claw can benefit people with rheumatoid arthritis, low back pain, and various other
rheumatic complaints.

In the June 2000 issue of *Phytomedicine,* French researchers reported
using devil's claw to successfully treat ninety-two people with osteoarthritis. The subjects were given either 435 mg of powdered devil's
claw or conventional drug treatment daily. By the end of the four-month

studies, people taking devil's claw had significantly less pain and greater mobility. They were also relying on fewer anti-inflammatory drugs and painkillers. Similar results were noted in a broader study, which included 122 patients with either hip or knee osteoarthritis or both.

Cat's Claw

Despite a similar name, cat's claw *(Uncaria tomentosa)* is unrelated to devil's claw. Cat's claw is native to South America and known as *una de gato* in Peru. Its use as an anti-inflammatory herb dates back hundreds of years, to the Inca civilization.

A recent series of experiments detailed the anti-inflammatory properties of cat's claw. Manuel Sandoval-Chacon, Ph.D., and Mark J. S. Miller, Ph.D., of Albany Medical College, New York, conducted cell and animal experiments to investigate the herb's specific biological properties. In one of the experiments, human cells were exposed to peroxynitrite, a powerful free radical that can destroy cells. When the cells also were exposed to cat's claw, they were protected from the peroxynitrite radicals.

Peroxynitrite also increases levels of pro-inflammatory prostaglandin E_2, and cat's claw would theoretically lower its levels. According to Sandoval-Chacon and Miller, cat's claw also inhibits the activity of NF-kappa B, a protein that turns on inflammation-causing genes. Such findings, the researchers noted, are consistent with the herb's traditional uses. Effective dosages range from 250 to 1,000 mg of cat's claw extract daily.

Chamomile

Chamomile (*Matricaria* species) was used as an herbal remedy by the ancient Egyptians and Romans, and the herb's mild-flavored tea has been recommended for menstrual cramps, stomach pain, indigestion, and fever. The tea, made with a tiny bit of honey, is excellent for treating an upset stomach. Used topically, chamomile poultices, lotions, and creams can have cosmetic and dermatologic benefits as well.

In Germany, which makes extensive use of pharmaceutical-grade herbs, chamomile is regarded as the first choice for treating mild skin problems, such as rashes, in infants. A human study of nine healthy women found that topically applied chamomile was absorbed deeply into the skin. Not surprisingly, then, many cosmetics (such as the Camo-Care brand) use chamomile.

The active components of chamomile include blue azulene (an essential oil), glycosides (carbohydrate-based compounds found in many medicinal plants), and many acids and esters. It is also rich in antioxidants. In an unpublished study allergist Holger Biltz, M.D., of Bad Honnef, Germany, reported that a chamomile-containing cream reduced reddening after UV exposure, and reduced skin roughness.

Green Tea

Green tea and, to a lesser extent, black tea are rich sources of antioxidant flavonoids known as catechins. These catechins include three closely related antioxidants: epigallocatechin-3 gallate (EGCG), epigallocatechin (EGC), and epicatechin-3 gallate (ECG). Together they form about 30 percent of the dry weight of tea leaves. The sheer quantity of catechins in green tea point to their remarkable antioxidant power.

Dozens of studies by Japanese researchers—avid drinkers of green tea—have shown that catechins can prevent free-radical damage to cholesterol and lower the risk of heart disease and cancer. Population-based studies have shown that tea drinkers have a lower than average risk of heart disease, stroke, and several cancers, including esophageal, stomach, and lung cancers.

The protective properties of green tea can be traced, at least in part, to the anti-inflammatory properties of catechins. These substances can inhibit the formation of pro-inflammatory compounds, and they have mild analgesic effects as well. In one study Japanese researchers reported that EGCG could inhibit the release of histamine, the compound that causes the itchy feeling in allergies.

A separate study, conducted at Case Western Reserve University, Cleveland, Ohio, tested the effects of green tea in arthritic laboratory mice. Only about half of the mice drinking green tea developed a serious form of arthritis, and the other animals in the green-tea group had only a mild form of the disease. In contrast, all but one of the mice drinking only water developed arthritis. In other words, green tea (in amounts comparable to what a person might drink) significantly reduced the likelihood of developing and the severity of arthritis in mice.

Bromelain

Bromelain is an enzyme found in pineapple stems, and it has been widely used to treat athletic injuries. It seems to reduce the sense of pain and heat in inflammation, and it may be of use in other conditions, such as colitis and arthritis.

This enzyme has some anticlotting properties, which may be why it has sometimes been recommended in the treatment of coronary artery disease. In fact, some pro-inflammatory eicosanoids (by-products of omega-6 fatty acids) promote clotting, whereas anti-inflammatory eicosanoids (by-products of omega-3 fatty acids) reduce blood clotting. Bromelain is best taken on an empty stomach, and 600 mg daily are worth trying for inflammation.

Boswellia

Boswellia is the common name for the resins of *Boswellia serrata,* a tree that grows in India. These resins have been used in traditional Ayurvedic medicine, and they are rich in a group of anti-inflammatory compounds described as boswellic acids.

Boswellia inhibits 5-lipoxygenase, one of the enzymes needed for the body's production of inflammatory compounds. It also seems to break some of the links in the inflammatory chain reaction involving what physicians know as "complement." While complement is an essential part of our immune defenses, its overactivity can contribute to chronic inflammation.

Several studies have used 200 mg of boswellic acid extracts three times daily to treat rheumatoid arthritis, osteoarthritis, and associated inflammation. These studies have shown a reduction in symptoms, such as pain and morning stiffness, as well as in inflammatory markers. Preliminary research also suggests that these extracts may ease asthma as well.

Feverfew

The herb feverfew *(Tanacetum parthenium)* was used in ancient Greece to treat headaches and, as the name indicates, fevers. It is currently approved as an over-the-counter product in Canada for the specific treatment of migraine headaches. Like other herbs, it is sold in the United States and other countries without a specific therapeutic claim.

Its active ingredient, parthenolide, stabilizes blood vessel tension. Although it is of limited use during an actual migraine headache, the herb's long-term use does reduce the frequency of migraine headaches. Dosages of feverfew products vary among brands, but one of the most

reliable brands (available at health food stores) is MygraFew, made by
Nature's Way.

In 2001 researchers at Yale University (New Haven, Connecticut) determined that parthenolide had potentially far-reaching anti-
inflammatory properties. They identified the molecular basis of the herb,
showing that it disrupts the function of "IkappaB kinase beta," an inflammation-triggering compound.

Elder

Elder leaves and elderberries (*Sambucus nigra* and other species) have a
long history of medicinal use. Hippocrates, regarded as the father of medicine, wrote about elderberries in the fourth century B.C. Shakespeare
mentioned them in his play *The Merry Wives of Windsor.* They were
viewed as so potent that during the 1600s, many people hung elderberry
branches and leaves by their doors to keep away the evil spirits that were
believed to cause illness. Among Native Americans, various species of
elder leaves were used to treat rheumatism and fever.

Laboratory experiments have confirmed the anti-inflammatory properties of elder leaves. Leaf extracts reduce levels of several pro-
inflammation cytokines. Meanwhile, a syrup made from elderberries was
reported, in a double-blind study, to significantly reduce flu symptoms. In
the study 90 percent of people taking the elderberry syrup (Sambucol) reported a "complete cure" of their flu symptoms in two to three days, compared with six days for most of the people taking a placebo.

Garlic

Many of the health benefits of garlic *(Allium sativum)* result from its anti-
inflammatory properties. For example, garlic is well known as a mild
blood thinner. It works by turning down the activity of thromboxanes,
which promote blood clotting. The same thromboxanes are also involved
in inflammation. Some studies also have found that garlic supplements
can lower blood sugar and cholesterol levels, though not all people seem
to benefit equally.

Because it is rich in sulfur, garlic also can boost the body's production
of glutathione. This food and condiment is a good example of some of the
health benefits of oxidation. The chemical constituents of garlic are relatively inert until it is sliced, diced, cooked, or chewed. Breaking up a

garlic clove begins a cascade of oxidation reactions (with oxygen), leading to the production of compounds very similar to sulfur-containing amino acids. All forms of garlic—supplements, powders, and fresh—appear to have benefits, though supplements and freshly prepared appear to be the most potent.

It makes sense to use ample garlic in your meals. Its adds tremendous flavor, even if it had no health benefits. Garlic supplements concentrate levels of some of the active constituents, but their advertising can be confusing. The major brands are Kwai, Kyolic, Pure-Gar, and Garlicin. Because each product is produced differently, each contains a slightly different group of compounds. Dosages of 500 to 1,000 mg daily may have an anti-inflammatory effect.

Ginger

Few spices besides gingerroot are versatile enough to flavor both entrées and desserts, from Oriental meals to gingerbread cookies. Native to South Asia, ginger *(Zingiber officinale)* has become a popular spice around the world.

Gingerroot has well-documented anti-inflammatory properties. It is rich in kaempferol, a flavonoid that functions in part as a mild Cox-2 inhibitor. In addition, ginger blocks lipoxygenase, another enzyme involved in the body's production of inflammatory compounds. Ginger also appears to contain trace amounts of melatonin, a hormone otherwise made by the pineal gland; melatonin has antioxidant and anti-inflammatory properties. (Pure melatonin has sleep-inducing properties, so it is not recommended as an anti-inflammatory supplement.)

Both ginger and ginger-containing supplements have been found helpful in osteoarthritis, rheumatism, and muscular pain. Ginger has the added benefit of reducing nausea. Although ginger is common in grocery stores, the best form (and most difficult to find) is fresh baby gingerroot, which is especially tender.

Curcumin and Turmeric Root

Curcumin, a bright yellow spice, is obtained from the root of turmeric *(Curcuma longa),* a member of the ginger family. Native to Asia, curcumin is one of the oldest and most cherished anti-inflammatory herbs in Indian Ayurvedic medicine.

Turmeric root and curcumin are mild Cox-2 inhibitors but are not as powerful and not as dangerous as popular Cox-2-inhibiting drugs. According to recent experiments, they block the activity of "NF kappa B," a protein that turns on inflammation-promoting genes. This effect and similar ones too complex to discuss here also suggest that the herbs also might reduce the risk of cancer. Animal studies have found that turmeric root and curcumin may reduce arthritic symptoms.

Plantain

The herb plantain *(Plantago lanceolata, P. major)* is used in Germany to treat upper respiratory inflammation and to reduce skin inflammation. It is an ingredient in some anticough and expectorant medicines.

One of its chemical components, ursolic acid, it a potent anti-inflammatory. In a study conducted at Uppsala University, Sweden, researchers reported that it was a highly selective inhibitor of Cox-2, the cyclooxygenase enzyme more involved in inflammatory reactions.

Oregano

This common culinary herb may be one of the overlooked reasons why the traditional Greek and Mediterranean diet is associated with a lower risk of heart disease. Oregano *(Origanum vulgare),* a member of the mint family, contains a large number of anti-inflammatory flavonoids and polyphenols, including rosmarinic acid, kaempferol, ursolic acid, and apigenin.

Widely used in Greek and Italian cooking, oregano adds a wonderful flavor to foods. Greek oregano has a stronger smell and flavor than Mexican oregano. Dried oregano is fine as a culinary herb, but it is best when freshly dried.

In this chapter we have explored a variety of vitamins, vitaminlike nutrients, and herbs that have documented anti-inflammatory and healing properties. These nutrients and herbs should be added to the core Anti-Inflammation Syndrome Diet Plan and supplement recommendations, but obviously you cannot take or use all of them all the time. In the next section we will focus on preventing and reversing some of the most common inflammatory disorders.

PART IV

Putting Anti-Inflammation Syndrome Nutrients to Work for You

CHAPTER 12

The Inflammation Syndrome, Diseases, and Specific Conditions

Up to this point we have focused on the leading dietary causes and solutions for the Inflammation Syndrome. In this chapter we shift to specific diseases and conditions that are caused or exacerbated by inflammation—and remedied by improvements in diet and anti-inflammatory supplements.

Inflammatory disorders frequently follow a progression, beginning with mild symptoms that, if the underlying causes remain uncorrected, progress to more serious and difficult-to-treat diseases. For example, gastritis can lead to stomach ulcers and increase the risk of stomach cancer. Similarly, athletic injuries can set the stage for osteoarthritis and chronic musculoskeletal pain. Although symptoms may seem to be mild or transitory during the early stages of an inflammatory disease, it is easier to heal them at this time. In contrast, it is more difficult to reverse established diseases because of the extent of tissue damage.

In addition, inflammatory disorders often occur in clusters, one disorder being linked to another, and often forming the Inflammation Syndrome. These clusters point to similar underlying causes, though the common causes may be overlooked. For example, periodontitis increases the risk of heart disease, making some physicians believe that both diseases have a common infectious cause. Rather, people with the two conditions more likely share a common inflammatory pattern resulting from a pro-inflammatory diet and inadequate intake of vitamins E and C. As another example, people with asthma frequently suffer from depression. The depression does not result from the unfortunate diagnosis of asthma but, instead, may be symptomatic of the same fatty acid imbalance affecting body and mind.

You might wonder why, if most people are eating essentially the same pro-inflammatory diet, one person develops a particular set of symptoms, such as rheumatoid arthritis, whereas another suffers asthmatic attacks, and yet another person has heart disease. The diseases to which you are susceptible reflect your individual biological weaknesses, which are the result of your genetics, overall lifestyle, stresses, age, and diet. To understand this, it helps to see your genes and biochemistry as a series of chainlike links. Everyone has their own set of weak links (as well as strong links), and the number of weak links increases with age, poor diet, stress, and other insults. Your major weak links may be your heart, your joints, or your stomach or some other tissue. Good nutrition reinforces these links and may be more important to health than genetics; this has been borne out by recent research. As you read early in this book, genes themselves depend on adequate levels of nutrients for optimal functioning.

In general, the following sections place more emphasis on conditions affecting larger numbers of people and less emphasis on those affecting fewer people. It would be impossible to cover the full spectrum of inflammatory diseases in this type of book. Still, the Anti-Inflammation Syndrome Diet Plan should have a positive impact on virtually all inflammatory diseases. So if you suffer from a disorder that is not described here, it would be worthwhile trying the diet plan and some of the supplements.

Age-Related Wear and Tear

What Is Age-Related Wear and Tear?

Throughout life, old or damaged cells are broken down and replaced. However, after about age twenty-seven, the rate of cell damage begins to outpace the body's natural repair processes. With poor nutrition, this shift toward greater cellular breakdown may begin at an earlier age. Old cells are not as efficient as new ones, and the accumulation of old cells is what is recognized as aging.

Causes

Wear and tear is a normal part of living and aging. Much of it results from damage by free radicals, according to Denham Harman, M.D., Ph.D., professor emeritus at the University of Nebraska, Omaha. In the 1950s Harman proposed the free-radical theory of aging—that these hazardous molecules chip away at the deoxyribonucleic acid (DNA), proteins, and fats in cells. The cumulative effect is less efficient cell performance and decreased activity of organs, reflected in a weaker heart and weaker lungs, as but two examples. Sometimes free-radical mutations of DNA lead to vastly different cell behavior, such as that of cancer cells.

Most of these free radicals are generated by normal metabolic processes in the body, such as the burning of glucose for energy or the detoxification of dangerous chemicals, such as cigarette smoke. Normally, most of these free radicals are contained in specific chemical reactions, but some do leak out—and additional free radicals may be formed when a person consumes inadequate levels of antioxidants.

Some people seem to age faster than others, a process strongly linked to excessive levels of free radicals. A good example is a woman who maintains a beautiful tan in her twenties and thirties, either by sunning herself on the beach or by using tanning booths. By the time she turns fifty, she will likely have far more facial wrinkles and tougher skin than a person who has minimized exposure to the sun. That's because tanning increases exposure to ultraviolet radiation, which creates free radicals and speeds the aging of skin cells. Athletic injuries also can accelerate the aging process, particularly of joints and bones, and injuries have been documented to create free radicals. The chemicals in cigarette smoke are dangerous in part because they stress the body's ability to detoxify them, generating still more free radicals in the process.

In addition, poor nutrition and leading a hard life increase wear and tear. For example, malnourished people often look ten to fifteen years older than their chronological age. Good nutrition should provide compounds that maintain a normal aging process or, ideally, even slow it down. Inadequate nutrition hurts our natural defenses against a variety of stresses, such as UV radiation, air pollution, and noxious chemicals.

How Common Is Age-Related Wear and Tear?

The sad fact is that everyone ages, and everyone will experience some degree of age-related wear and tear, even while remaining in "good health" late in life. Frailty late in life is one sign of wear and tear.

The Inflammation Syndrome Connection

Much of the cleanup of old cells is performed by the immune system, chiefly various types of white blood cells. Increased wear and tear activates more white blood cells, which are a double-edged sword because they secrete more inflammation-producing chemicals. Immune cells may target specific sites in the body, such as joints, the heart, or bronchi, or migrate and cause more systemic inflammation. A study in the November 11, 2002, *Archives of Internal Medicine* described a strong relationship between frailty in elderly men and women and high levels of C-reactive protein and other signs of chronic inflammation. In addition, frail elderly people also had elevated prediabetic levels of glucose and insulin. All of these factors contribute to the breakdown and aging of tissues—that is, age-related wear and tear—which evolves into a wasting syndrome among many elderly people. Disturbingly, the researchers noted that the 4,700 seniors in their study were healthier on average than most other people in the same age group.

Standard Treatment

There is really no treatment for the normal process of aging, though some hormones may restore many aspects of youthfulness, such as muscle and sexual vigor. Some medications also may improve cognitive function, but nearly all drugs possess undesirable side effects. For example, many hormones can increase cancer risk.

Nutrients That Can Help

Antioxidants such as vitamins E, C, and others often have been described as "antiaging" nutrients because they quench many of the excess free radicals. Consuming a lot of vegetables and fruits and taking antioxidant supplements strengthen the body's defenses against free radicals. Antioxidants also have potent anti-inflammatory properties.

What Else Might Help?

High levels of two hormones, insulin and cortisol, appear to speed the aging process. Insulin is usually regarded as the hormone needed to burn blood sugar, but it is actually a primary anabolic hormone that can increase either muscle or fat. Elevated insulin levels seem to speed the aging process and increase the risk of coronary artery disease. A diet relatively low in refined sugars and carbohydrates, such as the diet described in this book, can help lower blood sugar and insulin levels, which in turn lower inflammation levels.

Cortisol is one of the body's primary stress-response hormones, and high levels stress the body itself, leading to wear and tear. Cortisol also increases the risk of heart attack. The body cannot maintain a biological red alert without paying the price. Stress-reduction techniques as well as the B-complex vitamins can lower cortisol levels.

Allergies, Food

What Are Food Allergies?

Various types of food allergies or food sensitivities (characterized by symptoms, but not confirmed by laboratory tests) can maintain the body's inflammatory response at a high idle. These allergies can exacerbate symptoms of other inflammatory diseases, such as asthma and rheumatoid arthritis, or raise blood pressure and blood sugar levels. Occasionally they can completely mimic the symptoms of other diseases.

Causes

There are several leading causes of food allergies, and they may intertwine. Physicians have traditionally recognized only acute allergic reactions, such as when a person develops a rash after eating shellfish or strawberries. However, most cases of food allergies may be more subtle and difficult to diagnose.

Food Addictions

As ironic as it might seem, some people actually become addicted to a food that causes an allergic reaction. This allergy/addiction may develop as part of the body's response to a commonly consumed allergen. During these reactions, the body releases endorphins, substances that create a natural "high." Any substance that creates a temporary sense of euphoria can become addictive, and in this case people can develop an addiction to the allergenic food, initiating the high.

Often, eating a lot of any particular food (even healthy foods) can create an allergy to it because, inexplicably, it triggers an immune response or it stresses specific digestive enzymes. It is as if too much of any single type of food overloads the body's ability to continue to break it down in the gut. Furthermore, any food can be the source of an allergy/addiction, whether it is junk food or a healthy food. One clue to an allergy/addiction is a food that a person craves. Foods containing chocolate, dairy, wheat, corn, tomatoes, and soy are among the most common food allergens.

Celiac Disease

Wheat, rye, barley, and most (but not all) grains contain gluten, a term used to describe a family of about forty proteins. People who are gluten-sensitive often develop celiac disease, but nonceliac gluten sensitivity may be common. The immune response to gluten can damage the wall of the intestine, resulting in explosive bowel movements, poor nutrient absorption, and a consequential increased risk of dozens of diseases. Celiac disease also can trigger immune responses without any gastrointestinal symptoms. For example, British researchers reported in the journal *Neurology* that gluten sensitivity was the cause of headaches and the likely cause of inflamed brain tissue. Another study, published in the October 2001 *Rheumatology,* reported that 40 percent of subjects eating a gluten-free diet had a reduction in rheumatoid arthritis symptoms.

Specifically, celiac disease significantly increases the risk of a skin condition known as dermatitis herpetiformus, gastroesophageal reflux disorder, iron-deficiency anemia, irritable bowel syndrome, lactose intolerance, osteoporosis, and thyroid disease.

Leaky Gut Syndrome

Leaky gut refers to an abnormal permeability of the stomach and intestine wall, allowing incompletely digested proteins to enter the bloodstream. When such proteins move into the bloodstream, they trigger an immune response. Leaky gut is common in people with celiac disease, and it also may increase the likelihood of a variety of nongluten-related food allergies. A leaky gut can be caused by nutritional deficiencies, stress, stomach flu, antibiotics, and just about anything else that irritates the gut wall.

Nightshade Sensitivity

Some people, including an estimated 20 percent of people with rheumatoid arthritis, react to one or all nightshade foods, which include tomatoes, potatoes, eggplant, peppers, tomatillos, and tobacco (which is chewed or smoked rather than eaten). The reaction may be allergic in nature, or it may be that some people are very sensitive to small amounts of toxins in these foods.

How Common Are Food Allergies?

No one has precise numbers of the prevalence of food allergies and allergy-like sensitivities. Conventional allergists will often say they are rare, whereas physicians who routinely treat them may claim that 90 percent of people have at least one food allergy. The numbers of people with celiac disease are more precise, with the disease affecting about 1 in every 111 people—approximately 3 million Americans and 1 percent of the world population. Nonceliac gluten sensitivity, with often subtle symptoms, may affect half the population, according to some estimates.

The Inflammation Syndrome Connection

Food allergies with documented elevation of IgE and IgA antibodies reflect an immune system that has been unnecessarily stirred up. However, not all food allergies trigger these specific immune responses. It is possible that other types of immune reactions will eventually be identified, or that a person's symptoms occur through some other mechanism.

Allergic reactions may be greatest in one part of the body, such as in the gut or nasal area, but activated immune cells migrate throughout the body and frequently attack healthy cells, causing a wide variety of symptoms. In a sense, an allergic reaction shifts the normal biochemistry to a status resembling a military yellow or red alert. Such a heightened state boosts levels of other substances, such as adrenaline and the stress hormone cortisol. All of these stressful changes take a toll on the body and help deplete nutrients, so it is wise to reduce the symptoms of food allergies to relieve immediate discomfort and to lessen long-term wear and tear.

Standard Treatment

Conventional treatment of food allergens, when recognized, consists of avoidance.

Dietary Changes and Nutrients That Can Help

It is best to avoid foods that trigger allergic reactions. In addition, a rotation diet, in which the same food families are eaten only once every four days, may reduce the chances of future allergies developing. Avoiding an allergenic food for six months to a year sometimes allows the immune system to recover and not react to the problem food, as long as it is not consumed too often.

Several studies have found that low intake of fish and fish oils, or high intake of refined oils (such as margarine) are associated with a wide range of allergylike symptoms, rheumatoid arthritis, and asthma. Eating more fish and taking omega-3 fish oil supplements are likely to help, assuming that you are not allergic to the fish.

Sometimes concomitant allergies magnify a reaction. Concomitant allergies are a little like binary weapons, both parts being relatively innocuous until they are combined. Corn and banana, egg and apple, pork and black pepper, and milk and chocolate are common concomitant allergens. So are a variety of pollens and foods, such as ragweed and egg or milk, juniper and beef, elm and milk.

What Else Might Help?

Because damage to the gut wall is often involved in food allergies, several supplements might be useful in healing the digestive tract. Glutamine, an amino acid, plays important roles in gut-wall integrity. Probiotics, the term used to describe supplements of "good" gut bacteria, also might be helpful. Various digestive aid supplements, containing pancreatic or plant enzymes, might promote the complete digestion of food. Serenaid, a supplement that breaks down gluten, might help people deal with small and occasional amounts of gluten in the diet; it is available from Klaire Laboratories (800-859-8358).

When it is not possible to avoid a food, "neutralization" therapy might help. Minute amounts of an extract of an allergenic food are held under the tongue, from where they rapidly enter the bloodstream. It appears that the right dosage can inhibit the body's response to the allergen. The dosage has to be determined through *provocation* testing, which is done by a type of allergist known as a *clinical ecologist.*

Allergies, Inhalant

What Are Inhalant Allergies?

Inhalant allergies are immune system overreactions (hypersensitivities) to any type of otherwise innocuous substances, such as pollens, molds, and cat dander. These types of allergies typically elevate blood levels of immunoglobulin E (IgE), which is part of the immune response. Pollen allergies tend to be seasonal, causing reactions only when a specific grass or tree blooms, though some people react to many different pollens throughout much of the year. The most common symptom is rhinitis, which, in practical terms, means nasal inflammation, an itchy and runny nose, sneezing, and nasal congestion.

The term *atopic disease* is often used to describe inhalant allergies, but it is often inappropriate. Atopic suggests that such allergies are inherited. While people with allergies are likely to have allergic children, it is now common for children to develop pollen allergies although their parents and grandparents never experienced them.

Causes

When an immune system reacts to something, such as ragweed pollen, when it shouldn't, it is obvious that something serious has gone awry. Pollens or dander are misidentified by immune cells as threats, triggering a massive and physically uncomfortable response. While medical and drug researchers are trying to figure out the molecular details of what goes wrong, they miss the obvious: allergies, on the scale that they now exist, are a recent phenomenon. So what has changed?

Research conducted by Francis Pottenger, M.D., during the 1930s offers a clue about how modern dietary changes have led to significant increases in the prevalence of allergies. Pottenger conducted a variety of dietary studies on more than nine hundred cats. He found that when the quality of their diets declined, health problems developed and grew worse, with each subsequent generation eating the same poor diet. By the third generation 90 percent of cats eating poor diets had developed allergies and skin diseases (which were usually manifestations of allergy). Many vitamins and minerals are needed for normal functioning of the immune system, and suboptimal levels of nutrients and deficiencies impair the normal programming of immunity.

Pottenger found that this trend could be reversed in the second generation, but that it took four generations of normal feeding to once again yield healthy nonallergic cats. That reversal was not possible by the third generation of cats eating a nutritionally deficient diet. Furthermore, the cats became incapable of reproducing by the fourth generation, the last.

If you see parallels between the lives of Pottenger's cats and people today, you are on the right track. Based on the prevalence of allergies, many people (and families) are in the equivalent of second and third generations eating poor diets; one of every five American couples is infertile.

How Common Are Inhalant Allergies?

Inhalant allergies have become very common in Western industrialized nations and rare in less developed countries. Approximately 20 percent of Americans have allergies, which translates to almost 60 million people. As many as 17 million Americans also have nonallergic rhinitis, and 22 million have a combination of allergic and nonallergic rhinitis. Nonallergic rhinitis refers to the symptoms but without any identifiable allergic cause. According to Robert S. Ivker, D.O., of Denver, Colorado, 40 million Americans suffer from sinusitis, one manifestation of rhinitis.

The Inflammation Syndrome Connection

The first phase of allergic rhinitis involves sneezing and a runny nose after exposure to an allergen. This is followed by an increase in eosinophils, immune cells that promote inflammation, and, importantly, set the stage for a hair-trigger immune response after further exposures to the allergen.

Researchers believe that a shift in the ratio between two types of immune cells, Th_1 and Th_2 cells, which increases production of IgE and certain cytokines, predisposes people to allergies. But what causes the shift? The evidence is growing that a diet high in pro-inflammatory omega-6 fatty acids is largely to blame. Finnish researchers compared twenty allergic and twenty nonallergic mothers and found that both groups of women consumed the same amounts of omega-6 and anti-inflammatory omega-3 fatty acids in their diets. However, breast milk from the allergic mothers contained less of the omega-3 fatty acids, which would predispose their infants to allergies.

Long-term, inhalant allergies maintain a steady inflammatory state in the body, generating free radicals that further fuel inflammation. People with inhalant allergies often have food allergies as well. Allergies are a serious stress on the body, causing unnecessary wear and tear.

Standard Treatment

Avoidance of allergens is the best way not to have allergic reactions, but it is easier accomplished when the allergen is cat dander rather than pollen. Over-the-counter antihistamine products block allergy symptoms, but at a cost: drowsiness and an increased risk of cancer. Some prescription antihistamines (Claritin, Allegra, and Zyrtec) are safer than over-the-counter varieties. Immunotherapy—allergy shots—also can blunt symptoms, as can corticosteroid drugs.

Perhaps the best and safest over-the-counter allergy medication is cromolyn sodium, sold under the brand name NasalCrom. Cromolyn sodium is actually a synthetic flavonoid. It works by desensitizing cells in the nasal cavity that would otherwise react to an allergen and appears to have no systemic side effects, an effect that has similarities to the natural flavonoids in vegetables and fruit. NasalCrom is a nasal spray, and it is most effective when used several times a day, starting two weeks before pollen exposure. It also may help in dealing with allergies to cats and dogs. Other advantages to NasalCrom are that it is nonsedating and its activity appears limited to nasal tissues.

Nutrients That Can Help

Some physicians have become receptive to nutritional therapies because vitamin supplements relieved or eliminated their own allergies. For example, Robert Cathcart III, M.D., was impressed by how vitamin C supplements relieved his hay fever, and he went on to become one of the leading experts in the clinical use of vitamin C to fight infections.

A large variety of nutritional supplements might help, but you will have to experiment to find the best combination for your particular body and allergies. Vitamin C (1 to 5 grams daily), quercetin (300 to 1,000 mg daily), and omega-3 fish oils (1 to 3 grams daily) make a good start. Several B vitamins, including niacinamide, pantothenic acid, and vitamins B and B_{12}, also may help relieve allergies; a B-complex supplement may be better than individual supplements. Again, do whatever you can to reduce exposure, such as using air conditioning and high-efficiency air filters.

What Else Might Help?

Many people swear by honey as a way to reduce pollen allergies. It is very likely that honey produced in your region contains small amounts of pollen that serve as a "neutralizing dose," blocking larger amounts of pollen from triggering immune reactions.

Many foods seem to exacerbate allergic reactions to pollens, and it is probably worthwhile testing such foods by avoiding them for a week or so. Wheat, other grains, and dairy products, because of their own allergenic potential, often can aggravate pollen allergies.

Considerable research indicates that a disruption of the normal bacteria inhabiting the gastrointestinal tract can increase the likelihood of allergic sensitization during infancy. Taking antibiotic treatments for ear infections is a common method of destroying normal gut bacteria. Taking probiotic (good bacteria) supplements can reduce the damage when antibiotics must be taken.

Alzheimer's Disease

What Is Alzheimer's Disease?

Alzheimer's disease is the most common type of dementia. (The second most common form is caused by blood clots from ministrokes, a cardiovascular problem.) Alzheimer's is characterized by a serious impairment and worsening of memory, plus a decline in at least one other cognitive function, such as in perception or language skills. As Alzheimer's progresses, it leads to a loss of motor skills and reduced independence in daily activities, such as grooming and going to the bathroom.

Causes

Alzheimer's is characterized by deposits of beta-amyloid protein, as well as beta-amyloid tangles between brain cells. The beta-amyloid protein is believed, in some way, to choke brain cells.

How Common Is Alzheimer's Disease?

An estimated 4 million Americans have some degree of Alzheimer's disease. The Alzheimer Foundation projects that more than 14 million people will develop it by 2050, largely a consequence of 76 million aging baby boomers. Although these numbers may be inflated, the number of Alzheimer's cases is likely to increase because of the aging population and a decline in dietary quality.

The Inflammation Syndrome Connection

A major clue is that both animal and human studies have shown that use of ibuprofen, a common anti-inflammatory drug, reduces the risk of developing Alzheimer's disease. In animals the drug reduces the amount of beta-amyloid plaque. People who take ibuprofen are less likely to develop the disease.

Free radicals are known to stimulate the accumulation of beta-amyloid protein, and antioxidants have been suggested by Denham Harman, M.D., Ph.D., of the University of Nebraska, as one means of counteracting the process. Of course, free radicals promote the activity of adhesion molecules in inflammation. Unfortunately, it has been difficult for researchers to document the presence of specific immune cells in the brain, which would confirm the role of inflammation.

Standard Treatment

Several drugs are used to slow the progression of Alzheimer's disease, including selegiline. However, vitamin E appears to be slightly more effective than selegiline.

Nutrients That Can Help

The role of free radicals in promoting brain damage points to the potential benefits of antioxidant supplements. Indeed, a range of studies with cells, animals, and people have found antioxidants to be of benefit. The most dramatic study, published in the *New England Journal of Medicine,* found that very high doses of vitamin E (2,000 IU daily) extended the ability of late-stage Alzheimer's patients to care for themselves. Researchers are currently investigating whether the same dosage of vitamin E can slow or reverse the early stages of Alzheimer's. However, if your mind is in good shape, 400 to 800 IU is probably sufficient for long-term prevention.

A number of other antioxidant supplements might also be protective, including vitamin C, coenzyme Q_{10}, and alpha-lipoic acid. Specific dosages are hard to determine because of the limited amount of research on these antioxidants and Alzheimer's disease. Extracts of the herb Ginkgo biloba also might be beneficial, though the research has been conflicting. Ginkgo serves as both an antioxidant and as a dilator of blood vessels in the brain, improving blood circulation to neurons.

Some research indicates that the anti-inflammatory properties of omega-3 fish oils also can reduce the risk of neuroinflammation. Given the progressive nature of Alzheimer's disease, the emphasis should be on prevention or reversing its early stages. It is not likely that advanced Alzheimer's disease can be reversed because of extensive damage to brain cells.

What Else Might Help?

Several other nutrients also might protect against cognitive decline and Alzheimer's disease. Acetyl-L-carnitine, 2 grams daily, has been found to improve attention spans, long-term memory, and verbal abilities in some Alzheimer's patients. Phosphatidyl serine, a phosphorus-containing fat, is essential for the health of cell membranes, particularly brain cells. Dosages of 300 mg daily have been found helpful in improving memory, but 100 mg also might work in mild cases of memory impairment.

Difficulty concentrating—that is, fuzzy thinking—is often an early sign of diabetes. Elevated blood sugar levels and full-blown diabetes accelerate the aging process and, presumably, that of the brain as well. The Anti-Inflammation Syndrome Diet Plan is a low-glycemic, glucose-stabilizing diet, and it should improve glucose tolerance.

Arthritis, Osteoarthritis

What Is Osteoarthritis?

Of more than one hundred types of arthritis, osteoarthritis is by far the most common. Osteoarthritis refers specifically to a breakdown of the cartilage pad in at least one joint, such as the fingers, knees, or elbows. It also can affect the neck, hips, and lower back, even resulting in a decrease in height. These pads, known as articular cartilage, cushion the impact and lubricate the movement of bones in a joint. When articular cartilage is thin or completely gone, bones grind directly against each other. Signs of osteoarthritis include inflammation, swelling, pain, stiffness, and difficulty moving one or more joints. Nearly every person over age sixty has some degree of osteoarthritis, though the disease progresses at different rates from person to person.

Causes

For the most part, osteoarthritis is a disease of wear and tear; the more you use your joints, the more you lose them. Overuse, such as in athletics, and athletic injuries can accelerate the breakdown of articular cartilage. Sometimes immune cells inflaming tendons can spread out and affect a nearby joint.

Being overweight, even by as few as ten pounds, also can increase the risk of osteoarthritis. One reason is that the extra weight puts more stress on joints. Another is that fat cells secrete large amounts of pro-inflammatory interleukin-6 and C-reactive protein, which increase inflammation throughout the body.

An often overlooked cause is that relatively few people nowadays consume cartilage, which contains the building blocks of our own joints. In the past it was common to make soups using chicken or beef bones, with cartilage (and other nutrients, such as calcium) dissolving in the broth. Cartilage attached to the bones releases glucosamine and chondroitin, two important building blocks of our own cartilage. It is very possible that people would have less need for glucosamine and chondroitin supplements if they had regularly consumed homemade soups.

The omega-3 fatty acids found in fish oils inhibit some of the enzymes involved in breaking down articular cartilage, so eating less fish also may increase the risk of developing osteoarthritis. Allergylike food sensitivities also may influence symptoms of osteoarthritis. Exposure to allergens often varies, and this could explain why many arthritics feel better or worse from day to day.

How Common Is Osteoarthritis?

About three times as many women as men have osteoarthritis, and about one in every fourteen people (21 million in the United States) suffer mild to crippling symptoms. That number is expected to rise to 30 million by 2020. Overall, one in seven people has some form of arthritis, 40 million in the United States. That number is expected to increase to one in six by 2020.

The Inflammation Syndrome Connection

Immune cells are drawn to sites of injury, where they release powerful inflammatory compounds. Immune cells help clean up damaged cells, such as in torn ligaments, strained tendons, and flakes of bone and cartilage. Many mild injuries may not even be noticed, or their complete healing may be wrongly assumed. Injured tissue is more susceptible to repeated injury, and this situation may lead to chronic inflammation.

Standard Treatment

More than 250 different drugs are used to treat arthritis, including aspirin and other nonsteroidal anti-inflammatory drugs (NSAIDs), corticosteroids, and Cox-2 inhibitors. All have undesirable side effects. Some NSAIDs, such as ibuprofen, actually increase the breakdown of cartilage. Replacements of hip and knee joints are surgical treatments for severe cases of osteoarthritis.

Nutrients That Can Help

For osteoarthritis, supplements of glucosamine and chondroitin, about 1,200 to 1,500 mg of each daily, have been shown to reduce pain and inflammation. One excellent study found that glucosamine supplements can help rebuild articular cartilage, and chondroitin appears to have some anti-inflammatory properties. (For more details, review chapter 10.) Vitamin C is needed for the formation of collagen and cartilage, as are manganese and sulfur. A minimum of 500 mg of vitamin C may be needed. Additional sulfur, also essential for cartilage formation, can be obtained in glucosamine sulfate, chondroitin sulfate, or methylsulfonylmethane (MSM), and small amounts of manganese can be obtained in a multimineral supplement.

What Else Might Help?

A variety of other nutrients, herbs, and habits also may reduce inflammation and pain associated with osteoarthritis. The least expensive change is to drink more water. According to Hugh D. Riordan, M.D., of the Center for the Improvement of Human Functioning International, Wichita,

Kansas, poor hydration is a common problem. Sufficient water intake helps cushion cells and tissues.

Vitamin D may indirectly reduce the risk of osteoporosis, according to research by Timothy E. McAlindon, D.M., a medical doctor and rheumatologist at Boston University Medical Center. Vitamin D is necessary for normal bone development, and low levels may affect bone structure and stability underneath the cartilage pads in joints.

Another study, by Margaret A. Flynn, Ph.D., professor emeritus at the University of Missouri, Columbia, found that supplemental vitamin B_{12} and folic acid could improve hand-grip strength in men and women with osteoarthritis of the hands.

The herb ginger also may be helpful. A study in *Arthritis & Rheumatism* found that patients taking a ginger extract benefited from moderate improvements in knee pain. The study confirmed ginger's use as an anti-inflammatory agent in Chinese medicine, dating back more than twenty-five hundred years.

Two topical treatments also can help. Several studies have found that creams containing capsaicin, the pungent component of hot peppers, can reduce the pain of osteoarthritis. Capsaicin blocks the transmission of pain chemicals to the brain. The effect appears to be strictly symptomatic, but other than a local sensation of heat, it is far safer than acetaminophen and other nonsteroidal anti-inflammatory drugs. Creams containing the herb arnica also may relieve joint pain.

Lastly, mild movement therapies such as walking, yoga, and swimming may improve flexibility and reduce pain. It is very important, however, not to overdo such exercises because they may further break down articular cartilage.

Arthritis, Rheumatoid

What Is Rheumatoid Arthritis?

Rheumatoid arthritis is an autoimmune disease, which means that the immune system mounts a full-scale attack on the body's own tissues. In rheumatoid arthritis the attack is centered on connective tissue near joints. Early symptoms include inflammation, pain, stiffness, tenderness, and swelling. However, this disease also has wide-ranging systemic effects including fever, reduced appetite, weight loss, and fatigue.

Rheumatoid arthritis is generally progressive—it gets worse with time. There may be periods of remission when symptoms decrease or even temporarily disappear. Long-term, it can be disfiguring and turn fingers into stiff, twisted digits. About 20 percent of people with rheumatoid arthritis develop lumpy nodules under the skin. In some cases it becomes completely disabling.

Causes

It is possible that some cases of rheumatoid arthritis are triggered by an immune response to a viral infection. Whatever the triggering event, the severity of the disease reflects a highly disturbed immune system that cannot distinguish friendly cells from foes. To many observers it looks as though immune cells are chasing after biochemical ghosts.

Considerable research has shown that people with rheumatoid arthritis are commonly deficient in multiple nutrients. These deficiencies can impair immune function, and the benefits of nutritional supplementation have been confirmed by numerous studies. Several cases of scurvy (extreme vitamin C deficiency) have been reported with rheumatism as the most obvious symptom. Low levels of vitamin C lead to a weakening of blood vessel walls, allowing red blood cells to leak into surrounding tissue, where they trigger an immune response. Vitamin C supplementation resolved the symptoms in these patients.

How Common Is Rheumatoid Arthritis?

An estimated 2.5 million Americans (about 1 percent of the U.S. population) have rheumatoid arthritis. It affects twice as many women as men.

The Inflammation Syndrome Connection

Levels of several pro-inflammatory cytokines—interleukin-1, interleukin-6, and tumor necrosis factor alpha—are typically elevated in people with rheumatoid arthritis. These cytokines instruct immune cells to unleash a powerful attack. The tenderness, pain, and swelling are byproducts of chronic, intense inflammation.

Standard Treatment

Most medications—more than 250 different kinds—are designed to relieve pain. But none of them treat the underlying disease process.

Nutrients That Can Help

Many people benefit from the anti-inflammatory effect of omega-3 fish oils. However, it may take several months to see an improvement. A Scottish study of sixty-four men and women found that supplements containing about 3 grams of omega-3 fish oils daily resulted in a significant reduction of arthritic symptoms and less need to take conventional medications. Other research has shown that omega-3 fish oils reduce levels of the pro-inflammatory cytokines interleukin-1 and tumor necrosis factor alpha.

Gamma-linolenic acid (GLA), an anti-inflammatory omega-6 fatty acid, may be even more effective in rheumatoid arthritis. GLA boosts levels of anti-inflammatory prostaglandin E_1, which suppresses pro-inflammatory prostaglandin E_2. Human trials with GLA (approximately 1.4 grams daily) have shown consistent benefits over several months, reducing symptoms by roughly one-third to one-half. Of course, results will vary from person to person, and a combination of supplements will likely have greater benefits.

Increased intake of olive oil also can reduce symptoms of rheumatoid arthritis. Olive oil reduces the activity of adhesion molecules, which enable white blood cells to attach to and attack normal cells.

People with rheumatoid arthritis tend to have low antioxidant levels, and two studies so far have found that natural vitamin E supplements significantly reduce symptoms of the disease. The dosage used in these studies was relatively high, 1,800 IU daily. Vitamin E also lowers levels of interleukin-6 and C-reactive protein, both of which promote inflammation. Selenium, another antioxidant, also might help, but the research has not been consistent. The mineral boosts production of glutathione peroxidase, one of the body's main antioxidants.

People with arthritis have low levels of numerous other nutrients, such as vitamins B_2 and B_{12}, folic acid, calcium, and zinc. Deficiencies of folic acid and vitamin B_{12} are often exacerbated by methotrexate, one of the drugs used to treat rheumatoid arthritis. Methotrexate interferes with the metabolism of these two B vitamins.

What Else Might Help?

Many studies point to the apparent role of allergylike food sensitivities in rheumatoid arthritis. These adverse reactions to food can ramp up immune activity and inflammation. Dairy products and gluten-containing grains (such as wheat, rye, and barley) are among the most common food allergens, and studies have found that their avoidance eases arthritic symptoms, including morning stiffness and the number of swollen joints in many people, as well as reducing C-reactive protein levels. The elimination of allergenic foods may explain why fasting and gluten-free vegetarian diets help some people with rheumatoid arthritis.

According to Loren Cordain, Ph.D., a researcher at Colorado State University, lectins also might trigger symptoms of rheumatoid arthritis in some people. Lectins are a family of plant proteins found primarily in legumes, but also in wheat and rice. Like gluten, lectins may cause an inflammation of the gut, leading to a more generalized immune response. Temporarily avoiding lectin-containing foods may confirm a sensitivity to them.

Two additional supplements also might be of benefit: An animal study found that the antioxidant extract of green tea blocked the activity of several pro-inflammatory compounds, protecting against rheumatoid arthritis. Other research suggests that supplemental cetyl-myristoleate also might lessen symptoms of rheumatoid arthritis.

Asthma

What Is Asthma?

During asthmatic episodes, or attacks, the body's airways (bronchi and bronchioles, which deliver air to the lungs) overreact to pollen, cat dander, cigarette smoke, cold air, or other stimuli. The airway wall muscles begin to spasm, narrowing the opening and allowing less air to reach the lungs. An inflammatory response results in a rapid thickening of mucus, which further narrows the airway. An asthma attack may begin with wheezing, coughing, or shortness of breath; suffocation can occur in rare cases.

Causes

Ask ten different allergists about the cause of asthma and you may get twenty different explanations. A nearly mind-boggling number of causes have been proposed: dust, dust mites, cockroaches, house mice, wall-to-wall carpeting, central heating, gas stoves, overly sealed (insulated) buildings, candida yeast infections, pollen, and food allergies. In addition, some people blame urban air pollution. While air pollution certainly can trigger asthmatic attacks, urban air pollution has generally declined, while the number of people with asthma has increased. The same pattern is true with secondhand cigarette smoke, which can increase the risk of asthma in children—but fewer people are smoking, and the rate of asthma continues to rise. Others point the finger at the widespread use of antibacterial cleansers or antibiotics, both of which might reduce routine exposures to bacteria and interfere with the normal programming of immune systems.

All of the above factors can trigger asthmatic reactions in sensitive people. So can a host of other factors, including exercise, cold air, aspirin, sulfites (a preservative used in wines, beers, and some salad bars), and tartrazine (a yellow coloring used in some foods and drugs). In addition, emotional stress can induce asthmatic reactions in some people, and being overweight predisposes some people to asthma.

Like a fish that does not realize it is living in polluted waters, many people with asthma and many allergists don't understand that they are essentially swimming in a polluted diet. The modern diet, which is high in pro-inflammatory omega-6 and trans fatty acids and low in antioxidants, sets the stage for asthmatic reactions. In effect, asthma is one of many diseases of modern civilization and modern eating habits.

People with asthma tend to have higher than normal levels of free radicals, which stimulate inflammatory reactions and also indicate low intakes of antioxidant nutrients. Several studies have found that both children and adults have better lung function and are less likely to wheeze when they eat a lot of fruits and vegetables, the main dietary sources of antioxidants. Breast-feeding also may reduce the risk of asthma and other respiratory illnesses. J. Stewart Forsyth, M.D., of Ninewells Hospital, Dundee, Scotland, noted in the *British Medical Journal* that "nutritional deficiencies at critical periods of fetal and infant growth may induce permanent changes in physiological function."

Other research points to inadequate levels of anti-inflammatory omega-3 fish oils in the diet. A study of almost six hundred children by Ann J. Woolcock, M.D., of the Royal Prince Alfred Hospital, Australia, found that those who regularly ate fresh fish rich in omega-3 fatty acids had one-fourth the risk of asthma, compared with children who ate little or no fish. In a separate article, Jennifer K. Peat, Ph.D., a colleague of Woolcock's, noted that the increase of childhood asthma corresponded with a fivefold increase in the use of vegetable oils (rich in pro-inflammatory omega-6 fatty acids) and a shift to using margarine instead of butter. Similar changes have occured in New Zealand, England, and the United States.

How Common Is Asthma?

Asthma is the most common *obstructive airway disease*. Several decades ago, it was a rare respiratory disorder. Today it affects 17 million Americans, one-third of them children. Its prevalence in the United States has doubled since the 1970s, and African Americans and Hispanics experience particularly high rates of the disease. In Britain the incidence of asthma in children doubled during the 1990s.

The Inflammation Syndrome Connection

Asthma usually begins when the immune system becomes sensitized to an allergen, which may be a food, tobacco, proteins from cockroaches, or dander from pets. The immune system responds whether the trigger is a real threat or not, releasing a variety of inflammatory molecules. An upper respiratory tract reaction may cause little more than a runny nose (rhinitis), but asthma develops when the bronchi or bronchioles (which branch out from the bronchi) start overreacting to inflammatory molecules. One relationship is clear: the increase in asthma is related to the overall increase in allergies—that is, inflammatory reactions to generally innocuous substances.

Standard Treatment

A wide variety of medications are used to lessen asthmatic reactions, including corticosteroids and bronchial dilators. Most have long-term consequences. For example, corticosteroids increase the risk of cataracts and weak bones.

Nutrients That Can Help

Several studies have shown that large amounts of antioxidant nutrients can greatly reduce the frequency and severity of asthmatic reactions. Herman A. Cohen, M.D., of Rabin Medical Center, Israel, gave 2 grams of vitamin C or a placebo to twenty men and women, ages seven to twenty-eight, all with exercise-induced asthma. An hour after taking the vitamin or placebo, their lung function was measured as they walked or ran on a treadmill. Half of the patients had milder asthmatic reactions after taking the vitamin C, while those taking placebos experienced a significant decline in lung function.

Similarly, researchers at the University of Washington, Seattle, gave vitamin E (400 IU) and vitamin C (500 mg) daily to patients with asthma who were exposed to ozone (an air pollutant) and asked to run on a treadmill. After taking the antioxidants, the patients tolerated the ozone and exercise with considerably less breathing difficulty and, sometimes, with improvements in lung function.

Two studies have found that the antioxidants beta-carotene and lycopene, found in vegetables and fruit, can ease asthmatic reactions. Ami Ben-Amotz, Ph.D., of Israel's National Institute of Oceanography, and his colleagues measured lung function in thirty-eight people with asthma, then asked them to run on a treadmill. The subjects had an average decrease of at least 15 percent in their lung function. Next, Ben-Amotz gave them 64 mg of natural beta-carotene (derived from *Dunaliella* algae) daily for seven days. After taking the supplements (equivalent to about 100,000 IU daily), they went back on the treadmill. This time, twenty (53 percent) of the subjects had significant improvements in their postexercise breathing. In particular, these twenty patients initially had an average 25 percent decrease in lung function after exercising, but only a 5 percent reduction after taking beta-carotene supplements.

In the other study, Ben-Amotz asked twenty people with exercise-induced asthma to take either 30 mg of lycopene (the amount found in seven tomatoes) or placebos daily for one week. All of the subjects taking placebos had a 15 percent decline in lung function after exercising. But 55 percent of those taking lycopene had improvements in lung function after exercising.

Ozone, a common component of urban air pollution, is toxic to the respiratory system, and it increases the inflammatory response in people with asthma. However, in a study at the University of Washington, Seattle, supplements of vitamin E (400 IU) and vitamin C (500 mg) daily greatly improved breathing in seventeen adults with asthma after they were exposed to ozone.

In addition, research has found that omega-3 fatty acids—3 grams daily—can significantly reduce bronchial reactivity in asthmatic patients. Other studies have found similar benefits, though the results have not always been uniform. Rather than relying only on omega-3 fatty acids, people with asthma might have greater success by also taking gamma-linolenic acid, vitamin E, and other nutritional supplements.

What Else Might Help?

Many other nutrients help ease asthmatic reactions, and it is worth trying them—in addition to strictly following the Anti-Inflammation Syndrome Diet Plan. People with asthma commonly have low levels of magnesium, a mineral involved in more than three hundred biochemical processes in the body. Magnesium also is a mild muscle relaxant, so it may directly reduce the frequency and severity of reactions. Zinc and selenium also might be of benefit, along with quercetin (which inhibits some types of inflammation-promoting adhesion molecules) and the herb boswellia. A study published in the *Journal of Medicinal Food* reported that the herbal antioxidant Pycnogenol (1 mg per pound of body weight, up to 200 mg daily) improved lung function in patients with asthma. It is also important to maintain a normal weight, because overweight increases the risk of asthma. (See "Overweight and Obesity" in this chapter.)

Athletic and Other Injuries

What Are Athletic Injuries?

Athletic injuries can damage tissues so severely that they ultimately lead to chronic inflammation and pain and a complete breakdown of those tissues. The same can happen for any type of nonathletic physical injury as well, such as a broken bone from a fall or a muscle strain from lifting too heavy an object. Pain and discomfort long after an injury are signs of its incomplete healing.

Most athletic injuries and other types of physical injuries affect the skin, cartilage, muscles, and bones. Muscles strains and sprains, tendinitis, and bone fractures are the most common injuries. Repeated stress to the cartilage pads in joints, particularly in the knees, can weaken these cushions and set the stage for osteoarthritis. Physical stresses also may bruise internal organs such as the kidneys or the brain. For example, many boxers develop neurological damage years after they were fighting in the ring and absorbing punches. Even marathon runners exhibit elevated levels of inflammation-causing substances after a long-distance run.

Causes

Serious single injuries, repeated bruising, and overuse injuries are physical stresses to the body. They crush, tear, or break tissues, and healed tissue may not be quite as sturdy or resilient as tissue that has never been injured. Granted, accidental injuries are sometimes unavoidable, regardless of whether a person is a well-conditioned athlete or an average person who happens to trip over a crack in the sidewalk.

Injuries generate large numbers of free radicals released by activated white blood cells. Studies have found that broken bones and damaged cartilage increase free-radical levels, even without the presence of white blood cells. In addition, ischemic-reperfusion injuries also boost free-radical levels and tissue damage. Ischemia refers to a reduction of blood flow, often the first phase of an injury, which is followed by an influx of red blood cells; both phases generate large quantities of free radicals.

In general, the risk of injuries and painfully slow healing increases with age. Everyone knows that children tend to bounce back from injuries, but adults heal much more slowly. As was discussed earlier, our bodies experience an age-related deterioration. Bones, skin, and other tissues become thinner, and muscle mass declines—these are, after all, some of the signs of aging. It is important to keep in mind that fifty-year-olds don't have the physical attributes of twenty-five-year-olds. The chances of being injured can increase when a person denies the reality of aging and its concomitant decreases in strength, flexibility, reflexes, and coordination. When injuries occur, it is imperative that chronic inflammation be prevented and healing be supported nutritionally.

How Common Are Athletic Injuries?

Every person involved in athletic activities risks some type of injury. Professional athletes are conditioned and trained to minimize the risk of such injuries, but injuries still occur. For example, professional baseball pitchers usually rest for at least three days after starting a game. Weekend warriors, people who engage in sports only occasionally, are often neither conditioned nor trained. They run a high risk of developing overuse injuries, such as tennis elbow, golf elbow, or sore knees, as well as far more serious injuries. "Boomeritis," a term used to describe athletic injuries in the middle-age baby boomer generation, has increased dramatically in recent years. During the 1990s, medical office visits for boomeritis jumped by 33 percent among people between ages thirty-five and fifty-four. During the same time, emergency room treatment of sports-related injuries shot from 276,000 to 365,000 in the United States.

The Inflammation Syndrome Connection

Inflammation is the body's immediate response to injury. It enables a variety of blood cells to flood the site of the injury—platelets to stop bleeding, red blood cells to nourish healthy cells, and white blood cells to clear up damaged cells and fight infections. However, without adequate levels of many nutrients, healing cannot be completed and the inflammatory response cannot be turned off.

Standard Treatment

NSAIDs are commonly used to reduce inflammation and pain, but they can lead to excessive bleeding and ulcers. Some injuries must be treated surgically.

Nutrients That Can Help

Søren Mavrogenis, a physiotherapist in Copenhagen and the physical therapist for the Danish Olympic team, uses a combination of fatty acids and antioxidants to treat injuries among Olympians and other elite athletes. The fatty acids include omega-3 fish oils (706 mg daily), gamma-linolenic acid (670 mg daily), and modest amounts of antioxidant vitamins and minerals.

In one of several controlled studies, Søren and Norwegian physicians treated forty recreational athletes, men and women eighteen to sixty years old, with the fatty acid/antioxidant supplement or placebos for one month. All of the subjects had suffered overuse injuries in sports activities, experiencing chronic inflammation for at least three months before entering the study. In addition to the supplements and placebos, the subjects also received physical therapy. Nearly all of the participants had significant reductions in their inflammation and pain.

Exercise is well documented for increasing levels of free radicals, which can damage DNA. This DNA damage may account for the weathered looks of many serious athletes. Clinical trials have found that vitamin E supplements can reduce or prevent such DNA damage. Vitamin C quenches free radicals as well, and also is crucial for forming new collagen and cartilage during the healing process.

What Else Might Help?

Pycnogenol, a complex of natural antioxidants obtained from the bark of French maritime pine trees, has impressive anti-inflammatory properties. It also increases the body's synthesis of collagen and elastin, another tissue protein. Anthony Martin, D.C., of Montréal, has advised many professional Canadian athletes who have been injured. In one case, a hockey player who had injured his knee was told by his team's physician that he would probably need surgery and be on the sidelines for eight weeks. Martin recommended that the player take 400 mg daily of Pycnogenol. His knee stopped swelling, and after a week he no longer needed crutches.

He was also able to avoid surgery and was playing hockey again after just three weeks.

Several other nutrients may be especially helpful in healing injuries. Methylsulfonylmethane (MSM), 1,000 to 2,000 mg daily, has been found very effective in reducing muscle and joint pain. S-adenosyl-L-methionine (SAMe) stimulates the body's production of collagen. Both nutrients likely work at least in part because they donate sulfur to key biochemical processes. In addition, the B vitamins have an analgesic effect and are required for the production of new, healthy cells.

Cancer

What Is Cancer?

Cancer refers to the growth of abnormal cells, which can displace the normal cells composing tissues. Cancers are often distinguished by their ability to metastasize, spreading to and attacking other organs. There are many different types of cancer, but all arouse fear because of how they cut life expectancy and because of the pain associated with cancer and with conventional therapies (surgery, radiation, and chemotherapy). Although some cancers affect children, they are usually age-related: the older you are, the greater your risk of cancer. In general, cancers take years to develop, and many cancers go undiagnosed until autopsy.

Causes

Cancers are caused by mutations, or changes, in the deoxyribonucleic acid (DNA) that programs cell behavior. These mutations generally occur in two ways: through random transcriptional errors when cells normally replicate, and through free-radical damage to DNA. These errors permanently alter the cells' genetic instructions—analogous to being told to turn right on a street instead of left. The immune system recognizes and destroys most abnormal cells, but some are able to evade normal immunity. As a person gets older, a larger number of cell mutations and poor immune surveillance increase the likelihood of cancer.

How Common Is Cancer?

Cancer is the second leading cause of death in the United States and one of the most common causes of death worldwide. A little more than five hundred thousand Americans die of cancer each year. By far, cancers of the lungs and bronchi are the leading causes of cancer-related death in the United States, and they also are a common cause of death among non-smokers. Breast cancer in women, prostate cancer in men, and colorectal cancer are the next most common types of cancer.

The Inflammation Syndrome Connection

According to Bruce N. Ames, Ph.D., a leading cell biologist at the University of California, Berkeley, about 30 percent of all cancers are related to chronic inflammation or chronic infections. Both inflammation and infections generate free radicals, which can damage DNA, and the level of damage increases when these conditions are chronic. In addition, viruses also can mutate cells.

Standard Treatment

Conventional medical treatments of cancer are generally aggressive and designed to eradicate cancerous cells. They include surgical removal of the tumor mass or affected organ, radiation, and chemotherapy. Despite the many claims of advances in cancer treatment, the cure often seems worse than the disease. Indeed, an analysis published in the *Journal of the American Medical Association* found that improvements in the so-called five-year survival rate in cancer patients had more to do with better (earlier) diagnosis than with successful cures.

Nutrients That Can Help

Good nutrition and high intake of most micronutrients help preserve the integrity of DNA. Because of this, nearly every nutrient can play an important role in reducing the risk of cancer. However, some nutrients may be more important than others.

Antioxidant nutrients curb the activity of free radicals and, as a consequence, can reduce DNA damage. Selenium, part of the potent antioxidant glutathione peroxidase, has been shown to inhibit dangerous mutations to the flu and coxsackie viruses; vitamin E also prevents mutations to the coxsackie virus. Based on this research, it is highly plausible that selenium and vitamin E also might block virus-induced mutations that could give rise to cancer cells.

In general, vitamins E and C and flavonoids are potent antioxidants that can reduce DNA damage from various types of free radicals. Contrary to some news reports, vitamin C does not increase DNA damage or the risk of cancer. In one case, scientists corrected their warning and apologetically stated that vitamin C actually reduced DNA damage. Another study, performed in test tubes, showed no cancer-causing effect, though newsletter headlines claimed that vitamin C did.

Large dosages of vitamin C (10 grams or more daily) do have some benefit in treating cancer, particularly if the vitamin C is delivered intravenously. Many studies also have found that high-potency supplementation can extend the life expectancy of cancer patients, though these studies are often ignored by oncologists. In terms of prevention, vitamin E and selenium supplements are probably the best supplements for reducing the overall risk of cancer.

The B vitamins play crucial roles in the body's synthesis and repair of damaged DNA. Folic acid, vitamin B_{12}, vitamin B_3, and vitamin B_1 may be particularly important, especially in ensuring accurate gene transcription and repair. Some research also suggests that the omega-3 fatty acids reduce inflammation in the digestive tract and may reduce the risk of colon cancer.

Many anti-inflammatory nutrients have been directly linked to lower rates of specific cancers. For example, fish oils are associated with a lower risk of colon cancer. Lycopene lowers the risk of prostate cancer, and one study found that it reduced the size of prostate tumors in men scheduled for surgery.

What Else Might Help?

Cigarette smoke and other pollutants do their damage in large part by disrupting normal DNA transcription and by causing free-radical damage to DNA. Some of the free radicals may be part of the chemical pollutant, other free radicals may be produced when the liver tries to break down the pollutants. Thus, it helps to avoid tobacco smoke, live in a city that does not have serious air pollution, and to minimize exposure to cancer-causing chemicals at work and at home. If avoidance is not possible, the evidence suggests that supplemental vitamin E, selenium, and B vitamins—along with a diet with a diverse selection of vegetables—might rank toward the top of a cancer-prevention strategy.

Several aspects of diet are especially relevant in this context. First, high-fat diets promote the growth of many cancers, such as those of the breast and prostate. For prevention and during cancer treatment, it is worthwhile to reduce and, especially, to alter the ratios of specific types of fats. Several compelling studies have shown that fish oils have a cancer suppressive effect. In contrast, corn, safflower, and other vegetable oils high in omega-6 fatty acid promote the growth of cancers.

In addition, researchers at the University of Utah, Salt Lake City, had determined that diets high in trans fats are associated with significant increases in the risk of colon cancer. Given the fundamental roles of fatty acids in health, it would be prudent to avoid a synthetic fat that interferes with other fatty acids. Thus the ideal approach during cancer treatment might be to drastically reduce overall fat intake while emphasizing dietary fish and fish oil supplements. Under these circumstances it might also be best to avoid red meats and even to limit consumption of chicken and turkey.

Chronic Obstructive Pulmonary Disease

What Is Chronic Obstructive Pulmonary Disease?

Chronic obstructive pulmonary disease (COPD) is a chronic blockage of the airways, resulting from chronic bronchitis or emphysema. Chronic bronchitis is defined as a persistent cough with sputum, without a medically identifiable cause. Emphysema describes an enlargement of minute air sacs, called alveoli, and the destruction of their walls, which impair lung function. When the lungs cannot take in adequate oxygen, the body's cells become oxygen-deprived.

Causes

The leading cause of COPD is smoking, though extreme air pollution can degrade lung capacity. COPD may start to develop within five to ten years after a person starts smoking. Smoker's cough is one sign of COPD, as is the tendency for a head cold to move to the chest. By the time a person reaches his or her late fifties or early sixties, reduced lung function may result in shortness of breath, making washing, cooking, and dressing difficult.

How Common Is Chronic Obstructive Pulmonary Desease?

In the United States an estimated 14 million people have COPD, and approximately 104,000 die from it each year.

The Inflammation Syndrome Connection

Almost five thousand chemicals have been identified in cigarette smoke. Many of these release free radicals, which damage the proteins (elastin and collagen) that form the matrix of lung cells. In addition, white blood cells collect in aveoli, causing inflammation and further destruction of lung tissue. One cannot overstate the damaging effects of cigarette smoke—it is like living in a burning building and breathing in all of the noxious chemicals.

Standard Treatments

Prognosis and treatments are poor, though moderate exercise may improve overall quality of life.

Nutrients That Can Help

Compelling evidence indicates that a number of antioxidants and omega-3 fish oils may reduce the impact of air pollutants on lungs and help maintain normal lung function. This does not prove that these nutrients might help reduce the risk or severity of COPD. However, it is likely that these nutrients would exert some benefits in COPD, as long as they were consumed long before lung damage became irreversible.

N-acetylcysteine (NAC) is sometimes used by physicians to break up mucus in the lungs. Used on a long-term basis, NAC may help protect lung cells. A number of other antioxidants also might be helpful. Studies of smokers and beta-carotene have shown contradictory effects, but a modest intake of this carotene (10,000 IU or 6 mg) *in combination with other antioxidants,* such as vitamins E and C, is likely to be helpful. There appears to be a threshold of benefits from beta-carotene *in smokers,* so the above dosage should not be exceeded.

In a study of street workers in Mexico City, regarded as the most polluted large city in the world, men were asked to take 75 mg of vitamin E, 650 mg of vitamin C, and 15 mg of beta-carotene or placebos daily for 2½ months. When ozone levels were elevated, lung function in all of the men declined. However, men taking the antioxidant cocktail maintained better lung function throughout the study.

Still other research has found that lung function throughout life is related to intake of fruits and vegetables and high blood levels of antioxidants. One study found that vitamin E and beta-cryptoxanthin (found in papaya, peaches, tangerines, and oranges) were most strongly associated with good lung function.

James E. Gadek, M.D., of Ohio State University Medical Center, found that respiratory distress syndrome in hospitalized patients had significant improvements after they were fed a low-carbohydrate formula with vitamins E and C, beta-carotene, omega-3 fatty acids, and gamma-linolenic acid.

What Else Might Help?

There is no pill, natural or pharmaceutical, that will protect a person from the health effects of smoking. If you smoke, try your best to stop. Short of that, eat as many fruits and vegetables as you can. Smokers typically eat few fruits and vegetables, a rich and diverse source of antioxidant nutrients.

Coronary Artery (Heart) Disease

What Is Coronary Artery (Heart) Disease?

Coronary artery disease is characterized by a narrowing of the major arteries in the heart, a situation that leads to reduced blood flow and, in effect, slow starvation of cells forming the heart. The narrowing is caused by several factors, including lesions made up of cholesterol, abnormal growth of smooth muscle cells, and accumulated platelet cells. A heart attack occurs when a lesion grows large enough to completely block blood flow to the heart, or when part of a lesion breaks off and blocks an artery.

Causes

Theories describing the cause of coronary artery (heart) disease often become fashionable and then, after a number of years, unfashionable. Elevated levels of cholesterol were long seen as a major cause of heart and other cardiovascular diseases. The cholesterol theory oversimplifies the multifactorial causes of heart disease, and is being replaced by other theories, though you could not tell that by the large numbers of cholesterol-lowering drugs prescribed.

The two best explanations involve nutritional deficiencies and inflammatory injury to artery walls, and it is likely that both processes occur simultaneously. (They are not mutually exclusive.) One theory, proposed by Kilmer McCully, M.D., in 1969, argues that lack of certain B vitamins (chiefly folic acid and vitamin B_6) disrupts a fundamental biochemical process known as methylation. As a consequence, blood levels of homocysteine increase, damaging blood vessel walls. The body's response, meant to heal the damage, actually leads to the deposition of cholesterol and other substances.

The other theory, which dates back in part to clinical work by Evan Shute, M.D., in the 1940s and research by Denham Harman, M.D., in the 1950s, argues that oxidized LDL cholesterol is swallowed by white blood cells, which become lodged in the matrix of cells in artery walls. More recent clinical research by a variety of researchers, including Ishwarlal "Kenny" Jialal, M.D., of the University of Texas Southwestern Medical Center, Dallas, has clearly shown that *oxidized* but not normal LDL cholesterol is attacked and engulfed by white blood cells. What makes this research so intriguing is this: LDL is the medium through which fat-soluble nutrients such as vitamin E are carried in the blood. Oxidized LDL cholesterol is a sign of inadequate vitamin E intake (or, conversely, excessive intake of oxidized fats, such as in fried foods). Just as the B vitamins reduce homocysteine levels, so vitamin E reduces oxidation of LDL cholesterol.

How Common Is Coronary Artery (Heart) Disease?

An estimated 60 million Americans have coronary artery disease, and approximately 725,000 die each year from it, making it the leading cause of death in the United States. It is also the leading cause of death in Canada and England. Stroke accounts for another 116,000 annual deaths in the United States, with ischemic stroke (in effect, a "heart attack" in the brain) being the most common type.

The Inflammation Syndrome Connection

Research on the inflammatory nature of homocysteine and oxidized LDL cholesterol has helped establish coronary artery disease as an inflammatory process. The role of inflammation in heart disease has become better understood by the commercialization of a highly sensitive C-reactive protein (CRP) test and a shift in the medical perception of CRP. In the past high blood levels of CRP were seen as a marker of the body's inflammatory response after traumatic injury. The view today, which is more accurate, is that CRP is also a promoter of inflammation. It is a direct by-product of interleukin-6, perhaps the most inflammatory of the cytokines.

Although CRP levels reflect a general level of inflammation in the body, elevated CRP levels are a far more reliable predictor of heart disease than either cholesterol or homocysteine. People with high CRP levels are 4½ times more likely to experience a heart attack than are people who have normal levels. Arterial lesions containing CRP are unstable and highly likely to lead to breakaway fragments and clots. It is this relationship between CRP and heart disease, perhaps more than any other recent event, that has raised the medical consciousness of the role of inflammation in heart disease and other diseases.

Standard Treatment

The most common treatment for coronary artery disease consists of a class of cholesterol-lowering drugs known as statins. These drugs currently include Lipitor (atorvastatin), Mevacor (lovastatin), Pravachol (pravastatin), and Zocor (simvastatin). However, elevated cholesterol is more a symptom than a cause of coronary artery disease, so these and other drugs merely alter symptoms without addressing the underlying causes. Surgical treatments such as bypass and balloon angioplasty also are used to correct blocked arteries but do not change the underlying disease process.

Nutrients That Can Help

Many nutrients inhibit the inflammatory process in blood vessel walls and provide a variety of improvements in heart function. Several B vitamins lower homocysteine levels and appear to reduce the risk of heart attack. One study, published in the November 29, 2001, *New England Journal of Medicine,* found that modest supplements of folic acid, vitamin B_6, and vitamin B_{12} significantly lowered homocysteine levels and clearly reversed coronary artery disease in heart patients. Reducing homocysteine levels eliminates a major cause of blood vessel inflammation.

As discussed in chapter 9, vitamin E supplements lower CRP levels and, several clinical trials have found, reduce the risk of heart disease and heart attack. Vitamin E also reduces the tendency of LDL cholesterol to oxidize, which in turn keeps white blood cells from attacking LDL. In addition, vitamin E prevents the stiffening of blood vessel walls (endothelial dysfunction), which reduces blood flow and increases the risk of heart disease. Vitamin E also turns off the gene that programs the growth of excess smooth muscle cells, which also narrows blood vessels.

The omega-3 fatty acids found in fish oils and other sources, have diverse benefits to the health, stemming in part from their anti-inflammatory and cytokine-modulating properties. Research has found that the omega-3 fatty acids can reduce heart irregularities known as cardiac arrhythmias and also can lower blood pressure. In 2001 Danish researchers reported in the *American Journal of Cardiology* that heart patients with extensive narrowing of blood vessels had elevated levels of CRP and had low levels of omega-3 fatty acids. Supplements of omega-3 fatty acids should always be taken with vitamin E to protect them against oxidation.

Vitamin C and the B vitamin niacin (a form of B_3, which causes a temporary flushing sensation) have been found to lower cholesterol levels and to lower levels of lipoprotein (a), a cholesterol fraction that increases the risk of heart disease. In addition, magnesium plays a crucial role in heart rhythm, and supplements can sometimes reduce arrhythmias.

What Else Might Help?

It is of utmost importance to follow a diet that emphasizes nutrient density, such as the Anti-Inflammation Syndrome Diet Plan, which emphasizes fish, lean meats, and large amounts of fresh vegetables. Diets high in refined carbohydrates, sugars, and partially hydrogenated vegetable oils set the stage for insulin resistance and overweight, which increase the risk of pre- and full-blown diabetes and heart disease. Such a dietary approach, combined with anti-inflammatory nutritional supplements, also should reduce the severity of phlebitis, varicose veins, and blood pressure.

Finding some means of stress reduction or stress management is important as well. Stress raises levels of cortisol, which in turn boosts insulin levels—contributing to an increased risk of both abdominal obesity and heart disease. Removing yourself from the stress, even temporarily, can have an extraordinary effect. Consider a daily walk (which also lowers glucose and insulin levels), meditation, a hobby, recreational reading, or sightseeing as stress-reducing activities.

Dental Inflammation

What Is Dental Inflammation?

Three common dental disorders involve significant levels of inflammation: gingivitis, periodontitis, and temporomandibular joint (TMJ) syndrome. Chronic gingivitis refers to inflammation in the gum tissues visible near teeth. If your gums bleed when you floss or brush your teeth, there is a good chance that you have gingivitis. Periodontitis describes inflammation that is much deeper and involves the supporting bone of the teeth, and it is often missed in casual examinations. Periodontitis erodes the bone forming teeth. TMJ syndrome is generally recognized as a misalignment of the temporomandibular joint, located near the ears, which hinges the jawbone to the skull. This misalignment generates free radicals, which can fuel inflammation.

Causes

Each of these disorders has a different cause. Gingivitis results in large part from poor dental hygiene, which allows plaque-causing bacteria to proliferate and attack the gums. Periodontitis is associated with a different type of bacteria, but it is also often an age-related condition because some bone loss increases with age. TMJ syndrome is generally considered a consequence of malocclusion (crooked teeth). However, educator and author Malcolm Riley, D.D.S., of Tucson, Arizona, believes that TMJ syndrome is caused largely by stress, which leads to TMJ muscular spasms and pain.

How Common Is Dental Inflammation?

Dental caries (cavities) and periodontitis affect nearly every person at some point in life. For example, three out of four people develop some degree of gum disease by age thirty-five. The American Dental Association estimates that 10 million people in the United States might suffer from some degree of TMJ disease.

The Inflammation Syndrome Connection

In gingivitis, inflammation develops in response to bacterial infiltration of the gums. Similarly, in periodontitis, the breakdown of bone triggers an inflammatory response, which leads to additional destruction of bone. The inflammatory response activates a number of pro-inflammatory cytokines, which tell more white blood cells to get involved. If these cytokines leak into the bloodstream—a very likely event—they can prompt white blood cells throughout the body to react. In TMJ syndrome the sheering of bone generates large numbers of free radicals, which amplify pain and promote inflammation. All of these disorders are made significantly worse by smoking, which directly exposes oral tissues to large quantities of free radicals and which depletes antioxidants such as vitamin C.

People with periodontitis have a higher than normal risk of heart attack and stroke; people with any of these conditions commonly have elevated levels of C-reactive protein, a sign of inflammation. In addition, people with diabetes and rheumatoid arthritis—diseases with strong inflammatory components—have a higher risk of developing periodontitis and gingivitis.

Standard Treatment

Conventional dentistry takes a mechanical approach to what is a biological issue. Many dental procedures entail digging into tissues, filing away teeth, and building new structures. For example, the standard treatment for periodontitis in the United States is to clean teeth and then to cut away inflamed tissue. This contrasts with the approach of European dentists, who clean teeth and then allow the tissues to heal over many months. For gingivitis, conventional treatments involve better oral hygiene. TMJ disease is often corrected with a plastic cover over the teeth to separate the upper jaw and the lower jaw.

Dentists know that nonsteroidal anti-inflammatory drugs (NSAIDs) such as ibuprofen can slow the loss of bone in periodontitis. So this question arises: Why not use natural anti-inflammatory nutrients? Unfortunately, the answer is that most dentists are probably less knowledgeable than most physicians about the importance of nutrition in health.

Nutrients That Can Help

For long-term improvements in dental health, it is essential that you start with diet. Nearly everyone is taught that sugar-laden foods feed the bacteria that cause cavities. It is not as well known that sugary foods increase gingival inflammation. Cutting consumption of sugary foods and soft drinks reduces gingivitis, just as increased intake of protein and lower consumption of refined carbohydrates, combined with a multivitamin/multimineral supplement, reduce gingivitis.

Vitamin C intake also is important. In one study researchers found that intake of 65 mg of vitamin C daily eased gingival inflammation and bleeding, compared to when subjects received only 5 mg daily. However, much larger dosages (605 mg daily) led to even greater improvements in gingivitis and bleeding.

Low vitamin C intake is related to larger periodontal "pockets" (spaces around teeth where bone has been lost). While there are strong parallels between symptoms of gingivitis and periodontitis and the dental ramifications of scurvy (an extreme life-threatening deficiency of vitamin C), there also are major differences. In scurvy, bleeding from the gums is common, and vitamin C can reduce it. However, scurvy does not lead to the formation of fibrous scar tissue deep inside the gums, a sign of periodontitis. In addition, lower levels of inflammation are found in periodontitis than in scurvy.

Two other nutrients play key roles in controlling dental inflammation. In an animal study, vitamin E supplements reduced bone loss, very likely because it reduced inflammation. In several small human trials topical application of coenzyme Q_{10}, a vitaminlike nutrient, greatly improved periodontitis. To achieve the same benefits, break a soft gelatin capsule of CoQ_{10} (30 to 100 mg), massage its contents into the gums, and swallow the remainder.

What Else Might Help?

Although there has not been any research on the protective roles of omega-3 fish oils or gamma-linolenic acid in dental inflammation, supplements would likely have benefits. In addition, zinc supplements might promote healing of injured tissues. Calcium and magnesium might help maintain normal bone, and one study has found that glucosamine and chrondoitin reduce symptoms of TMJ disease when the joint is affected.

None of this information should negate the value of oral hygiene, but the best hygiene cannot make up for a poor diet and insufficient anti-inflammatory nutrients. Daily flossing and brushing along with periodic professional cleanings should be part of the best approach to dental health.

Diabetes

What Is Diabetes?

Diabetes is characterized by chronic elevated levels of blood sugar (glucose) and insulin. Glucose is the body's principal fuel, and insulin helps shuttle it into cells where it is burned for energy. However, high glucose levels are toxic to the kidneys, and diabetes is associated with a significantly increased risk of heart disease, cancer, kidney failure, blindness, and other diseases. In essence, diabetes accelerates the aging process, so diseases associated with old age occur during middle age.

Causes

Although glucose is blamed for many of the complications of diabetes, growing evidence also points to insulin. For example, people with diabetes who receive large amounts of insulin injections develop vascular disease more rapidly and extensively than do people who use less insulin.

Compelling research suggests that insulin is the oldest, or one of the oldest, hormones in living creatures on Earth. As such, its role is far more fundamental than simply regulating blood sugar levels. It turns on and off various genes and increases the production of body fat and, under different conditions, muscle.

What messes up things? People evolved eating low-carbohydrate foods, which only moderately raise glucose and insulin levels. The consumption of refined carbohydrates and sugars rapidly boosts glucose levels, and the body responds by secreting large amounts of insulin to move the glucose from the blood to cells. However, after a number of years of dealing with large amounts of glucose, cells become resistant to insulin's actions, with the consequence being chronic elevation of both glucose and insulin levels. Insulin resistance is the chief characteristic of diabetes.

Some genetically related groups of people, such as Native Americans, are especially sensitive genetically to insulin resistance and diabetes. But this genetic propensity only means that they develop the disease sooner rather than later when exposed to modern Western-style food. Genes aside, the real cause of type 2 (adult-onset) diabetes is dietary.

How Common Is Diabetes?

Full-blown adult-onset diabetes affects an estimated 15 million Americans, about half of whom have not been officially diagnosed with the disease. (Juvenile-onset diabetes is an autoimmune disease that is rarely reversible.) However, as many as 70 million Americans have some degree of insulin resistance or Syndrome X. Syndrome X refers to a cluster of insulin resistance, high blood pressure, abdominal obesity, and elevated cholesterol and triglycerides. (For more information see my previous book *Syndrome X.*) Basically, anyone eating the typical American diet is consuming foods that increase the risk of insulin resistance, Syndrome X, and diabetes.

The Inflammation Syndrome Connection

High levels of glucose autooxidize—that is, start a chain reaction that produces large amounts of free radicals and "advanced glycation products," both of which damage the body. Free radicals stimulate inflammatory responses and, in this way, people with diabetes develop high levels of inflammation. This situation has been well documented in several studies that have found sharp elevations of CRP and interleukin-6 in people with diabetes. Because of the ability of inflammatory cytokines to stimulate one another, people with diabetes typically have a strong undercurrent of inflammation, which increases the risk of other diseases, such as heart disease.

Standard Treatment

Glucose-lowering drugs such as metformin are usually prescribed to people with adult-onset diabetes. In severe cases insulin injections might be added to help lower glucose levels. As you might expect, side effects are common. Metformin interferes with the body's use of B vitamins, and insulin increases body fat, blood pressure, cholesterol levels, and arterial disease.

Nutrients That Can Help

Many supplements can lessen the inflammation in diabetes, but in this case, supplements can be like bailing water in a sinking boat: It is essential that the underlying diet be corrected.

That said, a key objective of supplementation should be to lower glucose levels and improve insulin function, which should in turn reduce inflammation. The chief supplements for improving glucose tolerance and insulin function are alpha-lipoic acid, chromium picolinate, vitamin E, vitamin C, and silymarin (an antioxidant extract of the herb milk thistle). If you are taking any drug for controlling glucose, be aware that your medication requirements may decrease.

Alpha-lipoic acid, a natural substance made by the body and found in beef and spinach, is used extensively in Germany to treat diabetic nerve disorders. In daily dosages of 600 mg it can improve insulin function and lower glucose levels in people with diabetes. It also is a powerful antioxidant.

A lack of chromium results in diabetes-like symptoms. Not surprisingly, therefore, supplements of chromium picolinate, a common form of chromium, have been shown to improve insulin function and lower glucose levels. Sometimes the effects can be significant after several months. In one U.S./Chinese study diabetic subjects were described as having a "spectacular" improvement after taking 1,000 mcg daily of chromium picolinate for several months. Diachrome, a proprietary combination of chromium picolinate and biotin, a B vitamin, have been shown to further enhance glucose control.

Vitamins E and C improve glucose tolerance and have the added benefit of lowering levels of CRP and interleukin-6. The effect of these vitamins on easing diabetic complications may be greater than their glucose-lowering properties.

Silymarin can have significant glucose-lowering effects in people with diabetes. An Italian study found major improvements in blood sugar levels and many other symptoms of diabetes after patients took silymarin supplements for one year.

By their nature, antioxidants have anti-inflammatory properties. Some antioxidants also influence the production of cytokines, so they reduce inflammation via another means. Based on insulin's fundamental role in biology, it is likely that the hormone controls the activity of some pro-inflammatory cytokines. It is worthwhile targeting a fasting glucose of between 75 and 85 mg/dl and a fasting insulin under 7 mcIU/ml.

What Else Might Help?

A person with diabetes must recognize that he or she has a potentially terminal disease, but one that usually can be modified and even reversed through diet. A relatively low glycemic diet, such as the Anti-Inflammation Syndrome Diet Plan, can moderate the spikes in glucose and insulin that result from refined carbohydrates and sugars. Protein will stabilize glucose and insulin levels, and the fiber in vegetables will have a similar effect because it blunts the absorption of carbohydrates.

It would be worthwhile as well for people with adult-onset diabetes to undergo testing for allergylike food sensitivities. For example, in one case, a person had no significant rise in glucose after eating ice cream, but had a several hundred point increase in glucose after having Scotch whiskey. A rise or decline of more than 50 points (mg/dl) in one hour is a sign of serious glucose-tolerance problems.

Gastritis, Ulcers, and Stomach Cancer

What Are Gastritis, Ulcers, and Stomach Cancer?

Gastritis refers to an inflammation of the stomach wall, as well as of the uppermost part of the small intestine, the duodenum. An ulcer, such as a peptic ulcer, is a lesion on the wall of the stomach. The most serious ulcers form deep craters or bleed. Gastric cancer is a growth of abnormal cells on the stomach wall. Sometimes, but not always, gastritis will evolve into an ulcer and both conditions increase the risk of gastric cancer.

Causes

For many years physicians believed that gastritis was the result of excess stomach acid, and drug treatments were designed to reduce the secretion of gastric juices or to make them more alkaline. In 1983 researchers identified a type of bacterium, *Helicobacter pylori,* in the stomach, and in the 1990s it was recognized as the leading cause of gastritis, ulcers, and stomach cancer. Conventional treatment now focuses on antibiotics and drugs that reduce the secretion of gastric juices.

However, there is a wrinkle to this story. With the successful use of antibiotics in eradicating *H. pylori* infections, a new leading cause of gastritis and ulcers has emerged: nonsteroidal anti-inflammatory drugs (NSAIDs) such as aspirin, ibuprofen, and coxibs. All NSAIDs, including the so-called Cox-2 selective drugs, disrupt the activity of cyclooxygenase-1 (Cox-1), an enzyme critical for fatty acid production and for maintaining the health of the stomach wall.

How Common Are Gastritis, Ulcers, and Stomach Cancer?

Gastritis affects roughly 3 million Americans, and an estimated 5 million people have gastric ulcers. Although stomach cancer does not garner many headlines, it is the second most common fatal cancer in the world, and in most countries the five-year survival rates are less than 20 percent. Chronic *H. pylori* infections boost the risk of stomach cancer by up to 80 percent.

The Inflammation Syndrome Connection

H. pylori irritates the stomach wall, but the immune response to this infection may wreak most of the damage. White blood cells are mobilized to the site of the infection, where they release free radicals and pro-inflammatory eicosanoids such as prostaglandin E_2. *H. pylori* is often highly resistant to this immune response, which can inflame the stomach wall and may eventually lead to an ulcer. Free radicals damage the DNA in stomach wall cells, increasing the chance of mutations, some of which could seed cancers.

The high levels of free radicals in the stomach rapidly deplete antioxidant levels in gastric juices and the wall, and numerous studies have found that gastritis and gastric ulcers are associated with low levels of vitamins E and C and beta-carotene. The situation is made worse when people consume relatively few fruits and vegetables, the principal dietary sources of antioxidants. In a Scottish study, researchers reported that *H. pylori* infection interfered with the body's utilization of vitamin C. When people infected with *H. pylori* ate few fruits and vegetables, their vitamin C levels dropped to one-third less than normal. Another study, conducted at the University of Auckland, New Zealand, found that people with *H. pylori* infections had only one-fifteenth the vitamin C in their gastric acid, compared with healthy subjects. Similar research has found that *H. pylori* compromises levels of vitamin E and the carotenoids, a situation that increases the risk of nearly every disease.

Standard Treatment

Antacids and drugs that alter the osmotic flow are commonly prescribed for gastritis and ulcers. A course of antibiotics is typically prescribed for people with gastritis or ulcers caused by *H. pylori* bacteria. Gastric cancer is treated with surgery or radiation.

Nutrients That Can Help

An impressive body of research, including clinical trials, has found that antioxidants strongly influence whether an *H. pylori* infection leads to gastritis, ulcers, or stomach cancer. Antioxidants can sometimes eliminate an *H. pylori* infection, though it is probably more judicious to use them in conjunction with antibiotics.

The most dramatic study investigated both antioxidant supplements and antibiotic therapy. Pelayo Correa, M.D., of Louisiana State University, New Orleans, asked 631 people with precancerous changes in their stomach-wall cells to take 30 mg of beta-carotene (50,000 IU) or 2 grams of vitamin C daily, a combination of both antioxidants, or a placebo for six years. Some of the subjects also underwent standard two-week antibiotic treatment for *H. pylori,* and others received both antioxidants and antibiotics. Changes to the gut were examined through endoscopy or biopsy after three and six years.

Correa found that three treatments—beta-carotene, vitamin C, and antibiotics—resulted in significant reversals of the precancerous stomach cells. In the treatment of nonmetaplastic atrophy, one type of precancerous condition, people receiving beta-carotene, vitamin C, or antibiotics were about five times more likely to improve than those receiving no treatment. Similarly, people with intestinal metaplasia, another type of precancerous condition, were almost 3½ times more likely to improve. In both cases the benefits of beta-carotene edged out vitamin C, and vitamin C edged out antibiotics. A combination of beta-carotene and vitamin C provided no additional benefits. However, 15 percent of the people taking antioxidants alone (no antibiotics) were cured of their *H. pylori* infection.

Two other studies have found that vitamin C supplements are beneficial. In a small trial sponsored by the World Health Organization, researchers gave 5 g of vitamin C daily for four weeks to thirty-two people with chronic gastritis and *H. pylori* infections. The supplements eradicated *H. pylori* infections in 30 percent of the patients. In Italy fifty-eight patients were treated with antibiotics, followed by either 500 mg of vitamin C daily for six months or no further treatment at all. Precancerous gastric cells were reversed in about a third of the patients taking vitamin C. In contrast, only one patient (technically 3.4 percent) from the other group improved.

What Else Might Help?

Other antioxidants also may offer protection against *H. pylori* infections and their consequential damage to the stomach. Among these are the herb Ginkgo biloba and garlic. Lycopene, a carotenoid that gives tomatoes their red color, has been associated with a relatively low risk of stomach cancer, though this association does not directly prove prevention. In addition, animal experiments suggest that food allergies also might irritate the stomach and lead to gastritis and ulcers.

An estimated 30 percent of people over age sixty-five suffer from atrophic gastritis, a chronic inflammation of the stomach associated with a wasting away of stomach tissues. The condition sharply increases the likelihood of vitamin B_{12} deficiency, which is significant because low levels of these vitamins can cause senile symptoms. It is important to keep in mind that the risk of atrophic gastritis does not suddenly appear at a certain age, but that it is a consequence of more subtle changes to stomach tissue and function. Although research in this area has focused on vitamin B_{12}, it is likely that atrophic gastritis and other forms of gastritis interfere with the absorption of many other nutrients. In addition, antiulcer drugs that inhibit the secretion of gastric juices could conceivably increase the long-term risk of atrophic gastritis.

Hepatitis

What Is Hepatitis?

Hepatitis literally means liver inflammation. It is usually, though not always, caused by a viral infection. Symptoms of acute hepatitis, which generally lasts fewer than six months, tend to appear suddenly and include fever, nausea, vomiting, and a general feeling of being ill. Many cases of acute hepatitis evolve into chronic low-grade liver infections.

Sometimes people with chronic hepatitis may be asymptomatic, and at other times they may experience extreme fatigue and loss of appetite. In both acute and chronic hepatitis liver enzymes become elevated—one sign of liver disease. Noninfectious hepatitis may result from drug or alcohol abuse. Often, the stress of hepatitis reduces levels of glutathione, one of the body's principal antioxidants, which is made in the liver. The viral and inflammatory stresses, combined with low glutathione levels, compromise liver function and may lead to cirrhosis or liver failure.

Causes

Viral hepatitis is caused by one of several viruses that attack this organ. The different types of hepatitis are referred to by a letter, as in hepatitis A or hepatitis B. Transmission of the different viruses occurs in a variety of ways. For example, hepatitis A is usually transmitted through fecal contamination of food, whereas hepatitis B is typically transmitted through sexual contact or shared needles. Hepatitis C is passed through blood, such as through shared needles or through pre-1991 blood transfusions. There are still other forms of hepatitis. One laboratory indication of hepatitis infection is an elevation in liver enzyme levels.

How Common Is Hepatitis?

Hepatitis C has received the lion's share of attention in recent years, and an estimated 4 million Americans have chronic hepatitis C infections. Many people have the disease without symptoms, and it may take decades of chronic hepatitis for it to become clinically apparent. Approximately ten thousand Americans die each year as a result of hepatitis C infections.

The Inflammation Syndrome Connection

Inflammation is the body's normal response to infection. But in chronic infection, the sustained immune activity may cause as much damage as, if not more than, the infection itself. From a biological standpoint, inflammation is very costly—stressful—to an organ. The liver is the body's largest organ, and it functions as a chemical processing plant, building needed molecules and breaking down toxins. This is a complex and diverse job, and the stress of a liver-specific infection is tantamount to a worker strike. When tissue damage and scarring become extensive, cirrhosis or liver failure may be the end result. Hepatitis results in more cases of liver failure than any other cause.

Standard Treatment

The most common pharmaceutical treatment is interferon, a synthetic version of a natural immune compound. However, interferon is expensive and frequently results in flulike symptoms that last for months.

Nutrients That Can Help

Burton M. Berkson, M.D., Ph.D., of Las Cruces, New Mexico, has found that a combination of three liver-supporting nutrients can control and reduce symptoms of hepatitis C. These nutrients are alpha-lipoic acid (discussed in chapter 11); selenium (also discussed in chapter 11); and silymarin, an extract of the herb milk thistle.

In the 1970s and 1980s Berkson used large doses of alpha-lipoic acid to treat *Amanita* mushroom poisoning, which often precipitates liver failure and death. Alpha-lipoic acid boosts the liver's production of glutathione, which aids the breakdown of *Amanita* toxins and promotes the synthesis of new liver cells. Similarly, selenium is needed for the liver to make several glutathione peroxidase compounds, all potent antioxidants. The herb milk thistle has been used for thousands of years as a liver tonic, and its silymarin extract is now recognized as a powerful antioxidant.

As with *Amanita* toxins (and many other toxic substances), the liver carries the burden of breaking down the poisons. Berkson has found that the combination of alpha-lipoic acid (600 mg daily), selenium (400 mcg daily), and silymarin (900 mg daily) is especially effective in lowering liver enzymes and restoring liver function.

What Else Might Help?

If you received a blood transfusion before 1991, when blood banks began testing for hepatitis C, it might be worthwhile to be tested. Even if the test provides bad news, it enables you to take steps to deal with the infection instead of allowing it to quietly run its destructive course.

Infections

What Are Infections?

Infections result from an attack on the body by pathogenic (disease-causing) bacteria, viruses, parasites, or prions. There are many ways to group infections, but for our purposes it is best to view them as either acute or chronic. Acute infections occur suddenly, such as in the case of colds and flus, followed by recovery. Chronic infections such as hepatitis or HIV/AIDS last many years and may be the ultimate cause of death. That said, acute infections can be very dangerous in themselves—the flu kills approximately twenty thousand Americans each year.

Causes

Most pathogens need a warm body to flourish. When they enter the body, typically through the mouth or the nose, and sometimes via the blood (such as through a cut or a transfusion), they trigger an immune response designed to destroy bacteria or virus-infected cells. However, many viruses and parasites can evade the immune response. A person's ability to resist infection, as well as to moderate symptoms of the infection, relates in large part to the health and efficiency of the immune system. The state of one's nutrition has a direct bearing on immune efficiency.

How Common Are Infections?

Everyone contracts an infection from time to time, whether it's a cold or an infected cut. Worldwide, infections have always been and are still the leading cause of death. If all of the infection-caused deaths in the United States were combined, they would add up to the third leading cause of death there, after heart disease and cancer.

The Inflammation Syndrome Connection

The immune system's inflammatory response is designed to kill pathogens. In colds, flus, and other acute infections, inflammation accounts for many of the symptoms, such as rhinitis, tenderness, and aches and pains. The consequence of this inflammation may last beyond the actual infection. As one example, Robert Cathcart III, M.D., of Los Altos, California, has pointed out that the stress of a cold or flu can lead to symptoms of an extreme vitamin C deficiency. That lack of vitamin C limits the body's ability to "clean up" excess free radicals produced by the immune system. These unquenched free radicals can cause considerable wear and tear on the body.

In many respects chronic infections, whether low-grade (such as parasitic infections) or more serious infections (such as HIV/AIDS), are more insidious. They force the immune system to remain at a heightened state of stressful activity, draining many of the body's nutritional and biochemical reserves. For example, people with HIV/AIDS often experience chronic diarrhea, which is likely the result of inflammatory bowel disease. The diarrhea limits absorption of essential nutrients, and high levels of vitamins and mineral supplements may be needed to achieve normal blood values.

Standard Treatment

Most over-the-counter treatments relieve symptoms, but often with undesirable side effects. For example, antihistamines may reduce nasal congestion, but they cause drowsiness and, long-term, they may increase the risk of cancer. Antibiotics can kill many types of pathogenic bacteria, but they disrupt some aspects of immunity and cause gastric disturbances. Some antiviral drugs reduce flu symptoms, but so far not to the extent of vitamin C or N-acetylcysteine (NAC). More powerful antiviral drugs can cause genetic damage.

Nutrients That Can Help

In general, the supplements that reduce symptoms of colds and flus can, in higher dosages, reduce symptoms and extend the lifespan in people with much more serious infections, such as HIV/AIDS. These nutrients do not have direct antiviral activity. Rather, they enhance the immune system's ability to confront the infection, as well as to prevent nutritional deficiencies that further compromise health.

Beginning in the 1970s Robert Cathcart III, M.D., started using large amounts of vitamin C, orally and at times intravenously, to treat patients with a variety of infections, including colds, flus, mononucleosis, hepatitis, and HIV/AIDS. Sometimes the dosages are truly massive, such as 100 grams or more daily. Cathcart found that people usually can tolerate large oral amounts of vitamin C without developing diarrhea when they are ill. As people recover, such large dosages of vitamin C become excessive and cause diarrhea, a sign that the dosage should be reduced. However, huge dosages of vitamin C may not always be necessary. In a review of twenty-one studies on vitamin C and the common cold, Harri Hemila, Ph.D., a professor at the University of Helsinki, Finland, found that 2 to 6 grams of vitamin C daily reduced the duration and severity of symptoms by about a third.

NAC is a potent antioxidant that, despite an unpleasant sulfur odor, has a significant effect on the symptoms and course of infections. It may, in fact, be superior to vitamin C. In a study of 262 elderly people, supplements of 600 mg of NAC daily reduced the occurrence of flu symptoms by two-thirds, and many people with laboratory-confirmed flu infections had no symptoms at all. In addition, researchers at Stanford University have reported that high dosages of NAC significantly extend the life expectancy of AIDS patients.

NAC also can help people with sepsis and septic shock. Sepsis, an infection of the blood, often pushes hospitalized patients to a life-or-death situation—not by a pathogen but by an overwhelming immune response to the infection. Researchers reported in the journal *Chest* that NAC reduced recovery times in patients with septic shock. NAC works in part by boosting glutathione, the most powerful of the body's own antioxidants. Selenium, part of the antioxidant enzyme glutathione peroxidase, increases survival among patients with a condition that has similarities to sepsis, severe system inflammatory response syndrome.

What Else Might Help?

To reduce the risk of contracting colds and flus, it is important to exercise caution when interacting with infected people. For example, wash your hands after touching a person (or touching objects the person has recently touched) who has such an infection. To reduce your risk of HIV and some types of hepatitis, avoid unprotected sexual contact or other exchanges of body fluids, such as through the use of unsterilized syringes.

Supplements of the herb echinacea stimulate immunity and appear to boost resistance to infections. It is possible that, as with NAC, echinacea does not protect against infections so much as it enhances immunity and renders symptoms negligible. Similarly, one clinical study unexpectedly found that people taking vitamin E supplements had 30 percent fewer colds. Lozenges containing zinc, a mineral needed for immunity, can significantly reduce cold and flu symptoms in many people, though the clinical findings have been mixed. The list of nutrients can go on, but it is important to remember that any deficiency impairs many aspects of health, including the degree of symptoms during an infection.

In children food allergies can increase the risk of ear infections. Allergies lead to fluid retention in the ears (which do not drain as well in infants and children as they do in adults), forming a breeding ground for bacteria. Eliminating the most likely food allergens, such as dairy and wheat products, can reduce the risk of ear infections.

Reduce the inflammatory stress caused by both acute and chronic infections. By doing so, you reduce the long-term damage—wear and tear, if you wish—from activated immune cells acting against their host.

Inflammatory Bowel Syndrome

What Is Inflammatory Bowel Syndrome?

Ulcerative colitis and Crohn's disease are the two types of irritable bowel syndrome (IBS). Both ulcerative colitis and Crohn's disease have similarities, and often it is difficult to distinguish between the two. As a general rule, ulcerative colitis is an inflammation limited to the wall of the colon (bowel). Its symptoms include abdominal cramps, fever, and bloody diarrhea. Similar symptoms, generally affecting the ileum (a portion of the small intestine) and without blood in the stools, are generally suggestive of Crohn's disease.

Causes

Officially, medicine does not know the cause of ulcerative colitis and Crohn's disease. However, the fact that IBS affects the digestive tract strongly points to an interaction with food.

How Common Is Inflammatory Bowel Syndrome?

An estimated 500,000 to 1 million Americans have either ulcerative colitis or Crohn's disease. People of Jewish descent are more likely than Gentiles to develop IBS.

The Inflammation Syndrome Connection

The abdominal cramps, which may come on suddenly, are spasmodic responses to an irritant. Various pro-inflammatory cytokines are elevated in people with IBS. The combination can lead to a "leaky gut" in which undigested food proteins move into the blood, causing a broader immune response.

Standard Treatment

A variety of drugs, including corticosteroids, may be prescribed for IBS. The role of diet is often ignored.

Nutrients That Can Help

It should come as no surprise that anti-inflammatory omega-3 fatty acids are helpful in relieving IBS. In a study published in the *New England Journal of Medicine*, researchers described how they gave 500-mg fish oil capsules or placebos daily to thirty-nine patients with Crohn's disease for one year. Only 28 percent of the people taking fish oil capsules had relapses of Crohn's disease, whereas almost two-thirds of those taking placebos experienced relapses. A much higher dose—7 to 15 grams daily—might prove more helpful.

Low levels of antioxidants also might hinder the body's ability to ease the inflammation. Canadian researchers have reported that people with Crohn's disease have elevated levels of "oxidative stress," a sign of inadequate antioxidants—even when symptoms are controlled by medication. For example, compared with healthy subjects, people with Crohn's disease had low selenium levels.

What Else Might Help?

It is essential that a person with IBS investigate the possibility of food sensitivities. The most likely dietary culprits are gluten-containing foods (wheat, rye, barley, and nearly every type of processed food) and dairy products. Eliminating these foods should improve symptoms within one to two weeks, if they were a cause of IBS.

One recent report by French researchers found that half of a group of 171 patients with Crohn's disease had elevated levels of homocysteine, a sign of folic acid and vitamin B_{12} deficiency. This does not necessarily mean that these B-vitamin deficiencies cause Crohn's disease, though they could be involved. Rather, the deficiencies may be a consequence of Crohn's disease that, over many years, could increase the risk of heart disease or stroke.

Lupus Erythematosus

What Is Lupus Erythematosus?

Lupus erythematosus is an autoimmune disease, meaning that the inflammation-causing immune cells attack the body's own tissues. It can affect different parts of the body, such as the skin, joints, kidneys, lungs, and cardiovascular system, and cause a wide variety of symptoms. Some cases are very mild, whereas others may be disabling or fatal. Ninety percent of people with lupus experience inflammation of their connective tissue, with symptoms often similar to rheumatoid arthritis, another autoimmune disease. Other common symptoms include rashes, sensitivity to sunlight, and kidney disorders.

Causes

No one really understands the cause or causes of lupus. Fever is common at its onset, suggesting that a bacterial or viral infection initiates the immune response (although inadequate vitamin B_1 also may cause fever). The hormone estrogen may influence lupus because it is most often diagnosed in women between their late teens and thirties. However, a hormonal link is tempered by the fact that estrogen therapies have not been useful as a treatment. It is conceivable that a woman's immune systems is simply biologically different in some ways from that of a man.

How Common Is Lupus Erythematosus?

Lupus affects approximately 1.6 million people in the United States, ten times as many women as men.

The Inflammation Syndrome Connection

As with other inflammatory diseases, particularly rheumatoid arthritis and multiple sclerosis, some factor or event turns immune cells against their host. Periods of remission are common, though lupus symptoms and tissue damage typically become worse with time.

Standard Treatments

Conventional treatments are intended to reduce inflammation and include corticosteroids as well as a variety of other immune-suppressing medications.

Nutrients That Can Help

Omega-3 fatty acids and vitamin E may help in controlling lupus. The evidence is more derivative than direct, based on the anti-inflammatory nature of these nutrients. A clinical trial published in *Arthritis and Rheumatism* found that large dosages of the hormone dehydroepiandrosterone (DHEA) may be beneficial. Supplements, which are available at health food stores, reduced the frequency of flare-ups. However, DHEA should be used under a physician's guidance.

One intriguing European study, published in *Phytotherapy Research,* found that supplements of the flavonoid-containing Pycnogenol significantly reduced markers of inflammation and disease activity in patients with lupus. Patients taking corticosteroids to suppress inflammatory symptoms benefited from greater reductions in symptoms after adding 120 mg daily of Pycnogenol, and they also had reductions in their sedimentation rate, a general indicator of inflammation. It is possible that grape seed extract and other flavonoids might be beneficial as well.

What Else Might Help?

While there is no clinical evidence to document its usefulness, it might be worthwhile to adopt (at least for a few weeks), a Paleolithic-style diet similar to the Anti-Inflammation Syndrome Diet Plan, as well as eliminating nightshade plants (such as tomatoes, potatoes, peppers, and eggplants). Such a diet provides high-quality protein and antioxidant-rich vegetables and fruit. At the same time such a diet eliminates calorie-dense carbohydrates, highly refined cooking oils, and trans fatty acids.

In addition, it might be helpful to take vitamin D (400 to 800 IU daily) supplements. Researchers at the University of Utrecht, Netherlands, reported that vitamin D deficiency is common among patients with lupus, either because they spend little time in the sun or because of how some medications interfere with the vitamin.

Multiple Sclerosis

What Is Multiple Sclerosis?

Multiple sclerosis (MS) is generally considered an autoimmune disease, in which immune cells attack the myelin sheaths wrapped around nerve fibers. Sclerosis is the medical term for lesion, and in MS multiple scar-like lesions form on the myelin, which is akin to the plastic insulation surrounding electrical wires. When the myelin becomes inflamed, it literally begins to fray, short-circuiting nerve signals and leading to the disease's physical and neurological symptoms.

Different MS symptoms are related to the location of specific nerve damage. They can take the form of extreme fatigue, weakness, a lack of balance, difficulty walking, double vision, speech problems, and depression.

Causes

Officially there is no known cause of MS. However, it is clearly related to an immune response that goes seriously awry. This immune reaction might be triggered by allergylike sensitivities, viral attack, physical injury, or any number of other insults, but the sustained damage appears related to the immune system. Although people with MS may have periods of remission, symptoms typically become worse—and crippling—over the years. On average, the life expectancy of people with MS is about a fourth less than that of people without the disease.

How Common Is Multiple Sclerosis?

MS affects an estimated 350,000 to 500,000 Americans. For reasons that remain mysterious, it strikes more women than men, most often between ages twenty and forty, and people of northern European descent (in contrast to Asians and Africans). According to a study at the University of California, San Francisco, the stress of daily hassles and major life events can exacerbate MS symptoms.

MS researchers have long recognized that the incidence of MS generally increases farther north and south from the equator, correlating to less sunlight. Sunlight activates the body's production of vitamin D, and people living farther from the equator would, over the course of a year, make less vitamin D. This relationship doesn't confirm that a lack of vitamin D increases the risk of MS. But there are other tantalizing data. According to a report by C. E. Hayes, Ph.D., and his colleagues at the University of Wisconsin, Madison, vitamin D can prevent experimental autoimmune encephalomyelitis, the mouse version of human MS.

The Inflammation Syndrome Connection

In autoimmune diseases most tissue damage is caused by immune cells rather than the event (if it is even identifiable) that triggered the immune response. For example, a form of the herpes virus known as *human herpes virus 6* seems to promote MS flare-ups, though most people harbor the virus without developing the disease.

What causes the immune overreactivity? It often seems to be related to a lack of anti-inflammatory nutrients in the diet. The modern diet, with a lopsided intake of fats, particularly highly refined fats and oils, may set the stage for MS in genetically susceptible people.

Although the prevalence of MS increases at extreme northern and southern latitudes, people living along the coast of Norway and throughout Japan have a relatively low incidence of MS. Such populations eat large amounts of fish, which are rich in anti-inflammatory omega-3 fatty acids.

Standard Treatment

Medications include short-term use of corticosteroids to suppress immune activity as well as interferon.

Nutrients That Can Help

Physicians at Trondheim University Hospital, Norway, have reported that 0.9 gram daily of omega-3 fish oil supplements significantly reduced MS symptoms in sixteen patients. In general, gamma-linolenic acid, found in borage seed oil, evening primrose oil, and olive oil enhance the anti-inflammatory effects of omega-3 fatty acids, so a combination of supplements might be ideal.

The perplexing increase in MS in extreme northern and southern regions might be explained by inadequate vitamin D. The body makes vitamin D when exposed to sunlight, but extreme latitudes have long winters and relatively few daylight hours. Recent research by Colleen E. Hayes, Ph.D., a biochemist at the University of Wisconsin, Madison, has shown that vitamin D suppresses the autoimmune reaction underlying MS. In experiments with laboratory mice Hayes found that vitamin D raised levels of two anti-inflammatory compounds (interleukin-4 and transforming growth factor beta-1) and stopped the progression of the animals' version of MS.

Brief exposures to sunlight (fifteen to thirty minutes daily) stimulate the body's production of vitamin D, and people living or working in sunny climates may produce more than 10,000 IU daily. According to Hayes, a very high dose—4,000 IU daily—may be required to achieve normal levels of the vitamin among people who do not receive sunlight.

This dose is ten times higher than the Recommended Daily Value, and because large, chronic doses of vitamin D may be toxic, it's best to take it under the guidance of your physician. He or she can monitor your blood levels of vitamin D, which should be about 100 nmol/L (nanomoles per liter of blood).

What Else Might Help?

Several other nutrients might reduce MS symptoms. Antioxidants such as vitamin E, flavonoids, and alpha-lipoic acid might ease inflammation. Vitamin B_{12} also might be of value. Several years ago E. H. Reynolds, M.D., of King's College Hospital, London, found that MS patients were almost always deficient in vitamin B_{12}, which is needed for normal nerve function. Japanese researchers gave MS patients huge dosages of vitamin B_{12} (60 mg, not mcg, daily) for six months. Their visual and auditory symptoms improved, but muscle function did not.

Because dietary fats have been so skewed by refining and processing, it might be worthwhile to adopt a Paleolithic-style diet similar to the one described in this book. Emphasizing anti-inflammatory fats and studiously avoiding pro-inflammatory trans fatty acids might have benefits.

Overweight and Obesity

What Are Overweight and Obesity?

By clinical definition, a person is obese when he or she is thirty or more pounds over his or her ideal weight. Simply being overweight is characterized by being a few pounds to up to thirty pounds over his or her ideal weight. Of course, a well-trained muscular person might be incorrectly considered overweight because muscle tissue is more dense and heavy than fat tissue. Therefore, accurate assessments should calculate fat-to-muscle or hip-to-waist ratios. From a practical standpoint, a look in the mirror can make much of the testing unnecessary. Most people who are overweight or obese know that they are, though they might want to deny the obvious.

Causes

Overweight and obesity usually are diseases of overeating, although metabolic factors affect some people. The traditional view is that people gain weight when they consume more calories than they burn. This is partly true because many people are not as physically active as their ancestors, but it fails to explain everything.

Often ignored is that diet can serve to exacerbate or moderate a preexisting metabolic disorder. In addition, the source of calories is at least as important as the overall quantity of calories. That is because protein is far less likely than carbohydrate to be stored as fat. In general, high-sugar and high-carbohydrate foods trigger a stronger insulin response, compared with protein-rich foods, and insulin helps promote the accumulation of body fat. High-sugar and high-carbohydrate foods also tend to be short on fiber, protein, omega-3 fatty acids, and vitamins and minerals that either buffer the absorption of carbohydrates or aid in the body's metabolism of them.

Several animal studies have found that some dietary fats are more likely than others to become body fat. For example, some research shows that consumption of monounsaturated fat results in less body fat than does saturated fat, even when both provide the same number of calories. Similarly, evidence suggests that consumption of omega-3 fatty acids, calorie for calorie, might result in relatively less body fat.

How Common Are Overweight and Obesity?

The prevalence of obesity and overweight have, without exaggeration, skyrocketed in recent years. In 2001 David Satcher, M.D., then surgeon general of the United States, described it as an "epidemic." He predicted that the health consequences of overweight and obesity would soon overtake the effects of tobacco. Thirty-one percent, or almost one-third, of North Americans are now obese. They are part of the 65 percent—two-thirds—of North Americans who are now overweight. The number of overweight children also is disturbing. Estimates of overweight children range from 13 to 20 percent.

These increases in weight result largely from the increased consumption of junk foods consisting chiefly of refined sugars, carbohydrates, and fats. A major source of dietary sugar is soft drinks, which the consumer-oriented Center for Science in the Public Interest has described as "liquid candy." A 64-ounce bottle of any calorically sweetened (in contrast to artificially sweetened) soft drink contains approximately ½ cup of sugar! Children have essentially been weaned on soft drinks and calorie-dense fast-food restaurant fare. "Super-size" meals lead to super-size children and adults.

Some physicians have noted that the rapid increase in the prevalence of overweight followed public health recommendations in the 1980s to eat low-fat diets. Low-fat diets usually translate into high-calorie, high-carbohydrate diets that, again, scrimp on protein, vitamins, and minerals.

Being overweight is the number one risk factor for developing adult-onset diabetes, and overweight children and teenagers now account for half of all new diagnoses of diabetes. The prevalence of type 2 diabetes among children has increased by an estimated fifteen to twenty-five times since 1980. Being overweight also increases the risk of hypertension, heart disease, gallstones, colon cancer, and (in men) stroke.

The Inflammation Syndrome Connection

The high-sugar and high-carbohydrate diets that lead to obesity raise glucose levels, and elevated glucose spontaneously generates large numbers of free radicals. These free radicals stimulate the inflammatory response, which can increase the risk of coronary artery disease, cancer, Alzheimer's, and many other diseases. In addition, abdominal fat cells secrete large quantities of pro-inflammatory interleukin-6 and C-reactive protein. In overweight and obese people both of these substances help maintain a state of chronic inflammation.

Increases in body fat are often associated with disturbed hormone levels such as elevated cortisol and insulin and decreased thyroid hormones. Sometimes figuring out which came first is like the chicken-or-the-egg story. However, being overweight leads to hormonal shifts that make it easy to gain still more weight. Because of their cell-regulating actions, it is very likely that weight-promoting hormones increase the activity of pro-inflammatory cytokines.

Standard Treatment

Conventional wisdom holds that people should eat fewer calories and exercise more to lose weight. Exercise helps because it creates more muscle cells, which burn calories for energy. But compelling research indicates that calories from protein and good fats are far better than those from carbohydrate-rich foods such as pasta, bread, and pizza. It makes no sense to build a diet around empty calories. Instead, follow a nutrient-dense diet such as the plan described in this book.

Nutrients That Can Help

The many fat-burning, fat-blocking, or carbohydrate-blocking supplements sold may help a small number of people, but they skirt the bottom-line issue: people cannot take a simple pill to compensate for bad eating habits. At best it is naive to believe that supplements (or medications) can combat a diet full of high-calorie, high-carbohydrate refined foods.

Persuasive research by Harvard Medical School scientists has shown that diets rich in refined carbohydrates and carbohydrate-dense vegetables and grains increase CRP levels and inflammation. In the study, potatoes, breakfast cereals, white bread, muffins, and white rice were most strongly associated with elevated CRP levels. As with diabetes, it is essential that a person exercise the responsibility to choose healthier foods, such as those recommended in the Anti-Inflammation Syndrome Diet Plan. Such a diet should emphasize nutrient-dense lean meats (such as chicken and turkey), fish, and vegetables, while deemphasizing calorie-dense sugary foods and grain-based carbohydrates. The simple rule is to get as much diverse nutrition as possible in every bite of food. That is more easily accomplished with fish and vegetables than with pasta or pizza.

What Else Might Help?

A number of supplements might enhance weight reduction, but they are by themselves unlikely to burn off pounds of fat. Such supplements as alpha-lipoic acid, coenzyme Q_{10}, and carnitine play key roles in the cellular breakdown of glucose and fat. Supplements containing ephedra, a stimulant, may help as well—but they carry risks that include higher levels of anxiety and nervousness and increased blood pressure, and I do not recommend them.

Skin Disorders

What Are Skin Disorders?

Your skin is your body's largest and most direct interface to the world around you. As such, it is exposed to a wide variety of insults, including air pollution, chemicals, sunlight, bacteria, and viruses. Under these circumstances, a vast number of conditions can cause transitory or chronic inflammatory skin disorders. Only a few examples of inflammatory skin disorders will be described here as proof that anti-inflammatory nutrients can be beneficial. Among these disorders are contact dermatitis, sunburn, psoriasis, and eczema.

Causes

Dermatitis literally means skin inflammation, and the term is usually interchangeable with eczema. Both are generally descriptions, not specific diseases. Dermatitis can take a variety of forms anywhere on the body, including itchiness, inflammation, swelling, and flaking skin. Many people consider dandruff a hair-related disorder, but it is actually a skin condition known as seborrheic dermatitis.

Contact dermatitis is often caused by direct handling of an irritating chemical. The body can often adapt to the exposure, which is what happens to people regularly working with chemicals. However, many people pay a physiological price—complete intolerance of the chemical—after a number of years. Some types of contact dermatitis are also caused by specific naturally occurring compounds in a variety of foods. Dermatologists refer to this as "balsam-related contact dermatitis." The term comes from a plant extract called balsam of Peru, which contains allergenic substances, which are also found in tomatoes, citrus, cola drinks, chocolate, and various spices (including vanilla).

Mild sunburn, known as erythema, is actually an inflammation of the skin. It is caused by damage from ultraviolet (UV) rays in sunlight, which split apart water molecules in cells and create free radicals. Tiny blood vessels rupture, and white blood cells respond to the damage. Regular sunburn or more severe sunburn can increase the long-term risk of skin cancers. That is because free radicals damage the DNA in skin cells.

Psoriasis is a chronic skin disease that often begins during a person's teenage years. It is characterized by thick, red skin patches. These patches are covered by white or silvery scales. These skin lesions itch, burn, crack, and sometimes bleed. About 15 percent of people with psoriasis also have arthritic joints, a condition known as psoriatic arthritis. Psoriasis tends to be worse during the winter months, when the air is drier and people have less exposure to sunlight.

Finally, wrinkling reflects age-related changes in the skin, including free-radical damage to the proteins forming skin and a thinning of the skin. Wrinkling can be accelerated by smoking and by excessive exposure to the sun.

How Common Are Skin Disorders?

Everyone experiences some type of dermatitis from time to time. Psoriasis, one of the most common chronic skin disorders, affects more than 7 million Americans. Many people enjoy the darker complexion afforded by a tan, but sun worshipers usually develop premature wrinkling and an increased risk of skin cancer, consequences of skin-cell damage from ultraviolet light.

The Inflammation Syndrome Connection

Research by Lester Packer, Ph.D., and Jens Thiele, M.D., of the University of California, Berkeley, has shown that the skin contains a reservoir of fatty acids and antioxidants. When the skin is exposed to ozone (a common air pollutant) or UV radiation, free radicals are generated, depleting these antioxidants and oxidizing fatty acids. UV-generated free-radical damage to the skin occurs in only two minutes. The inflammatory response occurs much as it does elsewhere in the body, but it is far more visible. A blistering sunburn (or skin burns from chemicals and fire) is a sign of much more severe skin damage and cell death. Also important to note, skin levels of antioxidants decline with age, possibly increasing the rate of damage.

Standard Treatment

Treatments for psoriasis include corticosteroid drugs, both oral and topical. Corticosteroids also are used topically to treat many types of skin inflammation. Sunscreens can block some exposure to ultraviolet radiation, but they are often improperly used. For example, sunscreens protect the skin for short periods, and they are easily washed off.

Nutrients That Can Help

The classic signs of fatty acid deficiency (omega-6, omega-3, or both) are dry and flaking skin. Such symptoms can develop when people are malnourished or eat low- or zero-fat diets. Eating fish and taking fish oil capsules can provide omega-3 fatty acids, and olive oil is an excellent source of omega-9 fatty acids. Adequate amounts of omega-6 fatty acids can be obtained in olive oil and raw nuts such as almonds, or pumpkin seeds.

Several antioxidants have been shown to be helpful in reducing the effects of sunburn. Combined with omega-3 fatty acids, antioxidants can likely ease other forms of skin inflammation through an inside-out approach: take oral supplements and use a topical cream with antioxidants. Vitamin E is the body's principal fat-soluble antioxidant, meaning that it protects against free-radical damage in fatty parts of cells such as membranes. Topical applications are well absorbed through the skin, with some of the vitamin also entering general circulation. In addition, topically applied vitamin E blocks UV damage to DNA. In a recent study Bernadette Eberlein-König, M.D., of the Technical University of Munich, measured how daily oral supplements of vitamin E (1,000 IU) and vitamin C (2,000 mg) increased resistance to UV rays. She found that subjects taking the vitamins were about 34 percent more resistant to sunburn, compared to people taking placebos.

Vitamin C also can reduce the damaging effects of UV radiation. A study by Steven S. Traikovich, D.O., of Phoenix, Arizona, found that a vitamin C–containing lotion was able to reduce fine wrinkles, roughness, and skin tone compared to a similar lotion without the vitamin. Vitamin C is essential for the body's production of collagen and elastin, two of the key proteins forming skin. In addition, several studies have found that beta-carotene supplements enhance the protective effects of sunscreen, illustrating the benefits of an inside-out approach to skin care.

Pycnogenol, a complex of antioxidant flavonoids extracted from the bark of French maritime pine trees, has been shown to reduce inflammation and, specifically, protect skin cells. Laboratory experiments have shown that Pcynogenol decreases the activity of two genes, calgranulin A and B, which are overactive in psoriasis and some other skin disorders. Pycnogenol decreased the activity of calgranulin A and B by twenty-two times. Other researchers have shown that Pycnogenol helps prevent the breakdown of elastin from inflammation and free radicals.

What Else Might Help?

Like many herbs, chamomile *(Matricaria chamomilla)* is rich in antioxidants. In Germany it has a rich history of use in treating skin disorders and also is found in many modern cosmetics. Allergist Holger Biltz, M.D., of Bad Honnef, Germany, found that a chamomile-containing cream reduced reddening after UV exposure and reduced skin roughness. One high-quality line of chamomile-containing skin products is CamoCare, available at many natural foods stores and pharmacies. Green tea also is a powerful antioxidant and may be helpful in some skin disorders.

A wholesome diet, similar to the Anti-Inflammation Syndrome Diet Plan, can help preserve the skin. Australian researchers have reported that people eating diets with large amounts of olive oil, fish, and vegetables experienced less facial wrinkling compared with people who ate more red meat, processed deli meats, soft drinks, and pastries.

Lastly, it is paramount not to smoke tobacco products and not to be in the sun long enough to get sunburned. Smokers develop a particular type of facial wrinkling, which is related to their premature aging in general. Approximately fifteen minutes of sun exposure daily are sufficient for the body to make large amounts of vitamin D, but not enough to result in sunburn (for most individuals). Longer sun exposure should be accompanied by the use of sunscreen or UV-blocking clothing.

Staying Healthy for Life

The prevalence of inflammatory diseases has clearly increased over the past several decades. Part of this increase is related to the overall aging of the population. After all, inflammation is one consequence of age-related wear and tear on the body. Millions of people already suffer from a variety of inflammatory diseases. And in the United States alone, almost 80 million baby boomers (born between 1946 and 1963) are entering middle age, a time when even the healthiest people are likely to notice some deterioration in their health.

However, I am convinced that the increase in inflammation has accelerated as a consequence of eating a poor or unbalanced diet, a situation others have described as malnutrition on a full stomach. For example, fat cells produce large amounts of inflammation-causing substances, such as interleukin-6 and C-reactive protein. With two-thirds of the population now overweight, it is easy to see how large numbers of people have set the stage for chronic inflammatory diseases.

Physicians and biomedical researchers are starting to appreciate the significance of the Inflammation Syndrome—how many different inflammatory diseases are interrelated. As one example, being overweight significantly increases the risk of developing diabetes, a disease with a strong undercurrent of inflammation. Both overweight and diabetes increase the risk of coronary artery disease, now recognized as being inflammatory in origin.

What many health professionals have missed, however, is that early signs of inflammation—whether a minor condition, such as gingivitis, or an asymptomatic elevated C-reactive protein level—stimulate inflammation throughout the body, increasing wear and tear and boosting the risk of far more serious inflammatory disorders. Recognizing the early signs of inflammation can be as valuable to us as canaries in cages were to miners a century ago. The canaries provided an early warning of poisonous gas, allowing miners to escape to the surface with their lives. Similarly, paying attention to—and taking action to reverse—minor types inflammation can help us reduce the risk of very serious diseases such as arthritis, heart disease, Alzheimer's disease, and some types of cancer.

Throughout this book, a key message has been stated and restated: our physical bodies, and our health, are directly related to the quality and diversity of nutrients we consume. The situation is analogous to the construction of a house. When quality building materials are used, the house has a sound foundation and structure. When shoddy building materials are used, the foundation and structure are weak and won't last as long.

We can control the quality of nutrients we consume—the building materials of our bodies. We can consume foods that stimulate inflammation, which is unfortunately what the majority of people seem to be doing, or we can eat foods that naturally reduce inflammation.

The Inflammation Syndrome is about making choices that can improve our health. As individuals, we hold our futures in the palms of our hands. We can choose to ignore the evidence and take our chances with long-term health. Or we can take many steps to improve our chances of having a long and healthy life.

Medical Tests to Assess Inflammation

If you would like more precise, medically supervised testing for inflammatory disorders, it might be worthwhile to consult a nutritionally oriented physician. (See appendix B for referral services.) Such a physician is often willing to do a number of tests beyond those of many conventional physicians. Although health maintenance organizations (HMOs) are not likely to cover such services, standard insurance policies may cover part of the costs.

Among the tests that would be helpful are:

- high- or ultrasensitive C-reactive protein to measure systemic inflammation and cardiovascular risk;
- oxidative-stress panel to measure levels of antioxidant vitamins and free radicals;
- fatty acid profile to determine levels of pro- and anti-inflammatory fats;
- food allergy profile, including IgE and IgG reactions, to indicate allergies;
- fecal microbiology test to evaluate pathogens and beneficial bacteria in the gastrointestinal tract;
- intestinal permeability to determine whether leaky gut is contributing to allergylike sensitivities;
- fasting and two-hour glucose and insulin levels to determine whether impaired glucose tolerance and hyperinsulinemia (diabetic and prediabetic condition) are factors in inflammation.

Sources of Anti-Inflammatory Products

Nutritional Supplements

Many companies market a variety of anti-inflammatory supplements. Although these companies are not allowed to make a therapeutic claim for nutritional supplements, many of their product names are often very suggestive, and clerks in health food stores and pharmacies can often provide guidance.

Some products are formulated as general anti-inflammatory supplements with many ingredients, whereas others are stand-alone products such as omega-3 fish oil, gamma-linolenic acid (GLA), glucosamine, and vitamin E supplements. The following companies produce and market high-quality products.

ABKIT, Inc.

Abkit manufactures the CamoCare line of skin-care products with chamomile and AlphaBetic, a once-a-day supplement for people with diabetes. Many of these products are available at health food stores, natural foods groceries, and pharmacies. For more information call 800-226-6227 or go to www.abkit.com.

Advanced Physicians Products

Founded by a nutritionally oriented physician, APP offers a broad line of excellent vitamin and mineral supplements, including omega-3 fish oils, natural vitamin E, and many other products. APP also is a source for Coromega fish oils. (See ERBL below.) For more information call 800-220-7687 or go to www.nutritiononline.com.

Bioforce

Bioforce is a Swiss maker of herbal products—mostly tinctures, but also some tablets and ointments. The products are not standardized in the conventional sense, but the company's manufacturing controls ensure consistency and high-quality products. For more information call 877-232-6060 or go to www.bioforce.com.

J. R. Carlson Laboratories

Carlson Laboratories offers the widest selection of natural vitamin E products, including supplements, creams, ointments, suppositories, and more. The company also sells a wide range of other vitamin and mineral supplements, including omega-3 fish oils, GLA, and glucosamine. For more information call toll-free 888-234-5656 or go to www.carlson labs.com.

ERBL

Erbl, Inc., markets Coromega, an orange-flavored omega-3 fish oil supplement that comes in squeezable foil packets, a taste and form factor that often appeals to children. For more information call 877-275-3725 or go to www.coromega.com.

Nature's Way

Nature's Way is a leading herb supplement company, with most of its 350 products sold in capsule form. Some of the company's products are standardized; others are whole herb products. For more information call 801-489-1500 or go to www.naturesway.com.

Nordic Naturals

Nordic Naturals markets a line of high-quality varied fish oil capsules, with slight differences in formulation designed to support joints, the cardiovascular system, and brain function. Some of the products are flavored to mask the "fishy" quality of omega-3 fatty acids. For more information call 800-662-2544 or go to www.nordicnaturals.com.

Nutricology/Allergy Research Group

Nutricology/Allergy Research Group is often at the cutting edge of original and useful nutritional supplements. Its main anti-inflammatory products are Enzocaine and Inflamed. Like most of the other companies listed in this section, it is known for exceptional quality. For more information call 800-545-9960 or go to www.nutricology.com.

Nutrition 21

This company supplies "raw materials" for more familiar brands of supplements. Nutrition 21 is the maker of Chromax chromium picolinate, the form of chromium best documented in clinical trials with diabetic subjects. The company also manufactures Diachrome, a proprietary combination of chromium picolinate and biotin (a B vitamin), which also helps control blood sugar levels. You may find the name Chromax in fine print on the back of supplements. The Nutrition 21 brand of Diachrome can be purchased by calling 800-343-3082 or 914-701-4500, ext. 517.

PharmaNord

This Scandinavian company markets Bio-Sport, which contains anti-inflammatory fish oils and antioxidants. The product has been used extensively in Europe, particularly by the Danish Olympic team to ease inflammatory injuries. It is currently available through limited distribution in the United States. For more information go to www.pharma nord.com.

Pure Scientific

This company markets an expanding line of Advantig brand supplements that preventively target different aspects of inflammation, such as joint, heart, and gastrointestinal health. These are innovative products that address some of the major focal points of inflammatory disorders. For example, the Advantig product for joint health includes many anti-inflammatory nutrients and herbs, including MSM, curcumin, ginseng, quercetin, N-acetylcysteine, green tea, grape seed extract, bromelain, alpha-lipoic acid, carotenoids, and flavonoids. For more information go to www.advantig.net (note the .net address, not .com) or call toll-free 877-877-4566.

Thorne Research

Thorne is one of the most morally ethical supplement companies, and product quality is exceptionally high. The company sells primarily to physicians, but it also accepts orders from consumers (mail order only). Thorne has a broad line of products, including many anti-inflammatory nutrients. Its MediClear product provides nutritional support for inflammation, allergies, and gastrointestinal integrity. For more information call 208-263-1337 or go to www.thorne.com.

UltraBalance Medical Foods

UltraInflamX, which is distributed by Metagenics, Inc., *only to physicians,* is a meal supplement designed with many anti-inflammatory nutrients. Ask your physician to obtain information directly from the company at 800-843-9660 or go to www.ultrabalance.com.

Vitamin Shoppe

This mail order company sells most (not all) leading health food brands of supplements discounted by 25 to 30 percent, which can lead to substantial savings. For more information call 800-223-1216.

Natural Grocers

The Anti-Inflammation Syndrome Diet Plan recommends eating fresh and natural foods. Your best bet for finding meat from range-fed animals and organic fruits and vegetables is a natural foods grocery store such as Wild Oats, Whole Foods, or one of the many independent stores. One of the best independent chains (but without fresh meat or fish) is Vitamin Cottage, with about a dozen stores in Denver and Colorado Springs. Trader Joe's grocery stores also have many high-quality meats, fish, fruits, and vegetables, though they are not always organically produced.

Trader Joe's

Trader Joe's is a chain of offbeat but high-quality "specialty retail" grocery stores, with many organic, gluten-free, and wholesome products.

You won't find the selection of a large supermarket, but the meats, vegetables, and seafood (frozen) are of exceptional quality and at comparatively reasonable prices. For more information and the locations of Trader Joe's stores go to www.traderjoes.com.

Wild Oats

This national chain emphasizes natural and gourmet foods. Wild Oats' meat departments offer free-range meats. For more information call 800-494-WILD or go to www.wildoats.com.

Whole Foods

Like Wild Oats, the emphasis is on wholesome, natural foods, including free-range meats, organic produce, and a wide variety of other healthful food products. For more information go to www.wholefoods.com.

Specialty Foods

Australian Mac Nut Oil

Macadamia nut oil is rich in oleic acid, a beneficial anti-inflammatory omega-9 fat. This product, sold under Dr. Pescatore's Healthy! for Good label, is cold-processed without chemicals. It has a high smoke point, so it can be used (if necessary) at very high stir-frying temperatures. Because of its subtle, nutty aroma, it can be used as an alternative to olive oil. For more information call toll-free 888-350-8446.

Czimer's Game and Seafood

If you live in the Chicago area, you are lucky to be near one of the most venerable purveyors of game meat. Czimer's has been in the retail business for more than thirty-five years, selling venison, bear, antelope, and other game meats. It's open Monday through Saturdays and is at 13136 West 159th Street, Lockport, IL 60441. For more information call 708-301-0500.

Earth Song Whole Foods

Earth Song makes several whole grain (some gluten-free) snack bars that redefine the meaning of a wholesome sweet. Among the bars are apple-walnut and cranberry-orange. In addition, Earth Song blends an excellent gluten-free muesli, known as Grandpa's Secret Omega-3 Muesli, which makes for a tasty and quick breakfast (if you take about five minutes to prepare it the night before). For more information call 877-327-8476 or go to www.earthsongwholefoods.com.

Eggland's Best

Eggland's Best is one of several egg producers that feed their chickens extra vitamins and fatty acids and, as a consequence, get eggs with higher levels of vitamin E and omega-3 fatty acids and lower levels of saturated fats. For more information call 610-265-6500 or go to www.eggland.com.

Greatbeef.com

Greatbeef.com is supported by more than a dozen independent family farmers who humanely raise livestock and chicken. Most of the animals are free-range or pasture-fed, with the result being meat with a natural balance of fatty acids and less saturated fat. Members of Greatbeef.com are in Arizona, California, Colorado, Iowa, Minnesota, Missouri, Nebraska, Nevada, Oregon, Pennsylvania, Tennessee, Texas, and Virginia. For more information about specific ranchers and how to buy meat from them go to www.greatbeef.com.

Lotus Foods

Lotus Foods offers a variety of original and tasty rice and rice flour products, including Bhutanese Red Rice and purple Forbidden Rice. The different rices will enhance your appreciation of rice, and the flours can be used to "bread" fish and chicken as well as to make gluten-free crepes. This company's products are truly exceptional. If your health food store does not carry Lotus Foods' rice and rice flours, ask it to order these products. For more information call 510-525-3137 or go to www. lotusfoods.com to order or to find recipes.

Northwest Natural

Northwest Natural makes frozen salmon burgers, halibut burgers, and tuna with pesto medallions, which can be pan fried or microwaved for a quick lunch (with a side vegetable dish). The company's products are sold by Wild Oats and other natural foods grocers. For more information call 360-866-9661.

Omega Nutrition

Omega Nutrition produces a broad selection of unrefined, organic, and minimally processed cooking oils, which can be shipped directly to your home. For information call 800-661-3529 or go to www.omega flo.com.

Pilgrim's Pride EggsPlus

Pilgrim's Pride, one of the largest egg producers in the United States, offers eggs fortified with omega-3 fatty acids. For more information call 800-824-1159.

Van's International Foods

Van's makes several excellent (and some wheat-free) waffles that can be part of a breakfast or dessert. For example, at breakfast, butter a Van's apple-cinnamon waffle with almond butter. For more information go to www.vansintl.com.

Wild Salmon Sources

Wild salmon contains a higher portion of anti-inflammatory omega-3 fatty acids compared with farmed salmon. By 2004, labeling laws will require distributors to identify the country of origin and whether the salmon was wild or farmed. For now, all types of Alaskan salmon—including king, coho, and sockeye—are always wild. You can also order wild salmon online from takusmokeries.com, alaskafoods.com, copperriver seafood.com, and ilovesalmon.com.

Nutritionally Oriented Organizations and Physicians

American College for Advancement in Medicine
www.acam.org

International Association for Orthomolecular Medicine
www.orthomed.org

American Association of Naturopathic Physicians

www.aanp.org

Health Practitioners Mentioned in This Book

Burton M. Berkson, M.D., Ph.D., Las Cruces, NM; phone: 505-524-3720

Ashton Embry; e-mail: AEmbry@NRCan.gc.ca; Web site: www.direct-ms.org

Abram Hoffer, M.D., Ph.D., Victoria, BC, Canada; phone: 250-386-8756

Ronald E. Hunninghake, M.D., Wichita, KS; phone: 316-682-3100

Judy A. Hutt, N.D., Tucson, AZ; phone: 520-887-4287

Robert S. Ivker, D.O., Denver, CO; phone: 888-434-0033; Web site: www.thrivinghealth.com

Richard Kunin, M.D., San Francisco, CA; phone: 415-346-2500

Shari Lieberman, Ph.D., New York, NY; phone: 212-439-8728

Søren Mavrogenis, Copenhagen, Denmark; phone: 45-33-33-8009; e-mail: cph@centrumfys.dk

Hugh D. Riordan, M.D., Wichita, KS; phone: 316-682-3100

Hunter Yost, M.D., Tucson, AZ; phone: 520-219-5060; Web site: doctor.medscape.com/HunterYostMD

Laboratories for Testing Nutrient Levels

The most scientific way of supplementing is to start by having your levels of vitamins, minerals, and fats measured. In that way you know exactly which nutrients you should increase. Most testing laboratories prefer to work with physicians. These three laboratories are well respected for their analytical capabilities. Physicians can prepare blood for shipment to them.

Bright Spot for Health
316-682-3100
www.brightspot.org

Great Smokies Diagnostic Laboratory
800-522-4762
www.greatsmokies-lab.com

Pantox Laboratories
619-272-3885
www.pantox.com

Newsletters, Magazines, Books, and Web Sites

Many publications provide excellent information on diet and supplements, though sometimes you may have to navigate contradictory information or ignore information inconsistent with the Anti-Inflammation Syndrome Diet Plan.

Newsletters and Magazines

The Nutrition Reporter

This monthly newsletter, produced by Jack Challem (the author of this book), summarizes recent research on vitamins, minerals, and herbs. The annual subscription rate is $26 ($48 CND for Canada, $38 U.S. funds for all other countries). For a sample issue, send a business-size self-addressed envelope, with postage for two ounces, to *The Nutrition Reporter,* P.O. Box 30246, Tucson, AZ 85751. Sample issues also are available at www.nutritionreporter.com.

Let's Live

This monthly magazine focuses on how diet, nutrition, and supplements help maintain health and reverse disease. The annual subscription is $15.95. To order, call 800-365-3790.

Natural Health

Natural Health eclectically covers the entire range of natural health— supplements, herbs, home remedies, diet, food, and lifestyle. Its articles are well researched and thorough. The annual subscription is $17.95. To order, call 800-526-8440.

Books

Syndrome X: The Complete Nutritional Program to Prevent and Reverse Insulin Resistance by Jack Challem, Burton Berkson, M.D., Ph.D., and Melissa Diane Smith (New York: John Wiley & Sons, 2000; $14.95). With a diet program similar to the Anti-Inflammation Syndrome Diet Plan, *Syndrome X* focuses more on preventing diabetes and heart disease, as well as losing weight.

The Paleo Diet by Loren Cordain, Ph.D. (New York: John Wiley & Sons, 2001; $24.95). Cordain, one of the leading experts on the Paleolithic diet, describes that diet, which can be considered the original Anti-Inflammation Syndrome Diet Plan.

Why Grassfed Is Best!: The Surprising Benefits of Grassfed Meat, Eggs, and Dairy Products by Jo Robinson (Vashon, WA: Vashon Island Press, 2000; $7.50). This small book (128 pages) is worth every penny. It makes a powerful case for eating grassfed meats and other foods, most of which are compatible with the Anti-Inflammation Syndrome Diet Plan. Included is a list of sources for meat from free-range and pasture-fed animals. Order it from Vashon Island Press, 29428 129th Avenue SW, Vashon, WA 98070. For more information call 206-463-4156. You also can order it from www.thestoreforhealthyliving.com. Add $4.50 for shipping and handling.

Going Against the Grain: How Reducing and Avoiding Grains Can Revitalize Your Health by Melissa Diane Smith (Chicago: Contemporary Books, 2002; $14.95). This book explores how the cultivation and consumption of grains led to a deterioration in people's health. Smith provides dietary plans for having low-grain and zero-grain diets.

Know Your Fats: The Complete Primer for Understanding the Nutrition of Fats, Oils, and Cholesterol by Mary G. Enig, Ph.D. (Silver Spring, MD: Bethesda Press, 2000; $29.95). Though technical, *Know Your Fats* may be the most comprehensive consumer book on making sense of the many dietary fats. For more information e-mail customer@bethesda press.com or go to bethesdapress.com.

Web Sites

The Official Anti-Inflammation Syndrome Diet Plan Web Site
www.stopinflammation.com

The Nutrition Reporter
Dozens of articles on vitamins and minerals.
www.nutritionreporter.com

Consumerlab.com
Independent reports evaluating whether specific nutritional supplements contain what their labels say. Although Consumerlab.com performs fair and independent evaluations, it tests only a small percentage of the nutritional supplements on the market, and it identifies only those that pass (not those that fail) testing.
www.consumerlab.com

Medline
The world's largest database of medical journal articles, providing free abstracts (summaries) of more than 8 million articles.
www.ncbi.nlm.nih.gov

Melissa Diane Smith
Nutrition consultant and expert on the health hazards of grains, including information from the book *Going Against the Grain.*
www.melissadianesmith.com

Merck Manual
The online edition of your physician's standard medical reference book.
www.merck.com

Nutrient Data Laboratory Food Composition
Type in nearly any food or food product and you instantly get its nutritional breakdown per cup or 100 grams.
www.nal.usda.gov/fnic/foodcomp/

Paleo Diet/Recipes
Most of these modern verions of Paleolithic recipes are compatible with the Anti-Inflammation Syndrome Diet Plan.
www.panix.com/˜paleodiet/list/

Price-Pottenger Foundation
A Web site dedicated to two twentieth-century nutritional pioneers.
www.price-pottenger.org

SELECTED REFERENCES

1. Meet the Inflammation Syndrome

Lindmark, E., et al. "Relationship between Interleukin-6 and Mortality in Patients with Unstable Coronary Artery Disease: Effects of an Early Invasive or Noninvasive Strategy." *JAMA* 288 (2001): 2107–2113.

Page J, and D. Henry, "Consumption of NSAIDs and the Development of Congestive Heart Failure in Elderly Patients: An Underrecognized Public Health Problem." *Archives of Internal Medicine* 160 (2000): 777–784.

Shield, M. "Anti-Inflammatory Drugs and Their Effects on Cartilage Synthesis and Renal Function." *European Journal of Rheumatology & Inflammation* 13 (1993): 7–16.

Zhang, R., et al. "Association between Myeloperoxidase Levels and Risk of Coronary Artery Disease." *JAMA* 286 (2001): 2136–2142.

2. Your Inflammation Triggers

Espinola-Klein, C., et al. "Impact of Infectious Burden on Extent and Long-Term Prognosis of Atherosclerosis." *Circulation* 105 (2002): 15–21.

Hadjivassiliou, M., et al. "Headache and CNS White Matter Abnormalities Associated with Gluten Sensitivity." *Neurology* 56 (2001): 385–388.

Kirjavainen, P., and G. R. Gibson. "Healthy Gut Microflora and Allergy: Factors Influencing Development of the Microbiotica." *Annals of Medicine* 31 (1999): 288–292.

Léone, J., et al. "Rheumatic Manifestations of Scurvy: A Report of Two Cases." *Revue du Rhumatisme* (English ed.) 64 (1997): 428–431.

Purba, M., et al. "Skin wrinkling: Can Food Make a Difference?" *Journal of the American College of Nutrition* 20 (2001): 71–80.

3. The Dietary Causes of Inflammation

Choy, E. H. S., and G. S. Panayi. "Cytokine Pathways and Joint Inflammation in Rheumatoid Arthritis." *New England Journal of Medicine* 344 (2001): 907–916.

Cohen, H. A., I. Neuman, and H. Nahaum. "Blocking Effect of Vitamin C in Exercise-Induced Asthma." *Archives of Pediatric and Adolescent Medicine,* 151 (1997): 467–470.

Darlington, L. G., and T. W. Stone. "Antioxidants and Fatty Acids in the Amelioration of Rheumatoid Arthritis and Related Disorders." *British Journal of Nutrition* 85 (2001): 251–269.

Enig, M. G. *Know Your Fats: The Complete Primer for Understanding the Nutrition of Fats, Oils, and Cholesterol.* Silver Spring, MD: Bethesda Press, 2000.

Grimble, R. F. "Modification of Inflammatory Aspects of Immune Function by Nutrients." *Nutrition Research* 18 (1998): 1297–1317.

———. "Nutritional Modulation of Cytokine Biology." *Nutrition* 14 (1998): 634–640.

Heller, A., et al. "Lipid Mediators in Inflammatory Disorders." *Drugs* 55 (1998): 487–496.

Hu, F. B., et al. "Dietary Fat Intake and Risk of Coronary Heart Disease in Women." *New England Journal of Medicine* 337 (1997): 1491–1499.

Hwang, D. "Essential Fatty Acids and Immune Response." *FASEB Journal* 3 (1989): 2052–2061.

Kankaanpaa, Sutas Y., et al. "Dietary Fatty Acids and Allergy." *Annals of Medicine* 31 (1999): 282–287.

Neuman, I., H. Nahum, and A. Ben-Amotz. "Prevention of Exercise-Induced Asthma by a Natural Isomer Mixture of B-Carotene." *Annals of Allergy, Asthma, and Immunology* 82 (1999): 549–553.

———. "Reduction of Exercise-Induced Asthma Oxidative Stress by Lycopene, A Natural Antioxidant." *Allergy* 55 (2000): 1184–1189.

Toborek, M., et al. "Unsaturated Fatty Acids Selectively Induce an Inflammatory Environment in Human Endothelial Cells." *American Journal of Clinical Nutrition* 75 (2002): 119–125.

Wu, D., M. G. Hayek, and S. N. Meydani. "Vitamin E and Macrophage Cyclooxygenase Regulation in the Aged." *Journal of Nutrition* 131 (2001): 382S–388S.

4. Balancing a Diet That's Out of Balance

Cordain, L., et al. "Plant-Animal Subsistence Ratios and Macronutrient Energy Estimates in Worldwide Hunter-Gatherer Diets." *American Journal of Clinical Nutrition* 71 (2000): 682–692.

de Vegt, F., et al. "Relation of Impaired Fasting and Postload Glucose with Incident Type 2 Diabetes in a Dutch Population." *JAMA* 285 (2001): 2109–2113.

Gerster, H. "Can Adults Adequately Convert A-linolenic Acid (18:3n-3) to Eicosapentaenoic Acid (20:5n-3) and Docosahenxaenoic Acid (22:6n-3)?" *International Journal of Vitamin and Mineral Research* 68 (1998): 159–173.

Hall, R. S. *Food for Nought: The Decline in Nutrition.* New York: Harper & Row, 1974.

Howell, W. H. "Diet and Blood Lipids." *Nutrition Today* 32 (1997): 110–115.

Khaw, K. T., et al. "Glycated Haemoglobin, Diabetes, and Mortality in Men in Norfolk Cohort of European Prospective Investigation of Cancer and Nutrition (EPIC-Norfolk)." *BMJ* 322 (2001): 15–18.

Subar, A. F., et al. "Dietary Sources of Nutrients among U.S. Adults, 1989 to 1991." *Journal of the American Dietetic Association* 98 (1998): 537–547.

5. What's Wrong with Anti-Inflammatory Drugs

Angell, M. "Is Academic Medicine for Sale?" *New England Journal of Medicine* 342 (2000): 1516–1518.

Chew, L. D., et al. "A Physician's Survey of the Effect of Drug Sample Availability on Physician's Behavior." *Journal of General Internal Medicine* 15 (2000): 478–483.

Bliznakov, E. G., and D. J. Wilkins. "Biochemical and Clinical Consequences of Inhibiting Coenzyme Q_{10} Biosynthesis by Lipid-Lowering HMG-CoA Reductase Inhibitors (Statins): A Critical Overview." *Advances in Therapy* 15 (1998): 218–228.

Bodenheimer, T. "Uneasy Alliance: Clinical Investigators and the Pharmaceutical Industry." *New England Journal of Medicine* 342 (2000): 1539–1544.

Bombardier, P., et al. "Comparison of Upper Gastrointestinal Toxicity of Rofecoxib and Naproxen in Patients with Rheumatoid Arthritis." *New England Journal of Medicine* 343 (2000): 1520–1528.

Brandt, K. D. "Should Nonsteroidal Anti-Inflammatory Drugs Be Used to Treat Osteoarthritis?" *Rheumatic Diseases Clinics of North America* 19 (1993): 29–44.

Gamlin, L., and J. Brostoff. "Food Sensitivity and Rheumatoid Arthritis." *Environmental Toxicology and Pharmacology* 4 (1997): 43–49.

Hoffer, L. J., et al. "Sulfate Could Mediate the Therapeutic Effect of Glucosamine Sulfate." *Metabolism* 50 (2001): 767–770.

Hollon, M. F. "Direct-to-Consumer Marketing of Prescription Drugs: Creating Consumer Demand." *JAMA* 281 (1999): 382–384.

Horton, R. "Lotronex and the FDA: A Fatal Erosion of Integrity." *Lancet* 357 (2001): 1544–1545.

Lazarou, J., B. H. Pomeranz, and P. N. Corey. "Incidence of Adverse Drug Reactions in Hospitalized Patients." *JAMA* 279 (1998): 1200–1205.

Lichtenstein, D. R., and M. M. Wolfe. "Cox-2-selective NSAIDs: New and Improved?" *JAMA* 284 (2000): 1297–1299.

Lockwood, K., et al. "Progress on Therapy of Breast Cancer with Vitamin Q_{10} and the Regression of Metastases." *Biochemical and Biophysical Research Communications* 212 (1995): 172–177.

Mendelsohn, R. S. *Confessions of a Medical Heretic.* Chicago: Contemporary Books, 1979.

Mukherjee, D., S. E. Nissen, and E. J. Topol. "Risk of Cardiovascular Events Associated with Selective Cox-2-Inhibitors." *JAMA* 286 (2001): 954–959.

Overvad, K., et al. "Coenzyme Q_{10} in Health and Disease." *European Journal of Clinical Nutrition* 53 (1999): 764–770.

Page, J., and D. Henry. "Consumption of NSAIDs and the Development of Congestive Heart Failure in Elderly Patients: An Underrecognized Public Health Problem." *Archives of Internal Medicine* 160 (2000): 777–784.

Phillips, D. P., N. Christenfeld, and L. M. Glynn. "Increase in U.S. Medication-Error Deaths between 1983 and 1993." *Lancet* 351 (1998): 643–644.

Portakal, O., et al. "Coenzyme Q_{10} Concentrations and Antioxidant Status in Tissues of Breast Cancer Patients." *Clinical Biochemistry* 33 (2000): 279–284.

Rao, C. V., H. L. Newmark, and B. S. Reddy. "Chemopreventive Effect of Squalene on Colon Cancer." *Carcinogenesis* 19 (1998): 287–290.

Relman, A. S. "Separating Continuing Medical Education from Pharmaceutical Marketing." *JAMA* 285 (2001): 1009–1012.

Ridker, P. M., et al. "C-reactive Protein and Other Markers of Inflammation in the Prediction of Cardiovascular Disease in Women." *New England Journal of Medicine* 342 (2000): 836–843.

Shield, M. J. "Anti-Inflammatory Drugs and Their Effects on Cartilage Synthesis and Renal Function." *European Journal of Rheumatology & Inflammation,* 13 (1993): 7–16.

Shorr, R. I., and W. L. Greene. "A Foodborne Outbreak of Expensive Antibiotic Use in a Community Teaching Hospital." *Journal of the American Medical Association* 273 (1995): 1908.

Simon, L. S., et al. "Anti-Inflammatory and Upper Gastrointestinal Effects of Celecoxib in Rheumatoid Arthritis: A Randomized Controlled Trial." *JAMA* 282 (1999): 1921–1928.

Stolberg, S. G. "Now, Prescribing Just What the Patient Ordered." *New York Times,* August 10, 1997, E3.

Vane, J. R., Y. S. Bakhle, and R. M. Botting. "Cyclooxygenases 1 and 2." *Annual Review of Pharmacology and Toxicology* 38 (1998): 97–120.

Washington, S. O. "Drug Company Lies about Celebrex in *JAMA*." *Washington Post,* August 5, 2001, A11.

Wolfe, M. M., D. R. Lichtenstein, and G. Singh. "Gastrointestinal Toxicity of Nonsteroidal Anti-Inflammatory Drugs." *New England Journal of Medicine* 340 (1999): 1888–1899.

Woodman, R. "*Lancet:* FDA Far Too Cozy with Drug Industry." Reuters News Service, May 18, 2001.

6. Fifteen Steps to Fight the Inflammation Syndrome

Blacklock, C. J., et al. "Salicylic Acid in the Serum of Subjects Not Taking Aspirin: Comparison of Salicylic Acid Concentrations in the Serum of Vegetarians, Nonvegetarians, and Patients Taking Low-Dose Aspirin." *Journal of Clinical Pathology* 54 (2001): 553–555.

Eberhardt, M. V., C. Y. Lee, and R. H. Liu. "Antioxidant Activity of Fresh Apples." *Nature* 405 (2000): 903–904.

Guillemant, J., et al. "Mineral Water as a Source of Dietary Calcium: Acute Effects on Parathyroid Function and Bone Resorption in Young Men." *American Journal of Clinical Nutrition* 71 (2000): 999–1002.

Liu, S. et al. "A High-Glycemic Diet in Relation to Plasma Levels of High-Sensitivity C-Reactive Protein in Middle-Aged Women." *American Journal of Epidemiology* 153, supp. 11 (2001): S97.

Pauling, L. "Orthomolecular Psychiatry." *Science* 160 (1968): 265–271.

Szent-Gyorgyi, A. V. *On Oxidation, Fermentation, Vitamins, Health, and Disease.* Baltimore: Williams & Wilkins, 1939.

Travis, J. "Mice Reveal the Off Switch for Inflammation." *Science News* 160 (2001): 388.

Yudkin, J. S., et al. "C-Reactive Protein in Healthy Subjects: Associations with Obesity, Insulin Resistance, and Endothelial Dysfunction: A Potential Role for Cytokines Originating from Adipose Tissue?" *Arteriosclerosis, Thrombosis, and Vascular Biology* 19 (1999): 72–78.

8. Good Fats That Rev Up Your Body's Natural Anti-Inflammatories

Bagga, D., et al. "Dietary Modulation of Omega-3/Omega-6 Polyunsaturated Fatty Acid Ratios in Patients with Breast Cancer." *Journal of the National Cancer Institute* 89 (1997): 1123–1131.

Bell, R. R., M. J. Spencer, and J. L. Sherriff. "Voluntary Exercise and Monounsaturated Canola Oil Reduce Fat gain in Mice Fed Diets High in Fat." *Journal of Nutrition* 127 (1997): 2006–2010.

Belluzzi, A., et al. "Effect of an Enteric-Coated Fish-Oil Preparation on Relapses in Crohn's Disease." *New England Journal of Medicine* 334 (1996): 1557–1560.

Conner, W. E. "N-3 Fatty Acids from Fish and Fish Oil: Panacea or Nostrum?" *American Journal of Clinical Nutrition* 74 (2001): 415–416.

Curtis, C. L., et al. "N-3 Fatty Acids Specifically Modulate Catabolic Factors Involved in Articular Cartilage Degradation." *Journal of Biological Chemistry* 275 (2000): 721–724.

Dewailly, E., et al. "N-3 Fatty Acids and Cardiovascular Disease Risk Factors among the Inuit of Nunavik." *American Journal of Clinical Nutrition* 74 (2001): 464–473.

Ernst, E., T. Saradeth, and G. Achhammer. "N-3 Fatty Acids and Acute-Phase Proteins." *European Journal of Clinical Investigation* 21 (1991): 77–82.

Faarvang, K. L., et al. "Fish Oils and Rheumatoid Arthritis: A Randomized and Double-Blind Study." *Ugeskrift for Lager* 156 (1994): 3495–3498.

Ferrara, L. A., et al. "Olive Oil and Reduced Need for Antihypertensive Medications." *Archives of Internal Medicine* 160 (2000): 837–842.

Hubbard, N. E., D. Lim, and K. L. Erickson. "Alteration of Murine Mammary

Tumorigenesis by Dietary Enrichment with n-3 Fatty Acids in Fish Oil." *Cancer Letters* 124 (1998): 1–7.

Iso, H., et al. "Intake of Fish and Omega-3 Fatty Acids and Risk of Stroke in Women." *JAMA* 285 (2001): 304–312.

James, M. J., R. A. Gibson, and L. G. Cleland. "Dietary Polyunsaturated Fatty Acids and Inflammatory Mediator Production." *American Journal of Clinical Nutrition* 71 (Suppl.) (2000): 343S–348S.

Jolly, C. A., et al. "Life Span Is Prolonged in Food-Restricted Autoimmune-Prone (NZB x NZW) F(1) Mice Fed a Diet Enriched with (n-3) Fatty Acids." *Journal of Nutrition* 131 (2001): 2753–2760.

Kunin, R. A. "Snake Oil: A Potent Source of Omega-3 EFA." *Journal of Orthomolecular Medicine* 4 (1989): 139–140.

Lau, C. S., K. D. Morley, and J. J. F. Belch. "Effects of Fish Oil Supplementation on Nonsteroidal Anti-Inflammatory Drug Requirement in Patients with Mild Rheumatoid Arthritis: A Double-Blind Placebo-Controlled Study." *British Journal of Rheumatology* 32 (1993): 982–989.

Leventhal, L. L., E. G. Boyce, and R. B. Zurier. "Treatment of Rheumatoid Arthritis with Gammalinolenic Acid." *Annals of Internal Medicine* 9 (1993): 867–873.

Linos, A., et al. "Dietary Factors in Relation to Rheumatoid Arthritis: A Role for Olive Oil and Cooked Vegetables." *American Journal of Clinical Nutrition* 70 (1999): 1077–1082.

Lorgeril, M. de, et al. "Mediterranean Diet, Traditional Risk Factors, and the Rate of Cardiovascular Complications after Myocardial Infarction." *Circulation* 99 (1999): 779–785.

Mantzioris, E., et al. "Biochemical Effects of a Diet Containing Foods Enriched with n-3 Fatty Acids." *American Journal of Clinical Nutrition* 72 (2000): 42–48.

Prakash, C., et al. "Decreased Systematic Thromboxane A2 Biosynthesis in Normal Human Subjects Fed a Salmon-Rich Diet." *American Journal of Clinical Nutrition* 60 (1994): 369–373.

Requirand, P., et al. "Serum Fatty Acid Imblanace in Bone Loss: Example of Periodontal Disease." *Clinical Nutrition* 19 (2000): 271–276.

Rose, D. P. "Dietary Fatty Acids and Cancer." *American Journal of Clinical Nutrition* 66 (1997): 998S–1003S.

Shapiro, J. A., et al. "Diet and Rheumatoid Arthritis in Women: A Possible Protective Effect of Fish Consumption." *Epidemiology* 7 (1996): 256–263.

Stoll, A. L., W. E. Severus, and M. P. Freeman. "Omega-3 Fatty Acids in Bipolar Disorder: A Preliminary Double-Blind, Placebo-Controlled Trial." *Archives of General Psychiatry* 56 (1999): 407–412.

Terry, P., et al. "Fatty Fish Consumption and Risk of Prostate Cancer." *Lancet* 357 (2001): 1764–1766.

Visioli, F., and C. Galli. "The Effect of Minor Constituents of Olive Oil on Cardiovascular Disease: New Findings." *Nutrition Reviews* 56 (1998): 142–147.

Wolk, A., et al. "A Prospective Study of Association of Monounsaturated Fat and Other Types of Fat with Risk of Breast Cancer." *Archives of Internal Medicine* 158 (1998): 41–45.

Wu, D., et al. "Effect of Dietary Supplementation with Black Currant Seed Oil on the Immune Response of Healthy Elderly Subjects." *American Journal of Clinical Nutrition* 70 (1999): 536–543.

Yaqoob, P., et al. "Effect of Olive Oil on Immune Function in Middle-Aged Men." *American Journal of Clinical Nutrition* 67 (1998): 129–135.

Zurier, R. B., et al. "Gamma-Linolenic Acid Treatment of Rheumatoid Arthritis: A Randomized, Placebo-Controlled Study." *Arthritis & Rheumatism* 11 (1996): 1808–1817.

9. Vitamin E to Extinguish the Flames of Inflammation

Chan, A. C. "Vitamin E and Atherosclerosis." *Journal of Nutrition* 128 (1998): 1593–1596.

Darlington, L. G., and T. W. Stone. "Antioxidants and Fatty Acids in the Amelioration of Rheumatoid Arthritis and Related Disorders." *British Journal of Nutrition* 85 (2000): 251–269.

Devarai, S., and I. Jialal. "Alpha-Tocopherol Decreases Interleukin-1b Release from Activated Human Monocytes by Inhibition of 5-Lipoxygenase." *Arteriosclerosis Thrombosis and Vascular Biology* 19 (1999): 1125–1133.

———. "Alpha-tocopherol Supplementation Decreases Serum C-Reactive Protein and Monocyte Interleukin-6 Levels in Normal Volunteers and Type 2 Diabetic Patients." *Free Radical Biology & Medicine* 29 (2000): 790–792.

———. "Low-Density Lipoprotein Postsecretory Modification, Monocyte Function, and Circulating Adhesion Molecules in Type 2 Diabetes Patients with and without Macovascular Complications: The Effect of A-Tocopherol Supplementation." *Circulation* 102 (2000): 191–196.

Edmonds, S. E., et al. "Putative Analgesic Activity of Repeated Oral Doses of Vitamin E in the Treatment of Rheumatoid Arthritis: Results of a Prospective Placebo-Controlled Double-Blind Trial." *Annals of the Rheumatic Diseases* 56 (1997): 649–655.

Fogarty, A., et al. "Dietary Vitamin E, IgE Concentrations, and Atopy." *Lancet* 356 (2000): 1573–1574.

Helmy, M., et al. "Antioxidants as Adjuvant Therapy in Rheumatoid Disease: A Preliminary Study." *Arzneimittel-Forschung/Drug Research* 51 (2001): 293–298.

Islam, K. N., S. Devaraj, and I. Jialal. "Alpha-Tocopherol Enrichment of Monocytes Decreases Agonist-Induced Adhesion to Human Endothelial Cells." *Circulation* 98 (1998): 2255–2261.

Jialal, I., M. Traber, and S. Deveraj. "Is There a Vitamin E Paradox?" *Current Opinion in Lipidology* 12 (2001): 49–53.

Jiang, Q., and B. N. Ames. "In Vivo Anti-Inflammatory Effect of Gamma-Tocopherol." *Free Radical Biology & Medicine* 31 (Suppl.) (Abstract 123) (2001): 47.

Kennedy, M., et al. "Successful and Sustained Treatment of Chronic Radiation Proctitis with Antioxidant Vitamins E and C." *American Journal of Gastroenterology* 96 (2001): 1080–1084.

Meydani, S. N., et al. "Vitamin E Supplementation and in Vivo Immune Response in Healthy Elderly Subjects." *JAMA* 277 (1997): 1380–1386.

Sano, M., et al. "A Controlled Trial of Selegiline, Alpha-Tocopherol, or Both as Treatment for Alzheimer's Disease." *New England Journal of Medicine* 336 (1997): 1216–1222.

Stephens, N. G., et al. "Randomized Controlled Trial of Vitamin E in Patients with Coronary Disease: Cambridge Heart Antioxidant Study (CHAOS)." *Lancet* 347 (1996): 781–786.

Uomo, G., G. Talamini, and P. G. Rabitti. "Antioxidant Treatment in Hereditary Pancreatitis: A Pilot Study on Three Young Patients." *Digestive and Liver Diseases* 33 (2001): 58–62.

Upritchard, J. E., W. H. F. Sutherland, and J. I. Mann. "Effect of Supplementation with Tomato Juice, Vitamin E, and Vitamin C on LDL Oxidation and Products of Inflammatory Activity in Type 2 Diabetes." *Diabetes Care* 23 (2000): 733–738.

Valigra, L. "Vitamin E May Stop Alzheimer's Cell Death." UPI newswire, August 27, 1999.

van Tits, L. J., et al. "Alpha-Tocopherol Supplementatin Decreases Production of Superoxide and Cytokines by Leukocytes ex Vivo in Both Normolipidemic and Hypertriglyceridemic Individuals." *American Journal of Clinical Nutrition* 71 (2000): 458–464.

Zheng, K. C., et al. "Effect of Dietary Vitamin E Supplementation on Murine Nasal Allergy." *American Journal of the Medical Sciencies* 318 (1999): 49–54.

10. Glucosamine, Chondroitin, and Vitamin C to Rebuild Your Tissues

Adams, M. E. "Hype about Glucosamine." *Lancet* 354 (1999): 353–354.

Challem, J. J. "Did the Loss of Endogenous Ascorbate Propel the Evolution of Anthropoidea and *Homo sapiens?*" *Medical Hypotheses* 48 (1997): 387–392.

Challem, J. J., and E. W. Taylor. "Retroviruses, Ascorbate, and Mutations in the Evolution of *Homo sapiens.*" *Free Radical Biology & Medicine* 25 (1995): 130–132.

Cumming, A. "Glucosamine in Osteoarthritis." *Lancet* 354 (1999): 1640–1641.

Das, A Jr., and T. A. Hammad. "Efficacy of a Combination of FCHG49 Glucosamine Hydrochloride, TRH122 Low Molecular Weight Sodium Chondroitin Sulfate, and Manganese Ascorbate in the Management of Knee Osteoarthritis." *Osteoarthritis and Cartilage* 8 (2000): 343–350.

Hoffer, L. J., et al. "Sulfate Could Mediate the Therapeutic Effect of Glucosamine Sulfate." *Metabolism,* 50 (2001): 767–770.

Johnston, C. S., and L. L. Thompson. "Vitamin C Status of an Outpatient Population." *Journal of the American College of Nutrition* 17 (1998): 366–370.

Langlois, M., et al. "Serum Vitamin C Concentration Is Low in Peripheral Arterial Disease and Is Associated with Inflammation and Severity of Artherosclerosis." *Circulation* 103 (2001): 1863–1868.

Leffler, C. T., et al. "Glucosamine, Chondroitin, and Manganese Ascorbate for Degenerative Joint Disease of the Knee or Low Back: A Randomized, Double-Blind, Placebo-Controlled Pilot Study." *Military Medicine* 164 (1999): 85–91.

Leone, J., et al. "Rheumatic Manifestations of Scurvy: A Report of Two Cases." *Revue du Rhumatisme* (English ed.) 64 (1997): 428–431.

Reginster, J. Y., et al. "Long-Term Effects of Glucosamine Sulphate on Osteoarthritis Progression: A Randomised Placebo-Controlled Clinical Trial." *Lancet* 357 (2001): 247–248, 251–256.

Ronca, F., et al. "Anti-inflammatory Activity of Chondroitin Sulfate." *Osteoarthritis and Cartilage* 6 (Suppl. A) (1998): 14–21.

Rovati, L. C., M. Annefeld, and G. Giacovelli. "Glucosamine in Osteoarthritis." *Lancet* 354 (1999): 1640.

Russell, A. I., and M. F. McCarty. "Glucosamine in Osteoarthritis." *Lancet* 354 (1999): 1641.

Shankland, W. E. II. "The Effects of Glucosamine and Chondroitin Sulfate on Osteoarthritis of the TMJ: A Preliminary Report of 50 Patients." *Orofacial Pain* 16 (1999): 230–235.

11. B Vitamins and More to Reduce Inflammation

Bayeta, E., and B. H. S. Lau. "Pycnogenol Inhibits Generation of Inflammatory Mediators in Macrophages." *Nutrition Research* 20 (2000): 249–259.

Berkson, B. M. "A Conservative Triple Antioxidant Approach to the Treatment of Hepatitis C." *Medizinische Klinik* 94 (Suppl. 3) (1999): 84–89.

Bernard, M. A., P. A. Nakonezny, and T. M. Kashner. "The Effect of Vitamin B_{12} on Older Veterans and Its Relationship in Health." *Journal of the American Geriatrics Society* 46 (1998): 1199–1206.

Blacklock, C. J., et al. "Salicylic Acid in the Serum of Subjects Not Taking Aspirin: Comparison of Salicylic Acid Concentrations in the Serum of Vegetarians, Nonvegetarians, and Patients Taking Low-Dose Aspirin." *Journal of Clinical Pathology* 54 (2000): 553–555.

Chantre, P., et al. "Efficacy and Tolerance of *Haroagophytum procumbens* versus Diacerhein in Treatment of Osteoarthritis." *Phytomedicine* 7 (2000): 177–183.

Cho, K. J., et al. "Inhibition Mechanisms of Bioflavonoids Extracted from the Bark of *Pinus maritima* on the Expression of Pro-inflammatory Cytokines." *Healthy Aging for Functional Longevity* 928 (2001): 141–156.

De Flora, S., C. Grassi, and L. Carati. "Attenuation of Influenza like Symptomatology and Improvement of Cell-Mediated Immunity with Long-Term

N-acetylcysteine Treatment." *European Respiratory Journal* 10 (1997): 1535–1541.

Eberhardt, M. V., C. Y. Lee, and R. H. Liu. "Antioxidant Activity of Fresh Apples." *Nature* 405 (2000): 903–904.

Erlinger, T. P., et al. "Relationship between Systemic Markers of Inflammation and Serum Beta-Carotene Levels." *Archives of Internal Medicine* 161 (2000): 1903–1908.

Haqqi, T. M., et al. "Prevention of Collagen-Induced Arthritis in Mice by a Polyphenolic Fraction from Green Tea." *Proceedings of the National Academy of Sciences* 96 (1999): 4524–4529.

Jurna, I. "Analgesic and Analgesia-Potentiating Action of B Vitamins." *Schermz* 12 (1998): 136–141.

Kritchevsky, S. B., et al. "Serum Carotenoids and Markers of Inflammation in Nonsmokers." *American Journal of Epidemiology* 152 (2000): 1065–1071.

Kwok, B. H., et al. "The Anti-Inflammatory Natural Product Parthenolide from the Medicinal Herb Feverfew Directly Binds to and Inhibits IkappaB kinase." *Chemistry and Biology* (2001): 759–766.

Li, W. G., et al. "Anti-Inflammatory Effect and Mechanism of Proanthocyanidins from Grape Seeds." *Acta Pharmacologica Sinica* 22 (2001): 1117–1120.

Middleton, E., and Anne S. "Quercetin Inhibits Lipopolysaccharide-Induced Expression of Endothelial Cell Tracellular Adhesion Molecule-1." *International Archives of Allergy and Immunology* 107 (1995): 435–436.

Panasenko, O. M. et al. "Interaction of Peroxynitrite with Carotenoids in Human Low-Density Lipoproteins." *Archives of Biochemistry and Biophysics* 373 (2000): 302–305.

Ringbom, Segura L., et al. "Usolic Acid from Plantago Major, a Selective Inhibitor of Cyclooxygenase-2 Catalyzed Prostaglandin Biosynthesis." *Journal of Natural Products* 61 (1998): 1212–1215.

Sandoval-Chacon, M., et al. "Antiinflammatory Actions of Cat's Claw: The Role of NF-kB." *Alimentary Pharmacology and Therapeutics* 12 (1998): 1279–1289.

Srivastava K. C., and T. Mustafa. "Ginger *(Zingiber offinale)* in Rheumatism and Musculoskeletal Disorders." *Medical Hypotheses* 39 (1992): 342–348.

Stefanescu, M., et al. "Pycnogenol Efficacy in the Treatment of Systemic Lupus Erythematosus Patients." *Phytotherapy Research* 15 (2001): 698–704.

Wegener, T. "Devil's claw: From African Traditional Remedy to Modern Analgesic and Anti-Inflammatory." *HerbalGram* 50 (2001): 1047–1054.

Weisburger, J. H. "Tea and Health: A Historical Perspective." *Cancer Letters* 114 (1997): 315–317.

Zakay-Rones, Z., et al. "Inhibition of Several Strains of Influenza Virus in Vitro and Reduction of Symptoms by an Elderberry Extract *(Sambucus nigra L.)* during an Outbreak of Influenza B Panama." *Journal of Alternative and Complementary Medicine* 1 (1995): 361–369.

12. The Inflammation Syndrome, Diseases, and Specific Conditions

Altman, R. D., and K. C. Marcussen. "Effects of a Ginger Extract on Knee Pain in Patients with Osteoarthritis." *Arthritis & Rheumatism* 44 (2001): 2531–2538.

Anderson, R. A., et al. "Elevated Intakes of Supplemental Chromium Improve Glucose and Insulin Variables in Individuals with Type 2 Diabetes." *Diabetes* 46 (1997): 1786–1791.

Angswurm, M. W., et al. "Selenium Replacement in Patients with Severe Systemic Inflammatory Response Syndrome Improves Clinical Outcome." *Critical Care Medicine* 27 (1999): 1807–1813.

Anon. "The Scourge of Boomeritis." *My Generation* (September/October 2001): 14.

Beck, M. A., et al. "Rapid Genomic Evolution of a Nonvirulent Coxsackievirus B_3 in Selenium-Deficient Mice Results in Selection of Identical Virulent Isolates." *Nature Medicine* 1 (May 1995): 433–436.

Bell, R. R., M. J. Spencer, and J. L. Sherriff. "Voluntary Exercise and Monounsaturated Canola Oil Reduce Fat Gain in Mice Fed Diets High in Fat." *Journal of Nutrition* 127 (1997): 2006–2010.

Berkson, B. M. "A Conservative Triple Antioxidant Approach to the Treatment of Hepatitis C." *Medizinische Klinik* 94 (Supp. III) (1999): 84–89.

Brinkeborn, R., et al. "Echinaforce in the Treatment of Acute Colds." *Schweizerische Zeitschrift für Ganzheits Medizin* 10 (1998): 26–29.

Burger, R. A., A. R. Torres, and R. P. Warren. "Echinacea-Induced Cytokine Production by Human Macrophages." *International Journal of Immunopharmacology* 19 (1997): 371–379.

Chan, A. C. "Vitamin E and Atherosclerosis." *Journal of Nutrition* 128 (1998): 1593–1596.

Cheraskin, E. "How Quickly Does Diet Make for Change? A Study in Gingival Inflammation." *New York Journal of Denistry* 58 (1998): 133–135.

Chongviriyaphan, N., X. D. Wang, and R. M. Russell. "The Effects of a Combination of Antioxidant Vitamins on Lung Squamous Metaplasia and Lipid Peroxidation in Ferrets Exposed to Tobacco Smoke." Presented at the 42nd annual meeting of the American College of Nutrition, October 4–7, Orlando, Florida.

Clark, L. C., et al. "Effects of Selenium Supplementation for Cancer Prevention in Patients with Carcinoma of the Skin: A Randomized Controlled Trial." Nutritional Prevention of Cancer Study Group. *JAMA* 276 (1996): 1957–1963.

Cohen, H. A., I. Neuman, and H. Nahaum. "Blocking Effect of Vitamin C in Exercise-Induced Asthma." *Archives of Pediatric and Adolescent Medicine* 151 (1997): 467–470.

Cohen, M. E., and D. M. Meyer. "Effect of Dietary Vitamin E Supplementation and Rotational Stress on Alveolar Bone Loss in Rice Rats." *Archives of Oral Biology* 38 (1993): 601–606.

Cook, D. G., et al. "Effect of Fresh Fruit Consumption on Lung Function and Wheeze in Children." *Thorax* 52 (1997): 628–633.

Cordain, L., et al. "Modulation of Immune Function by Dietary Lectins in Rheumatoid Arthritis." *British Journal of Nutrition* 83 (2000): 207–217.

Correa, P., et al. "Chemoprevention of Gastric Dysplasia: Randomized Trial of Antioxidant Supplements and Anti-Helicobacter Pylori Therapy." *Journal of the National Cancer Institute* 92 (2000): 1881–1888.

Cowley, H. C., et al. "Plasma Antioxidant Potential in Severe Sepsis: A Comparison of Survivors and Nonsurvivors." *Critical Care Medicine* 24 (1996): 1179–1183.

Curtis, C. L., et al. "N-3 Fatty Acids Specifically Modulate Catabolic Factors Involved in Articular Cartilage Degradation." *Journal of Biological Chemistry* 275 (2000): 721–724.

De Flora, S., C. Grassi, and L. Carati. "Attenuation of Influenzalike Symptomatology and Improvement of Cell-Mediated Immunity with Long-Term N-Acetylcysteine Treatment." *European Respiratory Journal* 10 (1997): 1535–1541.

Eberlein-Konig, B., M. Placzek, and B. Przybilla. "Protective Effect against Sunburn of Combined Systemic Ascorbic Acid (Vitamin C) And D-a-tocopherol (Vitamin E)." *Journal of the American Academy of Dermatology* 38 (1998): 45–48.

Festa, A., et al. "Chronic Subclinical Inflammation as Part of the Insulin Resistance Syndrome: The Insulin Resistance Atherosclerosis Study (IRAS)." *Circulation* 102 (2000): 42–47.

Field, A. E., et al. "Impact of Overweight on the Risk of Developing Common Chronic Diseases during a Ten-Year Period." *Archives of Internal Medicine* 161 (2001): 1581–1586.

Flynn, M. A., W. Iirvin, and G. Krause. "The Effect of Folate and Cobalamin on Osteoarthritic Hands." *Journal of the American College of Nutrition* 13 (1994): 351–356.

Fraser, A. G., and G. A. Woollard. "Gastric Juice Ascorbic Acid Is Related to *Helicobacter pylori* Infection but Not Ethnicity." *Journal of Gastroenterology and Hepatology* 14 (1999): 1070–1073.

Gadek, J. E., S. J. DeMichele, and M. D. Karlstad. "Effect of Enteral Feeding with Eicoapentaenoic Acid, Gamma-Linolenic Acid, and Antioxidants in Patients with Acute Respiratory Distress Syndrome." *Critical Care Medicine* 27 (1999): 1409–1420.

Gamlin, L., and J. Brostoff. "Food Sensitivity and Rheumatoid Arthritis." *Environmental Toxicology and Pharmacology* 4 (1997): 43–49.

Giovannucci, E. "Tomatoes, Tomato-Based Products, Lycopene, and Cancer: Review of the Epidemiology Literature." *Journal of the National Cancer Institute* 91 (1999): 317–331.

Giovannucci, E., et al. "Intake of Carotenoids and Retinol in Relation to Risk of Prostate Cancer." *Journal of the National Cancer Institute* 87 (1995): 1767–1776.

Golding, D. N. "Is There an Allergic Synovitis?" *Journal of the Royal Society of Medicine* 83 (1990): 312–314.

Gollnick, H. P. M., et al. "Systemic Beta-Carotene plus Topical UV-Sunscreen Are an Optimal Protection against Harmful Effects of Natural UV-Sunlight: Results of the Berlin-Eilath Study." *European Journal of Dermatology* 6 (1996): 200–205.

Gonzalez N. J., and L. L. Isaacs. "Evaluation of Pancreatic Proteolytic Enzyme Treatment of Adenocarcinoma of the Pancreas, with Nutrition and Detoxification Support." *Nutrition and Cancer* 33 (1999): 117–124.

Guochang, A. "Ultraviolet Radiation-Induced Oxidative Stress in Cultured Human Skin Fibroblasts and Antioxidant Protection." *Biological Research Reports from the University of Jyväskylä* 33 (1993): 1–86.

Hadjivassiliou, M., et al. "Headache and CNS White Matter Abnormalities Associated with Gluten Sensitivity." *Neurology* 56 (2001): 385–388.

Hafstrom, I., et al. "A Vegan Diet Free of Gluten Improves the Signs and Symptoms of Rheumatoid Arthritis: The Effects on Arthritis Correlate with a Reduction in Antibodies to Food Antigens." *Rheumatology* 40 (2001): 1175–1179.

Haney, D. O. "Tomato Nutrient May Fight Cancer." Associated Press, April 13, 1999.

Hanioka, T., et al. "Effect of Topical Application of Coenzyme Q_{10} on Adult Periodontitis." *Molecular Aspects of Medicine* 15 (1994): S241–S248.

Haqqi, T. M., et al. "Prevention of Colagen-Induced Arthritis in Mice by a Polyphenolic Fraction from Green Tea." *Proceedings of the National Academy of Sciences* 96 (1999): 4524–4529.

Hayes, C. E., M. T. Cantorna, and H. F. DeLuca. "Vitamin D and Multiple Sclerosis." *Proceedings of the Society for Experimental Biology & Medicine* 216 (1997): 21–27.

Hemila, H. "Does Vitamin C Alleviate the Symptoms of the Common Cold? A Review of Current Evidence." *Scandinavian Journal of Infectious Diseases* 26 (January 1994): 1–6.

Herzenberg, L. A., et al. "Glutathione Deficiency Is Associated with Impaired Survival in HIV Disease." *Proceedings of the National Academy of Sciences of the USA* 94 (1997): 1967–1972.

Hodge, L., J. K. Peat, and C. Salome. "Increased Consumption of Polyunsaturated Oils May Be a Cause of Increased Prevalence of Children Asthma." *Australia and New Zealand Journal of Medicine* 24 (1994): 727.

Hodge, L., et al. "Consumption of Oily Fish and Childhood Asthma Risk." *Medical Journal of Australia* 164 (1996): 137–140.

Hoffer, A., and L. Pauling. "Hardin Jones Biostatistical Analysis of Mortality Data for a Second Set of Cohorts of Cancer Patients with a Large Fraction Surviving at the Termination of the Study and a Comparison of Survival Times of Cancer Patients Receiving Large Regular Oral Doses of Vitamin

C and Other Nutrients with Similar Patients Not Receiving These Doses." *Journal of Orthomolecular Medicine* 8 (1993): 157–167.

Hogan, S. P., et al. "A Pathological Function for Eotaxin and Eosinophils in Eosinophilic Gastrointestinal Inflammation." *Nature Immunology* 2 (2001): 353–360.

Hosseini, S., et al. "Pycnogenol in the Management of Asthma." *Journal of Medicinal Food* 4 (2001): 201–209.

Hutter, C. "On the Causes of Multiple Sclerosis." *Medical Hypotheses* 41 (1993): 93–96.

Huisman, A. M., et al. "Vitamin D Levels in Women with Systemic Lupus Erythematosus and Fibromyalgia." *Journal of Rheumatology* 28 (2001): 2535–2539.

Jacob, R. A., et al. "Experimental Vitamin C Depletion and Supplementation in Young Men: Nutrient Interactions and Dental Health Effects." *Annals of the New York Academy of Sciences* 498 (1987): 333–346.

Jarosz, M., et al. "Effects of High-Dose Vitamin C Treatment on *Helicobacter pylori* Infection and Total Vitamin C Concentration in Gastric Juice." *European Journal of Cancer Prevention* 7 (1998): 449–454.

Kira, J., S. Tobimatsu, and I. Goto. "Vitamin B_{12} Metabolism and Massive-Dose Methyl Vitamin B_{12} Therapy in Japanese Patients with Multiple Sclerosis." *Internal Medicine* 33 (1994): 82–86.

Kirjavainen, P., and G. R. Gibson. "Healthy Gut Microflora and Allergy: Factors Influencing Development of the Microbiotica." *Annals of Medicine* 31 (1999): 288–292.

Kjeldsen-Kragh, J., et al. "Controlled Trial of Fasting and One-Year Vegetarian Diet in Rheumatoid Arthritis." *Lancet* 338 (1991): 899–902.

Krohn, J. The *Whole Way to Allergy Relief & Prevention*. Point Roberts, Wash.: Hartley & Marks, 1991.

Lamm, D. L., et al. "Megaose Vitamins in Bladder Cancer: A Double-Blind Clinical Trial." *The Journal of Urology* 151 (1994): 21–26.

Lau, C. S., K. D. Morley, and J. J. F. Belch. "Effects of Fish Oil Supplementation on Nonsteroidal Anti-Inflammatory Drug Requirement in Patients with Mild Rheumatoid Arthritis: A Double-Blind Placebo-Controlled Study." *British Journal of Rheumatology* 32 (1993): 982–989.

MacNee, W., and I. Rahman. "Oxidants and Antioxidants as Therapeutic Targets in Chronic Obstructive Pulmonary Disease." *American Journal of Critical Care Medicine* 160 (1999): S58–S65.

Madsen, T., et al. "C-Reactive Protein, Dietary n-3 Fatty Acids, and the Extent of Coronary Artery Disease." *American Journal of Cardiology* 88 (2001): 1139–1142.

Maire, F., et al. "Factors Associated with Hyperhomocysteinemia in Crohn's Disease." *Gastroenterologie Clinique et Biologique* 25 (2001): 745–748.

McVean, M., and D. C. Liebler. "Inhibition of UVB-Induced DNA Photodamage in Mouse Epidermis by Topically Applied A-tocopherol." *Carcinogenesis* 18 (1997): 1617–1622.

Messetti, A., et al. "Systemic Oxidative Stress and Its Relationship with Age and Illness." *Journal of the American Geriatrics Society* 44 (1996): 823–827.

Milam, S. B., G. Zardeneta, and J. P. Schmitz. "Oxidative Stress and Degenerative Temporomandibular Joint Disease: A Proposed Hypothesis." *Journal of Oral and Maxillofacial Therapy* 56 (1998): 214–223.

Miller, A. L. "The Etiologies, Pathophysiology, and Alternative/Complementary Treatment of Asthma." *Alternative Medicine Review* 6 (2001): 20–47.

Nair, S., et al. "Micronutrient Antioxidants in Gastric Mucosa and Serum in Patients with Gastritis and Gastric Ulcer." *Journal of Clinical Gastroenterology* 30 (2000): 381–385.

Nelson, H. K., et al. "Host Nutritional Selenium Status as a Driving Force for Influenza Virus Mutations." *FASEB Journal* 15 (2001): 1481–1483.

Neuman, I., H. Nahum, and A. Ben-Amotz. "Prevention of Exercise-Induced Asthma by a Natural Isomer Mixture of B-Carotene." *Annals of Allergy, Asthma, and Immunology* 82 (1999): 549–553.

———. "Reduction of Exercise-Induced Asthma Oxidative Stress by Lycopene, a Natural Antioxidant." *Allergy* 55 (2000): 1184–1189.

Nordvik, I., et al. "Effect of Dietary Advice and n-3 Supplementation in Newly Diagnosed MS Patients." *Acta Neurologica Scandinavica* 102 (2000): 143–149.

Nsouli, T. M., et al. "Role of Food Allergy in Serous Otitis Media." *Annals of Allergy* 73 (1994): 215–219.

Patavino, T., and D. M. Brady. "Natural Medicine and Nutritional Therapy as an Alternative Treatment in Systemic Lupus Erythematosus." *Alternative Medicine Review* 6 (2001): 460–471.

Patterson, R. E., et al. "Vitamin Supplements and Cancer Risk: The Epidemiological Evidence." *Cancer Causes and Control* 8 (1997): 786–802.

Purba, M., et al. "Skin Wrinkling: Can Food Make a Difference?" *Journal of the American College of Nutrition* 20 (2001): 71–80.

Romieu, I., F. Meneses, and M. Ramirez. "Antioxidant Supplementation and Respiratory Functions among Workers Exposed to High Levels of Ozone." *American Journal of Critical Care Medicine* 158 (1998): 226–232.

Salam, T. N., and J. F. Fowler Jr. "Balsam-Related Systemic Contact Dermatitis." *Journal of the American Academy of Dermatology* 45 (2001): 377–381.

Sano, M., et al. "A Controlled Trial of Selegiline, Alpha-Tocopherol, or Both as Treatment for Alzheimer's Disease." *New England Journal of Medicine* 336 (1997): 1216–1222.

Schnyder, G., et al. "Decreased Rate of Coronary Restenosis after Lowering of Plasma Homocysteine Levels." *New England Journal of Medicine* 345 (2001): 1593–1600.

Schünemann, H. J., et al. "The Relation of Serum Levels of Antioxidant Vitamins C and E, Retinol and Carotenoids with Pulmonary Function in the General Population." *American Journal of Respiratory and Critical Care Medicine* 163 (2001): 1246–1255.

Shankland, W. E. II. "The Effects of Glucosamine and Chondroitin Sulfate on

Osteoarthritis of the TMJ: "A preliminary Report of Fifty Patients." *Orofacial Pain* 16 (1999): 230–235.

Sivam, G. P., et al. "Protection against *Helicobacter pylori* and Other Bacterial Infections by Garlic." Presented at Recent Advances on the Nutritional Benefits Accompanying the Use of Garlic as a Supplement, November 14–17, 1998, Newport Beach, Calif.

Slattery, M. L., et al. "Trans-Fatty Acids and Colon Cancer." *Nutrition and Cancer: An International Journal,* 39 (2001): 170–175.

Stefanescu, M., et al. "Pycnogenol Efficacy in the Treatment of Systemic Lupus Erythematosus Patients." *Phytotherapy Research* 15 (2001): 698–704.

Symons, M. C. R. "Radicals Generated by Bone Cutting and Fracture." *Free Radical Biology & Medicine* 20 (1996): 831–835.

Tixier, J. M., et al. "Evidence by in Vivo and in Vitro Studies That Binding of Pycnogenol to Elastin Affects Its Rate of Degradation by Elastases." *Biochemical Pharmacology* 33 (1984): 3933–3939.

Trenga, C. A., J. Q. Koenig, and P. V. Williams "Dietary Antioxidants and Ozone-Induced Bronchial Hyperresponsiveness in Adults with Asthma." *Archives of Environmental Health* 56 (2001): 242–249.

Vaananen, M. K., et al. "Periodontal Health Related to Plasma Ascorbic Acid." *Proceedings of the Finnish Dental Society* 89 (1993): 51–59.

Wang, Q., W. Z. Zhao, and C. G. Ma. "Protective Effects of Ginkgo Biloba on Gastric Mucosa." *Acta Pharmacologica Sinica* 21 (2000): 1153–1156.

Welch, H. G., L. M. Schwartz, and S. Woloshin. "Are Increasing Five-Year Survival Rates Evidence of Success against Cancer?" *JAMA* 283 (2000): 2975–2978.

Wendland, B. E., et al. "Lipid Peroxidation and Plasma Antioxidant Micronutrients in Crohn Disease." *American Journal of Clinical Nutrition* 74 (2001): 259–264.

Wilson, A. C., et al. "Relation of Infant Diet to Childhood Health: Seven-Year Follow-up of Cohort of Children in Dundee Infant Feeding Study." *British Medical Journal* 316 (1998): 21–25.

Woodward, N., H. Turnstall-Pedoe, and K. McColl. "*Helicobacter pylori* Infection Reduces Systemic Availability of Dietary Vitamin C." *European Journal of Gastroenterology & Hepatology* 13 (2001): 233–237.

Zuerier, R. B., et al. "Gamma-Linolenic Acid Treatment of Rheumatoid Arthritis: A Randomized, Placebo-Controlled Study." *Arthritis & Rheumatism* 11 (1996): 1808–1817.

Zullo, A., V. Rinaldi, and C. Hassan: "Ascorbic Acid and Intestinal Metaplasia in the Stomach: A Prospective Randomized Study." *Alimentary Pharmacology and Therapeutics* 14 (2000): 1303–1309.

INDEX

ABOUT THE AUTHOR

Jack Challem, The Nutrition Reporter, is one of the leading health reporters in the United States. He has been writing about advances in vitamin and mineral research since 1974 and is the lead author of the best-selling *Syndrome X: The Complete Nutritional Program to Prevent and Reverse Insulin Resistance* (New York: John Wiley & Sons, 2000). Challem writes and publishes *The Nutrition Reporter* newsletter (www.nutritionreporter.com) and is a contributing editor to many health and consumer magazines, including *Natural Health, Let's Live,* and *Modern Maturity.* His scientific articles have appeared in *Cosmetic Dermatology, Free Radical Biology & Medicine, Journal of the National Cancer Institute, Journal of Orthomolecular Medicine, Medical Hypotheses,* and the *New England Journal of Medicine.*

CPSIA information can be obtained at www.ICGtesting.com
Printed in the USA
BVOW010048060313

314737BV00007B/144/A